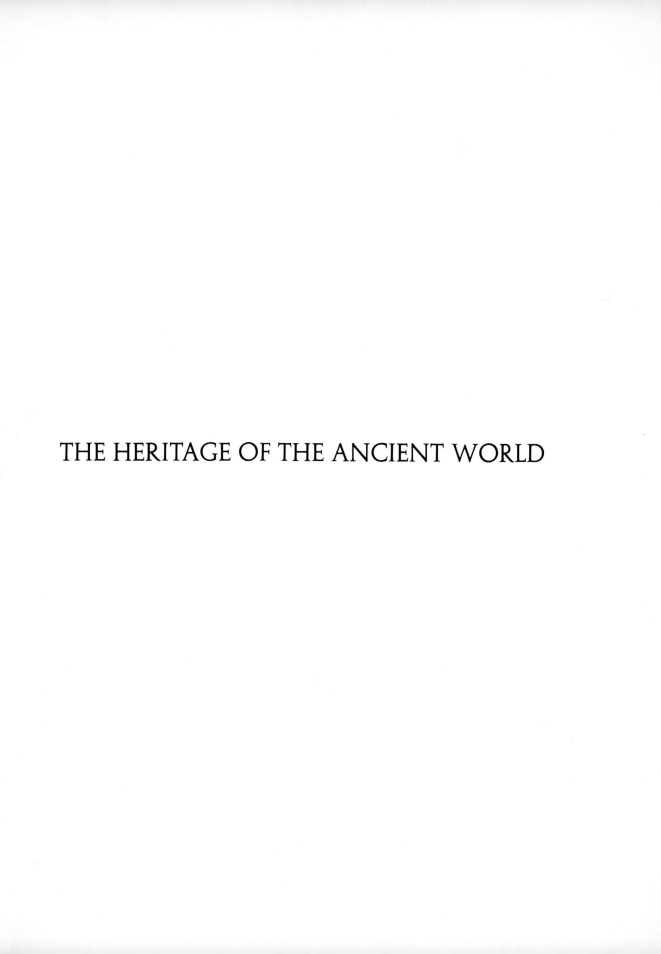

THE HERITAGE OF THE ANCIENT WORLD

SECOND EDITION

THE HERITAGE
OF THE
ANCIENT WORLD

STEWART C. EASTON

HOLT, RINEHART AND WINSTON, INC.

NEW YORK   CHICAGO   SAN FRANCISCO   ATLANTA   DALLAS   MONTREAL   TORONTO   SYDNEY

MAPS BY VINCENT KOTSCHAR

PREFACE

The Heritage of the Ancient World which is now being published in a second edition consists of the first fourteen chapters of the author's *Heritage of the Past: Earliest Times to 1500*, the third edition of which will appear at the same time. The changes made in both the second and third editions of the parent book are therefore now being incorporated into *The Heritage of the Ancient World*. The first chapter has been revised and it has an entirely different reading list devoted to the problems of historiography. The second chapter on prehistory has been rewritten in order to bring it into line with modern archaeological findings, the chapter on Mesopotamia has been reorganized, and the sections on Greek philosophy have been largely rethought and rewritten, as has the chapter on Christianity. In other respects the book remains more or less as it was, but many of the pictures have been changed, the maps, still by Vincent Kotschar, have been redrawn and restyled, and the reading lists at the end of each chapter have been brought up-to-date. The chapter on the contrasts between the Western world and the Far East has been retained, even though some of the material covered in this chapter is not contemporary with the Ancient World in the West.

A text which covers both Greece and Rome, as well as the ancient Near East, in a single volume of some 450 pages has two obvious uses: for those courses which cover these civilizations in a single semester; and for those two-semester courses where the emphasis is on reading the original sources, but which need a basic text to provide the necessary continuity. In view of the ever increasing demands made on the students' time, and the increasing emphasis being given, for excellent reasons, to the study of modern history, there has been a noticeable tendency to place the break in the standard Western Civilization course at a date later than used to be customary. Whereas a decade ago the date to 1500, representing the end of the Middle Ages, was regarded as a natural breaking point, today the more likely break is in 1648, 1715, or even 1815. With these later dates the study of the ancient world is likely to be completed in little more than two or three weeks, with the result that the ordinary student, whose only course in European history is Western Civilization, will acquire little beyond a smattering of ancient history. To my mind this is a serious loss in view of the great cultural and religious debt we owe to antiquity, and the fact that until recently a study of the great works of antiquity formed the basis of all liberal education. Yet to devote a whole year to a detailed study of the ancient world may seem excessive to many students in view of the limited time they have available. But it may not be too much for students who are not necessarily majoring in history but are anxious to have a broad liberal education to spend a single semester in obtaining a more detailed knowledge of the ancient world, especially if their appetite has been whetted by the cursory survey offered to them as part of the general course in Western Civilization.

It is for such single semester courses that *The Heritage of the Ancient World* will be found useful, especially since it has been organized on a topical basis, with an attempt to present each civilization as a whole rather than to provide all the historical details of what happened in the distant past. At least as much attention is devoted to the cultural achievements of the ancient peoples as to their actual history, while the chronology of events can be followed by using the chronological charts that appear in each of the historical (as distinct from the purely cultural) chapters. The scaled maps, with their names of places most of which have disappeared in the course of the centuries, can orient the students in space, and he may come to realize how greatly the world has changed from the days when Egypt, Mesopotamia, and Greece were the centers of the Western world, whereas today the United Arab Republic, Syria, and Iraq are among the poorest of the world's nations, and Greece is among the least developed states of Europe.

Now, fifteen years since the first publication of the parent book, so many historians have contributed suggestions, that only a comprehensive acknowledgment of all the help the author has received can be made here. For the errors that still remain the author naturally takes full responsibility; and to those students and instructors who prefer other interpretations than those given here, the hope is expressed that they will not be constrained by them, but will use them more effectively to develop their own. The interpretation of Egypt, and the Near East in general, which owes so much to the work done by scholars at the Oriental Institute in Chicago may not be the last word on the subject, but it still seems to this author to make more sense of Egyptian civilization, in particular, than any other interpretation known to him; and some interpretation is surely more helpful than merely trying to list what happened. No inconvenient facts have been turned up in the last two decades which would make it necessary to abandon this interpretation, so it is retained here for another generation of students to mull over, as a contribution to the understanding of a civilization totally different from ours which nevertheless in its days was the greatest that the world had yet known.

STEWART C. EASTON

St. Gaudens
France
November 1969

CONTENTS

ILLUSTRATIONS

MAPS

THE HERITAGE OF THE ANCIENT WORLD

PART I

BEFORE HISTORY

CHAPTER 1

THE FOUNDATIONS
OF AN ORGANIZED SOCIETY

► ## The economic and political foundations of a society

ECONOMIC REQUIREMENTS

In all ages and in all societies the human being has had certain fundamental needs. These arise from the very fact that he is a human being, living in a society. No man can live for more than a limited period by himself; even if he could survive alone for his own lifetime, he could not reproduce his kind. He must therefore have some relations with his fellow men, and these relations are necessarily regulated by custom and usually by law. As a producer and consumer, he has an economic part to play in the life of his society. Lastly, he has certain nonmaterial needs, which he pursues with greater or lesser intensity in accordance with his own personal wishes and with the demands made upon him, and the opportunities provided for him, by his society.

The basic economic requirements of human beings are food, shelter, and clothing. In prehistoric societies their pursuit must have consumed such an enormous proportion of available human energies that there was little left for other activities. Food could be obtained from animals and wild plants, which were hunted or harvested in accordance with the skills and techniques available to the society. Such an economy may be termed a natural one—man was dependent entirely upon what was provided for him by nature, especially if he clothed himself in animal skins and lived in caves, and human energy was the only motive power available to him. When nature failed him he moved on to a more favorable location, where he continued to live in a natural economy.

At the next stage of development, called the "Neolithic Revolution,"[1] man ceased to be totally dependent upon nature and began in some degree to control it. He learned to breed and tend animals, so that they were always available to him for food when he needed them, and he taught them to work for him

---

[1] It may be noted that the term "Neolithic Revolution" in recent years has fallen into some disrepute as specialists have begun to stress its "evolutionary" nature. This is in some degree true also of the "Industrial Revolution" of the eighteenth to the twentieth centuries. Both terms will continue to be used in this book because they are convenient labels; and whether or not these stages of development were "revolutionary depends at least to some extent on how one defines a revolution.

and supplement his own labor. He learned to plant crops and harvest them, laying down seeds in some spot cleared for the purpose and in which such plants did not grow by nature. He learned to build himself a home where none had been provided by nature, and he even discovered how to grow special crops such as flax from which he could make himself clothing.

Having learned in some degree to control and harness nature, man at last found himself both with leisure to produce luxuries that made life more pleasant and comfortable, and with a surplus of crops beyond the consuming needs of his society. He was able to offer these surpluses of manufactured luxuries and of crops for human consumption in exchange for goods produced by other men outside his immediate group. This *trade*, evidences of which have been found as early as the Neolithic age, was ultimately supplemented and fed by the products of *industry*. Industrial production is characterized by a more extensive division of labor under which some members of the society, freed from direct agricultural work, specialize in manufacturing a varied assortment of articles to be consumed at home or to be traded in exchange for foreign products. An economically advanced society is characterized by the diversity of products manufactured and by effective organization of production to take advantage of specialized human skills and to minimize the waste of human energies in unnecessary labor.

POLITICAL REQUIREMENTS

Protection through government and law

In the seventeenth century it was often assumed that man in a state of nature was forced to compete with all other human beings for his very subsistence, or, in the famous words of Thomas Hobbes, that his life was "solitary, poor, nasty, brutish, and short." In the nineteenth century many held the view that human survival depended on success in the "struggle for existence" among human beings. From this struggle only those who were best fitted to survive did so—as seemed to be true in the case of all other species in the natural world. However much a strong individual might have succeeded in impressing himself upon his fellow men, it seemed scarcely possible to imagine that any individual could have survived without help from them. An essential element in survival must always have been the willingness of human beings to cooperate in overcoming the dangers of a hostile environment.

Such cooperation must have involved banding together for the purposes of mutual protection, as well as for the daily activities of providing sustenance for the group. If a social unit, even one as small as a family, is unable to evolve an acceptable system, under which the authority to maintain internal order and resist external aggression is vested in one or more of its members, it will soon disintegrate. The first requirement of any government is, therefore, that it should possess power to enforce its will on individuals. This coercive power inherent in all governments may be backed by police forces for general use and military forces to repel external aggression. Whatever the form of government it must also possess some moral authority and be acceptable either to a majority of the people or to a minority that commands enough material or moral resources to enable it to coerce the majority. No government, whether by one man or by many, can survive without some support and acceptance.

Although we can have no certain knowledge of how governments in prehistoric times maintained their authority, it seems safe to assume that some social behavior must have been forbidden by custom, and that infringement upon this code of behavior was punished by the group through its government—as indeed happens today in preliterate "primitive" societies. The earliest known literate societies, the Sumerian city-states, already had their codes of law which, like all such codes, stated the kinds of behavior that were forbidden and prescribed penalties for them, while at the same time attempting to regulate commercial and other transactions among the citizenry. The Sumerian and later Mesopotamian rulers also promulgated new laws as their societies became ever more complex, culminating in the major codification of the laws known as the Hammurabi Code. Egypt, by contrast, did not have a written law until a very late date. But the ancient Egyptians did have a concept of justice, which was supposed to be of divine origin and was administered by the Pharaoh. As a god able to "know the hearts of men" he could administer justice in the light of his divine knowledge, and thus had no need for law codes. Hammurabi of Babylon shared the Egyptian view that it was the task of the ruler to administer justice, and that his laws in consequence must be "just." He pictured himself as having "received" his laws from the Babylonian god of justice. Moses, who according to the Bible received his laws directly from Yahweh, was in the same tradition, and even the Athenian lawgiver Solon consulted the oracle of Apollo at Delphi before promulgating his laws.

Thus from the very earliest times it was believed that laws should be in accord with the ideal of justice; that men who promulgated, administered, and enforced them were above the common run of humanity; and that behind them stood the gods ready to punish with their own sanctions all who presumed to break them.

Evolution of political institutions—From clans and tribes to the national state

It is possible that in the far distant past the self-sufficient family may also have been the political unit, with one member exercising an authority recognized and accepted by the other members. This state of affairs, however, presupposes the self-sufficiency of the one family, and such self-sufficiency is unlikely at any time or in any place. An historically known social and political unit is the clan, which unites a small number of families, connected by a close blood relationship and possessing a common ancestor. The clans of the Scottish Highlands were of this type. A larger unit is the tribe, composed of several different clans. Still larger units of government are city-states, of which the first examples known to history were in Mesopotamia. City-states continued to exist until very recent times, and even now have not altogether disappeared. The Republic of San Marino in Italy is an example. Almost everywhere city-states have now given place to the national state. Both city- and national states have in the course of history ruled over wide areas conquered in warfare and have thus become empires. But few empires have ever succeeded in winning the loyalty of the subjected peoples, a loyalty which is usually given spontaneously to the smaller units of clan, tribe, and nation, and helps to keep them together as social and political units.

The forms of government are many and varied. The Greek philosopher Aristotle recognized three types of what he thought of as "good" governments: monarchy, aristocracy (rule by "the best"), and constitutional government. These could degenerate into tyranny, oligarchy (rule by the few, not necessarily the best), and democracy (rule by the propertyless many). In modern times hereditary absolute monarchy has usually given way in the West to constitutional monarchy, in which the king has very limited powers but is a symbol of unity. The king's advisers have become representatives elected by the people and responsible to them. "Tyrannies" continue, most of them dependent for their power on the acquiescence or active support of professional armies, while oligarchies of varying kinds hold power in many areas of the world. These no longer rule by virtue of noble birth but because of their control of their countries' wealth, as in many states of Latin America, or because they control the state bureaucracy, as in the Soviet Union and other Communist states.

Whatever the form of government, its first task is to govern. If it cannot do this it will inevitably be replaced by one that can, since no modern state, however ill developed, can function for long without at least a modicum of governmental services, the most important of which remains the protection of its citizens.

THE "CULTURE" OF A SOCIETY

The common elements of all cultures—The accumulated heritage from the past

Together the social organization, political institutions, technology, economic activities, law, science, art, religion, and thought are called the culture of a society. The cave paintings of the Old Stone age and the mass-production techniques of the twentieth century are equally an expression of the cultural creativeness of these particular societies. They are the work of men living in the society, making use of the physical environment provided for them by nature. Their creativeness is limited by the natural conditions, but not determined by them. The men of the Old Stone Age could hardly have progressed at a single leap to the mass-production technique of the twentieth century or to its representative political government, since cultural inventiveness had first to traverse all the intermediate stages, and the institutions of society had to be modified with each innovation. Men had first to live in settled communities and develop institutions fit for such communities; they had to make the necessary technical inventions for communication, transportation, and production, and again slowly develop social institutions that could release and take advantage of natural human inventiveness.

But it is not necessary for each society to start again from scratch, inventing its techniques from the beginning. It can take advantage of the achievements of its predecessors. Once the Neolithic Revolution had taken place and agriculture was seen to be an improvement over the earlier food gathering, this fundamental invention became a part of the permanent possession of mankind, and any new society could build on the foundations laid by Neolithic man. Cultural change, therefore, is cumulative. The thoughts of mankind have been, as it were, built into the world—and the world has been changed by them, forever. Only if all knowledge of human deeds in the last seven thousand years were lost, would it be necessary for mankind to return to the conditions of the Old Stone Age and start again.

The uniqueness of each culture

Although each society does build on the foundations laid by its predecessors and exploits its cultural heritage, it is also, in a sense, unique. The men of ancient Egypt developed a political institution, the divine kingship, that they were unwilling to abandon, yet which was not successfully copied by other societies; they developed an art that had relatively little influence on subsequent art in other countries but is in perfect consonance with what we know of the Egyptian attitude toward life and death.

The Egyptians seem to have regarded death as having an unbroken continuity with life, and for this reason spent much of their earthly substance in preparing for their "life" in the "hereafter." The Hindus and Buddhists, believing that earthly incarnation is the result of deeds in a former life on earth which require them to reincarnate in order to make compensation, naturally look upon all life as suffering, and earthly striving for betterment as useless labor. The Muslims, believing that their earthly task is to submit to God's will, naturally tend toward fatalism. For a man of the European Middle Ages it was self-evident that the afterlife which would last through eternity was more important than the short span of life he endured upon earth, and he would have been surprised, even shocked, by our belief in earthly progress. Even the Greeks, whose ideas were in so many ways similar to ours, lacked that sense of the importance of building for the future that is characteristic of modern Western civilization.

While the ancient Egyptians denied the fact of change, regarding it as illusory, we in the twentieth century not only recognize the fact of change but try to take advantage of it. We set ourselves goals that we try to achieve, then, having achieved them, we set ourselves ever more distant goals and strive toward them. To the Egyptians the moon was a goddess, not an area for potential human colonization. No society of the past had our belief in and attitude toward what we think of as progress, and a considerable number of those societies looked back to some golden age in the past when man, if not in paradise, was at least happier and more fortunate and better endowed than in the present "age of iron." To us such a notion is an illusion based on no historical evidence since those peoples knew little of their own past. But when we study ancient civilizations it may be wise to look upon their achievements in the light of their beliefs and the limited goals they set themselves, and not as if the ancients had been men like ourselves determined to increase the sum of human knowledge and to use it for the material betterment of themselves and of mankind.

The diffusion of culture

Cultural advances first made within a particular society may be taken up by other societies and spread throughout the entire world. But they must be able to find their proper place in the receiving society; they must find a fertile ground for reception and propagation. The divine kingship of Egypt would not have fitted into the existing contemporary society in Mesopotamia, and even if the Mesopotamian peoples had known of it, they would hardly have tried to graft it onto their existing native institutions. On the other hand, the Christian and other religions have been diffused through many countries where they supplied answers to the problems that the inhabitants of those countries had been trying to solve and where they fitted in with the psychological predisposition of the peoples. The system of parliamentary government whose origins are to be found in medieval England was gradually diffused throughout Europe and, especially after World War I, spread into many countries of the world that desired to accept a form of government that had apparently proved itself to be effective in the war itself. But in other places it has so far failed to take root because of the tenacity of existing institutions.

Technical inventions do not, as a rule, meet with the same opposition as religious or political innovations and can be passed from one society to another with less disturbance. There are thousands of examples of such diffusion of inventions from the earliest times to the present. Probably the idea of food growing and the domestication of animals spread throughout most of the Old World from some center in the Near East, though the possibility of the separate invention of such a fundamental idea cannot be ruled out. Although writing was probably diffused from the Sumerians to the Egyptians, it was almost certainly invented more than once in different areas, for example in China. The Egyptians modified and improved on the Sumerian practice, using their own pictures and symbols, and developing new writing materials available to them but not to the Sumerians. The languages of peoples in historic times have many resemblances to each other, but this fact is best explained by the known movements of peoples, rather than by the "diffusion" of language itself. The diffusion of technical inventions such as gunpowder, printing, and paper can be traced with some certainty by the historian from their first use in one country to their full development in another.

Each society, then, receives by diffusion some of its cultural heritage, to which it adds the products of its own genius. A society may even invent for itself things that have already been developed elsewhere, unknown to it, which it could have received by diffusion if it had enjoyed wider cultural contacts. On the other hand, not all knowledge available to any one people has been preserved or transmitted to others. The ancient Sumerians knew all the basic forms of architecture, but the Egyptians and Greeks did not make use of them; medieval European technical knowledge—as, for instance, of the rotation of crops—was in many ways markedly inferior to that of several earlier peoples. The Renaissance Italians had to reinvent many commercial aids known to the Hellenistic world. Each civilization does not accept the entire cultural heritage of its predecessors and build on it; it accepts only what fits its own environment and its own way of living. The immense technical achievements of the modern age are available to even the most technologically backward peoples of today's world. But few are as yet prepared to make full use of such achievements for improving their own living conditions. Their use would necessarily involve changes in social and political organizations, which may be strongly resistant to such change—even if the new nations possessed adequate natural resources to permit effective use of the new technology. Lastly, the values taken for granted in most Western nations are not necessarily acceptable in the new nations; there are in some countries cultural and religious objections to the use of new techniques. Even non-Western leaders who have been educated in the West may not accept Western technology wholeheartedly once they return to their own countries.

► The work of the historian

HISTORY: SCIENCE OR ART?

As the aforementioned considerations will make clear, the subject matter of the historian is virtually unlimited, since he must concern himself with the totality of events in the past, including those realms covered in more detail by specialists in the various social "sciences." What limits him in practice is his ignorance of those facts about which no one has written, perhaps because they were not considered, by contemporary record keepers or by other historians, to be of historical significance. He can engage in intensive research into sources, such as tax rolls and parish registers, which were written for immediate practical purposes and with no eye to posterity. But this process will bring him no enlightenment that he can communicate to his readers unless he himself has some idea of the wider significance of the facts he has uncovered, and unless he tries to explain this significance to others. The writing of history is, therefore, always an effort to select such facts as seem meaningful to the historian. This very act of selection places his craft outside the canons of science, and denies him the title "scientist," to which some members of the historical fraternity aspire. The his-

torian may use some scientific procedures in his examination of documents and his marshaling of evidence. But, although the study of history is often classed as a social science, the historian can never hope to make predictions and verify them with the accomplished ease of the physical scientist, a defect which ought in itself to place history outside the ranks of the sciences.

Indeed, the historian has a greater affinity with the artist than with the physical scientist. The sculptor, faced with a mass of inert marble, has to give it an aesthetically pleasing form. Before his work begins, as Aristotle used to point out, the marble is all potentiality; it can be molded into anything the sculptor desires within the limitations of his material. The painter, faced with a blank canvas, can paint a madonna or a devil or a simple geometrical design. The novelist has nothing whatever to create with except the letters on his typewriter, which he can order in any way he pleases for the purposes of communicating the contents of his mind and imagination. The historian is limited by his material and by his dedication to truth; he is not entitled to go beyond the facts, but even the facts known to him or knowable by him are myriad, and it is his task to impose an order and pattern on them. So we can speak of the rise and fall of civilizations because we or our predecessors have chosen to regard the separate facts that we know about a particular people as an indication that the civilization in question did "rise" and "fall," and because we have chosen to write the history of that particular people from its own point of view and not from the point of view, for example, of the peoples it enslaved who might not have seen the matter in the same light. When the historian Arnold Toynbee tried, in *A Study of History*, to write a comparative history of civilizations, drawing certain moral lessons from the failure of all historically known civilizations to meet the various challenges that had been presented to them, his list of "civilizations" appeared to many of his colleagues to be an exceptionally arbitrary one. But it is impossible to exclude arbitrariness from the study of history; and perhaps Toynbee was in this no more arbitrary than his critics, even though the latter were fortified by long-standing convention.

THE PURPOSES OF HISTORICAL STUDY

If history is primarily an art and not a science the main purpose for studying it may well be, like the practice of any art, for the enrichment of the whole human being, not for any incidental usefulness it may have in practical life. It is no doubt useful for the statesman to know how some of the problems he faces today had their analogues in the past, and to know how his forebears attempted to solve them. A knowledge of history may, therefore, prevent him from making mistakes similar to those made by his predecessors. A statesman with an intimate knowledge of how peace was made at Vienna in 1815 and at Versailles in 1919 should be able to profit from that knowledge when he himself sits down at a "peace table." If he has an intimate knowledge of the events that culminated in the conference of Munich in September, 1938, he may not be tempted to regard all peacemaking as "appeasement" of the kind practiced by Britain and France at that conference. It is even possible that a knowledge of the Confederation of Delos in the fifth century B.C., and the manner in which the Athenians converted it into an empire and thereby contributed to the outbreak of the war which proved to be their ruin, might be of practical aid to modern statesmen tempted to follow a similar path in the twentieth century A.D. But these are somewhat rare bonuses to be wrested from the study of history.

A much more important benefit lies in acquiring an historical perspective, the recognition that the human race has survived numerous crises in the past, however dangerous they may have appeared at the time; that at different times different peoples have been leaders in world evolution and have spread their influence widely, but that none has ever had the monopoly of world wisdom; that even the achievements of Western Civilization to which this book is devoted rested upon the achievements of earlier peoples whose civilizations fell into decay; and that even if world leadership should one day pass out of the hands of Westerners, Western civilization would still have been one of the mightiest and most creative of civilizations while it lasted, and would have contributed more, at least to the advancement of technology and science and to the material betterment of mankind, than had any of its predecessors.

A student can also learn through the study of history that all peoples have not had the same ideals or the same goals as he and his own people. Through such knowledge, he may acquire a greater tolerance of diversity; he may gain some comprehension of the conservatism of all societies, and may come to realize how slowly social changes have been incorporated into them, how few permanent changes were brought about by even the most radical of revolutions, and how certain outstanding human beings expressed ideals which, after numerous backslidings, at last became a part of the general thinking of mankind—in the process providing at least some evidence for the moral evolution of the human race. With such an historical background a student is better able to judge some of the aberrations of the last decades and to measure them against the other achievements of his own age as well as those of the more distant past.

Since history is the story of all that men have done in the past, the institutions they have built, the thoughts they have harbored, the works of art and literature they have created, and the technology they have put into operation, nothing is foreign to it that was ever done in the past, even as recently as yesterday. Its primary purpose is to make *sense* out of our world, a sense that is missing if we view each existential fact without knowledge of its antecedents or its context. As such, history needs to borrow no prestige from physical science, nor has it any interest in prescribing for the ills of society or in building a better world. This task it gladly leaves to the specialists, each in his own realm, having staked out its own realm as the great provider of information and understanding for such specialists and for all others who wish to know how humanity reached the present moment of time, and lived to tell the tale.

► Suggestions for further reading

PAPER-BOUND BOOKS

Bagby, Philip. *Culture and History: Prolegomena to the Comparative Study of Civilizations.* University of California Press.

Becker, Carl. *Detachment and the Writing of History: Essays and Letters of Carl Becker,* ed. P. Snyder. Cornell. By one of the most renowned of modern American historians, this book is well worth reading for his ideas on his craft.

Bloch, Marc. *The Historian's Craft.* Vintage. Unfinished work by a leading French historian killed in World War II. Thoughtful consideration of the tasks of a historian, especially useful for its evaluation of the different kinds of historical sources.

Bury, John Bagnell. *The Idea of Progress.* Dover. A classic study, first published in 1920, of how men have come to the belief that some progress is to be discerned in history. Mostly concerned with the idea of progress during the eighteenth-century Enlightenment, but including a good section on the nineteenth century.

Carr, Edward Hallett. *What is History?* Yale. Important and stimulating series of lectures, entertaining as well as instructive, on the tasks of the historian, and the different viewpoints held on such matters as historical causation, the idea of progress, and the like. This book and that of Bloch are two of the most useful books on the subject as introductions for the would-be historian and the student.

Clough, Shepard B. *The Rise and Fall of Civilization.* Columbia University Press. Interesting and well-written interpretation, stressing heavily the material advancement of man and its influence on his culture.

Collingwood, R. G. *The Idea of History.* Galaxy. The author's contributions to the philosophy of history, as collected in this posthumous volume, have been both much discussed and influential. Collingwood emphasizes the relativity of all historical judgments.

Gustavson, Carl G. *A Preface to History.* McGraw. Interesting introduction to the study of history, its meaning and purpose.

Hegel, G. W. F. *Lectures on the Philosophy of History,* trans. from the German by J. Sibree. Dover. Seminal lectures by the early nineteenth-century German idealist philosopher, virtually the founder of the modern philosophy of history. The least formidable of Hegel's writings for the beginner. Examples are stimulating and interesting.

Hughes, H. Stuart. *History as Art and Science: Twin Vistas on the Past.* Torchbooks. Discusses in detail the problem dealt with at the end of this chapter. Stimulating and well-written.

Muller, Herbert J. *The Uses of the Past.* Mentor and Galaxy. A series of brief, sympathetic studies of several past societies and their enduring achievements. Examples chosen to illustrate differences between past civilizations and the modern West. Provocative on the issue of what may really be learned from the past. See also Muller's *The Loom of History* (Mentor).

Stern, Fritz, ed. *The Varieties of History: from Voltaire to the Present.* Meridian. Useful anthology of historical writing from earliest examples to the present.

Tholfsen, Trygve. *Historical Thinking: An Introduction.* Harper and Row. A very substantial work, but by no means easy reading.

CASE-BOUND BOOKS

Highet, Gilbert. *The Migration of Ideas.* New York: Oxford University Press, 1954. Stimulating little book on how culture and ideas are diffused, with thought-provoking illustrations from all periods of history.

Namier, Lewis B. *Avenues of History.* New York: The Macmillan Company, 1952. Influential British historian's essays on his specialty. First essay especially valuable on the task of the historian and the functions of historical study.

CHAPTER 2

PREHISTORY

▶ **The changing picture of prehistoric man**

The sciences of archaeology, paleontology, and anthropology on whose findings the historian has to draw for his presentation of prehistory are not very old, and their techniques have been changing rapidly during the twentieth century. Moreover, these findings have had to be modified with almost every major discovery of prehistoric men and their tools and refuse. Even now everything said in this chapter is in the nature of an interim report.

During the period of history covered by written records such difficulties seldom arise. New and original interpretations may become fashionable. Important new documents may cast a different light on hitherto unchallenged assumptions in limited areas. But the basic facts remain true; no new discoveries will change them or alter the fundamental picture of an age in the way in which the picture presented by earlier prehistorians has been modified by the patient labors of archaeologists in the last decades. The major reason for the changing picture of prehistoric man is of course the recent discoveries,

especially in Africa. Scarcely less important has been the increasing use of the carbon 14 technique for dating organic matter. This technique was still in its infancy when the first edition of this book was written.[1] It has now been greatly improved in itself, and it has been used to find the approximate date for almost every important discovery within the limits of its usefulness. Other techniques such as the determination of fluorine content and, more recently, the measurement of radioactive potassium that decays to

[1] Briefly stated, the method is as follows: All living organisms incorporate a very small amount of radioactive carbon 14, but obviously cease to assimilate it when they die. This carbon has a half life of 5568 years and disintegrates according to a consistent and predictable time schedule. It is now possible to detect on a sensitive Geiger counter the amount of carbon 14 that still remains in a long-dead organism and thus calculate the period during which it died. The older the organism the more difficult exact calculations become and thus the less certain the dates. There is always a margin of error, sometimes considerable, in all dating by this method; but, on the whole, results obtained from the use of the technique have checked fairly closely with dates known from historical records, giving scientists encouragement to think that dates not to be checked by other means are reasonably accurate also. The most sensitive of Geiger counters at the present time are limited to about 25,000–30,000 years.

► chronological chart

Ages of Prehistory (Approximate Dates B.C.)

Types of Men	Tool Cultures	Geological Epoch	
(Proconsul Ape)		Miocene	20,000,000
Zinjanthropus (Paranthropus— Africa)	Lower Paleolithic	Pliocene	1,750,000
Homo habilis (Australopithecus— Africa)			1,750,000
Homo erectus (Java, China, Africa)		Early Pleistocene	500,000
Neanderthal and Neanderthaloid		Late Pleistocene	150,000
Homo sapiens (Cromagnon— Europe and others)	Upper Paleolithic	Late Pleistocene (sometimes called Holocene or Recent)	40,000
	Mesolithic (Natufian, Maglemosian)		8,000
	Neolithic (Near East)		7,000
	Copper Age		4,500

These dates, as indicated in the text, are all disputed, and are likely to be disputed for an indefinite period. But the above approximations would probably be accepted by a substantial number of scholars at the present time.

argon gas have served to supplement the carbon 14 technique.

Until lately much was written about the way of life of prehistoric men, derived from analogies with present-day "primitive" men, such as the South African Bushmen and Hottentots, and the Australian aboriginals. This approach has been finding fewer exponents and has been largely replaced by imaginative efforts to reconstruct the life of prehistoric men on the basis of examination of the actual debris left behind them. Lastly, the science of comparative anatomy has continued to make great strides, and it is now possible to construct from even relatively meager anatomical finds, such as a part of a jawbone, a generally acceptable picture of its owner. Anthropologists may engage in lengthy and heated controversies over a particular find and its significance, but an ever-increasing body of knowledge is becoming acceptable to all. Thus new finds can be fitted within this accepted framework; and it now seems unlikely that any such fraud as the famous Piltdown skull, unmasked in 1953, would be accepted by any substantial body of anthropologists as a part of a genuine early man. Indeed, when this skull was finally shown to have been manufactured (obviously by or under the instructions of an experienced anthropologist) from an ape and an ordinary man of the Neolithic age, artificially aged by chemical means, remarkably few anthropologists needed to be convinced, and many had already expressed their reservations on the genuineness of the skull, on the sole basis of anatomical and historical considerations.

▶ **The first beginnings of man**

THE EVOLUTION OF MAN AS A SPECIES

The evolutionary theory of the origin of man has been greatly modified since Darwin first propounded it in crude form in the middle of the nineteenth century and it explains reasonably well what we know of early man. According to this theory those species of living organisms that were best fitted to survive in their environment did survive and were gradually modified in form by the process of mutation, a process that can be observed in the laboratory in the case of certain animals. The ancestors of man were not those most specialized and suitable for a particular environment. On the contrary, they were more "generalized" and adaptable. From time to time new mutations appeared in the species, and those of them that could survive best in a changed environment did so and propagated, while the older, less adaptable species died out. The huge animals became overspecialized and incapable of adaptation, perhaps in a modified environment, and so became extinct; while the smaller, unspecialized creatures, forced to adapt themselves or perish, developed mutations with survival value. Thus, it is hypothesized, the ancestors of man first came on to dry land from the ocean, lived for countless aeons in trees, and at last descended to the earth and began to walk upright, in the process increasing their brain capacity.

It may also be noted that the prevalent opinion today is that those early types of man who are not regarded as the direct ancestors of present-day man (*homo sapiens*), likewise became overspecialized. Being unable to take the step forward in evolution that could have converted them into *homo sapiens*, they continued without change on the same path as their ancestors and became extinct, either destroyed by *homo sapiens* or unable to survive in the new climatic conditions that favored a more adaptable creature. Nevertheless there is no direct evidence for the forcible destruction of Neanderthal man by *homo sapiens;* and Neanderthals had survived similar climatic conditions at least once before in their history. Thus their swift collapse, unless *homo sapiens* evolved from them, remains one of the great unsolved problems of prehistory.

▶ **Geological and climatic changes in man's habitat**

Geologists divide the immensely long history of the earth into four (sometimes five) well-defined eras. The most recent of these is the Cenozoic (dominated by the mammals) that is itself subdivided into the Eocene, Oligocene, Miocene, Pliocene, and Pleistocene epochs. We are still living in the later part of the Pleistocene epoch, though some geologists have preferred to speak of the Holocene, or Wholly Recent epoch to describe the interval since the last glaciation, an epoch covering the last 10,000 years.

The Pleistocene has been marked by continual upheavals in the earth's crust for reasons that are still imperfectly understood. Extensive mountain building and volcanic activity have continued throughout this age, and glaciers have advanced and receded several times. As a result of these changes lands now separated by sea have been connected by land bridges, for example, Siberia with Alaska, England with the Continent, and others. The glacial ages of the Pleistocene bear the European names of Günz, Mindel, Riss, and Würm, with different names for the American phases that closely correspond to them. The beginning of the Pleistocene epoch may be placed at about 1,000,000 B.C., and the onset of the last (Würm) glaciation as about 70,000 B.C. The glaciers finally receded about 10,000 years ago (ca. 8000 B.C.), and we have been living in an interglacial period ever since. It may be noted that the last interglacial period (Riss-Würm) lasted for about 30,000 years(100,000–70,000 B.C.), and that all the glacial periods have been marked by an increase of rainfall outside the glacial areas, giving rise to a named series of "pluvial" periods, especially in Africa.

▶ **Earliest men**

THE BEGINNINGS IN AFRICA

There now seems little doubt that the earliest human beings (hominids), all of which have become extinct, emerged in Africa during the late Pliocene epoch. Apes had already evolved in Africa as early as the Miocene period, some of them quite flexible and adaptable, and therefore regarded frequently as the direct ancestors of man (notably a type called Proconsul, now extinct).

Numerous other species developed in succeeding epochs and spread elsewhere in the world. Important finds in central and southern Africa have revealed the existence of a hominid who is now called Australopithecus as well as other creatures of about the same age, known as Paranthropi (ca. 2,500,000 B.C.). Among the latter must be counted Zinjanthropus, who was discovered by L. S. B. Leakey in the Olduvai Gorge in present day Tanzania in 1959, and who was for several years regarded as the first true man. However, later discoveries by Leakey in the same site included several specimens of what is almost certainly a true man, and probably a direct ancestor of present day man.[2] These latter finds, all of Australopitheci of a kind similar to others found in southern Africa, revealed a type of man who made tools, and was therefore named *homo habilis* by his finder. The appearance of this hominid marks the beginning of the Lower Paleolithic culture that lasted until the appearance of *homo sapiens* on the scene in considerable numbers about 40,000 B.C.

WAS HOMO SAPIENS CONTEMPORARY WITH THE EARLY APE-MEN?

The Olduvai Gorge proved to be exceptionally rich in prehistoric finds. In recent years many strata have been excavated, revealing a progressive development of tools

---

[2] The anatomical dividing line between man and ape will probably always be a matter for dispute. Although recent investigations of chimpanzees have shown that these animals make use of some aids to food gathering that may be thought of as tools, the use of tools in general, and above all their improvement in the light of experience, is preeminently a human activity, and the easiest way of determining whether fossilized primates were indeed men and not animals is by determining if they used tools. When no tools can be associated with a particular fossil, then a study of the anatomical structure can provide information, such as the capacity of the brain case, the size and massiveness of the jaw, whether the creature walked upright, and similar important details that may in total amount to a strong probability that it was a man and not an animal. *Pithecanthropus erectus* or Java Man has been classified as a man although no tools are associated with him. But obviously a man can better be judged by his artifacts than by his physical structure.

from primitive pebbles to true hand axes obtained by the process of flaking, all of which represents a culture that continued throughout the Middle Pleistocene until comparatively recent times. In addition to these tools, which were presumably used by Australopithecus, specimens of another human species have been discovered which have no significant variations from the hominids of Asia, who have been known for many decades. These hominids, who walked erect, have now all been classified by the general name *homo erectus*.

THE ASIAN HOMINIDS—JAVA AND PEKING MEN

For several years from 1890 onward a Dutch surgeon named Eugene Dubois began to discover specimens of a hominid who was believed to stand upright and who was named *Pithecanthropus erectus javanenesis*. It was many years before these discoveries were recognized as genuine, and Dubois himself had to undergo much ridicule. Some confirmation was provided for the genuineness of his finds when another hominid, named *Sinanthropus pekinensis* was discovered near Peking in China. This hominid definitely used tools, of the "chopper–chopping" type, not flaked tools like those found in Africa. Peking man knew the use of fire, and the evidence is strong that he was, like some Neanderthal men, a cannibal. Both these Asian types of hominid, like *homo erectus* of the Olduvai Gorge, are believed to have lived in the Mid-

Neolithic dwellings (Scotland). (MINISTRY OF PUBLIC BUILDINGS & WORKS, EDINBURGH, CROWN COPYRIGHT RESERVED)

dle Pleistocene era, or the later part of the early Pleistocene, and a convenient approximate date for them all is 500,000 B.C.

EARLY TOOL CULTURES
OF PRE-NEANDERTHAL MEN

Although fossilized men are very scarce indeed for the period of the Early and Middle Pleistocene prior to the arrival on the scene of Neanderthal man, this does not apply to their cultures. In Africa, especially east-central Africa, there are numerous finds of pebble tools and hand axes. It now appears probable that the hand-axe technique spread from Africa into Europe, western Asia, and southern India. In Europe this tool culture is known as Abbevillian and Acheulian from the European areas where it was first identified. Sharper flaked tools,

especially useful for skinning animals, became prevalent in northern Europe during the second (Mindel) glaciation and remained for millenniums afterward. This Clactonian culture gave place to the Levalloisian culture, marked by the more sophisticated use of flakes during the subsequent Riss glaciation. It is generally believed that the Acheulian hand axe people retreated to the south during the glaciations, retaining their old hand axe tradition with an admixture of flaked tools. This attempt to trace the comings and goings of prehistoric man during these long ages is necessarily a tentative reconstruction based solely on the age and type of tools they employed. With the coming of Neanderthal man in the interglacial period following the Riss glaciation, far more information becomes available (*ca.* 150,000 B.C. onward).

Tools of prehistoric men, showing various phases of development, and revealing why some of these tools were called "coups de poing" [blows of fist]. (COURTESY AMERICAN MUSEUM OF NATURAL HISTORY)

▶ Neanderthal man and the Neanderthaloids

PHYSICAL STRUCTURE AND DISTRIBUTION

The first Neanderthal man was discovered in the Neanderthal Gorge in Germany in 1856, and enough skeletons have been discovered in the last century and enough sites have been unearthed to give us what must be a fairly substantial picture of both the men and their culture (most of it Mousterian, after the French site of Le Moustier). Neanderthal men, it is safe to say, spread into southwestern Asia and North Africa, and at least as far to the northeast as Turkestan. Their brain capacity in some instances comes close to that of modern men, but in other respects they resemble the ancient pithecanthropi of Asia more than they resemble *homo sapiens*. Their skulls were large, thick walled, and low vaulted, with huge brow ridges, a broad nose, massive chinless jaws, large teeth, and clumsy legs and arms, suggestive of a not fully upright posture—not unlike the general picture of cave men as popularized in so many comic strips. Though they lived mainly in the open, at least until the onset of the Würm glaciation, during the latter period they stayed in the colder north, and either lived in caves or retreated frequently to them for shelter. A number of finds have also been made of men classed as Neanderthaloid hominids, who were contemporary with Neanderthal men and resemble them strongly in many respects. Nevertheless, there are some outstanding differences between the two species, leading some anthropologists to think that they and not Neanderthal man himself evolved into the *homo sapiens* who appeared during the Würm glaciation and thereafter peopled most of the earth. At the onset of this glaciation, perhaps about 70,000 B.C., Neanderthal men had reached their widest geographical distribution. Some samples of the species survived to as late as 40,000 B.C., but no reliable evidence has ever been uncovered of their survival later than this, and it is not known whether any of them persisted into the interglacial period that followed.

NEANDERTHAL CULTURE

Neanderthal men used flaked tools, scrapers, and small hand axes, seeming especially to favor the triangular or heart-shaped forms. Their tools were strictly utilitarian and, unlike the tools of their successors, show no signs of having been modeled with any esthetic purpose in view. They made very little use of bone or antler, but in their successful hunting, which enabled their species to survive, they probably used wooden spears, stone balls, and pit traps to destroy their prey. In spite of his failure to make any significant innovations in tool technique, Neanderthal man for the first time, as far as we know, paid considerable attention to the burial of his dead. Corpses have been discovered on which elaborate care was expended. Tools and funeral offerings were found with them, and the bodies in some instances were painted with red ochre. A Neanderthaloid child was buried in Siberia together with horns from mountain goats, which appear to have been placed upright around the corpse. Though such practices clearly indicate the growth of ceremonial customs and rituals of the kind we associate with religion, it is hazardous to leap to the conclusion, as some commentators have done, that Neanderthal men believed in a future life. Other explanations might equally fit the observed facts. The burial of tools may indicate no more than that the tools were inseparably connected with a man during his lifetime and that it was considered dangerous for any other to use them after his death. The wedding ring, sometimes buried today with its wearer, does not imply a belief that it will continue to be worn in the hereafter. Ceremonial burials today are surely more a gesture of respect to the dead than the result of a belief in either the immortality of the soul or the resurrection of the body. Even so, the funerary customs of

Neanderthal men, coupled with the very considerable variety of similar customs among Upper Paleolithic men as well as other practices suggestive of magic and ritual among the latter, certainly may suggest to us that there was a widespread belief in the unseen world among both peoples—as indeed exists without exception among all "primitive" peoples today.

▶ Upper Paleolithic Age—The arrival of *homo sapiens*

During the course of the Würm glaciation, *homo sapiens*, as already noted, suddenly appeared in large numbers and within a short time had peopled most of the earth. Not only did he appear in the Old World, but also in the New World, where no evidence of pre-sapiens types has ever been uncovered. As yet the earliest date given by the carbon 14 technique for the existence of man in America is a little before 20,000 B.C., or during the glaciation called Wisconsin in America (Würm in Europe). It is assumed that he came over the land bridge between Siberia and Alaska, which existed at that period. Evidence has been found of his presence as far south as the Straits of Magellan by 6700 B.C., a really prodigious journey if he really came over from Siberia by the Bering Straits and only by that route. Since prehistoric man in America lies outside the scope of this book, it need only be noted here that many difficulties still remain to be cleared up in connection with the peopling of America in prehistoric times and the rise of the many ancient cultures, especially in Mexico and Peru. Archaeological research is relatively new on this continent but is progressing rapidly, and it may be that future excavations and discoveries will present a more coherent picture of American development than has so far been achieved.

THE DIFFERENTIATION OF HUMAN RACES

There are no really significant anatomical differences between *homo sapiens* of the Upper Paleolithic age and men as they exist today in different parts of the world—with the exception of a few types such as the pygmies and bushmen. But a sufficiently long period has elapsed since the beginning of this age for *homo sapiens* to have been differentiated into the separate races of today, with their relatively minor anatomical differences. It was almost certainly during the early milleniums of the Upper Paleolithic period that what we think of as the races of today were differentiated. All belong to the species of *homo sapiens*. But in different parts of the world certain variants of the species have lived and continue to live today, perhaps because of their superior adaptation to climatic and other conditions of their environment. The major races such as the Caucasoid, Negroid, and Mongoloid have themselves been subdivided, even though there is no consensus on the subdivisions. The Mediterranean branch of the Caucasian race, for example, is better fitted to survive in the sun drenched areas of their habitat than the Nordic group with its fair skin and lesser pigmentation. The peoples of northern India, also a subdivision of the Caucasian race, are now regarded as brown men. It has been suggested that in India the peoples with darker pigmentation were better fitted to survive in that area, and thus through intermarriage with their own kind they became progressively darker.

However this may be, it remains true that no substantial difference has ever been discovered that might enable it to be said that one race is in any way superior mentally or physically to another, though each may have become better adapted to living in its own particular environment and may not be so well suited to living in another. Nevertheless, account should be taken of the great adaptability of mankind, which has made it possible for men of all races to survive in any environment, and for later generations descended from them to become completely adapted and acclimatized.

TOOL CULTURES

It seems probable from present evidence that the first of the Upper Paleolithic peoples appeared in western Asia, especially in Palestine, and from there spread to Europe. In Europe so many sites have been uncovered that it is possible to distinguish a number of successive cultural periods, all marked by the appearance of the superior stone knives that are the hallmark of the Upper Paleolithic age. These separate cultures, called after their French sites, all tentatively dated by the carbon 14 method are as follows: Châtelperronian (32,000 to 28,500 B.C.), Aurignacian (28,000 to 22,000 B.C.), Gravettian (22,000 to 18,000 B.C.), Solutrean (18,000 to 15,000 B.C.), and Magdalenian (15,000 to perhaps as late as 8000 B.C.). A skeleton found at Combe Capelle was probably the bearer of the Châtelperronian culture. He was soon followed by Cro-Magnon man with his large brain and anatomical characteristics similar to those of present-day Europeans, and then, perhaps, followed by Chancelade man who is represented by too few examples to enable his anatomical type to be strictly determined. These two types were the bearers of subsequent Upper Paleolithic cultures. The differences between them, as far as can at present be ascertained, are no more than exist between the present surviving races of man. Discoveries of Upper Paleolithic men in China suggest that Mongolian characteristics were already noticeable in that area. This is also true of the earliest American finds.

The Aurignacian tool culture was far more sophisticated than the Châtelperronian and was so distinctive and widespread that it strongly suggests a single migrating people. The Aurignacians appear also to have been the first people who began to decorate caves with drawings and engravings, a tradition carried on with increasing skill for over 20,000 years. The Gravettians seem to have arisen, or soon concentrated, in southern Russia and western Siberia, whence they spread westward as far as France and England. The Solutrean culture was notable for a special kind of pressure flaking, a technique later practiced by the historical Egyptians, used especially for spearheads and dagger blades. Lastly, the Magdalenian culture, which flourished in a limited geographical area of southern France and northern Spain, brought all these earlier tendencies to their peak of perfection and was responsible for the best of the cave paintings, shortly to be described, and for numerous other forms of art. It should be added that the Upper Paleolithic culture moved into Africa during the late Magdalenian period, creating the Capsian culture at the end of the Upper Paleolithic age; the rock art of northern and central Africa is believed to have been derived in this way from Europe.

All Upper Paleolithic peoples lived primarily by hunting, to which they devoted far more inventiveness than did earlier peoples. In addition to stone, they made extensive use of bone and antler, from which barbed spears, fish gorgets and harpoons with detachable heads and barbs like curved teeth (Magdalenian) were made. From stone they manufactured chisels, gouges, and awls which could be used to work the bone and for carving and engraving. The tools themselves were often made in an artistic manner. The Magdalenian peoples used an eyed needle made of bone. Several of these peoples made the first mechanical aids to hunting, a spear thrower and the bow and arrow, both of which permitted hunting from a distance, thus revolutionizing their way of life. The Gravettian cultures produced carved figurines commonly called "Venuses," which are widespread throughout the area of this culture.

THE EARLIEST BUILDINGS

The earliest man-made buildings date from the Upper Paleolithic period and probably belonged to mammoth hunters of the Gravettian culture in Czechoslovakia, Russia, and Siberia where suitable natural caves were scarce. The houses so far excavated appear to have been each used by several families. One was oval in shape, measuring about 40 feet in length with five hearths. It is not known what was used for roofing material, if anything, possibly skins weighed down by branches much like a tent.

Another house was surrounded by a wide circular wall made of limestone and clay. In Czechoslovakia coal, which was close to the surface in that area, was already in use for fuel. Other houses of the same period were made by digging a kind of cellar and apparently using logs both for the roof and as support for the sides.

CAVE ART

The outstanding feature of Upper Paleolithic culture is its cave art, an art that compares not unfavorably with any art man has produced in the centuries since. It begins in the Aurignacian period with black and white drawings and engravings, and culminates in the tremendous polychrome paintings of the mid-Magdalenian epoch, which are familiar to us from the numerous reproductions that have been published, especially from Lascaux in southern France and Altamira in northern Spain. The pig-

ments used were mineral oxides that have survived in all their freshness in the special conditions of the caves until the present day (though in 1963 French authorities felt compelled to close down the caves temporarily since exposure to air and human breathing had begun to damage them).

This cave art has posed numerous problems to those of us who wish to understand as well as esthetically appreciate it. Some facts require explanation. In almost all cases paintings are superimposed upon others, and upon still earlier drawings and engravings. The caves in which they were painted show few signs of human habitation. Often the paintings are hundreds of yards from the entrance of the caves; and sometimes, as in the Cave of the Two Brothers and Tuc d'Audoubert in the department of Ariège (southern France), the inner chambers where the paintings were made are almost inaccessible, requiring the visitor in some instances to inch along a narrow passage on his stomach. Other paintings are made high up on the walls, which must have necessitated either the building of a scaffolding or the use of a ladder, unless the artist stood on the shoulders of a companion. The earlier engravings were sometimes of human hands, both imprints filled in by the artist ("positives"), and others ("negatives") with the paint apparently sprayed around the hand while it was held in position. There are very few human beings portrayed at any time; there are rather composite figures of human beings and animals. The vast majority of paintings are of animals, sometimes extraordinarily vivid and lifelike, stressing power and movement. Many of

The "Venus of Willendorf," a carved limestone figurine, perhaps as much as 25,000 years old. The lack of importance given to the head and the stress laid upon the sexual characteristics strongly suggest that it was a cult-object of magico-religious significance, similar to much later figurines used in the worship of the great Earth-Mother. (ERICH LESSING, MAGNUM)

these animals have spears, darts, and other weapons transfixing them. Though light was certainly provided by torches made from animal fat, no great amount of light can have been available in the utter darkness of these caves. It is safe to say that no modern artist could conceivably paint these animals in similar conditions.

What then do the paintings seem to reveal about the capacities of our Upper Paleolithic ancestors and their purposes and beliefs? First, surely, that they had an extraordinarily accurate visual memory, as no models could possibly have been used. Second, they must have acquired, probably from long living in caves, the ability to see clearly, if not in total darkness, then at least in very dim light. It may also not be too far-fetched to suggest that they identified themselves imaginatively with the animals they hunted and livingly experienced their vitality and strength. The few human figures painted or sculpted have no such vitality and give the impression of being cult objects emphasizing fertility, rather than naturalistic representations. However, there are some stylized, almost abstract, drawings dating from the Mesolithic period in eastern Spain, which have much charm. It seems clear that the paintings were not there to be looked at and admired—unless perhaps on the occasions of special festivals—or more effort would have been made to expunge the previous picture instead of painting over it. Some of the caves, for example Cave of the Two Brothers, suggest that they were regarded as temples. The long journey to the heart of this cave is concluded at a dead end, where after passing animal guardians, the beholder is suddenly brought face to face with the terrifying figure known as the Sorcerer, a part animal part human creature with human legs and thighs and an animal head with powerful staring eyes. It is hardly possible to doubt that this being presides over the whole and that the journey toward him is a journey of initiation wherein the guardians are passed one by one until the initiate reaches the Presence. Yet in other caves there is no suggestion of anything comparable.

The usual explanation for the drawings of animals transfixed by weapons is that a hunting magic was involved; that the artist, whether or not he was also a hunter, painted his pictures underground, with the approval of his people, while his fellows hunted them above. This explanation certainly would account for the freedom allowed the artist to paint in a society dependent on the success of the hunt and in need of all its members to help in it. On this hypothesis the act of painting would be of more importance than contemplating the finished product, as evidently was the case. But this explanation would not wholly account for the excellence of the paintings nor their continued improvement through the millenniums unless there was a very

Archers painted in the rock shelters of eastern Spain (late Paleolithic or Mesolithic). (AMERICAN MUSEUM OF NATURAL HISTORY)

close connection in the Paleolithic mind between the artistic merit of the painting and the success of the magic. What does seem clear is that in the widest sense of the word the paintings were religious in inspiration, and that the caves in which they appear were to some degree shrines. It is probable also that the caves were visited on several ceremonial occasions, since there are imprints still extant in the clay of feet that appear to be dancing. In the absence of written records a full explanation will certainly never be available to us. But we may still be permitted to marvel at the accomplishment of these ancient ancestors of ours who were able to do so much with such primitive techniques and, within the limits of their subject matter, to achieve a mastery that, in the opinion of many, has never been equalled in the centuries since.

▶ Mesolithic Age

Between the Neolithic Revolution, marked by the domestication of farm animals and the planting and harvesting of agricultural crops, and the Upper Paleolithic age just described, prehistorians now recognize an intermediate period when the preliminary steps which led to the Revolution were taken. In many respects this is an exceptionally interesting epoch. The Würm glaciation had come to an end, and the more favorable climatic conditions made for easier living. *Homo sapiens* was slowly peopling the earth, and a great variety of new occupations became possible, notably those connected with the sea. Cave art had virtually come to an end in the area occupied by the Magdalenian peoples. But in certain other areas such as eastern Spain and Palestine other artistic techniques were being born, and the range of tools was widening, even though few were now decorated in an artistic manner.

As far as can be determined at the present time, the two major centers of Mesolithic culture were in the lands to the east of the Mediterranean, especially Palestine (Natufian culture), and the northern plains of Europe (Maglemosian culture). Southern Europe appears to have contributed little that was new in this period, and it was several millenniums before the Neolithic Revolution spread to Europe from its places of origin in western Asia. The Natufian culture appears to have been originally based on hunting. But as time went on the Natufians, as is evident from their sickles and reaping knives, began to harvest natural grasses that grew in the area. No evidence as yet suggests that these grasses were planted or that grain was ever stored. But pestles and mortars, and querns have been found in which the grain was pounded and beaten. Both the Natufians and Maglemosians domesticated the dog, the first animal known to have been tamed as a helper of man. Probably the first dogs were scavengers around the Mesolithic settlements, and were later utilized in the hunt.

The Natufian, like other Mesolithic cultures, is marked by the wide use of microliths (apparently invented during the Upper Paleolithic age), small sharpened stones used with weapons such as spearheads and reed arrows. The blades of Natufian bone sickles contained several such microliths set in grooves in the bone. Late Natufian culture, which shades over into the Neolithic, has been brought to light in the successive deposits of the ancient "city" of Jericho, built around an important desert oasis. Here at one period the people lived in round huts with sunken floors and walls built of brick, the whole surrounded by a stone wall with inner stairways and round towers obviously used for defensive purposes—even though here as elsewhere there is very little evidence for much warfare either in Mesolithic or Neolithic times. At a later stage the houses were made up of rectangular rooms set around a courtyard, and it is estimated that Jericho may have had a population as large as 3,000. There is some evidence that the Natufian villages also kept herds of goats, in which case it is likely that wild goats were the second species of animal to be domesticated. Funerary customs included the making of death masks from the skulls of the dead men. These were filled with clay and modeled in a human likeness with the eyes inlaid with shells. The people were frequently buried with fine head-dresses and necklaces of delicate stone beads.

By the carbon 14 method the date of this Natufian culture is the eighth millennium B.C., and represents a transitional stage to the Neolithic. The Jericho area, indeed, is certainly one of the centers where the Neolithic Revolution began, though whether it holds absolute priority in time has yet to be determined.

The Maglemosian culture (Denmark) in northern Europe was a hunting culture like its predecessors, but far more use was made of maritime resources, possibly because in the changed climate hunting in the forests had become more difficult. It is evident that large numbers of these Mesolithic men lived by fishing as well as by hunting. The use of microliths for hafting axes and similar tools as well as for harpoon barbs is well authenticated, and the hafted axes must have been very valuable for the necessary work of felling the forests. Hard igneous rocks were worked for the first time to obtain sharp points and cutting edges. Far more tools were now made of bone and antler, including improved fish spears and harpoons and fish-hooks not too different from those used today. The Maglemosian peoples also used fish nets and fish traps, and some of their neighbors already used a sleigh. A dugout canoe dated at 6250 B.C. by carbon 14 has been found in Holland. These peoples also decorated their tools and implements, sometimes with intricate geometric patterns; they carved animals in amber and made many different kinds of pendants and amulets. The Maglemosians domesticated a dog which was smaller than that domesticated by the Natufians. It resembled a chow. But as yet there is no evidence that this Mesolithic culture of the Maglemosians developed any agriculture. The Neolithic Revolution, by which we mean the domestication of animals and the planned growth of plants, arrived in these hunting areas of northern Europe several milleniums after it had been spread throughout much of the East.

► Neolithic Revolution

BEGINNINGS OF AGRICULTURE

Some anthropologists today are inclined to play down the "Neolithic Revolution" on the ground that it was more in the nature of an "evolutionary" outgrowth of previous developments. It must be admitted that the name "Neolithic Revolution" is somewhat loosely applied, since the "revolution" began in the Near East at a time when tools characteristic of the Neolithic age had not yet been developed. If a Mesolithic age is recognized for the Near East, as it is not by all anthropologists and prehistorians, then the "Neolithic Revolution" presumably began in this "Mesolithic age," and reached Europe when Europe was in its Neolithic age. However, these considerations are not of great importance to the nonspecialized student, and the "Neolithic Revolution" is a term hallowed by time. This historian, at least, regards it as possibly the most important "revolution" in all history in the sense that it changed the way of life of the peoples of the world in a fundamental manner, making possible all subsequent civilizations. Yet, as will be recognized from our account of the Mesolithic, it was not truly a sudden change but grew gradually out of the practices of those peoples who had settled down in communities even before they had learned to plant and harvest crops. Nevertheless, it was a tremendous intellectual advance that was at the root of the revolution.

If we consider the matter, it is not obvious that a plant grows from a seed. It is possible that many of us would never notice the way in which plant life is propagated if we were not first shown the process. If we lived in a land where the only plants were perennials or where the plants were naturally fertilized year by year by wind, birds, or bees, we would take these phenomena for granted, as no doubt did the Mesolithic peoples who for hundreds of years harvested grain without learning how to plant it. Like them, we would harvest what we needed each year; then when the soil from this constant self-seeding and monoculture became exhausted, we would take this as a natural thing and pass on to new lands still unspoiled.

It requires acute observation to see *how* a plant grows, to perceive the sequence of cause and effect between the seed and the plant. Then it requires experiment to take a seed, plant it, and at last to see it grow, fulfilling the presumption of the experiment. This was the act of someone whom we may legitimately think of as the first practical scientist, some nameless leader. From the evidence at present available, it seems likely that the idea spread by diffusion from its original center in the Near East, being first taken up by local communities and gradually penetrating further afield, reaching parts of eastern Europe soon after 5000 B.C. and Britain about 3000 B.C. In some parts of Europe the older food-gathering, hunting culture persisted until much later times. It still seems probable that the Neolithic Revolution in America took place independently of the Old World, and as early as at least 5000 B.C., a date when diffusion from Siberia is regarded as unlikely.

DIFFUSION OF THE REVOLUTION

The Jericho culture, already mentioned, is at present the earliest known Neolithic culture (about 7000 B.C.). Two other centers, the Belt Cave culture in Iran just south of the Caspian Sea and the Jarmo culture near the source of the Tigris in the Kurdish hills, appear to have originated somewhat later than Jericho. However, these centers had become full Neolithic cultures by 6000 B.C., with at first domesticated sheep and goats and no evidence of agriculture, then shortly afterwards pigs and cows and a wide range of domesticated plants including wheat and barley. The Belt Cave peoples lived in two large caves, whereas the Jarmo and Jericho peoples lived in substantial villages. These three centers are the major sites excavated so far, and it seems extremely likely that others will be found in this general area where it appears most probable that the Neolithic Revolution originated. Three important sites, two in Iraq (Tell Hassuna and Tell Halaf) and one in Iran

(Sialk) from a rather later period have revealed the existence of an extensive hand-made pottery industry. Similar pottery is known from other Neolithic sites, including the later phases in Jericho, from about the beginning of the sixth millennium B.C. Both the Iranian and Iraqi sites are not believed to be by any means the oldest in their areas, and it is probable that older sites will yet be uncovered. At Sialk were found the first known tools made of beaten copper, which was produced no doubt from local copper deposits not available elsewhere. From Asia Minor comes the first evidence of weaving, followed by the rapid growth of textiles in Egypt and the Near East.

From such excavations as have been made to date it would therefore appear that the domestication of animals and planned agriculture originated in the area of Western Asia and were quickly diffused locally. The island of Cyprus had a Neolithic culture from the beginning of the sixth millennium, but Egypt did not acquire it, as far as is known, until the middle of the fifth millennium.

Fired pottery became a widespread industry throughout the Asiatic and later the Egyptian Neolithic areas. Since it is quite possible for the art of firing clay to be discovered by chance, it may be that it was invented in several centers, as it almost certainly was in America. The Neolithic mode of life required the use of storage facilities and containers of all sizes. Once the technique had been invented the potters quickly began to improve the form of their wares and to paint and decorate them. It is generally believed that women were the first potters and during the later stages of the Neolithic period were the bearers of such artistic traditions as there were. There is no certain evidence of the use of a potter's wheel until several millenniums later; but some mechanical method of turning the pottery while it was being molded was probably in use. Plain figurines exist from as early as Upper Paleolithic times, almost invariably of women, suggesting to some that a cult of a "Mother Goddess," represented also in much larger carved figures, was widespread.

The great art of the Upper Paleolithic was never repeated. Only in the production of exceptionally beautiful battle axes, some of them decorated, and in the painting of pottery, usually in abstract and geometrical patterns, did Neolithic man display much artistry.

Textile weaving and basketry were the new crafts of this age. Rope nets had long been used for fishing, but weaving was new and required the prior invention of spinning. In most of the earlier examples of weaving flax was used as the raw material, leading in dynastic Egypt to the production of beautiful linen garments, though wool was preferred in Sumer. Basketry, which made use of whatever local materials were available, appeared even before Neolithic times, but was greatly developed during this age when the need arose for containers for the new farming life. Tools were not greatly changed except for the addition of reaping knives, sickles, and hoes. The digging stick was used for preparing the ground. The ox-drawn wooden plow appeared at least as early as 3000 B.C. in Mesopotamia, Egypt, and probably in India, when it is mentioned in written records. None has survived from an earlier date than this.

In the city-states of Sumer, to be discussed in Chapter 4, a new and more complex style of living was being developed by the beginning of the fifth millennium B.C., which has been called, somewhat dubiously, an urban revolution. While bronze was coming into use and written records were for the first time being produced in Mesopotamia, the Neolithic Revolution was gradually being diffused throughout Europe, most of which remained Neolithic (that is, without metal and without written records) for several millenniums more. Nevertheless, the European Neolithic is of considerable interest since the cultures that have been examined developed further along their own lines. We have, for example, especially detailed knowledge of a series of communities known as the Lake Dwellers of Switzerland. It was formerly thought that these people built their houses on piles and dropped their refuse in the water, where it was preserved far better

than in most excavated sites on dry land. This theory has now been abandoned, and it is currently believed that the houses were built close to the marshy shores of lakes and were merely raised when the water rose too high for the comfort of their inhabitants. However this may be, the accumulated debris gives us a remarkable picture of the life of these Lake Dwellers. It is clear from the number and quality of the hafted stone axes—and indeed this might be inferred from the nature of the countryside—that a major job of clearing the forests had to be done first and the forests kept in check. Wheat, barley, peas, beans, and lentils were grown; plums and apples were eaten. They wore linen clothes which were woven from the flax they grew; they also wore skins and furs in the winter. They kept cattle, pigs, sheep, and goats, and these early farmers already knew the use of manure. The farming was supplemented with fishing rather than with hunting. Containers were made from birch bark, and the same bark was used to cover some pottery, no doubt for insulation as well as for decoration. Many different kinds of baskets were made from local materials, as well as pottery painted or incised with geometrical forms. Though metals and writing were not known to the Neolithic peoples of the third millennium B.C., their way of life was very far from being "primitive" and may well have compared favorably with what followed in literate ages many millenniums later.

MEGALITHIC CULTURE OF THE NEOLITHIC AGE

A strange movement spread in Neolithic times throughout much of Europe, which is still imperfectly understood for lack of written records. This was the building of monumental tombs that made use of huge dressed stones. This tomb building probably spread westward from the eastern Mediterranean. Nevertheless, it is difficult to explain all Megalithic architecture as an outgrowth of tomb building; nor can we explain, as solely burial places, the great Megalithic temples, for example, of Malta, together with such open air monuments as Stonehenge in southern England and the circles of Carnac and other sites in Brittany, although burial remains have been found associated with some of the megaliths. It is indeed difficult to resist the interpretation that some of these monuments were connected in some manner with sun worship, with the shadows cast by the sun creating a kind of temple. Any visitor to Brittany, Wales, or Salisbury Plain is sure to have seen these menhirs, large single pillars of stone, and the circles of such stones, which are called cromlechs. Stone slabs or blocks, with other slabs serving as a roof, making a kind of chamber of stones, are not uncommon; these are known as dolmens. At Carnac there are long avenues of stones, often stretching for several hundred yards. It is surely not farfetched to believe that an ancient priest stood at the head of the avenue to welcome the new day when the sun appeared on the horizon or greeted the reappearance of a star long absent from the heavens.[3] It has also

[3] The Egyptians, for example, kept watch for the annual reappearance of Sirius (Sothis), and the Aztecs for the rising of the stars during the five days regarded as unlucky which brought their year to an end, and gave assurance that the world was not to come to an end also.

been noted that the shadows thrown by some of the stone groups make complex geometric figures, and at certain times of the day and of the year the shadows cast seem to create "buildings" of their own.

Far the most impressive of all the Neolithic monuments is Stonehenge on Salisbury Plain in England. This is a circle of megaliths close to which are burial places that probably antedate the stone circle itself. The bodies were cremated and the remains buried in these pits. These remains have been dated by carbon 14 as about 1850 B.C., a date which, in England, falls within the early Bronze age. Many problems are connected with this famous circle, not all of which have yet been solved. Some of the smaller stones ("blue stones") used for the outer circle of the monument are of a kind not found locally, and it seems that Bronze Age man transported them more than three hundred miles, presumably, for the most part, by sea and river. Why was this particular stone believed to be so sacred? The lintels (cross pieces) are secured with very great care to the uprights by tenons and sockets, and to one another by mortise joints. How did early man attain such precision with his primitive tools? Though the megaliths had to be dragged a shorter distance than the

The Alignments of Carnac in Brittany. Their significance has not been determined for certain, but it seems most probable that they were in some way connected with sun-worship. (WESTON KEMP)

This striking picture of Stonehenge, a Bronze Age monument in southern England, with the sun shining through one of the dolmens, emphasizes the now generally accepted belief that the monument had an astronomical significance. (WESTON KEMP)

smaller "blue stones," the distance was still upwards of fifty miles and through soft, pathless uncleared country. How did they accomplish such a feat?

Interesting though it would be to know the answers to these technical questions, a much greater mystery evidently lies behind Stonehenge, namely how much astronomical knowledge was available to these Bronze age peoples. In recent times many astronomers have studied the problem, and all have been greatly impressed by the evidence, even though they are naturally reluctant to admit the extent of the knowledge possessed by the builders or designers, a knowledge which appears to have died with them. Fred Hoyle, one of the most famous of English astrophysicists, has concluded from a detailed study of the monument that Stonehenge was not only an advanced astronomical computer, enabling Bronze age man to plot the movements of the sun and moon, but that the great circle around the monument was a giant protractor, of which each ditch is a division. Under this hypothesis the stones were built as high as

they were to enable the observer to compute with greater accuracy. Other astronomers have found that the ancients were able to use Stonehenge to predict eclipses without the necessity for complicated calculations—which in the absence of writing and a system of arithmetical notation would have been difficult indeed. If these conclusions stand the test of time and further investigations, it is clear that our estimate of the achievements and capacities of preliterate men will have to be drastically revised.

SIGNIFICANCE OF THE NEOLITHIC REVOLUTION

The Neolithic Revolution may surely be thought of as one of the two most important revolutions in the history of man. The other revolution of comparable importance was the Industrial Revolution, which began in the eighteenth century and is still continuing today with ever increasing momentum. The Industrial Revolution has in it the potentiality of freeing man from drudgery and providing all men everywhere with the necessities of life and the leisure to enjoy it. From Neolithic times to the Industrial Revolution a condition of universal plenty was never possible, even if man had been able to achieve the social organization required. Every human being can do only a limited amount of work himself in a day. He can produce only a limited surplus which cannot keep any very large number of people fed and clothed who are not themselves engaged in actual production. The leisured classes in such circumstances must always be strictly limited in number. Improvement in transportation and organization can distribute very widely the surplus of the many producers. But this total surplus can never be very great. This inconvenient fact has conditioned all civilization between the Neolithic and Industrial Revolutions. A small class of leisured people, with their needs and even luxuries provided for, have been the intellectual and cultural leaders in civilization. In our own times, with machines capable of performing so many tasks formerly done by human energy, plenty for all has at last and for the first time become theoretically possible.

Before the Neolithic Revolution man was condemned to live from hand to mouth. He had no means for preserving his food, which had to be killed and eaten as he needed it. He took whatever crops were provided for him by his environment. With the Neolithic Revolution it was possible for some favored people to be spared the manual labor of farming, because each farmer could now produce a small surplus over and above his immediate needs. Moreover, it was possible even for the farmer himself to spend a part of his time in private enjoyment without filling every hour of the day in manual labor. He could spend at least some of his time in thinking and in cultural activities not immediately connected with his bodily sustenance; and many producers could spare enough so that an occasional man need not work with his hands at all. What was needed now was better organization of production, an improved social order, and the technological equipment and understanding for the production of a new range of materials and manufactures.

► The beginnings of metallurgy

Traditionally three metals have given their names to successive ages in history—the Copper (Chalcolithic), the Bronze, and Iron ages. With these we leave the Paleolithic and Neolithic ages behind us. But it should be recognized that metal tools and weapons, which were much more expensive, did not at once replace stone tools. All were used for special purposes, and not until iron metallurgy, making use of a cheap and plentiful raw material, had become extremely widespread did the use of stone tools die out.

Recent investigations have made a convincing case both for the areas where the different phases of metallurgy began and the means by which the necessary discoveries were probably made. Copper is in short supply in the river valleys, which are the sites of the great early civilizations. But it was readily available in immediately usable form from the mountains of Anatolia eastward into Iran. By the middle of the fourth millennium B.C. copper tools were known, hammered out of raw copper by stone tools. Such tools had several advantages—as well as some disadvantages—over contemporary stone tools. It is no doubt a matter of taste whether copper or stone is preferred for decoration and ornamentation. In order to smelt copper a temperature of slightly over 1000 degrees centigrade is necessary. Such a temperature cannot be obtained in a camp fire or even an ordinary charcoal pot. But the heat in a pottery kiln certainly exceeds this figure, and it seems extremely likely that copper would at some time be dropped into such a kiln, with the result that it would be smelted and become much more amenable to hammering and molding into tools. Gold became widely used at the same time as copper. All the earliest gold finds, however, are of alluvial gold hammered and beaten without having been smelted. But the smelting techniques involved in copper working were soon applied to both gold and silver.

The peoples who did not possess copper within their home territories but came to desire it were compelled to trade their surplus goods and food in exchange for it; and there can be little doubt that the desire for metals gave a considerable impetus to foreign trade—which indeed was already growing during the Neolithic Age. It seems likely that the discovery of bronze was due to the fortuitous fact that the copper obtained by the city-states of Sumer from Oman on the Persian Gulf contained as much as 14 per cent tin. If such copper ore was smelted in a kiln, bronze would be the result; and though for many years tin, mostly obtained later from cassiterite, was probably not recognized as the necessary component for the bronze alloy, in due time major efforts were made to discover cassiterite, and its sources were mined on behalf of the Bronze Age peoples. There is evidence that early mine prospectors were sent out from Europe and western Asia looking for the metal (as well as for new sources of copper), and thus brought new ideas and spread the discoveries of civilization to the Neolithic peoples, within whose territories the metals were to be found. The island of Cyprus even took its name from the rich copper deposits worked there.

Ancient tradition credits the Hittites with the discovery of iron smelting, and archaeology suggests that the metal was first smelted in the Hittite homeland of Anatolia. Elsewhere meteoric iron was used when available long before smelting. But early in the second millennium B.C. the Hittites had learned its secret and established a tight monopoly both over the process and over the export of iron products. Iron, however, has no advantages over bronze until it has been smelted at higher temperatures than copper and bronze, and carbonized. Moreover, it is a longer process requiring heating and reheating as well as hammering and beating. The "steeling" of iron can be achieved in a charcoal fire by the use of a blast of air of a certain strength; it can also be achieved by the use of a wooden pole charred by immersion in a fire. Both of these processes could be discovered by chance and repeated at will once the cause and effect sequence was observed, as long as an efficient bellows was also available (blowpipes were used earlier) to raise the heat of the charcoal fire.

But it is not surprising that it took several centuries before the technique was mastered, and another two or three before the secrets were learned outside its country of origin. But iron making spread eventually throughout Europe. The Peoples of the Sea who invaded Egypt in the time of Rameses III possessed it. So did the Philistines on their arrival in Palestine. So also did the Dorians who destroyed the Bronze Age civilization of Mycenae. The accessibility of iron ores and their cheapness eventually brought the Bronze Age to an end, giving place to the Iron Age, which has lasted until our own century.

▶ **Language and writing**

At the beginning of this discussion the distinction between prehistory and history was based on the possession of written records. It is therefore fitting that it should conclude with the invention of writing which almost certainly first came into use in Mesopotamia in the Sumerian cities. It is impossible from the evidence to say when prehistoric man first began to speak with fully formed words in language; indeed, all that may be said on that subject must lie in the realm of hypothesis. Moreover, the various opinions of authorities are so diverse that it seems best to add no further speculation here, except to remark that the possibility of telepathy in earlier times as a precursor of speech appears to have been neglected by authorities. If this were present, then speech would follow as another example of the advance of consciousness exemplified in the planned improvement of tools and the development of art in the Upper Paleolithic age and later.

On the question of the origin of writing, however, we are on firmer ground; and though it is still not entirely established that Sumerian writing is prior in time to the Egyptian, still less that the Egyptians took over the *idea* of writing from the Sumerians, both these suppositions appear probable. The Sumerians, who will be discussed further in

Chapter 4, required that records be kept in their temples to confirm the ownership of property by the temple-god. Many of these records still exist, as do business records from a slightly later period; and it seems quite probable that the pictures originally used for this purpose soon became stylized. These stylized symbols in Sumer, however, did not usually represent separate words. The crucial invention of the Sumerians was the devising of symbols to represent *sounds* in their language, rather than words. A two-syllable word could, for example, be represented by two separate symbols, as in the English word "belief," which could be represented by separate stylized pictures of "bee" and "leaf." Whenever the sound appeared in any word the same symbol could then be used. Though the Egyptians made use of different pictures from those of the Sumerians, they used the same principle (known as the rebus principle).

It is still not known whether the Egyptians borrowed the *idea* of writing—though not the cuneiform symbols—from the Sumerians and adopted it for their own totally different language. At all events, both peoples had their own written languages, and thus their history thereafter became a matter of written records, which we have supplemented by archaeological discoveries—just as the archaeologists themselves have also found that early Egyptian and Sumerian written records supplement and confirm their own findings in their specialized field.

▶ Suggestions for further reading

PAPER-BOUND BOOKS

Braidwood, Robert. *Prehistoric Man.* 7th edit. Scott Foresman. This is perhaps the most useful book for the beginner. It has passed through many editions and is kept as up-to-date as feasible, but it lacks detail which should be supplied from the other books recommended.

Childe, V. Gordon. *Man Makes Himself.* Mentor. Written as long ago as 1936, this little book by a pioneer archaeologist and prehistorian is still useful, though the information in it needs to be supplemented from other sources. The same author's *A Short Introduction to Archae-*

ology (Collier) and *What Happened in History* (Penguin) are also useful.

Clark, Grahame. *World Prehistory: An Outline.* Cambridge University Press. Up-to-date (1961) survey in brief compass, with a minimum of interpretation.

Clark, Wilfred E. *Antecedents of Man: The Evolution of the Primates.* Torchbooks.

Cleator, P. E. *Lost Languages.* Mentor. Concerned with the origin and development of writing and language, containing many useful illustrations.

Hawkes, Jacquetta, and Woolley, Leonard. *History of Mankind: Cultural and Scientific Development.* Vol. 1 Part 1 *Prehistory* (Hawkes); Vol. 1 Part 2 *The Beginnings of Civilization* (Woolley). Mentor. These two books constitute Volume 1 of the UNESCO *History of Mankind,* originally published in 1963 by Harper and Row. The section by Woolley is more useful for later chapters, but there is much useful information in it on the beginnings of technology touched upon in this chapter.

Leakey, L. S. B. *Adam's Ancestors: The Evolution of Man and His Culture.* Torchbooks. By the archaeologist who excavated most of the recent sites on the African continent. Especially good on the way prehistoric man made his stone tools, but more limited in scope than Clark. By the same author with others, *Adam or Ape* (Schenkman) includes Leakey's more recent thoughts on the subject.

Oakley, K. P. *Man the Toolmaker.* Phoenix.

Tylor, Edward. *Researches into the Early History of Mankind and the Development of Civilization,* ed. P. Bohannan, Phoenix. An old but still interesting classic (1865) by a pioneer English anthropologist.

Woolley, Leonard. *Digging Up the Past.* Penguin. Useful introduction to the work of archaeologists.

CASE-BOUND BOOKS

Ceram, C. W. *Gods, Graves and Scholars.* New York: Alfred A. Knopf, Inc., 1951. Ever popular work on the achievement of archaeologists.

Coon, Carleton, S. *The Story of Man: From the First Human to Primitive Culture and Beyond.* 2d ed., rev. New York: Alfred A. Knopf, 1962. An anthropologist's account of early man and his society. One of the best in the field, solidly based on our knowledge of the prehistoric finds, but not free from illegitimate inferences from our knowledge of present-day "primitive" man.

PART II

EAST OF THE MEDITERRANEAN- THE FOUNDATION OF CIVILIZATION

CHAPTER 3

EGYPTIAN CIVILIZATION

▶ **General considerations—Reason for extended study**

Before coming to the history of ancient Egypt a few words of explanation should be given for the order in which this history is treated in this book and for the amount of space devoted to it. Egypt was probably not the "cradle of civilization"; that honor, as far as we know now, belongs to Mesopotamia. In a strictly chronological history of civilization, therefore, Mesopotamia ought to be studied first. Moreover, the Egyptians, of all great peoples, left fewest traces upon subsequent civilizations. The legacy of Egypt cannot, in our view, be in any way compared in depth or magnitude with the legacy of Mesopotamia and Israel. Why, then, should such a long chapter be devoted to Egypt?

This chapter has also followed a procedure different from that adopted in the rest of this book. Instead of treating the civilization as a whole and listing its contributions systematically under various topics,

an attempt has been made to show the close connection between the political and economic events and the very slight changes to be observed in the attitude toward life on the part of the Egyptian people as expressed in their religion and art. This procedure has necessitated the mention of some historical facts which in themselves would have been of little interest to twentieth-century students but are of importance in their Egyptian context. An effort has been made to introduce only those historical facts which have a bearing on the changes in the Egyptian attitude toward life, while others, doubtless of equal importance to a professional historian or student of Egyptian history, have been omitted.

Egyptian civilization seems to the author to be unique in history for several reasons. It was a very long-lived civilization, lasting more than 2,500 years. It changed very slowly indeed during this span of time; but it did change, as we shall see. All the great discoveries made by the Egyptians were the result of work done during the first few centuries of the existence of that civilization. Its forms and its art were evidently found satisfactory by the Egyptian people, who felt no need to change them. Thus it was a stable civilization, more stable than any other known to us, with the possible exception of China. This stability was reflected in Egyptian religion as well as in its art forms.

Western civilization has at no time been notable for its stability. It has at all times been a dynamic civilization, and in its latter centuries has been accompanied by an idea of continual progress toward something new and better. This has meant constant disorder and constant wars. But it has also meant that the people, even while living in the midst of these uncertainties, have at least had the hope that something better would come out of them—and indeed it cannot be said that we have been unsuccessful in our aims. We in America have produced for ourselves by our efforts a world in which we enjoy a far higher standard of material comfort than was known in, say, the Middle Ages in the early days of Western civilization.

The Egyptians felt no urge toward progress. On the contrary, the consistent rising and setting of the sun was the inspiration for their idea of human life. The sun rises and sets in almost the same quarter on the same day each year. Change, to the Egyptians, was the same thing as disorder, and they did not enjoy it. Yet in spite of this, or more probably just because of this, the Egyptian civilization lasted longer than the civilization of the Greeks or the Romans, and longer than any Western civilization has lasted since. In this chapter, therefore, we shall make the effort to study this unique civilization as a whole, trying to show how everything in it contributed to the stability of the entire civilization, symbolized by the pyramids, which may well outlast any physical manifestation of our own era.

Yet, as we shall see, Egypt did change underneath. After such political disturbances as the collapse of the centralized monarchy at the end of the Old Kingdom, it was not possible to restore completely the old divinely ordained social order which the

people believed was a reflection of the unchanging cosmic order. As the centuries passed it was increasingly difficult to deny the obvious *fact* of change, and it was found impossible really to restore the past. The last Pharaohs, diligently copying ancient inscriptions while barbarians threatened, and even at times ruled, their kingdom, are a pathetic reminder to us of the truth that there can be no standing still in history without falling back, and may serve to reconcile us to our world of disorder and progress. But the history of Egypt may also remind us that there was one great people which tried to hold back the clock, which developed and maintained a set of values altogether alien to ours, and yet survived for so long a time that we have difficulty in imagining it. If we count backward the time span of Egyptian civilization from the middle of the twentieth century A.D. we shall reach the dawn of Greek civilization. Solon had not yet been born, and Homer had not been long in his grave. How much of history and change have we encompassed in almost 2,600 years since then, and how restricted a space do we give to the study of the history of Egypt from the First Dynasty to the last inglorious defeat by the Persians in 525 B.C.!

The Egyptian civilization is a working model of a truly homogeneous culture, affected very little indeed by other cultures. Yet, successful as it may have been from its own point of view, it bears almost no resemblance to ours, and its influence on the whole stream of civilization has been so slight that very little intensive study has been given to it except by specialists. The general student receives a vague impression of pyramids and tombs and otherworldliness; but it all seems so alien to him and so unworthy of serious attention in these modern days that he quickly passes on to Greece, whose people are recognizably like ourselves, and whose governments and philosophies have served as foundations for our own. Much of this misunderstanding, indeed, may be laid to the door of the Greeks themselves, who admired Egypt greatly because of its age and general impressiveness, but had little understanding of the Egyptian achievement, nor why the Egyptians had become as the Greek traveler and historian Herodotus described them (see p. 73).

Yet it is possible to gain some understanding of Egypt if the effort is made. And the effort, in the view of this writer, is eminently worth while because it may teach us that our own type of society and civilization is not the only possible one, that people can pass their lives satisfactorily without any idea of progress, without aggression against their neighbors at least until the civilization was falling into decay, without those drives and urges which we have been led to consider as natural and inevitable for survival in a cruel and competitive world. It is not impossible that the human psyche has evolved since the days of the ancient Egyptian civilization; but, if so, it is surely worth while to consider at some length, before dealing with the main stream of civilization, the nature of man and his psyche as they were in those long-past days, if only to gain some perspective, and even some greater knowledge of ourselves by contrast with what we have evidently ceased to be.

In view of the fundamental differences between the Egyptian beliefs and way of life and our own, it is of the utmost importance for us to try to enter imaginatively into Egyptian beliefs and values, and not to contrast them with ours, except momentarily. It has therefore seemed to the author that it would be improper in this chapter to be content with listing Egyptian contributions to *our* civilization. Such a procedure would distort the facts and conceal their meaning. We should notice the period *when* any particular contribution was made, we should examine when a particular event took place and what its effect was upon the people. We are looking for real changes underneath an appearance of stability. The divine monarchy suffered a relapse at the end of the Old Kingdom, and it was restored during the Middle Kingdom; then again Egypt was ruled by foreigners during the so-called Second Intermediate Period, but the monarchy was restored for a new period of brilliance during the New Kingdom. But was Egypt fundamentally changed in spite of the façade?

Thus a chronological framework is essential to the understanding of the process of change. The Old, Middle, and New Kingdoms must be distinguished from one another, and the so-called religious revolution of Akhnaton, the period most familiar to modern students by reason of the popular novels written about it (for example, Mika Waltari's *The Egyptian*) will be dealt with in some detail as an important symptom of this process of change. The last part of Egyptian history, on the other hand, when there were no changes of consequence, will require very little space in comparison. The gradual sinking into a cultural coma can safely be taken for granted when the end is known.

► ## River-valley and maritime civilizations

Three of the first civilizations known to us began in the valleys of great rivers where agriculture was comparatively easy, and a surplus of produce could be made available for those who did not themselves work on the land. By the Nile in Egypt, by the Tigris and Euphrates in Mesopotamia, and by the Indus in northwestern India, civilizations sprang up at an early date. There is still no agreement upon which of these was first, though it is virtually certain that the Indus civilization was the latest of the three. Evidence suggests that its technology originated in the west. The Indus civilization will be discussed briefly in Chapter 6; meanwhile the other river valleys will be handled here in some detail, since their influence on Europe was more marked.

Slightly later than the river-valley civilizations are those which were from the first primarily dependent on the sea. These maritime civilizations lived by trade. The land available to them was limited, as in Phoenicia; nevertheless some agriculture was indispensable to provide a basis for subsistence. These maritime civilizations have throughout history been in a dangerous economic position. They have been forced to protect their lines of commerce, and for this purpose to build navies or arm their merchantmen. Their livelihood has depended upon their ability to trade successfully; they have always imported more food than they exported and they have paid for these imports by the products of industry and by their services as distributors.

Mere geographical proximity to the sea does not necessarily mean that the people live by maritime trade. The Hebrew people usually had a fairly long coast line under their control; they remained primarily but not exclusively a pastoral people. Lower Egypt and Crete had enough land available to make their economies a mixture of agriculture and maritime commerce.

▶ ## Contrast between Egyptian and Mesopotamian river valleys—Physiography, government, outlook on life

Of all the river-valley civilizations, Egypt was the most clearly dependent upon its great river, the Nile. A glance at a conventionally colored map of Egypt will show the thin strip of green bordering the Nile Valley, with the uncultivable desert hemming it in on both sides. Egypt is an almost rainless land, and the annual inundations of the Nile provide it not only with all its usable moisture but with great quantities of new fertile soil which are deposited in the fields. If the flood were allowed to run its natural course without any human interference, the area of land fertilized by it would be small indeed. In ancient times the uncivilized peoples to the south of Egypt made no effort to control the floods, and the areas bordering the Nile remained, for the most part, uncultivated. They were the home of waterfowl and animals and lush semitropical water plants rather than of industrious peasants; and we can infer from this natural condition what would have been the fate of Egypt if it had not been for the efforts of man.

The birth of Egyptian civilization, then,

was the result of the labor of those unnamed men and women who first cleared and drained the land and then learned to understand and control the floods, building dikes to hold the water for a longer time than it would have been held in the course of nature, leading it by canals and projects of irrigation beyond the natural boundaries of the flood into adjoining areas of what had previously been a desert, but could be made to bear fruits by human labor and ingenuity.

We know nothing of these early human efforts but we know that they must have been made. Early pictures exist showing the abundant life of the marshes, and the tangle of reeds and brush that called forth the efforts of generations of prehistoric men. Once completed, the work did not need to be done again; and the valley of the Nile from that day to this has remained one of the great fertile regions of the earth. But it did require eternal vigilance and endless toil to make the most of the gift of the great river; and above all it needed cooperation between the peoples inhabiting the valley. The flood was not uniform; it did not always arrive at a given place on the same day each year, and the flood might be high or low, depositing a greater or lesser amount of water and soil. If the Nile was low one year, it might be high the next. Sooner or later there has always been a return to normal. But there might be years when marginal fields could not be cultivated and the dry desert winds would blow away the topsoil. These would be years of famine such as those described in the Bible when Joseph advised the Pharaoh to build granaries and store supplies.

All these dangers could be overcome by good government and organization. The approach of the inundation could be signaled all the way from the Fourth Cataract beyond the boundaries of Egypt right to the Delta. The labor of the peasants could be coordinated, manpower quickly transferred to the areas where it was most needed. The height of the flood, when it was known in advance, could be communicated to workers nearer

▶ chronological chart

Neolithic Age	*ca.* 5000–3000
Old Kingdom: Dynasties i–iv	*ca.* 3000–2200
Unification of Upper and Lower Egypt	*ca.* 3000
"Stepped" pyramid of Zoser	*ca.* 2700
Great Pyramid of Khufu	*ca.* 2600
Memphite Theology	*ca.* 2600
Instructions of Ptah-hotep	*ca.* 2600
Pyramid Texts	2350–2175
First Intermediate Period: Dynasties vii–xi	*ca.* 2200–2050
Prophecies of Ipuwer	*ca.* 2100
Reconquest by Theban prince of north	2050–2000
Middle Kingdom: Dynasty xii	*ca.* 2050–1792
Coffin Texts	2150–1700
Second Intermediate Period:—Dynasties xiii–xvii	*ca.* 1800–1550
Hyksos Domination	1680–1570
Reconquest of Egypt by Theban princes	1580–1550
New Kingdom: Period of Empire—Dynasties xviii–xx	1570–1090
Hatshepsut	1501–1480
Thutmose iii (minor till death of Hatshepsut)	1502–1448
Battle of Megiddo—Conquest of Syria and part of Mesopotamia	1478
Book of the Dead (present form)	*ca.* 1400 onward
Religious revolution of Akhnaton	*ca.* 1377–1360
Restoration by Tutankhamon	*ca.* 1360
Horemhab	1349–1319
Rameses ii (captivity and exodus of Israelites?)	1301–1234
Battle of Kadesh and treaty with Hittites	1297
Rameses iii	1195–1164
Victory of Rameses over the "Sea Peoples"	1190
Tomb Robberies	1120
New Kingdom: Post-imperial period—Dynasties xxi–xxx	*ca.* 1090–525
Conquest by Assyria	*ca.* 670
Conquest by Persia	525
Conquest by Alexander the Great	332

All dates are before Christ. Most of them are taken from J. A. Wilson, *The Burden of Egypt* (Chicago: The University of Chicago Press, 1951), pp. vii–viii.

---

to the mouth, and preparations made accordingly. The prosperity of Egypt was bound up with the efficiency of its governmental organization to a degree hardly equaled anywhere else in the world, and this fact, as we shall see, was appreciated by the ancient Egyptians themselves. If it would be too much to say that the form of government of ancient Egypt was determined by the river and the necessities connected with it, it is not too much to say that the extraordinary worship given to the Pharaoh and the prestige of his government can best be explained by the intimate connection between its efficiency and the prosperity of the Egyptian people.

In the river valleys of Western Asia all this was different. The Tigris and Euphrates overflowed, but less predictably than the Nile; there were torrential rains (the Egyptians said Asia had a "Nile in the sky") and hurricanes. There were terrible sandstorms as well as uncontrollable floods. The peoples of Mesopotamia could not look upon their rivers as the source of all life when they were as destructive as they were beneficent. Though irrigation was practiced, as in Egypt, it necessarily took on a different character; a strong government was not required with such urgency as in Egypt. The contrasts between Mesopotamia and Egypt are almost as great as the similarities, as we shall see; the kind of river is as important in the study of these civilizations as the mere fact of the river and its valley. If we are only studying the predominant manner of making a living, that is, by agriculture on irrigated land, then the classification is important and valid. If, however, we are studying the whole civilization and its accomplishments, then the contrasts must be equally examined. And at once the inadequacy of the geographical and environmental explanation becomes apparent.

It would be going too far in a work of this nature to try to produce a philosophy of history adequate to cover the vast material. Clearly no single factor or even complex of many factors *determines* history. The peoples of the Upper Nile could have produced a civilization comparable to that of the Egyptians, but they did not; the Egyptians produced a certain kind of civilization because of their particular kind of river, but they need not have produced a civilization at all, and it could have taken different forms. It survived so long because the original ideas were found adequate for thousands of years, though, as we shall see, they were in important respects modified. The Mesopotamian peoples knew more different kinds of government than did the Egyptians,

and none of them survived as long as the Egyptian. But what are we to say of the Hebrews? Could only a people such as this have given birth to monotheism and maintained it? Other peoples were in a similar position of insecurity, continually in danger of extinction from their neighbors, but they remained polytheists or "idol worshipers"; they did not conceive of themselves as specially chosen by God and protected by him.

These spiritual achievements were not determined by environment, though it may be true to say they were limited by it. If they had known a different environment the ideas might not have survived because they did not fit their experience. The Egyptian idea that the king, or Pharaoh, was a god manifest on earth, all-wise and all-powerful, could not survive the earthly experience that he was obviously not all-powerful because he was defeated by his enemies. The experience had to be explained away if the belief was to be retained, or, if it could not be explained, the religion must be modified accordingly. The Hebrews explained their own defeats in spite of their position as the chosen people of God in different ways at different times, as we shall see. God was trying their faith, God did not value earthly victories as man did, God punished man for his sins. Ultimately, when all other explanations had failed, they thought that God would redress the balance of this world in the next. The Egyptians might say that their Pharaoh was not the true one, that his power had grown weak and needed reviving by magical means; or they could abandon interest in this life in favor of the next. The Mesopotamian peoples could and did give up all attempt at explanation of their misfortunes, regarding themselves as incapable of understanding what the gods wanted of them. The gods were arbitrary, perhaps unjust, and certainly not behaving in a rational manner toward them in accordance with any such contract as the Hebrews believed they possessed with their God. For all these beliefs one can see some justification in the life experience and environment of these peoples. But can one say that the beliefs were *necessarily* such as they were, and that no other was possible?

Mention has already been made in Chapter 1 of Toynbee's theory of challenge and response. According to Toynbee, all peoples at all stages of their careers have certain challenges to meet. A people may meet such a challenge by accepting it and producing a response which will carry them one stage further in civilization, until another challenge is presented. If a people do not respond in a creative manner, then their civilization will decay; or they may respond in such a way as to use up all their creative energies without making further progress. In the latter case they respond continuously, but they cannot move onward. The study of history, in Toynbee's view, consists in trying to determine the nature of the challenges and of peoples' responses to them; and in trying to find lessons in history by discovering what are our own challenges, and whether we are responding or can respond in a creative manner.

There can be no question of the existence of these challenges and responses. At every moment in the life of a human being or a people there is some insistent problem that requires solution. This is so obviously true as to be hardly worth stating as a contribution to the understanding of history. But it has the supreme value of directing our attention to the human element in history as distinct from the environmental factors that shape it. History is the story of how human beings reacted to their environment and changed it; only human beings have history and only human beings make and record it. The story of the animal world, as of the earth itself, is an account of the external environment and its effects. But man has always had the choice of reacting creatively or being driven by forces beyond his control. For the thousands of years of prehistory dealt with in Chapter 2, man was like the animals insofar as he accepted his environment and lived as they did; he began to act like a human being when by thinking and planning and consciously willed action he changed that environment.

▶ Prehistoric or predynastic Egypt

The early Egyptians in the time called prehistoric or predynastic[1] had already laid the foundation for their later civilization under the Pharaohs. There is no evidence of planned irrigation before the union of Upper and Lower Egypt, but the inhabitants had cleared and drained the areas adjacent to the Nile, they lived in villages, and they had learned agriculture and the domestication of animals. There was already fine pottery in predynastic times, though apparently without the use of the potter's wheel; this art, however, had reached a climax and deteriorated before the First Dynasty. The Neolithic settlements in Egypt show much the same characteristics as elsewhere. There were crude oval huts of mud followed by houses of shaped mud bricks with small windows. Since they knew the use of flax and cultivated it, the people wore clothes of linen. They had hoes made of wood and sickles with flint teeth. They were not cut off from the outside world, since there were already sailing ships on the Nile; indeed, Egyptian goods of the period have been found as far away as Persia. In the last centuries before the union of Upper and Lower Egypt and the great creative act of "Menes"[2] the unifier, metal began to be used in Egypt and the copper mines to be exploited. Ivory, myrrh, lapis lazuli, and other foreign products were known and used.

---

[1] A dynasty is the period of time during which one particular family held the throne of Egypt. Conventionally the First Dynasty of Egypt refers to the period immediately following the unification by Menes. The term "dynasty" or its equivalent, however, was unknown to the ancient Egyptians themselves, and the conventional division stems from the work of Manetho, a late Egyptian priest.

[2] It may perhaps be significant that there is much doubt as to whether any king of Egypt ever possessed the name "Menes" or "Mena," for kings of other names seem to have performed the deeds ascribed to him. If the linguistic connections could ever be established, the consonants M-N might be found to constitute the essential parts of the names of many mythical founders of kingdoms and civilizations, from Mannus of Germany mentioned by Tacitus to Minos of Crete and Manu of India.

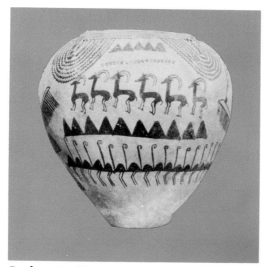

Predynastic Egyptian jar, decorated with gazelles and ostriches. Note the considerable skill of the artist at this very early stage of Egyptian history. (COURTESY THE METROPOLITAN MUSEUM OF ART)

Predynastic Egypt has left no writings, and we cannot know for certain about much of the religion and government of the people. Various figurines and symbolic objects have been found in graves dating back to this period, and from the considerable numbers of warlike implements we can assume that warfare was not unknown. It is probable that, until very late predynastic times, the basic governmental unit was the tribe, and that this unit gradually increased in size, containing different peoples not related by blood, until rather suddenly it became possible for local rulers to extend their authority by agreement and conquest, thus laying the basis for the remarkable unification of all Egypt that marks the beginning of Egyptian history proper.

It was believed until very recently that the Egyptians adopted a solar calendar and a year of 365 days as early as 4241 B.C. and therefore well within the predynastic period. This theory has now been abandoned and the adoption of this calendar placed within the period of the first three dynasties. But before it could be adopted there must have been many years of recorded observations. Probably these observations extended back into the predynastic times, though not necessarily very far into them. Writing appears also in a developed state early in the dynastic period, suggesting that its first elements were laid down before. Most modern opinion inclines to the view that in late predynastic Egypt there was quite extensive borrowing from Mesopotamian civilization, which in some respects was further developed at an earlier date. Monumental architecture, the cylinder seal, the potter's wheel, various artistic motifs, and, above all, writing, were known in Mesopotamia before there is any evidence for their use in Egypt. It is therefore probable that the last achievements of the predynastic age took place under foreign influence and provided the necessary stimulus for the great step forward which occurred as soon as the political conditions for further advance came into being.

SOURCES—OUR CHANGING KNOWLEDGE OF EGYPTIAN HISTORY

It should be stated at once that the intensive study of Egyptian history is comparatively new. Until the early nineteenth century the Egyptian language was unknown to us. In 1798 the Rosetta Stone, bearing an inscription in Greek and two forms of Egyptian writing, was discovered by an officer in the army of Napoleon. Some thirty years afterward the French scholar Champollion had progressed so far in his comparison of the unknown language with the known Greek that he was able to produce an Egyptian grammar and dictionary. But great numbers of Egyptian texts are now known, and more are discovered every year. Even today it cannot be said that all the important ones have been read and analyzed. Moreover, in addition to the written texts, archaeologists have provided and are still providing us with an enormous mass of new material, all of which needs to be evaluated by modern criticism in the light of existing information. It is a far cry now from the days when the information given by Greek tourists and historians, who themselves lived thousands of years after the Pyramid Age and obtained their information from priests often as ignorant as themselves, was regarded as accurate. Indeed it can be said definitely that we, with access to the contents of tombs unknown to the Greeks and with a knowledge of the Egyptian language not possessed by them, have a far greater and more accurate knowledge of ancient Egypt than they had, even though we are living more than two thousand years after the inquiries of Herodotus. And, to complete the paradox, we probably know more about the history of ancient Egypt than did the later Egyptians themselves, since they did not have access to the tombs, which have been entered and examined by modern archaeologists and evaluated by modern scholars with modern tools of research.

It was natural that histories of Egypt should be written in the nineteenth and early twentieth centuries on the basis of insufficient information, since the interest in ancient Egypt outstripped the research of early Egyptologists. It is not to be wondered at that much of what these pioneers wrote must be modified by later discoveries and more thorough criticism. Even the best translations made during the period prior to World War I must be used with great caution, so great has been the progress since that time in our understanding of the language. These older histories were the best available in their time, however, and served as a useful stimulus for further study. But, as in the field of anthropology discussed before in Chapter 2, even now there is little that can be taken for granted as unquestionably true, and the histories to be written a hundred years hence should be incomparably better than ours. There are still very few competent Egyptologists today, and the findings of each cannot be dissociated from his subjective prejudices. The most famous of American Egyptologists, the late Professor Breasted, with his Christian predilections, was too anxious to discover Hebrew thought in Egyptian documents to be completely objective; and, with our predominantly Christian and Jewish heritage, too many of us are inclined to use terms belonging to this heritage and apply them to ancient Egypt. Sin, evil, righteousness, and such terms all stem from this background, and a translator is hard put to it to discover neutral synonyms and often cannot do so. Perhaps, after all, there are some advantages in a picture language where the reader is free to clothe the symbols with whatever emotional content he pleases rather than try to extract the whole weight of his tradition from the finished words presented to him.

▶ The Old Kingdom

THE CREATIVE ACT OF "MENES"—UNIFICATION OF UPPER AND LOWER EGYPT

Through the whole land of Egypt, as has been said, flows the life-giving Nile. The fertile area is bounded on the east and the west by the desert, sparsely peopled by groups of nomads, who, for lack of numbers, are incapable at any time of conquering the settled groups in the valley. To the north is the sea, over which invaders could come, but were not likely to come in sufficient numbers to overpower a united people. To the northeast again is the desert of Sinai which could be crossed, but nevertheless constituted a formidable barrier to invasion. To the south are the six cataracts of the Nile, the first, at the usual boundaries of Egypt, easily navigated or bypassed in ancient times, while the remainder presented serious barriers to navigation, and thus to invasion by river. Potential enemies to the south, the Nubians and the Ethiopians, could be held in check by small frontier forces which needed only to patrol the narrow fertile area, since the desert was a sufficient protection on the flanks.

Egypt thus formed a compact and defensible unity against invaders from every direction. On the other hand, within itself it was not a unity. There was the sharpest distinction between the Delta, the mouth of the Nile in Lower Egypt, which faced the sea and maintained contact with foreigners, and Upper Egypt, which lived in natural isolation. In Lower Egypt also the fertile land of the Delta is many miles wide, while in Upper Egypt the desert hems the cultivable land within closely confined barriers. The whole life of Upper Egypt was dependent on the river and the small area watered by it.

Before the creative act of "Menes" the Upper and Lower areas were under separate jurisdiction, with the geographical advantages manifestly on the side of the north. But it was nevertheless a prince of Upper Egypt who united them, presumably by conquest, and established the capital of the new kingdom at Memphis in Lower Egypt. By the time of the Third Dynasty this kingship of the Two Lands was regarded as a peculiar gift of the gods to Egypt and the king himself (Pharaoh or Great House, as he was later called) was the god manifest on earth, which he remained throughout the whole of Egyptian history. Though the capital changed several times during the course of this history, it was a fixed dogma of the religion that the Pharaoh was always "Ruler of the Two Lands," and he wore the double crown of Upper and Lower Egypt, even though there was no longer any geographical or administrative distinction. At the coronation of the king, all rituals and ceremonies were performed for each land, and separate offices for each were maintained for the king's use in spite of the fact that he performed no separate duties.

There is no mention in Egyptian documents of any armed conquest of Lower Egypt by "Menes." The unification is always stated as a divine act performed by him; the natural divine order was manifested on earth by the deed of "Menes," though this essential unity had always existed even before it was made manifest. We are thus left in doubt as to the means employed; but in physical terms we are bound to assume that the unification did not take place without some struggle; indeed, the records give some signs of rebellion against the new rule. But it is certain that the consolidation was ultimately accepted by all, and endured essentially throughout all Egyptian history, in spite of the topographical differences between Upper and Lower Egypt. There can be no doubt that this union of Upper and Lower appealed to the Egyptian sense of symmetry so noticeable in both Egyptian art and religion—the conception of an underlying unity manifested in dual form. Egyptian gods always come in pairs, the right and left banks of the Nile balance each other, the eastern mountain range balances the western; so no doubt divine monarchy was a unity, but manifesting itself in rulership over the Two Lands.

THE DIVINE KINGSHIP

The conception of the divine king is not peculiar to Egypt, and indeed is still to be

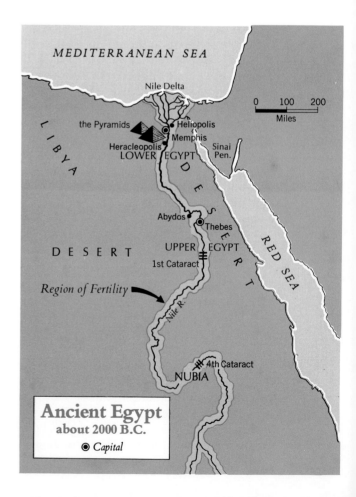

found among certain African tribes, possibly a decadent survival of the once-great Egyptian civilization of that continent. But the god who appears on earth, as distinct from the king who becomes a god at death (as under the Roman Empire) or the representative of the gods on earth (the Mesopotamian notion), was, as far as we know, unique in that age. Since it had the most profound consequences for Egypt, and was indeed her key institution, it needs a more detailed treatment than is usually given in textbooks.

In our culture we are accustomed to think in monotheistic terms of a transcendent God who is apart from the world, however much he may have been responsible for its existence and however great the interest he takes in it. Such a conception would have been completely alien to Egyptian thinking and feeling, as it is to most Oriental peoples today. The polytheism of the Egyptians is as natural a belief and even as intellectually respectable as monotheism, provided the conception is appraised not from our point of view but from theirs. At times the Egyptians thought of all their gods as manifestations of an underlying unity and thus approached closely to monotheism; at other times they laid more stress on the functions and powers of the gods, and then each function was represented by a personified god, or, in our terms, a natural force. The modern civilized man whose feelings are turned in awe toward the wonderful works of God thinks first of one divine power or attribute and then of another. He cannot encompass them all at the same moment. Where he thinks of the power of God as manifested in creation, the Egyptian might think of Hathor the cow-goddess; where he might think of death and resurrection the Egyptian would think of Osiris; where he might think of the first great creation by the divine mind the Egyptian would turn to Ptah, who created the world by giving utterance to the thought that was in his heart. An Egyptian would personify all these powers by the names of gods and goddesses; but these powers were experienced doubtless as powers in which the Egyptians saw the activities of the gods.

It is a mistake to think of all polytheism as "idol worship" in the sense used by the Hebrews.

The ruler of Egypt was pre-eminently a Horus, the son of Osiris, who had been conceived by his mother Isis after the death of his father Osiris, who had been killed by his own brother Set, the power of darkness. The myth of the great struggle between Osiris and Set, the birth of Horus and his rise to manhood, and the drawn battle between him and his uncle in which Horus lost his eye—this fundamental myth is found in different forms at different periods in Egyptian history. But the basis remains the same. Osiris fought with Set and was killed; his sister-wife found him after a long search and either revived him sufficiently to enable her to bear Horus, or she conceived Horus after his resurrection. At all events, Osiris thereafter reigned as king in the world of the dead and Horus was his successor on earth. Thus each new king of Egypt was a Horus, but by the proper ritual burial he became an Osiris after death. When the old king became an Osiris through burial, then a Horus could be born again upon earth.

But the king was not only a Horus, son of Osiris; he was also the son of Re, the great sun-god, and at times this is the emphasis given to his divinity. The point to be understood is that these titles are not mutually exclusive. The fact that he was the son of Re or of Amon did not mean that he was not also the son of Osiris. To us a son has only one father and one mother, and this is of course true in a physical sense. But a king may be a son of many gods, for all have their share in him, and the worshiper or subject may emphasize now one aspect of his divinity and now another. By giving him more titles the worshiper enhances the god's dignity and his power, and enriches the conception of the king-god rather than detracts from it. The Egyptians had several different stories of creation and to them all were true; they were not alternative hypotheses only one of which could be true. The heavens were created by the action of a huge cow who stood up. The heavens were supported by four posts. Shu and Tefnut, air and moisture, gave birth to earth and sky and to Geb and Nut, the gods of earth and sky—and, as we have seen, all were created also by the mouth of Ptah. All of these conceptions were true, from their separate point of view, to the ancient Egyptian—not, as has sometimes been supposed, at different stages of Egyptian history, but at one and the same time. They were not hypotheses framed by the thinking mind to account for, to *explain* the how of creation, but an intuitive perception of the infinite depth and breadth of the creative process.

So the Pharaoh of Egypt partook of all the possible aspects of divinity; yet even he was not as great as the all-encompassing "total" deities; he had something of the nature of Osiris, something of Re, something of Atum and Amon and Ptah in him; but, being on earth, he was limited, and thus is usually spoken of as the son of Re or Amon rather than these great gods in their entirety. It was not until the limiting restrictions of the body had been cast off that he would become a true Osiris and go around the heavens in the boat of the sun-god as himself now an aspect of the sun-god. But he was also not simply one of the gods, a minor god who was given charge over the land of Egypt, or a representative of God who had to make petition to higher gods. As a god he was possessed above all of three supreme powers, authoritative utterance or creative command (*hu*), perception or understanding (*sia*), and *Ma'at*, an untranslatable word which will be discussed more fully later. These powers enabled him to rule the land of Egypt with infallible judgment and unquestioned authority. His command was not limited to command over men. He was himself responsible by his divine powers for the inundation of the Nile. He made the Nile rise and did not merely predict it; if the Nile overflow was insufficient or excessive, it was the Pharaoh who was responsible. When the king grew old and had been long on the throne, a special festival (the Sed festival) was celebrated for him, a kind of thirty-year jubilee for the renewal of his powers.

Rameses ii of the Nineteenth Dynasty celebrated the festival not only after thirty years of rule but at frequent intervals thereafter, perhaps because he felt his own life-forces to be in need of renewal.[3]

THE DIVINE GOVERNMENT ON EARTH—*Ma'at*

As a consequence of his position as a god, all Egypt was naturally subject to him, and all authority derived from him. His viziers and ministers only held office at his pleasure, and all spoke in his name. He owned all the land, though in most periods he did not exercise his right to ownership, and land was bought and sold as if it belonged to the "tenants." In theory he could, however, always resume his ownership, and in the New Kingdom there is evidence that he did so and had the land worked through nominees. In theory he even owned all that existed in foreign countries, so that an ordinary commercial transaction would have to be disguised as a "gift" or "tribute" even when the foreign country was in fact entirely independent and the goods were bought and paid for.[4]

It was of course possible for a Pharaoh to abuse his position. Such overwhelming power in our more self-conscious age would be an intolerable tyranny, however paternally the power was administered. It would be an affront to the dignity of the human individual. We could not conceivably allow any man, however wise and however saintly, to possess such power as of right, simply by what we would call the "accident of birth." The whole political history of recent centuries has been a struggle to take power away from the hereditary autocrat and di-

[3] Certain African tribes today perform a similar rite for their kings.

[4] The system was that the Pharaoh's servants would send gifts to the foreigner on behalf of their master, and the equivalent "gifts" from the foreigners would then be left for the Egyptians to collect and record on their monuments as "tribute." In an informal account of an expedition to the stone quarries, on one occasion when a remarkable incident occurred which revealed the presence of a fine block of granite, the incident was recorded as having "happened to his majesty," although the Pharaoh was hundreds of miles away at the time.—H. Frankfort, *Ancient Egyptian Religion* (New York: Columbia University Press, 1948), p. 58.

vide it among the people. Such an idea would have been inconceivable at any stage of Egyptian history, simply because the Pharaoh was believed to be a god, with all the attributes that divinity entails. Our fear would be that the autocrat would use his power arbitrarily, consulting only his own whims and pleasures. The Egyptians did not have this fear because a god would not do this; hence they were secure, while we would be insecure, with a "divine" king.

The record of Egyptian monuments, from the beginning to the end of their history, never allows the idea to appear that the kings are fallible individuals. If there were arbitrary and unjust individuals among them, we do not know of them. We know of Akhnaton, who changed the religion of Egypt and tried to destroy the old one, but though the priests opposed him they do not seem to have questioned his *right* to make the change. Even the records of victory are rarely fully individualized. They follow a certain type and in some cases even the names of the conquered reappear in different inscriptions hundreds of years afterward. Pharaohs with but a few exceptions did not take pride in their personal exploits.

In all the sculptures of royal victories the contests appear unfair to us. The Pharaoh is depicted as of superhuman size, while his enemies are dwarfs cringing before him. And while it is true that the personal prowess of some Pharaohs is extolled by the sculptor, this is only because the latter wished to emphasize the Pharaoh's power and glory and the good fortune of Egypt that she had a powerful god to lead her to such smashing victories. Even Amenhotep ii, who took such evident pride in his achievements as athlete and hunter, was clearly never in danger from man or beast; his prowess was only to be expected.

Such power carries truly awful responsibilities, and in all ages of Egyptian history we have no indication that they were not fully realized by the rulers.[5] The king con-

sulted his advisers but the decisions were all his. As a god he was expected to have the knowledge necessary to make them wisely. The records always speak merely of the offerings of opinion by the counselors, followed by the revelation of the king and the acclaim of the counselors. "The king took counsel in making disclosures," or "The king made his appearance [the same word is used as for the rising of the sun] with the double crown, and gave commands." The counselors answer, "Authoritative utterance is in thy mouth. Understanding follows thee . . . it is thy plans which come to pass."

The reason that the Pharaoh alone was able to make decisions, the reason that he "made disclosures" was that he alone knew the true nature of the universe. The order of the universe, the static perfected universe of the Egyptians, not subject to change and established from the beginnings of time, was called in the Egyptian language *Ma'at*. The Egyptians did not deny apparent change, the recognized recurrent change, the return to the starting point as of the eternal sequence of day and night. Such change was part of the established order. But no fundamental change was possible. The union of Upper and Lower Egypt had not taken place in time, but was a permanent fact. Only creation was a real change; but even at the time of creation divine monarchy had existed. *Ma'at*, then, in its original meaning was the divine order of creation, order created out of chaos. But this is only one kind of order. Falsehood is manifestly disorder; so is injustice. *Ma'at* can therefore mean also both truth and justice. When the Egyptians claimed that they lived by *Ma'at*, this only means that they were living in accordance with the divinely established order. A rebel against the Pharaoh would have ceased to live by *Ma'at*, as he wished to substitute chaos for order. When the Pharaoh made a decision, he made it by virtue of his knowledge of what the right order was—not for moral reasons, or because such an action was useful. Rather,

[5] A wonderfully evocative and, as far as can be ascertained, accurate imaginative picture of the position of the divine monarchy in Old Kingdom Egypt

may be found in a recent novel by Frederick Heckel, *A Tale of Ancient Egypt* (New York: Philosophical Library, 1963).

The New Kingdom Pharaoh Thutmose III destroying his enemies. Note the gigantic size of the Pharaoh and the conventional puniness of his enemies.

Amenhotep II (New Kingdom) was evidently very proud of his skill as a lion hunter. Here the convention is observed of showing the Pharaoh as far larger and more powerful than his enemies, animal and human alike. Hence the lion is rather a puny beast and, as in all Egyptian conventional art depicting the fighting of a Pharaoh, the hunt is strictly "no contest." (COURTESY THE METROPOLITAN MUSEUM OF ART)

because it was *harmonious*. As a god he also knew naturally what was just. It was not necessary for him to listen to evidence, and seek out where the truth lay; his decree was infallible for he was the source of justice. He could not of course decide upon every case throughout the land of Egypt, and thus his power devolved upon his representatives; but it was always clear that they only held their power, and indeed their knowledge, from him.

This conception of justice as known only by the Pharaoh effectively accounts for the complete absence in Egypt of any codified law.[6] No doubt it was customary law that was administered in practice, as it has always been. But precedents, even cited from the decisions of the Pharaoh, could never be officially quoted since the decision could only naturally hold for the particular case, and, as far as we know, there was never any reference made to earlier cases or decisions rendered by earlier Pharaohs. As the sole possessor of *Ma'at*, the sole *knower* of what was just, orderly, and right, his word was law and against it there could be no appeal.

As god the Pharaoh was, of course, both head of the religion and the object of worship. But he was not high priest as has sometimes been stated. The high priest was theoretically subject to the Pharaoh and appointed by him, though in later times, at least, the office tended to remain semihereditary in certain families. In the later New Kingdom during the decline of the monarchy there is no doubt that the priesthood held tremendous power and was perhaps the real governing body of the country. Nevertheless it was possible for the autocrat Akhnaton to abolish the whole priesthood of the ruling god Amon for at least the duration of his reign without producing a

rebellion. But in early times we hear little of the high priests and can only assume their effectively subordinate position.

Thus the king combined in himself enough functions to make him the most completely absolute monarch of any civilized people in history. He was the supreme ruler whose word was law beyond any questioning; he was the fount of all power in Egypt, natural and political; he owned all the land, appointed all officials, and was the source of justice. He acknowledged no authority whatsoever, not even that of the gods whose equal and partner he was. And in the Old Kingdom, as far as we can tell from the records, only he possessed certain immortality and only he was able to ensure immortality for those of his subjects who served him to the end and were buried under his protection.

From all this it follows that the only danger for the people of Egypt was that the new king might not be a god as his predecessors were. He always did become a god at his coronation, when the old king was mummified and buried. But he had not been born as a god, and there was always a period of uncertainty from the moment of the death of the old king to the coronation of the new. The new king came to the throne as the sun rose on the day following the death of the old. There was an impressive ceremony for this accession and a mystery play was performed. But at the accession of the new king, the dead king had not yet become an Osiris; consequently the new king was not yet a Horus. For the all-important coronation the appropriate season in nature had to be awaited, some decisive moment when there was a beginning in nature—either the beginning of the season of the inundation, the rising of Sirius (Sothis) which heralded the subsequent rising of the Nile, or the beginning of what the Egyptians called the Season of Coming Forth when the crops were sown. Since the successful enthronement of the new king as a Horus depended on the successful transfiguration of the late king as an Osiris, tremendous importance was attached to the funerary rites of the old. In this understanding may lie the key to the

[6] It was once thought that forty scrolls of the law lay before the vizier when he tried a case on behalf of the Pharaoh. But these are now recognized as forty leather thongs, the symbol of his authority.—J. A. Wilson, *The Burden of Egypt* (Chicago: The University of Chicago Press, 1951), p. 172 and note references, also published in paper back as *The Culture of Ancient Egypt* (Phoenix) with the same page numbers as those cited throughout this chapter.

great monuments of the Old Kingdom, the ever-impressive pyramids of this age.

THE PYRAMIDS—SYMBOL OF EQUILIBRIUM AND STABILITY

Not all the pyramids were built during the Old Kingdom, but all the more impressive ones, including the so-called Great Pyramid of Khufu (Cheops in Greek) at Gizeh. Although they have almost all been fully excavated and examined and measured, there is still no general agreement either on how they were built or their real purpose. Though later Egyptians built some smaller pyramids and there was another whole age of pyramid building far to the south by the Ethiopians who controlled Egypt during her last years, there have been few attempts to imitate them by other peoples. To our taste they are not particularly beautiful nor do they serve a useful function. With modern machines they could probably be built with only a tithe of the manpower used by the Egyptians, but we do not want to build them, although it is possible they will outlast any other buildings at present existing in our world. The Greeks, and even the Egyptians of the New Kingdom, visited them as tourists, and were given such information as the priests then possessed. But there is no reason to believe these priests knew even as much as we do about them, since they were without our scientific curiosity and, moreover, had no means of examining them as thoroughly as we have examined them. The descriptions of the Greek historian Herodotus are only valuable insofar as they give us the knowledge of what existed in his day and has disappeared since, and his explanations are only as valuable as the tradition from which they were taken. The Muslim Caliph Mamun in the ninth century A.D. authorized an expedition to examine the Great Pyramid in search of treasure. It was successfully broken open, but the treasure was missing if it had ever been there. There is no certain knowledge that there ever was enough to repay the labor of stealing it.

The kings of the First and Second Dynasties were buried in mastabas, a kind of better-built version of the contemporary house, and intended as the everlasting home of the incumbent. It was not until the Third Dynasty that the first pyramid was built, and this was built in steps or layers. It is not now generally believed that the pyramid was an improved form of the mastaba, as was once held, but rather that the pyramidal form represented some change in the solar religion and the beliefs in the afterworld, so that the pyramid became a suitable form for the body of the dead king to inhabit. None stood by itself in lonely grandeur as the pyramids appear today. Each was part of a complex, including a mortuary temple where rites for the dead king were celebrated. More simple tombs for the queens, nobles, officials, and women of the household were erected in the same area, presumably in order that they might continue to serve the king in the hereafter.

After the stepped pyramid of Zoser in the Third Dynasty began the erection of the great pyramids of the Fourth. These were

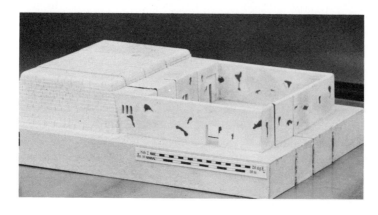

Model of a mastaba constructed by The Metropolitan Museum of Art. (COURTESY THE METROPOLITAN MUSEUM OF ART)

The stepped pyramid of Zoser at Sakkarah (IIIrd Dynasty). This shows the earliest form of a pyramid. (PHOTO BY LEKEGIAN)

Model of the Great Pyramid complex, constructed by The Metropolitan Museum of Art. Note the impressive mortuary temples leading up to the pyramid itself. (COURTESY THE METROPOLITAN MUSEUM OF ART)

true pyramids, made of huge granite blocks, all encased in limestone, so that the surface of the whole pyramid was smooth and regular. This surface has now been removed or worn off, exposing the granite blocks, and giving an appearance of irregularity unknown in ancient times.

The Great Pyramid of Khufu stands on a square base whose sides trace exactly the four points of the compass with a tiny margin of error. The longest side of this square is only 7.9 inches longer than the shortest. The east side is 5'30" west of north, the greatest variation of the four sides. It is not known how this almost incredible precision was attained with the instruments then known to the Egyptians, for it could not be achieved merely with the use of the North Star. The Egyptians, of course, did not have the magnetic compass. The height of the pyramid when complete rose to 481.4 feet and the area covered by its base was 13.1 acres. This, it has been estimated, would give room for the cathedrals of Milan, Florence, and St. Peter at Rome, as well as Westminster Abbey and St. Paul's Cathedral, and still leave some space to spare. There are more than two million separate blocks of granite in the structure, weighing two and a half tons each. Inside the pyramid, which is entered 55 feet above the ground, there is a great gallery leading upward to a spacious chamber called the King's Chamber by the Muslims, while there is another gallery leading downward to what is certainly erroneously known as the Queen's Chamber. There is no evidence whatsoever that a queen was buried there.

The engineering and labor problems involved in the erection of these gigantic structures raise many questions, not all of which can be satisfactorily answered. Herodotus' statement of the hundred thousand men employed for three months for twenty years is only a nice round estimate given to tourists of his day by Egyptian priests and may be no truer than statements now given to wide-eyed tourists by professional guides. We do know from quarry marks on stone transported to other pyramids that the laborers worked in gangs with popular names such as "Boat Gang," "Vigorous Gang," "Craftsmen Gang," and so on, and we know of the later use of ramps, along which the stones were propelled up a fairly gentle slope and then eased into position. The pulley principle was unknown in ancient Egypt. Presumably all the dressing for the stones was done by skilled craftsmen below. The stones were finished with incredible precision, fitting into position with but one hundredth of an inch out of alignment from the true square.

The quarrying of these quantities of granite must have presented problems almost as difficult as the problems of construction, though the river, which at full flood at Gizeh closely approached the base of the pyramids, could be used for transportation. The amount of labor expended was, of course, enormous, when the whole project is considered, though not necessarily as large as the estimate of Herodotus, since so much would depend upon intricate and careful planning and organization. That a state should have reached such an extraordinarily high degree of efficiency in organization still excites the admiration of our technical age.

There is no reason to suppose that the labor was provided by slaves. We are too often misled by the Biblical stories of the Children of Israel who thousands of years later labored for the Pharaoh. The monuments of the Ramessids of the Nineteenth Dynasty were far inferior in craftsmanship and precision to those of their great predecessors in the Pyramid Age, and most of these monuments rest on comparatively feeble foundations; on the other hand, everything connected with the Great Pyramid was carried out with the utmost honesty, clearly by true craftsmen who had a real feeling for the work they were doing and strove to make it as perfect as possible. It is not only in the finish but in the unseen parts of the structure that this scrupulous honesty was observed. In the Old Kingdom of Egypt there were few foreign wars and thus few opportunities to win slaves.

The building of the pyramids was done in the period of the year when work on the land was impossible. Probably, as in the case of the ancient Peruvian peasants working for the Incas, their king-gods, every Egyptian also had the obligation to spend part of each year in the service of his king-god, service which was given gladly or reluctantly according as he believed in the purpose of the work or did not.

There remains the question of the purpose of the monuments. Unfortunately inside the pyramids of the Fourth Dynasty there are no carved reliefs or texts of an explanatory nature. In those of the Fifth and Sixth Dynasties, however, there are numerous writings, mostly in the form of spells. There can be no doubt that some of them are very old and refer to conditions long before these later pyramids were built. So we are reasonably justified in regarding them as in some degree applicable to the pyramids of the Fourth Dynasty, those of Gizeh. It would seem from these spells, as also from the design of the pyramid, that a pyramid was regarded as a kind of ladder to the heavens, upon which the dead king might ascend to his final resting place. No more perfect symbol of equilibrium between heaven and earth has ever been devised than a pyramid whose summit —and there is some evidence to show that the Egyptians sometimes finished theirs in gold—catches the rays of the sun before they reach the earth beneath.

Yet we also know that the Egyptians, both before and after the Great Pyramid, believed that the afterlife was spent in the tomb. The *ba* (perhaps the nearest Egyptian equivalent to the soul, or principle animating the body) is shown in some pictures as hovering over the body and descending the tomb shaft to visit it, presumably attracted back to its earthly habitation, preserved by the piety of its descendants. The blessed afterlife was indeed in all periods ensured by proper burial rites and mummification. The presence of a mortuary temple right against some pyramids, with its sanctuary adjoining it and a false door leading from the pyramid, suggests also that the dead king, like his subjects, could return to his tomb. It is possible also that two shafts leading from the king's burial

place in the pyramid to the outer air, the purpose of which is still unknown, might act as a passageway for the *ba*.

The foregoing considerations therefore suggest to the author that the pyramid had two functions to perform. One was to act as the means of ascent for the dead king so that he might join his colleagues and ancestors in the circumpolar stars, which was one of the greatest hopes of the Egyptian. This would account for the extreme precision used in the erection of the pyramid and its astronomical accuracy. But when he had ascended he had become an Osiris, superior to the rank he had attained on earth and to the present incumbent of the throne. We know from other sources that it was hoped that the dead king would still be able to help his people after death. If, then, he had become as powerful as the pyramid spells tried to make him, then he might indeed be able to help them if he could be given some means of returning to earth. What above all did he need most, the one thing he had used in life but now no longer possessed in death? His body. If his *ba* could be attracted back into the pyramid to animate his mummy and come into the sanctuary kept ready for him by his priests who were specially endowed for the purpose, what blessings would such a powerful being not be able to bestow upon the land of Egypt?

It must be admitted that there is no positive evidence in the texts that such a future was hoped for; indeed, the pyramid spells do not suggest it. On the other hand, the spells perhaps perform only one part of the process. Their purpose was to ensure the Pharaoh's power in the next world as an Osiris, a prerequisite for his assistance in this. If it were well known at the time that the pyramid would ensure the continued presence of the Pharaoh, there would be no need to stress it in the texts. If such a hypothesis is tenable, then all the other facts fit into place. The people of Egypt would not be building the pyramids to satisfy a megalomaniac desire on the part of their king to force his way into immortality by sheer physical force, as Breasted suggested, nor would it even be an act of gratitude on the part of the people for the lifetime deeds of a great king. On the contrary, it would be for their own benefit, to ensure that his power, immensely enhanced by his presence among the gods, would remain with them during the lives of his successors. Then the labor would be, as Moret suggests, an "act of faith" indeed, but also an act of faith that looked for a reward in the present life, with which the people of the Old Kingdom were so well satisfied. It would be comparable to the devotion of the medieval men who built the great French cathedrals by an enormous cooperative effort, and no more a reluctant and forced labor than theirs.[7]

ASPECTS OF OLD KINGDOM CREATIVITY

Technical advances—Improvement in stoneworking, architecture, and sculpture

It has already been suggested that an extraordinary technical advance took place between the Third Dynasty pyramid of Zoser and the Great Pyramid of Khufu. This advance was not confined to technical accomplishment but found expression in all fields

[7] There are, of course, many other theories on the purpose of the pyramids and the meaning of their symbolism. It is certain from the texts that the dead king did ascend from the pyramid to the sky, and there he was greeted by his divine colleagues. It is not known whether he returned to the pyramid after death, as other *bas* were believed to return in later times. It has been suggested that the pyramid is an enlarged version of the primeval hill on which the Creator-God stood when he made the world (Henri Frankfort, *Kingship and the Gods* [Chicago: The University of Chicago Press, 1948], pp. 152–154), or that it was a simple copy of the solar symbol at Heliopolis (James H. Breasted, *Development of Religion and Thought in Ancient Egypt* [New York: Charles Scribner's Sons, 1912], p. 72). It used to be commonly held that the pyramid evolved naturally as a piece of funerary architecture from the earlier mastaba through the stepped pyramid to a true pyramid. For the whole problem see I. E. S. Edwards, *The Pyramids of Egypt* (Baltimore: Penguin Books, 1947), pp. 232–241. It may be added that Osiris at this period was also the god of the Nile and of vegetation. The ascent of the Pharaoh and his reception as an Osiris may therefore have been regarded by the Egyptians as a means of enlisting heavenly assistance for the inundation of the Nile and the growth of crops.

of Egyptian activity, and the people seem to have been aware of it. This period of less than a century seems to have been one of those rare, almost incredibly creative eras in the history of mankind comparable to fifth-century Athens. Unfortunately for Egypt, we do not possess the roster of great names, and few besides those of the Pharaohs are known to us. There is no accounting for these eras by noting the presence of certain determining factors; the historian can only suggest conditions favorable to them. The union of Upper and Lower Egypt was by now thoroughly accepted, the belief in the king-god protecting Egypt gave her people an unprecedented sense of security, foreign enemies gave them no trouble, and the frontiers could be maintained with a minimum of effort, so that no standing armies were necessary; harvests were good, the bountiful land, aided by its beneficent river, gave three crops regularly every year—these no doubt were contributing factors. Responsible and creative leadership and patronage by the Pharaohs assured the artisan of a

Diorite statue of Khafre, with the Horus Falcon behind him. The statue depicts the Pharaoh with the majesty of a god and no sign of human failings. This statue should be contrasted with the statues of Middle Kingdom pharaohs which appear on the following pages.

market for his output, and his worship called forth the highest efforts of his skill.

But not even the combination of these things can account for the tremendous outburst of energy, discovery, and advance in all fields that characterizes this age. The engineering and technical advances have already been described. In Zoser's time the stepped pyramid was certainly built in stone, unlike the earlier and contemporary mastabas of brick. But the stone was cut up into small blocks, which were laid as if they were bricks. The potentialities of stone itself as a material in its own right were not realized until this age. The sculptured figures of the earlier dynasties were cylindrical, giving place in the Pyramid Age to the cubic; sculpture in the round and relief sculpture came into their own. The familiar flat planes skillfully twisted, with head and shoulders in full frontal view while the rest of the body was in profile, belong to this period of experimentation. The art forms in the earlier dynasties were to a large degree conditioned by their material, and the Egyptians before the Fourth Dynasty could not handle stone, though they were successful with ivory. Stone statues were merely massive. But the royal statues of Fourth Dynasty Khafre—whether in diorite or in softer stones—all alike give the desired impression of majesty as well as any in the whole period of Egyptian history. One statue, carved from diorite, a hard and difficult stone to work, was probably never equaled again for the monumental majesty it expresses; it is one of the most reproduced of all Egyptian sculptures.

The relief carvings of this age show unbounded energy, life, and apparent optimism. The Egyptian is already preoccupied with death, but his death promises only, at this time, a fuller life. Harvest scenes, hunts, games, and festivals are abundant. The tomb scenes, so different from those of the New Kingdom, really show a denial of death and the future by projecting the present into the hereafter.[8] It may seem unfortunate to

us that Egypt gained a high degree of artistic mastery so early in her history, since nearly all later Egyptian art consists of elaborations of these earlier art forms. To us, therefore, Egyptian art lacks variety. The early establishment of basic art forms is a phenomenon to be found elsewhere in the ancient world; for instance, some observers have noted it in China. But it is nowhere so striking as in Egypt. There may be more exquisite workmanship in the Middle Kingdom, as there is certainly a more finished literature; but the same general standards and forms, once having been found and approved, persisted. They became, in Egyptian terms, part of "the right order of the world established from the beginning," and so not to be changed. Only the heretic Akhnaton offered a new standard, but his reforms did not survive his dynasty.

It might be argued that in a static society presided over by a king-god, from whom all authority stemmed, there would be a social rigidity that would be hard to endure. But it does not seem that such a rigidity ever existed in the Old Kingdom. We possess several autobiographies of self-made men, some of them reading like modern success stories. Even a peasant could rise to high position if he showed ability. Where all were equal under the king, it was within his

---

[8] One might be tempted to say that the Egyptian at no time ever *doubted* his immortality itself. He hoped it would be better than this life in the sense of being more abundant and full, but essentially unchanged. We should beware of reading into Egyptian thought the idea that immortality must be *won*. In the Old Kingdom nobles were buried with the Pharaoh so that they might continue to serve him afterward. But this was the established order of things and it was good. They could not be supposed to desire immortality as lonely individuals, not integrated into any social system, when they had never been individuals in this sense in life. Likewise the masses of the people, unable to conceive of life without their lords, could equally not conceive of death without them. The *kind* of immortality to be won became of the greatest importance in later Egypt when the old peaceful static order had disappeared and the kingship had decayed and belief in the god-king was shaking—when, as the Egyptian said, *Ma'at* was no longer in the land. Then personal immortality, without assistance from the king, and outside the disintegrating social order, naturally became more important, and mummification and proper burial rites were emphasized.

power to raise anyone by his favor, as Joseph in the Biblical story was raised out of prison to be the chief steward of the realm. We know of one Uni, keeper of a modest government storehouse, who rose to be Governor of Upper Egypt and ultimately—an even higher post—royal Tutor. An architect tells how the king's favor raised him from the position of a common builder to be Royal Constructor and Architect. Though giving due credit to the Pharaoh, he nevertheless implies that it was his own ability which was justly rewarded. Within the framework of this completely unquestioned Pharaonic government a man might strive for his own wealth and fortune and succeed. In the extant documents of this age, no gloomy fears and no doubts were voiced. There was, on the contrary, everywhere an air of bustle and achievement, as if the people knew they were living in a great age and gloried in it. The book of Instructions written by Ptah-hotep, a vizier in the Old Kingdom, gives clear advice to his son on how to get on in the world by striving for personal improvement—and explains the rules which must be kept. In his words *"Ma'at* is great and its appropriateness is lasting; it has not been disturbed since the time of him who made it, whereas there is punishment for him who passes over its law."[9] This was the eternal and unchanging social order within the framework of which a man should progress.[10]

---

[9] J. B. Pritchard, ed., *Ancient Near Eastern Texts Relating to the Old Testament* (J. A. Wilson, tr.; Princeton, N. J.: Princeton University Press, 1950), p. 412. Extracts from this source are used by permission of Princeton University Press.

[10] Though all the teachings of Ptah-hotep and similar sages may be interpreted as simple advice on how to get on in the world, there can be little doubt that this interpretation does not exhaust their meaning. If this is all that they were, it would be hard to account for the great veneration in which they were held in later years. It would probably be more accurate to say that they were primarily useful as teachings concerning the established order, or *Ma'at*, and wherein it consisted. Hence their importance when *Ma'at* was no longer in the land, and it was the duty of teachers to try to restore it. On this point see, especially, Frankfort, *Ancient Egyptian Religion*, pp. 61–76.

Religious speculation—The "Memphite Theology"

Another aspect of the special creativeness of the Pyramid Age is to be seen in the remarkable and original document commonly known as the Memphite Theology, which, though only known in a late copy, can be dated with certainty to the Old Kingdom. There is very little indeed in Egyptian religion that can be called speculative. As suggested earlier, the Egyptian was inclined to enrich his conceptions of the divine by the multiplication of symbols rather than by trying to understand the essential nature of divinity. He concentrated upon the multiplicity of divine manifestations rather than seeking to discover an underlying unity. But in the Memphite Theology the priestly writers really tried to come to grips with the problem of the nature of divinity as both cause and continuous effect. This account does not deny the other stories of creation, but goes much more deeply into the matter than do other extant Egyptian documents.

Ptah, the Great One . . . gave birth to the gods. There came into being as the heart and there came into being as the tongue, something in the form of Atum. The mighty Great One is Ptah, who transmitted life to all gods. . . . Thus it happened that the heart and tongue gained control over every other member of the body, by teaching that he, Ptah (as heart and tongue), is in every body and in every mouth of all gods, all men, all cattle . . . by thinking and commanding everything that he wishes. . . .

Thus all the gods were formed . . . all the Divine Order really came into being through what the heart thought and the tongue commanded. . . . Thus were made all work and all crafts, the action of the arms, the movement of the legs, and the activity of every member, in conformance with this command which the heart thought, which came forth through the tongue, and which gives value to everything. . . . Thus it happened that it was said of Ptah: "He who made all and brought the gods into being."[11]

[11] Pritchard, *Ancient Near Eastern Texts*, p. 5.

Medicine and surgery

It is probable that the so-called Edwin Smith Surgical Papyrus, the finest Egyptian medical document, also describes medical knowledge from this period, although the document itself dates from the Middle Kingdom. In this papyrus there is a curious physiological parallel to the Memphite teaching about Ptah. Instead of the usual account of home remedies and herb lore which constitutes most Egyptian medical documents, this papyrus explains how the heart "speaks" in various parts of the body, and how the doctor may "measure for the heart" in these parts. Most of the treatise is concerned with how to set fractures and which of them were curable. In the manner later used in the Greek Hippocratean corpus the writer denies demoniacal force, "the breath of some outside god," as the reason for partial paralysis as a result of some fractures. No later Egyptian medical document adopts such a scientific attitude.

► First Intermediate Period

DECLINE OF CENTRALIZED GOVERNMENT

It has already been remarked that the Fourth Dynasty pyramids are the largest, the most impressive, and the most solidly and accurately built of the pyramids. In the Fifth and Sixth Dynasties the pyramids are smaller, though the total pyramid complex reaches almost the same proportions, with more space devoted to the temple buildings than in the Fourth Dynasty. And the new pyramids possess the texts and spells which were presumably considered unnecessary by the Fourth Dynasty monarchs Khufu and Khefren. Was this already the beginning of a doubt? The realm was still prosperous, but it is usually suggested that its resources had been overtaxed by the immense labor expenditure and wastage of materials required for the pyramids, and even rich Egypt could not afford a pyramid for every king. At all events, during the long reign of Pepi II in the Sixth Dynasty, signs of decay began to appear, and suddenly after his death the Old Kingdom disintegrated.

The period that followed the collapse of the Old Kingdom used to be called the Feudal Age (Seventh to Eleventh Dynasties). It is now more usually given the name of the First Intermediate Period. There is no doubt that it possessed elements of feudalism in that the central government had broken down, and the nobles, for want of a better authority, usurped the local governments[12] and refused to recognize the weak kings of Memphis who exercised jurisdiction only over small areas. When the capital was transferred for two dynasties to the city in central Egypt called Heracleopolis by the Greeks, the kings of this city expanded their sway until it embraced more than half of Egypt. But the land as a whole was still disunited, and local nobles were still the effective rulers in most of the country. With the breakdown of the central government, foreigners from the north penetrated into Lower Egypt and the Delta lands, and settled there, although there is no indication of any armed invasions. The trouble was of internal origin and seems to have been altogether due to the breakdown of the old way of life and the security that went with it.

The texts of this period are of special interest in that they reveal so clearly the characteristically Egyptian way of reacting to such troubles. In the first place there is no sign whatever of any revolutionary attempts by the common people to obtain any share in the government. It is true that all social values were overturned, that the poor man now lived where his master lived before. But he did not seem to like it. What he gained was nothing in comparison with the loss of his physical and psychological security, or, as he put it, the fact that "*ma'at* has disappeared from the land." The prophet Ipuwer said: "Why, really, the land spins round as does a potter's wheel . . . all maidservants make

---

[12] Traditionally Egypt had been divided into forty-two nomes or provinces.

free with their tongues; when the mistresses speak it is burdensome to the servants . . . the children of nobles are dashed against the walls . . . noble ladies are gleaners, and nobles are in the workhouse. . . . He who never slept on a plank is now the owner of a bed. . . . Behold the owners of robes are now in rags . . . he who never wove for himself is now the owner of fine linen." A harpist sang: "The gods who lived formerly rested in their pyramids; the beatified dead also, buried in their pyramids, and they who built houses—their places are no more. Foreign trade has ceased." Ipuwer again said: "No one really sails north to Byblos today. What shall we do for cedar for our mummies . . . ? How important it now seems when the oasis people come carrying nuts and plants and birds." And it is all due to the absence of kingship. "Where is he today? Does he sleep perchance? Behold his might is not seen."[13]

There was no voice of triumph arising from the people whose day might seem to have come. And though this conclusion may simply be due to our lack of records from this side, it does not seem likely. There was certainly no organized attempt on the part of the people to gain more rights, and there was certainly great rejoicing when Upper and Lower Egypt were once more united in the Middle Kingdom. But from what we know of the importance of order and stability to the Egyptian, from the way in which these values were re-established and endured after this period, and from the complete dependence upon this order in the Old Kingdom, it seems impossible to believe that this people, with its lack of individual self-reliance, could have relished the change.

For the nobles it was a different matter. The great change for them was that they now appropriated for themselves the rituals and ceremonies hitherto reserved only for the king. The pyramid texts are now to be found, substantially unchanged, within the coffins of the nobles. They used the same

spells and looked forward to the same future. Commoners who had the wealth also sought similar privileges. From this time onward their own life in the afterworld was ensured by their own funerary ceremonies, and this age marked the beginning of that extraordinary preoccupation with death that we associate with Egypt and that attained its fullest expression in the relatively late New Kingdom compilation of spells that constitutes the Book of the Dead, and the ascendancy of the priesthood that resulted from that preoccupation. Egypt would never be quite the same carefree land again. Anxiety had entered into Egyptian psychology for the first time.

DAWN OF THE IDEA OF SOCIAL JUSTICE FOR ALL

But there is another side to this tale of the disintegration of old values. The loss of *Ma'at* is the responsibility of the Pharaoh, as it is his duty to restore it. Ipuwer, a commoner, stands up to the great Pharaoh himself and accuses him of misrule, and the Pharaoh apologizes and excuses himself, almost humbly. "Authority, perception and *Ma'at* are with thee," Ipuwer tells him, "but it is confusion thou wouldst set throughout the land together with the noise of contention."[14] And the Pharaoh answers that he had tried to protect the people but failed for lack of resources. One Pharaoh confesses to his son: "Behold, a misfortune happened in my time; the Thinite regions were hacked up. It really happened through what I had done, and I knew of it only after it was done." The king is no longer infallible and conscious of his relationship with the gods.

From this period also comes the famous Tale of the Eloquent Peasant in which the peasant, despoiled of his goods by trickery, makes appeal to the king's steward for restitution, reminding him that he is the custodian of *Ma'at*, and it is his duty to see that justice is done, even to a poor peasant. *Ma'at*, from being merely "right order," has now become justice, for the poor man as well as for the rich. Though, of course, the earlier

[13] Pritchard, *Ancient Near Eastern Texts*, pp. 441–442, 467.

[14] *Ibid.*, p. 443.

conception of *Ma'at* had included justice of this kind, it is not until the Intermediate Period that it is emphasized and insisted on from the point of view of the poor man who needs it. Under the earlier administration the king-god "listened to it with his heart," and spoke it forth in infallible pronouncements, and we hear nothing of the *right* of anyone else to receive it.

FIRST IDEA OF A "LAST JUDGMENT"

Finally we have the first suggestion of a judgment after death. Re, the sun-god, will "count up character" and "weigh *Ma'at*." He will see whether a man has lived in accordance with the right order of the universe. If so, that man will then be permitted to dwell in the Field of Rushes or go round the earth in the boat of the sun-god or in some other way become integrated with the life of nature and the universe.

A word is necessary here on the difference between the Egyptian conception of wrongdoing and the Hebrew idea of sin, a distinction also important in our study of Mesopotamia. Sin, as moral misdeed, is a distinctive Hebrew and late Oriental idea and is not to be found in Egypt, as far as we can tell from studying the texts as they are written. Translations which use the words "evil" and "sin" are as misleading when they deal with Egyptian thinking as they are in Greek thought. Evil to the Egyptian seems to have been a failure to integrate himself with the harmonious workings of the universe. Like the Greek, he could lack restraint and so bring misfortune upon himself; or he could lack understanding, and thus make foolish mistakes which would draw down upon him the anger of the gods. As Ptah-hotep says: "It is the heart that makes the owner into one that hears or one that hears not. His heart is a man's fortune. . . . As for a fool that hears not he can do nothing at all. He regards knowledge as ignorance and good as bad. He lives on that of which one dies; his food is untruth."[15]

So at all stages of Egyptian history it is disharmony that is the only evil; and to be out of harmony with the universe is a long way from the Hebrew or Christian conception of sin and moral evil.[16] But at least the relationship between a man's deeds on earth and a happy life in the next world is suggested at this period. This, to our way of thinking, is a distinct moral advance. The idea of a divine sanction for human misdeeds was, of course, to bear fruit in the later thinking of the Hebrews and Christians. When we bear in mind that the greatest hope of the Egyptian was to be permitted after death to join the stars or circle the earth with the sun-god, and when we think also that harmony with the divine order was the only true moral good for the Egyptian, then it is perceived that the Egyptian conception possesses an inner logic. An understanding of this point will help also to show why the famous Declaration of Innocence or Negative Confession, so often quoted as evidence of Egyptian moral thinking, should not be taken as seriously as it has been by writers permeated by the Hebrew and Christian tradition of sin and punishment.[17]

▶ **The Middle Kingdom**

RESTORATION OF THE DIVINE ORDER OF SOCIETY (*Ma'at*)

The First Intermediate Period was brought to an end by the conquest of the whole of Egypt, presumably largely by force of arms, by princes of Thebes in the Eleventh Dynasty; hence Thebes, hitherto an unimportant provincial town, now became the capital of the Two Lands. War, however, was resumed after the death of Eleventh Dynasty Mentu-hotep, and the real founder of the Middle Kingdom was Amenemhet I, who had been a vizier under his predecessor.

---

[15] *Ibid.*, p. 414 (abbreviated).

[16] The Greek idea of *Hybris,* discussed in the Greek section below, is closer to Egyptian thought than it is to Hebrew or Christian. It was primarily an error of judgment, in that man, through his excessive prosperity, came to believe it was his own doing, thus misunderstanding and underestimating what he owed to the gods.

[17] See below, Chapter 5.

THE COMING OF AGE OF EGYPTIAN CIVILIZATION

Mature idea of social justice

In many ways the Middle Kingdom was the period of Egypt's maturity. The divine monarchy was re-established, but all the lessons of the Intermediate Period had not been lost. We now hear of the king as the good shepherd of the people. He himself is now aware of his responsibilities even more than before. Amenemhet claims: "I gave to the destitute and brought up the orphan. I caused him who was nothing to reach his goal, like him who was somebody." It has frequently been pointed out in what a marked manner the portrait statues of these Middle Kingdom monarchs differ from the serene majesty of those of the Old Kingdom. We learn from the records about much of the unceasing activity on behalf of the people, the renewal of foreign trade and the cultural rather than military imperialism, of these Pharaohs—treaties made, records kept of the height of the Nile and its approach, even as high up the river as the Second Cataract. They adopted a strong frontier policy to the south against the penetration of the Nubians and erected fortresses. The conditions of the Old Kingdom seemed to have been restored. The documents of the time all show a renewed dependence upon the king-god. His favor was required for advancement and the people were happy and contented. For a while these Pharaohs even built pyramids again, though never of such size and magnificence as those of the Old Kingdom. Perhaps the Pharaohs themselves now thought of them as an anachronism; if they knew of the original purpose of the pyramids, this purpose had patently not been fulfilled during the period of anarchy. They and their successors quietly turned to elaborate funeral rites and tombs, more sumptuous and magnificent than those of nobles or commoners as befitted their rank, but still of the same kind, and not unique, like the great pyramids.

The Middle Kingdom was a beneficent despotism. It re-established ownership of all the land by the king; but the people within this framework seem to have had their rights more fully maintained. Peasant cultivators did not need to fear eviction from their lands or other arbitrary acts. The way of the scribe was a way that offered advancement to anyone who cared to learn, for once a scribe he could become a government official. The highest officials in the Old Kingdom had usually been members of the royal family; in the Middle Kingdom they were bureaucrats who had reached their position through merit.

"Democratization of the hereafter," equal rights in the next world

But, probably even more important for the Egyptian, his rights in the next world were equalized. All classes of society from Pharaohs to peasants are found in the great Middle Kingdom necropolis of Abydos, though, of course, the wealthy and the notables could afford more elaborate funerals.

Head of Amenemhet III (Middle Kingdom). Note the more humanized features as contrasted with the statue of Old Kingdom Khafre. (COURTESY THE METROPOLITAN MUSEUM OF ART)

Granite statue of Senusert III (Middle Kingdom), showing careworn features of the monarch. (COURTESY THE METROPOLITAN MUSEUM OF ART)

This naturally meant the increase of the influence of the priesthood, even though it never attained at this time, as far as we know, any power to dictate to the king, as it did in late New Kingdom days. Amon, originally the special god of Thebes, was eminently fitted to become the supreme god of Egypt. His name meant "the Hidden One"; he was formless and invisible, immanent everywhere. With such a scope it was possible to graft him onto all other gods. In his form of Amon-Re, king of the gods, he became later the great imperial god of the Empire. As breath and wind he was the source of all life in man or beast. "He is too mysterious for his glory to be revealed, too great for questions to be asked of him, too powerful to be known. . . . One hears his voice but he is not seen, while he lets all throats breathe." While there is doubtless a considerable element of political and religious imperialism in his rise to be god of all, and without the rise of Thebes he would never have received such a promotion, it is theologically sound that it should be he and no other, and perhaps helps to explain the continued allegiance of the people to him even under the heretical Pharaoh Akhnaton.

Since the Pharaoh had ceased to be the sole user of funerary equipment and his subjects now sought to fill their tombs with as much magnificence as they could afford, the market for such objects naturally increased. And it was not unnatural that the high standards set for such materials in the Old Kingdom could no longer be maintained. The craftsmen still produced exquisite objects especially for the kings and rich nobles, and they were greatly assisted by the new use of bronze. However, it was no longer possible to devote so much time to their work as had their predecessors in the Old Kingdom, and

Model of a Middle Kingdom weaving shop. Such models are often found in graves of Egyptian manufacturers. (COURTESY THE METROPOLITAN MUSEUM OF ART)

the temple reliefs are never superior to, and were frequently less conscientiously executed than, those of earlier times. There was no experimentation with new forms except insofar as the temple replaced the pyramid. It seems that the Egyptians were living on their heritage rather than trying to make progress toward new forms and experimenting creatively as in the great age of Khufu and Khefren. As has already been suggested, change was never looked upon as natural or desirable, but as a departure from the harmony of the established universe. But in the Middle Kingdom this idea had not yet become a dogma. There was as yet no conscious archaism as in the declining years of the civilization.

SECOND INTERMEDIATE PERIOD—CONQUEST BY THE HYKSOS

We know little of the last Pharaohs of the Middle Kingdom, but we can guess that the administration suffered from some complacency, as at most periods of prosperity.

Scene from the tomb of a nobleman in the New Kingdom necropolis of Kurna (Thebes). The god, Anub is shown bending over the dead man who presided over burial rites in Egypt. (ELLIOTT ERWITT, MAGNUM)

For it is clear from what happened that there must have been considerable laxity in the guarding of at least the northern frontiers. The Egyptians were always contemptuous of foreigners, and their dogma of the divine king bestowed only on Egypt supported their attitude. The "wretched Asiatic" was plagued with rain and storms, they said, unlike the favored land of Egypt, where everything was as it should be. It was all right to trade with barbarians, because Egypt could use their products; but it must always be remembered that Egypt was the one land protected by the gods, and all other peoples were naturally subject to it. Other countries, however, could not be expected to accept this viewpoint, and while Egypt was standing still the peoples to the north were making progress. They were no longer so small and disorganized as they had been in the old days. They had begun to use the horse and chariot, and had made other military improvements unknown to the Egyptians. And at the end of the long-lived Twelfth Dynasty there were signs that there were internal troubles in Egypt and disputed successions.

It has already been mentioned that even before the Middle Kingdom foreigners had infiltrated into the Delta lands. But now it seems that there were more organized expeditions, and the Egyptians were at last forced to take notice of them. Various documents "cursing" foreign enemies are extant from the late Middle Kingdom. So when there was internal trouble in Egypt and the foreign people called the Hyksos pressed in on the land from the north, they apparently met less resistance, and were in sufficient numbers not to become absorbed easily and at once into the superior Egyptian culture.[18]

The Hyksos, invading from the north with horse and chariot, first subdued Lower Egypt and built fortresses to keep it in subjection; then they gradually pushed south.

[18] The Hyksos were a conquering people who swept down into Canaan a few decades before they conquered Egypt. Their exact origin is unknown, but many evidences of their progress through Canaan have been uncovered in recent years. They built a fortified city in lower Egypt called Avaris (Tanis), and made it their capital.

Necklace of drop beads of gold, carnelian, lapis lazuli, and green feldspar. This necklace belonged to an Egyptian princess of the Middle Kingdom. (COURTESY THE METROPOLITAN MUSEUM OF ART)

Probably they never occupied the whole of Upper and Lower Egypt, though they did establish their leaders as Pharaohs, and the Fourteenth to Seventeenth Dynasties are credited to them. The native Egyptians always regarded them with abhorrence as barbarians "ruling without Re," and their national pride was deeply wounded. But the remains from this period do not show them in quite the same light as their victims regarded them. At least they used the Egyptian language and adopted Egyptian names and customs. But the Egyptians never accepted them, and gradually beyond the reach of their power the more defiant among the Egyptians learned to use their weapons and military technique against them. Again a prince of Thebes, who had been permitted some degree of independence, led the war of liberation, and his successor Ahmose I drove their remnants out of Egypt and founded the great Eighteenth Dynasty.

▶ The New Kingdom—Period of expansion

IMPERIALISM

The conquests

The first task of the new dynasty was the restoration of internal security. The expulsion of the Hyksos by princes of Thebes was a clear sign that Amon-Re was the chief of gods and these princes were his colleagues. So in the so-called New Kingdom the dogma of the king-god was reinforced more strongly than ever, though we suspect it needed centuries of success to make much impression on the people. All the old rituals were reestablished. With the accession of imperial wealth from trading expeditions and conquests, these ceremonies could be and were more magnificent than ever. But this is also the age of the Book of the Dead, and of the great *fear* of the afterlife. Gone is the old security and isolationism, gone is the certainty of Egyptian superiority over all other peoples and cultures. Now Egypt's power rests at least as much on the sword as on divine right, and the king-god's position is dependent primarily upon his success. Not all the magnificent temples of Thutmose III and his successors nor the great tombs of their nobles can conceal the evidence of internal decay. And the kingship had a competitor, potentially as strong as itself, in the priesthood of Amon.

Thutmose III was certainly a successful imperialist. In a series of victorious campaigns he penetrated as far as the Euphrates, pacifying Syria and maintaining it as a tributary province under his own governor, and breaking up at Megiddo the coalition of Asiatic peoples which was the only serious threat to Egypt. After the initial conquests he thoroughly reorganized his army on a professional basis and established military posts throughout the empire. At the first sign of rebellion he would send a lightning raid against the rebels with unvarying success.

His power of retaliation was so greatly feared that ridiculously small garrisons were sufficient to keep prosperous cities in check and ensure the payment of the tribute, upon

Obelisk of Thutmose III (New Kingdom) found at Heliopolis and transported to Central Park, New York, where it still stands. (COURTESY THE METROPOLITAN MUSEUM OF ART)

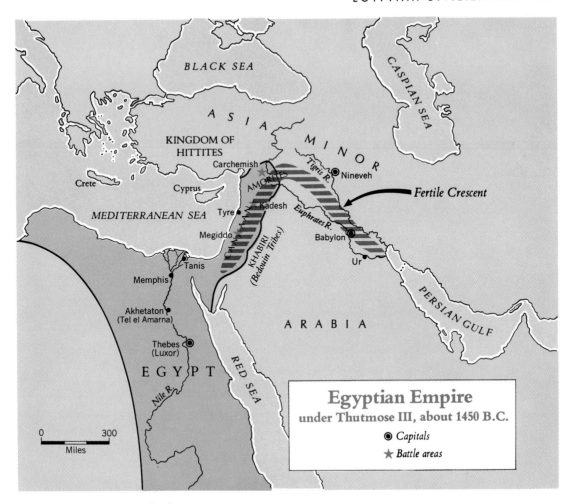

BLACK SEA

CASPIAN SEA

A S I A

M I N O R

KINGDOM OF
HITTITES

Carchemish

Tigris R.

Nineveh

Fertile Crescent

Crete

Cyprus

AMORITES

Kadesh

Euphrates R.

MEDITERRANEAN SEA

Tyre

Megiddo

KHABIRI
(Bedouin Tribes)

Babylon

Ur

Tanis

Memphis

PERSIAN GULF

Akhetaton
(Tel el Amarna)

A R A B I A

Thebes
(Luxor)

E G Y P T

RED SEA

Nile R.

0   300
Miles

Egyptian Empire
under Thutmose III, about 1450 B.C.

◉ *Capitals*
★ *Battle areas*

which the economy of Egypt was henceforth to be based. Thutmose III must indeed have seemed like an invincible god not only to his own people but to those far beyond the borders of Egypt.

Consequences of the conquests

*Social cleavage between rich and poor— foreign slaves—*The results of these conquests were momentous for Egyptian society. There could be no returning to the old cultural isolationism. As in the later Roman Empire, the Egyptians, like the Romans, preferred to avoid the hardships of army life, and the less civilized Asiatic peoples took their place. Asiatics rose to high position not only in the army but in the state. Foreign cultures,

though less advanced than the Egyptian, nevertheless made their influence felt, especially in the vulgarization of the old austere tradition. Foreign slaves, prisoners of war, became an essential part of the economy, and many of these, as in Rome, held positions superior to those of poor native peasants. But the latter, unlike the Roman proletariat, had no political rights and were dependent upon the divine justice of the Pharaoh, who became clothed in an even greater majesty than before. The enormous public buildings of the Eighteenth and Nineteenth Dynasties were now in fact, as Herodotus believed they always had been, built by forced slave labor, driven by overseers. And even native Egyptians lost their freedom for various rea-

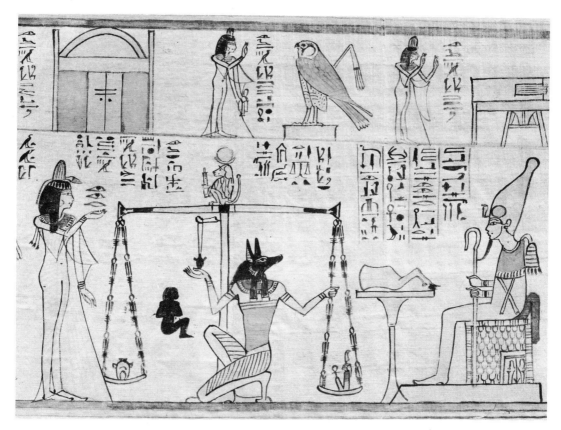

Funerary papyrus of an Egyptian princess of the XXIst Dynasty. The heart of the deceased is shown being weighed in the scales before the god Osiris. On the opposite side of the scale are the symbols for truth and life. The god Anubis performs the weighing ceremony. (COURTESY THE METROPOLITAN MUSEUM OF ART)

sons, and were forced to work on these projects. The conditions described in the Book of Exodus were those of the New Kingdom.

A great cleavage became noticeable between rich and poor. Theoretically the Pharaohs continued to dispense impartial justice, and the country as a whole was wealthy. But this influx of wealth did not apparently penetrate down to the masses, who had lost their security but gained nothing comparable in return. Most of the land now in actuality as well as in theory belonged to the Pharaoh, who farmed it as his own estate, with the peasants as his serfs, or foreign slaves, working the land. And again the result is to be seen in an increasing hope for a better future life, and its accompaniment—the fear of death and the unknown.

Religions—Rise of religious imperialism and early monotheism—Influence of the priesthood—The Book of the Dead—The priesthood gained from the empire in two directions. On the one hand the Pharaoh appears now less as an infallible and ever-successful god in his own right than as a nominee of the gods, supported by Amon-Re but definitely subordinate to him. Amon-Re gives him his victories, Amon-Re dictates to him when to go to war and "lends him his sword," and in return the rewards of empire also go to Amon-Re. Extensive lands and all other forms of wealth are given to the priesthood on behalf of Amon, thus laying the foundation for its extraordinary wealth which it retained long after the decline of the empire. And from the opposite side we see the people more and more dependent upon the priesthood for their one hope of a blessed hereafter, and enriching it by purchasing spells and funeral services. The next world is no longer a beautiful repetition of life on earth, for life on earth is no longer so delightful to them. In the Book of the Dead, the great collection of spells and information concerning the next world, which no doubt incorporates beliefs already thousands of years old, we are given the final Egyptian thought on the nature of the hereafter, and we can see all the gross superstition that had been allowed to grow up—the means of cheating Osiris, the god of the netherworld, the means for overcoming all the monsters set in the path of the dead man. The originally austere Osirian religion, now the one hope of the masses, has itself become vulgarized. The trials and dangers of the dead man lost all dignity in this atmosphere, calm and beautiful though some of the descriptions remain. One of these trials was the passing before the forty-two judges and the Declaration of Innocence, the weighing of the heart against *Ma'at*, which by this time had become the regular symbol for truth. Other trials of perhaps equal importance in this journey of the dead man were the encounters with monsters armed with knives and with bullying porters and ferrymen; and his fear that he might forget his name, or that he might have to walk upside down, or eat dirt, or be forced to work.[19] All such enemies could be overcome by possessing the right spells written on a piece of papyrus, by having access to the right magic; and it was only the priests who could provide these.

THE RELIGIOUS AND POLITICAL REVOLUTION
OF AKHNATON

The new "teaching"—Supremacy of Aton, the sun-disk—Artistic naturalism

So the ground was laid for the revolt of the Pharaoh Akhnaton, who preached a new and purified religion, who defeated the priesthood for the duration of his reign, but whose work, un-Egyptian as it was in many respects, and necessarily unpopular, could

not endure. In the reign of his father, Amenhotep III, the civilization of the New Kingdom reached its height and betrayed at the same time its innate weaknesses. The reign of Amen-hotep III was long, and the nobles and upper classes enjoyed many years of peace and prosperity. Like his predecessors, he built many imposing monuments, including the two great colossi which even in Roman days used to sound forth at the rising of the sun and attracted the curiosity and interest of Roman tourists. He gave costly gifts to foreigners, and he made an important marriage alliance with an Asiatic princess; he built immense temples at Karnak and Luxor. But toward the end of his reign he was faced with a rebellion in Syria, and Semitic nomads began to enter Palestine without hindrance. When he died all Palestine was in revolt, and appeals from the Egyptian governors had already begun to pour in upon the capital. But Akhnaton, when he succeeded to the throne, paid very little attention to his empire. His interests were concentrated elsewhere.

Egyptian culture and religion had already been greatly affected by the new imperial and international contacts. From the time of Thutmose III there had been a tendency to make Amon-Re no longer the exclusive god of Egypt but a god of the whole world. No doubt this was a form of religious imperialism on the part of the Pharaoh and his god Amon.[20] But there was also a tendency in the opposite direction to equate the native Egyptian gods with foreign gods found in the empire. Egyptian governors even erected temples to these under their foreign and Egyptian names. And for at least forty years before Akhnaton a hitherto unknown god, Aton, the disk of the sun, had been accorded worship. The Aton had fought on the side of Thutmose IV "to make the foreigners to be like the Egyptian people, in order to serve the Aton for ever." This

---

[19] On this point see especially Frankfort, *Ancient Egyptian Religion,* pp. 118–119.

[20] In one document Amon is greeted with these words: "Jubilation to thee from every foreign country, to the heights of heaven, to the width of earth, to the depth of the great green sea."—Quoted by Wilson, *The Burden of Egypt,* p. 211.

The goddesses Isis, Neith, and Selkit, part of the funnerary equipment from the tomb of Tutankhamon discovered in 1922. (METROPOLITAN MUSEUM OF ART, PHOTO BY HARRY BURTON)

Aton was now to become the center of a religious and political revolution unique in Egyptian history.

The new Pharaoh seems to have acted as co-regent during the last years of his father before coming to the throne as Amenhotep IV, and he had already built temples to the god Amon. Then suddenly he announced a new revelation, called himself Akhnaton—"He who is serviceable to the Aton"—and proposed to build himself a new capital, Akhetaton—"The place of the effective glory of the Aton" (now known as Tel-el-Amarna). We do not know the immediate reasons for this break, but no doubt the political and religious were closely intermingled. As Pharaoh, Akhnaton was a divine king and was entitled to receive a revelation. This the priests of Amon, whatever they may

have thought privately about the divinity of the king, could not publicly deny. He must have realized the political and economic strangle hold of the priesthood of Amon on the resources of Egypt, and at the same time the gross superstitions of the Osirian cult of the dead. At all events he tried with all his power to overthrow both these religions and substitute the far purer worship of the Aton, the sun-disk, usually represented in Egyptian art as holding outstretched hands over the land of Egypt. It is a measure of the extraordinary power that a Pharaoh still exercised that he was able to accomplish this revolution apparently without bloodshed or armed protest. He was able to retire to his new capital and supervise its building without hindrance for many years, even though his empire itself and its sources of income were disintegrating through his neglect.

There will always be something appealing about this piece of "modernism," and in our day we may prefer the extreme naturalism and vivacity of the art forms of the new movement above the static splendor of traditional religious art. The hymns to the Aton, who never seems to have been anything beyond the solar disk in all its splendor and simplicity giving life, as it does, to all creatures on the earth, are usually considered by modern taste as the most beautiful poems in Egyptian literature. Yet what a supreme certainty Akhnaton must have had in his revelation and his belief in his chosen mission that he should have attempted to overthrow the faith of almost all his people and substitute not a truly monotheistic ethical religion but a kind of intellectual nature worship. And the supremacy of the Aton by no means diminished his own position as god-king. On the contrary, the Aton was his own personal father, only to be worshiped by himself and his own immediate family. For all others the only approach to the Aton was through himself. His title always included the words "the good god." The scenes in the tombs of the new city all show him serving the living sun-disk, while his courtiers bow in adoration before their Pharaoh,

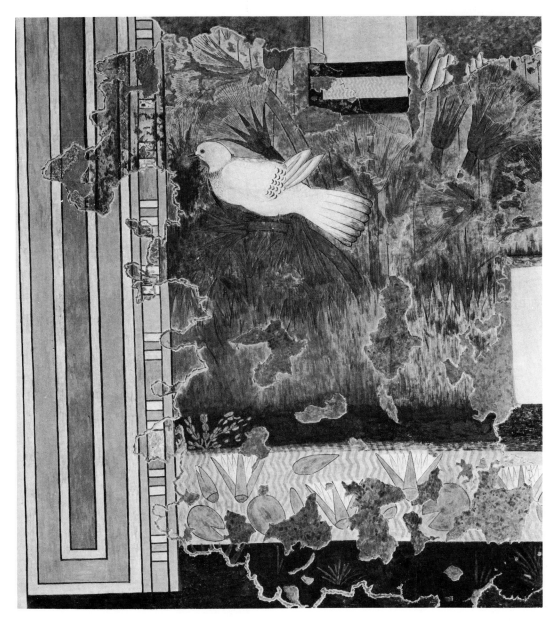

Copy of an original painting from the time of Akhnaton. Note the fresh naturalism of the bird and plants typical of this period. (COURTESY THE METROPOLITAN MUSEUM OF ART)

to whom they pray in such words as these: "May I continue in the service of the good god (Akhnaton) until he assigns to me the burial that he gives. Let him remain here until the swan turns black, until the raven turns white, until the mountains stand up to walk, until the sea runs up the river." Another courtier prays that he may "hear thy sweet voice in the sanctuary when thou performest that which pleases thy father, the living Aton." And in one hymn Akhnaton himself says to the Aton: "Thou art in my heart and there is no other knows thee except thy son (Akhnaton) whom thou hast initiated into thy plans and into thy power."[21]

[21] Quoted by Wilson, *op. cit.*, pp. 223–224.

The Pharaoh Akhnaton worshiping. Note how he himself offers worship to the sun god Aton, whose rays enfold him, while his family, at a lower eminence, appear to be worshiping the Pharaoh rather than Aton. (COURTESY CAIRO MUSEUM)

All this, however, did not mean that the Pharaoh held himself in austere seclusion from his people. Though he made a vow that he would never leave his new city, and those who came to live there and built it were his own followers and owed their positions to his favor, he and his sister-wife showed themselves continuously to the workers, driving through the rising city in their chariot, with their daughters around them, showing their affection publicly—all in the highest possible degree repugnant to Egyptian tradition. His religion was naturalistic (in accordance with *truth*, if the *Ma'at* of Akhnaton can bear this meaning) as Amarna art is also naturalistic—both apparently foreign to Egyptian feeling and filling no great need in their lives. This is evidenced by the speed with which it was overthrown, and the failure in nearly another thousand years of history to revert to anything similar. The naturalistic art left its imprint upon later Egyptian art, it is true. But it was quietly absorbed as Egyptian artists returned to their old well-tried forms; later art was all slightly changed, a little more naturalistic than it probably would have become without the inspiration of the new revelation and the new city.

Persecution of the priesthood of Amon— Lack of popular support

But, however much we may sympathize with the reformer, it cannot be denied that the new religion offered to the Egyptian people even less than the religion of Amon and Osiris. If it were true, if Akhnaton had really received a new revelation of *Ma'at*, if the truth were as he declared it to be, then all the preparations they had made for the next world and all their hopes were doomed; and everything they and their ancestors had spent was wasted. And, even theologically, it cannot be asserted categorically that the monotheism of Akhnaton was necessarily superior to contemporary polytheism. As suggested earlier, it depends on the way in which the many gods are accepted and viewed by the worshiper. And Amon was not just one imperial god among many; as Amon-Re he was immanent in all nature and the whole universe. The Aton could be incorporated into the pantheon of

the Egyptian gods where there was room for him, for the sun-disk undoubtedly represents one manifestation of Amon-Re. But Akhnaton denied all other gods but the Aton, and this meant the abandonment of the whole manner of worship of the Egyptians. It is not surprising, then, that only a few intellectuals and courtiers could be found to support the Pharaoh. Only if there had been a deep ethical content in this religion—and no such ethical content is discernible in any of the extant writings—could it have sufficed to take the place of the comfortable secure world of Egyptian polytheism—and the whole story of the Old Testament is a commentary on the difficulties facing the reformer who wishes to introduce an ethical monotheism into such a world. If Egyptian polytheism had not been so decadent under the New Kingdom, even such a single-minded autocrat as Akhnaton would hardly have felt the necessity of trying to destroy it.[22]

[22] It has sometimes been urged that Moses knew of the Akhnaton "monotheistic" worship. But not only had it died out as an official religion long before the earliest acceptable date for Moses' birth, but it is the ethical content of the Hebrew religion that is paramount and this could not have been gained from Akhnaton. The verbal similarity between some

Relief sculpture of the period of Akhnaton. Note the naturalism of the horse, and the strained appearance of the workers—unlike the usual conventional pose depicted in most Egyptian reliefs. (COURTESY THE METROPOLITAN MUSEUM OF ART)

Restoration of Amon—Strengthened hold of priesthood

Probably political reasons primarily caused the downfall of the new religion. Though the army under Horemhab was still favorable to the Pharaoh and antagonistic to his priestly enemies, the whole monarchy had lost prestige from its failure to support the army in Syria. But there is evidence to show that a younger brother of Akhnaton returned to Thebes before the end of his reign, and Queen Nefertiti seems to have fallen into disfavor. Perhaps the Pharaoh realized that the power of the priesthood of Amon was too strong to break. At all events we know that his successor Tutankhamon, who had at first been a devotee of the new religion and had married a daughter of Akhnaton, made a full submission when he himself became Pharaoh. In restoring the worship of Amon he says: "The temples of the gods and goddesses . . . had gone to pieces. Their shrines had become desolate, and had become overgrown mounds. . . . The land was topsy-turvy and the gods had turned their backs upon this land. . . . If one prayed to a god to seek counsel from him, he would never come. If one made supplication to a goddess similarly she would never come at all. Their very hearts were hurt, so that they destroyed that which had been made." So Tutankhamon "expelled deceit throughout the Two Lands and Ma'at was set up, and lying was made an abomination as in its first time."[23]

The revolution was over. The Pharaoh had been exhibited as one who had no longer the right to receive revelations and to decree *Ma'at*. He had become only the interpreter of the will of the gods, the head of the state, but to be guided by the priests. He had become almost what the kings in Mesopotamia

had always been. And although he remained in appearance king-god and the same age-old ceremonies were carried on throughout the rest of Egyptian history as if he had been a god, he had become a prisoner of the priests, except insofar as his power rested in his command of the army like any other absolute ruler. It was no accident that the restorer of order after the revolution was the army general Horemhab and that he was recognized by the priesthood as the first legitimate Pharaoh since Amen-hotep III.

▶ The New Kingdom—Period of decline

PARTIAL RESTORATION OF EMPIRE UNDER HOREMHAB AND EARLY RAMESES PHARAOHS

The rest of Egyptian history is soon told. Horemhab restored internal order in the country and all vestige of the revolution was destroyed. The Nineteenth Dynasty undertook to restore the empire and was partially successful. The smaller empire continued to pay enough taxes to Egypt to enable Rameses II to sustain the enormous building program, the results of which are so evident today to any visitor to Egypt.[24]

---

of the Psalms and the hymns of Akhnaton, which probably shows borrowing, reveals no connection with Akhnaton. The nature hymns were not exclusive to Aton and could well have remained part of Egyptian literature. For a fuller treatment of this problem, see Wilson, *op. cit.*, 224–228.

[23] Quoted by Wilson, *op. cit.*, p. 216.

[24] A theory was put forward in the early 1950's by Alexandre Varille and others which excited great interest and controversy, especially in French archaeological circles. He produced some evidence, and a closely knit theory based on observation and examination of the temples themselves, to the effect that the temples of Rameses and other late monumental structures have deliberately used materials from those of their predecessors for astronomical reasons. Into the temples had been built all the secret knowledge of the universe possessed by the Egyptian priests; they were not built casually to symbolize power and magnificence. As the heavens changed in the course of time, so new temples were required which would continue to be true pictures of the heavens in stone. Especially the highest parts of the old temples, representing the future movements of the heavens, were now the present, and so could be incorporated into the new temple, so that it would always be an accurate representation of the heavens. Even the old materials were used as the foundation out of which the new picture of the heavens could grow. If such is ever shown to be the case it will mean at least that true astronomical secrets were still known to the Egyptian priesthood of the time of Rameses, and of course it will dispose of the modern theory that the older temples were despoiled to glorify the new temples

The immense temple of Amon at Karnak was built over many years by pharaohs from the XVIIIth Dynasty to almost the end of Egyptian independence. Sometimes parts of the structure were used as a reservoir of building materials for others. The imposing entrance (above), with its avenue of sphinxes, was built by Rameses II; the lower picture shows part of the temple court, with the statues of the gods, built by Rameses III. The whole temple complex is in the process of being restored by the Service des Antiquités and the Egyptian government.

HUGE BUILDINGS OF KARNAK AND LUXOR

His buildings at Karnak and Luxor are large and impressive, colossal in size, and still today overpowering to the visitor. But he built too quickly, and his craftsmen were no longer what they had been in the past. The foundations of the magnificent buildings were too often only rubble, suggesting the commercial contractor rather than the conscientious religious builder. He built a new capital at Tanis in the Delta which was renamed Rameses and no doubt inspired the Biblical tradition of the forced labor of the exiled Children of Israel. After almost losing a battle with the Hittites followed by the first known treaty of antiquity, there was peace throughout most of the rest of Rameses' reign. But new and distant tribes were beginning to challenge Egypt's position in Palestine. Rameses III of the Twentieth Dynasty was the last Pharaoh to win a substantial victory abroad for many centuries. He defeated the so-called Peoples of the Sea in 1190 B.C.

FOREIGN CONQUEST BY ETHIOPIANS, ASSYRIANS, PERSIANS

Thereafter the Pharaohs were content to retire within their own boundaries. There are indications of temporary interruptions in the kingship, and even usurpations by foreign officials. Later there was widespread anarchy, followed by invasions from the south by Ethiopians who took over the monarchy and called themselves Pharaohs and divine. It was only a question of time before the still rich but slowly disintegrating Egypt would fall prey to the rising empire of the invincible Assyrians. Esarhaddon of Assyria

Stone statue of Rameses II from the temple of Amon in Luxor, dated about 1250 B.C. (HIRMER)

conquered Egypt in 670 B.C., but a few years later, with the aid of Greek mercenaries, she recovered her independence. There was a brief renewal of life for a century, and she feebly tried to intrigue in Palestine, incidentally serving, by her alliance with the kingdom of Judah, to bring down the armies of Babylon upon Jerusalem. With the conquest by the Persian Cambyses in 525 B.C. her independence was over for almost 2,500 years until our own twentieth century A.D. As Ezekiel had prophesied, "there shall be no more a prince of the land of Egypt.[25]

GRADUAL SENESCENCE OF EGYPTIAN CIVILIZATION—ANTIQUARIANISM

It was inevitable that the decline of national spirit should be reflected in all aspects

and their creators. But it is unlikely that convincing proof could ever be obtained for such a theory, which is based so much on perception and esthetic considerations. If the Egyptians possessed astronomical knowledge of the quality suggested, it must have been kept secret by its possessors.

After the accidental death of Varille and the difficulties attendant on the Egyptian revolution of Naguib and Nasser, archaeological investigations slackened and no further speculation along the above lines has appeared in recent times.

[25] Ezekiel 30:13.

of Egyptian life. Even up to the time of Rameses II, though there had been more fear and less emphasis on the joyous nature of the hereafter during the empire than in earlier days, there had been at least some emphasis on the continuance of the excellent life known on earth. But with the Twentieth Dynasty a great change is visible. Death suddenly became a welcome release. Autobiographies of the owners of the tombs, characteristic of earlier times, disappeared almost entirely. Their place is taken by hymns, rituals, and ever longer magical and religious texts used for protection against the dangers and terrors of the afterlife. There is an em-

phasis on humility and piety, and there are even confessions of inadequacy, closely resembling our Judaeo-Christian conception of sin, and mercy is sought from the gods: "Come to me, thou who protectest millions, and rescuest hundreds of thousands, the protector of the one who cries out to him."

There is an extraordinary return to the old documents of their ancestors as if these had known a truth hidden from themselves. Many of the important documents of the Old Kingdom are known to us only from copies made in the last centuries of Egyptian independence. There is apparent a gradual fossilization into the set forms described by Herodotus, including even the mummification of animals, which had never in earlier times been actually worshiped.[26] The *power* in animals, their changeless part in the cosmic scheme was no doubt what made the Egyptians revere them and use the animals as symbols of some power associated with them. But in these last days the form was retained without the living substance of their religion. As Herodotus succinctly puts it, "They keep the ordinances of their fathers and add none others to them."

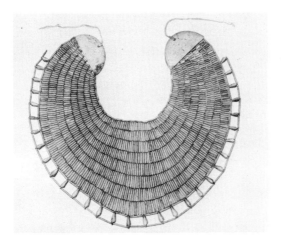

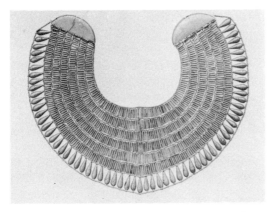

Two collars of beads. The one at the top dates from the XIth Dynasty, the one at the bottom from the XVIIIth. More than seven hundred years separate these two collars, yet the design is the same, suggesting something of Egyptian conservatism. (COURTESY THE METROPOLITAN MUSEUM OF ART)

▶ **General summary of Egyptian achievements**

WRITING, MATHEMATICS, MEDICINE, ARCHITECTURE

The form of exposition adopted in this chapter has emphasized throughout the intimate connection between the social and religious history of Egypt and the political. In the course of recounting this history we necessarily have taken account of the changes in religion, art, science, and technology in response to the social and political experience of the people. We believe that our procedure was necessitated by the fact that in

[26] Herodotus, Plutarch, and other Greeks were misled by Egyptian animal worship into believing that the Egyptians thought that human souls passed after death into animals. This idea, however, is certainly incorrect.

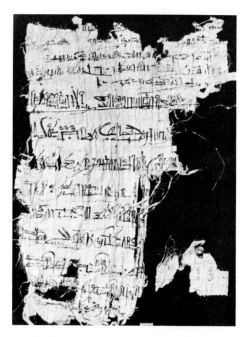

At the left is a fragment of an Egyptian legal document written in hieratic, the common official script. At the right is a fragment of an Egyptian papyrus of the Roman period written in demotic, the common Egyptian writing for everyday use. Contrast these two writings with the hieroglyphic used for sacred texts, as shown on the obelisk of Thutmose III, which appears earlier in this chapter. (COURTESY THE METROPOLITAN MUSEUM OF ART)

ancient Egypt religion, art, and science were inseparable as they have not been in later civilization. In Greece, science becomes emancipated from art, though art remains tied to religion. In the later Western civilization all three have become separate and can be treated separately. Art for art's sake in either Egypt or Greece was unthinkable. It only remains therefore here to summarize in a more convenient form the major discoveries and contributions to the history of civilization made by the Egyptians.

The Egyptians almost certainly did not invent writing; this honor rests with the Sumerians, as was noted in the last chapter. It seems probable, though it cannot be proved, that the *idea* of writing was taken over by the Egyptians from the Sumerians, together with their stylized pictures and syllabic system, and then altered to fit their own very different language. In the process they approached very closely to the idea of an alphabet of consonants, but they never at any time in their history made any signs to represent vowels, which are, of course, inserted by the speaker when the language is spoken. The determinative (initial consonant) in a word was sometimes used for a particular sound, and thus could obviously have been used as a letter in an alphabet—if they had taken this crucial step forward. The step was taken later by other peoples within the field of their cultural influence, as we shall see in Chapter 5. The Ugaritic alphabet, at present the most ancient known, consonantal, like the Hebrew and Phoenician alphabets, and dating from the middle of the second millennium B.C., uses three different signs with its consonants to show what vowels follow them.

The earliest Egyptian writing, which dates from at least as early as the First

Dynasty, was the hieroglyphic, a highly decorative writing mostly used on official monuments. By the Fourth Dynasty a cursive script called the hieratic, written with a brush or reed pen on papyrus came into use. A more simplified writing, the demotic, became popular about the eighth century B.C. Paper made from papyrus, a reed found near the Nile, and the pointed reed pens and inks made from various gums were greatly superior to the cumbersome Sumerian and Babylonian writing materials. It is not surprising that the European peoples adopted implements similar to those of the Egyptians and that the cuneiform system, though it lasted for several millenniums, eventually died out everywhere.

The Egyptian system of arithmetic seems clumsy to us, but it was used with modifications in certain parts of Eastern Europe and Asia until comparatively recently. Being unable to multiply or divide by more than two, they combined these two procedures in an ingenious manner in such a way that they were able to do a complicated multiplication slowly but quite accurately. The two numbers to be multiplied are written in separate columns; then one column is multiplied by 2 and the other divided by 2. Disregard all even numbers on the side divided, and add only those in the other column opposite the odd numbers. The answer will be the required number.

Example: To multiply 44 by 28.

44	28
22	56
11	**112**
5	**224**
2	448
1	**896**
	1,232.

The Egyptians could not use complex fractions and, like all peoples before the last few centuries of Western civilization, were hampered by an inadequate system of notation. For fractions they reduced all the numerators to one, and then added.

This, of course, does not exhaust the mathematical, as distinct from the arithmetical, ability of the Egyptians, since, as we know, they were remarkably efficient at surveying and could build such precisely calculated figures as pyramids. It has been pointed out by a mathematician that in order to build the Great Pyramid they must have known both the G ratio (the ratio between the side of a regular decagon and the radius of its circumscribed circle, the formula for which was a nineteenth-century discovery) and the Golden Section (a line segmented into two unequal parts so that the smaller part has to the larger part the same ratio as the larger part has to the whole). The Great Pyramid has the G ratio between its triangles and the base.

As far as our present knowledge goes, the Egyptians had no theoretical knowledge of mathematics at all in the modern sense. Their notebooks are filled with practical examples, but the universality of a mathematical principle was unknown to them. They did not invent a single geometrical proposition, e.g., *all* triangles have such or such a property, whereas the first Greek mathematicians were able to *abstract* the universal principles from the particular examples, and thus could formulate valid theorems or propositions.

In medicine the Edwin Smith Surgical Papyrus has already been mentioned as an example of the best Egyptian medical knowledge of the Old Kingdom. And we know from the developed Egyptian mortuary practices how skillful they were in preserving the human body after death. The Ebers Medical Papyrus, probably dating from the Middle Kingdom, possesses much herbal lore, too many magic formulas, and strange magical medicines; but it also has a fairly accurate account of the workings of the human heart.

In architecture the Egyptians were the first people to make a really successful use of mass when dealing with stone. Their structures, it has been pointed out, imitate the solid mass of the desert cliffs and mountains, and they planned that their buildings, like these cliffs, would last for eternity. There can be little doubt that classical Greek architecture borrowed the idea of floral capitals from Egypt, but it is not as clear why the Egyptians themselves used them, as they are singularly inappropriate functionally. Why should a powerful stone column sprout flowers and buds? It has been suggested that they are a survival from the days when bundles of reeds with flowers or tufted heads would appear at the top of the pillar, being used as supports instead of timber which was lacking. The explanation, however, seems hardly convincing. The obelisk as well as the pyramid is a distinctive Egyptian form, copied self-consciously by other peoples for purposes of self-glorification. But they always seem native to and at home only in Egypt.

NATURE OF EGYPTIAN LITERATURE—ABSENCE OF MUCH NARRATIVE IN A CHANGELESS WORLD

Egyptian thought and literature have been sufficiently dealt with in the main body of this chapter not to require much further mention here. It may only be pointed out that the Egyptian, at least in the written literature that survives, was only very slightly interested in narrative. In such a tale as The Eloquent Peasant, the bulk of the story is taken up with what we consider tedious and repetitive teachings and platitudes. Yet these were what gained it its popularity; not the brief story of the loss of the peasant's goods and their eventual restitution, which is what we should relish. Modern digests of this tale too often give the wrong impression by omitting all but the few lines of "story." It would seem probable that this lack of interest in mere events is connected with the Egyptian sense of time and eternity. The "platitudes" were timeless truths, while the events were ripples in the ocean of eternity. For the same reason, the Egyptian lacked a sense of history and too often did not bother to record it, or record it accurately. As we know, the same deeds are repeated of different monarchs, and interest is directed away from these mere details to the—to us—monotonous record of victories which were only to be expected of a divine monarch and recurred whenever he took the field. There

is nothing that can possibly be called an epic in the whole of Egyptian literature.

THE VALUES OF EGYPT

The Greeks considered Egypt the repository of all ancient wisdom, and they accorded to her a respect which was perhaps undeserved. While we may now admire the civilization of the Egyptians, it sometimes makes us impatient that they made so little progress, that the great achievements of the Old Kingdom were not treated as the beginning of an ascending path, a fine start to be built upon rather than a Golden Age of glory to be looked back upon and forever imitated.

What we have tried to present in this chapter is a picture of a civilization that looked backward and decayed, as distinct from the picture familiar to us of a Western civilization that looks forward and strives forward, but is chaotic and unstable, and is even now able to destroy itself and all its

Composite capital from an Egyptian temple of Amon. Capital represents papyrus plant. (COURTESY THE METROPOLITAN MUSEUM OF ART)

works by the destructive use of a science which was brought to its present perfection through that very desire to progress which is the essential feature of this civilization. If we assume that it is an inborn characteristic of man to wish to advance, it is perhaps as well to realize that it was not a characteristic of the ancient Egyptians. Toynbee, in studying Egyptian civilization, was hard put to it to discover his challenges and responses and succeeded in devising a pattern satisfactory to him only by doing grave violence to the facts of Egyptian history, as has already been pointed out by many historians. We are thus left with a phenomenon which seems ultimately to be explained only in terms of itself—that the Egyptians, unlike ourselves, neither wished to advance nor succeeded in doing so after a brilliant start. Yet their civilization did not die until twenty-five centuries had elapsed.

We wish to point no moral and to draw no conclusions. We have merely presented the phenomenon. To study it should be an exercise in that historical imagination spoken of in the introductory chapter, without which there is neither understanding nor appreciation of history; and it may serve to help us view our own civilization in perspective. We, like the Greeks, must respect the Egyptians for what they accomplished in the light of their own ideals and their own aims, with so little, and so early in the world's history. And even though we may not share their ideals nor respect their aims, we can hardly deny that it was one of the few great civilizations of the world.

▶ Suggestions for further reading

PAPER-BOUND BOOKS

Aldred, Cyril. *Egypt to the End of the Old Kingdom.* McGraw. Valuable survey of the period from the third to the sixth dynasties.

Breasted, James Henry. *A History of Egypt.* Bantam. Still the best general history of Egypt in English, though in several respects out-of-date and not in accord with more recent interpretations.

Cottrell, Leonard. *Lost Pharaohs. Universal.* A study of Egyptian archaeology.

Edwards, I. E. S. *The Pyramids of Egypt.* Penguin. Contains valuable details on the pyramids, explaining how they must have been built and indicating the as yet unsolved problems.

Emery, W. B. *Archaic Egypt.* Penguin. Fascinating study of what is known about the first two dynasties.

Erman, Adolf. *The Ancient Egyptians: A Sourcebook of their Writings.* Torchbooks.

Frankfort, Henri. *Ancient Egyptian Religion: An Interpretation.* Torchbooks. Many stimulating and original insights, though several are disputed by other students of ancient Egypt.

Frankfort, Henri, *et al. Before Philosophy.* Penguin. This symposium by scholars of the Oriental Institute of Chicago contains an article by John A. Wilson which he enlarged in his *Culture of Ancient Egypt.* The book is available in hard cover as *The Intellectual Adventure of Ancient Man* (Chicago: University of Chicago Press, 1946); the paperback edition omits the article by W. A. Irwin on the Hebrews.

Frankfort, Henri. *Birth of Civilization in the Near East.* Anchor. Makes effective use of recent archaeological finds both in Egypt and other areas.

Gardiner, Alan H. *Egypt of the Pharaohs.* Galaxy. Scholarly and rather difficult work for beginners, presupposing some knowledge of Egyptian history. In presenting a relatively brief account of Egyptian history, accompanied by fuller discussion of Egyptian historiography, the book is especially useful for its reminder of how little we know for certain of the events of ancient Egypt.

Gyles, M. F. *Pharaonic Policies and Administration.* University of North Carolina. Important book on Egyptian government.

Hawkes, Jacquetta, and Woolley, Leonard. *Prehistory and the Beginnings of Civilization.* Vol. I of the UNESCO *History of Mankind.* New York: Harper & Row, Publishers. 1963. The second half of this book by the noted archaeologist, the late Sir Leonard Woolley, contains much useful material on the prehistoric and Bronze ages in Egypt.

Heckel, Frederick. *A Tale of Ancient Egypt.* New York: Philosophical Library, Inc., 1963. Imaginative picture of life in Old Kingdom Egypt, couched in the form of a novel concerning a modern man who returned to Ancient Egypt in a time-machine. The Egyptian scenes, unlike those in almost all modern novels on the subject, are true to our knowledge of that age and the contrast between our age and the Old

Kingdom is thought provoking. The novel is especially successful in depicting through a presentation of one Pharaoh the role of the king-god in ancient Egypt.

Mercer, Samuel A. B. *Pyramid Texts in Translation and Commentary.* 4 vols. New York: David McKay Company, Inc., 1952. May be consulted to give a flavor of these unique texts. These literal translations may show why there is wide difference of opinion on their meaning.

Moret, Alexandre. *The Nile and Egyptian Civilization.* New York: Alfred A. Knopf, Inc., 1928. Written by a French scholar. Some of the material is out-of-date but still worth reading, especially for the detailed account of the life of a typical Pharaoh.

Pritchard, James B. *Ancient Near Eastern Texts Relating to the Old Testament,* rev. ed. Princeton, N.J.: Princeton University Press, 1955. Excellent selection of readings from the ancient world, including all the most important ones from Egypt. The editor has interpreted his mandate liberally and not tried to confine his selections to those with immediate bearings on the Old Testament. Translated by leading scholars in each area, with valuable notes. An illustrated selection from this book is also available in paperback, called *The Ancient Near East: An Anthology of Texts and Pictures* (Princeton).

Steindorff, G., and Steele, K. C. *When Egypt Ruled the East.* Phoenix. Attempts to bring Breasted's pioneer history of Egypt up-to-date, especially the period of the Egyptian Empire.

Wilson, John A. *The Culture of Ancient Egypt.* Phoenix. This interpretation of ancient Egyptian culture and the relation between Egyptian religion and politics has been used extensively in the chapter above. A uniquely valuable work published also as case-bound book under the title of *The Burden of Egypt* (Chicago: University of Chicago Press, 1951).

CASE-BOUND BOOKS

Frankfort, Henri. *Kingship and the Gods.* Chicago: University of Chicago Press, 1948. Another valuable work from the Oriental Institute in Chicago. The first half is concerned with Egypt and should be read in conjunction with Wilson mentioned above. Concentrates on concepts of kingship in Egypt. By a practicing archaeologist who devoted many of his last years to pondering the significance of the material he and others had uncovered.

CHAPTER 4

MESOPOTAMIA

▶ **General characteristics of Mesopotamian civilization**

Throughout the country today known as Iraq two great rivers, the Tigris and the Euphrates, flow southeastward to the Persian Gulf. To the north and east of these rivers are mountains, to the south is the great Arabian desert. The fertile valleys of the Tigris and the Euphrates form the eastern arc of what is usually called the Fertile Crescent, the western arc of that crescent stretching down through Syria and Palestine to the borders of Egypt. In both these areas of fertility civilizations sprang up in ancient times, but the Tigris-Euphrates valleys hold priority. For here, in all probability, is the real cradle of western civilization.

Though there are still some scholars who argue for Egypt, the weight of the evidence seems almost conclusive that any early borrowing of cultural elements was by Egypt and not vice versa.

There is no one name which can be applied to the whole area drained by the Tigris and the Euphrates rivers. The word "Mesopotamia" really refers to the northern area only, while "Babylonia" refers to the southern part.

But neither of these is an exact term, though during the long period of Babylonian supremacy the whole southern part of these valleys was under the control of Babylon. The ancient land of Sumer and Sumerian civilization, which was the parent of all other civilizations in this area, were absorbed, and even the Sumerian language died out. Our only justification, then, for using the word "Mesopotamia" to cover all the area in question is that its use has become conventional. The word itself means "the land between the rivers" and this is the general meaning we wish to convey.

The area, unlike Egypt, does not form a natural entity, and the boundaries are not clearly defined. No warrior could ever say he had conquered Mesopotamia; he would never be able to boast that he had reached its natural frontiers and was prepared to defend them, as an Egyptian could say of his country. Yet the continuity of culture in this area is remarkable. All the conquerors and successors of the Sumerians until the Persians adopted the main features of Sumerian culture, their gods, their festivals, their writing, their art and architecture. The late Assyrian was in all respects far closer to his Sumerian forebears than to his Egyptian contemporaries.

This total civilization, in fact, stands out in marked contrast to that of the Egyptians. The Egyptian civilization was grand and magnificent; but, as was shown in the last chapter, it was isolated, and it was totally alien to us. It was therefore studied as a whole for itself, rather than for its "contributions" to world civilization. Mesopotamian civilization, on the contrary, seems far closer to ours. The line of descent from ancient Sumer to ourselves is clear. Though the Children of Israel were in bondage in Egypt, their Egyptian heritage was small. And though they were not taken into captivity in Babylon until their civilization had flourished for hundreds of years and had taken on its most characteristic forms, there can be little doubt that it was influenced by Mesopotamian ideas and institutions. Even Hebrew religion itself is concerned with questions raised by the Mesopotamian peoples and in its own special way gives answers to them. The Egyptian idea of a static universe found no adherents in Mesopotamia, nor was its supreme self-confidence or its king-god found acceptable.

In this chapter, therefore, it will be possible to adopt a more conventional treatment of the material than was suitable for Egypt. The rise and fall of Mesopotamian culture does not present a similar object lesson to us, for it merged gradually into the whole cultural stream of mankind and never collapsed with its foundations undermined, as happened in Egypt. For in Mesopotamia there never were any fixed foundations, there never was any psychological security to be destroyed. The Mesopotamians had no great expectations of good to be obtained in life; they expected change on earth and were prepared to endure it. They had no expectation of a blessed hereafter. The Mesopotamian view of life was more in keeping with our own view of life than with the Egyptian view. Their relatively pessimistic attitude toward life was certainly more appropriate for them than the naïve optimism of the Egyptians. At all events, their view of life as a vale of tears has almost always prevailed since their time.

It has already been pointed out that the kind of river rather than the mere fact of a river should be considered when attempting to trace the effect of a river valley upon its civilization. Both the Tigris and the Euphrates rise in flood each year in the spring, but the floods are unpredictable and vary greatly from year to year. Sometimes they are very severe and break the dikes, wreaking havoc upon the lands and submerging the crops and villages. At other times they are insufficient to ward off drought. Famines due both to flood and to drought are therefore not uncommon. There are scorching winds and smothering dust storms which wrack the throat and may even suffocate. There are occasional torrential rains which turn the ground into mud, making travel impossible. The sun in summer has no appearance of being a beneficent force giving life to the crops. It is savage, fierce, and blistering, and the land often lies parched under it, or blows away in dust. The sublime, life-giving sun of cloudless Egypt could never have become the all-pervasive god of Mesopotamia, however strongly the people might be impressed with its power and force. In addition to these doubtfully benevolent forces of nature, the land was militarily indefensible as an entity, and time and again was conquered, either by outside invaders or by one or another of the Mesopotamian peoples. At any time a city might be destroyed in war if it did not take care of its defenses; or if, as the Mesopotamians themselves put it, the gods were for any reason angry with them and wished to destroy it. This complex of forces, as we shall see, tended to breed in these peoples a deep sense of insecurity and inadequacy, which found expression in a pessimistic view of life utterly at variance with the Egyptian optimism, and in a religion which stressed man's helplessness against the arbitrariness and unpredictable wrath of the gods. But it did not prevent them from creating an earthly civilization which, from our point of view, compares favorably with that of the Egyptians.

▶ chronological chart

Neolithic Age	*ca.* 6000–4500
Invention of writing	*ca.* 3500
Temple communities of Sumer	*ca.* 3500 onward
Beginning of the Bronze Age	*ca.* 3000
First Dynasty of Ur	*ca.* 2600
Empire of Sumer and Akkad (Sargon of Agade)	*ca.* 2400–2300
Guti	*ca.* 2300–2200
Gudea of Lagash	*ca.* 2200
Third Dynasty of Ur	*ca.* 2150
Amorite rule in Babylon	*ca.* 1900–1600
Reign of Hammurabi	1792–1758 (?)
Conquest of Babylon by Hittites	*ca.* 1600
Kassite rule in Babylon	*ca.* 1560–910

Assyrian Empire

Conquest of Babylon	910
Conquest of Samaria and deportation of Ten Tribes	721
Conquest of Egypt by Esar-Haddon	670
Library of Assurbanipal	660
Fall of Nineveh to Medes, Chaldeans, and Scythians	612
Battle of Carchemish—End of Assyrian Empire and annihilation of Assyrians	606

Chaldeans and New Babylonians

Conquest of Jerusalem by Nebuchadnezzar	586
Reign of Nabonidus	555–538
Fall of Babylon to Persians	538

Persian Empire

Zoroaster the Prophet	*ca.* 600
Cyrus of Persia accepted as king by Medes	549
Conquest of Lydia by Cyrus	547
Conquest of Babylon	538
Conquest of Egypt (Cambyses)	525
Reorganization of Persia by Darius I	522–486
First Persian expedition to Greece (Darius)	490
Second Persian expedition to Greece (Xerxes)	480–479
Persian influence in Greece	410–338
Conquest of Persia by Alexander the Great	330

Dates are before Christ. All earlier dates are approximate and much disputed; later dates may be a year off.

▶ The Sumerians

ORIGINS.

Mesopotamia, as has been said, was indefensible against invaders. In discussing the Mesopotamian civilization we shall therefore be dealing with several distinct peoples who ruled the territory, though without necessarily displacing those who had settled there before. The origin of the Sumerians themselves, who always called themselves simply the "black-headed people," is still uncertain. Their language was neither Semitic nor Indo-European in type, and though similar in form to Turkish and Chinese, is in other respects unlike any other language and has no relation to them. They settled in southern Mesopotamia, probably coming from the east in the early part of the fourth millennium B.C., and mingling peaceably with the advanced Neolithic peoples, to whom they contributed products of their own genius, notably writing. There is evidence that some time before 3000 B.C. another people from the east penetrated into the same area. The "Sumerians" must therefore properly be thought of as an amalgam of these three peoples.

Other peoples were at the same time in possession of the less developed northern Mesopotamia, the Assyrians, Hurrians, Subaraeans, and others, all of whom in due course fell under the powerful cultural influence of the Sumerians. The non-Semitic Hurrians learned to write in the cuneiform script of the Sumerians, and probably aided in spreading it westward into Asia Minor, especially to the Hittites who will be dealt with separately in the next chapter. The kings of the Sumerian city of Ur also subjected to their rules parts of northern Mesopotamia both before and after the great empire of Sargon of Agade.

EARLY GOVERNMENT—"PRIMITIVE DEMOCRACY"

From the beginning of the present century there have been many archaeological investigations in Sumer, and we now have a considerable amount of information about the great Sumerian "city-states" of Ur,

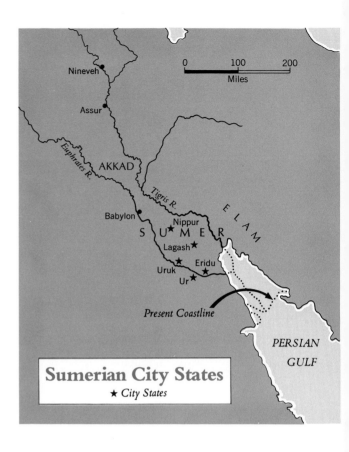

Sumerian City States
★ City States

Lagash, Uruk, and others, though the evaluation of this information is still very far from complete. As in the case of Egypt, we lack information on the transitional stage from primitive village life to the civilized life of the larger villages and cities, and to the organized government that knew how to direct the large-scale irrigation. For in these early days in the first cities of Ur there already were irrigation and canals, together with fine art work and craftsmanship, facts which presuppose a previous period of technical development of which we know little. But it is now believed by many that the earliest government in the independent "city-states" characteristic of the Sumerians was a kind of democracy.

Although there is little direct evidence for the existence of what has been called by some scholars a "primitive democracy," the inferences to be drawn from the myths and legends concerning the behavior of the gods are so strong as to amount to a virtual certainty. As we shall see later, what happened in the Sumerian heaven was always the counterpart of what happened on earth. This is the fundamental notion behind the religious thoughts of the Sumerians and of all the successive peoples that adopted them. When therefore the early legends tell of an assembly of the gods in which the superior gods asked the opinions of all, then adopted the prevailing opinion and gave effect to it, it is unthinkable that the Sumerians attributed such an assembly to their gods without having experienced it themselves on earth, though whether the procedure just outlined amounts to a "democracy" may be more questionable. As it happens, a document exists that deals with an assembly which was convened about 2800 B.C., composed of both a Council of Elders (or Senate) and an assembly of all the fighting men. In this "bicameral congress" the Elders advised the ruler Gilgamesh against going to war, whereupon he called on the assembly of fighting men for their opinion. When these voted for war, Gilgamesh accepted their decision and went to war.[1]

It is therefore extremely probable that the Sumerian assemblies, either single or double chamber, had survived from much earlier times. The system may well have persisted during the period of the temple communities since it was not abandoned even when the cities were ruled by kings.

The first strictly historical Sumerian records tell of simple communities, ruled by a *sangu*, or steward of the gods. Larger communities, with several temples, are ruled by an *ensi*, who is also a steward of the gods, but he is responsible to the god of the whole community, whereas the earlier *sangu* was responsible only to the god of his particular temple. The last form of this development is the emergence of a king or *lugal*, who was usually the ruler of many cities, or at least of a considerable number of temple communities. The *lugal* ruled a fairly advanced type of community which may, not improperly, be called a town or a city. It is no longer merely an agricultural community; and though the temple may be the principal building, the whole life of the community no longer centers around it, as in the more primitive society. But the *lugal*, like the earlier rulers, remains only the chief representative on earth of the gods, who are the theoretical owners of all the land. There is therefore no such thing as a secular state, nor does a truly secular state at any time develop in any Mesopotamian country. The reason for this will become clear if we now turn to the relation between men and gods, and how this relation was reflected in the political and social institutions of the Sumerians.

Relation between Sumerian religion and the social order

It is clear from all the evidence that the Mesopotamian peoples feared their gods, while they worshiped them as beings commanding respect and submission. They did not love them, as the Hebrews in later times were taught to love their God, and they did not regard them as just and powerful protectors, looking after their land and seeing that it was prosperous, as did the Egyptians. The reason for this Mesopotamian view has already been hinted at. The gods of the Mesopotamians in fact did not protect their land, nor could the people think their gods behaved justly to them. Instead, these deities made demands upon them, while giving them little in return, and this little was given quite arbitrarily. The bounty of the gods depended upon the sacrifices given to them by the people and the duties performed in their behalf. Yet the gods did not tell man unequivocally just what they wanted of him; man had to find out for himself and he might be wrong. Herein lies the profound difference between the Sumerian and the Hebrew conceptions of the divinity. Both required man to perform certain duties; but the Hebrew God told his people in no uncertain manner what these duties were. He gave them the Law, and thus provided the He-

<hr/>

[1] S. N. Kramer, *History Begins at Sumer* (New York: Doubleday Anchor, 1959), pp. 30–31. An exact parallel may be found in the history of the Roman Republic, when the consuls wished to make war on Carthage. On the refusal of the Senate to authorize it, the consuls summoned the military assembly, the *Comitia Centuriata*, which gave its consent. See below, page 321.

brews with a sense of security always lacking in Mesopotamia.

Moreover, the Mesopotamian gods not only omitted to tell their people what was required of them but punished them for their ignorance. This was the arbitrary act of an unpredictable and unjust master—in short, the behavior of a human master to his slave. This master-slave relationship, once the early primitive democracy was over, was the central feature of the theology in Mesopotamia, and was adopted first by the Sumerians, and then by all the peoples who followed them in the Land of the Two Rivers. Man was born to be the slave of the gods. This conception permeates not only the religion and myths of these peoples, but their whole social order.

The Mesopotamian peoples, unlike the Egyptians, did not have many different stories of creation, all giving a different point of view. Creation was not to them the one supremely important fact, the only thing in history which could properly be called an *event,* as it was in Egypt with its static conception of time. It was certainly not a theme for religious meditation. There is, in fact, nothing really religious in the Mesopotamian story of creation; it did not inspire awe or reverence, but was merely true, something to be accepted and taken into consideration by man in all his earthly actions. Like all Mesopotamian religious stories, it represented conditions in heaven as being the exact counterpart of what occurred on earth, a conception which, as we shall see, permeated Mesopotamian thinking and ultimately gave birth to the great Chaldean science of astrology.

We have a fairly complete account of creation dating from the period of Babylonian supremacy, and we have others from Assyrian records. The Babylonian god Marduk is the hero in the Babylonian story and Assur in the Assyrian.[2] The Babylonian

version, known as the *Enuma Elish* (When Above), tells how Marduk, or Assur, supplanted the older gods by conquering Tiamat, the goddess of primeval chaos. The earthly position corresponding to this is clear. As soon as a conqueror took over a new city, his conquest was in a very real sense the victory of his god as well as of himself. When Babylon extended its rule over the Sumerian cities, this was the supplanting of the older gods of Sumer by Marduk of Babylon. As we shall see, the city-god was entirely responsible for the welfare of his city, and his power rose and fell with the success or failure of his city.

In the beginning there is primeval chaos, Tiamat, says the story; with her is Apsu her consort (the sweet waters) and attendant hosts. They beget the earliest gods, and in two generations the sky, Anu, comes into being, the supreme lord of the world above. And Anu engenders En-ki, or Ea, the earth, the most cunning and skilled of the gods. But the gods have to work with pick and shovel on this small piece of earth because as yet there is no man, and no place for man to live. The movement of the gods, however, upon the belly of Tiamat disturbs her and Apsu, so that she proposes to destroy them "that peace may reign and we may sleep."

It is clear that the begetting of these gods is also a nature myth explaining how land is indeed created in Mesopotamia "upon the bosom of the deep" by the meeting of the sweet waters (Apsu) and the salt water (Tiamat) and the formation of silt. But this aspect need not be treated in detail here.

---

[2] No similar creation myth has yet been discovered dating from Sumerian times. In one fragment En-ki, the god of wisdom, in obedience to the suggestion of the superior gods that some way should be found to relieve them of the task of having to provide for their daily bread, created man from clay with the cooperation of Nammu, the

primeval deep. But it remains possible that another version will yet be discovered as the prototype for the Babylonian story, since Enlil is described in other Sumerian legends as the god who divided heaven and earth, and Enlil alone of the Sumerian gods does not appear in the Babylonian version. In any event the myth illustrates so well the attitude of the Mesopotamian peoples as a whole toward their gods that it is discussed here with other Mesopotamian religious concepts, since present knowledge is insufficient to enable us to isolate the Babylonian and Assyrian cosmological concepts from those of the Sumerians. Some clearly later religious developments attributable to the Babylonians and Assyrians will be discussed in the course of the chapter.

So Tiamat prepares for war, and the gods, disturbed, send En-ki down to forestall trouble. He is successful in killing Apsu by a word of command (the sweet waters now held immobile forever afterward). Tiamat is furious, but temporarily quiescent until her attendants rouse her again to action. Meanwhile she marries a new consort, Kingu. The gods again send En-ki down to deal with Tiamat, but this time he is impotent. Even the great Anu finds he can do nothing against her. The gods are now in despair until En-ki proposes that his son Marduk (in the Babylonian version) be authorized to do battle with her. The gods are at first doubtful but, having tested Marduk's power, are willing to concede him authority on his own terms, namely, that thereafter he shall be the executive power of the gods.

Marduk, thus fortified, then marches against Tiamat, and envelops her and her hosts in a net. When Tiamat, pictured as a great sea monster, opens her mouth to swallow him, he sends in the force of the winds, preventing her from closing her mouth while he shoots an arrow which pierces her heart and kills her. Her followers are held in the net and taken captive. Marduk returns to the upper world and claims his position, which is conceded. Then he takes the body of the dead Tiamat, cuts it in two, and lifts half of it up to form the sky, making sure that the water above the earth is guarded by locks to prevent its escape. The lower part of her body exactly corresponds to the upper, and on it Marduk makes his own dwelling. He sets stars in the sky to determine the days and months of the year and special openings for the daily entrance and departure of the sun, moon, and planets.

Finally comes his last task, how to relieve the gods of their toil "that they may freely breathe," and he says: "Arteries will I knot, and bring bones into being. I will make a savage, 'Man' be his name. I will form a savage—man. Let him be burdened with the toil of the gods." So Kingu, the defeated consort of the dead Tiamat, is executed, and "they condemned him, severed his arteries, and from his blood they formed mankind."[3] And Marduk divides the gods, assigning some to heaven under the direction of Anu and assigning others to earth. The gods take pick and shovel in hand for the last time to build Marduk a city; then they confirm his titles and status, and the poem ends by a recounting of his many names.

So mankind was created out of the blood of the defeated consort of the forces of chaos, than which there was nothing lower in the universe; and he was created as a slave to perform the menial tasks of the gods, relieving them of their work. This conception of the place of man in the universe permeates Mesopotamian thought. The king is the chief human representative of the gods upon earth, but even he is a slave of the gods. He may be all-powerful in earthly things, but he is not himself a god, and his titles in early days mean steward or governor. He is a viceroy rather than a true king. He is the head of an underprivileged group in the cosmic state, rather than the giver of rights to the people.

The temple-community

In theory, then, it is clear that the gods were the owners of all the land, with the king or *ensi* their steward or bailiff. In practice we find that the temple had the first call upon the services of all the people, but those services were strictly defined by law and custom. And the temple had a large portion of the land under its direct control. Nevertheless the king was not subordinate to the priestly power as he was in later Egypt, except in matters considered purely religious; and these matters were carefully defined according to a prescribed set of rules. The kings appointed the high priests and not vice versa, though in some Sumerian cities the high priest is, in the absence of an *ensi* or steward of the gods, himself the chief secular authority also. From Assyrian documents to be discussed later it is clear that the religious knowledge of the priesthood could have lent itself to consid-

[3] These quotations are from J. B. Pritchard, ed., *Ancient Near Eastern Texts Relating to the Old Testament* (tr. E. A. Speiser; Princeton, N. J.: Princeton University Press, 1950), p. 68.

erable abuse. But there was always the safe-guard that the king also knew the rules to be observed in determining the will of the gods, and the priests had to point to specific omens which required a certain line of conduct from the king before he would agree to abide by their decisions. This was one of the great advantages of a written law in curbing the power even of those who administered and executed it.

The temple estates in the Sumerian cities were really conceived of as the estates of the gods who owned them, who themselves had subordinate gods under them, even to the divine bailiffs in charge of operations, divine inspectors of fisheries, and divine gamekeepers. Only the menial labor was done by human beings, organized under the chief human overseer, the *ensi*. His position was that of a steward in relation to the god. He was supposed, like an earthly steward, to consult the god on all important and even unimportant occasions, and to administer the law for him, according to contracts entered into with the god. He had to negotiate with the *ensi* of other city-gods, since each city had its own particular city-god. These city-gods, as a rule, were comparatively minor deities. The great gods had more to do than bother with one city-state, but their power extended through all of the communities according to their particular functions in the universe. The wife of the *ensi* had similar duties to perform for the wife of the god.

At once this question arises: How did each god communicate with his *ensi?* Was it left entirely up to the priesthood to decide what the gods wanted?

The chief method was through the interpretation of omens. However, these were not interpreted according to the judgment of individual priests, but from long catalogues in which all possible omens and their meanings were listed. In other cases, when a particular question had to be answered, the liver of some sacrificial animal would be inspected. The liver of a sheep, for example, has certain markings on it, which, like the lines of the human hand, differ widely from each other. Most personal of all methods of communication with the god was the dream. The king would go to the temple, sacrifice and pray, then lie down to sleep, and the god would appear to him and give him his orders. From these methods it can be seen that the priesthood, though it acted as interpreter, remained the servant of the god and the king, and could not abuse its power readily. And the duty of obedience to the gods' wishes seems to have been so deeply impressed upon all Mesopotamian peoples that a manipulation of these wishes for political purposes was probably at most periods unthinkable. If even the Assyrian kings with their militarist peoples behind them could not act against the will of the gods, much less would the priests have had the audacity to do so.

The whole conception of the close relationship between the processes of nature (as represented by the gods) and the activities of man seems to have been the ruling thought of Mesopotamian culture at all times. What happened in heaven was the counterpart of what happened on earth. The heavens and natural events could be consulted to see what must happen on earth, and, if possible, human beings might try to avert dangers and disasters foretold there. Nothing in nature happened casually. Any movement of birds or animals, any eclipse or conjunction between one star and another —these did not happen by chance, but by design of the gods, as the earth itself was created as the direct counterpart of the heavens. When astrology largely took the place of divination by omens, the conception was in no way changed. Chaldean astronomy and astrology belonged to the same view of the world, and were just as natural. It is clear that astronomy was an incidental by-product of astrology and must have been so, for astrology itself was only a more scientific method of discovering the will of the gods and coming events on earth than the earlier techniques. The dream was the least effective of these methods because it could not be compelled, and there could be no interpretation until there was a dream to interpret. But when every natural event could be read as an omen, and every movement of the heavens portended some event on earth, it is clear there was no lack of information on the will of the gods for their earthly slaves to carry out.

The chief figure, then, in the Sumerian city was the god, and his chief human attendant was the *ensi*. In human terms title to the greater part of the land would be vested in the temple of the city-god. If the city were a large one there might be several estates belonging to different local gods and their families, together with the larger estate of the chief city-god, which would exercise some jurisdiction over the estates of minor gods. In the case of administrative units of two or three towns and villages, the chief god of the chief city, and his *ensi*, would be the paramount authority of the unit. Each temple had its own serfs and tenants working on a sharecropping basis, with the lion's share of the produce going to the temple-landowner. The temple also had its own servants, the priests and their assistants, who were devoted to the strict service of the god. The work of a temple community might be directed either by the *ensi* if there was one, or by the high priest of the particular god in person as the chief local temple authority. In practical terms this seems to have meant that the land was owned by the community and that everyone within the city-god's estate had a definite position with definite duties to perform for the community. The serfs had no rights except that they were protected by their master, in this case the temple, and the tenants had a certain amount of land whose produce they could keep for themselves. The rest they cultivated on behalf of the temple-community. Other land seems to have been rented out by the temple-community for money. Everyone, whatever his status, was liable for certain community services, e.g., for building temples, public works, roads, and irrigation projects.

In larger communities, in addition to the *ensi* there was a real king, a *lugal*. As servant of the god of the city or groups of cities, he had an overriding authority over both minor *ensis* and the high priests. But his position, in theory and apparently, at least in the early days, in practice, was only temporary. If the gods gave a sign that he should be replaced or that kingship should cease in the area, then it was his duty to retire or submit to being deposed; or as a last resort, in the Sumerian phrase, he could be "smitten by weapons." No doubt this deposition would be carried out if the king had lost the support of the community; or, if the religion had sufficient hold on the minds of the people, this loss of support by the community would result from his having been abandoned by the gods.

Attitude of the people to the gods

These gods of the Sumerians were so closely identified with the civil administration that they must have commanded little worship from their adherents beyond formal obedience and submission. They could not be approached by individuals for help. So the individuals also had personal gods, usually some minor deities who were believed to have shown personal interest in the worshiper by some special mark of distinction. Believing as deeply in his own powerlessness to change events as the Sumerian did, he could only hope that his personal god would be influential enough to achieve something in his behalf in his own field of activity. There are many examples of letters written to these personal gods by their adherents, asking for their assistance in ordinary worldly affairs. And these gods are even threatened with desertion by their worshipers if they do not lend their aid. Naturally the great gods would be chosen as helpers if they were available. But the Sumerian was only too well aware of the remoteness of such deities. So it was safer to choose some minor god and try to persuade him to use his influence with those higher up. Unhappily, in spite of law codes and the paraphernalia of justice, it seems probable that this practice also reflects contemporary experience. For it is often only elementary justice that the worshiper petitions from his god; and if he needed a god to influence other gods to obtain it, and this god could be bribed, threatened, or cajoled into exercising it, the inference is clear!

Once the basic premise has been grasped, it is not too difficult to understand this world of the Sumerians. If we abandon the belief that heavenly affairs are the counterpart of earthly—a belief abandoned by the Hebrews with their conception of a righteous and transcendent god—we shall readily find the substrata of our Judaeo-Christian heritage, especially the powerlessness of man in the face of God. The Mesopotamian religion certainly offered few grounds for optimism. If the gods are arbitrary and man is created only to do their will, everything in life is made to hinge upon the knowledge of what the gods want from man; they do not instruct man in this, so that at any time he is liable to make a mistake. Disagreements in heaven are decided solely on the basis of rank; and man has to pay the price for it. When the city of Ur was destroyed by foreign invaders, it was because the gods in council had so decreed it; and the protective goddess of Ur had herself been forced to acquiesce in the decision. In the description of the destruction of Ur the goddess mourned, but was unable to save it; and the decree is carried out by Enlil, the executive of the heavenly state. Nowhere is the crime imputed to the actual invading armies, who were only the earthly tools of the gods. Had the gods not decreed it, these tools would have been powerless. The Hebrews also looked upon their enemies in this manner. The Babylonians could not have destroyed Jerusalem if God had not so decreed it. But the Hebrews had a consolation denied to the Sumerians. They knew that the reason for the destruction was that they had committed sins and were being punished for them. The Sumerian had no such faith. The best he could hope to do was to discover in advance that the gods were contemplating destruction; and then try his utmost to appease them, and so prevent it. But there was never any certainty that he had correctly diagnosed the situation or understood what the gods required of him to avert it.

The position of the Mesopotamian kings as representatives of gods

This uncertainty affected the position of the king in a remarkable manner at all stages of Mesopotamian history. We have evidence on this point from the middle of the third millennium B.C. right down to the age of the Assyrian conquerors. Being the chief representative of the gods on earth, he had also the chief responsibility. When Lagash was defeated, the responsibility was at once placed on the personal god of the king who had proved too weak to protect it. It was the king's duty above all to discover what the gods wanted and then do it, at whatever personal cost and inconvenience to himself. No one but the king could stay the anger of the gods, though there is evidence that his mantle, and even a substitute king, could function for him on occasions. King Gudea of Lagash, when the gods had indicated that a new temple should be built, had to look in all directions for a sign as to where it should be built and the exact moment for it. An extant cylinder seal records the extraordinary precautions taken by the king before he could be certain that he had correctly understood the message. Then at last he had to purify himself thoroughly and then mold the first brick with infinite care. Correspondence exists from the Assyrian kings to their priests, in which a powerful king complains that the gods' demands seem unreasonable, and requests them to examine the omens again. He is made to undergo ritual shaving, a considerable ordeal for men who had beards such as are shown in the Assyrian reliefs and paintings. On another occasion he was made to live in a reed hut in the desert for several days in order to avert a threatened disaster to his people. When an eclipse took place he prayed: "In the evil eclipse of the moon which took place in the month of Kislimu, on the tenth day; in the evil of the powers, of the signs, evil and not good, which are in my palace and my country, I fear, I tremble, and I am cast down in fear! . . . At thy exalted command let me live, let me be perfect, and let me behold thy

Head of Gudea, ensi of Lagash. (COURTESY THE METROPOLITAN MUSEUM OF ART)

divinity. Whenever I plan, let me succeed! Cause truth to dwell in my mouth."[4] When the Assyrian King Sennacherib impiously destroyed rebellious Babylon, he forgot that he was destroying a city of his empire, for which he was responsible to the gods. His successor, realizing the fact, humbly rebuilt the city and built new shrines for the god of the city, hoping to appease him. In all the great festivals of the year the king had to be present, performing his ritual part, especially in the great spring festival of the New Year, which begins with the special Day of Atonement for the king, and is followed by his ritual humiliation. It was clearly no light burden to be a king in Mesopotamia.

GENERAL PESSIMISM OF SUMERIAN AND MESOPOTAMIAN PEOPLES—EPIC OF GILGAMESH

We have no evidence that the Sumerians were disturbed by the arbitrary nature of their gods to the extent of repudiating them or criticizing them. But their later suc-

4 Quoted by H. Frankfort, *Kingship and the Gods* (Chicago: University of Chicago Press, 1948), p. 248.

cessors within Mesopotamia have left several documents in which the gods are shown as unjust, oppressing man on earth, demanding service, and giving nothing in return. And when man dies there is no hereafter to compensate. All go alike to Irkalla, the abode of shades. Why must this be? Although the two best examples of this thought are not Sumerian, they are of interest as revealing the insoluble nature of the problem within the framework of Mesopotamian religion, and so will be discussed here. But it should not be thought that such ethical emphasis as appears in these texts is as early as the Sumerian civilization.

In one dialogue, which may have been the prototype for the later Hebrew Book of Job, a sufferer is afflicted by the gods, but can see no reason for it. He has sacrificed, prayed, and worshiped; he has performed his duties for the king, and looked after the prescribed ritual. Yet he is suffering from a loathsome disease, he has been whipped with a lash, and his enemies rejoice over him. There should be a reason, he feels, but in typical Mesopotamian fashion he is simply bewildered, until, without any explanation, Marduk heals him and all is well again. So he praises the Lord of Wisdom, but has gained no understanding of why it happened in the first place. However, it is clear that this thinker believed that there should have been some clear connection between his suffering and his life on earth, during which he had always correctly performed his duties to the gods.

The Epic of Gilgamesh, the earliest known poem to deal with the adventures and trials of a great hero, has had many successors, from the *Odyssey* to *Parzival*. In its extant form it is not a Sumerian poem, though a Sumerian poem exists which implies that Gilgamesh was troubled by the question of death, and why the human being does not have immortality. In the Babylonian and Assyrian versions of the epic, Gilgamesh seeks the plant of immortality because his friend has died without apparent reason, and he wishes to know why he has been taken from him.

Gilgamesh hears of an ancestor of his who did indeed have eternal life, one Utnapishtim, who now lives beyond the waters of death. So he sets out on his quest, wanders through the mountains, goes where the sun travels at night. But everyone tells him of the uselessness of his journey. He will never find Utnapishtim, for he lives beyond the waters of death; he might as well abandon the quest. But at last Gilgamesh gains passage over these waters and finds his ancestor. But Utnapishtim has no hope for him. The only reason he himself lives on is because he had saved himself, his wife, and pairs of all living things when Enlil decided to destroy the earth by flood. Then Enlil had repented of his act and, though angry with Utnapishtim at first, granted him immortality for his deed. After the conversation Gilgamesh falls into a magic sleep, which would have turned into death had not Utnapishtim's wife awakened him just in time. She then persuades her husband to give him a parting gift. This gift turns out to be information about a plant which grows on the bottom of the sea and would bring renewed youth to anyone who should eat it. With the aid of Utnapishtim's boatman Gilgamesh discovers the whereabouts of the plant, dives down beneath the sea, and brings it up. Without eating it himself he makes haste back to the city of Uruk. But, as he nears it, he sees a pool and, being tired, he goes for a swim, leaving the plant on the bank. There a snake smells it and snatches it away, thus winning the power of everlasting renewal by shedding his old body and growing a new one. There is, however, no happy ending for Gilgamesh. He bewails his loss and all the trials he has undertaken. He has found no answer; and man cannot gain immortality.

Fundamentally this is the mood of Mesopotamian civilization. There *is* no answer. Man is the plaything of the gods; there is no reason in anything. Man's duty is only obedience and submission to the inevitable in this life, and there is nothing to be looked for beyond the grave.

OTHER SUMERIAN ACHIEVEMENTS

Language and writing

Right at the beginning of Sumerian history, perhaps even before they entered Mesopotamia, the Sumerians invented the so-called cuneiform writing; at the same time were developed the characteristic Mesopotamian art and architectural forms which persisted throughout the whole civilization. The evolution of writing from the original pictures can easily be traced in Mesopotamia, these pictures becoming more and more conventionalized and stylized as time progressed. So it is impossible to determine the earlier forms from the later writing, as in the case of our own writing, without first examining the intermediate stages between the picture and the conventional sign. The accompanying diagram will illustrate the transition.

The writing was not done by scratching some form of pen over a paperlike material, as in Egypt, but was made by impressing soft clay with a square-tipped reed, and then baking the clay into a kind of brick. This made a permanent record of considerable bulk. This method of writing determined the form, as it was impossible to use much artistry with such tools. The writing is called cuneiform ("wedge-shaped"), from the form of the finished characters. Enormous quantities of these tablets have been found in the ruins of Mesopotamian cities, not all of which have even now been read. The language was phonetic, each of the 350 or so signs representing either a syllable or an entire word. The rebus principle described in chapter 2 was first developed by the Sumerians. There was, however, never at any time a cuneiform alphabet, as far as we know.

The language was not deciphered until the middle of the nineteenth century. A huge rock inscription at Behistun in western Iran, written in three cuneiform scripts—Old Persian, Elamite, and Assyrian—had long been known; but the ascent to this rock was difficult, and would have been useless until some progress had been made at the ground level in the knowledge of what to look for in the inscription. When Sir Henry Rawlinson, an Englishman, had discovered three names of kings in the simplest of these writings, the Old Persian script, and thus identified fourteen Persian characters, he climbed the Behistun rock and made copies of the inscription. On his descent to the ground he was able to complete his Persian investigations and turn to the more complex Mesopotamian writings. With the aid of other investigators who were able to note the similarity to the later Hebrew and Arabic languages, he was at last able to complete the knowledge of Assyrian. From this it was a short step to understand the Akkadian language. But it was not as yet even recognized that either the Sumerian people or a Sumerian language had ever existed. The discovery of the library of Assurbanipal in ancient Nineveh, however, provided the world with a host of new cuneiform tablets. Among these were many in an unknown non-Semitic language.

The translation of these tablets, as it turned out, did not present scholars with the same obstacles as had been experienced with Babylonian and Assyrian. The Sumerian language was evidently regarded by the later inhabitants of Mesopotamia as a kind of classical language, as Latin was by our medieval forefathers. Long after it had ceased to be spoken it was studied—and many docu-

Sumerian stone stela of the third millennium B.C. This stela is a legal "document" recording the transfer of land, animals, and a dwelling by Ishnun-gal to his priestess daughter and three other legatees. (METROPOLITAN MUSEUM OF ART)

ments are extant that describe the training of scribes in Mesopotamia. As an aid to this study interlinear translations were made, and the Sumerian equivalents for the Babylonian and Assyrian signs were systematically listed. With such a key, scholars had no difficulty in learning the basic elements of the Sumerian language and grammar. However, with so few specialists working in the field, it has

Sumerian	Babylonian	Assyrian

The cuneiform symbol for a bird, showing its evolution from the picture of a bird. The original bird symbol, however, is not actually known, but the later forms as shown above allow us to presuppose that in very early times a definite picture of a bird, similar to this, was used.

taken many decades to arrive at full agreement on all the details of meaning and syntax, and translations even of the same documents are constantly being improved.

ART AND ARCHITECTURE

All architecture, domestic and monumental, was limited in this region by the nature of the only available building mate-rial, mud and clay baked into bricks. Since this material is not permanent and is easily damaged and made shapeless by the elements, nothing has survived to our time in its original form; in fact, in ancient times there was constant replacement of buildings. Cities are found superimposed upon one another, and Mesopotamian cities have to be carefully excavated to see traces of each suc-

These two pictures show the mound of Tepe Gawra in Assyria at different stages of excavation. Tepe Gawra, in the words of Dr. Speiser, the director of the excavation project, "furnishes the longest continuous record of superimposed occupations known to science." The latest of the settlements was abandoned at least 3,500 years ago, and the great majority of the settlements date from the third and fourth milleniums B.C.; over half are demonstrably prehistoric. (COURTESY OF E. A. SPEISER)

cessive city. Before excavation a buried city is nothing but a sand-covered mound in the desert.

The characteristic form of monumental architecture in Mesopotamia is the ziggurat, built of brick, unlike the Egyptian temples. A ziggurat was usually built on an artificial mountain of sun-dried bricks rising out of the plain. Upon this base was erected the temple itself, a kind of tower with several stories, or terraces, each stepped back and smaller than the one on which it rested. A great stairway led to the summit. On the shrine itself all the resources of the country could be used. As early as the First Dynasty of Ur[5]—a city now far inland, but then close to the Persian Gulf—there were fine friezes in relief and inlay work of the highest craftsmanship. The brick columns were overlaid with copper and mother of pearl. The architects used their ingenuity not only in solving the technical problems of building in sun-dried brick, but in suggesting the central nature of the temple by making all the lines lead up to the shrine at the top. It was not possible to use the post and lintel, as in Egypt, with this material; when trying to span large openings with small pieces of material they developed the arch with its blocks of different shapes to take the stress. The vault and dome were also used by the Sumerians, but in their private architecture rather than in the conventional ziggurats.[6]

The craftsmen of ancient Sumer must have been by far the most skilled in the world of their day. They carved gems, and understood a great deal more about alloys and the casting of metals than did any of their contemporaries. The graves at Ur are full of finely sculptured ornaments, usually in precious metals and stone. These are imaginative and varied, excelling in the representation of human and animal life.

[5] 2600 B.C., or earlier.

[6] It is not known whether there is any direct relationship between the Mesopotamian ziggurat and the Egyptian pyramids, including the step pyramid of Zoser, which in many respects resembles the former. The ziggurat, at all events, was never a tomb, and thus lacked those elements in the pyramids which were present because they were tombs as well as solar monuments.

PRACTICAL INVENTIONS AND THE ECONOMY—MATHEMATICS

The Sumerians seem to have been an eminently practical people, and they developed many useful devices for use in their economy and daily life. Their calendar suffered from the disadvantage of all lunar calendars in that it needed to be adjusted to the solar year at irregular intervals by intercalating an extra month when necessary. In this practice, too, they influenced later peoples. The Hebrews and the Muslims later adopted a lunar calendar rather than the more effective Egyptian solar one. At an early date the Sumerians had already achieved skill in practical mathematics, adopting a positional notation for the use of large numbers which influenced indirectly even our own system. They used 60 as their basic number, instead of 10 (the decimal system). Since 60 has more factors than 10, especially 3, which presents so much difficulty in our decimal system, this had some practical advantages. To use this system one must remember that each position counts for 60 and not for 10. Thus 123 in our system $= 1 \times 10^2$ plus 2×10^1 plus $3 \times 10^0 (1)$. A similar notation in Mesopotamia $'$ $''$ $'''$ would give 60^2 plus 2×60^1 plus $3 \times 10^0 (1)$ $= 3,723$, while 123 would be written in two positions as $''$ $'''$ or 2×60^1 plus 3. For numbers under 60, however, the notation is clumsy, as a dividing line had to be used for the tens and integers:

$$'' < ;;; = 26.$$

Fractions, however, could be handled by the use of another sign, it being understood that the denominator in each case would be 60:

$$' \leqq '' \ ' = 1 \text{ plus } \frac{2}{60} \text{ plus } \frac{1}{60^2}.$$

Later Mesopotamian civilizations, using the same method, divided the circle into 6×60 degrees, which has remained the standard to this day. The unit of weight was the mina (or pound) which was divided into 60 shekels.

Model of the City of Ur about 2000 B.C.; constructed by the American Museum of Natural History. (COURTESY AMERICAN MUSEUM OF NATURAL HISTORY)

The remains of a ziggurat in the Assyrian religious capital of Assur. (EDITORIAL PHOTO-COLOR ARCHIVES)

Jewelry from the graves of two ladies-in-waiting of the Queen of Ur, 3500–2500 B.C. Made of gold, carnelian, and lapis lazuli, this jewelry is the oldest known in the world up to the present time, but the skill shown presupposes long development in craftsmanship from prehistoric times. (COURTESY THE METROPOLITAN MUSEUM OF ART)

Steatite (soapstone) vase carved in relief. Sumerian, about 3000 B.C. (COURTESY THE METROPOLITAN MUSEUM OF ART)

White gypsum figure from a Sumerian temple, about 3000 B.C. (COURTESY THE METROPOLITAN MUSEUM OF ART)

A flourishing trade exchanging the surplus agricultural and industrial produce of this usually fertile area especially for metals not found in Mesopotamia was the basis of the prosperity of the Sumerian cities. Almost all the simple methods of transacting business known today were already in use—bills, receipts, notes, and letters of credit. Such large quantities of this commercial material have been preserved that much of it has never been read. The investigator can at once see that a tablet concerns a business transaction of a familiar kind, and he needs to go no further. For a comparatively small sum the private collector can buy such a tablet, thousands of years old, knowing that, even if he could read it, it would change nothing of our knowledge of this ancient civilization.

Extensive regulations for international and domestic trade were early developed, and there is no doubt that the famous Hammurabi Code, to be discussed later, had its basis in Sumerian law, and was issued as a new code by Hammurabi only because his dynasty had conquered Babylon and Sumer, and he wished to establish a common law for all his dominions. But since all the extant Sumerian law codes are far from complete, detailed discussion of the Sumero-Babylonian system of law will be deferred to later in the chapter, where the Hammurabi Code will be analyzed in some detail.

▶ ## Conquests of Mesopotamia

By the middle of the third millennium B.C. most of the old temple communities had been converted into city-states ruled by a single *lugal* or king. About 2,600 B.C. the First Dynasty of Ur was established and ruled far beyond the confines of that city for a period, spreading its cultural influence, in particular, over northern Mesopotamia. In the twenty-fifth century B.C. Ur lost its political supremacy. All the independent city-states were unable to withstand the imperial ambitions of a Semitic king of Agade named Sargon, who subjugated all Mesopotamia to his rule and extended his power westward to the sea, perhaps even to Cyprus.

Our information about this first great empire of antiquity is dependent on too few written records for us to know fully either its boundaries or its system of administration. But it was evidently underpinned by extensive trading, and the merchants in the empire expected Sargon to support their interests, which he did to the best of his ability. The empire was overrun after perhaps a century by the Guti, a barbarian people of whom little is known. Ur then reasserted its supremacy under its Third Dynasty (*ca.* 2150 B.C.). By this time the Sumerian and Semitic populations had intermingled, and the Akkadian language of Sargon had probably replaced Sumerian as a spoken language, leaving Sumerian as a dead language to be studied only in schools, as noted earlier.

About 1900 B.C. the Elamites and Amorites (Amurru), nomadic peoples from the desert, invaded Mesopotamia, and sacked and destroyed Ur, dividing the country between them. The Amorites made Babylon, hitherto an unimportant village, their capital. The sixth king of the Babylonian Amorite dynasty, Hammurabi or Hammurapi, defeated the Elamites, and became the undisputed ruler of an empire, which he called Sumer and Akkad, the same name given by Sargon to his empire five centuries earlier. The dynasty did not long survive his death, as his successors were unable to cope with the barbarian invasions that had probably begun fairly early in the millennium.

From still unidentified areas to the north and east the Indo-European peoples gradually moved into Mesopotamia, Asia Minor, Persia, India, and, at a later date, into Europe. These peoples belonged to a totally different language group and had a different culture, which included the use of the horse in warfare. They were probably responsible for the overthrow of the older Bronze Age civilization of India based on Mohenjo-Daro and Harappa, to be discussed in Chapter 6, and introduced the culture called Aryan into that country. A branch called the Mitanni became powerful in northern Mesopotamia where they absorbed the earlier Hurrians,

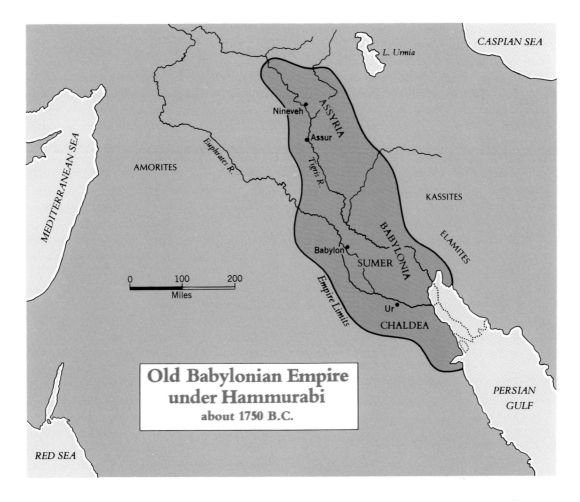

Old Babylonian Empire under Hammurabi
about 1750 B.C.

and at times penetrated far down into Syria where they came in contact with Egypt. Another branch, the Hittites, took over Anatolia and Syria, possibly leaving colonies behind in northern Mesopotamia, since their influence continued strong in that country. All were indebted in greater or lesser degree to the Sumerian culture that they found in their new homes.

The Hittites (or Hatti), a warlike people given to raids on the territories of their neighbors, turned eastward into Babylonia early in the sixteenth century B.C. and captured Babylon, putting an end to the, by this time, nominal rule of the Amorite dynasty. This destruction made it possible for another barbarian group, the Kassites, possibly affiliated with the Indo-Europeans— though the names of their kings are not Indo-European—to conquer Babylon somewhat later. They exercised sovereignty there for the remainder of the millennium, even though they do not appear to have fully subjugated the country. The Kassites in turn were overthrown in 910 B.C. by the Assyrians, who will be discussed later in the chapter.

▶ **Mesopotamia under Hammurabi— The Hammurabi Code**

The rule of Hammurabi in Babylonia and the elevation of Marduk, the god of Babylon, to the chief position in the celestial universe were marked by no great cultural advances. But we are well informed about the life of the times, and the political and economic administration of the period, through our possession of the great Hammurabi Code and some of the official correspondence of the great king.

The code was given to him by Shamash, the god of the sun and of justice. It was therefore this god who inspired him; but Shamash is not given credit for the authority to execute the laws, which is specifically ascribed to the old Sumerian gods Anu and Enlil, and to Marduk, who had just replaced the latter. "When lofty Anu . . . and Enlil . . . determined for Marduk, the first born of En-ki, the Enlil functions over all mankind . . . called Babylon by its exalted name, made it supreme in the world . . . at that time Anu and Enlil named me to promote the welfare of the people, me, Hammurabi, the god-fearing prince, to cause justice to prevail in the land, to destroy the wicked and the evil, that the strong might not oppress the weak . . . ."[7]

[7] Pritchard, *Ancient Near Eastern Texts,* tr. T. J. Meek, p. 164.

A stela showing Hammurabi receiving his code of laws from the sun god Shamash, who was also the god of justice. The code itself is inscribed on the stela. (COURTESY THE LOUVRE)

If we translate these theological terms into earthly conceptions, we shall find that this is a very accurate description of the nature of the code, which is a mixture of old barbarous custom and more modern attempts at administering an evenhanded justice. Hammurabi, who now ruled an empire made up of many peoples, wished no doubt to use his code as a means of unification and to fortify his royal power. He could not, even if he had wished, have abolished the more barbarous provisions that appear in the code, since these were hallowed by long usage. It remains noteworthy that Hammurabi acknowledged that the laws ought to be just in response to the wishes of the gods. He was still the representative of the gods on earth. From the epilogue to the code, which calls down horrendous curses on any who might presume to change the laws in later times, it is clear that he believed that laws once sanctified by the gods should remain valid in perpetuity. No allowance was made at this early time for the possibility of social change in the empire that would require the application of a different code.

Much of the code was, even from our point of view, extremely enlightened and often marked by good common sense, having regard for the nature of Babylonian society. The rights of soldiers on campaign were carefully safeguarded. Officers who withheld their pay or in other ways exploited them were severely punished, in some cases by death. Provisions were made to have a soldier's land looked after in his absence and his feudal dues paid. His city had to ransom him if he were taken prisoner. If there was no money to support his wife, she could remarry temporarily, returning to her former husband when he came back from his campaign, leaving any children of the second marriage to her temporary husband. False witnesses or plaintiffs who could not prove their claims were subjected to the punishment that would have fallen to the lot of the defendants. If a city was unable to bring a robber to justice, it had to compensate the victim. Carelessness in maintaining dikes entailed the payment of compensation by the man who had neglected his duty. If he could not make payment, he could be sold into slavery.

There are detailed provisions regulating commerce, and much attention was given to the proper attestation of all commercial documents, including deeds of sale. Merchants were punished for dishonesty more severely than were their employees. Prices were regulated to discourage profiteering. The right to disinherit a legal heir was hedged about by many restrictions, and permitted only in the event that the son had grievously failed in his filial duty or been seriously delinquent. Children of marriages between persons of different classes usually were raised to the status of the higher ranking parent, and slaves could become free by marrying above their class. Doctors' fees are regulated in the code, but severe penalties were prescribed for negligence and failure to perform what was promised. What is, however, noticeable in all these provisions is the absence of any attempt to temper justice with mercy, and no account is taken of possibly sincere motives and genuine accidents. Nor are the special circumstances of a particular case given any consideration. It is, of course, possible that the judges were given some leeway in making their decisions and decreeing penalties, but we do not have much reliable information as to how the cases were decided in practice. Perhaps Babylon was like Rome, whose citizens for hundreds of years were always permitted to choose exile instead of death. Indeed, when Julius Caesar as high priest tried to revive some of the old laws and their strange penalties, it outraged the feelings of even the most conservative senators. In the early nineteenth century in England, capital punishment could be inflicted for the theft of property worth more than a shilling. But we also know that juries refused to convict when the law made such penalty mandatory.

Certain features of Babylonian society emerge clearly from the code. Justice was unequal. The population was divided into three classes, nobles, free commoners, and serfs and slaves. Crimes against nobles were dealt with more severely than those against the lower classes; but nobles themselves were also in many cases dealt with more severely if it was they who committed the crime. Capital punishment was very common, both for crimes against the person and against property. Aliens were treated liberally, women held a relatively high position, and there were extensive regulations for industry and trade, as might be expected in a commercial civilization. Noteworthy is the fact that private tenure of land seems to have been the rule, unlike the system described for the Sumerian city-states. Peasants were sharecroppers or serfs as before; but, in addition to the priests, the government and nobles now owned the land. This probably reflects the changed conditions under a conquering house of invaders who would not necessarily respect the arrangements made by deities for their sustenance, even while they accepted the general divine order decreed by them. The sharecroppers were protected by law against eviction before the end of the contract year—as before under the regime of the gods—and against obligation to pay full rent if the crop failed.

There are many provisions governing marriage in the code. Evidently it was a legal contract in Babylonia. Though the wife was the legal property of her husband and brought a marriage gift to him, she had some rights, being permitted to return to her father if ill treated by her husband. Although marriage was ordinarily for life, divorce was permissible; the bridal gift would be returned with her, and she would keep the custody of the children. Women were allowed to engage in business, and had as many business rights as the men. However, if the husband fell into debt the wife could be sold as payment for it. There are severe penalties for adultery and other sexual offenses.

The most barbarous feature of the code, from our viewpoint, is the so-called *lex talionis*, applied in a manner which hardly seems to accord with any abstract conception of justice. If a man kill another man's son, his son shall be put to death. If a house collapses, killing the owner's daughter, then the builder's daughter, not he himself, is to be put to death. No doubt such provisions reflect the fact that sons and daughters were regarded as the property of their parents, although they may also be survivals from a more barbarous age and society.

Although we know enough about the earlier Sumerian codes to say that at least some of the penalties for similar crimes were less severe than in the Hammurabi Code, and that the commercial practices described in the latter had been in existence for many centuries in the Sumerian cities, it is still not possible to state how far the code represents an advance upon earlier thinking and practice. We do not know enough about how it was administered, though the correspondence of Hammurabi shows that he took his own duties very seriously. He himself investigated quite trivial disputes, and there are several instances of his sending back cases for retrial, as well as handing down decisions himself, always based on a strict interpretation of the code. It may, however, be noted that even among the Greeks those who proposed to modify the basic legislation handed down by their great lawgivers ran the risk of severe penalties if the proposals were turned down. Not until the Romans was there any truly secular legislation, subject to change by duly authorized legislators.

Both the Hammurabi Code and the whole Mesopotamian legal tradition had a marked influence upon the Hebrew law of a far later epoch, especially upon those parts of the Hebrew codes which seem to be the most ancient. Here no fewer than thirty-five provisions out of fifty are similar. Even the language in both has marked resemblances. The probable explanation is the influence the legal tradition had upon Canaanites and other peoples of Palestine rather than any direct borrowing by the Hebrews. The Hebrews would naturally adopt some of the customs of the Canaanites; and if, as seems probable, there were already Israelites in Palestine before the exodus of the captives from Egypt, during the reunion of the two branches of the people after the exodus each would absorb customs and laws from the other.

▶ The Empire of the Assyrians

THE RISE OF THE ASSYRIANS TO POWER IN THE NEAR EAST AND IN EGYPT

When Babylon fell about 910 B.C. to the Assyrians, the conquerors were not a newly established people, but had been settled in northern Mesopotamia as early as 3000 B.C. During the period of Sumerian and Babylonian ascendancy they had been a pastoral, and then a trading, people, but had always been in danger from their neighbors. We know of wars they fought against Babylonians, Hittites, and Mitanni, as well as against mountaineers and Aramaeans who overran their defenseless frontiers.

The whole history of Assyria is relatively well documented from the records of the great library of Assurbanipal at Nineveh, and inscriptions which have been excavated since the middle of the nineteenth century in other Assyrian cities. From these records we can see the gradual turning of a peaceful people into a nation of warriors, sudden periods of domination over their neighbors followed by periods of quiescence when their enemies were too strong for them. Then, at last, the building of the greatest empire the world had yet seen by the use of methods that have made the Assyrians the byword in later times for ruthless and unprogressive militarism and imperialism. In the Assyrian records there is no attempt to hide the ruthlessness of the conquerors. On the contrary, they boast of it, evidently considering it to be the most effective imperial policy.

We also have the records of the Hebrew prophets and chroniclers, who seem to have looked upon Assyria as the necessary scourge of God, and with a kind of horrible fascination at their wickedness. The delirious delight of Nahum at the destruction of Nineveh, unmatched anywhere else in the Bible, gives some measure of the hatred it had inspired: "Woe to the city, bloody throughout, full of lies and booty. I will strip off your skirts to your face. . . . I will throw vile things at you. And treat you with contempt and make you a horror; so that everyone that sees you will flee from you."[8]

Once the Assyrians had embarked on their aggressive policy they went into it thoroughly. By devoting all their capacities to military invention they far surpassed the technical abilities of their opponents. Few as they were in numbers, they were never defeated in battle until the very end, when their resources were too thin to permit defense on all fronts. Conquered countries were

[8] Nahum 3:1, 5–7. This and other Biblical translations in this text are taken from J. M. P. Smith, E. J. Goodspeed, and others, tr., *The Complete Bible, an American Translation* (Chicago: University of Chicago Press, 1939).

made to pay tribute; if the tribute was not forthcoming at the proper time a lightning expedition would be made against the defaulters, who would pay dearly, as an example to other would-be offenders. All rebellions were crushed ruthlessly, Sennacherib razing the great city of Babylon to the ground and turning the waters of the Euphrates over the site. In the Assyrian records there is mention of wholesale massacres, terrible tortures, public exhibition of the bloody heads of corpses on the battlements of conquered cities, even by those kings, like Assurbanipal, who devoted themselves also to peaceful pursuits. They used iron on an extensive scale for weapons, the first nation to do so; they made use of a mounted cavalry, they invented the battering ram and special

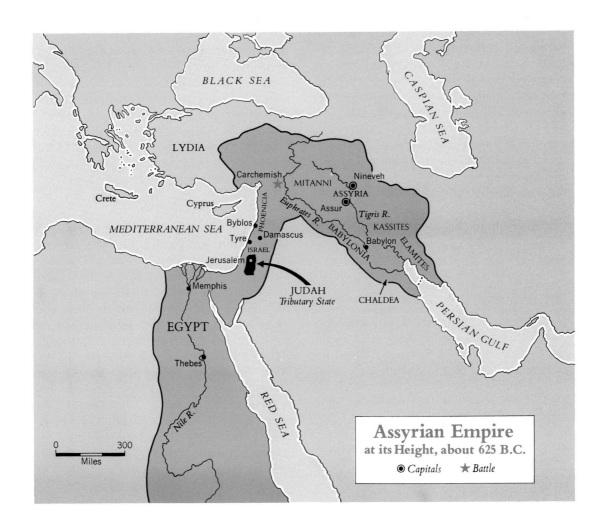

Assyrian Empire
at its Height, about 625 B.C.
◉ *Capitals* ★ *Battle*

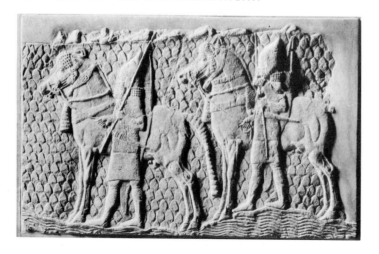

Wall slab (alabaster) from the palace of Sennacherib at Nineveh, showing the king's cavalry in the mountains. (COURTESY THE METROPOLITAN MUSEUM OF ART)

siege machinery capable of overcoming the brick cities of Mesopotamia and Palestine without too much difficulty. They conquered the whole of Mesopotamia and most of Palestine, deporting the inhabitants of Samaria and sending in immigrants from elsewhere so that there would be no further disturbance—a policy used by them frequently elsewhere. They did not conquer Judah, however, the deliverance being ascribed to the angel of the Lord who destroyed the Assyrian army of Sennacherib. Judah did, nevertheless, become tributary to Assyria, as the records show. Esarhaddon also conquered Egypt, as already related, but the Assyrians could not rule such a vast land with so few men, and they had to abandon it soon afterward.

ORGANIZATION OF THE EMPIRE

The rule of the Assyrians was not, however, entirely without its compensations for the conquered peoples so long as they submitted and continued to pay tribute.[9] Local

---

[9] Their work has also been valuable for *us,* in that they carefully collected the records of earlier civilizations of Mesopotamia, preserving them in their libraries. Once destroyed, Nineveh, their capital, unlike Babylon, was never again refounded, as the very site was cursed; and their records remained there intact until they were uncovered by archaeologists more than two thousand years later.

wars between their subjects came to an end, an efficient provincial administration was developed to keep a close watch on governors and subject kings, who had to keep in continuous correspondence with the capital. Roads were built, and a regular royal postal service was inaugurated. A considerable amount of self-government was permitted to the subject cities, and, in particular, trade, in which the native Assyrian of imperial times took little interest, flourished, mainly in the hands of the Aramaeans, a people who will be briefly discussed in the next chapter.

CULTURAL ACHIEVEMENTS

The Assyrian kings were great builders, living in fine palaces with pleasure gardens, and constantly building and rebuilding temples. There was little original in their work, and they did not make much use of stone, although it was abundant in their empire. Their whole culture and religion were as already mentioned, Babylonian, and, through Babylon, Sumerian in their origin. In fact, toward the end of the Assyrian imperial age Marduk seems to have been almost as important as their native god Assur. They made use of Babylonian science and patronized it, altering the cuneiform script by the addition of more symbols. Their many reliefs in their monumental architecture were well executed but Sumerian in inspiration.

It would seem that the Assyrian rulers were more conscious of the past of the Mesopotamian peoples than were the Babylonians whom they supplanted. It has already been mentioned how many of the old stories are known to us only through Assyrian versions, and how frequently the Assyrians copied them. The Babylonian kings of the Hammurabi Age were far less attached to the idea of the king as the representative of the gods on earth and responsible to them than were these even more powerful monarchs. Never were the temples in Mesopotamia so prosperous as under the Assyrian despots. Perhaps the more civilized of their kings may have felt the hatred of the conquered peoples and realized the weak foundations of their empire, and desperately tried to ward off the evil day. Military conquerors in all ages, not excluding the twentieth century A.D., have been superstitious, playing their luck and looking to omens and astrologers for reassurance.

Slab (alabaster) from a pavement in the palace of Sennacherib at Nineveh. The design shows lotus blossoms, palm cones, and rosettes. (COURTESY THE METROPOLITAN MUSEUM OF ART)

FALL OF THE ASSYRIAN EMPIRE

However this may be, the final destruction of the Assyrians was sudden and merciless. It was believed impossible to defeat them in battle if the numbers were at all equal. An exiled prince from Babylonia tried to raise a coalition against them but failed repeatedly. Nevertheless the peoples to the east of Mesopotamia were able to advance slowly and relentlessly, Medes and Chaldeans, and Scythians from the north—all sure of the support of the conquered peoples if the Assyrian hold should weaken. The Assyrians fought back, still winning every local engagement, until suddenly the coalition took Nineveh and razed it to the ground, thus destroying the basis of the state. Still the Assyrian remnants fought on from the old capital of Assur until Nebuchadnezzar, son of the new Chaldean king of Babylon, defeated them and their Egyptian allies decisively in 606 B.C. at the battle of Carchemish. The Assyrians received no mercy as they had shown none. The very people disappeared from history, killed or absorbed into the population of their conquerors.

Subsequent peoples from that day to this have pointed to the fate of the Assyrians as an object lesson for imperialists, and as a people they have had few admirers. Nevertheless they did prepare the way for a great flowering of civilization in Mesopotamia, first under the Chaldeans, then the Medes, and finally the Persians. The East had moved into an era of great empires, and the civilization thus built up was absorbed into the heritage of the West when Alexander the Macedonian three hundred years later conquered the last feeble Persians and founded the Greco-Oriental civilization which exercised such a profound influence on the Romans, and through them and through Christianity upon ourselves. By uniting the Mesopotamian people after a long period of disunity the Assyrians blazed the way for their more constructive successors.

▶ The Chaldeans and New Babylonia

PIETY, ANTIQUARIANISM—ASTROLOGY

The new empire of the Chaldeans at Babylon quickly showed signs of wishing to inherit the mantle of Assyria. Nebuchadnezzar tried to take Tyre and failed, but he succeeded in defeating Egypt severely in several battles, though he did not conquer it. He was at first content with installing a tributary king in Jerusalem; but after repeated rebellions he took the leading Jews captive to Babylon, and Judah was incorporated into his empire. Thus he became overlord of almost all Palestine, and for the rest of his reign retired to his capital of Babylon, which was then enjoying a cultural renascence, in many respects the most brilliant of all.

The people who controlled Babylonia at that time were called Chaldeans, both by the Hebrews and by the Greek historian Herodotus. In Mesopotamian records the name appears only toward the end of the Assyrian Empire. As far as can be judged they do not seem to have been a people different from the Semitic Babylonians of earlier times, though it is possible that exiles from the Assyrian domination now returned to Babylonia from regions to the East, bearing with them astronomical knowledge which gave a new impetus to the study of the stars, which increased greatly in this period of Chaldean rule. The Chaldean kings made every effort to restore the ancient Mesopotamian heritage, and there was a pronounced trend toward antiquarianism. The Chaldean attitude toward religion bears a strong resemblance to the piety of the later Egyptians. It was as if all life had left it, and the only thing that remained was to try to blow upon the old fires and hope to revive them. The result, as in Egypt, was formalism—the revival of the form without the living substance.

Submission to the gods had always been a characteristic of Mesopotamian religion. But now it became a simple matter of resignation and humility before the unalterable decrees of fate. It was still not an ethical religion such as the one the Hebrews developed; sin, as before, was the failure to behave in the manner prescribed by the gods, and had little relation to moral behavior on the earth. As explained earlier, the study of astrology would fit in naturally with the Mesopotamian world-conception; but it was even further removed from the reach of the people, since no one could understand the star lore without instruction. In earlier days they could at least recognize omens. But with the enthronement of astrology as the supreme science the ordinary people were too far removed from the gods to do more than offer humble submission to their decrees. So arose the conception of fate and destiny which was to play such a large part in Oriental thought thereafter.

Chaldean interest in astrology, however, did give rise to the science of astronomy, which reached heights far beyond anything previously achieved by the Mesopotamian peoples. They charted the entire heavens, they worked out a system for the recording of time which was the best so far achieved, and they calculated the length of the year with an error of only twenty-six minutes. All celestial occurrences were recorded with meticulous care. The planets were equated with the old Babylonian gods, and given their names. All this work was continued under the Persians, Greeks, and Romans; from the ancient Chaldean astrologers has come not only all subsequent astrology, especially as developed by the Muslims, but also our own astronomy.

THE CITY OF NEW BABYLON

The absence of a living religion did not prevent the building of great temples in the new Babylon of Nebuchadnezzar. The great temple of Marduk excited the enthusiasm of Herodotus, the Greek tourist and historian, and his description of the ziggurat in the temple and the whole city corresponds very exactly to the results of modern archaeological investigation. It was probably the largest ziggurat ever built. Nebuchadnezzar's palace, with its Hanging Gardens, was for the Greek one of the seven wonders of the world. The famous gardens were a terraced roof garden high above the ground with tropical plants growing in it in great profusion. The city of this king, devoted to peaceful arts and a thriving trade, was one of the greatest, perhaps the greatest city in the world of the day, larger by far than any previous Mesopotamian city. This was the city where the final ethical religion of the Jews was developed, the city whose luxuries tempted them so sorely, the city whose inhabitants to the more puritan among them seemed to symbolize everything they must avoid, the very essence of wickedness and worldly vice. "Daughter of Babylon who art to be destroyed, happy shall he be that rewardeth thee as thou has served us. Happy shall he be that taketh and dasheth thy little ones against the stones."[10]

[10] Psalms 137:8.

The great Persian empire

CONQUEST OF BABYLONIA

To the northeast of the new Babylonia a warlike power was gathering strength. The Medes, an Indo-European people, had already joined forces with the Chaldeans in the destruction of Assyria. But thereafter friendly relations had not been maintained, and the Medes extended their empire further east, bringing another Indo-European people, the Persians, under their rule. The Persians, however, under a young and adventurous prince who went down in history as Cyrus the Great, revolted from the Medes in 549 B.C., and the Medes, apparently without serious opposition, accepted him as king. Thus was formed a strong imperial power, a potential threat to the rapidly weakening Chaldean regime. The story of the "conquest" of

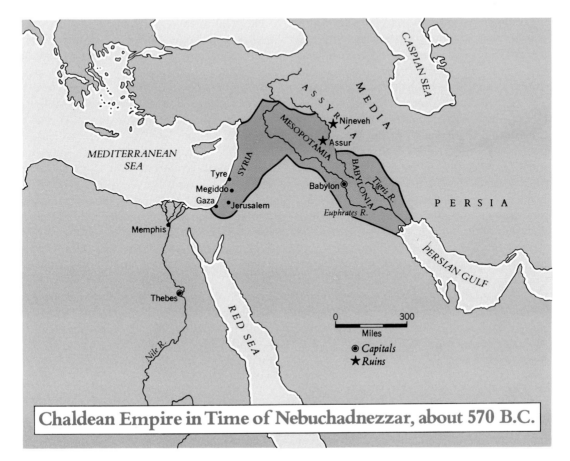

Chaldean Empire in Time of Nebuchadnezzar, about 570 B.C.

Babylon by Cyrus is told in the Book of Daniel—how Belshazzar the king was feasting when he saw the writing on the wall which told him that his kingdom was to be divided and given to the Medes and Persians; and "the same night" Cyrus entered the city and fulfilled the prophecy. However this may be, Cyrus in his own records declared that he took Babylon "without a battle and without fighting," and there can be no doubt that he experienced little opposition from the Chaldeans. The incorporation of Babylonia into his empire made it the greatest that the world had yet seen, stretching as far east as the borders of Turkestan and India, and west to the Aegean Sea. For before proceeding against Babylon Cyrus had conquered Lydia, the chief power in Asia Minor, and expanded his power equally in Central Asia.

In Babylon Cyrus was hailed as a deliverer by the influential classes as well as by the Jews, who were permitted to return to Jerusalem and build their temple. Although his religion was quite different from the one he encountered in Babylon, he had the political good sense to proclaim himself the servant of Marduk and accepted the throne as a gift from Marduk and his priests. The city became henceforth one of the capitals of the Persian Empire. It had to pay taxes to the Great King (as the Persian emperor was always called) like all the conquered lands; but in return the whole of Mesopotamia for the first time enjoyed the benefits of a comparatively enlightened administration and an internal peace which endured until the conquests of Alexander the Great. These benefits, however, were not, for the most part, the work of the great conqueror Cyrus, who was killed in battle while still a fairly young man, nor of his successor Cambyses, who conquered Egypt, but of Darius the Great who usurped the throne when Cambyses died on the way home from Egypt.

GOVERNMENT AND PROVINCIAL ADMINISTRATION

The problem of organizing this vast empire presented many great difficulties. Sardis, the capital of Lydia, an outpost of the empire, was fifteen hundred miles from Susa, the chief imperial capital—a tremendous distance when the difficulty of communication is considered. And though the Persians did not attempt to interfere with local customs, they were still a conquering people and regarded as such. A show of force was necessary to ensure obedience and payment of the taxes required from their subjects. Persians, moreover, had special privileges in the matter of taxation and officeholding in the imperial administration. Nevertheless, the organization set up by Darius did endure for two hundred years in spite of local rebellions by dissatisfied subjects and disobedient governors.

For administrative purposes the country was divided into provinces, each under an official called a satrap. He was head of the civil administration and led the king's armies in the province in the event of war. But the military establishment in other respects remained under the direct authority of the king. The satraps also had to submit to inspection by other officials who were appointed by, and were directly responsible to, the king and who were supposed to keep him informed on the efficiency and loyalty of the satrap. The satrap was responsible for collecting the taxes of the province, which were realistically set at a figure which enabled the satrap to remit to the monarch less than he collected. The system, therefore, was a mixture of local and centralized government like the republican provincial administration of Rome. The chief difference, however—and it is perhaps in favor of the Persian system—was that the satrap could remain in office only as long as he performed his duties capably, and he was always liable to dismissal by the king; whereas the Roman official was restrained only by the threat of legal proceedings by the provincials *after* he had laid down his office, when he had the proceeds of his tenure at his disposal to bribe the juries.

THE ARMY

The army commanded by the Persian king was formidable in size, but motley in its

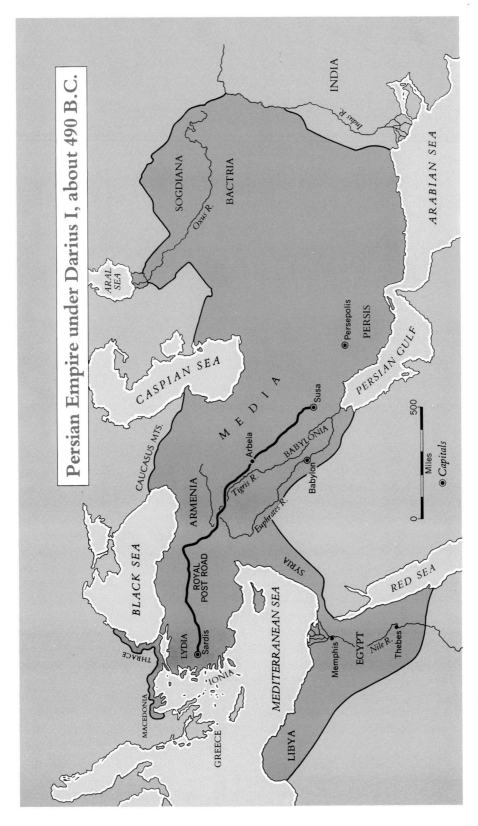

Persian Empire under Darius I, about 490 B.C.

General view of the remains of the palace of Darius I in Persepolis. (ORIENTAL INSTITUTE, UNIVERSITY OF CHICAGO)

composition and of doubtful loyalty outside the famous band of Immortals—a picked body of Persian nobles—and the standing army of native Persians who formed the personal bodyguard of the Great King. The difficulty experienced by the Persians in their wars with Greece, especially when attacked by Alexander the Great, was that the levies liable for service belonged to all the subject peoples of the empire, with different military customs and different traditions. Moreover, they could not be assembled at a moment's notice, but required time both for assembly and for training together. It was possible for Xerxes to recruit a mighty army when he was the aggressor and could choose the moment for his expedition; but even so the army was seldom a match for the smaller numbers of well-trained, disciplined, and patriotic Greeks. But it was not possible for the later Darius who had to face Alexander to assemble his army all together at one time

when he was on the defensive against the vastly smaller Macedonian forces. So Alexander was able to defeat him piecemeal. One thing, however, the Persians always possessed —money; and with this they could afford to hire Greek and other foreign mercenaries, and could intrigue, as the later Persian kings did, to prevent the union of Greek city-states in a possible offensive alliance against themselves. They were also able to mobilize a large fleet, manned for the most part by Greeks and Phoenicians, some of whom were in the empire and some of whom were hired as mercenaries. With this fleet the Persians explored the southern Asiatic coast to the borders of India and restored the canal, newly built by one of the last Egyptian Pharaohs, between the Nile and the Red Sea.

Darius also restored and greatly improved the postal system of the Assyrians. He built new roads to connect with the imperial capital, and along these he stationed relays of fast horsemen to carry messages. By this means the time for news to travel from Sardis to Susa was cut from three months to less than two weeks. The new roads were also a great assistance to trade and general intercourse within the empire. Therefore, in spite of the local variations within this empire the culture became authentically Persian over the centuries, though the dominant language in its western half was Aramaean, with its alphabet from which a new Persian alphabet of thirty-nine letters was formed. The cuneiform languages gradually died out under this competition.

RELIGION

Zoroaster and the traditions of the Avesta

While for the most part the Persians adopted and developed the culture of their predecessors, as was to be expected of a people only recently emerged from barbarism, and while in Mesopotamia and Palestine they did not interfere with local religions, adapting their religious policies as required, they brought with them an entirely new religion of their own, many features of which were in the course of time to supplant the older ones and to exercise a profound influence upon all later religions, including Christianity and Islam.

The origins of what is called Zoroastrianism lie far back in the remote past, and it is impossible to determine how much of the Persian religion was of recent origin, how much was due to the influence of the prophet Zoroaster or Zarathustra, who lived perhaps as late as the sixth or seventh century B.C., and how much came from remote antiquity. The prophet himself was always a mysterious figure, and the teachings of his religion, as propounded by himself and enlarged by the Magian priests of the Persian religion, were not collected in one book, the *Zend-Avesta*, until the early Christian Era. As with the religion of India, there was a considerable religious tradition handed down by word of mouth for centuries before it was found necessary to record it in writing. Even in the *Zend-Avesta* itself there is so much that is

mysterious and difficult to comprehend and so many apparent contradictions in the different sections of this composite work that it is almost impossible now to state with confidence what were the exact teachings of the prophet. The difficulty in determining the date of his mission is compounded by the information given by the Greek writer Plutarch, who tells us that the Persians believed that a Zarathustra had lived many millenniums before the seventh century B.C. In the *Zend-Avesta* itself it was predicted that Zarathustra would return at the end of time as a Savior with the task of renewing all existence. He would raise the bodies of the dead and unite them with their souls preparatory to the Last Judgment.

It is clear that Zoroastrianism in the form in which we find it during the Persian Empire and in its many important successors was a religion that was well suited to supplant the older Mesopotamian religions which, as has been seen, were already in their death throes. For this reason alone, if for no other, the existence of a comparatively late prophet, who at the very least refounded and reinterpreted the traditional religion, would seem probable. For Zoroastrianism was clearly an ethical religion, one that appealed to the developing spiritual capacities of mankind, and fitted to command the faith and allegiance of individuals rather than the devotion of the state and the people as members of the state. It was deeply concerned, as the older religions were not, with the problem of good and evil, ethical good and evil, and not merely with the failure to observe prescribed ritual practices or to understand what the gods required of man and his integration within the order of the universe.

Dualism—The spirit of light and the spirit of darkness

The world had been created by Ahura-Mazda, the god of light. But though he would ultimately triumph, he was not omnipotent and was engaged in a constant struggle with the god of darkness, Aingra-Manu, or Ahriman, who was the embodiment of all wickedness, treachery, and deceit and possessed of almost equal powers. Each of these gods had his attendant host of spirits ceaselessly working for him. It was man's duty—within limits he had free choice—to aid the god of light in his struggle with the god of darkness and help to overcome him. The Persian kings all claimed their position by the grace of Ahura-Mazda and conceived it as their duty to support the rule of light upon earth, administer justice, and rule according to righteousness. Darius expressed this ideal in the Behistun inscription referred to earlier. The priests of Zarathustra, usually called the Magi, kept alive the sacred fire, the symbol of Ahura-Mazda in their temples.

Ethical system and the belief in immortality

Zoroastrianism contained a definite and clear belief in a future life. In the process of time the good powers would overcome the evil, and then Zarathustra would return to prepare the end of the world. The last great day would then come when Ahriman would be finally vanquished, and the souls of the dead would be judged according to their deeds, the justified would at once enter Paradise, while the wicked would be cast into Hell with their master Ahriman. There they would serve him until they too would be redeemed in a far distant future. There can be little doubt that the Christian story of the Wise Men of the East who visited the infant Jesus in Bethlehem to worship him was intended to show that the priests of Zarathustra had recognized in him the Messiah whom they too awaited.

The sins which lead to damnation are catalogued—pride, gluttony, sloth, and other of the Christians' "deadly sins"—as are also the virtues—keeping contracts, obeying rulers, tilling the soil, showing mercy, giving alms, and not doing to others what one did not wish done to one's self. Early Zoroastrianism, unlike the later religions which developed from it and stressed the evil nature of the material world, did not approve of asceticism, self-inflicted suffering, and excessive fasting or grief.

Influence of Zoroastrianism on later religions

The relationship between Zoroastrianism and later religions has been much disputed. Mithraism, which became so strong in the early Roman Empire as to threaten the growing influence of Christianity, has a clear Persian origin, but is far removed from the teachings of Zoroaster himself. It is believed to owe more to pre-Zoroastrian pagan traditions than it does to the prophet. Two elements in Zoroastrianism have been stressed by later religions: the resurrection of the body and life after death, which entered Judaism and orthodox Christianity; and the struggle between good and evil for the mastery of the human soul, a struggle the outcome of which was in doubt because of the great strength of evil, an independent force not created by God but in opposition to him. This doctrine, known as dualism, was a strong component of many Christian heresies, including Manichaeism, which arose in Persia in the third century A.D. and was accepted for a time by St. Augustine, one of the most influential of the fathers of the Christian Church. However, even before the Persian prophet Mani preached his religion and founded his heretical church various Christian teachers who were condemned as heretics by the orthodox had adopted Dualism, especially the Gnostics.

It is natural for thinking men to ponder the great question of why God permitted evil to come into the world. Dualism adopts the position that God was not all-powerful, but had to struggle against an evil god and needed the help of man to overcome him—a notion clearly to be found in Zoroastrianism. In the view of some heretical sects, especially the medieval Cathars (see Chapter 18) matter itself has been created by the evil god. It is therefore man's task to free himself from the dominion of the material world through asceticism, a notion that, as we have seen, was frowned upon by Zoroaster. By contrast the Hebrew tradition, followed by the Christian Church, holds that evil was permitted to enter the world by God, who could have prevented it. It is man's task thereafter to resist the lures of evil and to do good. But this by itself did not settle for the early Christian theologians the question of the origin and purpose of evil. Their answer, which became the orthodox teaching of the Church, was that the world had indeed become a prey to evil, and it would have overcome man's puny strength if God had not sent his Son to redeem men from "original sin," thus making it possible for them to receive "grace," and thereby know good and do it. Much of this formulation was worked out by St. Augustine, who as a Manichaean had felt the force of the dualistic arguments.

Hebrew thought, as we shall see, was concerned with the question of why evil flourished, and why the evil man prospered, but never considered the possibility that God was not omnipotent. By contrast Zoroastrianism raised the question of God's omnipotence by stressing the role of the evil god, Ahriman. Although this religion itself gave the victory to Ahura Mazda rather than to Ahriman, others, wrestling with the same problem, came to different conclusions. Zoroastrianism has the merit of having at least drawn attention to the problem which has concerned thinking men ever since.

► **Conclusion—The influence of Mesopotamia**

We have now traced the history of Mesopotamia until the coming of the Greeks. The greatest direct contribution of these peoples to Western civilization was probably their science, which became mingled with Greek science and so was passed on to the West after the conquests of Alexander. The art of writing was discovered by them, they did important work in mathematics, and they laid the foundations of astronomy. Indirectly their work was of the greatest importance for the Hebrews, since they gave them their basic law, and from them sprang the whole tradition of submission and obedience to the gods who ruled the universe. The Persians added an ethical emphasis which affected both later Hebrew thought and Christianity, with their conception of the Last Judgment and rewards and punishments in the next

world, and new thoughts on the nature of good and evil. The Assyrians provided a great object lesson on the dangers of undiluted imperialism which was appreciated and profited from by the Persians and Greeks who followed them.

In bulk the contribution of Mesopotamia does not begin to compare with the legacy to the West of the Greeks and Romans, though it probably surpasses the legacy of Egypt; but in the depth of its influence it is surpassed by few civilizations. Without the pioneer work of the Mesopotamian peoples in science and religion the lives of all later peoples would have been substantially different. And Mesopotamia itself did not cease to be a center of civilization, but again rose to power and influence under the Parthians, the Sassanid Persians, and the Muslim Abbasids. But by this time the independent civilizations of the West were growing up and the civilizations of the Near East had only a minor influence upon them. When Harun-al-Rashid of Bagdad and Charlemagne of Aachen exchanged courtesies in the eighth century A.D., each knew almost nothing of the other. The East and West had embarked on their independent journeys.

► **Suggestions for further reading**

PAPER-BOUND BOOKS

Chiera, Edward. *They Wrote on Clay.* Phoenix. An older work (1938) by one of the pioneer cuneiform scholars. Well-written general account, brief but good introduction to the subject.

Cleator, P. E. *Lost Languages.* Mentor. See *Suggestions for further reading* at the end of Chapter 2.

Contenau, Georges. *Everyday Life in Babylonia and Assyria.* Norton. Based on archaeological investigation, with excellent illustrations.

Frankfort, Henri, *et al. Before Philosophy.* Penguin. The article on Mesopotamia by Thorkild Jacobsen in this volume is stimulating and provided the basis for much of this chapter, but some of the conclusions should be regarded as more disputable than the article admits.

Frankfort, Henri. *Birth of Civilization in the Near East.* Anchor. Useful introduction to the subject by a distinguished archaeologist.

Frye, R. N. *The Heritage of Persia.* Mentor. A good introduction, with excellent photographs.

Gelb, Ignace J. *A Study of Writing.* Phoenix. Careful analysis of early writing, including the first alphabets.

Gordon, Cyrus H. *Hammurabi's Code: Quaint or Forward-Looking?* Holt, Rinehart and Winston. Topical study of the major provisions of the code, with commentary by the author, an expert in Babylonian language and history.

Hawkes, Jacquetta, and Woolley, Leonard. *Prehistory and the Beginnings of Civilization.* See *Suggestions for further reading,* Chapter 2.

Kramer, Samuel N. *History Begins at Sumer.* Anchor. A list of the contributions of the Sumerians to history and the various fields in which they were the pioneers, written by one of the few living Sumerologists, who was himself the first to read many of the documents analyzed here.

Kramer, Samuel N. *Sumerian Mythology.* Torchbooks. An earlier book (1944) than the author's *History Begins at Sumer;* the myths and legends are more fully described.

Mallowan, M. E. *Early Mesopotamia and Iran.* McGraw. An excellent book for the interested student.

Moscati, S. *Ancient Semitic Civilizations.* Capricorn. A good introductory book.

Olmstead, Albert T. *History of the Persian Empire; Achaemenid Period.* Phoenix. Well-written work, best on history and political organization, somewhat weak on Zoroastrianism.

Roux, Georges. *Ancient Iraq.* Penguin. Political history of ancient Mesopotamia.

Sanders, Nancy, trans. *The Epic of Gilgamish.* Penguin. A prose translation of the famous epic.

Saggs, H. W. F. *The Greatness that was Babylon.* Mentor. A fascinating account of everyday life in Babylonia based on the cuneiform inscriptions.

CASE-BOUND BOOKS

Bottero, et al. *The Near East: The Early Civilizations.* New York, Delacourt, 1967. Probably the best general survey of ancient Mesopotamia.

Huart, Clement. *Ancient Persian and Iranian Civilization.* New York: Alfred A. Knopf, Inc., 1927. Readable analytic account of the organization of the Persian Empire.

Kramer, S. N. *The Sumerians.* University of Chicago Press, 1963. The most comprehensive of the books by this eminent Sumerologist.

Neugebauer, Otto. *The Exact Sciences in Antiquity.* 2d ed. Providence, R.I.: Brown University Press, 1957. Re-evaluation of Babylonian contributions to science. Somewhat difficult and technical, but well worthwhile for students with a knowledge of modern science.

Olmstead, Albert T. *History of Assuria.* Charles Scribner's Sons, 1923. New York. Well-written standard work, perhaps too favorable to imperialism for most modern tastes.

Pritchard, Joseph B., ed. See *Suggestions for further reading* at the end of Chapter 3.

Zaehner, Robert C. *The Dawn and Twilight of Zoroastrianism.* New York: G. P. Putnam's Sons, 1961. By far the best available work in English on the subject, careful and thorough, though most of the book is concerned with the later history of the religion.

CHAPTER 5

MARITIME AND OTHER CIVILIZATIONS OF THE ANCIENT WORLD

▶ General contrast between Hebrew and other civilizations

This chapter, the last to be devoted to the Near Eastern precursors of Western civilization, necessarily lacks the geographical unity of the two preceding ones. Most of the civilizations to be dealt with here grew up in close proximity to the sea, though only the Cretans (Aegean civilization) and Phoenicians were dependent upon it for their livelihood and built powerful navies. The Canaanite peoples, including the Hebrews, enjoyed an extensive trade outside their borders, but relatively little of it was carried by sea. Though all the peoples to be considered in this chapter developed cultures of importance in their own day, none of them preserved their identities in post-Christian times except the Hebrews to whom most attention will therefore be given.

The story of this people, indeed, is unique in the world's history. Their independence lasted for only a few centuries. The northern half of the country was conquered by the Assyrians in the eighth century B.C., whereupon the people were scattered throughout the Assyrian territories and disappeared as a separate entity from history.

The southern half, the kingdom of Judah, though conquered by the Chaldeans who deported most of the population to Babylon, nevertheless preserved its religion, and with it a sense of its separate identity. When the exiles were permitted by the Persians to return to their former country and capital, they retained their religion and rebuilt their state as a virtual theocracy. In a later century they were conquered once more by Alexander the Great and became a part of the Hellenistic world under his successors. After a successful rebellion they reestablished their independence. Conquered again by the Romans, who put an end to their state, they were scattered throughout the Roman and Christian world. But the Jewish religion was now too strong to be suppressed and continued to maintain itself separate from the religion which had stemmed from it and which became the religion of Western civilization. Now in the twentieth century by an astonishing and unique effort of the will, the Jews against all obstacles have created their own national state of Israel, which is open to immigration to all Jews. They have made the language of the ancient Hebrews their national language, which the young are required to learn and which is the sole nationwide language of com-

► chronological chart

Hittite Empire	Aramaeans	Phoenicians
		In Palestine before 2000 B.C.
Migration into Asia Minor *ca.* 2200 B.C.		
Largest extent of Empire Suppiluliumas I (1375–1355)	Largest Empire in Palestine 1500 B.C.	Conquest by Egypt (Thutmose III) 1447
Battle of Kadesh and treaty with Rameses II of Egypt 1297		
Fall of Hittite Empire (remnants around Carchemish) 1200		Independent Phoenician cities 1200–1000
		Leadership of Tyre —maritime supremacy of Phoenicians *ca.* 1000–774
	Kingdom of Damascus *ca.* 1000–732	
	Fall of Damascus to Assyrians (Tiglath–Pileser III) 732	Phoenicians tributary to Assyria 774–625
Lydian Empire *ca.* 950–547 B.C.		Phoenicians tributary to Persia 538–332
Fall of Sardis to Cyrus the Persian 547		Conquest of Phoenician cities by Alexander the Great 332

Hebrews

Abraham in Palestine	*ca.* 1450*
Family of Jacob migrates to Egypt	*ca.* 1350*
Exodus of Hebrews from Egypt (?)	1260*
Period of Judges in Israel	1225–1020
Saul, king of Israel	1020–1004
David	1004–965
Solomon	965–926
Division of kingdom of Israel	926
Fall of Samaria to Assyrians	721
Fall of Jerusalem; Exile in Babylon	586
Return of Jews to Jerusalem	538
Building of the new temple	520–516
Conquest of Palestine by Alexander the Great (part of Ptolemy I's domain)	332
Palestine conquered by Antiochus III of Syria	198
Revolt of Maccabees against Antiochus IV	167
Conquest by Romans under Pompey, ruled by family of Herods, clients of Romans	63
Direct rule by Romans A.D.	6–41
Jewish revolt against Romans	66–70
Destruction of Jerusalem by Titus	70
Jerusalem rebuilt under name of Aelian Capitolina; Jews not permitted to live in it; Judaea remains Roman province	135

Aegean Civilization

Neolithic Age in Crete	*ca.* 3000 B.C. onward
Early Minoan Civilization	2500–2000
Middle Minoan Civilization	2000–1550
Mycenaean civilization on mainland	before 1600
Mycenaean rule in Crete	*ca.* 1400
Conquest of Crete by Dorians	*ca.* 1200
Fall of Troy to Achaeans and others	*ca.* 1184
"Dark Age" in Crete and on mainland	1100–800

* These much disputed dates follow those given in Cyrus H. Gordon, *Introduction to Old Testament Times* (Ventnor, N. J.: Ventnor Publishers, Inc., 1953), pp. 102–103.

munication between its disparate groups. However, unlike the history of the Jews, the history of other Canaanite peoples became merged in that of their conquering successors.

► The Hittites

DISCOVERY OF THEIR CIVILIZATION

Little was known about the Hittites until the twentieth century, and a hundred years ago no one considered them to be of any consequence. They were mentioned occasionally in the Old Testament, always as if they were a minor people; for this great empire had fallen into decay before any of the Hebrew records were committed to writing.

The first indication of the Hittites' importance came from a few chance finds in Syria written in an unknown language in 1870, which excited the interest of archaeologists and stimulated the search for more. By 1907, when a great Hittite city was discovered near Boghazköy in Anatolia, there was enough information available to show something of the scope of this Hittite empire; and with the excavation of the city and the finding of extensive documents in the ruins, the stage was set for an archaeological development as promising as that of Crete, which was simultaneously being unearthed for the first time.

The great obstacle in both cases was the deciphering of the writing, which in the case of the Hittites was both cuneiform and hieroglyphic. The Hittite cuneiform documents were deciphered without too much difficulty, since a knowledge of the widely used Akkadian—a language already understood by scholars—contributed the necessary clues. Many of the Hittite documents, indeed, were in a form of Akkadian, apparently modified by Hittite usage, whereas the hieroglyphic documents were in the Indo-European Hittite language. After the finding of a bilingual document (Hittite and Old Babylonian) in 1946, most of the relatively few hieroglyphic inscriptions have now been successfully read, and we have for the first time a fairly complete picture of Hittite history and civilization.

In some respects the study of the Hittites has proved disappointing, since only in a few fields did they produce anything truly original and their art was derivative and without great interest. From another point of view, however, their importance is only now beginning to be appreciated. The Hittites, not so much a nation as a confederation of peoples, dominated not only Asia Minor but most of Palestine during a period of pre-Biblical history of which little was previously known. Their traders were at home in this area and founded many settlements—as, for example, at Hebron, where Abraham purchased his burial plot. The whole transaction, as recorded in the Bible (Genesis 23) took place in strict accordance with Hittite law.[1]

More important still, the Hittites were basically an Indo-European people, though greatly influenced by the civilization of Mesopotamia. Thus, in company with the Hurrians, with whom they mingled, and with the Mitannians, from whom they adopted some of the Aryan deities of India, they acted as a kind of cultural bridge with Greece, where they undoubtedly had contact with the Mycenaeans (to be discussed later in this chapter) in the archaic period of Greece. The Hittite story of the creation of the gods is almost identical with that given in Hesiod's *Theogony*, with only the names changed; it is also very possible that the Epic of Gilgamesh which was very popular among the Hittites was transmitted to Greece by them and thus influenced the *Odyssey* directly. A ceremony for the cremation of a Hittite monarch bears a marked resemblance also to the funerals of Patroclus and Hector described in the *Iliad*. Such ceremonies were possibly a part of the joint Indo-European heritage of the Hittites, Aryan Indians, and the Greeks. Even if their civilization was not of the greatest in its own right, it may have had importance as a cultural transmitter—a

[1] Cyrus H. Gordon, *Before the Bible* (New York: Harper & Row, Publishers, 1962) p. 94.

field which in the case of the Hittites is only now beginning to be explored by scholars.

HISTORY

The Hittite people began soon after 2000 B.C. to move into Asia Minor and Mesopotamia and founded their capital of Hattusas in Anatolia. By the early seventeenth century B.C. a Hittite confederation had been formed, ruled by an elected monarch, and it soon began to expand to the east and west. By the end of the century the Hittites were the leading power of the Near East. Early in the sixteenth century Babylon was captured and the Amorite dynasty overthrown. The Hittite king Suppiluliumas I (1375–1335) conquered the short-lived Mitannian kingdom and made northern Syria into a vassal state, thus coming into direct contact with imperial Egypt. An Egyptian embassy was received by the Hittite king, as a result of which the king agreed to send one of his sons to marry an Egyptian princess, probably the widow of Tutankhamon. But when the son was killed on the way to Egypt the project for an alliance collapsed. The interests of Hittites and Egyptians constantly clashed until the battle of Kadesh in 1296 between the Hittite king Muwatallis and

Hittite hieroglyphs, recently deciphered. (COURTESY THE METROPOLITAN MUSEUM OF ART)

Rameses II of Egypt. The Hittites appear to have won the battle itself, but the Egyptians were saved from complete disaster by the personal valor of Rameses II. Soon afterward a treaty was concluded, under which the new Hittite king Hattusilis III (1275–1250), a king who wrote an autobiography generally called the *Apologia,* to be discussed later, gave one of his daughters as a wife to Rameses. The latter welcomed her with great honor and made her his chief wife. The treaty, the first in history whose full text is known to us in both the Hittite and the Egyptian versions, was honored for the next seventy years and peace ensued between the two great empires.

The Hittite empire, however, had by now passed the peak of its power. The new series of Indo-European invasions, which were also responsible for the peopling of Greece by Dorians and others, put an end to it. The advance guard of the invasions even penetrated as far as Egypt and was only with difficulty repelled by Rameses III in 1190. Hattusas, the Hittite capital, was destroyed, and though some of the Hittite outposts survived for several hundred more years (especially at Carchemish on the Euphrates), the last traces were absorbed in the Assyrian empire, while the furthest western vassal territories became the independent kingdom and empire of Lydia.

RELIGION

The Hittites borrowed most of their religion from the peoples with whom they mingled, and the Sumerian legends were very popular with them. But as far as can be ascertained, the sun goddess Arinna seems to have been the most important deity of the state in the original Hittite religion, though her spouse, the Storm or Weather god, was evidently more important for the people, since each city had its own private storm god named after the city. The king, who remained for several centuries an elected monarch—or at least one who had to be approved by the assembly of nobles and warriors after being nominated by his father—was the chief priest, responsible for the cult of the Sun Goddess. Even he was not permitted to be absent from the annual great festival of the goddess. The king in the extant inscriptions is almost always shown wearing his priestly garments. It is clear that the gods desired both justice, sincerity, and righteous dealing, and the well-being of the country was apparently dependent upon this. One of the most astonishing of ancient documents is the *Apologia* of Hattusilis III, who made the famous treaty with Egypt. In this autobiography the monarch confesses that he had usurped the throne but claimed he could not have won it without the favor of Ishtar (the Babylonian goddess to whom he was dedicated in his youth), and that the revolt was successful only because of the divine help promised to his wife in a dream. He urges that he lacked the material means for his victory, which could therefore only have been won by divine approval, and he had not been vindictive afterward. Such an apology for what he had done is unique in Near-Eastern annals and seems closer to the thought of an Indian such as the Buddhist monarch Asoka (see the next chapter).

LAW

Perhaps the most notable achievement of the Hittites was the legal system. The extant laws, which do not constitute a complete codification, date probably from the fifteenth and fourteenth centuries B.C. and are therefore much subsequent to the Hammurabi Code. But though the Hittite code has many features in common with Babylonian law, it is crucially different in that aspect of the Hammurabi code which was criticized in the last chapter. The Hittite code makes distinctions between different kinds of murders and takes some account of extenuating circumstances, lack of premeditation, and the like. In no respects is it inferior to the code of Hammurabi. The death penalty is reserved for rebellion, rape, and black magic—though in the case of premeditated murder the family of the victim may decide on whether to accept compensation or to decree the death penalty. All cases of

capital punishment had to be confirmed by the king, and local justice was final only in minor cases. The general principle of Hittite law was that justice consisted in making proper restitution rather than that it was the task of the state to enforce retribution. This principle with its detailed lists of compensations runs through the entire code. Mutilation, which appears in the Hammurabi Code and was very common in the Assyrian code as known to us—almost contemporary with that of the Hittites—is completely absent from the Hittite law.

We have some knowledge of the actual legal procedure among the Hittites and how cases were handled in practice through the fortunate survival of some sworn statements and minutes of cases tried in the courts. Cross examination was permitted, the defendant was granted full freedom to say anything he wished on his behalf, and the magistrates took great care in sifting the evidence, especially when the charge was embezzlement or neglect of duty. Military representatives of the king were entrusted with the task of enquiring whether any crimes had been committed locally or civil cases were up for decision. They were empowered to conduct trials, even suits brought by slaves and servants. One set of extant instructions to such a commander includes the words, "Do not make the better case the worse or the worse case the better. Do what is just." Petitioners, no doubt, then as now, might be afraid to bring a case that would be judged by local magistrates, or might think that they would be unlikely to obtain justice if the defendant were a man of importance in the community. This procedure (adopted by Britain for the same purpose when Henry VII set up the Court of Star Chamber in 1487) certainly tended to exalt the authority of the king, but in the Hittite empire, as under the Tudors, it may have made also for a fairer judgment.

DEVELOPMENT OF IRON

The single great achievement of the Hittites for which they have always been known is the development of iron, already briefly discussed in Chapter 2. In fact the Hittites themselves, though they probably developed iron and perhaps kept the monopoly on it, used bronze weapons like the other peoples of the time. Iron remained a rarity, used mainly for ceremonial purposes and for gifts to foreign potentates. The mountains of Anatolia were rich in metals, especially silver, which was used as currency and exported throughout the Near East, and lead and copper. But it is not for their iron that they should be remembered. Their importance lies rather in the fact that they established a relatively enlightened empire. Their kings were aware of their responsibilities to the gods, and as rulers they tried to mete out justice on earth. Though they lacked any original art, in political matters they at least equaled and in some respects surpassed all their contemporaries. It is fitting that the empire they once ruled should have been rescued in the twentieth century from the oblivion in which it had rested for so many centuries; and it is possible that their role as cultural transmitters may yet entitle them to a far from lowly place in the heritage of Western civilization.

▶ The Lydians

The Lydians grew to power in Western Asia Minor at a time when the great ancient empires were in decline and the newer and more efficient empires had not yet arisen. They may have migrated from Europe and intermingled with the existing peoples, probably after the fall of the Hittites. They became prosperous by the exploitation of the natural mineral wealth of the country, which

The earliest coined money in the world. Invention attributed to the Lydians, three of whose coins are shown here. (COURTESY THE METROPOLITAN MUSEUM OF ART)

included gold and electrum, an alloy of gold and silver found in river sands. Electrum gave them the opportunity to make their greatest contribution to civilization, for which they are chiefly remembered—the coining of money. Prior to this time precious metals were usually weighed and the currency unit corresponded to a given weight. Now the Lydians began to stamp the electrum with its value and used it as money in our modern sense. The practice was quickly adopted by other countries which used gold and silver, thus considerably helping international trade. The Lydians established a strong and wealthy state based on Sardis, their capital, and extended their empire into the Greek (Ionian) coastal cities, but apparently without disturbing too much local self-government, as long as the subject cities paid their taxes regularly. The great age of Ionian science began during the Lydian rule. The last great king of Lydia was the famous and fabulously wealthy Croesus, about whom the Greeks wove many legends; and the sudden loss of his empire to Cyrus the Persian was the theme of many moral stories. Sardis, the Lydian capital, fell in 547 B.C. and the Lydian Empire was absorbed into Persia.

▶ The peoples of Palestine and Syria

The Hebrew prophet Ezekiel in one of his more striking "oracles" told his people: "By origin and birth you belong to the land of the Canaanites. Your father was an Amorite and your mother a Hittite." (Ezekiel 16:3) Such a passage would have been incomprehensible before the discovery of the history of the Hittites, but it must now be recognized that Ezekiel was in large measure correct. It is impossible to separate the Hittites, who for so long dominated northern Syria, from the desert Amorites whose rule in Babylon was overthrown by the Hittites and who transmitted so much of their culture to the Hebrews. The Canaanites, however, cannot be distinguished as a separate people, and the word is best used to describe all the peoples from Syria southward to the borders of Egypt without distinction, as it was customarily used by the Hebrews. Except for the Hittites and for the Philistines, who entered Palestine perhaps as early as 1500 B.C. but came in force only later during the invasions of the "Peoples of the Sea" at the beginning of the twelfth century, all the Canaanite peoples were Semitic, as were the languages of the country. The Phoenicians may have settled in Palestine in relatively recent times, but scholarly opinion on the whole is against the tradition recorded by Herodotus that they came from the Red Sea area. At all events it is impossible to confirm the tradition, nor can it be determined when they entered Palestine. They may well have been there before the end of the third millennium B.C.

An important distinction should be made between the peoples who settled to the east and the west of the coastal mountain range. To the east lies the desert, broken only by a few oases and by the valleys of the small rivers. At the confluence of two of these rivers was founded the great city of Damascus, the capital of the Aramaean state in the first millennium B.C. Most of the desert peoples were nomads, including the Amorites, many of whom, as noted in the last chapter, migrated at the beginning of the second millennium into the fertile river valleys of Mesopotamia. To the west of the mountains were founded the great coastal cities, such as Tyre, Sidon, Byblos, Ugarit, and others. These cities were usually completely independent and self-governing. They lived largely by sea trade, though they possessed some fertile lands of their own as a hinterland, and were able to exploit the cedars of Lebanon and export this valuable timber across the Mediterranean and southward to Egypt. Most of these cities enjoyed long periods of peace and prosperity, and it is now fairly certain that it was among them that the idea of the alphabet was brought to fruition.

The oldest known alphabet, dating from about 1400 B.C. was discovered in the coastal city of Ugarit. The alphabet was probably invented much earlier, but the Ugaritic version is clearly the ancestor of the Phoenician and Hebrew alphabets. True vowels were still missing, as they were in the Phoenician and Hebrew alphabets. Not until the Greeks took over the Phoenician alphabet and added symbols for vowels did an alphabet of the modern type come into existence. The Etruscans may have taken an early version of the Greek alphabet to Italy and transmitted it to the Romans, whose alphabet we use today. The Greeks adopted the same order and signs as were used both in Ugarit and by the Phoenicians.

The coastal cities of Palestine possessed a common basic culture and the same pantheon of gods, but all adopted some alien elements, including a few from the Indo-European peoples who lived in these areas. It has been pointed out that the romantic theme of the recovery by a king of his abducted wife is a common Indo-European motif. The Ugaritic story of the abduction of King Kret's wife is the earliest version known to us. In addition to its appearance as the Helen of Troy story in Homer, it appears in the Biblical story of Abraham, who had twice to recover his abducted wife Sarah (Genesis 12:15–20; 20:2–14).[2] Numerous figures of speech discovered in Ugaritic literature, including some of the most striking images in the *Psalms,* the instructions of Baal to his people to build him a temple because he alone of the gods did not have a house to dwell in, are all to be found, sometimes in unchanged form, in the Old Testament.

What is, however, completely missing in all this literature is any ethical content; nor is there any striving after justice, such as can be found in the Hittite law codes. It is therefore not in the least surprising that the Hebrews, with their single god and their emphasis on morality, should have reacted so strongly against the Canaanite peoples from whom their Twelve Tribes sprang. Though the Old Testament incorporates a not inconsiderable amount of Canaanite lore, the Hebrews were instructed by their god to hold Canaanite customs in abomination. Throughout Hebrew history it was always

[2] For this and other examples see Gordon, *Before the Bible,* chapter 5.

the task of their prophets to recall to them their duty to avoid contamination with Canaanite ideas, and their kings were urged not to join them in marital alliances, lest their queens bring in the hated Canaanite religion. The great attention given to the marriage between the Phoenician Jezebel and the Hebrew Ahab by the Hebrew chronicler, and the public test between Elijah the prophet and Jezebel and her priests of Baal are sufficient reminders of the temptations to which the Hebrews were always subjected after their conquest of Canaan.

Among the peoples of Canaan only the Aramaeans and the Phoenicians need some attention here. Though both were ancient peoples, both rose to their height of power and prosperity after the great invasions of the early twelfth century B.C. had put an end to Hittite domination, and before the rise of imperial Assyria to power. The Aramaeans, a desert people who had always been engaged in trading over the caravan routes to the east, established a state centered on Damascus early in the first millennium B.C. Biblical records tell us much of the relationship of the Hebrews with the kings of Damascus; on one occasion the prophet Elisha was even sent by God to instigate the murder of one king and anoint his murderer as king to the vacant throne. At all events, the kingdom of Damascus was very useful to the Hebrews, acting as a buffer state to absorb the shocks from Assyria and the north. It was not until Damascus had been taken that the full fury of the Assyrian onslaught was felt in Israel. The influence of the Aramaean language, Aramaic, continued to spread—thus anticipating by a millennium the comparable achievement of the Arabic language, which was also the language of desert nomads—until it became virtually the common language of the Near East. Jesus of Nazareth spoke Aramaic. Some of the latest books of the Old Testament were written in this language, which displaced Hebrew even in Palestine itself. The Aramaeans are an interesting example of a people which made all its conquests by

peaceful means after it had lost its national independence, thus providing a precedent for the later history of the Jews.

After the fall of the Hittite empire those of the Phoenician cities that survived or were rebuilt—not including Ugarit which was permanently destroyed by the invaders—entered into a federation for a period under the rulership of Tyre. It was during this period that Hiram, king of Tyre, helped Solomon to build his temple. The Phoenicians are usually credited with having sailed as far as Britain in search of tin for bronze, and it is certain that they traded with Spain. By tradition they were hired by one of the last Egyptian Pharaohs to circumnavigate the African continent, and according to Herodotus they accomplished the mission successfully.[3] They founded colonies throughout the Mediterranean, the most important of which, Carthage, survived the fall of its founder and dominated the western Mediterranean until destroyed by Rome. They were evidently still the chief sea power in the Aegean and Mediterranean area in the Homeric epoch, and their wealth and skill in manufacture were proverbial.

In addition to their seafaring and their function as distributors of goods, especially the luxury products of Egypt, they had a thriving industry of their own, for the most part learned from Egypt. They were especially noted for their dye, the Tyrian purple, which was exclusive to them, being made from a Mediterranean mollusk. They also excelled in glassware, textiles, and metalwork, ornamented with designs mostly borrowed from Egypt.

In spite of a desperate resistance against the Assyrians, the union of Phoenician cities was unable to maintain its independence, and they passed under the Assyrian yoke. They were also conquered by the Chaldeans of New Babylon, and by the Persians. Alexander captured Tyre after a long siege, then after the Phoenicians made another effort at independence one of his successors recaptured the city. The Phoenicians always re-

[3] *Persian Wars*, IV, 42.

tained their maritime skills, and their sailors and ships were always put to use by their conquerors. But they never again recovered the trade they had possessed before the Assyrian conquest. The Greeks who had remained free, and the Greek cities in Asia Minor in the Lydian and Persian empires, captured the bulk of Phoenician trade and never again lost it.

▶ The Hebrews

The persisting significance of Hebrew history

There is little doubt that the Hebrews would have occupied but a small place in Western history if the impression they made upon the external world in their own time were the sole criterion for their importance. Yet this history is familiar to us in the Western world probably beyond that of any ancient people. The names of outstanding Hebrew individuals are familiar to us as household words, and a modern encyclopaedia boasts that it contains every Biblical character with an appropriate Biblical reference. Medieval scholars with their love of allegory tried to extract a secondary religious meaning from numerous events recorded in the historical writings of the Hebrews.

This astonishing success of Hebrew historians arises not merely from the fact that they were the great pioneers in the historical art and may rightfully be considered as the first true historians. It is above all the result of their way of regarding history as having an intelligible meaning. To a Hebrew historian there was no such thing as a chance event. If a pestilence decimated the people this was an act of God, arranged by God either to teach them a lesson, or to punish them for some sin against him. God was ceaselessly watchful, tirelessly guiding his chosen people on their path. The peoples of Mesopotamia, as we have seen, attributed their disasters to divine powers who had been insufficiently courted and appeased; but the Hebrews tried to make sense of every event, even of some that might seem to us

trivial or resulting from quite adequate natural causes, and always as revealing some new facet of the relationship between man and God. And because man likes to think that his sojourn on earth has significance, the Hebrews' belief in divine Providence has permeated the writings of numberless historians since their day, and even those in our time who merely search for laws of history are in their debt for having been the first to deny that it is just a tale "told by an idiot, signifying nothing."

It will, of course, at once be realized that a history designed with the purpose of setting forth the relationship between man and God, intended to instruct the people in their duties toward God, and in what happens when man disobeys the divine injunctions, must be treated with some caution, since both events and their interpretation are inextricably interwoven, and events selected for recording will be those that lend themselves best to this particular interpretation. And if we must regret the shortage of information on the lives of kings, such as Omri of Israel, who played an important part in the external affairs of their time but were unimportant in religious history, this is a small price to pay for the incomparable color and life imparted to their historical writings by the fervor and conviction of these ancient Hebrew writers.

A great deal of the early history of the Hebrews has by this time been subjected to considerable checking, both with the archaeological record and with the literature of their predecessors and contemporaries. On the whole the result has been to confirm the Biblical stories far more than to discredit them; and even the most obscure chapters, such as Genesis 14, have in recent times begun to receive confirmation. The sale of the cave of Machpelah to Abraham by the local Hittite community has already been noted as being in full accord with Hittite law. But while this subject is still so much under discussion it seems reasonable here to recount the story just as the Hebrews themselves told it. We shall adopt the same procedure with the early Christian stories recorded in the Gospels and the Acts of the Apostles, adding only a few explanations where necessary. A further reason for refraining from criticizing the probabilities in the case of both Hebrews and Christians is the undoubted fact that the very belief of these peoples that their own history was true served itself to mold their later history. The teachings and actions of Jesus Christ and of medieval Christians would surely have been different had they not believed, for instance, in the sojourn of the Hebrews in Egypt and their miraculous escape through divine intervention, just as Christian history would unquestionably have been different had there been any doubt in Christian minds of the absolute truth of the Gospel story.

EXTERNAL HISTORY OF THE HEBREW PEOPLE

The scriptural tradition of the Hebrew people, or, as they called themselves, the Children of Israel, begins with the patriarch Abraham to whom God promised that his seed would endure for ever. Abraham who came from "Ur of the Chaldees" (probably not the original Sumerian city of Ur, but, according to recent scholarly opinion, one of the northern colonies of Ur, which fits the circumstances better) migrated into Palestine perhaps late in the fifteenth century B.C. with his flocks, setting up altars to his God, Yahweh, and digging wells. It is very likely that this tradition is true, and that Abraham did indeed found the worship of Yahweh in Palestine. His son Isaac and his grandson Jacob, also called Israel, continued his work, digging the wells again and finding "living water," growing prosperous and powerful in the land through alliances with the local Canaanites. Joseph, one of the sons of Jacob, was "sold into Egypt," where he became later the vizier of the Pharaoh, from which office he was able to befriend his brothers and father when they emigrated there to escape a famine in Canaan. The descendants of Jacob in Egypt were all enslaved by a subsequent Pharaoh "who knew not Joseph," and made to work on his extensive building program. From this servitude they were rescued by Moses, who led them back into

Canaan after they had spent forty years in the wilderness of Sinai. Moses taught them to worship Yahweh and welded them into a powerful and united fighting force capable of conquering the country. Moses himself did not live to lead them personally into the promised land, this task falling to his successor Joshua.[4]

The "promised land," though Yahweh had granted it to his people, was by no means uninhabited. However it was far from unified and incapable of presenting a united opposition to the invaders. It required several centuries of fighting before the Israelites were able to conquer it, subduing first the peoples of Moab and Ammon across the Jordan, then the various Canaanite peoples who resisted them, and ultimately the Philistines. The Israelites themselves were rarely united, preferring to fight by tribes in a loose alliance. The Song of Deborah, perhaps the earliest document in the Old Testament, celebrates the victory of one such alliance, and treats with contempt those Children of Israel who had been too timorous to join it.

The early Israelites were ruled by judges, who were religious leaders with only a local authority. In the course of the wars with the Philistines, who for many years kept most of the Hebrews in subjection, it was realized that a king would best serve as a rallying point for the whole people. The prophet and judge Samuel therefore chose a certain Saul, of the tribe of Benjamin, as king, and anointed him as the chosen of Yahweh, thus conferring upon him both a secular and a religious responsibility. Throughout Hebrew history the king had a special task in that he had to set an example

[4] There is nothing inherently improbable in this tradition, since the Egyptians certainly were accustomed to enslaving foreign peoples and setting them to work in Egypt. But it cannot at present be substantiated unequivocally from Egyptian records. Controversy is centered around the question of whether the Apiru who appear several times in Egyptian documents actually constituted a distinct people in Palestine; were a class of persons, such as merchants; or were, simply, aliens. None of the references clearly point to any particular people, and the latest of them occurs sixty years after the Israelites had been recorded in Egyptian documents as already in Palestine.

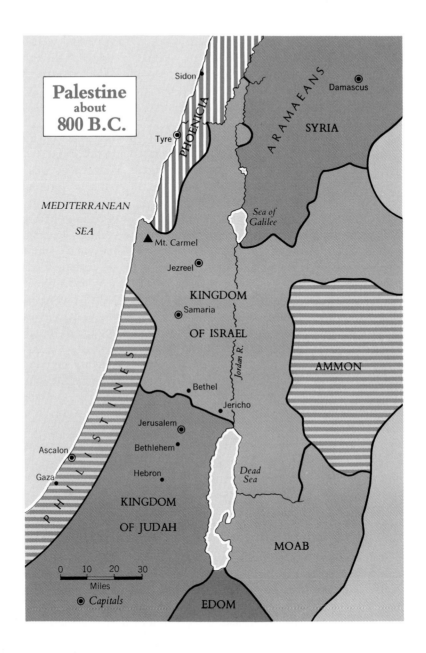

in worshiping Yahweh as well as leading the people in their secular affairs.

According to the Biblical narrative Saul failed in his religious duties, and was abandoned by Samuel in favor of a young man named David of the tribe of Judah, who was anointed king even before he had reached manhood. Thereafter David went to the court of Saul, and acted for a time as Saul's armor-bearer and married Saul's daughter. But Saul became jealous of the military prowess that David showed and forced him to go into exile, where he engaged in guerrilla warfare against the common enemy the Philistines. When Saul was killed in battle against the Philistines, David was proclaimed king. In this new capacity he broke the Philistine yoke for good, cap-

MARITIME AND OTHER CIVILIZATIONS OF THE ANCIENT WORLD   125

tured Jebus, which he made into his new capital of Jerusalem and founded a strong unified kingdom stretching as far as the Aramaean and Phoenician cities in the north and in the south to the borders of the Arabian desert. The Canaanite peoples of Moab and Ammon and Edom in southern Palestine were kept under control, though retaining their nominal independence. This Israelite kingdom lasted through the reigns of David and his son Solomon.

But the price was heavy. Solomon tried with his limited resources to live like an Oriental despot, and at the same time to engage in an extensive building program, including the famous temple of Yahweh in Jerusalem. His resources were not sufficient, and he was compelled to enter into an agreement with the Phoenician king of Tyre to send Israelites to work in the forests there in exchange for materials and assistance in the building program at Jerusalem. The result was a rebellion of the northern tribes of Israel on the accession of Solomon's son.

Thereafter there were two kingdoms, the north, which took the name of Ephraim or Israel, and the south, which was composed of only two tribes, Judah and Benjamin, and which centered around what had been the national capital of the united kingdom. The northern kingdom was the more prosperous and sophisticated, but at the same time more subject to foreign influence and penetration. It enjoyed several periods of prosperity, even though the priestly chronicler denies that even a single king "did what was right in the sight of the Lord." All of them walked in the ways of the first king of the north, Jeroboam the son of Nebat "who made Israel to sin." In other words they adopted most of the customs of the local religion and deserted Yahweh. But it was the northern kingdom that fell first (in 721 B.C.) to the conquering Assyrians, while the southern, which was more defensible and not so close to the great conquering powers of the age, maintained a precarious and usually only nominal independence. It, too, fell to the

Chaldeans, in 586, after its rulers had vainly allied themselves with the decadent and powerless last Pharaohs of Egypt. The Chaldeans deported to Babylon first the leaders and then most of the Jewish (as it was now called) population. There under the inspiration of at least one great prophet they kept alive the worship of Yahweh and probably intrigued against their captors. When the Persian Cyrus took Babylon, they received their reward, and were allowed to return to Jerusalem, where, after encountering much opposition but supported by their Persian overlords, they were able to rebuild the temple as a center for their religion.

Palestine remained in Persian hands until its conquest by Alexander, after whose death it fell to Seleucus, one of his generals. When Antiochus Epiphanes, a descendant of Seleucus, tried to enforce the Hellenization of the country, he encountered stiff opposition from the more orthodox Jews who, under the leadership of the family of the Maccabees, asserted their independence until the whole country fell to the Romans. Thereafter the land was ruled by client kings of the Romans until it was converted into an imperial province A.D. 6. When it rebelled against the Roman rule, Jerusalem was captured by Titus A.D. 70 and the inhabitants dispersed. There was no Jewish nation again until the middle of the twentieth century.

▶ **The Hebrew contribution to civilization**

THE EVOLUTION OF HEBREW THOUGHT

This account of the external history of the Jews, bald though it is, does serve to bring out one remarkable, almost unique phenomenon—the extraordinary persistence of the national and religious tradition, and the tenacious refusal of the Hebrews to be absorbed permanently into any other culture. Though thousands of them—no doubt an enormous majority of those born into it through the centuries—abandoned their heritage, nevertheless a nucleus always remained who "remembered the god of their fathers." So when Jesus of Nazareth was born a few years before Judaea became a Roman province, he was able to sum up the whole Hebrew and Jewish heritage in such a way that it could be passed on by his followers as the foundation for the great militant religion of the West. Even if the Jewish religion itself had not survived, this transmission to Christianity alone would justify the tremendous efforts and concentrated thought devoted by generations of Hebrew prophets and priests to the great problems of life, destiny, and the duty of man toward God.

We have purposely refrained from treating the evolution of the Hebrew religion in terms of the changing social experience of the Hebrew people partly because there is still so much controversy about it, especially concerning the dates of the various documents which comprise the Old Testament, and partly because this religion has never died and is still regarded by millions of Christians and Jews as permanently true: there *is* one God not many; he *is* just and righteous and omnipotent; he *did* create the world; and he does rule it through his Providence. In such circumstances it is needlessly offensive to suggest that the Bible was arrived at by addition and subtraction, a kind of Darwinian process of the survival of the fittest—this idea having been pilfered from Babylon, this from Egypt, and this from Persia—or that the Hebrews, having suffered so much, wanted so urgently that a god should punish their enemies that they came to believe in a God of the whole earth, using even the terrible Assyrians as his tools. Yet it is clear that there are such differing concepts of Yahweh in the Old Testament that it is impossible to believe that the concept in the Book of Isaiah, for instance, was held at the same time as the concept in the Book of Exodus or the Book of Numbers. So it would seem best to attempt to trace Hebrew thought in regard to the same great problems with which their contemporaries also contended,

and to see what solutions were worked out by different Hebrew writers at different times, without relation to the events that may be supposed to have suggested these solutions. In this way we shall treat the thought as a whole, dating the writings from the standpoint of maturity and richness of conception, instead of trying to relate this thought to particular social experiences. The student will have enough material at his disposal to enable him to judge this relevance for himself.

THE NATURE AND UNITY OF GOD

Monotheism versus polytheism

The Hebrews are, of course, credited above all with the formulation of monotheism, the worship of one God; and this monotheism has been transmitted both to Christianity and to Islam, so that it is the fundamental religious belief of the West. But it is not always recognized that they are also responsible for the precise definition of the nature of sin; and their thought upon the question of sin and punishment has permeated Western thought as deeply as has the concept of monotheism itself. The evolution of Hebrew thought on these two subjects will therefore be treated in some detail in this chapter.

The Hebrews did not come all at once to their idea of a transcendent God ruling the universe. In the period of the desert wanderings we find them given the commandment that they are to have no other gods beside Yahweh, but there is as yet no suggestion that other gods do not exist. He is their special God, their protector and rock of defense, who will keep his promises to his chosen people; but as yet nothing more. It is only in relatively late times that the great prophets picture him as the God of the universe, with all peoples alike subjected to him, and the gods of other peoples as nothing but idols of wood and stone. They were perhaps driven to this conclusion through their belief that God used foreigners to punish his own people and thus must control these foreigners also.

In early times also it is clear that the Hebrews believed in a rather primitive anthropomorphism, that Yahweh could walk the earth and talk to men, and that he needed an earthly habitation. By the time of the end of the kingdom of Judah the priests were emphasizing that God could neither be seen nor heard by human beings, but that he was a spirit, infinitely remote from man, though caring for him like a father, dwelling in heaven and not on earth. Ultimately both these concepts—the unity and the spiritual nature of God—were fully accepted by the Jews, and it was in this form that the Hebrew ideas about God were transmitted to posterity.

It should be pointed out, however, that there is no reason to assume that this evolution from polytheism to monotheism is a necessary progress in religious thought, as has already been suggested in connection with the Egyptians. The best Hindu religious thought is far from primitive; yet it is polytheistic, and it shows no signs of developing into monotheism. To a Hindu all gods are an aspect of the great whole which is Brahma; but this does not mean that the others do not have a separate existence. The process of subtracting from the powers of lesser gods and adding them to Brahma is not considered necessary to the Hindus, as it was by the Hebrews—and it is perhaps not surprising that ancient legend should have attributed the invention of mathematics to Abraham. For Hebrew thought on God was eminently logical and, in a sense, mathematical; whereas the Hindu approach to religion, as was the case also with the ancient Egyptians, is emotional, enriching their feeling for the Divine by indefinitely multiplying their gods, in accordance with their reverence for all the works of God. Monotheism conceives of God primarily as a person, on the analogy of an omnipotent and omniscient ruler, whereas the Hindu thinks of Brahma as present in all the works of his creation, a divine element in all phenomena, rather than differentiated from them and responsible for their existence.

Importance of monotheism for morality— Contrast with Mesopotamian polytheism

The supreme consequence of the Hebrew concept is in the field of human morality. Because God is a person, he can take part in human affairs, guiding them, rewarding and punishing his children, thus upholding the moral order.[5] This monotheism is clearly an advance on Mesopotamian thought, since the many gods of the Babylonians were conceived of as so many arbitrary but powerful beings competing for man's worship. Each man had a personal god who was expected to use his influence with the higher gods on behalf of his protégé, as human beings use political influence to ensure personal favors. And among the higher gods it was impossible for a man to choose which to petition. He could not tell which one he had offended, nor did he know what was demanded of him.

Polytheism cannot escape the dilemma that the different gods may issue contradictory demands; unless these gods may be said to have agreed among themselves on what to demand from man, their different commands will necessarily at some time conflict with each other. The separate gods can only reward and punish in accordance with their limited power, and thus cannot command obedience from man and insist upon it on pain of punishment. Shamash, the Babylonian god of the sun and of justice, might give Hammurabi a code of laws, but it was only by virtue of his function as lawgiver among the numerous Babylonian gods. The Babylonian did not regard him as the enforcer of the laws, nor did he pray to Shamash to mitigate his severity. This was the task of the personal god of the Baby-

[5] The Hindu Brahma does none of these things. The moral order is conceived of as a part of the whole universe. The consequences of a man's deeds affect his life in the spiritual worlds after death, and determine the character of subsequent lives on earth (reincarnation). No transcendent God is needed to guide this process; the deeds themselves are the cause, and the character of subsequent lives is the effect.

lonian, who used his influence among his superiors in the pantheon.

But the Hebrew God, being one, not a force of nature but a transcendent being, separate from the world yet immanent in it, could act as ruler and governor, first of his chosen people and then of the whole world. He could issue a law which instructed the people as to exactly what he expected of them, could define disobedience to the law as sin, and could take steps to see that he was obeyed. The law thus removed any doubt in the sinner's mind as to what he was expected to do, and what was forbidden him, and held out the hope that if he fulfilled these duties toward God he would be prosperous and happy. We shall see in the next section how the Hebrews were forced to modify this simple conception in the light of their actual experience, but the following quotations from Babylonian and Hebrew documents will serve to point the contrast between the two attitudes, and reveal at the same time how greatly the Hebrew felt he had been privileged when God gave him his Law.

The Babylonian: "What is good in one's sight is evil for a god, what is bad in one's own mind is good for his god. Who can understand the counsel of the gods in the midst of heaven? Where has befuddled mankind ever learned what a god's conduct is?"[6] Again: "Man is dumb; he knows nothing. Mankind, everyone that exists—what does he know? Whether he is committing sin or doing good he does not even know."[7]

The Hebrew: "I have stored thy message in my heart that I may not sin against thee . . . . With my lips I recount all the ordinances of thy mouth. In the way of thy decrees I delight, as much as in all wealth. I meditate upon thy precepts, and I observe thy paths. I find joy in thy statutes, I will not forget thy word . . . . At midnight I rise up to give thee thanks because of thy righteous ordinances . . . the law of thy mouth is worth more to me than thousands in gold and silver."[8]

Hebrew monotheism, then, with its consequent belief that God rewarded and punished men in accordance with their deeds, has been of incalculable importance in the religious and psychological history of mankind. Nevertheless, the conception of morality, enforced by God in his capacity as judge, even tempered by mercy shown by him as a loving father who "rebukes and chastens" his children, is ultimately a sterile one, negative because it does not (indeed, cannot) prescribe goodness, and because it does not touch the more difficult matter of human ethics, or the art of right action.

This aspect too did not escape the best Hebrew thinkers. Some of the prophets saw that the commands of the Law limited morality within a too rigid framework. When Micah spoke of the task of man as to "do justice, love mercy, and walk humbly with God," he extended the boundaries of those actions favored by God to cover less circumscribed activities. And Jeremiah had an inkling of the need for escape from the bondage of the Law when he made this promise in the name of the Lord: "Behold I will make a new covenant with the house of Israel . . . . I will put my law in their inward parts and in their hearts will I write it . . . . And they shall teach no more every man his neighbor and his brothers, saying, 'Know the Lord'; for they shall all know me from the least to the greatest of them."[9] Paul, converted from Judaism to Christianity, but thoroughly conversant with the Law, explained that the Law was given to the people because of offenses, that they might know what was sin, and could strive to avoid it. The Law, he said, was a schoolmaster, to prepare the people for Christ: "A man is not made upright by doing what the Law commands, but by faith . . . the Law has nothing to do with faith; . . . We, by the Spirit, through faith wait for the

---

[6] Pritchard, *Ancient Near Eastern Texts*, p. 435. Translated by R. H. Pfeiffer.
[7] *Ibid.*, p. 392. Translated by F. J. Stephens.

[8] Psalms 119:11–16, 62, 72.
[9] Jeremiah 31:31–34.

Polychrome painting from the cave of Altamira, northern Spain. In this cave, which is not very far below the surface of the earth, there are irregularities in the surface of the wall which have been effectively used by the prehistoric artist to suggest the physical features of the animals he painted. (ELLIOTT ERWITT, MAGNUM)

RIGHT: *Hippopotamus in faience from a Middle Kingdom (Twelfth Dynasty) Egyptian tomb.* (METROPOLITAN MUSEUM OF ART, GIFT OF EDWARD S. HARKNESS, 1917)

BELOW: *Early New Kingdom painted linen shroud from Thebes depicting an offering.* (METROPOLITAN MUSEUM OF ART, FLETCHER FUND, 1944)

ON THE FOLLOWING PAGE: *The delicacy and beauty of Cretan painting is admirably displayed in this fresco from the throne room of the palace of Minos at Cnossos.* (ERICH LESSING, MAGNUM)

uprightness we hope for . . . . What the Spirit produces is love, joy, peace, patience, kindness, goodness, faithfulness, gentleness, self-control."[10] When we were children, he says, we needed such a schoolmaster, but when we become men we put away childish things.

This conception of the schoolmaster seems to suggest the true place of the Law in the history of human morality. It was an advance on the arbitrariness of the Babylonian gods who kept mankind in ignorance. When man did not yet know from within what he must do, then his behavior must be prescribed from without. When the Law was written within the heart, or was replaced by faith, then there was no longer need of the schoolmaster. Here, as we shall see, Greek and Hebrew thought meet, in Socrates' experience of the "little god" within, and in the search for the positive good carried out so unwearyingly by himself and his pupil Plato.

The idea of a Universal God

The third great development in Hebrew thought concerns the total activity of God in the world. In early times the whole conception of God expressed in Hebrew writings was as protector of the Children of Israel, his chosen and peculiar people. But if he was all-powerful, then he did not have to fight with other nations; he would deliver them into the hands of Israel. What, then, did this deduction mean, from the point of view of other nations? Was he not their god also? Once this problem was posed, and it did not arise so long as Yahweh was only one god among many, the answer must follow. But it did arise when the logical consequences of his supreme power were considered. If his power were not supreme, then he had to fight on behalf of Israel against the gods of their enemies. If he was supreme, then he was their *enemies'* protector too; or else they were unfortunately left without a true God at all, which would be unjust. There was no way out of the

[10] Galatians 2:15, 3:12, 5:5, 22–23.

dilemma; the other nations must somehow fit into the world order. It was all very well to denounce Assyria and Egypt, call their gods false gods, and prophesy destruction for them. But could any prophet with a sense of justice allow such a one-sided arrangement and say it was the work of a just God?

The answer might be, and was, given in terms of Israel's mission. God was using the foreign nations for purposes of his own, for the disciplining of Israel. He could have prevented the Assyrians from oppressing Israel, as he prevented them from taking Jerusalem in the time of Hezekiah; or he could use them to punish Israel's sin, as when the northern kingdom was deported. But to the more thoughtful among the prophets even this seemed rather a cavalier treatment of foreign nations. Were they not judged and punished for their sins; or did only Israel's sins count?

The question was no sooner posed in this manner than it must be answered in the only way possible. If Yahweh were indeed the God of the whole earth, then all the peoples were responsible to him equally, even if Israel had special tasks and special responsibilities as the only people of the earth to whom he had revealed himself and his Law. But the Assyrians were responsible when they broke the ordinary unrevealed natural law, and could be punished for it.

And so we have the Book of Jonah, which tells how the prophet was sent to Nineveh to urge the Assyrians to repent. It is nothing short of astounding how daring this thought was that a prophet from the despised nation of Israel should go up to the capital of the mightiest world empire at the height of its power and prophesy its destruction (if it did not repent). And the writer shows that Jonah was well aware of his temerity. For at first he did not dare to go, but took a ship going in the opposite direction. Then the Lord sent a storm upon the ship and did not calm it until the sailors had cast Jonah into the sea. Here he was swallowed by a whale, and not released from the belly of the whale until he had repented and promised to fulfill his mission. So at last he went up to Nineveh and preached. And, lo and behold, the Assyrians did repent, and the Lord spared them.

But the story does not end here. Jonah is angry because God has forgiven the Assyrians, thus making him a false prophet. So he sulks in the sun by the gate of the city. A gourd grows to protect him from the sun, and then, at God's command, the gourd withers, showing him by this sign that God has everything in his power, and that Jonah himself would not survive against God's will. And the book ends with the stern rebuke, "Should I not have compassion on Nineveh, that great city, in which are more than a hundred and twenty thousand people who know not their right hands from the left, and also many cattle?" Their ignorance saved them, for they had not been chosen and so had not known of God; when at last they were warned and heard, then God turned from his original purpose.

It should not be thought from this emphasis on the logical thought of the Hebrews that there was anything cold or abstract about their religion or their God. On the contrary, their whole thinking represented God as a person impossibly high above man, but recognizably akin to him, and with the feelings of man. It was thus possible not only to worship God but to love him, and God loved man in return. Man was in a real sense to the Hebrews the son of God, who must occasionally be corrected, but always with a fatherly hand. "Those I love I rebuke and chasten," says the writer of the Proverbs. But the emphasis was not always in the chastening. "I taught Ephraim to walk, I took him in my arms . . . with human bonds I drew him, with cords of love. How shall I give you up, Ephraim, how shall I let you go, Israel? My heart turns within me, all my tenderness is kindled. I will not perform my fierce anger. I will not turn about to destroy Ephraim. For I am God and not man."[11]

SIN AND PUNISHMENT

It has already been suggested that later Hebrew thought was disturbed by the dis-

[11] Hosea 11:3–8.

A medieval impression of Jonah praying to God for deliverance from the belly of the whale. Evidently the illustrator's knowledge of zoology left something to be desired! From a manuscript, Pseudo-Rudolf von Ems, Weltchronik, ca. 1400. (COURTESY THE PIERPONT MORGAN LIBRARY. Ms. 769, folio 223)

crepancy between the promises made by God to his people seen by the Hebrews as a special Covenant between God and his chosen people—and the experience of life on earth as they knew it. If they obeyed the Law they should have been rewarded, and if they ceased to obey it, then they should have been punished. But only rarely did this happen; and it was the apparent happiness of the ungodly, and the undoubted occasional suffering of the manifestly righteous that probably persuaded the later Hebrews to adopt the idea of a future life where justice would be vindicated.

It does not seem that the Covenant itself was ever seriously questioned. But later thinkers realized that it could not comprise the whole duty of man, nor could the simple theory of rewards and punishments on earth for keeping or breaking it suffice for them. More thought was needed on this central problem of the relationship between God and man, and much of the profoundest thought of mankind went into the effort to understand it—which thought, embodied in the Old Testament, became part of the imperishable heritage of Western man.

God had created man, not as a slave of God, but in the image of God. He had made man only a little lower than the Elohim (one of the Hebrew words for God, but sometimes translated by the timorous who do not appreciate the grandeur of the Hebrew aspiration, as "angels"); he was God's special favorite among all living creatures, a child of God. And God was for man a Rock of Defense. If this were so, and God was all-just, all-righteous, and all-powerful, demanding equal righteousness from man, how could he sometimes seem not to care, and deliver man over to destructive forces of nature or to his earthly enemies? Was this the protection to which he was entitled by the Covenant?

The answer varied in different stages of Hebrew civilization, and according to whether the fate of the Hebrew people or the individual man was being considered. But both problems were thoroughly explored.

The most prevalent early view, the one expounded by the priestly writers when they considered the history of the people of Israel, was that in fact the people had not obeyed the Law and were rightly punished for disobedience. The individual kings were also punished for leading Israel into sin. But this theory was far from accounting for all the facts. Jeroboam II of Israel and Manasseh of Judah, both wicked kings according to the priests, had long and apparently prosperous reigns. Josiah of Judah, in spite of his reform of the religion in accordance with priestly desires, met an untimely death in battle. These matters are not satisfactorily explained by the writers. But much is made of the miraculous prolongation of the life of King Hezekiah of Judah and his deliverance from the Assyrians because "his heart was right with the Lord." It can be seen, therefore, how great a temptation it was for these priestly writers to slur quickly over those reigns which pointed no moral lesson, thus in some degree distorting their history.

According to the priestly tradition, then, the sins of the people of Israel and Judah were responsible for the destruction of these independent kingdoms; but Judah, because it was the home of David, to whom God had made special promises, would not be destroyed forever, because of God's mercy and because of his oath to David. God therefore was able to act unilaterally on behalf of his people out of his mercy, though the people had not in fact deserved it. The people sinned and deserved punishment; God sometimes spared and sometimes condemned them. Yet this was still not arbitrariness on the part of God, as he was bound by his oath to spare the house of Judah. This tradition is naturally characterized by concentration upon the deeds of the kings because it was primarily they who led the people astray and "made them to sin." Though there were individual righteous men in Israel and Judah, and schools of prophets continuing to keep the First Commandment, they were far outnumbered by those who followed the king in his aberrations.

The great prophets, deeper thinkers than the priests, and gradually moving away from the strict tradition of the Law as comprising the sum total of human duties, would not accept the traditional answer; and some of them came to the thought that the sufferings of the people were not the result of sin, but a preparation, a testing, for an even higher destiny. At the time of the fall of Jerusalem to Babylon, and during the exile, this thought alone seemed to fit the circumstances. It was not only because of God's mercy that the remnant was saved; it was because God had need of them. Not all of them, but those who had continued to worship him in spite of all their disasters. From the idea of suffering as the due recompense for sin, it became instead a discipline, a purification in the fire, so that those who survived were fitted for this great destiny. And so ultimately, fully in accord with this thought, followed the idea of a Messiah who should redeem the world, sometimes conceived of as an earthly king who would inaugurate the rule of righteousness on earth, and sometimes as a suffering servant, "the man of sorrows and acquainted with grief," who would take upon himself the sorrows of the world. In both cases the mission of the whole Hebrew people had been to prepare themselves to be ready to receive the

Messiah, forming an elect body of righteous men to leaven the great masses of wicked humanity in the new age.

Once again it will be seen that these prophets returned the only answer that was logically possible unless the whole Hebrew tradition were to be abandoned as false. The suffering of a people, if it is to have a meaning—and the Hebrews could not deny meaning to it without abandoning their faith in the justice and righteousness of God—must be either punishment for the past or discipline for the future. There is no other alternative.

It did not, however, need a prophet to give the answer to the other parallel problem, the sufferings of the individual. To the logical mind, if the man who keeps the Law suffers, there must be some reason. Conversely, if the man who fails to keep the Law is not punished, why not? Here there are more possibilities, and the Hebrews explored all but one—the possibility of a future life of rewards and punishments—very thoroughly. And this last possibility as soon as it was suggested was abandoned by all the thinkers included in the canonical books of the Old Testament. Moreover, even when it was accepted by some Jews, it did not attain the dignity of a revelation, and was still not accepted by the priestly party at the time of Christ.

We see a suggestion of the problem very early; and already in the Law there is a typically primitive answer. The sins of the fathers are visited upon the children, an answer scornfully rejected by the prophets Ezekiel and Jeremiah: "The fathers have eaten sour grapes, and the children's teeth are set on edge." It is posed frequently in the Psalms: "Why do the ungodly flourish like a green bay-tree?" Look to the end of their life, suggests one answer. Their good fortune will change. But manifestly this is not always the case. They will suffer inwardly from the knowledge of their crimes; but no, there are instances where this does not happen. The problem treated from this point of view is insoluble. And the righteous man? The Psalmist stoutly affirms that he has never seen him in poverty and his seed begging their bread. But he must be honest with himself; he *has* seen them. And in case the conception of sin contained in the Law is too narrow, the Psalmist makes it clear that he is considering just dealing in its broadest sense, and not only as obedience to the Law. After wrestling with the problem without receiving an answer he goes into the sanctuary of the Lord, and there it appears he receives the only possible answer—he must just continue to believe and throw himself on the mercy and trust to the wisdom of God. And as for the ungodly man, he must believe that God will punish him "in the latter end."[12]

Substantially this is the same answer given in the Book of Job, an old Babylonian legend in a new guise, with all the depth of Hebrew thought built into it. Here the problem is presented in dramatic form. The book opens with the Devil boasting in Heaven of his accomplishments. There is, thanks to him, no righteous man upon earth. God asks him to consider "my servant Job," a man "after my own heart." The Devil complains that Job has never been properly tempted, and receives permission first to take away his wealth; then, when this has failed, to afflict him with "boils." Job's wife advises him to "curse God and die," but he refuses to accept such a counsel of despair. God remains just, and there is some reason for his action, but Job cannot find it. Three "friends" visit him, and with varying arguments they try to convince Job that he must have sinned, and must repent before God will forgive him. Job replies stubbornly that he is not conscious of any sin, either of breaking the Law or of sinning in any other way. He considers all the possible alternatives, including the possibility of an afterlife but rejects them all, finally being almost driven to the conclusion that God is ruled by caprice, that he is arbitrary and unjust, afflicting man without cause. And so at last he appeals to God himself to answer him.

God answers out of the whirlwind with the unanswerable argument. Job, he asks,

12 See especially Psalm 73.

can you make a crocodile—or a horse—or even a hippopotamus? And these chapters give the Hebrew poet a wonderful opportunity to describe these animals, the marvelous works of God. But Job can only answer no. "Can you make any of my works?" The answer is still no. So Job is at last convinced that man can find no answer, and God is so tremendously far above him that he cannot attempt to find understanding. And he "repents in dust and ashes" for ever having dared to question. At which God shows mercy to him, heals him, and gives him twice as much as he had before. So this magnificent book ends on a note of the deepest pessimism as far as man is concerned. There is an answer, but it is not to be understood by man's weak faculties. God remains just, but "his ways are past finding out."

THE CANONIZATION OF THE LAW

It should be emphasized that the bulk of Hebrew thought on the relationship between man and God was achieved by prophets and independent thinkers rather than by the priests. But in the last days of the kingdom of Judah a book of the Law was "found" in the temple and became the basis of a thoroughgoing religious reform carried out by King Josiah and the priests. This book has usually been thought to be the one called Deuteronomy, and from it we can see that as yet there has been no great change in the conception of sin and punishment held in earlier times, no emphasis on righteousness beyond the dictates of the Law. God will prosper the people if they keep his Law. "If you will but heed the commands that I am giving you today, to love the Lord your God, and serve him will all your mind and heart, he will give you rain for your land in due season . . . and he will produce grass in your fields for your cattle, and you will eat your fill."[13] This is the tone of the whole book, as was indeed to be expected in a religious reform carried out by the aid of the priesthood. The emphasis was on the

tribulations that had come upon the people because they had not kept the Law, and the material rewards that would be their lot if they returned to it.

A short time afterward the kingdom was conquered by the Chaldeans, and some of the leading Jews were taken captive and brought to Babylon. There, in spite of great prophets to lead them who laid little emphasis on the Law, they were held together as a people by the Law, and on their return to Palestine under Persian auspices, it was the priests who supervised the return and rebuilt the temple. As can be clearly seen especially from the book called *Ecclesiasticus*, or the *Wisdom of Sirach*, the Law had become the cement binding together both the Hebrew religion and the Jewish nation. The Law in its now conclusive form was sufficient for all human purposes. The Torah or Pentateuch (the first five books of the Old Testament) was canonized as the revealed word of God. It was not earthly but divine; and it was unchangeable. It remained for Jesus Christ and his followers to return the emphasis to the *spirit* of the Law as suggested by Jeremiah, and allow scope for human ethics beyond it.

THE INFLUENCE AND IMPORTANCE OF THE HEBREW RELIGION

The importance of the whole Hebrew religion to the world is incalculable. Once the problems of man's relationship with God and the resultant ethics had been wrestled with and certain conclusions reached, the world would never be the same again. One may deny the original premises[14] and ask for the evidence for the existence of any God at all; one may say that the Hebrews projected their own highest aspirations into their imagination of a supreme ruler of the universe. But one cannot deny the aspirations nor that the conclusions, as far as they go, follow from the premises. Not only did Christianity, the predominant religion in the West, base itself upon Hebrew thinking, but Islam also adopted the idea of the single

---

[13] Deuteronomy 11:13–15.

[14] The author of *Ecclesiastes*, a canonical book, even puts this point of view forward himself!

transcendent God and much of Hebrew social thought. The teachings of the Old Testament became the standard of conduct and even provided some of the law for the Protestant reformers in the sixteenth century, especially for those who followed the teachings of Calvin. And the Jews themselves have preserved their heritage and their belief in the promised land even thirty centuries after the death of Moses, and over nineteen hundred years after they ceased to exist as a separate nation. But more important than all this may have been their belief that man is answerable to God for his deeds on earth, that there is a divine sanction over man's activity. Whether we forget this, or believe with Aristotle that man cannot be happy unless he is good and that no divine sanction is necessary, since man must seek for happiness, we cannot deny that the concept has profoundly influenced all subsequent civilization, and that few men in the West have not at some time in their lives been forced to consider the possibility of its truth.

THE HEBREWS AS LITERARY ARTISTS

After this extended study of Hebrew religion it is hardly necessary to dwell further upon Hebrew literature. The Hebrew religious documents, with very rare exceptions, are couched in language of considerable beauty and are rich with concrete images; many of them, such as the Psalms, are the purest poetry. The ancient Hebrew clearly had a discerning eye, and took a delight in this world. The famous description of the horse in the Book of Job; the Psalmist's panegyric on the way God provides for the animals; Isaiah's prophecy of the heavenly world of peace among men and beasts; and even the Deuteronomic priest's lyric description of the land of Canaan—all spring to mind. The so-called Song of Songs is one of the most beautiful love lyrics in any language. "The time of the singing of birds is come and the voice of the turtle dove is heard in our land."[15] But

[15] The King James Version reads "turtle," the archaic word for turtle dove. Our turtle, unhappily, is no songster.

even this is included in the Old Testament. There is no secular literature known to us until a very late date, simply because only literature that concerned man and God was worth preserving in a canon of Scriptures, and to the Hebrew almost any poetry concerned some aspect of this relationship.

The Hebrews contributed little to political theory or practice outside what is implied in their religion. Kings, of course, could never be, or be made into, gods because there was only one God, and only one God was conceivable. The kings of Israel were chosen because they were needed for government and warfare; but they as well as, or more than, their people must obey the Law. They were not above the Law, and they could be and were frequently recalled to their duty by outspoken prophets, who were protected from kingly anger either by divine protection (as with Elijah) or by the prestige of their calling (Micaiah before Ahab). The priest Jehoiada kept a king of Judah from "sinning" as long as he was his guardian.

In all the other arts and in science the Hebrews were singularly lacking in accomplishment. The famous temple of Solomon was Phoenician in design and execution. It was a great wonder to the Hebrew chronicler, but it would hardly have ranked as a second-class building in Egypt. Sculpture was abhorred and forbidden by the law; no scientific invention is to be ascribed to the Hebrews. There can be no doubt that the whole of their creative genius was concentrated on their religion and thought and, incidentally, their literature. More could hardly be expected of one small people.

▶ Aegean civilization

MINOAN CRETE—A TRIUMPH OF ARCHAEOLOGY

The discovery and excavation of the Aegean civilization is one of the great romances of archaeology. It began when Heinrich Schliemann, a retired businessman and accomplished linguist, organized an expedition to Asia Minor to search for the site of Troy. In spite of discouragement from scholars, he firmly believed that the Troy of the

A reproduction of the Phaestus disk, a clay tablet with undeciphered hieroglyphic script, dating from about seventeenth century B.C. and probably containing a literary inscription. If so, it would be unique, but it may well not be Cretan, even though found on a Cretan site.

Iliad was not an invention of Homer and Greek bards, but a real city which had had a real war with the Achaean Greeks,[16] even if the war had not concerned the abduction of Helen from her husband's palace in Sparta. He succeeded in finding nine cities superimposed upon one another, the last dating from Roman times; and though he was too anxious to identify the Troy of Homeric fame, and chose the second instead of the seventh city, his work excited the imagination of the whole scholarly world. Homer was now taken much more seriously as historian as well as poet, and Schliemann himself turned his attention to the Greek mainland and to Mycenae, the supposed home of Agamemnon. New discoveries of tombs were made here containing great treasures belonging to a civilization then still unknown, which, it was believed, might be an offshoot of an older civilization based on Crete. In the later years of the nineteenth century the attention of several archaeologists from different countries was also drawn to Crete, and the Englishman Sir Arthur Evans, who had already published a book on Cretan seals, was granted the right

[16] See pages 137, 182–189.

to excavate under ideal conditions an ancient site on which he soon uncovered the so-called Palace of Minos at Cnossus. Since then excavation has continued under various auspices in all parts of the island, and the "Minoan" civilization with its unique art, its flourishing commerce, and its "modern" way of living has been laid bare.

Even so, there are numerous difficulties that remain to be cleared up. There are two Cretan scripts known as Linear Minoan A and Linear Minoan B, quite distinct from one another and both comparatively late. There are also some earlier hieroglyphic inscriptions, but it is not at all certain that these were either native to Crete or were used as a form of writing prior to the development of the Linear scripts. In any event there seems at present no likelihood of their translation. In 1953 an architect named Michael Ventris, who had devoted most of his spare time for years to efforts to decipher the Linear scripts, announced that he had succeeded in deciphering Linear Minoan B. He and his collaborators identified it as a form of archaic Greek. Though he himself remained for a long time doubtful of his success, and there are still numbers of scholars who do not accept the entire system as it was elaborated, most scholarly opinion inclines to the belief that the method is basically sound and that major conclusions to be drawn from it are justified. If it is accepted, then it is demonstrated that the Cretans from about 1450 B.C. onward were writing a form of Greek.

But the decipherment of Linear Minoan B has not so far offered any major clues to Linear Minoan A. Indeed, recent work by Cyrus H. Gordon has gone far to show that this language is closely allied to the Phoenician and other Semitic tongues; and it now seems likely that this will ultimately be demonstrated and the writings will be translated. But even if this proves to be the case, we shall still not know a great deal more about Minoan civilization. Not only is Linear Minoan A relatively recent, but the writings in both scripts are highly specialized, being made up mostly of lists, either of gods or household goods, and similarly unhelpful data. No historical documents or literature is known in either script. Though this may be due to ill luck in that nothing of the kind has yet been excavated, it seems now more likely that this kind of written literature simply did not exist in Minoan civilization.

There are many literary references to the island in classical Greek literature, both in Homer and in later writers, and many myths are concerned with it. Unfortunately archaeological and other investigations have on the whole been far from confirming any of the references. For example, the famous story of Theseus and the Minotaur and the maidens who were sacrificed to this monster in the labyrinth has little support from archaeology. Bull leaping as a sport engaged in by boys and girls is depicted on Cretan frescoes, and it may have been a part of the religion. But there is no reliable evidence of bull worship on the island, nor of any kind of cult connected with the bull, such as appeared in late Egypt and in the Near East. The great king Minos, if he existed,[17] cannot be identified as yet with any historical personality—though he may well have ruled in Cnossus during the reconstruction after the great earthquake around 1570 B.C., and he may have made the voyage to Sicily described by Herodotus and even have been killed there.

Thus the history of Minoan civilization still has to be reconstructed almost exclusively from archaeology, in much the same way as the societies described in Chapter 2; and though the remains are far more numerous and extensive than for any Neolithic society, the reconstructed history given here must be treated with considerable reserve.

Following Sir Arthur Evans the culture is conventionally divided into Early Minoan, Middle Minoan, and Late Minoan periods, each with three major subdivisions. The dates for these are now fairly widely accepted as about 2500–2000 B.C., 2000–1550 B.C., and 1550–1200 B.C., respectively. During the Late Minoan II and III periods (1400–1200) the Mycenaeans ruled in most of Crete, though

there is evidence that the native inhabitants gradually filtered back into the cities and may even have taken over the government of several during this period. Sometime in the next century the Dorians and other invaders from the mainland took over the island from the Mycenaeans, and for the next few centuries the now inferior art of the island continued under Greek mainland influence until the disintegration of the civilization just at the time when the great cities of the mainland were rising to the height of their culture.

It used to be thought that the Minoan civilization was a thalassocracy (an imperial power based on command of the sea), but this is not confirmed by archaeology. It is true that the Cretans were protected by their navy, and they did not need to defend their cities by building walls, as did some of the mainland cities. But there is little evidence that they ever imposed their will on their neighbors, and the Mycenaeans on the mainland were able to compete for trade effectively with the Cretans for several centuries before they actually ruled the island. Indeed, the evidence suggests that once they acquired the Cretan manufacturing techniques they proved to be more aggressive traders than their teachers and were steadily ousting them from their former markets. It is still not known why the Cretans succumbed to the Mycenaeans about 1400 B.C. Although Cretan palaces and houses were evidently looted, this might have been done by the Cretans themselves. The weight of evidence suggests, and scholarly opinion now inclines to the belief, that another natural disaster, probably an earthquake with tidal waves, overwhelmed the Cretans first, and the Mycenaeans took advantage of subsequent Cretan weakness to establish their supremacy in the island.

The probable history of Minoan civilization is more or less as follows. About 3000 B.C. or a little later the Neolithic Revolution made its way to the island, probably carried by peoples who came by sea from the Asian continent, especially Asia Minor. They may have been joined by Egyptians who left their own country about the time of the unifica-

[17] See footnote 2, p. 39.

tion of Upper and Lower Egypt. Trade relations which began early were always maintained with Egypt, though during the Old Kingdom of Egypt trade was relatively small. About 2200 B.C. copper tools are first found, but there is no evidence of bronze until the Middle Minoan period (2000 onward). The Middle Minoan and the first phase of Late Minoan were the great periods of Cretan prosperity, during which all the best and most original art was produced, the great palaces were built, and Cretan civilization became the equal of any in the world at the time. Though all metals were in short supply on the island and only copper is known to have existed, the Cretans, working with imported materials, became such excellent craftsmen and their manufactures were in such great demand, that they were able to sell enough luxury goods abroad to enable them to pay for all their imports.

Late in the first half of the second millennium B.C. the people usually known as Achaeans settled in Greece and began to build up their civilization, especially in the cities of Mycenae, Tiryns, and Orchomenus in the Peloponnese. By trading with the Cretans the Achaeans gradually learned the skills and came to compete with them. Although the Achaeans never equalled the best Cretan manufactures, they produced goods which were sold in the market that had been formerly in the hands of the Cretans. Soon after 1400 B.C. the Mycenaeans moved into Crete as rulers, where they stayed until they in turn were ousted by the Dorians. The latter seem to have come in several waves over a long period, beginning probably some time in the twelfth century B.C. From the time of the Dorian invasions both the Cretan and Mycenaean mainland civilizations rapidly declined, and for several centuries, marked only by the epic poetry of Homer, little of cultural importance arose in the Aegean area.

MINOAN GOVERNMENT, RELIGION, AND SOCIETY

Though the Cretan people of the Minoan civilization cannot be classed as Greeks, of whom the Achaeans were the earliest known, their art resembles in many respects that of the later Greeks as will be shown, even though it is perhaps more indebted to Egypt. The civilization therefore was an important link between ancient Egypt and classical Greece. Even Minoan government seems to have been much more similar to later Greek institutions than to Egyptian ones, though it is difficult to speak with much conviction in the absence of written records.

The kings of Crete seem to have held a position unparalleled elsewhere in early times. Attached to their palaces were great factories, which turned out pottery, textiles, and metal goods, suggesting to some scholars that they were merchants as well as kings; and that perhaps their power was based on their commercial position at least as much as on any reverence paid to the throne as such. But even in the large cities there were apparently private enterprises. Until Late Minoan times there was little centralized government, each city being at least partly self-governing. Only during Late Minoan I does Cnossus appear to have been a real capital, with its kings ruling the whole island. At this time the Cretan kings were shown in Minoan art together with symbols indicating that they were military and naval commanders, legislators, judges, and priests. A king is shown receiving a code of law from the gods, like Hammurabi in Babylon.

The chief deity of Crete, as far as we can tell, was not a god but a goddess, represented in art as the symbol of fertility, sometimes carrying a child in her arms, and accompanied by a serpent and a dove. Snake goddesses, however, are extremely common, and it is regarded as likely that the snake was viewed as the protector of the home, as is the case even in parts of modern Crete and elsewhere in the Eastern Mediterranean. No buildings are extant which can be definitely classified as temples, nor do there seem to have been any buildings devoted exclusively to religious purposes. The Cretans used high places open to the sky or sacred caves. There was certainly a tree and pillar cult, and there were altars and chapels in the palaces. Each house had its own corner

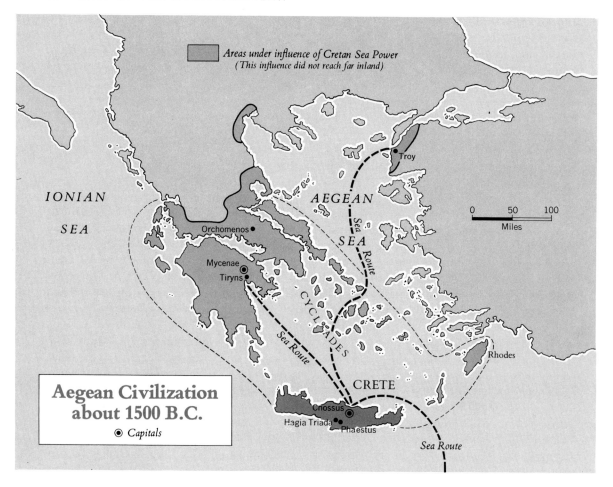

Areas under influence of Cretan Sea Power
(This influence did not reach far inland)

IONIAN SEA

AEGEAN SEA

Troy

Orchomenos

Mycenae
Tiryns

CYCLADES

Rhodes

CRETE

Cnossus
Hagia Triada
Phaestus

Sea Route

0 50 100
Miles

Aegean Civilization about 1500 B.C.

⊙ Capitals

devoted to worship, and miniature statues were kept in them. The dead were buried with all the articles they had used in life; the hunter with his spear, and the sailor with a miniature boat.

The Cretans seem to have been precursors of the Greeks in their love of athletics and all forms of games. One of the favorite was bull leaping in which the athletes, both men and women, would catch a horn of the animal, spring to his head and turn a somersault, and try to land on their feet to the rear of the bull. A comrade stood ready to catch the athlete in case of mishap. The Cretans engaged in boxing contests, running matches, and dancing, and they built fine stone theatres for their games, processions, and their music. In all these things they were far closer to the Greeks than to the Egyptians.

There seems to have been substantial social equality and relatively little slavery, although the Linear Minoan B script, if it can be trusted, lists a number of slaves from the Mycenaean period of rule in Crete. Women evidently occupied a social position superior to that held by them in classical Greece. Women took a prominent part in religious festivals as priestesses. In addition to engaging in the athletic contests, including prize fighting, we see them working side by side with the men in the factories and even hunting with them. But they remained feminine, as evidenced by the remarkable changes in fashion, puffed short sleeves and bare forearms, tiered skirts, even bustles, their many hats, and their attention to the art of

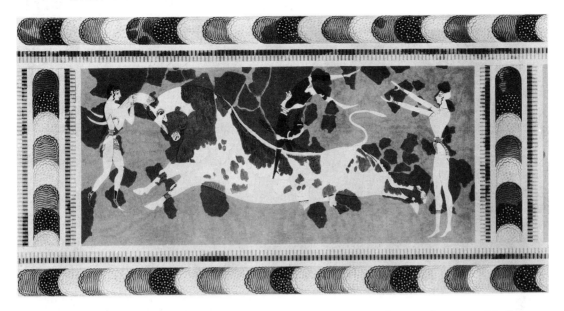

Reproduction of a Cretan fresco from the palace at Cnossus, showing the sport of bull leaping. Evidently the man uses the bull's horns as an aid in leaping over the bull, to be caught by his female partner on the other side. (COURTESY THE METROPOLITAN MUSEUM OF ART)

hairdressing. Though an Egyptian might not feel too strange in Crete, any stray visitor from Palestine or Mesopotamia might well find himself sadly out of place in this atmosphere; even a classical Greek straying back into the past would be unlikely to admire wholeheartedly what he found in Crete.

MINOAN ART

The greatest glory of Minoan Crete was its art, one of the few really great arts of the world. It was delicate, and at the same time spontaneous and natural, and continuously creative; beautiful objects, as in the Greek world, were to be found everywhere and not only in the houses and palaces of the great. As with the Greeks, art seems to have been a necessity of their lives. Though the Cretans learned much from the Egyptians, in certain respects they far surpassed their masters. While their architecture was not especially distinguished, even the great palaces being designed at least partly for comfort and utility, the interiors of their buildings were beautifully decorated, especially with paintings. Painting was

the supreme art of the Minoans, although sculpture and pottery were not far behind. It is typical of this culture that it developed sanitation more thoroughly than any Oriental people. Flush toilets were already known, and there was a sewage system, with main and subsidiary drains, for the streets as well as for the palaces. No ancient people surpassed the Minoans in such refinements until the Romans.

Minoan painting, mostly in the form of mural frescoes, shows a strong instinct for the dramatic, and for the naturalistic portrayal of plants, and of animals in action. Their wonderful pictures of the frightened deer and the stalking cat have become famous in reproductions in the Western world. Human figures appear only in late times, and they are largely stereotypes, and conventional. The sculptor did not make gigantic statues but concentrated upon miniature objects of exquisite workmanship in clay, ivory, and metal, which were used in individual homes. Only in very late Minoan times did the quality of these fall off, possibly with mass production, to fulfill the huge demand for domestic and foreign con-

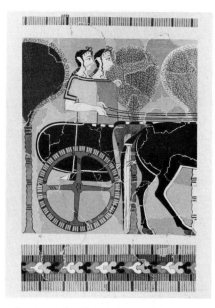

Reproduction of a fragment of a Cretan fresco, showing the head of a young girl. Note the elaborate hair styling, with a modern-looking "spit curl." (COURTESY THE METROPOLITAN MUSEUM OF ART)

Reproduction of a fresco from the mainland of Greece (Tiryns); two women watching a boar hunt. Note the mainland use of Cretan technique. (COURTESY THE METROPOLITAN MUSEUM OF ART)

sumption. In ceramics there was constant development and improvement in technique as well as creative inspiration, and new forms were continually produced until the late period, when the same decline is seen as in sculpture. The old forms were used again and again; and at last after the fall of Cnossus the workshops were reduced to the production in quantity of common ware. The art of the goldsmith and jeweler was as highly developed as sculpture and ceramics. Exquisite jewelry of all kinds has been found, and finely decorated swords and daggers; and gaming boards are known with inlays of gold, silver, and crystal.

It is difficult to appreciate the impression made by the remains of this ancient civilization, and the extraordinary enthusiasm kindled by it unless one examines a large number of its art objects. It was a civilization that remains all light and color and beauty, in the absence of written records which might contradict that impression. It is hard indeed to forgive the ruthlessness of those peoples who learned so much from it, if it was indeed they who destroyed it.

Reproduction of a Cretan jug exported to Egypt. (COURTESY THE METROPOLITAN MUSEUM OF ART)

A room in the so-called palace of Minos at Cnossus in Crete. (HIRMER)

For the art of the Mycenaeans is derivative and inferior by comparison, in spite of its own great superiority to what followed before the classical age of Greece. And their civilization, with its concentration on war and defense, bears no comparison at all. Marvelous gold weapons, crowns and swords belonging to the treasure of their kings, were found in the six shaft graves of Mycenae, as well as bracelets, cups, necklaces, and alabaster vases. But the art of making these was learned from Crete, and many of the best specimens were imported from there. Literacy seems to have been uncommon among the Achaeans, and it was the kings and princes for whose benefit the weapons

This picture of an ordinary Cretan household drinking cup shows how ancient is the design of cup and handle that we use today. (COURTESY THE METROPOLITAN MUSEUM OF ART)

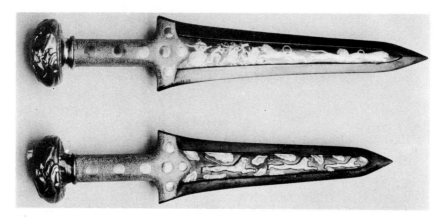

Reproductions of two inlaid daggers from Mycenae. This mainland center was especially noted for the fine bronze weapons it produced. (COURTESY THE METROPOLITAN MUSEUM OF ART)

and ornaments were made. It is therefore not necessary to go into the achievements of the Achaeans and Mycenae and Orchomenus and the mainland cities separately.

INFLUENCE OF AEGEAN CIVILIZATION

It is not possible to assess accurately the influence of Aegean civilization in general upon the world. The Achaeans remained in Greece and were absorbed or worked as serfs for their conquerors, especially in Laconia, the main center of Doric penetration, though some cities remained independent for a long time. The memory of Minoan and Mycenaean civilization was retained by the Greeks and found its echoes in Homeric poetry, and some Greek gods were known by Cretan names. Probably the festivals of Greece and certainly their devotion to athletics were derived from this earlier pre-Hellenic age. In spite of the dark age that followed the Dorian invasion, much of the past was retained without a distinct break, and this especially in the cities of Asia, peopled by Ionians and living for centuries under the mild rule of Lydians and Persians. Philistines who settled in Palestine introduced a few elements of Aegean culture into Palestine. As traders the Aegean peoples spread Egyptian culture as well as their own, and they formed a kind of cultural bridge between Egypt and Europe.

But, as far as our present information goes, the Aegean peoples were not thinkers, and their influence on Western civilization has been incomparably less than that of the Hebrews or the Mesopotamians—a fact which provides an interesting reflection on the requirements for cultural immortality. But it is good to think, unless and until written evidence suggests the contrary, that at least one people *enjoyed themselves* in antiquity.

▶ Suggestions for further reading

PAPER-BOUND BOOKS

Albright, William F. *The Archaeology of Palestine.* 5th ed. Penguin. Survey of various peoples who inhabited Palestine from earliest times from the point of view of an archaeologist. Contains little interpretation or reconciliation with Biblical material, for which see author's other books noted below.

Albright, William F. *The Biblical Period From Abraham to Ezra: A Historical Survey.* Torchbooks. The most recent and up-to-date of this author's books on the subject, precise, clear, and specific.

Albright, William F. *From the Stone Age to Christianity.* Anchor. A thought-provoking study of early religions in the light of archaeological investigation.

Butterfield, Herbert. *Christianity and History.* Scribner. Contains several superb chapters on the Hebrew understanding of history.

Chadwick, John. *The Decipherment of Linear B.* Vintage. Summarizes the discoveries of Michael Ventris and the work done in this field since his death.

Daniel-Rops, H. *Israel and the Ancient World Image*. A study by a leading Catholic scholar.

De Burgh, William G. *The Legacy of the Ancient World*. Penguin. The early part of this book provides an interesting survey of the influence of Hebrew thought in later times.

Driver, Samuel R. *An Introduction to the Literature of the Old Testament*. Meridian. Though the last edition of this famous pioneer work dates from 1914, it is still worth reading. Most of the interpretations have been incorporated into all later writings on the subject.

Ehrlich, E. L. *A Concise History of Israel: From the Earliest Times to the Destruction of the Temple*. Torchbooks. Excellent narrative history.

Goodspeed, Edgar J., trans., *Apocrypha*. Vintage. Contains the noncanonical Old Testament books. Of special interest for the study of the material in this chapter are *Wisdom of Sirach, Wisdom of Solomon* (on the concept of the future life), and the books of the *Maccabees*.

Gordon, Cyrus H. *Ugarit and Minoan Greece*. Norton. A study of the commercial and cultural contacts between Minoan Crete and the Asian mainland.

Gurney, O. R. *The Hittites*. Penguin. Reliable survey of all phases of Hittite culture, with illustrations.

Harden, Donald. *The Phoenicians*. Praeger. Most modern paper-bound study of this important trading people.

Hutchinson, R. W. *Prehistoric Crete*. Penguin. This recent (1962) survey by a practicing archaeologist is indispensable for the latest discoveries of Minoan civilization.

Kenyon, K. M. *Archaeology in the Holy Land*. Praeger. Interesting and up-to-date study.

Mellaart, James. *The Earliest Civilizations of the Near East*. McGraw. A good introduction with special attention to Anatolia.

Orlinsky, Harry M. *Ancient Israel*. Ithaca, N.Y., Cornell University Press. Short, clear, up-to-date account of Hebrew history by a Jewish scholar, taking good advantage of archaeological and recent biblical criticism.

Samuel, Alan. *The Mycenaeans in History*. Spectrum. A short study of what little is known about mainland Greece during the Bronze Age.

Webster, T. B. *From Mycenae to Homer*. Norton. Greece during the Dorian invasions.

Wellhausen, Julius. *Prolegomena to the History of Ancient Israel*. Meridian. Scholarly nineteenth-century work (1882), interesting as example of pre-archaeological commentary.

CASE-BOUND BOOKS

Ceram, C. W. *The Secret of the Hittites*. New York: Alfred A. Knopf, Inc., 1956. Well-written popular work, with extensive bibliography, mostly on how the Hittite civilization was discovered and interpreted, but needs to be supplemented with Gurney on details of Hittite culture.

Frankfort, Henri, *et al. The Intellectual Adventure of Ancient Man*. Chicago: University of Chicago Press, 1946. The essay by W. A. Irwin on the Hebrews was extensively used for the interpretation given in this chapter.

Glotz, Gustave. *The Aegean Civilization*. New York: Alfred A. Knopf, Inc., 1925. Old and still useful, though to be treated with caution in view of later discoveries and interpretations.

Gordon, Cyrus H. *Before the Bible: The Common Background of Greek and Hebrew Civilizations*. New York: Harper & Row, Publishers, 1963. Controversial and original work, with stimulating suggestions, including the importance of the Hittites as cultural transmitters.

Graham, W. C. *The Prophets and Israel's Culture*. Chicago: University of Chicago Press, 1934. Brief but stimulating study of the prophets, primarily as social reformers.

Lods, Adolphe. *Israel From its Beginnings to the Middle of the Eighth Century*. Napierville, Ill.: Alec R. Allenson, Inc., 1953. Reissue of a thoughtful book, first published in 1932, mostly concerned with Hebrew religious, social, and intellectual history, using primarily, but not exclusively, Old Testament records. By the same author—*The Prophets and the Rise of Judaism* (reissued 1955 by the same publisher).

Oesterley, W. O. E., and Robinson, T. H. *A History of Israel*. 2 vols. Oxford, England: Clarendon Press, 1932. Carefully planned, judicious, and readable study, using all the material available at the time of writing. Probably the best general history of the subject.

CHAPTER 6

FAR EASTERN CONTRASTS
WITH THE WESTERN WORLD

► **Reasons for inclusion of the Far East**

In a book intended to deal with the heritage of the West, there would at first thought seem no reason to discuss China and India, whose influence on Western civilization has been relatively slight, certainly not important enough to justify an extended treatment. These countries, however, are now influencing and being influenced by the West, with tremendous and far-reaching consequences for each. So it has seemed worthwhile to offer a brief study here, not of these civilizations as a whole, but primarily of the great differences between East and West which prevented any extensive diffusion of culture in either direction until the nineteenth century of our era. There was always some trade between East and West, sometimes on quite an extended scale as in the period of the Roman Empire. But such trade was almost entirely in scarce luxury goods, and the traders had only minor contacts with the peoples with whom they traded.

The Indian and Chinese civilizations, indeed, have been astonishingly self-sufficient, even to this day. It is barely a hundred years since the Chinese emperor learned to

his cost that Queen Victoria of England was not a tributary princess owing him allegiance; and though the Indian rulers bowed to the superior might of the British a century earlier, few Indians thought they had anything much to learn from their masters in any of the major arts of civilization and vice versa. Although China in earlier times occupied much less territory than now, it usually formed one political unit; the civilized part of China has always been one cultural unit, in spite of invasions, and even of rule by foreign conquerors. These conquerors, with few and short-lived exceptions, adopted the customs and language of the people they ruled, and quite consciously built their regimes upon the cultural foundations of the native Chinese they displaced. India has only rarely been a political unit, in part because of the presence of natural boundaries within the territory. When the Muslims conquered it in the sixteenth century, they did not attempt to impose their religion on it; but in the course of their rule which lasted over two centuries they did convert substantial numbers of Hindus, whose descendants have remained Muslim, and been joined by other converts in later years. Most of the converts formed their own Islamic islands in

► chronological chart

India		China	
Harappa civilization	*ca.* 2500–1500 B.C.		
Aryan invasions	*ca.* 1500		
		Shang dynasty	1450–1050 B.C.
		Chou dynasty	1050–256
Death of Mahavira	*ca.* 528		
Life of Gautama Buddha	*ca.* 563–483	Life of Confucius	551–478
Expedition to India of Scylax the Persian	*ca.* 518–517	Era of the "Contending States"	481–256
Alexander's invasion of India	327–326		
Maurya dynasty	322–185		
Chandragupta Maurya	322–298		
		Ch'in dynasty	256–207
		Reign of Shih Huang Ti	221–207
Kushan monarchs	*ca.* 40–A.D. 220	Han dynasty	206 B.C.–A.D. 220
		Reign of Wang Mang	9–A.D. 23
Gupta Empire	320–647		
Reign of Chandragupta II	380–415		
Reign of Harsha of Kanauj	606–647	T'ang dynasty	618–906
Era of Rajput princes	700–*ca.* 1100		
		Sung dynasty	960–1279
Muslim invasions	1175 on		
		Mongol conquest of northern China	1234
		Mongol conquest of China completed under Kublai Khan	1279
		Mongols driven from China	1368
		Ming dynasty	1368–1644
Sack of Delhi by Tamerlane	1398		
Conquest of India by Babur	1526		
The Great Mogul Empire	1526–1857		
Reign of Akbar the Great	1556–1605		
		Manchu dynasty	1644–1911

the sea of Hinduism, so that a partition along geographical lines was not impossible when Britain conceded independence in 1947. It proved to be difficult in some areas, and the partition was accompanied by much bloodshed when millions tried to join their co-religionists in India and Pakistan in preference to being ruled by men of a different faith. But neither Hinduism nor Islam was much changed by the other. Hinduism successfully resisted both Islam and Buddhism, and has not changed in its essentials since it was first brought to India by the invading Aryans in the second millennium B.C.

In this chapter, therefore, the history of the Indian and Chinese peoples will be kept to a minimum, only enough to give some indication of the greatness of these civilizations in the past, which is so often ignored by Westerners who know only of the drab present of most of the East at a time when it suffers from poverty, overpopulation, and exploitation. What will mainly be stressed are the social and cultural differences between the East and the West. This procedure, it is hoped, will bring out the self-sufficiency of the Eastern cultures and the limited nature and extent of their contribution to the heritage of the West.

▶ India—The land and its history

THE LAND

India is usually called a subcontinent, a fair description when it is recalled that her population is over 400 million, and her territory is as large as all Europe without Russia. The high mountains to the northeast, shutting India off from Tibet and western China, have served to keep contacts with China to a minimum, although the way into southeastern China is not so strongly protected by natural barriers. But the mountains to the northeast are not altogether impassable, and the northwest frontier, which was always guarded carefully by the British, has been the historic route for land invasions of India. The British, however, with their command of the sea, conquered India from over the sea, a feat that could hardly have been accomplished if India had been united against them, or if they had been compelled to bring land armies over the Khyber Pass from Afghanistan.

The land of India falls naturally into four well-defined sections—the northern hill country stretching up to the Himalayas; the north central plain, partly desert but mostly well watered by India's great rivers; the south central plain known as the Deccan, south of the hills called the Vindhyas which formerly were covered with thick jungle; and the southern maritime plains known as Tamil Land. In ancient times the small Vindhya Hills were sufficient to protect the Deccan from any but the best equipped and most militant of empire builders, and the Deccan was the first to be lost when the emperors of the north fell on evil times. The narrow southern plains have usually been ruled independently. At certain times in Indian history one language could be understood from coast to coast, and from northern mountains to the southern tip. But in modern times countless dialects are spoken throughout India, though scholars everywhere may be able to read Sanskrit, the language of Hindu learning and the Hindu scriptures. The great religions of India have their believers in the whole territory, and help to give the people an awareness of their cultural unity.

The land is a violent one, and there are everywhere violent contrasts. Many parts of the country are extremely fertile and have a very high rainfall; others are chronically short of rain, dependent upon a specially favorable monsoon, and much of the northern territory is semidesert. Except for the highlands, the climate is torrid and enervating, and there is always danger in India from animals and reptiles as well as from hunger and starvation. Nevertheless, before the last centuries of gross overpopulation, India was a relatively prosperous land. China and India were both envied by Westerners as lands of riches and luxury for most of the centuries of their history.

HARAPPA OR INDUS VALLEY CIVILIZATION (ca. 2500–1500 B.C.)

Not so many years ago there was no suspicion in the minds of historians that there had been a flourishing civilization in the Indus Valley before the invasions of the people usually called the Aryans in the second millennium B.C., and little was known of the pre-Aryan inhabitants. But in recent years two important sites have been excavated and thoroughly explored by archaeologists, and many others are known. These two sites are at Mohenjo-Daro and Harappa in the northwest of India, and the civilization is now usually called the Harappa after the name of the modern village over one of the ancient sites. It appears to have been a civilization at least as far advanced as those of its slightly older contemporaries in Egypt and Mesopotamia, with a bronze and copper technology, buildings made of a fired brick superior to that used in Sumer, and a pictographic script. The latter, however, has not yet been deciphered, though it is not now believed there was any extensive literature. All the records so far discovered are short, and probably concern details of personal property. There was clearly some trade with Sumer but little sign of any influence by either civilization on the other, and it is possible that the idea of writing, though not the script, was adopted from the Sumerians. But all the evidence points to the complete self-sufficiency and separateness of this urban civilization, and that the Dravidians, the older inhabitants of India, continued to live according to their old Neolithic pattern. Indeed, there is considerable dispute over the identity of the Harappa people, and some Indian scholars continue to believe that they were Aryans.

But it is not the details of this early civilization that concern us here. What is most suggestive is the discovery of the archaeologists that so many of the features of later Hindu society were found at these ancient sites and apparently survived the Aryan invasions. The area of the Harappa civilization was considerable, more than seven times the extent of Sumer. More than seventy towns and villages have been discovered in addition to the two main sites, which themselves were four hundred odd miles apart. Evidence tends to show that it was not a confederation of cities but an organized kingdom with a central government. Both cities were in all essentials similar, planned urban units, well built, rectilinear, and without any of the crooked narrow streets and slums characteristic of later Oriental (and Occidental) towns. What is of great interest is the quite extraordinary conservatism of these ancient Indians. Several times Mohenjo-Daro was actually destroyed by the flooding of the river Indus; but on each occasion it was rebuilt exactly as before, with no apparent changes, even the houses rising again on exactly the same spot as before. In the citadel at Mohenjo-Daro there was an open bath surrounded by verandahs, complete with disrobing rooms. The bath

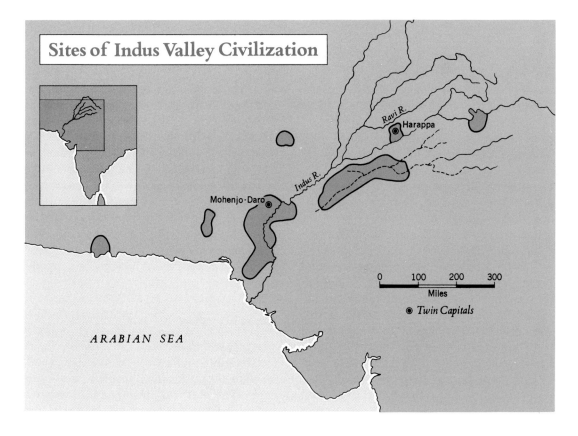

Sites of Indus Valley Civilization

Ravi R.

Harappa

Indus R.

Mohenjo-Daro

ARABIAN SEA

0   100   200   300
Miles

⊙ *Twin Capitals*

This picture of the site of the prehistoric Indian city of Mohenjo-Daro gives some idea of the size of this ancient center of the Indus Valley civilization. (COURTESY GOVERNMENT OF INDIA INFORMATION SERVICES)

was apparently the central feature of the building, just as in later sacred sites of India —suggesting the importance even to the ancient Indian of a ritual bath, which may indeed, as now, have been prescribed by his religion. The art and architecture of the Harappa civilization are quite distinctly Indian. There are several statuettes of gods and goddesses which resemble their later counterparts, especially one of a god which could easily be taken for the later Siva.

In the whole civilization there is no sign that there was ever any warfare. There are no war implements, no strong points for defense. The leading cities never went to war with each other. It seems to have been a truly peaceful civilization, and it was perhaps this very feature that made these early Indians incapable of defending themselves when at last they were attacked and defeated by invading Aryans. All this suggests that the authority wielded by the central govern-

ment was moral and religious, not military, and that already there were priest-kings who ruled by virtue of their sanctity and their connection with the gods. Such rulers, the basis of whose power was their moral ascendancy over their people, are less rare in Indian history than in any other known civilization, and the example of Gandhi in modern times shows that the tradition is not yet dead. However, such suggestions cannot yet be confirmed and must await further excavation and possibly a deciphering of the script.

THE ARYAN INVASIONS—THE VEDIC AGE

Invaders from the northwest began infiltrating into India early in the second millennium B.C. It seems difficult to resist the conclusion that the Harappan civilization and its cities were destroyed by the as yet barbarous Aryans, who, indeed, in their epics speak of destroying "walled cities."[1] They then moved gradually southward, driving many of the Dravidian peoples into the south of the peninsula, where their descendants have remained to this day. The Aryans are generally believed to have taken over some elements in their religion from the earlier inhabitants. They produced, however, a remarkable heroic literature, especially two long epic poems known as the *Mahabharata* and the *Ramayana,* which are comparable in many respects to the poetry of the Heroic Age in Greece to be described in the next chapter. This early poetry, which included also many hymns, was incorporated in the Vedas probably many hundred years later. These Vedas have given their name to the whole age, which is usually called the Vedic age.[2]

In due course the marauders settled down to a life of agriculture. They began to live in villages, as their descendants have lived until today. The larger Aryan towns were usually fortified, and wars were constant. To these invaders is ascribed the caste system, perhaps originally devised for the purpose of maintaining their separateness from the earlier inhabitants, though in early times the castes were not so highly stratified as they became later. It is not known whether the Aryans found a caste system already in existence among the people they conquered or whether they developed it themselves. At all events by the end of the Vedic age it had already crystallized into a closed system without freedom of movement between the castes. The system will be fully dealt with in a later section of this chapter.

[1] This may not be conclusive since the cities of Mohenjo-Daro and Harappa do not reveal evidence of walls, only of fortified citadels. Numerous bodies were discovered in the ruins. The only other possible explanation is that these people were killed in a natural disaster, of which nothing is otherwise known.

[2] It is difficult to tell in exactly what order these epics were composed since for a long time the Vedas were considered too sacred to write down, and in any case the great epics, the *Mahabharata* and the *Ramayana,* contain material evidently from different periods. The most sacred book of the Hindus, the *Bhagavad Gita,* is incorporated, for instance, into the *Mahabharata.* The poems and the hymns together give a fairly complete picture of early Aryan society.

PERSIAN AND GREEK INVASIONS—THE MAURYA DYNASTY (322–185 B.C.)

Under the Persian ruler Darius I, an expedition succeeded in entering India from the northwest, and a Persian satrapy was set up which did not survive for very long. The Persian admiral sailed down the Indus to the ocean, a feat duplicated by the next invader, Alexander the Great of Macedon in 327–326 B.C. Alexander defeated the local Indian chieftain at the battle of the Hydaspes, mentioned in a later chapter, but was forced to turn back when his troops refused to follow him further into the unknown. The expedition had no lasting effects on the Indian government or social structure, though some of Alexander's successors again penetrated into the Punjab and for brief periods set up independent kingdoms in that area. Greek influence, however, can be discerned in Indian art, and Alexander himself became a heroic figure of Indian legend under the name of Iscander.

The year after Alexander's death an Indian ruler named Chandragupta Maurya (322–298 B.C.), who is believed to have met Alexander and even fought against him, began to unify northern India, and ultimately was able to establish a firm rule over all India north of the Vindhyas. The dynasty that he founded was sometimes disturbed by Greek inroads from the Bactrian kingdom to the east of the Persian Empire, but those Greeks who penetrated to the court of Chandragupta were welcomed there. The new kingdom was peaceful and well organized, and extremely rich by comparison with any of the other kingdoms of that day. The Brahmin priests were influential and the Hindu religion, enriched some while earlier by the profound speculation of the Upanishads, was the official religion of the realm.

Chandragupta's grandson Asoka (273–232 B.C.), however, was converted to Buddhism, with its more ethical teachings and its charitable emphasis. This monarch deserves more than a passing attention.

After adding the Deccan in southern India to the lands that he had inherited,

Asoka underwent a conversion to Buddhism, as a result of which he realized that he had caused unnecessary suffering to millions of people. Thereafter he eschewed war and became a model ruler, tolerant in matters of religion in spite of his conversion, helpful and compassionate, determined to convert others to Buddhism by example rather than by coercion. Asoka, in this respect, is unique in history. India has had many rulers of high character, the mainspring in whose lives was the desire to put into practice the ethics of Indian religion, which insist upon nonviolence, peacefulness, and government in the interests of all, and who have believed that the king himself must set an example of humility and responsibility. But none appears to have equalled Asoka, and his attitude is an ideal which has been alien to the West, especially in his humility and tolerance. The best Western monarchs have had a deep sense of responsibility. But the dynamism and activism which are characteristic of the West have usually led to intolerance of opposition and to the attempt to gain adherents by force, rather than by love and compassion, so greatly emphasized by Asoka. It is difficult to imagine any Western ruler insisting that the poor serfs should be won over by kindness, as Asoka attempted to win over the jungle folk, comparing himself to a nurse. "The skilled nurse," he said, "is eager to care for the happiness of her child. Even so have my governors been created for the welfare and happiness of my country, and their task is to be pursued with patience and perseverance."

Asoka sent Buddhist missionaries into countries to the west, as well as throughout India itself. These missionaries converted Ceylon, which became and has remained to this day primarily a Buddhist country. Tibetans, Burmese, and Siamese similarly received his message and kept it. Difficult also is it to imagine a Western ruler, even a pope, insisting that "although a man injures him, the Emperor believes that as far as possible it must be patiently endured," although this has been the teaching of the Founder of Christianity. Asoka proclaimed the *Dharma*, or Law of Piety of Buddha, as the ideal to be followed, with its virtues of compassion, liberality, truth, purity, gentleness, and saintliness of life, and he endeavored himself to live up to it. Wars of religion were to be stopped, all religions were to receive toleration and even royal support, no more animals were to be slaughtered, and animal sacrifices were to be abandoned. The emperor abolished the royal hunt as an example.

Fundamentally the Buddhist ideal, preached and demonstrated by the emperor, rested upon the belief that all men equally lived many lives on earth and were subject to the law of *karma*. Life was suffering, as the Buddha had proclaimed. No man could escape from this suffering, which was the lot of men upon earth, but each man had the task on earth of helping others, alleviating and not adding to this suffering, knowing that he was in his present position on earth as the result of his former lives, and each equally was worthy of pity and compassion, as on the same path as one's self. Parenthetically, it may be added that, according to Western ideals, Asoka should

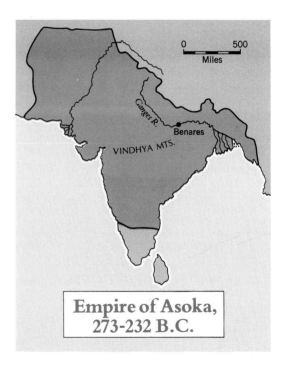

Empire of Asoka, 273-232 B.C.

have made an attack upon the caste system. But it is symptomatic that we should know of no such attempt. We know of his tolerance of the Brahmins, although they were not of his religion, and we know of his efforts to mitigate the hard lot of the lowest members of society. But the caste system, as we shall see, was not looked upon as discrimination, but rather as the conferring of a definite status and definite responsibilities upon all members of society; and the system was deeply rooted in all Indian religion of the time, whether Hindu or Buddhist. A man was in his particular caste in this incarnation because of his deeds in a previous life, and he encountered the opportunities and suffered the restrictions imposed upon him by it. In an individualist society which believes in "getting on in the world" this notion would be intolerable; but India of this age was not individualist. Indian philosophers and holy men did not even believe the world itself to be real, but an illusion, a *maya* which had to be endured and ultimately understood for the illusion that it was. The bond with earth had to be severed by the achievement of a state of being without desire for it; the thirst for existence had to be overcome.[3]

It can therefore be seen why even the most enlightened of reformers would not wish to interfere with a system believed to be part of the whole universal order. A man's place in life was not only divinely ordained, but was for the ultimate benefit of the individual man himself. For only by being tested and by suffering in the position he had merited by his deeds, and needed for his development, could he hope to rise into the state called Nirvana by the Buddhists, which would make unnecessary any further incarnation upon earth. This question has been entered into briefly by anticipation here because it invariably arises in a discussion of Asoka. Hinduism and Buddhism will

[3] This system was only fully developed in the Sankara school of philosophy about A.D. 800, but it is implicit in many of the Upanishads which had already been composed well before the time of Asoka.

be dealt with in more detail later in this chapter.

LATER INDIAN HISTORY TO THE ONSET OF ISLAM

The Maurya dynasty did not long survive the death of Asoka. The next period is poorly documented—the Indians themselves were not interested in writing history until a much later period—but it is certain that the control of the monarchy declined. The Deccan became independent for several centuries under one dynasty (Andra), and was never fully conquered again, in spite of sporadic campaigns from the north, until the coming of the Muslims. Invaders again poured into the north, including Greeks from Bactria who became Indianized, and in many cases accepted Hindu religion. A dynasty of nomads, called the Kushans (*ca.* A.D. 40–220), controlled much of the north fairly effectively for two centuries or so. As close neighbors of the Roman Empire to the west, the Kushans imitated Roman coins and engaged in trade with them. Many of the Kushan rulers became Buddhist, but under their rule Buddhism became a theist religion, in the form of Mahayana Buddhism, to be discussed briefly later. Buddha himself became a god and was represented as such in Indian sculpture.

Following the breakup of the Kushan Empire there was a further dark age that ended in the establishment of the so-called Gupta Empire (320–647), which under Chandragupta II (380–415) again became a benevolent despotism, with the country well ordered, peaceful, and prosperous. Though apparently an orthodox Hindu himself, he and his family always granted full and complete tolerance to the Buddhists. It was this circumstance that gives us our knowledge of his reign, since he was visited by a Chinese Buddhist pilgrim, one of many devoted and learned Chinese who made the difficult pilgrimage from China to visit the shrines and holy places and monasteries of their religion. Another glimpse of a great ruler of this time is given by a seventh-century Chinese pilgrim, who was also much impressed by the Emperor Harsha (606–647). He especially noted the excellence of the administration and the high standard of living enjoyed by all classes. Both Brahmins and Buddhists he found to be living up to the best precepts of their religions. During the Gupta Empire there was considerable trade with the West over the caravan routes, but much more with China. Occasional Indian merchants voyaged to the West by way of the Red Sea. But it seems that the voyages were mostly in the easterly direction, while the Indians themselves went east and planted colonies in Burma, Java, Sumatra, and Indo-China, taking both Hinduism and Buddhism with them.

During all this time southern India and Ceylon were entirely free from domination by the northern region, and they themselves did not expand, but seem to have been content with their own very fertile territory. The government usually seems to have been decentralized. Most of the people made their living by agriculture. But the tropical products which grew there in such profusion were much in demand in the West, and a very extensive trade was carried on with the Roman Empire. The Romans and Greeks, however, had little to offer to this prosperous people. The West, therefore, had an extremely unfavorable balance of trade with southern India, which had to be made up by the export of currency, of which there was a great shortage in the later days of the empire. About A.D. 900 southern India fell under the rule of an efficient but warlike series of monarchs who unified the whole of the southern region and maintained the unity for several centuries. They were great builders. Hinduism and Buddhism flourished together for a long time in the southern area, but in later times several rulers instituted persecutions of Buddhists and Jainists. The result was the eventual triumph of Hinduism except in Ceylon, which was ruled by native Sinhalese monarchs until the fourteenth century. Tamil invaders from southern India then entered Ceylon: they tried to extirpate Buddhism but only succeeded in driving it

from the coastal areas into the highlands, where it persisted until the present time.

THE MUSLIM INVASIONS AND THE ESTABLISHMENT OF THE MOGUL EMPIRE

After the fall of the Gupta Empire in the north the country fell into the hands of small princes until the Muslims began to make serious invasions in the twelfth century. Orthodox Islam detested the polytheism of the Hindus. By this time Hinduism had largely superseded Buddhism in India. The old Hinayana Buddhism of Asoka had, as has been seen, been replaced by Mahayana Buddhism with its personal gods, among whom was the Buddha himself. Perhaps this latter form of Buddhism seemed to be too little distinguished from orthodox Hinduism to be worthy of a separate existence in the country of its birth. The Buddhist monasteries, with their praying monks, may well have been a social evil, in addition to presenting a serious competition to the Brahmins who were dominant in Hinduism. At all events, it seems that the new Rajput princes who followed the Gupta emperors

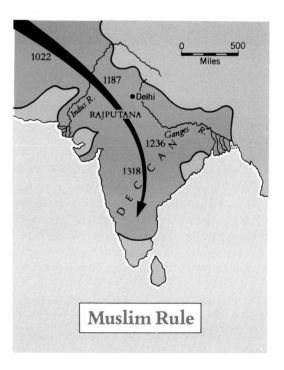

Muslim Rule

allied themselves with the Brahmins and together they vanquished Buddhism, so that today it is almost extinct in the territory of India. Hinduism was made more formal and ritualistic than ever and the caste system was defined and enforced. So the Muslims were faced with a polytheistic religion which was by this time marked by a number of rather horrible rites, which, incidentally, did not conduce to effective defense against a courageous and fiercely aggressive enemy. In particular the *jauhar*, a mass suicide of the vanquished, or those who believed themselves to be vanquished, became not uncommon. The Hindus, rather than allow themselves to be captured or defiled by ritually unclean peoples, cremated themselves on a gigantic funeral pyre. Suttee, or the suicide of a widow on her husband's funeral pyre, had always been expected of a Hindu woman who wished to stay with her husband in the afterlife. But during the ascendancy of the Rajputs and during the Muslim invasions it became ever more prevalent and was even enforced instead of being left to the choice of the widow. The Hindus invariably outnumbered their adversaries, but their military tactics were outmoded. The elephants, on which Hindu military rulers had always relied, were defeated time and again by mobile horsemen and were made to turn back upon their own army, as had already been done centuries before by Alexander at the battle of the Hydaspes. But the Indians did not change their tactics, and the numerous Hindu kingdoms refused to unite against the common enemy. The only breathing space they had against the Muslims was when the latter withdrew of their own accord, or there were internecine rivalries between Muslim rulers. Almost never did the Hindus win a battle, until at last the Muslims came to stay, and organized the enduring empire of the Moguls.

Although this period lies outside the scope of this book, a few words should be devoted to Akbar the Great (1556–1605). This extraordinary man, though an alien conqueror, ruled in the tradition of Asoka. If he was not quite as saintly in his private life, and if he sometimes lost his temper and meted out severe punishment to his enemies, he nevertheless stands out as a ruler with few equals in the history of the world. Like Asoka he realized that it was his duty as monarch to care for the interests of his subjects, Hindu and Muslim alike. Completely tolerant in matters of religion, and himself a striver after religious truth, he tried to devise an administrative system for his subjects that would be based upon the principles of order and justice. During his reign there can be no doubt that the Mogul Empire was the best-governed territory in the world, there was the least corruption, the greatest equality in matters of taxation and equality for all under the law. The administrative system that he devised lived for centuries after him. And it is said of him, too, that he loved children; and he is remembered for the saying "Children are the young saplings in the garden of life; to love them is to turn our minds to the Bountiful Creator."

For more than a century not all the vices and bigotry of his successors could destroy the structure that he had built. The dynasty itself did not officially end until after the so-called Indian mutiny in 1857, though the British had been virtual masters in India for a century before.

► China—The land and its history

THE LAND

China is a land of great contrasts. Larger than India, it stretches in the north into temperate and even cold climatic zones, while in the south it is subtropical. Thus the crops are varied, depending not only upon the differences in temperature, but upon the rainfall. Many parts of the north and northwest are arid, and the land needs more water than it obtains by nature. Though irrigation is practiced, China nevertheless suffers from famine because of insufficient rainfall and damage due to floods—sometimes both in the same year. Parts of the land, especially in the south, are rich, but on the whole it is not a rich country, and the soil is always in danger of severe erosion. But very careful attention to the land, the building of terraces, and controlled irrigation have always made possible a high yield per acre of cultivable land, whether of northern wheat or of southern rice. But it has also necessitated the hard and constant labor of many people, and at all times the very large majority of Chinese have been tied to the land. Until a few centuries ago China was underpopulated in relation to its resources, and the comparatively few inhabitants probably enjoyed as good a standard of living as anywhere else in the world. Only in these last few centuries has the population begun to mount, enforcing a grinding poverty only equaled by the similarly overpopulated India and parts of the Near East.

The two greatest rivers in China have not been an unmixed blessing. The Hwang Ho, or Yellow River, in the north has had to be heavily diked to spare the surrounding countryside the floods which would otherwise have overwhelmed it, and it is as a rule not navigable owing to the swiftness of its current; yet, when kept under control, it brings down with it enormous quantities of life-giving and soil-building mud. The Yangtze River is the main artery and waterway and means of communication in China, and upon it have grown up the great commercial cities which have always served as industrial centers and entrepôts of trade. Southern China has also its great river, the Si, on which is situated the great commercial city of Canton. The Chinese are not a homogeneous people. Most of them belong to the race classified as Mongolian; but there are large Turkish elements, Tibetans, and others which have been kept united by the all-pervading and absorbent Chinese culture, which, by any known criterion, must surely be considered to have been the greatest in the world for almost two thousand years of the world's history. At most periods in this history a considerable percentage of the area now called China has been ruled by a single "Son of Heaven," in this differing in a marked manner from India, which until modern times was never ruled entirely by any single government.

PREHISTORY

For various reasons which will be discussed later, the Chinese have always been very conscious of their history, and the historical records of China are more complete and continuous than those of any other nation. Yet the bulk of the earlier records are so seriously refuted by the evidences of archaeology that many scholars are inclined to abandon them as utterly worthless. There are legends of celestial emperors reigning for impossibly long periods of time, ruling over highly civilized peoples during ages when the archaeological records show little beyond small primitive Neolithic settlements. The earliest really historical records confirmed by archaeology only begin in the middle of the second millennium B.C., at a time when Egyptian civilization was already growing old and entering on its long period of decline, when Hammurabi had long been gathered to his fathers and the Sumerian language had already become extinct. About a millennium earlier the Neolithic Revolution had reached China. Though archaeological investigation has not been so active in China as elsewhere, the Yang Shao culture along the middle course of the Yellow River produced some of the finest painted jars of the age, and the people were already living in well built huts and engaged in ceremonial burials which strongly suggest ancestor worship. Yet the Chinese histories are extremely detailed on these prehistoric epochs. They name the kings and give anecdotes from their lives, even to the words they are supposed to have spoken. If these are only the results of the working of fertile human imaginations of later times, they still remain interesting; but their significance has yet to be established.

THE SHANG AND CHOU DYNASTIES
(*ca.* 1450–256 B.C.)

History proper, then, begins with the Shang dynasty, and with the first known use of writing. Yet this is already a highly developed civilization, with excellent glazed pottery which is very close to the later porcelain, an advanced bronze technology, and the use of that characteristic Chinese material, silk, which was woven into garments and material for decoration. All these things must have been developed in the earlier prehistoric times, and indeed there are traces of their use in excavated villages and towns belonging to an earlier epoch. There were already hundreds of gods, local deities attached to particular places, and gods of every element of nature from rivers to thunder and lightning. There was divination, especially by means of "oracle bones," that is, bones which were burned on one side in order to make cracks on the other and the cracks were believed to have significance. There were human sacrifices, apparently, for the most part, of captured prisoners of war. The ruler of the Shang state was already an emperor, who was chosen to rule by the "mandate of Heaven." All the names of the Shang rulers can be found on contemporary records as well as in history books, and the

historians of later ages have their names correctly. This suggests the careful work of the scholar, thus making the mystery of the earlier rulers whose existence has not been confirmed even more baffling. The Shang dynasty, however, did not rule over the whole of China, but primarily in the province of Shensi in the northwest, though their dominion was later extended farther toward the south. Rebellion brought the dynasty to an end about the year 1050 B.C., and the Shang dynasty was replaced by the Chou, which held the mandate of Heaven for over eight hundred years.

As has happened so often in China, the new ruling house does not seem to have been Chinese in origin, but rather nomad Turkish. However, the rulers soon identified themselves with their subjects. For the long centuries of their rule the Chou monarchs were rarely effectively in control of their lands. As a comparatively small group of interlopers, they were forced to share their rule with powerful lords, and sometimes the reigning monarchs were puppets of these

Two bronze vessels from the first historical dynasty of China, the Shang. The vessel below is called a kuang, that at the right a ku. (COURTESY THE METROPOLITAN MUSEUM OF ART)

lords, kept with an honorary title but without effective power. It was during the period of their weakness in the fifth century B.C. that Confucius taught his political and social ethics, elaborated on especially by his follower Mencius, and left substantially unchanged by generations of political theorists, though some schools of thought did develop that disagreed with a few of the basic tenets of Confucius. Confucius and his followers elaborated precepts of behavior for rulers and subjects that were based on conditions of the Chou period when there was no effective centralized state. Yet the rules for the moral behavior of emperors in name were not found to be too much different even when the rulers were effective absolute monarchs. All rulers, in Confucius' view, being dependent upon heaven for their thrones, should act with responsibility towards their subjects. Thus Confucian ideas, derived from the social experience of an earlier epoch, could be used in later centuries as a real limitation on the arbitrariness of absolute monarchs.

THE CENTRALIZED MONARCHY OF THE CH'IN (256–207 B.C.)

The last years of the Chou are known as the period of the "Contending States." In this period whatever authority the Chou had exercised collapsed, and more than a thousand petty Chinese states engaged in almost unending warfare. None of these states proved able to dominate the whole. Alliances were made and remade, war lords aligned themselves first on one side and then on the other; but gradually in the stress of military competition many war lords found they could no longer survive in independence. They offered their swords and services to others more powerful than themselves. By the middle of the third century B.C. there were only fourteen states left that could lay claim to and enforce any effective degree of independence. At the same time peaceful and military penetration into southern China increased, the natives of these regions putting up little resistance either to the merchants in search of new food supplies and ready to

provide their industrial wares in exchange or to the military adventurers in search of new land. The result was that the stage was set for the unification of all China under the short-lived military dictatorship of the Ch'in (256–207 B.C.).

The state of Ch'in in the northwest of China had been one of the "Contending States." However, it differed from most of the others in that a large proportion of the people of Ch'in were not Chinese but had a considerable admixture of Turks and Tibetans. The other states regarded the Ch'in as barbarians. Nevertheless before the final downfall of the Chou dynasty the Ch'in had put their house in order, and the state was ruled by real leaders who had effectively subordinated the feudal lords in their territory. For about thirty-five years the Ch'in waged an organized warfare against the feudal lords of the rest of China, until at last the emperor Shih Huang Ti became Emperor of all China (221–207 B.C.), ably assisted by an extraordinary minister, Li Ssu.

These able and energetic men, who had a few key ideas as to how the empire was to be administered, were backed by an efficient army and supported by a school of realistic political philosophers (the Legalists). They succeeded in the short period of less than twenty years in remaking China in such a way that the work was never undone in spite of the fall of the Ch'in themselves. The key policy was one of unlimited centralization in every field and the destruction, as complete as possible, of the decentralized feudal system. The entire administration of the country was to be carried out by officials in a graded hierarchy, the higher members appointed by the emperor himself, and the lower responsible directly to imperial appointees. Weights and measures were to be standardized throughout the country, and a uniform tax system instituted.

These plans were duly put into effect with considerable energy and brutality. Feudal lords were forcibly transferred from their previous domains when necessary. The greatest difficulty experienced was in finding enough competent officials, but the Ch'in did

A part of the Great Wall of China.

at least firmly lay the foundation for the bureaucratic rule which has been so characteristic of China ever since. In the effort to obliterate all memory of the destroyed feudal states and the philosophy that had underpinned earlier Chinese society, the Ch'in decreed a gigantic holocaust of books throughout the country, especially books of history and of Confucian philosophy, which latter had stressed the responsibility and virtue of rulers rather than the power politics of the Legalist School that was now in the saddle.

This literature had to be laboriously pieced together again by later rulers who returned to Confucian principles in their government; and there can be little doubt that this great burning has been in large part responsible for the unreliable nature of earlier Chinese history.

Finally the Ch'in built the so-called Great Wall, which already existed in part; it was a remarkable effort to keep out the constantly invading nomads from the north as well, perhaps, as to seal in Chinese civilization against disruptive forces from without. The huge rampart, made partly of brick and partly of stone, now stretched from the personal kingdom of the Ch'in in the northwest right to the sea. According to Chinese tradition, the loss of life in building the wall was enormous, but the Ch'in cared nothing for this and pursued the work with the utmost thoroughness and determination. The wall was completed before the dynasty fell.[4]

THE HAN DYNASTY—RULE BY THE BUREAUCRACY AND GENTRY (206 B.C.–A.D. 220)

The Emperor Shih Huang Ti was no sooner in his grave than the reaction came. But it was found impossible to reverse the centralizing process. The revolution, once made, could not be undone, and the new imperial system was so tempting for other autocrats that it is not surprising that the first ruler of the Han dynasty who came to the throne in 206 B.C. built his empire upon the foundations laid by the Ch'in and changed nothing of importance. It is true that the Han proceeded to give out new feudal estates to their friends and relatives. But the new independent landowners, who possessed both wealth from their land and valuable official positions in the state, were able to prevent the recrudescence of the old-style feudal system based solely upon landownership and the military power that went with it. The old system was completely dead within a hundred years of the accession of the Han. The new, independently wealthy landowners united with the emperors to form the real governing class of China from the time of the Han until the Chinese Revolution of the twentieth century. They became the scholars and officials of the empire, and their numbers were constantly augmented from others of the same class. These officials are usually called in Western literature the "gentry

class," although some Chinese historians have objected to the term as misleading. They have pointed out that these men were closely tied to the interests of their own local communities and did not in any way identify themselves with lords and officials in similar positions in other communities. They never took action as a class either for or against the emperors. However this may be—and some attention will be given to the matter later in the chapter—the scholar-bureaucrats did in effect become the mainstay of the Chinese throne for the remainder of Chinese history.

LATER CHINESE DYNASTIES TO THE COMING OF THE MONGOLS (220–1279)

In a chapter primarily devoted to contrasts between East and West it is unnecessary to go into the details of the successive dynasties of China after the Han. The Han dynasty was broken by a brief interlude under a usurper, Wang Mang (A.D. 9–23), who was backed by a powerful clique of gentry. But in spite of extreme measures to perpetuate his power (often termed "socialist," but erroneously, since the sole object was to strengthen the power of the monarchy), he failed after a few years of power and was replaced by more rulers of the Han dynasty.

Following the final fall of the Han in A.D. 220, the kingdom was divided into three independent domains and considerable territory to the south was added. Larger areas were penetrated by Chinese language and culture. From Han times onward there were continuous wars in the north, especially with the Hsiung Nu or Huns, a nomad people, about half of whom finally settled in China and became Chinese, while the remainder turned west and formed the nucleus of the Hun hordes that poured into Europe in the fifth century (see Chapter 14).

At last China achieved stability again under the T'ang dynasty (618–906), whose founder instituted a series of far-reaching administrative reforms which tied the gentry-bureaucrats more closely to his person and greatly improved the collection of taxes. In the T'ang period the famous Chinese civil

---

[4] It has, of course, often been remarked how similar the whole process was to recent twentieth-century revolutions, and efforts have been made to predict the future accordingly. There is no doubt that the Russians, certainly unconsciously, have used many of the techniques of the Ch'in, and the present Chinese revolutionaries are returning to the same tradition.

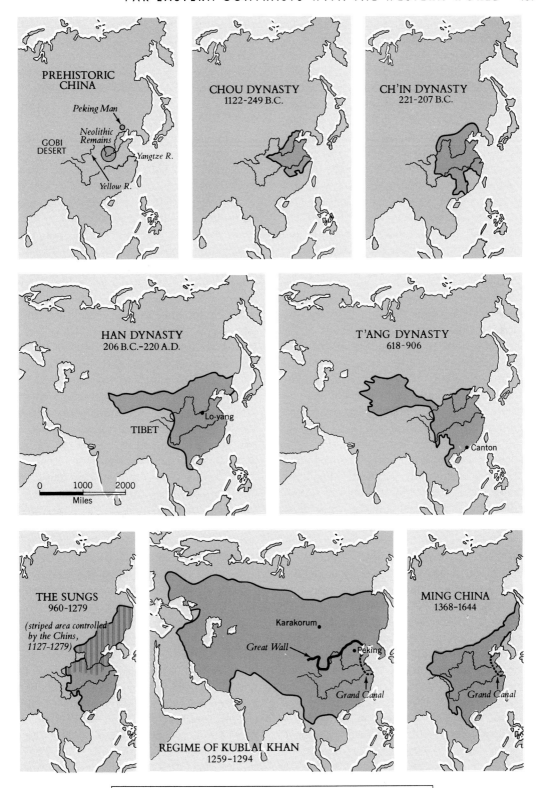

PREHISTORIC CHINA

Peking Man

Neolithic Remains

GOBI DESERT

Yangtze R.

Yellow R.

CHOU DYNASTY
1122-249 B.C.

CH'IN DYNASTY
221-207 B.C.

HAN DYNASTY
206 B.C.-220 A.D.

Lo-yang

TIBET

0   1000   2000
Miles

T'ANG DYNASTY
618-906

Canton

THE SUNGS
960-1279

*(striped area controlled
by the Chins,
1127-1279)*

REGIME OF KUBLAI KHAN
1259-1294

Karakorum

Great Wall

Peking

Grand Canal

MING CHINA
1368-1644

Grand Canal

The Growth of the Kingdom of China

service examination, already instituted by the Han, became the invariable method of recruiting new members of the bureaucracy. Theoretically all the people of China were entitled to sit for this examination, which was given in literary and philosophical subjects, the so-called Classics. But the examination was extremely difficult and was divided into three parts, all of which had to be passed successfully. Then the candidate was eligible for an imperial appointment, which was usually forthcoming, especially to those whose grades were highest. As few could afford the considerable time needed for the study and memorization required of the candidates, the highest positions in the state were virtually barred to the peasant class. But at least the system prevented purely hereditary appointments and thus kept the power of the bureaucracy from falling into the hands of the hereditary nobility. It may be added that even the passing of the first part of the examination conferred local prestige on the candidate, who had been forced at least to become literate in order to sit for the examination at all.

After a century and a half of power, during which the boundaries of the empire had been considerably extended, the T'ang dynasty had to cope with a number of serious revolts by their Turkish subjects as well as with invasions by foreigners. For a time these outsiders controlled the throne. Then, soon after the restoration of the T'ang, the dynasty was again threatened by a peasant revolt, the first in Chinese history, brought on by famine and military exactions. The revolt became a full-fledged civil war, with the government depending upon the alien Turks for support. Finally a Chinese leader emerged who successfully deposed the last T'ang and proclaimed himself Emperor Chu Chuan-Chung (A.D. 906). Again China became divided, with the south enjoying under a series of military rulers a greater prosperity than the north. This period was followed by the rise of the great Sung dynasty, which was able in the process of time to defeat the northerners who had set up a separate state under Mongol leadership. The Sung, however, never established any lasting and effective rule over north China. Their power was really consolidated only in the south, though they are officially credited with being the rulers of China from 960 to 1279.

MONGOL RULE (1259–1368)

The Chinese now had to face the onslaught of the Mongols, Jenghiz Khan and his successors. This nomadic horde, which is dealt with briefly in Chapter 15, was able with the aid of its central Asiatic resources, its tremendous army, and, for the day, its advanced military technique to conquer and subdue the whole of China for the first time. Kublai Khan (1259–1294), the final conqueror of China, who also attempted even to conquer Japan, was an efficient organizer and administrator as well as soldier. But his power could not rest upon anything but the sword in view of the racial policy he adopted. There were hundreds of thousands of Mongols and their allies to be supported, ultimately by the Chinese peasantry; and every Mongol employed in a supervisory capacity meant a Chinese bureaucrat disgruntled and out of work, a further burden to be supported by the same overburdened peasantry. However, as long as the Mongols had control of other areas in Central Asia and could be sure of military reinforcements and supplies, they were able to hold China in subjection. Legislation favoring Mongols, and adopting a generally racialist policy, was enforced. The capital was moved for the first time to Peking, which was laid out by the Mongols without regard for expense and with the aid of a forced corvée of the Chinese peasantry. It remains the most brilliantly planned capital of the world, not excelled by any European capital city, since it could be built without regard for any existing rights of the former inhabitants. Tremendous palaces and temples were erected, far larger than anything China had boasted previously. The life of the court of the Mongols, described by Marco Polo, was of a style and grandeur never before seen.

Yet Peking was not really the center of the country. It was in the wheat belt, whereas most of the Chinese were now subsisting on rice, and the land around Peking was not especially fertile. So again huge quantities of food for the capital had to be imported at great cost, and transportation had to be improved. Hence the Grand Canal, a tremendous engineering project of the sixth century A.D. which links the Yellow River with the Yangtze, had to be made fit for the heavy traffic of this age. All this was necessarily at the expense of the peasants; the bulk of the gentry accepted the inevitable and joined the Mongols. They were allowed to keep their estates but were deprived of their privileged political position, which was naturally reserved for the Mongols.

It was therefore not surprising that with the first signs of weakness in the Mongol rule the peasants again revolted against the oppressions of the tax collectors and the ever-increasing *corvée*. Whenever the Mongols tried to collect *corvées*, even when in the interests of the people as, for instance, when the dikes of the Yellow River burst, they were met by armed resistance. A peasant leader who in his youth had been a Buddhist monk finally organized these scattered revolts into a really national resistance movement. Such

of the Chinese gentry as had not been murdered by the peasants again switched sides and joined the adventurer, and the Mongols at last retired from China to their northern domains without attempting any serious resistance. The peasant leader Chu became the founder of the great Ming dynasty (1368–1644).

The last years of Mongol rule were embittered for the Chinese by stringent racial laws put into effect against them, with the consequence that what had started as simple resistance to Mongol exactions became in effect a war of national liberation. From this time onward the Chinese have had a certain sense of Chinese nationality, missing in earlier times, combined with a detestation of foreigners. The Mongol period of rule has always been distorted by Chinese historians, although in fact it left for the Ming rulers the heritage of a united China which the Chinese themselves had never been able to organize.

MINGS AND MANCHUS

After a brief brilliant period of rule, the Ming emperors became puppets of the court cliques, while the more virile Mongols and

The summer palace at Peking built by the Yuan (Mongol) dynasty. (COURTESY THE METROPOLITAN MUSEUM OF ART)

Manchurian tribes (Manchus) from the north began to penetrate China again. By the early part of the seventeenth century they were entering northern China almost with impunity, and in due course numbers of important Chinese war lords and gentry deserted to them. Invited to take part in the siege of Peking against a usurper who had forced the last Ming emperor to commit suicide, the Manchus stayed. Though few might have expected their rule to survive the century, especially as they revived the racial laws against the Chinese and forced them to wear the pigtail as a badge of servitude, the Manchus did manage to survive by skillful diplomacy and effective military measures until they, too, lost the "mandate of Heaven" in the late nineteenth century, assisted in their defeat by the "barbarians" from the West.

▶ Similarities between China and India—Contrast of both with the West

GENERAL SIMILARITIES

The two great countries of the East, with a population between them of over 800 million, not much less than half of the entire human race, are in many respects extremely similar. They have never fought with each other as nations, the only clashes between them occurring in districts in southeastern Asia in which both peoples competed for spheres of influence.[5] Each has at many periods of history admired and imitated the other. Numerous Chinese, in particular, visited India in ancient times, often for the purpose of worshiping at Buddhist shrines and holy places in the land of the founder of their religion. It is to Chinese pilgrims that we owe much of our knowledge of such paternal Indian monarchs as Asoka, Chandragupta II, and Harsha, all of whom these pilgrims greatly admired, and whose rule

[5] It now seems clear that the Chinese Communist attacks over the boundaries of northern India in 1962 had the limited objective of rectifying the frontier between the two countries, a frontier that had also been disputed by the earlier Nationalist regime, and were not a prelude to a full-scale war.

appeared to them to be in accordance with the moral principles they themselves accepted. Both countries are now heavily overpopulated. This overpopulation, however, seems to be a phenomenon only of the last few centuries, a fact which accounts for the relative prosperity of these countries in earlier ages.

The religions and patterns of social behavior of each country are based upon a different conception of time from those of the West, on an understanding of the continuity of human existence rather than of the importance of the self-realization of particular individuals in one incarnation upon earth. In all history they have lacked the dynamism and drive of the West, and their influence upon the West, if not quite negligible, is nevertheless very small indeed. Until recent times the influence of the West upon the East was likewise small. The Macedonian-Greek Alexander the Great was able to win victories in India,[6] but left little there beyond a legend; the Muslims, with their dynamic monotheistic religion which they wished to force upon the world, conquered India, but most of those they converted were casteless persons who were not accepted as equals in India itself. Thus the Muslims always remained a separate community, and under the present partition still inhabit a territory carved out of India, leaving the minority still as separate groups within India, though enjoying the same rights as their Hindu compatriots. The British were never more than a small company of administrators and soldiers who introduced India to the West but remained incurably alien. The Mongol conquerors of China lost their nomad dynamism under the Manchu regime and became as Chinese as their subjects, the same people having failed to hold the throne in an earlier century because they insisted on remaining alien and practicing racial discrimination. It is only now that both China and India—and of course Japan—are being forced by the manifest superiority of Western techniques and armaments, and the shrinking of the world under modern methods

[6] See Chapter 9.

of transportation and communication, to realize that they cannot remain isolated and insulated from the impact of the West.

Japan imitated the West with a forced march into the twentieth century. China is engaged in the same process, first under the influence of the Western democratic powers and presently under the influence of the alien ideology of Communism. India, after a long period of tutelage and preparation under the British, in her new independence is now trying to increase the tempo of change gradually, and hopes to accomplish the necessary revolution in cooperation with the West rather than being forced violently into a mold imposed upon her either by the West or by the Communist powers. Each country has reacted in its own way, but both have the same basic problem to solve—how to modify their ancient cultures without succumbing to the dynamic expansionism of the West.

THE SOCIAL STRUCTURE IN THE ORIENT

The village as center of the community

The basic social unit in China and India is the family, and the basic political unit is the village. This has been the case from the most ancient times, and is still true at the present time. The village is made up of a number of families, almost all of whose members are engaged in agriculture. The villages are largely self-sufficient. As in medieval Europe, but unlike modern Western countries, the farmers do not live in isolated farms in the middle of their land; on the contrary, the village is the center of the cultivated land. Each family owns or leases some part of the land and keeps it in cultivation, but the family actually lives in the village. Thus what affects one person in the village affects everyone else, though the family, or the several closely related families under one roof, has its own private life. And, especially in China, the houses, when possible, are built in such a way as to insulate this small community within its walls; the windows in many cases face inward onto a court and not outward to the street. But in almost all the affairs of life, community cooperation is a necessity,

and both Indian and Chinese societies are fundamentally uncompetitive. The individual person obtains his entire psychological security from his position in his own family and community rather than from the possession of wealth or a thriving business; and any prestige he may gain in the course of his life is worthless to him unless it is recognized by his family and community.

The possession of enough land for the family is, of course, required. Loss of land entails the breakup of the family. But a business—unless, as is so often the case in these countries, it is a family business based on the ownership of property—does not serve to keep the family together, and its loss is only a loss of money, not of security. A bankrupt merchant always has his family to fall back upon. The persistent conservatism of these peoples, which is the despair of the West, is primarily due to the lack of incentive provided by the society; whereas in the West, where prestige is bound up with success, and especially financial success, there is always a pressing incentive to "get on," which increases as small successes are won, and is, in the nature of things, ultimately insatiable. When a member of the Chinese family leaves the shelter of his home community to make his way in the world, any success is nothing to him unless he can return to the community, use his wealth to help his family, and can be pointed out in his town or village as a great man. It is no use merely being a great man at Peking or Nanking or Shanghai, for he can enjoy that success with no one whose good opinion he really desires.

The caste system in India

In these respects China and India are similar, in contrast with the West. In their methods of achieving this social control their methods are different, though the results are not too unlike. The caste system in India has been briefly referred to above, but will now be dealt with in more detail. As has already been said, the early Aryans do not seem to have had a fully developed caste system, though in the later Vedic age the lines of differentiation had already been established.

At about the beginning of the Christian Era the system was formulated clearly and written down in the so-called Laws of Manu, named after a mythical lawgiver of the ancient past. These laws, which prescribe the duties of each caste, making clear in particular the central position of the Brahmin, have been accepted since that time as authoritative until the present century, when the Indian government, under the inspiration of Gandhi, outlawed untouchability in its constitution.

The highest caste is the Brahmin, whose members perform all the priestly and religious duties of the society; the second is the Kshatriya or warrior caste; the Vaisya caste, the third, is made up of herdsmen, farmers, and tradesmen. The lowest caste is the Sudra, whose duty it is to perform the menial work for the others. But not all Indians belong to these four castes. There are others, in some cases composed of foreign slaves and their descendants, and the offspring of mixed marriages; and in other cases perhaps of people who had disobeyed the laws of their castes and have been expelled from their former castes. These—in recent times as many as one sixth of the whole population—were the outcastes, pariahs or untouchables, the very contact with whom by men of superior castes meant defilement. They carry on occupations which themselves are considered defiling and, unlike orthodox Hindus, can eat meat, and by this very act become defiled. The caste system has tended to divide and subdivide into rigid occupational groups, all distinguished from each other by the nature of their work, which it is impossible, or at least very difficult, for any members of the family to leave in order to better themselves.

It should be emphasized that the members of each caste have their duties and responsibilities as well as their privileges. The Brahmin performs all religious rituals for which he may receive payment as well as prestige from the rest of the community; but at the same time he must rigorously observe the regulations of his caste, and these are not simple or easy. He may not eat meat, he must constantly purify and repurify himself, especially from the slightest contact with untouchables, or even the shadow of an untouchable. He must bathe several times a day in running water; his clothes must always be scrupulously clean. There are thousands of things he is forbidden to do. He is not necessarily a professional priest, and there are holy men in India from every caste. But if he is not a priest, and is only called upon occasionally to perform priestly functions which he is entitled to perform by reason of his birth, he must still at all times act in such a way as not to defile himself or in any way disqualify himself from those duties for which he was born. It is doubtless in many ways more difficult for the Brahmin to live up to his high responsibilities than for members of the lower castes to live up to their lesser ones.

The religious system of Hinduism as developed by Hindu philosophers makes clear the basis of the caste system. Every human being holds his caste in this earthly life as a result of his acts in a previous life. It is not simply an arbitrary decision on the part of the gods. Over the course of many incarnations he has worked himself up to the position where it is possible for him to be born, for instance, as a Brahmin. And it is equally possible to degrade one's self by one's acts so that one may be born another time as a member of the lower castes or even as an untouchable. In honoring a Brahmin, therefore, a lower-caste Hindu is not honoring primarily the Brahmin himself, nor even paying tribute to his present holiness. He is honoring the whole process of development of the individual soul in previous incarnations which have led the Brahmin to his present position of social superiority.

The social consequences of the caste system have been immense. In such a system there was, of course, no equality of opportunity. Birth determined the nature of the career, and, whether in a village or in a great city, there was an upper limit beyond which one could not progress. As marriage between castes was forbidden, there was no free choice of marriage partners. This did not trouble the member of a higher caste, but it might be serious for a Vaisya or a Sudra (though there was at least one family of Sudras which occupied the throne). If there had been no subdivision of castes then there would have been plenty of opportunity, even within the caste. But with the proliferation of the castes in later centuries opportunity for promotion and social mobility became scarcer. Discrimination between castes worked enough hardship upon the lower castes, but it was serious indeed for the untouchables, who were kept in their lowly position by the united pressure of all the persons of caste. They could not enter a temple, they could not take part in festivals, they could not receive an education. It was these manifest disabilities and the visible evidence everywhere of their enforced degradation that made Gandhi undertake so many fasts on their behalf in the effort to force his fellow religionists to relax their laws. His triumph came when the Indian Constitution at last outlawed untouchability, though common practice has not as yet caught up with the provisions of the law.

Yet the caste system did have one redeeming feature besides its stress on responsibilities and duties. It gave each man and woman of caste a secure position in society, and it strengthened the bonds of community between persons of the same caste or sub-caste. When the bonds of family and village were broken, the city dweller could find fellow caste members who accepted him as one of themselves, and to some extent overcame the psychological disease of loneliness which may afflict a Western man in similar circumstances. The ordinary Indian, unprepared by the nature of his closely knit family life and the lack of stress upon individuality in his upbringing and education for living by himself in the alien world of the big city, nevertheless found a natural milieu in which he would be socially accepted.

The family in the Orient

The caste system, important though it is in India, is not as important as the family considered as a social and economic unit, both in India and in China. The caste system could probably be entirely abolished without disrupting the general social basis of Indian life. Not so with the family structure. Within the village the families, as has been said, tended to congregate under one roof or in several houses built close to each other. In both countries the chief element that served to keep the family together was the observance of ritual presided over by the male head of the family. The family property was held in common, that is, none of the land could be alienated or in any way disposed of without common agreement between the males. When the father died, if there was enough, the land would be divided, thus starting another family group, though the eldest son remained the head of the family. But under the Laws of Manu they had no right even to this division while the father still lived. Likewise all the earnings of individual members were considered to belong to the family as a whole. It was therefore of the utmost importance for every man to have sons to carry on his line, and especially to take care of his funeral rites. This applied in both countries in spite of the difference of actual religious beliefs. If there was only one house for the family, it was presided over by the head of the family; if the family was large enough to possess more than one house, then all members of the family would gather for common worship, as far as feasible, at the house of the head of the family. Women who married into the family were regarded as part of it, and therefore had to be chosen with the greatest care and found acceptable to the head of the family and its other more prominent members. Unmarried daughters remained in the parental home until they were married.

Modern conditions have wrought various changes in this stable social structure in both China and India, especially with the growth of industrialism, and the new opportunities offered for both men and women in factories and other establishments far from the control of parents. The Chinese Communists are trying by military and political means to force its destruction from above. But a structure that has endured for centuries can clearly be neither destroyed nor even radically changed in a few short years, much less in a moment.

For such a social order is very stable, and it presents certain advantages not always apparent to Westerners. And even though under the impact of the West it is bound to change, it is not yet certain that the whole structure will go. The child from his earliest years is under the influence of his elders of both sexes, by whom he is automatically accepted and from whom he learns. He does not look especially to one parent for protection; still less does he expect them to compete for his favor. He is just one of the family, a junior because he is its youngest. He is not encouraged to be an individual and to express himself, and no psychological problems arise from excessive competitiveness, as in the West. He is expected to show respect to his elders, and he sees others in his family doing the same. In China this even extends beyond the surviving parents to the ancestors who are now no longer on the earthly plane, but are believed to retain an interest in the affairs of their earthly family, and who are informed of these at regular intervals by the survivors. These members have only changed their form but continue close to their household as protecting spirits. When the child grows up he knows that his first duty is still to his elders, and above all to his father, who has no worries about being neglected in his old age, having to survive alone and unloved and uncared for. The old men and women have no need to seek for old-age pensions and retirement pay; they have the first call upon their children's earnings as these latter will be able to look to their children when they in turn come to their own old age. The Western isolation of the individual has no place in Oriental society. Unemployment and old age may be hardships, but old age holds the compensation of greater respect and attention, while unemployment is at least shared by the whole family, and in many cases by the whole community. It thus becomes more bearable, and any member who is able to find work will become the mainstay of the rest of the family. For this he will be repaid in prestige and gratitude—which for an Oriental may be better reward than "enjoying himself" with the fruits of his labor.

There is no outsider in an Oriental family. If there is only one house and fifteen persons to live in it, they at least know that there are always a few square feet available for them. If they have but one bushel of wheat, no stronger member will steal from the others and leave the weakest to starve. Clearly it is a system which gives little incentive to an individual to outshine the others, and this may be in part a reason for the grinding poverty of their lands. But it is also a system in which poverty can be more easily borne than in a society where it is regarded as a measure of ill success and of failure to make the grade in a competitive world, and is despised accordingly.

THE ROLE OF THE RULER IN THE ORIENT

It is no accident that both Oriental peoples should have produced thinkers who stressed virtue, above all, in their rulers. Perhaps the bulk of the rulers of these lands were in practice no more virtuous than rulers in the West. But it is significant that the ideal ruler in the theory of both peoples should have been pictured as a wise and benevolent father, and performing the functions of a father. It is hard to match the deeds of Asoka, Harsha, or Akbar anywhere in the West at any time. Asoka, as we have seen, after a destructive conquest of the people of the south, was horrified at what he had done and became a convert to Buddhism. Then he proceeded not only to preach the enlightened doctrines of Buddhism but to practice them. He actually did renounce war, he did execute justice as far as he could possibly conceive it, he did enforce upon his subordinates the same canons of morality as he obeyed himself. In the whole record of his reign after his conversion it is impossible for the most carping critic to find one act in which he was untrue to his ideals of justice, mercy, and humility, and even nonviolence to animals, the hunting of which had been the traditional royal pastime until his day. Harsha of Kanauj followed in his footsteps, granting tolerance to all, discharged all his duties with never-failing care and courtesy, tried to mitigate the rigors of the caste system, and gave away the surplus of the imperial treasury to the poor as an act of charity. When there was nothing to distribute it was said of him that he wore a secondhand garment until there was again a surplus. Akbar stated publicly that his gratitude to his God could only be shown by preserving a just government with due recognition of merit. Though an alien conqueror, he refused to treat his Hindu subjects as unequals, severely punished any attempt to humiliate them, and gave them complete equality of treatment in his appointments. He abolished the tax on pilgrims to the sacred shrines of India though he was not a Buddhist, and he not only devised an administrative system that was one of the most equitable ever yet put into practice, but he saw to it that each position, as far as was humanly possible, should be filled on the sole basis of merit.

The Chinese rulers, according to Confucian theory, held the "mandate of Heaven" only as long as they ruled well. It was always understood that revolution was justified if the ruler failed to maintain his own virtue. It was the theory of Confucius and his follower Mencius that virtue was handed down from the ruler to the people. He must rule by the force of his moral example, not by the use of crude force. "An intelligent ruler," says Mencius, "will regulate the livelihood of the people, so that they shall have enough to serve their parents, wives, and children." Then he "may urge them, and they will proceed to what is good, for in this case the people will follow this good example." Confucius says that the rulers, "when they wished to order well their own states, first regulated their families." In order to do this they must first "rectify their hearts, and be sincere in their thoughts."

We do not know of any Chinese rulers who were, in practice, the equal of the greatest Indian rulers. But constantly their scholars urged the path of virtue upon them; no Chinese ruler, under pressure from his society which believed that the gods would overthrow him if he ceased to follow it, could afford to be completely arbitrary if he hoped to maintain his position. Moreover, it was expected of the emperor that he would take the blame for any natural disasters that overtook the empire, and attribute them to his own lack of worth. Cases are known of emperors obeying this prescription. Alien conquerors such as the Manchus were early taught by their scholars and bureaucracy what was expected of them when they took over the "mandate of Heaven." Many of them did their best to live up to it. There is no instance in Chinese history of the restoration of any emperor who had ruled badly and thus lost than mandate. Once they had shown themselves to be lacking not only in power but in "virtue" they were never able to obtain the necessary support for their restoration. Apparent disloyalty to a particular ruler and wholesale switching of sides in China is not to be judged, therefore, altogether by the standards of the West. Recent history has tended to show that this ancient Confucian principle has not been forgotten even by men who have ceased to read the works of the sage himself.

While benevolence has sometimes been the Western kingly ideal, as in eighteenth-century monarchy,[7] on the whole, Western doctrine has taught rather the responsibility of the ruler to God, with an emphasis on the right to rule ("divine right of kings") rather than on the responsibilities entailed by the position. Moreover, the power to win the throne and the prestige attached to a particular family have generally been regarded as sufficient justification for the tenure of Western rulers. The Hebrews are a possible exception. But for Hebrew historians and religious theorists, the kings' responsibilities were primarily in the matter of religion. Hebrew history shows little evidence that the rulers themselves regarded the matter in the same light. The priests put pressure on them to observe the Law, and when the kings were unsuccessful they blamed it on royal disregard for the Law.

---

[7] In extolling the excellence of benevolent despotism, Voltaire used, in fact, the extensive Chinese literature on the subject, which was just being translated in his time, assuming for the purposes of his argument that the Chinese rulers had always lived up to the ideal.

But there is no sign that any priest threatened the king with divine displeasure or interpreted his failure as evidence of the lack of that "virtue" extolled by Confucius.

It should be added that one important school of Chinese political philosophers, the Legalists, rejected the theory of the virtue required of rulers. They insisted instead on the proto-Machiavellian theory that the king rules by rewards and punishments (one reward against nine punishments!) and impresses his will on the people by keeping them weak and the army strong and obedient. It is perhaps instructive to note that the only dynasty that ever officially adopted this philosophy was the Ch'in, which came to any untimely end, the shortest rule of any of the recognized Chinese dynasties.

ORIENTAL CONCEPTION OF TIME AND HUMAN LIFE—REINCARNATION

Chinese religion and philosophy

There are many important differences between Chinese and Indian religion and art, but both are based upon the conception of time and continuity held in the East. Each people expresses its time sense in different ways. Chinese art is impressionistic, suggesting tranquillity; even silk, the material used for the painting, enhances the effect. The painter or sage often paints himself in the picture as part of the landscape—not differentiated, however, as an individual, as in such Western masterpieces as the Rembrandt and Van Gogh self-portraits, but rather to suggest that the human being, too, is a part of the natural scene, any human being, not especially the painter. Chinese poetry has a similar tendency. Much of it is nature poetry, usually short and descriptive, not full of dramatic action, but pictorial, the images having no inner symbolism, making no connection with other allied thoughts in the reader's mind.

It is no accident that the Chinese symbol for time is a pool. A stone thrown into a pool spreads ripples ever wider and wider, and then the water is as it was before. To an Oriental, time is not something to be hoarded or spent, time is not money, and it is not something which is fast running out and must be enjoyed because it is going by so quickly. A life on earth is a short space in years, but it is a part of eternity, without beginning and without end except in some unimagined, far-distant future. It is not exactly true, as is so often said, that the Chinese worship their ancestors. Their ancestors are only an earlier phase of their continuing family, as the "celestial" emperors who gave China her first rulers are likewise a part of the continuity of China herself. The heavens are peopled by millions of gods under the Supreme Lord Shang Ti, who corresponds to the emperor on earth. The worshiper, as in ancient Babylonia, does not expect to interest the supreme god in his very minor affairs on earth. Rather he deals with minor functionaries who are chosen as his special protectors, who may be bribed and cajoled like men on earth. In China also it has always been important to find what these gods wanted and appease or placate them; hence the need for the ubiquitous soothsayers and diviners still to be found plying their trade in every Chinese village. The excellence or failure of harvests is due to interventions by the gods, who may be persuaded not to attack a particular community if their intentions are known in advance.

After death there are numerous rewards and punishments, but this life after death is not of unlimited duration, as in Western thought. Soon there will be a return to life on earth in a position commensurate with one's behavior in the previous life. Life is an endless cycle; to be born in a fortunate position is due either to one's own merits in a previous life or to the merits of one's parents who had deserved to have such a dutiful son. The ancestors then are only temporarily sojourning in the spirit worlds during the period between death and rebirth. Soon their imperishable spirit will return to inhabit a new body. But meanwhile they need sustenance during their period of death, and this must be provided for them by the living. If there are no living to provide for them,

Painting attributed to Ma Yuan (Sung dynasty). As often portrayed in Chinese paintings, the sage is shown in contemplation. Note the contrast between the suggestions of landscape in this picture and the care for detail shown in the flower painting (below) of the same period. Evidently the purpose of the second painting is to induce a mood, and the painting might therefore be termed "impressionistic." (COURTESY THE METROPOLITAN MUSEUM OF ART)

Flower painting of Sung dynasty, showing the Chinese exquisite care for detail. (COURTESY THE METROPOLITAN MUSEUM OF ART)

then death for them is a sorry affair. Hence the importance of having a dutiful family. These ancestors can reciprocate by helping the living.

There is thus no clear distinction between the living and the dead, as there also may not have been in ancient Egypt. But the Chinese are not depressed by this belief, nor by their ignorance of what the gods desire of them. For these spirits are not altogether arbitrary. The members of one's own well-loved family live as spirits in the spirit land, and it is possible to receive aid from them and to give them aid in return. This attitude seems to have taken away from the Chinese all horror of the hereafter and allowed them to concentrate their attention on earthly affairs. The orientation of the Chinese toward the earth, their philosophy of this world, and their religion are rooted in the belief that nothing changes fundamentally after death. Even a natural disaster such as an earthquake could affect the dead ancestors equally, and the living were expected to give them special aid and relief as if they were alive. At death only one change occurred: the body was dropped and the spirit pursued its path without it, needing sustenance as before but satisfied with food and paper models of furniture and other requirements of earthly life.

This folk religion is of immemorial antiquity and is almost universal in China except among the minority for whom one of the more highly developed religions such as Buddhism, Islam, or Christianity has been found acceptable. But, as we shall see, Buddhism in the form in which it was accepted in China (Mahayana Buddhism) was in no way contradictory to basic prevailing beliefs. For most Chinese, Buddha became merely one of the gods, as Christ and Mahomet were also accepted into the pantheon without grave difficulty. Every town, and nearly every village, has more than one temple, and the worshiper may use any or all of them as he wishes, in the hope of finding the solace and protection he needs from one, if not from another. Some temples will house Confucius, Buddha, and Lao-tzu as gods. This fact has one important conse-

quence, religious toleration. The Westerner may wish to oust all the other gods in favor of his single all-powerful one; but the Chinese is quite willing to be hospitable to the gods of other peoples. In his system there can never be too many gods. Any or all of them may work evil upon him at any given time and for any given offense; but they are not intrinsically evil except those demons whose business it is to cause natural catastrophes. Yet these, too, can be kept in order by their superiors.

It is never therefore as an enemy of any particular religion that the Chinese in history have sometimes shown signs of intolerance. Organized religions may lead to social abuses as did the increase of Buddhist monasticism in the ninth century A.D., with its attendant evils of idleness and celibacy. For the practices of Buddhist monks could only be considered by most Chinese as damaging to the whole of their society, not least because when the monks died their spirits wandered aimlessly with no descendants to take care of them, causing some disruption in the social order in the spirit worlds and consequent harmful effects on the living. Similar social and political disturbances followed the introduction of Christianity; but any persecution visited upon missionaries was the result of their Westernism, not of their religion. As emissaries, and sometimes the vanguard, of the hated Western powers in the nineteenth century they received the same treatment as their conationals, and thus they are treated today by the Chinese Communists.

Chinese religion, as this account has made clear, has been conspicuous for its dearth of any systematic theology or religious speculation. Indeed, most Chinese intellectuals have always tended toward ethical Confucianism, which has no place in it for a god, and despise popular religion in particular. There has, however, been at least one important Chinese religious philosophy, although its appeal was limited. This is the philosophy of Lao-tzu, usually called Taoism. Systematic Confucianism was a political and social teaching. When, many centuries after the death of Confucius, it became a

A Chinese Buddhist temple.

religion, it was absorbed into the popular cult and Confucius was accepted merely as one of the many gods. Lao-tzu was likewise received into their company, as was even Buddha himself, except among the sophisticated monks and philosophers, some of whom made the pilgrimage to India already mentioned.

The Taoist writers stressed the unity and transitoriness of all worldly phenomena. All things change their form but return in the process of time to their starting points to take up the ceaseless round. This is the "Tao," or the Way of the universe. Man who pursues the Way must give up striving and realize the relativity of all things in the universe, including action, and he must not strive to interfere with their harmonious workings. He must contemplate and become one with the world by direct experience, not trying to force change upon it by his puny efforts. The Taoists, therefore, wished to retire from active interference with nature, take no part in government, and, if possible, even avoid the ordinary social duties of private life. It is not surprising that in later centuries the Taoists became interested in the transmutation of elements, the science of alchemy. It became the chief concern of

many of the followers of the cult to find the philosophers' stone or the elixir of life; for this stone had the power of hastening the ceaseless process of the Tao. All things were slowly changing in their endless cycle. Base metals would certainly one day become gold. Why should a good Taoist not cooperate to his own profit?

This philosophy bears very remarkable resemblances to the Hinduism of the Upanishads and later Hindu philosophy, though apparently of independent origin. But both, as will be seen, derive from the same view of life and the same understanding that man's life on earth is but a small part of his sojourn in eternal duration.

Indian religion and philosophy

The wheel of rebirth—The Hindu thinkers from very early times gave serious attention to the fundamental problems of religion. Even in the Vedic hymns there is speculation on the nature and existence of the gods. In the popular religion of India there have always been many gods representing various powers of nature. Today, while there are still many gods, there are three who are almost universally worshiped: Brahma the all-embracing Lord of the Uni-

Indian god Vishnu, the preserver. (COURTESY THE METROPOLITAN MUSEUM OF ART)

of life that only mystics in the West have ever interpreted our earthly experience in similar terms.[8]

For to many Hindu thinkers, and not

[8] It should, perhaps, be noted that while the discussion in the text describes the general cast of Hindu thought, Hindu philosophy is so rich that it would be possible to cite other thinkers who have followed paths of thought less alien to ours, and more similar to certain schools of thought in the West. Nevertheless, these have not been the really influential schools of thought in India, perhaps in part, at least, because of the fact that the "illusionist" philosophies have been more in accord with traditional Hindu religion and the way of life based upon it.

Seated statue of the great god Brahma, represented in later Indian sculpture with three heads. Actually, in Indian philosophy Brahma is purely spiritual and impersonal, and thus could not have been represented in sculptured form. (COURTESY THE METROPOLITAN MUSEUM OF ART)

verse, Vishnu the Preserver, and Siva the Destroyer. But this did not prevent Hindu thinkers from striving to penetrate behind even these gods and speculate upon the nature of Brahma and in what way he was present in all created things, even in the other gods, and upon the universe of Brahma. The teachings of these thinkers are to be found especially in the Upanishads (written down from about the sixth century B.C.) and their numerous commentaries in later centuries. Their assumptions, which seem to have been shared by all the Indian peoples, even those far removed from philosophical and religious speculation, are extraordinarily alien to our own, and, indeed, appear to be so contradictory to the realities only to the thinkers but to some of the ordinary believers, the world itself is an illusion, a *maya*. Man is not an earthly being who may hope to win immortality in a different kind of existence after death, but a spiritual being who incarnates from time to time on earth, in exile from his natural heavenly abode. The eternal being of man is indestructible; it does not have to win immortality, for it is already immortal; it is the deeds of this being in earthly life which chain him to that life and make his reincarnation on earth necessary. At different times in Indian thought it has been held that this eternal being can also incarnate in the lower kingdoms of nature; probably at all times some people have believed this, though it has not been held by the greater teachers, who have always insisted that reincarnation must be into another human being, not into an animal or plant. The soul or spirit of man indeed creates for itself a new body when required and chooses those parents who can best help him to achieve his destiny.

If, then, the world itself is an illusion, the task of the man who would become wise is to try to understand the nature of the illusion, and at the same time free himself from dependence upon it. Man has become dependent upon the earth for his sustenance by being born on earth for the first time. This has certain inevitable consequences. He begins to desire earthly things for their own sake, and while on earth he performs certain deeds which bind him to other people and to the whole destiny of the earth. These deeds can never be undone, and they constitute man's *karma*. After his death when he is freed from his body these deeds are relived and spiritually understood; but they still must be compensated on earth, which is the only testing ground provided for man. So his *karma* attracts him back to earth to a milieu suitable for the task which he has to perform, which may be a particular family in a particular caste; or, indeed, he may be born as an untouchable if the task which he has to perform is one that demands persecution or enforced humility. He may also be required to compensate personally

for evil deeds he has performed toward a certain person, in which case he will be born close to a person with whom he has lived on earth before. Thus a Hindu can never be sure that he is meeting another person for the first time in this incarnation; on the contrary, he may have a special task to perform for any person he meets, a task which must be performed if he is to redeem himself from some important part of his *karma,* and thus continue on the path of spiritual progress. There is thus, according to Hindu thought, a long procession of births and rebirths, usually pictured as a kind of wheel. But in all these incarnations the eternal spirit of the particular man, which, incidentally, is not itself truly real but appears to be subjectively real for the duration of the incarnations, should continue to strive upward to reach *moksha* or enlightenment, by freeing itself as far as possible from the desire for earthly things.

It is at once clear how exactly the caste system fits into this scheme. The Brahmin and the untouchable equally hold their status by virtue of their previous lives on earth, and the task which has been laid upon them by their *karma* to perform in this particular life. Interference with the caste system, even the improvement of the lot of an untouchable, is, in this scheme, an interference with the destiny that the man has chosen on earth for himself, and which he really needs for his spiritual development. It is a scheme perfectly fitted for a static social order where man's task lies not in trying to improve his position on earth but in accepting his lot as unchangeable. Instead he must try to help others whom he may have wronged in a previous life, while in patience and resignation he now strives to build up less *karma* for himself to be redeemed in a later incarnation.

Though most Hindus are unaware of all these subtleties in their religion, nevertheless some elements of it are almost always understood in all classes of Indian society. This accounts for an atmosphere in India which is quite different from any known in the West, a kind of widespread gentleness and tendency toward resignation and nonviolence, a respect for holiness and moral purity, and a willingness to follow the example and advice of a holy man who really lives out his principles in daily life. The "go-getter" of the West rarely commands such admiration as is accorded to an apparently lazy holy man. And though Gandhi may have been a shrewd politician as well as a holy man, it was his holiness and not his shrewdness that gave him his unique hold upon Indian minds and hearts and made his spectacular fasts so effective. Few were prepared to take responsibility for his death if they had refused to do what he wanted, even though it meant adopting a policy of which, as political men, they disapproved. The extreme nationalists who at length murdered him had to replace in their own minds the old religion of India with their nationalism, a modern variety of religion which they themselves held fanatically before they could have dared to lay a hand upon him.

A further aspect of nonviolence should be noted which is equally bound up with Indian religion. All created things, as has been said, were considered an aspect of Brahma and thus sacred. Especially sacred are certain animals, above all the cow, which provides the perfect food for man in the form of milk. The cow, therefore, must not be killed. The strict Hindu must eat no food that comes from a dead animal, and the Hindu religion does not permit animals to be killed for food at all. The doctrine of nonviolence (*ahimsa*), though imperfectly observed at all times in Indian history, is the necessary consequence of the understanding of all nature as being one. "Thou art That," says the Hindu sage.

Escape from the wheel of rebirth—Yoga, Jainism, Buddhism—In their desire to dispense with the almost endless round of rebirths which put such a premium on resignation, many schools of thought in India have wished to speed up the process of acquiring enlightenment. One, very well known to the West because of its often spectacular manifestations, is the practice of Yoga, which has developed certain ancient Hindu practices to

an extreme, though its detailed regulations are of comparatively recent date.

The theory of Yoga is that a man must endeavor by special exercises to make himself as little dependent upon earthly things as possible. He must cultivate his latent spiritual powers, especially by intense concentration and exclusion of worldly thoughts. In this way the yogi achieves enlightenment by learning to understand the illusionary nature of the world; moreover, by developing his spiritual powers, he becomes less dependent upon his physical environment. He lives as simply as possible and fasts often; he may become a hermit, able to bear solitude and physical discomfort, or he may return to the world, be in it but not of it, giving advice and aid to others. There are different practices in Yoga according to the task which the yogi conceives to be his. Some practices are intended to fit him for prolonged work in the world, administering loving care to others, while different practices may fit him rather for a life of solitude. In all cases the yogi is expected to acquire control of his physical organism and dominate it through his developed spiritual powers. Since self-control, with its accompanying enlightenment, is admired by all those in India who have refrained from attempting it, the yogi is widely regarded as a holy man and honored accordingly. Not all holy men who are thus honored, however, have actually attained any degree of self-control or enlightenment, and there are many who prey upon the superstitions and beliefs of the people, and are sometimes willing to admit that fact to strangers. Many are simply charlatans, professional beggars who make their living performing feats of "magic," but the prestige accorded to them undoubtedly rests upon the general belief that the yogi has genuinely renounced the world for the purpose of attaining that freedom from earthly ties and the lessening of *karma*, which is the main task of all men upon earth.

But long before Yoga had been systematized there appeared about the same time (sixth century B.C.) the two chief "heretical" religions of India, Buddhism and Jainism.

Both built upon the earlier Hindu foundations and were based upon Indian life experience. Perhaps they are best thought of as reform movements in Hinduism which later became distinct religions. They arose at a time when Hinduism itself had not yet become as systematized and carefully formulated as it was later in the different Hindu schools of religious philosophy, though it was already filled with carefully prescribed ritual.

Jainism was founded by Mahavira, probably an older contemporary of Gautama Buddha, who after years of meditation emerged from his seclusion to become a prophet and teacher. While accepting the general religious ideas of Hinduism, including, of course, the doctrine of *karma*, he lowered the number of incarnations to be endured by human beings to nine provided that they were lived in strict asceticism, that certain vows were taken and kept, such as sexual abstinence and the renunciation of worldly goods, and that continuous attention was paid to the achievement of enlightenment. After nine such incarnations the soul could attain a state of desirelessness and freedom from earthly entanglements which was called *Nirvana*. But according to a Jainist teaching not all souls who had attained the right to Nirvana did in fact accept it. They could, if they so wished, return to the earth and help others toward the same salvation. Before long Jainism divided into two sects, the stricter one composed of ascetics who practiced nudism as part of the effort to separate themselves from earthly things and contact with matter (the "air-clothed"), the members of the other sect distinguished by white clothes, symbols of the purity they sought. The Jainists, as ascetics, were often persecuted in later times, and several rulers tried to extirpate the sect. Nevertheless, it still exists in India, with an estimated million and a half believers.

Buddhism, on the other hand, is almost extinct on the mainland of India, though, as has been seen, it is still strong elsewhere, if in a form that its founder would scarcely have recognized. Thousands of legends have sprung up about Gautama Buddha, which it is impossible at this late date to disentangle from the truth. But the main lines of his life are fairly well established.

He was the son of a ruler variously described as a king or a chieftain. Brought up in his father's palace, he was kept shielded from the realities of life until he was an adult. Then suddenly he was exposed to the sight of death and poverty, which made such a profound impression upon him that he spent the next years of his life wandering through India ministering to the poor and sharing their suffering. At last in his twenty-ninth year he fell into a deep meditation as he sat under a bo tree, from which he emerged as an "enlightened one," a Buddha. Soon afterward he went to Benares, where he delivered a famous sermon which laid down the teachings which became the core of what was later called Hinayana Buddhism (the "Lesser Vehicle"). It was this form of Buddhism that was accepted by the Emperor Asoka and spread by his missionaries. Thereafter Gautama Buddha spent the rest of his life as a wandering preacher and teacher, gathering around himself a devoted band of disciples who were the first Buddhist missionaries.

The fundamental teaching of Buddha was that all life is suffering, and that man's task on earth is to overcome it by following the Eightfold Path. The choice of these particular eight means of overcoming suffering shows how deeply indebted Buddha was to his Indian predecessors, and to the Indian view of the nature of the world. For one must not simply alleviate suffering, although this is a part of the task; one must perceive the illusion that it is. The Four Noble Truths of Buddha describe the nature of suffering: that all existence is suffering, that the origin of suffering is desire, that suffering ceases when there is no longer any desire, and that the way to overcome suffering is to follow the Eightfold Path. This path consists, in this order, of Right Belief, Right Resolve (to renounce all that leads to increased desire and to cultivate nonviolence), Right Speech, Right Conduct, Right Way of Living, Right

Effort, Right Contemplation, Right Meditation (or Ecstasy). The path thus leads from faith to action, and ultimately to Contemplation and Meditation, ever further away from the world into a mystic unity with the Divine. Thus each individual could progress in accordance with his own spiritual potentialities, first believing, then doing, ever moving upward to the highest form of earthly existence, to contemplation and meditation at which point he would be coming close to that desirelessness which was sought as an end. The end itself was Nirvana, the same state of being (or, more truly, nonbeing) which was pursued by the Jainists, when it would no longer be necessary to incarnate on earth, and all *karma* had been redeemed.

But Buddhism, by stressing the gentleness, compassion, and nonviolence which characterized the lower rungs of the ladder to Nirvana, put the emphasis more strongly upon ethical behavior than was customary in other Indian religions. Moreover, by emphasizing the fact that all human beings are equally born to suffering, the Buddhist paid less attention to the caste system, which may lead to pride in one's own status and in one's own spiritual achievements which have led to the present privileged position. For Buddha the lowest casteless man is as much a human being as the highest Brahmin; all alike are doomed to suffering and can only reach Nirvana in the same way as other men. Moreover, ritual held no importance in his teachings, nor was worship of the gods enjoined upon Buddhists. The only god in Buddhism was that divine essence (called Brahma in the Upanishads) which embraces every earthly phenomenon, living or dead, as the ocean embraces the waves.

It is one of the extraordinary ironies of religious history that this earlier Hinayana Buddhism should, in its later form of Mahayana Buddhism (the "Greater Vehicle"), have become theistic, that Buddha himself should have been metamorphosed into a god, and that statues of him should have been made in vast profusion in all the lands into which Buddhism penetrated. Though Buddha had not advocated asceticism, or separation from the world, Buddhist monasteries living under rules formulated by ascetics, grew up in India, and especially in Tibet, where they flourish till this day, even though the religion, as has been seen, was driven out of India. Mahayana Buddhism was far more active, seeking for converts in a dynamic manner not characteristic of its early adherents. There is no doubt that many of Buddha's teachings lent themselves to this treatment when in other hands than his. If one stresses the last steps on the Eightfold Path, then for meditation and contemplation it is clearly best to retire from the world; if the overcoming of all desire is the primary end to be pursued, then asceticism, the denial of all ordinary human desires, may seem to be the best way of achieving it: and if the Divine is present in everything, then it is not out of place to glorify the particular aspects of the Divine as manifested in Buddha himself and in such other great men as Confucius and Lao-tzu, especially when it is seen how human beings crave for something less abstract than Brahma for the exercise of the human feelings of reverence and desire to worship. Finally, when the Buddhists had realized that their own leader had progressed to the status of a Buddha by his life on earth, prepared for him in previous incarnations, the possibility that other men might do the same led the Mahayana Buddhists to look for new appearances of other men (called bodhisattvas, a lower grade of adept than a Buddha) who would become Buddhas in their turn. Thus they introduced the idea of a Maitreya Buddha, as a messiah who would appear at the appointed time.

Influence of Indian religions

On Indian life—There is no doubt that these religions of India are, as they have been called, "life-denying." They are all based on the assumption that the world is an illusion, a place for the testing of human souls, but not a field for human enterprise nor a territory to be mastered to yield a life that is to be enjoyed for its own sake—certainly not a place which is so beloved that the greatest wish of men is for heaven to be its replica, as in Old Kingdom Egypt. For the Indian, death is a welcome escape and release, a period between two lives when the soul can be truly itself.[9] When such beliefs are widely held, as they are in India, it is evident that there will be little incentive to earthly progress, little emphasis on personal success, and little earthly ambition. And yet India has many virtues which may be thought to compensate. Gentleness, compassion for men and animals, nonviolence to others and realization of the sacredness of all living things, gratitude to divine powers and recognition of their gifts to man, and above all the strongest of all incentives toward well-doing in the doctrine of reincarnation and *karma*, the impossibility of escaping judgment for one's evil-doing in the next life on earth—these are not virtues to be entirely disregarded in these days of the ascendancy of the Western way of life with its self-assertiveness and aggression. But one has to look no further than these teachings of resignation, humility, and renunciation to see why the West has been able to exploit and dominate the East from first contact until the revolutions of the twentieth century.

Influence on Western thought—It has always been a fascinating question as to how far, if at all, the West has been influenced by these Oriental teachings. No direct influence has ever been proved in any of the major Western philosophers. Yet Plato's teaching, and even more the philosophy of his later follower Plotinus, who certainly had access to Oriental philosophies, insisted upon the inferior if not illusionary nature of the physical body and the physical earth. Plato, indeed, called the body the prison house of the soul, and the world as an inferior copy of the heavenly reality. The myth of the cave in the seventh book of his *Republic* comes very close to the Hindu teachings on the nature of reality, though Plato draws different, and Greek, conclusions from his story. The thought of Plato deeply influenced Paul, and both Plato and Plotinus influenced Augustine. Stoicism, the late Hellenistic Greek philosophy, also stressed resignation and the equality of all men through suffering, as had Buddhism; and the Stoic teachers could certainly have been in direct contact with Buddhist missionaries or with Buddhism itself in India. Moreover, the Stoic god of Divine Reason bears a recognizable resemblance to the Brahma of the Indians. Probably there is some influence on these key philosophies of the West which has penetrated into much of Christian thought. We know also that Indian mathematics, with its numerals miscalled Arabic and its zero (often suggested as a typical Hindu conception, a consequence of Hindu desire to recognize and attain nonbeing), influenced the West through the Muslims, as we shall see in a later chapter.

But whatever the underlying influences on Western thought that have been accepted from the Oriental world, one can hardly deny that the Western attitude toward life on earth as a field for human activity is profoundly antithetic to the attitude developed in the East, and that the importance of individuality is emphasized in the West in a manner that is still unaccepted by the East. This chapter, in striving to bring out these contrasts, may therefore be found to have been justified in a book devoted to

---

[9] It is instructive to contrast the *Odyssey*, the great epic of the West, with the Indian *Ramayana*. The entire mood of the Indian epic is almost the polar opposite of the Greek. At the close of the *Ramayana* the heroine, Queen Sita, has been justified and it has been proved that she had, in spite of appearances, been faithful to her husband. But just at the moment of what for a Westerner would be triumph, Sita calls upon her Mother, the Earth, to take her back to herself, since she cannot bear the shame of having ever been doubted.

> If unstained in thought and action I have lived
>   from day of birth
> Spare a daughter's shame and anguish, and
>   receive her, Mother Earth!
> If in duty and devotion I have labored undefiled,
> Mother Earth who bore this woman, once again
>   receive thy child.
> If in truth unto my husband I have proved
>   a faithful wife,
> Mother Earth! relieve thy Sita from the
>   burden of this life!"
>   —Translation by Romesh Dutt (*ca.* 1880)

Western civilization, for we often see ourselves most clearly in contrasts.[10]

Suggestions for further reading

PAPER-BOUND BOOKS

Basham, A. L. *The Wonder That Was India*. Evergreen. Illustrated history of pre-Muslim Indian culture.

Bodde, Derk. *China's Cultural Tradition: What and Whither?* Holt, Rinehart and Winston. Interesting and up-to-date discussion of attitude to religion, gentry society and the role of the civil service examinations, the position of the ruler, and similar topics.

Burtt, Edwin A., ed. *The Teachings of the Compassionate Buddha*. Mentor. Selections from Buddhist scriptures and later writers.

Conze, Edward, trans., *Buddhist Scriptures*. Penguin. Selections with comments. By the same author is the useful *Buddhism: Its Essence and Development*. Torchbooks.

Creel, Herrlee G. *The Birth of China*. Ungar. By an authority on Confucius and Confucianism, this book is especially useful for its account of very early China.

Eberhard, Wolfram. *A History of China*, rev. ed. University of California.

Fairbank, John King. *The United States and China*. Compass. Several good, though compressed, chapters on ancient China.

Fitzgerald, Charles P. *China, a Short Cultural History*. Praeger. Interesting attempt to explain the relationship between Chinese history and culture.

---

[10] This account has purposely omitted more recent influences, which are numerous in the last two centuries even if they have not been very profound. New commodities, such as silk, muslins, brocade, and porcelain, and new foods such as tea, have been found desirable by Western countries. In a footnote to page 167 there is a mention of Voltaire's interest in the supposedly benevolent character of Oriental rule; other eighteenth-century thinkers, such as Rousseau and Montesquieu, were greatly interested in, and to some degree were affected by, Chinese thought, and they studied Chinese institutions. Western art has frequently admired and imitated some features of Chinese art. Finally, the importance of the wealth of India should not be underestimated, especially its effect on the rise of the British Empire. But these instances do not belong in a book which closes in the year 1500.

Goodrich, L. Carrington. *Short History of the Chinese People*. Torchbooks. The standard American short account by one of the leading authorities.

Grousset, René. *The Rise and Splendor of the Chinese Empire*. University of California Press. Colorful, but a little old-fashioned. Better on Chinese art than on history.

Humphreys, Christmas. *Buddhism*. Penguin. Good general account of Buddhist history, including much material on its various sects.

Mascaró, Juan, trans., *Bhagavad Gita*. Penguin. Hindu "bible," also available in numerous case-bound editions.

Northrop, F. S. C. *The Meeting of East and West*. Collier. Several interesting though controversial chapters contrasting Oriental and Western art, and the ideas that underlie both.

Radakrishnan, S. *Hindu View of Life*. Macmillan. Contrasts Western and Hindu attitudes to life. By leading Hindu philosopher and late president of the Republic of India.

Rawlinson, Hugh G. *India*. Praeger. Successful integration of Indian culture with Indian history. By the same author is a shorter work, *Concise History of the Indian People*.

Sen, K. M. *Hinduism*. Penguin. Standard account of growth and status of Hinduism.

CASE-BOUND BOOKS

Bagchi, E. C. *India and China: A Thousand Years of Cultural Relations*. New York: Philosophical Library, Inc., 1951.

Hsu, Francis L. K. *Americans and Chinese: Two Ways of Life*. New York: Abelard-Schuman, Ltd., 1953. Stimulating discussion of the numerous contrasts between Chinese and Americans, by an anthropologist who knows both cultures almost equally well and has divided his life between the two countries.

Lin Yutang. *The Wisdom of China and India*. New York: Modern Library, Inc., 1955. Selection of source materials with comments.

Needham, Joseph. *Science and Civilization in China*. New York: Cambridge University Press, 1954–1962, 4 out of 7 vols. published to date. Epoch-making work on Chinese achievements, counteracting usual underestimation of Chinese material civilization.

Taylor, Edmond. *Richer by Asia*. Boston: Houghton Mifflin Company, 1947. Sympathetic account of modern India by former O.S.S. officer during the war, suggesting many interesting contrasts with the West.

PART III

CLASSICAL CIVILIZATION IN THE WEST

CHAPTER 7

GREEK CIVILIZATION

▶ Physiography

CLIMATE AND TERRITORY

The mainland of Greece is a land of many contrasts, now, as in antiquity. There is wild mountain country, there are fertile river valleys and plains, and there are bustling seaports. Communication between the different areas has always been difficult, making for regional self-sufficiency and independence; political unity, though perhaps always desirable, was never essential for the maintenance of an orderly life, as it was in Egypt. Every city in classical times was at least partly dependent upon its local fertile area, while there were certain mountain districts where primitive conditions persisted throughout the whole period of Greek greatness. The fertile area of the country, however, amounts to hardly more than one fifth of the total acreage of the country, making poverty the general rule in the absence of nonagricultural methods of subsistence.

The pressure of poverty and population in Greece has always stimulated emigration; in classical times it also stimulated enterprise. In general, the valleys run in a southeasterly direction and the harbors face southeast. Hence there was no great open expanse of sea to be crossed before contact could be made with foreigners. There are chains of islands, welcome havens for the sailors of antiquity, each with its own harbor, inviting trade and transshipment. Before the Greeks became seafarers the Minoans and the Phoenicians came sailing into the Greek ports; when the Phoenicians declined in power it was natural for the Greeks to take their place.

The climate of Greece is equable; there are land and sea breezes to temper the heat of summer, and winter, except in the mountains, is not cold and remains sunny, as in all Mediterranean lands. As early as February the Athenians held an outdoor festival. There is little or no rain in summer, but in most areas there is sufficient rain in spring and fall. Severe storms, however, are known (the thunderbolt of Zeus was not only a poetic imagination); but they are local in incidence and never damage all the country's crops equally.

POVERTY OF THE NATURAL RESOURCES

The fertile areas themselves present contrasts. There is the lush plain of Boeotia, suitable for grain and cattle, and there is the stony soil of Attica, suitable for vines and olives but, as Solon insisted, not suitable for grain. The greater part of Greek soil was heavily eroded even in the time of Solon, perhaps because of excessive cutting of timber. There is a striking contrast between the comparative wealth of the life described by Homer and the life of an Athenian of the fifth century, still more with that of the Spartan. There were no oxen roasted whole in Athens; in fact, there was little meat at all, and even fish, despised in Homeric times, was a luxury. Timber was in short supply, metals were rare, and there was no iron. Gold, silver, copper and lead, though present, were not abundant; but there were many varieties of excellent building stone, and a good quality of clay for pottery.

In short, the most outstanding physical fact of Greece was and is the shortage of means of subsistence. Yet the Greek of antiquity was able to make such good use of what he had that extreme poverty was very rare, and he was able to build up a civilization on a fairly secure economic base. The process was a simple one, and has much to recommend it—learn to do without. If the Greeks had needed three meals a day with meat as a regular diet, they could not have had them; alternatively a favored few could have satisfied their own demands, but would have been forced to build a political organization that ensured their special position. In an equalitarian and democratic society all equally had to do without. Breakfast was unknown; two meals, both of them simple, sufficed. And the remarkable number of long-lived men in Greece suggests that the regimen did them no harm. Bernard Shaw outlived Sophocles, but only by three years; John Dewey outlived Plato by only seven; and the examples cited are exceptions in our society. Winston Churchill has to survive almost a decade if he is to reach the age of Isocrates. If the Greeks had needed luxurious houses, central heating, and spring beds they could not have had them. Fortunately their climate made the first two unnecessary, and their lack of taste for our kind of luxury spared them the other.

The grain that the Athenians had to import at the time when they were specializing in the culture of the vine and olive was paid for not only by these products but also by their craftsmanship. Clay was cheap and plentiful, but vases required skill and artistry. Taken into the right market by enterprising traders, they were worth much grain. But, even so, the only time Athens became really rich was when she was able to draw upon the surplus of her island confederacy. Then again, she provided skill in seamanship, and some political organization, as her invisible export to keep her economy balanced.

The Greek civilization then was far different from the material civilization of the Minoans, or of the modern Americans. But fourth- and fifth-century Athens nevertheless presents a roster of great names in every field of activity that would be hard to match in any civilization at any time in history, and we have continued to try to imitate her art with imperfect success to this day.

▶ The peoples of Greece

The Greeks called themselves Hellenes, and their land Hellas.[1] In historic times they regarded themselves as a peculiar people, different from the rest of the world, which indeed, as we shall see, they were. Others were "barbarians," a descriptive term originally used for those who spoke foreign languages, but certainly intended as a term of reproach. The Greeks were in no sense ethnically a pure "race," nor ever pretended to be. It was their customs that set them apart.

There is no consensus as to who the Greeks were, nor even where they came from. It used to be assumed that they migrated from central Europe, and this may be true of some of them. Modern research inclines toward accepting at least a partial Oriental origin in the more remote past, and is ready to accept more cultural connections with the Near East than had previously been admitted. It is also unknown who the original inhabitants of Greece were before the waves of immigrants arrived, nor what proportion

[1] The word "Greek" was first used by the Romans in referring to the civilization of southern Italy.

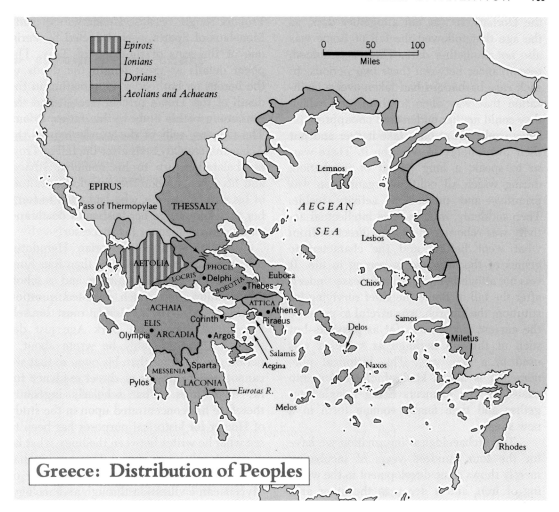

Legend:
- Epirots
- Ionians
- Dorians
- Aeolians and Achaeans

0 50 100
Miles

EPIRUS
Pass of Thermopylae
THESSALY
AEGEAN SEA
Lemnos
Lesbos
Chios
AETOLIA
LOCRIS
PHOCIS
Delphi
BOEOTIA
Thebes
Euboea
ACHAIA
ATTICA
Athens
Piraeus
ELIS
Corinth
Olympia
ARCADIA
Argos
Samos
Delos
Miletus
Salamis
Aegina
Naxos
MESSENIA
Sparta
Pylos
LACONIA
Eurotas R.
Melos
Rhodes

Greece: Distribution of Peoples

of the original stock survived. There is little doubt that the least civilized of the conquering groups, the Dorians, arrived last in Greece, as already described. Ionians, as well as Achaeans preceded them, together with smaller groups such as the Aeolians. The Dorians themselves were followed by the always imperfectly civilized Epirotes, who did not penetrate into southern Greece at all. It seems probable that the Ionians were contemporary with, or even earlier than, the Achaeans, but that the latter, being in closer contact with the Cretans, developed their civilization more quickly. The Ionians settled in Attica and southern Euboea. Then, either of their own accord at an early date, or later when driven to it by the Dorians, they populated the majority of the Aegean Islands and pushed across to Asia Minor, where they settled near the coast and maintained some contact with their Greek motherland at the same time as they absorbed some of the higher culture of the Orient.

The Athenians were proud of their Ionian heritage, and had many legends which boasted of its antiquity; in later days they regarded themselves as superior to the rude Dorians, whose virtues were certainly dissimilar to theirs. But both had great virtues, and these two were the leading peoples in Greece throughout the classical era.

▶ Homeric Age

INFORMATION FROM ARCHAEOLOGY

We have already spoken of a Dark Age that fell upon Greece with the fading of the Mycenaean civilization and the invasions of extent taken the position of bronze, that agriculture and sheepherding were the chief means of making a living, that the common method of distribution and exchange of goods was by barter, aided by war and plunder, that the Greeks were not as skilled as the Phoenicians at making industrial products, that slavery, except for domestic purposes, was relatively uncommon. And we can gather that family ties were strong, that respect for parents and age was the general rule, and that strangers were expected to be treated hospitably.

INFERENCES FROM THE HOMERIC POEMS

We are on less certain ground when we insist on the aristocratic nature of Homeric society. It is true that in the *Iliad* the common man is hardly mentioned, though he may be presumed to have done most of the real fighting against the Trojans, and even Thersites, who used to be cited as the one example of the common man, was not really one, but the son of a barbarian king. Eumaeus, the noble swineherd of the *Odyssey*, was also the son of a king, who had in his youth been enslaved by Phoenicians. But the purpose of Homer has to be considered before we can make inferences on the nature of the society of his day. He was not writing history, nor even a systematic story of the Trojan War. He does not begin at the beginning nor end with the fall of Troy. He is primarily interested in telling, as he himself informs us, of the wrath of Achilles and his quarrel with Agamemnon, and the evils to which they led. It was a moral poem, and was always recognized as such; and it is difficult to see where the common man could have been brought into it. Similarly in the *Odyssey* the story is of the cunning and craft of Odysseus, and the wickedness of the suitors who cared nothing for the gods nor for the traditional ideals of good faith and hospitality and common humanity, and so met with punishment from the returning master. Finally we must always remember that Homer's audience was probably largely aristocratic, interested in listening to the deeds of heroes and not of common men.

There are, nevertheless, some inferences that may safely be made. There is a complete absence in the Homeric poems of anything resembling the divine kings of the Orient, or even of absolute rule by a monarch. Agamemnon, "the king of men," is the leader of the expedition to Troy, and no one ever thinks of deposing him, in spite of the disasters brought upon the Achaean host by his willfulness. Achilles is able to retire and refuse to go into battle, though he cannot keep his prize, the maiden Briseis, once Agamemnon has decided to take her to compensate for the loss of his own prize. Achilles does not defend her by the might of his own sword because the goddess Athena counsels him against doing so, and he obeys rather than incur divine wrath. Put into secular terms, this sounds as if Agamemnon had a certain prescriptive right to rule which had nothing to do with his personal valor; and that he had a kind of overriding authority over the whole expedition which he was not expected to exercise in matters not affecting the expedition. He could, however, do so, even in the face of public opinion, which was all on the side of Achilles; no one except the aggrieved party could stop him, though all might counsel against a misuse of kingly power. On the other hand, there are many divine sanctions preventing Agamemnon's use of arbitrary power; the gods could punish his host, and prevent the success of the expedition. Indeed, he had been forced to give up his own prize because she was the daughter of a priest of Apollo, and Apollo knew how to protect his own.

In both the *Iliad* and the *Odyssey* we have examples of councils and assemblies called by the rulers. Here there is considerable freedom of speech, even against these rulers. Anyone is permitted to speak, but he must convince the whole assembly and the ruler if he is to have his policy adopted. Telemachus, son of Odysseus, has apparently the right to call a council in the absence of his father. The suitors may meet among themselves, but in the absence of the actual ruler they cannot call a council of all the people. These customs do not look unlike those of the Primitive Democracy discussed under Mesopotamia where the elders and heads of families were listened to with respect. But in Homeric times the chief elder has become a king, as we saw he did in Mesopotamia in historical times. But the king in Greece never developed into the absolute monarch of the Orient; on the contrary, he lost his power to the nobles and ultimately, as we shall see, to the people.

THE HOMERIC EPICS

The authorship of the poems

But the Homeric poems are far more important for what they are in themselves and for what they became in Greek culture than as source books for the history of the Dark Age in Greece.

There is no unanimity of opinion on who Homer was, when he lived, whether he wrote both the *Iliad* and the *Odyssey*, whether they were written in one piece or assembled at a later date—or even whether there was ever a Homer at all. The question will certainly never be settled to the satisfaction of everyone, and, on the whole, it does not seem necessary that it should. In spite of passages which seem to have been added to each poem, both have an impressive unity of idea; and this unity could best be attained by the activity of a great poet working over a considerable mass of earlier material. There is nothing immature about either poem; both are finished works of art, the despair of all later imitators. "Homer" would seem to come at the end of a long line of poets and minstrels rather than to have created both his epics out of nothing. But it was he who gave form to the material. Whether the *Iliad* and the *Odyssey* were written by the same poet is an even more thorny question. Longinus, the best critic of antiquity, did not doubt the authorship. His famous remark, "Homer in the *Odyssey* is like the setting sun; the grandeur remains but not the intensity; it is as though the Ocean had shrunk into its lair and lay becalmed within its own confines," has found many adherents among modern critics, while others are equally certain that the same poet could never have written both, so marked

are the differences. The arguments put forward by Samuel Butler trying to prove that the author of the *Odyssey* was a woman make an impressive total; and even these cannot be refuted on the basis of our information.

Homer as "the Bible of the Greeks"

But whatever the answer to this "Homeric Question" there can be no doubt of the enormous influence of the poems on all later Greek thought, and the remark that Homer was the Bible of the Greeks is apt. Above all he was their common heritage; in spite of the differences between the individual city-states, Homer served, like the great Greek festivals, to remind them that they were one people. Painters, poets, men of action, and philosophers alike turned to him for inspiration. Every schoolboy could recite long passages by heart, and any allusion to Homer would at once be understood, as any allusion to the King James Bible was understood by every educated Englishman and most Americans before the twentieth century.[2]

The *Iliad*—The first tragedy of destiny

Why did Homer become such a bible? The evidence shows it was not his language, magnificent though it is, but primarily his thought. Not that the later Greeks believed in the gods of Olympus in any literal sense —and there is no reason to believe that even Homer did. This was his conventional framework. He describes the activities of the gods, but he is really speaking about the human beings. When Achilles refrains from attacking Agamemnon and swallows the insult offered him, the good advice he receives is credited to Athena. But Achilles is not a puppet in the hands of Athena; it is he who receives the inspiration and acts upon it, and this is the impression gained by the reader. Achilles is the greater man for his self-control, and

---

[2] Toynbee in our day represents the tradition. There are few pages in his six volumes which do not have at least one Biblical allusion, which—alas, mistakenly—he seems to think will be appreciated at once by his readers, though he is careful to give the necessary chapter and verse, even for the most familiar passages.

this impression is undoubtedly intended by the poet. When Diomede is filled with super-human vigor in the fifth book of the *Iliad* and attacks and puts the goddess Aphrodite to flight, and even takes on the great god Apollo himself, the god first defends himself. When Diomede continues to try to dispatch Aineias the Trojan against the god's will, Apollo finally forces him to desist with the words "Be not so fain to match thyself with God. The immortal kind ranks not with mankind." This is the message to the reader. Man is not a god. Elsewhere we are shown Apollo pleading for the life of Hector against Athena, who claims it for Achilles. Zeus, though sorry for Hector as a human being, cannot override the Fates who have decreed his death. So even Zeus is not all-powerful. He, too, must bend to the unalterable law of fate.

What, then, Homer taught the Greeks was above all that man is not a god, that pride, especially pride that would make man equal with the gods, will lead to destruction; and that the laws of the universe are not of man's making but must be obeyed. Homer has an unsurpassed feeling for the tragedy of man's life, the *lacrimae rerum* never far from the Greek consciousness. Hector is portrayed with the utmost sensitivity, and his scenes with his wife Andromache are unsurpassed in all literature for their human tenderness. Homer understands what it will mean for her when Hector is killed and Troy captured. Yet Hector must die; we know, and the poet knows, that this is a decree of destiny and it is no fault of his. It is no sin of Hector's that is to bring him to destruction, and there is no moral to be taught. And Hector knows his fate, too, but he cannot avoid it. Because he, as a hero, must be true to himself. He cannot avoid the battle and play the coward, even at the entreaty of his beloved wife.

So in the *Iliad* we have the heart of Greek thinking already presented to us in a magnificently dramatic and human form. Man is living in a framework of necessity which he cannot change. It is his delusion that he should exult in his own strength, and believe it is his, when in reality it is given him by higher powers. He can always abuse it by making himself the equal of the gods, and this is the deadly error which will lead to his destruction. But within the given framework he has a duty also to be himself, to seek for the only immortality that he will ever know, a glory among men that will live after him. Then he will have played his part on earth with nobility. All classical Greek thought is included in this ideal. The gods disappear as persons, but the ideal remains. Socrates, refusing to go into exile rather than stand trial because his daemon has not counseled it, and drinking the hemlock because he is not above the law, is in the same tradition. Man's morality is not required of him by the gods. The gods make no demands upon him, and so have been thought immoral in Homer. But neither do they make demands in any Greek thought. The laws of the universe are there from the beginning, and the gods administer them. But it is man himself who creates his own ideal of what is befitting him as man, and his reward is on earth in the approval of himself and his fellow men. Even in Plato and Aristotle this humanism is present. The gods of Olympus have disappeared, but the search for the good remains human good. The duty toward one's self missing in Hebrew thought is balanced by the Greek ideal of humanism; and because it was present in Homer, he was never outmoded, even while the gods of Olympus disappeared into higher regions.

The Odyssey—The Greek mind in action

In the *Odyssey* we see revealed the second great gift of the Greeks to humanity, the means by which the ideal is attained—the Greek mind. Odysseus, above everything else, is a man of "many wiles." There is no future for Achilles, who belonged only to the old world of warriors, relying on his strength and fleetness of foot, remaining true to himself—for he had chosen a short life of glory in preference to a long life of ease—but a man of swift anger and without compassion, almost a force of nature, living by instinct rather than in full self-consciousness. It is Odysseus who *thinks out* how to take Troy, with the wooden horse. And it is noticeable that the inspirations of Odysseus are not provided him by the gods; they are his own. It is he who thinks out how to outwit Polyphemus, not Athena, though Athena does guide him on other occasions. We must, however, remember also that Athena is the goddess of wisdom, and sprang, fully armed, from the *head* of Zeus. Odysseus boasts of *his own* cleverness, and in so doing draws upon himself the vengeance of the god Poseidon, who leads him into so many unnecessary dangers and hardships. But he is also a mighty man of valor and strength. It is only he who can string his bow; all the suitors have tried and failed. So in Odysseus we have the combination of mind and body which became the ideal of the classical Greeks.

The *Odyssey* has been described as a novel, and many recent translators have had this in mind as they worked. But it is far more than this, or it could never have commanded a position in Greek thought equivalent to that of the *Iliad*. It is the story of a wandering hero who passes through trials of fortitude to reach his home and execute judgment upon those who had been eating up his substance and breaking the sacred customs of the land. The suitors are godless men who think they can treat his wife and son with contempt, and they are punished with death, even those who had shown some signs of common humanity. Those survived who remained faithful to the wanderer and would not believe him dead. And Odysseus himself is clearly chastened by his wanderings and his bitter experiences during his long time in disguise in his homeland, living as a beggar and submitting to humiliation at the hands of the suitors. He knows he will destroy them when the time comes, but he has to wait for the right moment. The plan is carefully laid and carried out; the goddess Athena plays her part in this finale, guiding him at every turn. It does not seem that all this framework is present just for the purpose of making an entertaining story though it is certainly that too.

What we have here is a story of the Homeric hero as a grown-up man, no longer ruled by elemental passions needing a god to control them; but ruled now by his own mind. And Homer shows how this cleverness and lack of moderation and wanton boasting destroyed his innocent companions, and led Odysseus himself to his trials and his humiliation. Only when this had been fully experienced could he take up his bow and with the help of Athena kill the suitors and recover his position as king. The divine framework is still there; man is still to beware of his pride which will bring destruction. He must still be true to himself and seek his ideal—which is not here conjugal bliss with Penelope but recovery of his rights as king, filched from him by the suitors and their families. Odysseus has all the qualities admired by the Greeks: valor, decision, presence of mind, and intelligence. Achilles lacked the last; he didn't need it in the world of the *Iliad*. But in the new world of the *Odyssey*, when the hero is cast alone on the deep, when at the last he is thrown up naked and without one companion on the shores of Phaeacia, then a man must rely upon his own inner strength, his mind, and not only his martial prowess. Though few would claim that the *Odyssey* is superior to the *Iliad* in passion, sublimity, or humanity, it is a worthy companion and complement; and it is a fitting prologue to the drama of Greek history, which is in essence the coming to maturity of the human mind.

▶ General characteristics of the Greek peoples

GREEK HISTORY AS A UNIVERSAL HISTORY ON A MINIATURE SCALE—THE STUDY OF EXTREMES

The mature ideal of the Greeks was *sophrosyne*, or moderation, a quality for which they strove, but which was comparatively lacking in their original make-up. We study the history of Athens and Sparta, the two most renowned of Greek city-states, because they were extremes. If we want to examine the nearest approach to a full democracy, completely logical, permeated through and through by the mind, we study Athens. If we want to study the opposite, the most completely logical example of a closed state, unwilling to accept a new idea, a civilization fossilized and arrested by intelligent design, we study Sparta. When Aristotle wanted to find a golden mean, a moderate state, neither too progressive nor too conservative, he looked for the halfway point between Athens and Sparta.

The Greeks impressed their minds on everything they undertook. Their political history is worth studying in some detail because it was an experiment in miniature with human nature. How much democracy and freedom can human nature stand? Or, on the other hand, how much self-sacrifice can it stand for an accepted ideal enforced on all members of the society? Though the conditions for each experiment were peculiar to the time and place and can never be exactly repeated again, we can learn something of the limitations of human nature from the efforts of these peoples. We can almost see the exact moment when the pressure of outside events proved too much for it—especially when we have with us as a guide a man who lived through the crucial times and recorded them with a self-consciousness and depth of understanding rarely, if ever, equaled in a historian.

The problems the Greeks had to deal with are universal problems, transcending the limitations of time and place. When we read in Thucydides' histories of the debate in the Athenian Assembly between Cleon and Diodotus on the efficacy of capital punishment as a deterrent to treason, we cannot say that times have changed or that human nature has changed essentially from the fifth century B.C. When we read Demosthenes' speeches in the same Assembly excoriating Philip of Macedon—warning against the dangers of self-delusion in the face of a determined enemy—we are transported forward to the 1930's. When we read of the deterioration of Athenian character under the influence of fear and desire for party gains, we are unhappily again in our own world of the 1960's. The only great difference is that today we are no longer living in a small *polis*, or city-state. The laboratory experiment has been transferred to the great world of superstates. So, necessarily, our particular problems are different, and the particular Greek solutions are not relevant as solutions to the problems of our world. But we can still return to the Greeks for an understanding of the dignity and the limitations of man; and the unanswered questions raised in the city-states of ancient Greece are with us still in our superstates. The refinements of a technical civilization, of which they never dreamed and which it is doubtful they would have appreciated, do not change the nature of the fundamental human problems with which man is confronted, today and twenty-five hundred years ago.

THE SEARCHING MIND OF THE GREEK

All knowledge, said the Greeks, begins in wonder, wonder about the world, and wonder about man. The Hebrews asked only one question about man, his relation to his God. The Greeks asked not only this question, but all other questions. They were the greatest people for questioning that the world has yet seen, or at all events until our own time. When Aristotle came to write his *Politics* he felt obliged to ask a great many fundamental questions before he dared to generalize. He had amassed material on 158 constitutions, constitutions evolved by generations of men struggling with the problem of how men could best be governed. None of the constitutions was perfect; all had failed in some respects. But the people themselves had discovered the defects, and by asking why and considering the alternatives they had tried to remedy them. So Aristotle conceived it to be his task to classify these constitutions, to see if he could evolve a system that would have the most merits and the fewest weaknesses even if it would not be ideal. Plato, on the other hand, was looking in his *Republic* for an ideal state. So it was necessary for him to inquire first on what principles an ideal state could be built, and then try to find institutions through which it could be expressed. This took him a long way. For, having discovered that it must be based on justice, he then had to find out what justice was. Neither Plato nor Aristotle ever thought for a moment that it was not the duty of man to improve his institutions, as the ancient Egyptians had thought. And it is this willingness to seek new knowledge and to stake their lives upon the result of ever-continuous experiment based on the best thinking of which they were capable that distinguishes the Greeks from their predecessors.

The Greeks wondered about the physical world. What was the underlying stable substratum in a world where everything appeared to be in flux—was it water, air, fire, or atoms? Clearly everything changed in appearance; but they did not doubt that this change was only an apparent change. Underneath was a unity. When Thales saw the Egyptian notebooks which told of the measurements of the angles and sides of a triangle, his mind leaped ahead to the universal idea underlying all these particulars. And he is credited with the famous *pons asinorum* theorem—in *all* triangles, the angles subtending equal sides are equal to one another.

They wondered about man—his nature, the seen body and the unseen soul that gave life to it. They assumed the existence of the soul, but they tried to find the relationship between soul and body. How does man acquire knowledge? What is the nature of the mind that knows it? What are the laws of thinking? How does one idea connect with another? What is an idea? What are the activities proper to man? What is morality?

In all these questions except the last, the Greeks were pioneers in human thinking; and even in the last they were different from the Hebrews in that at least the later Greeks accepted nothing, even the gods, as final arbiters. While they might admit that the fear of the Lord was the beginning of wisdom, this to them would only be one more reminder that they were men and not gods. The last thing a classical Greek would

do would be to enter the sanctuary and there receive a comfort which would save him the necessity of questioning further.

THE REVERENCE FOR MAN AND ALL HIS WORKS

But the Greeks were not a people of philosophers and questioners alone. Their interest in man excited not only their inquiry but also their reverence. The sudden panegyric of man voiced by the chorus in Sophocles's tragic drama *Antigone* seems ready to burst out of the Greek at any moment. What a wonderful thing is man, of all things most wonderful. He can navigate the seas, he can curb the horse, he can tame the wild beast; with his thinking mind he is the lord of creation. And so with loving hands they modeled man in stone and clay, the discus thrower and the athlete and the runner, sculptured him in movement, breathing the living activity into him as no people has ever done since; and they put crystals in his sockets for eyes, put color on his face and sheen on his limbs. And the victor in the games was crowned with a laurel wreath, and poets extolled him for his achievements and gave him immortal fame.

Believing in the dignity of man, the classical Greeks were singularly uncorrupt in everything they did; and though they were later corrupted by exposure to the hard facts of life and found it beyond their powers to retain the purity of their ideal, as artists it was impossible for them to be insincere and shoddy. Though they all worked equally for a wage of one drachma a day, the nameless artists of the Parthenon and the Erechtheum did work that has been the despair and admiration of later ages. High above the ground and only dimly illuminated by such light as filtered through the translucent marble roof, the Parthenon friezes were a worthy offering to Athena, while the foundations beneath the unique building are as honestly laid as anything in the temple that was visible. The artistry of the workmen, as well as the apparent ability of all the people to appreciate and understand the tragic drama, encourages us to

possible to revive the Greek ideal, save in certain local communities, as during the settlement of America.

The origin of the Greek polis is still a matter of opinion, since there are no written records. But it is assumed that during the invasions the clan, or group of families with a common ancestor, tended to settle in the same place; that clans united into brotherhoods, and brotherhoods into tribes; and that the union of tribes formed a nation—and we have Greek words for all these subdivisions. It is unfortunate for the theory that we have evidence of quite close kinsmen settling in different areas, but the rule may still have been as described. Coming into a certain area the tribes, or union of tribes, settled in scattered agricultural villages, and joined together around some fortified strong point, the *acropolis*. Here the leader of the clans, chosen, or holding his position by prescriptive right as the closest in kin to the common ancestor, would be the king. But other clan leaders would be as important as he, and these would form the class of nobles. The villages, needing a means for common defense, would need the fortress and with the gradual division of labor would come to require a common market. This market—the agora of all Greek cities—would soon grow beneath the acropolis and the fortified place would also be the natural center for assembly.

This general theory fits the circumstances well enough. We know of the hero or divine ancestor of the cities, we know of the division into clans and tribes which persisted even after the full organization of the polis. We know of the tradition of kings whose power was usurped by the nobles, and we know of the occasional assemblies for the consultation of all the people. What is not known is why the development, not a unique one, nevertheless stopped short at the polis. The physical barriers of Greece might favor the polis as the ultimate unit of government, but certainly did not determine it, because even when the barriers did not exist the polis persisted. On the whole it can only be stated that the Greeks found it favorable to their own particular genius,

and liked the small unit; and there was no external power at this time capable of forcing a larger unit upon them. Not all poleis, however, moved on to democracy—by progressively limiting the power of the king and the nobles and giving it to the people. Some were ruled by individuals who evidently satisfied their subjects, others were ruled by oligarchies (rule by the few) or aristocracies (rule by the best), or by the old nobles, more or less controlled or accepted by the people. Some had oligarchies, tyrannies, and democracies at different times. And all had parties favoring one or the other form of rule, the foundation for internal rivalries within the states themselves that almost ruined them.

So far we have been speaking only of freeborn citizens. In addition to these there were resident aliens (called at Athens *metics*) without full rights, and there were slaves. All the cities were too poor in resources to support a wealthy leisure class. Not even by extensive slave labor could enough surplus be produced to give this leisure to any substantial number. So it is entirely inaccurate to imagine any Greek city-state as composed of a small leisure class creating the high culture while slaves toiled to provide the means for it. Almost every Greek, slave or free, had to work for his living, with the possible exception of the inhabitants of Sparta, where the free citizens, or Spartiates, were heavily outnumbered by their slaves, and were required to do a large amount of unproductive supervisory work. There was almost no agricultural slavery outside Sparta. It was difficult enough on most Greek land for anybody to make much of a living, and the slave had to be fed. For the most part slaves worked in industry or in domestic employment. The well-to-do Athenian liked to have one or two domestic slaves, who could be more accurately described as his unfree servants. The Old Oligarch, a disgruntled aristocrat who did not like the Athenian democracy, complains in his work on the Athenian constitution that in Athens it was difficult to distinguish a slave from a freeman, so it may be assumed that slaves were not badly

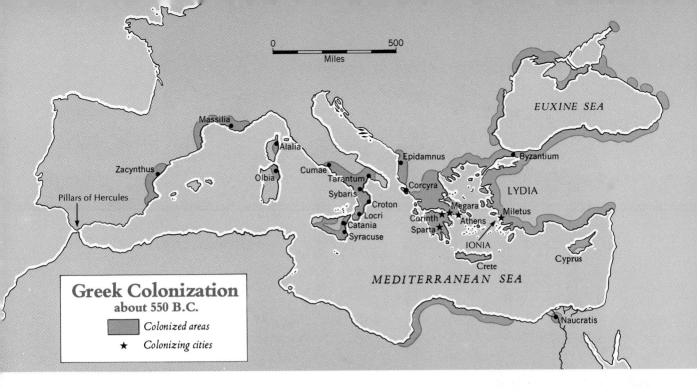

Greek Colonization
about 550 B.C.

Colonized areas
★ Colonizing cities

treated. Nearly all industry in Athens, as we shall see, was small, as was to be expected of a people all of whom liked to be in business for themselves. But factory owners employed slaves, a few each as workers. The slaves also were paid, and beating them was not permitted—another complaint of the Old Oligarch. So, on the whole, it is more accurate to regard the slave as a worker with no political rights, and under a permanent contract with his employer—which contract could be sold to another employer without consulting the worker.[4] While the slavery certainly detracted from the purity of the democracy, it was more of an economic evil, tending to keep the freeman's wage down to the level of that of the slave, than the social evil it has been elsewhere.

EXPANSION OF GREECE—EARLY COLONIZATION

Before proceeding to the internal development of the individual Greek polis, mention should be made of the great movement to colonize other lands in which all the peoples of Greece took part. This colonization antedated the political and social reforms in the cities which gave the latter their characteristic shape. Although we know little about the reasons for the colonization

[4] The only great exception to this rule was the worker in the mines, where conditions were terrible and few freemen could be found to do the work.

movement, we do know that at least the early colonies were not trade settlements like those of the Phoenicians but were the result of land hunger. This suggests the pressure of an expanding population which could find little outlet in Greece itself. With the nobles in possession of the land, and enslavement for debt the common result of failure to make a living, the younger sons of small farmers would be anxious to leave and try somewhere else. Moreover the polis was not yet the ideal place to live in, and for the poor there was as yet no participation in the community life. If they started again somewhere else, there was always more hope.

Along the shores of the Mediterranean and Black Seas, along the whole west coast of Italy, colonies were planted, each of them a little Greece beyond the sea. At first the ventures were rather haphazard, and organized by private enterprise. Then the mother cities themselves organized the emigrating parties, often inviting the participation of other cities in the venture. Before a colony was decided upon the participants usually took the precaution of consulting the Delphic Oracle, which acquired much knowledge and experience in colonization and so was able to give useful advice. A colony, however, did not remain subject to the mother city, though it had provided the

The temple of Poseidon at Paestum, one of the Greek colonies in Italy. In spite of being located in Italy, this temple is older than the Parthenon, and is the best-preserved Greek temple in the world. These Greek colonies were conquered by the Romans and absorbed into the Confederation of Italy at the close of the wars with Pyrrhus. (PHOTO BY MRS. JOSEPH E. WISAN)

colony with a human founder and its own gods. One or two cities, such as Miletus and Corinth, tried to keep some control of their foundations, but were never permanently successful. The ties between the colony and its mother city were religious and sentimental; and though these ties counted for much with the Greeks, they were never decisive, and colonies not infrequently in later years joined in wars against their founding cities. This action was never regarded as rebellion, even though Greek public opinion was against it as unnatural strife. At the beginning the colony always had every reason to maintain good relations with its sponsor, especially when it had been formed for trade purposes, since in its early years it had little energy to spare in seeking out new markets for its product.

Many of the colonies became greater and more prosperous than the motherland. The small rocky polis of Megara founded Byzantium on the Bosporus, and Chalcedon

on the Asiatic shore opposite; Miletus made the Black Sea area almost a Milesian lake, with ninety colonies in the area according to tradition. She even established a colony at Naucratis in the Egyptian Delta. Corinth founded Corcyra and Syracuse, the latter destined far to surpass her in prosperity. Even Sparta founded the chief city in southern Italy, Tarentum, though there were special reasons for this venture. Athens, however, developed later and took no part in the early colonization movement. She was more engaged in affairs at home. Having the territory of Attica, larger than that possessed by most cities, to settle, her energies were occupied with this during the formative period.

The results of the colonization movement, though not visible at once, were momentous for the future of Greece. Though the colonies were founded from land hunger, the immigrant Greeks, with their always keen business sense, soon entered into trade relations with their neighbors, who in most cases were inferior in culture to themselves, but had foreign products to sell. Thus a new trade sprang up, bringing prosperity to the motherland as well as to themselves, and providing more employment and stimulating movement to the cities from the overpopulated countryside. Some of the most lasting work of Solon in Athens was his stimulation of the Athenians to look overseas, produce goods suitable for export, and so relieve the pressure on the land. Being eminently fitted for this task, Athens was soon able to compensate for her late start.

SPARTA

The type of the closed society

It has been already remarked that the Greeks, in spite of their ideal of *sophrosyne* or moderation, tended to go to extremes, and that Athens and Sparta represent the extreme cases of their particular forms of government. The contrast between Athens and Sparta makes an eternally fascinating study. Sparta has been called a classical example of a fossilized static state, a militarist state, a communist state, a fascist state, even an imperialist state, and none of the terms is altogether inaccurate. Yet, on the other hand, such essentially humane non-Spartans as Plato, Aristotle, Xenophon, Plutarch, and Polybius all in some degree approved of her constitution on theoretical and even practical grounds. Did these men, then, approve of fascism, militarism, and the rest?

Toynbee in one of his finest studies presents the history of Sparta as a classical instance of an arrested civilization; and there is no doubt that it fits perfectly into this classification. Sparta was proud of the fact that she had not changed for centuries; she revered as a god her mythical lawgiver Lycurgus. She was ultimately forced by circumstances to emerge from her isolation, and she had to change her way of life when at last her state slaves, known as *helots*, revolted successively. But the changes were grudgingly made; and in spite of increas-

ingly difficult conditions the constitution was continuously restored, with only minor changes down to the time of Cleomenes III in the third century B.C. By this time the conditions that gave rise to it had completely disappeared.

For, as will be seen, it is clear for what purpose the supposed lawgiver "Lycurgus" issued his famous laws.[5] What is not quite so clear is on what earlier foundations he was building that the laws should take such a tenacious hold on the people. The Spartans were the most nearly pure Dorian stock in Greece. The Dorians penetrated to the southeastern portion of the Peloponnesus, where they had to contend with the old Myceneaean stronghold of Argos. The process of conquest seems to have been slow and arduous, but it was at last successful, and the Dorians finally subdued the whole of Laconia, a fertile plain bounded by mountains. They enslaved the native population, making them, however, not into domestic or industrial private slaves but into state slaves, working on the land and contributing half their produce to the citizens who had charge of them. The Dorians themselves lived in Sparta, and a ring of villages around Sparta was peopled by free inhabitants not belonging to the dominant group and of mixed ancestry. These were called perioeci (neighbors). They were not permitted to intermarry with the true Spartans, called Spartiates, and they had no political rights.

It will therefore be seen that long before the constitution of Lycurgus, Laconian society was increasingly stratified. It could, however, have developed more on the lines of other Greek cities had not events of supreme importance occurred—the Messenian Wars. At the time of these wars Sparta was well abreast of the other Greeks in artistic production. The Dorian style was more simple and severe than contemporary Ionian, but it was creative and beautiful. Poets and artists still lived in Sparta. There

[5] It has never been established by historians whether any man Lycurgus ever existed, even though Plutarch wrote his biography, which is mainly an account of the Spartan Constitution.

*Two views of a Spartan kylix (terra-
cotta). The painted interior depicts
the apotheosis of Heracles. This
piece shows that by 580 B.C., the
date of the kylix, the Spartans were
still able to produce works of craftsmanship comparable to that of
the other Greeks.* (COURTESY THE
METROPOLITAN MUSEUM OF ART)

were music and luxury in the city, and the
Dorian choral lyric was developed there.
Foreigners were welcomed who could enter-
tain and enliven the lives of the highborn
Spartiates.

The conquest of the Messenians— Establishment of a rigid militarism

But land hunger attacked the noble
lords of Sparta, as it attacked others in
Greece, and they were not content with
Laconia alone. Colonization was not her
answer—the only important colony she sent
out, to Tarentum in Italy, was peopled by
the offspring of Spartan women and perioeci,
an illegitimate union in Spartan eyes—for she
had a military tradition, and unlike other
Greek cities, a standing army. So she in-

vaded Messenia to the west, a country more
fertile and more thickly populated than herself, and conquered it. Many Messenians
fled and founded colonies elsewhere; and
Sparta was faced with the problem of what
to do with this new territory. She decided
to annex it, and made the whole population
into helots working for the Spartiate masters.
We have little knowledge of how this system
worked; but we do know that toward the
end of the eighth century B.C. the Messenians, allied with Argos and other Peloponnesian cities, revolted, and a desperate and
bloody war ensued. Victory at first went to
the allies, who pressed on into Laconia.
Then, with the death of the Argive leader,
the tide of battle turned, and the Spartans,
spurred on by Tyrtaeus, their last poet, won
the final victory. It had taken twenty years

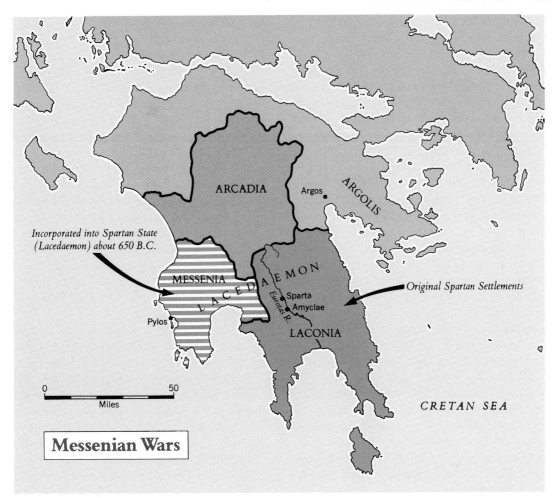

Incorporated into Spartan State
(Lacedaemon) about 650 B.C.

Original Spartan Settlements

ARCADIA

Argos

ARGOLIS

MESSENIA

LACEDAEMON

Eurotas R.

Sparta

Amyclae

Pylos

LACONIA

CRETAN SEA

0   50
Miles

Messenian Wars

of warfare. It seems almost certain that the laws of Lycurgus date from this time, and were directed to the problem of what to do about Messenia.

The Spartiates were now outnumbered by their subjects by about twenty to one. These subjects would be a constant menace to their masters unless held under tight control—or allowed self-government. In the latter case they would soon have slipped from Spartan jurisdiction altogether. The answer was, to our view, inhuman, but it was strictly logical. The Spartiates, according to the laws of Lycurgus, were to be supported as a professional military class by the helots and perioeci. The perioeci could live in Laconia as before and handle all the economic affairs of Sparta. They were not to become professional soldiers, nor inter-

marry with Spartans, nor have any political rights. They could make an adequate living, but not participate in any Spartan activity, except that in case of war they served with the Spartan heavy infantry. The remainder, the vast bulk of the population, was to be held down by the Spartiates by military force and secret police. Each Spartiate would be allotted a certain number of helots to work for him, and from their produce he and his family would live. The professional military class would devote itself to nothing but war and preparations for war. This class would be rigidly selected. Children who were weak and puny would simply be exposed at birth. Education for boys was to consist of all forms of athletics, military instruction, and physical exercise. Boys were made to go barefoot and ill-clad in winter, to sleep without coverings, and to prepare all their own meals. Girls being fitted to be mothers of Spartans had to undergo a similar regime of athletics and games, and were taught courage, endurance, and patriotism. Boys lived at home with their mothers till they were seven years old. Then they went into military training in groups under the charge of older boys, and lived in barracks. At the age of twenty marriage was compulsory, but the husband continued to live in barracks, and could visit his wife only on rare occasions. According to Plutarch, it was hoped that this continence would serve to procreate more healthy children, and in any case it protected the Spartiate from a possible weakening caused by contact with home comforts. From the labor of his helots each adult had to supply his share of the food eaten at the public mess. If a Spartiate for any reason could not supply his share, he lost status, and became an inferior citizen, with reduced political and social rights. To prevent contamination with foreign ideas and people, aliens were rarely admitted to the city; and those who received permits were periodically expelled. To prevent the accumulation of wealth the Spartans maintained a heavy iron currency which was not exchangeable anywhere else.

The helots were not personal but state slaves, as mentioned above. They were therefore possessed of certain elementary rights. They could not be put to death except by the state; though it was customary to allow the Spartiate youths approaching manhood to complete their education by spying on the helots. If the youths found any sign of conspiracy, they were armed with the authority of the state and could put the alleged conspirators summarily to death. A helot, provided he farmed well and furnished his particular master with the necessary supplies, could keep the remainder of his produce for himself. He was personally free, and could raise a family in the normal manner. Though in some respects his life appears less dismal to us than that of his masters, we do know that the helots were constantly seething with revolt. For

they were true Greeks, with a Greek detestation of any limitation on their freedom; and it must have been galling indeed to know that all other Greeks were living the full life of the polis, while they were kept under by a military state. Helots were naturally not permitted in the Spartan army except on rare occasions of danger, until the Spartiate population had dropped below the point where it could keep its position in Greek affairs without the aid of the helots. But by this time the helots were on the verge of freedom. It says much for the persistence of their independent spirit that when they were ultimately freed by the Thebans in the fourth century, they were able to set up a Messenian state independent of Sparta, and maintain it until all Greece was subdued by Macedonia.

This logical "Lycurgan" system fulfilled its purpose. The helots were kept under control for more than two hundred years, and Sparta possessed an army which was able to play a noble part in defeating the Persians. Its heavy infantry was unbeaten by any Greek city in battle until the rise of Thebes in the fourth century, and was the most highly disciplined and efficient body of troops in Greece. However, it should be understood that the main purpose of this army was for internal control, and not for foreign imperialist adventures. The Spartans were always hesitant to go to war abroad for the obvious reason that this would lessen their control over the helots. Besides, Sparta could not afford to lose many of her citizens, for they were irreplaceable. If any sizable body of Spartiate prisoners were taken, as at Pylos in the Peloponnesian War, she would at once sue for peace, and pay almost any price to gain it. Moreover, the leaders of the army, once outside the borders of Sparta, were in full control, away from the social sanctions of the city. Several Spartan generals showed initiative in their campaigns and came at once under suspicion. The Spartans preferred not to take the risk of military adventures away from the Peloponnese and not until after they had emerged as victors in the Peloponnesian War did they adopt any truly imperialistic policy. And then this policy led rapidly to the freeing of the helots and the breakdown of the Spartan state. The only consideration that could lead the early Spartans to make war was fear of encirclement, or aggression by others. Athenian democracy and the Athenian empire presented a grave threat, not only by reason of their dangerous ideas, but because of the possibility that Athens was aiming at the unification of all Greece. Oligarchies were much safer as neighbors than democracies. The Corinthian envoys who finally persuaded Sparta to make preventive war on Athens played shrewdly upon these Spartan fears; but that Corinth should have been compelled to produce such arguments is conclusive proof of Sparta's lack of interest in further expansion.

Institutions of Spartan state—Kings, ephors, Senate, Assembly

None of the Greek philosophers knew quite what to make of the Spartan constitution, as distinct from her social system. There were two kings from different families, relics of earlier times, who had little power at home but had the hereditary right to lead the army in the field. When with the army, the king had absolute power, unless the two kings were with the same army, in which case one had a veto on the other. In general each king served to limit the power of the other, but at home neither had very much authority, their function being primarily religious. So Sparta, though it had kings, was not a monarchy. The most important ruling body in the state were the five *ephors*, who were chosen annually by the Assembly. They had supreme power over the helots, handled foreign affairs, interviewed ambassadors, acted as censors of public and private morals, and could call anyone in Sparta to account for his actions, including the kings. The Council or Senate (*Gerousia*) was composed of twenty-eight members of old and noble families. The Senate acted as the supreme criminal court, and it prepared legislation for the Assembly. With the ephors, it also composed the exec-

utive of the state. The Assembly of all Spartiates (*Apella*) was the legislature; it also elected the ephors. It could not, however, debate, and it did not vote in the usual manner. Elections and legislation were carried by the loudest shout, as in modern radio programs. Aristotle gave up trying to classify this remarkable mixture of new and old constitutional elements, and called it a "mixed constitution." Broadly speaking, it had many of the characteristics of an oligarchy. But the Spartan constitutional forms are of minor importance in comparison with the social system—the laws, as the philosophers called them—which was the really effective control in Sparta.

Social pressures molding Spartan character—Approval of the philosophers

Why, then, did the philosophers approve of this system, and why did so many contemporary Greeks turn to it with a kind of envy, and at most with only a half-hearted disapproval? Probably few of the contemporaries knew of the historical reason for the system, and all believed in the laws of "Lycurgus." There is no reason to suppose that the enslavement of the helots was regarded as a particularly heinous offense. What they did see was the Spartan prowess in war, which, as warlike people themselves, they admired; at the all-Greek festivals, they saw the Spartans carrying off many of the honors; and they saw the Spartan girls and women, who were famous in Greece for their modesty, physique, and beauty. And they did not hear Spartan grumbling, if there was any. The Greeks of the other cities did not have as high an appreciation of their own art as we do, and the Spartan lack of artistic achievement probably was not considered specially blameworthy. Spartan heroism, however, was proverbial, and undoubtedly real. The social sanctions ensured it, for no Spartan dared go home in disgrace; he dared not even leave the battlefield to take news home. The Spartan anecdotes and sayings recorded by Plutarch illustrate the kind of reception his fellow citizens, and especially the women of Sparta, would give him.

The other Greeks, with their high ideal of civic virtue and duty, recognized that on this score the Spartans were their superiors. Civic duty, though in Sparta it was of a military nature, was nevertheless imposed by the polis and accepted by the citizens. This condition, to them, was not slavery, because obedience to laws was the whole ideal framework of the polis, as obedience to divine laws was a similar duty for the individual. The other Greeks did not think the Spartans lived under a tyranny, but under a regime chosen for them by Lycurgus, and accepted by them. The Athenian would not have accepted such laws for a moment, nor would he have put up with the Spartan food and frugality, which were the object of frequent jests among citizens of other states, frugal as they were themselves by our standards.

It was the privilege of the Spartans to choose their laws and to obey them; and to all appearances they did obey them. We do not hear of Spartans leaving their city to enjoy the delights of Athens or Corinth until after the Spartan victory in the Peloponnesian War (404 B.C.). It was perhaps the heroic nature of their extreme and narrow ideal and the heroic way in which they lived up to it that excited the admiration of their neighbors; while the philosophers admired the way they used their laws to form character and the logical nature of the laws themselves. The vulgarity, boasting, and propaganda of modern fascist states distinguish them effectively from Sparta. It was the Spartan's pride that he was a man of few words; and the word "laconic" has passed into our language. And a "Spartan" regime means, not an imperialist, fascist, communist, or oligarchic state, but a regime of simplicity and abstinence.

The Peloponnesian League

Sparta with her new professional army became the leading power in Greece after Argos had been defeated in the Second Messenian War. Her power in the Peloponnesus was beyond question. Her late enemies either joined voluntarily, or were forced into an alliance with her. The independent cities of northern Peloponnesus, including the trading center of Corinth, applied to her for protection, which she was willing to grant. Thus came into existence the first and the most long-lived of all Greek leagues, containing all the Peloponnesian poleis except the mountain areas, most of Achaea, and the city of Argos.

Within this league Sparta was the acknowledged leader; but when the members met for discussion, the Spartan vote counted for no more than any of the others. No member was allowed to secede, and there was a binding offensive and defensive alliance between all the states. There was no interference with local government, though most of the states were oligarchic. There was no common treasury and no funds, though all agreed to contribute in the event of war. It was in no sense a Spartan empire, and the variety of separate and largely complementary interests, plus the dominance of Sparta in prestige and military power, prevented most of the internal jealousies which broke up other Greek political organizations. Nevertheless there were weak links in it among the trading cities in the north. The secession of Megara, which put in a democratic government in the early days of the Periclean empire, and the defeat of Aegina in open warfare by Pericles, who forced her into the Athenian Confederation, gave the Spartans their first serious suspicions of Athenian imperialism, and were an important contributory cause of the Peloponnesian War, even though the seceding states returned to Sparta repentant before the actual outbreak.

THE ATHENIAN DEMOCRACY

The early beginnings—Rule by aristocracy

The difference between Athenian political development and that of all other Greek states, as far as we know, was the willingness of the Athenians to go forward to a complete democracy. If the landowners and nobles had insisted on being stubborn and recalcitrant, they might well have prevented this development; then there would have

This model of the Agora shows Athens in the second century A.D. rather than in the period covered by the text. Many changes were made during the period of domination by the wealthy Hellenistic monarchs; however, the model will serve to give some idea of the layout of the Agora. Although the buildings of the fifth century B.C. were less sumptuous and costly and the arrangement was less orderly, the style of architecture was not greatly different. (COURTESY AMERICAN SCHOOL OF CLASSICAL STUDIES AT ATHENS)

been no Athenian democracy, and probably no Athenian creative achievement. But time and again the aristocrats in Athens gave way, talked things over in a reasonable manner, abstained from violence to gain their own ends—and throughout the great period of Athens it was they who were the accepted, democratically appointed, political leaders. In all Athenian history there is but one real oligarchic revolution, and it lasted for barely a year. It came into existence only on Spartan insistence, when Athens had been disastrously defeated in war.

We do not know even in what century the small villages and poleis of Attica united into the one polis of Athens, nor do we know the name of the statesman responsible for this first constructive political act of the Athenians—though Athenian legend attributed it to Theseus. The union was celebrated by a festival in later times (*Synoikia*); though not remembered as vividly in Athens as the similar act of "Menes" in Egypt, it

was no less important. For it was the real foundation of Athenian greatness.

The date at which kingship disappeared from Attica is likewise unknown, but there was probably a gradual process under which the king became a civilian magistrate. We find a record of a king with a ten-year term of office; following this period there were chief officers of state called *archons*, one of whom was called a "king-archon," which title remained to the days of the democracy. Another was the *polemarch*, leader in war. The legislative and judicial body of the state became the Areopagus,[6] and though in these early times an assembly had a shadowy kind

---

[6] The Areopagus, a body made up of aristocrats and the wealthy, was all-powerful, and from its ranks all the magistrates of the state were chosen; the poor farmer was unrepresented and at the mercy of his superiors and creditors, who had the monopoly of the police power of the state. And there must have seemed no chance of improvement, for the land could not be made to produce enough for himself and his insatiable oppressors.

of existence it does not seem to have had much power. Only the nobles, heads of the traditional clans, were eligible to election for office. The next stage was the taking into political partnership of the more wealthy landowners, and a property qualification was substituted for the sole qualification of birth. The law was administered arbitrarily, the large landowners were squeezing out the small farmers, and economic depression was rife. In the absence of colonies the small farmers unable to make their living on the poor soil of Attica were becoming tenants and sharecroppers. They fell heavily into debt; unable to pay the debts, they sold themselves into slavery. Then, as slaves, these former freemen and citizens were kept on the same land which had once been theirs, or were even sold abroad.

The reforms of Solon

About 621 B.C. one of the causes of discontent was attacked when the nobles gave authority to a certain Draco to codify the law. The law he published was extremely severe (Draconian), but at least it was some check on the old blood-feud method of settling murder cases, and was the foundation of Athenian law. Distinction was made between voluntary and involuntary homicides. But none of the other important grievances was settled.

It was at this point that most Greek states, unable to work their way out of their troubles, allowed the situation to degenerate into bloody revolution. But in Athens the aristocrats and wealthier merchants who formed the powerful class in the state realized that something constructive must be done. So they called upon Solon, a merchant and much-traveled man, a poet who had written fiery attacks on greed and injustice and who was noted as a wise man. They elected him as archon in 594 B.C. with full powers to reorganize the state in any way he saw fit.

Solon was a remarkable statesman. He saw the close connection between the economic and social discontent, and set Athens on the path to curing both. Hitherto the Athenians had tried to make a living growing grain in the unsuitable soil of Attica; they had even exported grain for cash, though the price they obtained could hardly cover the cost of producing it. This was the basic reason why so many of the peasants had fallen into debt, why the large landlords had swallowed up the small ones. Unable to make a living on the land, they had been forced to borrow first on the security of their farms and then of their persons. Solon now realized that it was not only "greed and injustice." He at once prohibited enslavement for debt, but accompanied this with a prohibition of the export of grain. He brought back those who had been sold as slaves abroad and annulled all debts for which the security was either the land itself or the person of the borrower. He did not redistribute the land as the more radical reformers were demanding. While he dissuaded farmers from growing grain as unsuitable for Attic soil, his experience told him that the olive and vine could be cultivated successfully and required less space; and that the products themselves were more profitable. On the other hand, the specialized agriculture would release more men from the land, who would then, in company with the newly freed slaves and the farmers who could not make a living, need an alternative occupation. The production of wine and oil required containers, giving work to the potters, but not enough. There must be a large-scale expansion of industry, and foreign markets must be secured. So Solon promised Athenian citizenship to skilled foreign craftsmen if they would settle in Athens, and he decreed that every father must teach his son a trade. Finally he adopted or stimulated the use of the best coinage available in Greece at that time.

The economic reform of Solon therefore was designed to solve the agricultural problem and build up the city at the same time. Dispossessed farmers, or farmers who could no longer make a living because fewer men were needed for the new crops, could go to the city to learn a trade, and craftsmen were to be found who could teach them.

Slaves freed by their masters need not return to the country, but could become craftsmen in the city. And the traders would have more goods to sell and more incentive to seek foreign markets. Only the landed aristocracy might suffer, deprived of the easy sale of wheat, wrested from a starving peasantry; and even these might sometime hope to make profits from wine and olives. If they cared to, they, too, could become merchants and traders. That many of them did not become reconciled to Solon's "New Deal" is shown by the forcible ejection of large numbers of them from their land in the time of Pisistratus, as we shall see.

Though such reforms could not bear fruit at once, and few were immediately satisfied, they laid the basis for all later Athenian prosperity.

Having dealt with the economic problem Solon turned to the political. The new industrial and commercial class required political rights; and all the citizens needed a new status, and some sense of participation in the life of the community. The old Assembly was therefore put on a new basis, and apparently became a full legislature. Every male citizen, of whatever class in society, was entitled to sit in this Assembly. The archons, on the other hand, the executive of the state, retained their high property qualifications. But they were now to be elected indirectly by all the people. Each of the four traditional tribes elected ten eligible citizens, and out of these forty, nine were elected by lot as archons. The old Areopagus, which was recruited from former archons, was kept intact, but some of its legislative powers

Each of these three amphorae is from a different century. The one on the left is from the seventh century B.C. and is a product of inferior technique; also, note that the decoration still shows some Oriental influence. The center amphora is from the great age of Pisistratus when Athens was striving hard against severe competition in the export market. The amphora on the right is from the age of Pericles when Athens was secure and prosperous and these amphorae were often used for the home market; note the ornateness of this amphora. (COURTESY THE METROPOLITAN MUSEUM OF ART)

were taken away from it by the formation of a new Council, the *Boule* of four hundred chosen by lot from an eligible list elected also by the tribes. The poorest classes of the city were not as yet, however, eligible for the Boule. The chief business of the Boule was to prepare legislation for the Assembly.

Finally Solon introduced the popular law court, the *Heliaea*, which was a large body elected by the whole people to act as a court of appeal from the decisions of the magistrates. It could also try former magistrates for their activities while in office. Since this typical Athenian institution was naturally not used during the regime of the tyrants who followed Solon, it will be discussed more fully in its later form as revived by Cleisthenes.

The age of Tyrants—Pisistratus— Economic advance

Having produced this constitution, Solon then went into voluntary exile from Athens to see how the state would function without him. It soon became evident that this moderately democratic constitution had one serious defect, apart from the time required to put it in full operation with any chance of success. The tribal system of election was a relic of old clan days, and the tribal leaders were sure of election. Moreover, they were situated in definite geographical areas. Thus party politics based on economic interests were possible and to be expected. Two old clan leaders, both nobles, organized groups known as the Shore and the Plain, presumably the traders and the landowners. They then proceeded to engage in a political and family struggle, making government in Athens for a time impossible. A third noble, Pisistratus, then organized a new party of his own from the rural groups, which he called the Mountain; and with this he bid for the support of the Shore. By a number of ingenious devices he succeeded after several abortive attempts at making his political machine supreme and establishing himself in supreme power in Athens with the solid support of the Mountain and the Shore.

His first task was to silence opposition from the Plain. He did not try to liquidate his opponents, but he took hostages, and imprisoned and exiled others. Then he settled down to constructive work. His rule raised Athens to prosperity and laid the economic basis for the later political freedom; moreover he was careful also to behave in a scrupulously correct manner toward his fellow citizens, observe the laws, and keep to such forms of the constitution as could be permitted; and he died in his bed. The Greek word "tyrant" merely means one-man illegitimate rule, as distinct from a hereditary monarchy. It was the misrule of Pisistratus' son, not his own, that gave the word its later meaning which we have inherited.

Having disposed of the largest landowners, Pisistratus divided their lands among the landless and the small holders, stocking them with vines and olives with the aid of

Terra-cotta oil flask, recently discovered in Athens, in the shape of an athlete with much of the original paint preserved. The flask gives a good impression of how the Greeks looked in the age of Pisistratus. (COURTESY AMERICAN SCHOOL OF CLASSICAL STUDIES AT ATHENS)

funds obtained from new mines which he worked, and from a small income tax on the rich. By these means he satisfied most of his friends of the Mountain. The remainder he set to work on the first great beautification of Athens, with a huge temple of Olympian Zeus which was not finished until the time of the Roman Emperor Hadrian. Among other public works, he gave Athens a new water supply by building a new aqueduct. He patronized the drama, and supported its development into a popular spectacle with annual contests in tragedy.

For his friends of the Shore Pisistratus built a strong navy, entered into foreign commercial alliances, and sent out a few colonies to important strategic points. He maintained a policy of peace and alliance with the Peloponnesian League. Athens prospered under his rule, and fully recovered from her hesitant start. By the time of his death Athens was the recognized leader of the Ionian peoples, and one of the greatest—if not the greatest—polis in Greece.

The Constitution of Cleisthenes— Establishment of political democracy

Pisistratus was succeeded by his two sons, who for a time continued his policies. But when one was murdered in a private quarrel, the other, Hippias, hired mercenary troops, paid for them by levying high taxes, and became a tyrant in the modern sense. It was not long before a group of exiled nobles was able to enlist enough outside support, including Sparta, to overthrow him. But when these nobles attempted with Spartan help to establish an oligarchy and regain their old aristocratic privileges they were met with determined resistance from the Athenians. One of the noble leaders, Cleisthenes, turned against his fellow nobles and supported the people. The Spartan soldiers were expelled, and after some delay decided not to contest the issue further. So Cleisthenes was left supreme, supported by virtually the whole Athenian people. It was a magnificent opportunity for constructive statesmanship, and he grasped it to the full. The constitution of Cleisthenes remained the

fundamental constitution of the Athenians; and though it was modified in a few relatively unimportant points later, it survived all stresses for the rest of the period of Athenian independence.

What was primarily needed now was political reform, for the economic base had been securely laid by Pisistratus. The tribal jealousies and the possibility of political manipulation had to be overcome. Though the reform of Cleisthenes looks too ingenious to work, it was made to work by the public spirit of the Athenians and their desire to make it work. The finished system could be abused, and was greatly abused later. But in theory and practice it was probably the most democratic constitution ever devised and put into effect (if one disregards those who, like the women, the noncitizens, and the slaves, were always disfranchised). Its abuse is a commentary upon human nature in the difficult circumstances of later years rather than upon the constitution itself.

The four tribes were replaced by ten new ones, each with a mythical ancestor as patron. But not all the tribes were geographically next to each other any more. Each was made up of about ten *demes* (townships or parishes), a third of these coming from the Mountain, a third from the Plain, and a third from the Shore. The deme was the real local unit. Each would-be citizen and boy growing up to manhood would have his credentials examined by the demesmen, and they would probably know enough about the candidate to handle his application. But it was the tribe, that apparently theoretical organization with a fictitious ancestor and no fixed abode, that voted in the Assembly. The members of the tribe, which was composed of its widely scattered demes, would have to sit together in the Assembly.

The purpose of this reform was probably almost as much social as political. Citizens from different areas would learn to know each other, and they were united by their common aims and common citizenship in the Athenian polis. Moreover, the Athenians also now fought by tribes, and dramatic and other contests went by tribes. In spite of their artificiality, rivalry sprang up between them. Indeed the comparison with army regiments is a very accurate one. Regiments in modern wars contain members from every part of the country. Yet rivalry springs up between them and, with rivalry, loyalty.

The next step for Cleisthenes was to restore to full power the Assembly, the Council, and the law courts of Solon, and reform them to meet the new conditions.

The Boule was to be chosen by lot, fifty members of each tribe. It is not agreed whether this meant complete reliance upon the chance of the lot, as there is some evidence to suggest that the demes provided an eligible list to the tribes. But probably this only means that the eligible list contained the names of all who could be elected. Though we know of exceptions, ordinarily citizens did not sit in the Boule more than once in their lives, so that many each year would be ineligible. In practice, in any case, the result was that a considerable majority of all the citizens actually sat in the Boule during their lifetime. The Boule of five hundred was considered to be too large to transact business efficiently. So a committee, composed of all the fifty members of one tribal delegation (a *prytany*) did the work for one tenth of the year each. Every day a new chairman of the prytany was chosen by lot to be president of the Assembly and titular head of the state for that day. This means that thirty-six out of every fifty tribal delegates would be president of the polis for one day apiece in their lifetimes.

The Boule took care of all administrative matters, looking after shipping, foreign affairs, finance, and public works, and prepared legislation for the Assembly. Individual members would be chosen by lot from the Boule to occupy all the public positions in the state, with a few exceptions. These officers of the state, however, could be excluded from their position before entering on it by action taken against them in the law courts; they had to submit to examination in the law courts after leaving it; and all their accounts had to be audited before they could leave Athens or sell property.

The Assembly (*Ecclesia*) was the sovereign legislature. It could initiate legislation, but it did not often do so. It met at least once every prytany (later four times), and could be called specially by the Boule in matters of urgency. Though the chairman of the Boule for the day presided, anyone could speak, anyone could make a proposal, and the measure was decided upon by majority vote. The citizens, however, had to be present in person to vote.

The only control over the people was exercised by the *Heliaea*, or law court. Six thousand members were chosen by the demes each year, and of these the number required for the juries was chosen by lot as occasion demanded. The juries were very large, sometimes as many as 1001, and apparently never less than 101. In these courts the acts of magistrates and their characters were reviewed, private and public cases of all kinds were tried, and in later times even a law could be tried, and sustained or quashed, in spite of the fact that the Assembly had voted for it. There was no public prosecutor, and of course there could be no higher appeal than that to the sovereign people. Anyone was permitted to bring a case against anyone else, whether he was the aggrieved party or not; but he risked both losing his case and then being punished himself by the vote of the jury. There were no lawyers, and the parties to the case had to plead personally; though professional speech writers were available, the pleader had to learn his speech by heart and speak it himself. Since his case was decided by majority vote, and the jury decided both on the guilt of the accused and on the penalty to be imposed, much depended on the ability of the speaker to convince by his oratory. However unfair, this system is in full accord with the theory that the whole polis had the right to rule, and had the last word on everything in the state.

Two further innovations were introduced either by Cleisthenes or a successor. A board of *strategi*, or generals, came into existence; they were the official chief magistrates of the state, but their primary purpose was to take command of the army and navy.

Since these offices required special competence, appointment for them was not decided by lot but by election. The office, furthermore, though annual, could be held by the outgoing general. And indeed it became customary for the generals to be re-elected. No general, however, had the right to command the army or navy in any particular campaign. The Assembly made the decision on the military leader when the time came, but as a rule the command fell to the leading general. Pericles held the position of general for over thirty years, and during this time he was able by his personal control of the Assembly and this position to rule the Athenians almost as he liked. But at any time in the annual elections he could have been ousted, as indeed he was for a brief period at the beginning of the Peloponnesian War.

The other innovation was ostracism, a clumsy device to prevent any man from becoming too powerful and possibly becoming tyrant. Once a year the Assembly might hold a referendum to see whether any citizen should be sent into an honorable exile for ten years. No specific name was mentioned; and any citizen's name could be written on a potsherd, or *ostrakon*, by the voters. If any person or persons received more than six thousand such votes he had to go into exile, with no further penalty attached. The last ostracism occurred during the Peloponnesian War, when it was in fact used as a piece of political maneuvering. It was evidently clear to the Athenian people by this time that it was an ineffective weapon for the purpose for which it was intended, and it fell into disuse. Moreover, the people were so thoroughly accustomed to the rule of law by then that a tyrant could hardly be expected to be able to get into power by political manipulation. Far more effective weapons were now available to serve the same ends.

Characteristics of Periclean democracy

When Cleisthenes had finished his work, the democracy was still not quite complete. The Areopagus retained some power, and the archons who entered the Areopagus after

their year of office were still elected with minor property qualifications. They had some important duties to perform, especially the supervision of the law courts and the festivals. But it was in the hands of the Assembly to deprive them of these duties at its pleasure. In the years after the Persian Wars when the democracy was riding the crest of its success, the Areopagus was stripped of all powers except the right to try homicide cases, which were essentially religious offenses to the Greeks; the archonship, moreover, was opened to all but the poorest class in the state and election was by lot. Jurymen were now for the first time paid for their services, so that all citizens were equally able to serve on the juries if elected by their demesmen. Payment for attendance at the Assembly, however, was not instituted until some years after the death of Pericles. Everyone was, of course, eligible to attend and was expected to do so. But when the number of meetings was increased to between 30 and 40 a year, not including special sessions, attendance required a considerable expenditure of time. It seemed only fair to later Athenians to compensate the citizen for attendance.

Unfortunately for the democracy this well-intended reform meant that those to whom the small pay was attractive attended regularly, while busier persons with greater means often stayed away. The regulars included not only retired farmers and others unable to work, but also the city proletariat who knocked off work for the day when the Assembly was sitting. This group of unemployed and low-paid workers in time came to dominate the Assembly, especially during and after the Peloponnesian War, ensuring some class legislation and exploitation of the propertied classes. Moreover, all the evidence would seem to show that the Assembly took an excessive interest in policies which could be made the basis of emotional appeals, such as imperialistic adventures. The philosophers and conservatives alike regarded the Assembly's susceptibility to emotional appeals as a radical defect in democracy itself. However, during the regime of Pericles, the masses were willing to follow

Ostraka, or ballots, used for ostracism in Athens in the fifth century B.C. Note the names of prominent Athenian statesmen written on them: Kimon, Themistokles, (A)risteid(es), Perikles, Miltiades. (COURTESY AMERICAN SCHOOL OF CLASSICAL STUDIES AT ATHENS)

him—but then, as well as being an enlightened statesman, he was also an imperialist; and his empire paid handsomely.

The last feature worthy of mention in this account of the Athenian constitution was the writ of illegality (*graphe paranomon*), an effective device that was destined to take the place of ostracism. As suggested earlier, the Athenian did not regard his fundamental laws as alterable for any temporary reasons of expediency. His respect for law was too great, for the laws of a polis were the expression of its ideals. Anyone who proposed a law could be attacked in the courts for proposing an unconstitutional law. If he were acquitted, the law was passed; if not, the proposer was fined or otherwise punished according to the will of the jury. This procedure not only effectively discouraged rash innovators but gave the people a chance to think again, since the law could not be put into execution until the case had been decided. It should be understood that there was no definite criterion as to whether the law was really unconstitutional or not, though the proposer would also try to produce evidence that it was not contrary to previous laws and customs. Such evidence would be weighed by the jury together with all other considerations and the verdict rendered accordingly; the device therefore amounted substantially to a judicial review and a trial of the law itself.

The details of the constitution of the Athenians have been gone into at such length because this was the system under which Athens in the great "Classical Age" of Pericles lived, and the system survived for several hundred years. Even under the Macedonians the Athenians still kept substantial self-government though the franchise was restricted. During the Classical Age all the great Athenian masterpieces of art and literature were produced. Such a constitution would be unthinkable in the modern world; indeed, except in the special circumstances of the polis it could not succeed at any time. In spite of its defects even in Athens—and there were many, especially during the Peloponnesian War and in the fourth century B.C.— its many virtues probably outweighed them.

The constitution was predicated upon the belief that every citizen both wished to take, and was capable of taking, an active part in political life, that the judgment of one citizen was as likely to be right as that of another, that nearly all offices of state could be administered as easily by one citizen as another. It gave no consideration to the specialist—and indeed the Athenian ideal was of the gifted and versatile amateur rather than the specialist, as being nearer to the whole man. At least a majority of the citizens under this system held administrative office in the Boule at some time in their lives. It has been estimated that at any given time at least one sixth of the citizen body was engaged in public activity of some kind, either in the Boule, in the juries, or in one of the numerous minor administrative positions in the state—apart from the Assemblies, where all citizens were expected to be present. This political activity was the real breath of life to the Athenian citizen; it was something that suited his temperament, with his love of talk and social intercourse. And this explains his extreme attachment to the form of the polis, and why no other kind of state was thinkable for a freeman, as Aristotle understood. It also explains why the polis could not absorb other poleis, and why no representative system could be developed, as this would rob the citizen of what he valued most.

It made for strength under adversity, as a general rule. Though the Assembly might be subject to occasional emotional sprees every man in it knew that his decisions in the Assembly would affect him personally. There was no idea of "they" and "we" about his attitude toward the government. Time after time in the hard years of war we see Athens recovering from a defeat, even after the disastrous Syracusan expedition—though on this occasion there was a brief period of fear and a brief suspension of full democracy. Almost miraculously she then produced a fleet and citizen sailors to man it, aristocrats and slaves rowing together. Even in the decadent fourth century B.C., when Athenian fighting was mostly done through mercenaries, the eloquence of Demosthenes, his strong sense of patriotism, and the democratic tradition of responsibility were able to recall the Assembly to its duty, and create a citizen army. Though the errors of judgment of the period were enormous, and Athenian power had dwindled, the soul of the city remained. It took defeats by Philip, Alexander, and Antigonus Doson to quell the democratic spirit; and even then it died slowly, and never altogether until the coming of the Romans.

The usual criticism of the Athenian democracy—that it rested on foundations of slavery—is based upon a misunderstanding, as is also the second line of attack—that women were disfranchised. The theory of the Greek polis was that it was an enlarged family, an association of kinsmen. A Greek slave could therefore ultimately hope to be freed and become a citizen, while a barbarian slave—in the Greek view—could never understand the working of a polis. If the latter were freed, he must remain an alien. The slave could not exercise the functions of a citizen until he had been freed and educated. If slavery had been abolished, in spite of the economic conditions that bred it, then political rights for the Greek freedmen would have followed as a matter of course. Slavery cannot therefore be regarded as a blot on Greek democracy as a political ideal, whatever we may think of slavery as an economic and social evil. *Metics*, or resident aliens, could win full citizenship on occasion, but to do so was difficult. As foreigners they were not expected to understand the concept of the polis as an enlarged family until they had been resident in it for a considerable time. They had rights, but they could not perform the duties of a citizen without understanding very fully the relationship of these duties to the whole ideal of the polis. The enfranchisement of women was, of course, unknown in the Greek world, though we can infer from the fact that Aristophanes devoted a whole play to a lampoon on women in government (*Ecclesiazusae*) that it was an issue of some interest to the citizens. The position of women in Athens will be discussed later. Here it need only be said that the duties of men and women were rigorously circumscribed. If the status of women had been different, the logic of the situation would have demanded that they be given a vote; but it was their social status that determined their political position. It would have been quite alien to Greek political conceptions that the vote should be, or could be, used to improve social status, as in our own age.

It is fortunate that the entire ideal of the Athenian polis and political life can be inferred from the institutional evidence without touching what is perhaps the most eloquent expression of a political ideal ever made—the Funeral Speech put into the mouth of Pericles by Thucydides. In this speech in honor of the citizen soldiers who have been killed in the first year of the Peloponnesian War, Pericles, instead of praising the dead as was the custom, praises the ideal for which they have died. So his speech becomes a panegyric of the Athenian polis. An Athenian citizen, he says, "does not neglect the state because he takes care of his own household; and even those of us who are engaged in business have a very fair idea of politics. We alone regard a man who takes no interest in public affairs, not as a harmless, but as a useless character; and if few of us are originators, we are all sound judges of policy. . . . When a citizen is in any way distinguished, he is preferred to the public service, not as a matter of privilege, but as the reward of merit. Neither is poverty a bar, but a man may benefit his country whatever be the obscurity of his condition."[7]

It is impossible to deny that these virtues are to be found in the developed Athenian constitution. Within all Greek states there were oligarchic and democratic factions, even in Athens; though in the days of her greatness the aristocrats, on the whole, supported the democracy, and one of its most outstanding members led it. During the Peloponnesian War the oligarchs twice came to power briefly, as we shall see; but only because the democracy had discredited itself through failure in the war. There was always a natural antagonism between the cities with democracies and those with oligarchies, the latter tending to concentrate in the Peloponnesus. The other cities and colonies usually had their parties fairly equally balanced. The result was frequent revolutions, with the oligarchies appealing to Sparta and the democracies to Athens, for help, which was usually given. This situation accounts partly for the divisions and antagonisms between the cities. Trade and other rivalries also caused local wars. Spartan fears of encirclement and Athenian imperialist policies in the fifth century also made for dissension, and local, followed by general, war. There is hardly any period when the Greek cities, each claiming and maintaining full freedom of action on foreign policy, were not engaged in some hostilities against other cities. These intercity rivalries and quarrels are a sad commentary on the Greek political systems which gave rise to them, but they do not compel us to say that the form of government was a failure when it obviously had so many merits in the eyes of its own citizens, enabling them to manage its internal affairs with such marked success. The national state also has not so far succeeded in abolishing wars.

▶ **Intercity relations**

UNIFYING FORCES IN GREEK LIFE—THE
RELIGIOUS LEAGUES AND FESTIVALS

But there were also unifying forces in Greek life. All Greeks looked with contempt upon barbarian kingdoms as unfit for free men, and, as we shall soon see, some unity of purpose was achieved against the attacks of Persian "barbarians." There were several all-Greek festivals, the best known of which were the Olympic games. Here Greeks forgot

[7] Thucydides, II, 39 ff.

they were citizens of different poleis, and sat together in amity. Though each city had its patron god or goddess, the great gods were gods of all the Greeks equally, as were the Orphic and other mysteries. The great oracle of Apollo at Delphi in Phocis was a neutral, giving advice impartially to all comers, protected by its sacred position, with even its treasure safe until the late fourth century B.C. Though the Delphic Oracle was in Phocian territory, a league called the Delphic Amphictyony made up of the different states and tribes of Greece was responsible for its protection, and a kind of international law prevailed, neutralizing the sanctuary in the event of war. Even this Amphictyonic League, however, was later manipulated for political purposes, especially by the non-Greek Philip of Macedon. Another league of Ionians protected the sanctuary of Apollo at Delos. On the whole, the political leagues accentuated the division between the states rather than helped to unite them. The great political failure of the Greeks was unquestionably in interstate relations, and it was not until more than a century after the conquests of Macedonia that there appeared any serious likelihood of unification brought about by the free efforts of Greeks themselves.

UNITY IN FACE OF EXTERNAL DANGER—
THE PERSIAN WARS

The only occasion in classical times that a majority of Greeks made an important united effort was in the early fifth century against the Persians.

The campaign of Marathon

The struggle began with the revolt of the Ionian cities of Asia Minor against Persian expansion under Darius the Great. Darius and his Persians had already expanded into Europe and conquered Thrace, and suppressed some of the liberties of the Ionian cities conquered from Lydia by Cyrus.[8] The moment for the revolt was badly timed. Though the war lasted a long time, Darius at last was able to bring his superior forces to bear, especially the Phoenician

[8] See above, Chapter 4.

navy, and defeat the cities. He destroyed the ringleader Miletus; but the remainder he treated leniently, even allowing them to have democratic governments if they desired them. But he did not forget that the Athenians and Euboeans had sent a small expedition to help their Ionian kinsmen. The expedition had returned home after aiding in the destruction of the local Persian capital, Sardis; but, according to Herodotus, the historian of the Persian Wars, Darius cherished thoughts of revenge. Urged on by Hippias, the exiled tyrant of Athens who was at his court, Darius prepared an expedition against Athens and Euboea, and sent heralds to other Greek cities demanding submission. Several, including Thebes, sent the token earth and water to the Persian king.

In 490 B.C. the expedition set sail for Athens across the Aegean Sea, under the command of the generals Datis and Artaphernes. After chastising the Euboeans the Persians anchored in the Bay of Marathon, only a few miles to the northeast of Athens, intending to land troops and march directly to the city. Few preparations had been made to meet the Persians, though the young Athenian democracy had a well-trained citizen infantry under the polemarch Callimachus, with an experienced general, Miltiades, a hater of Persia, as strategic adviser. When they heard of the landing at Marathon, and apparently not before, the Athenians sent a runner to Sparta requesting aid, which was duly promised. Unfortunately, however, the omens in Sparta were not favorable and the army was not sent immediately. The result was that Athens had to face the Persian host with the aid only of fewer than a thousand men from the neighboring city of Plataea. The total army facing the Persians was at the most ten thousand; and the Athenians might not have even engaged in battle if they had not thought that Spartan help would soon arrive.

However, the Persians were so sure of victory that they did not trouble to throw in their whole force. It has also been suggested that the account given by Herodotus can be explained only on the assumption that the Persians were awaiting a signal from traitors in Athens sympathetic to the exiled Hippias. However this may be, it seems that the Persian fleet with a large part of the army watched the battle without taking part in it, prepared at the first sign of victory to make for Athens by sea. Nevertheless, the Athenians, assisted by superior knowledge of the terrain, and superior tactics, inflicted an overwhelming defeat on the Persians; then, immediately the battle was over, without waiting to bury the dead, they returned to Athens and marched straight through to Piraeus, the port of the city, a few miles to the southwest. They arrived just as the Persian fleet made its appearance, and the latter, not anxious to engage the victors of Marathon in battle so soon after their own defeat, returned to Persia. Darius died soon afterward, and the Greeks had a breathing space of ten years before Xerxes, his son, could prepare a really formidable expedition, this time not only to punish Athens but to conquer the whole of Greece.

The interval was marked in Athens by the rise to power of Themistocles, who realized the extent of the danger and the only way to combat it. He persuaded the Assembly to use the profits of a new silver mine for the expansion of the navy. Thus, when the Persians struck, Athens had an efficient, well-trained navy, which was to prove one of the decisive factors in the war.

The full-scale invasion of Xerxes

In 480 B.C., Xerxes, at the head of a huge, motley army, and accompanied by a navy, partly Phoenician in origin, which hugged the coast ready to lend support, marched through Thrace to the borders of Greece. Sparta, for once taking the initiative, called a congress to consider a joint defense. Thebes followed her previous policy of immediate submission to the Persians (called "Medizing" by the Greeks), other cities wavered, and ultimately submitted when the Persians approached. Nevertheless this congress at Sparta was attended by delegates from almost all the major cities of Greece, an impressive demonstration of unity never again duplicated. The results, however, were not equally impressive. In view

of her naval commitments, Athens found it impossible to spare men to help defend the passes into Greece. Ultimately only three hundred Spartiates with some auxiliary helots, and several more or less unwilling allies, marched to Thermopylae under the leadership of Leonidas, king of Sparta. This army nevertheless withstood the Persians for several days until a traitor revealed a side path which was inadequately guarded. Sending most of the allies home, the Spartiates fought to the last man[9] in one of the most famous and heroic defenses of history. The army of Xerxes poured through the pass, the Spartans and the Peloponnesian League proceeded to build a wall across the Isthmus of Corinth, and Themistocles and the Athenians prepared to evacuate Athens and Attica and take to the ships. The army of Xerxes entered Athens, sacked and looted it, and burned the temples.

The navy, meanwhile, under the command of Athens but not manned entirely by Athenians, was having trouble in arriving at a decision. The allies wanted to retire to the Peloponnesus, as did the Spartans. But Themistocles threatened to take the Athenian part of the fleet and sail to the west and found a new colony. This sobered the Spartans and the allies, and Themistocles was reluctantly given permission to engage in naval battle with the Persians at once. Baiting a trap with a supposed traitor who succeeded in deceiving Xerxes, he lured the Persians into the narrows of Salamis, where the Greek fleet won a resounding victory. Xerxes returned home, leaving Mardonius, his brother-in-law, to carry on the campaign. He retired north for the winter, but again advanced on Attica in the spring. Athens appealed frantically for help to the Spartans, who were now safely holed up in the Peloponnesus; and after much delay the Greeks decided to take the offensive north of the Peloponnesus. At last a really representative allied army brought the army of Mardonius to battle on fairly equal terms.

---

[9] According to Herodotus, one man alone escaped, who was held by the Spartans in such infamy that he sacrificed his life in ostentatious deeds of valor later at Plataea.

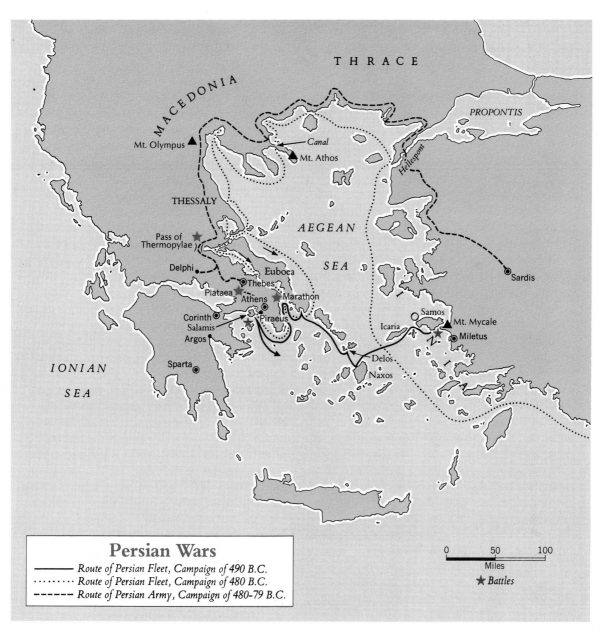

Persian Wars

—————— *Route of Persian Fleet, Campaign of 490 B.C.*
················· *Route of Persian Fleet, Campaign of 480 B.C.*
- - - - - - *Route of Persian Army, Campaign of 480-79 B.C.*

0   50   100
Miles

★ *Battles*

The discipline and valor of the Spartan hoplites won the battle of Plataea (479 B.C.) and Mardonius and almost the whole of his army were killed. This was the decisive battle. The allied fleet won, traditionally on the same day, the final victory of the war at Mycale, off the coast of Ionia, and the Ionian cities were freed.

The Persian Wars revealed, as usual, the prevalence of local jealousies and the extreme difficulty of obtaining any kind of unity, even in the face of the overwhelming threat of submersion within a barbarian empire and the loss of all Greek liberties; nev-

ertheless, by the end of 479 B.C. there had been an impressive cooperation and a unified command. Although more than half of it was Athenian, the allied navy had submitted to the control of a Spartan admiral, and won the final victory under his leadership. But no one in Greece after Mycale would have dared to prophesy a permanent unification of all the city-states for any purpose; and indeed, as far as we know, not one man ever thought of such a thing. The nature of the polis, as we have seen, precluded any more effective arrangement than glorified leagues; the kingdom or empire was universally regarded as a barbarian form of government. The Spartans were only anxious to go home; they had done their duty and had won their glory, but more pressing needs were now paramount.

THE CONFEDERATION OF DELOS—ATHENIAN IMPERIALISM

In general all the other mainland city-states except Athens were of the same opinion; but the Ionian cities of Asia Minor, just freed from Persian rule, and the islands of the Aegean did not feel themselves so secure. All Greeks knew that an expedition of the type manned by Xerxes was impossible for years to come, and in any case could probably be beaten off by improvisation as before. But it was not too difficult for Persia, with its immense financial resources and the seamen of Phoenicia at its disposal, to put together a fleet which could do severe damage in the Aegean. So when the Athenians proposed to keep the maritime part of the recent league in being, the islands were willing. The guiding spirit behind the naval policy was undoubtedly Themistocles, the hero of Salamis. He alone among the statesmen of Greece had a clear vision of the future and prepared for it, converting the Athenian democracy in the years after the wars to the understanding that its future lay on the sea. But the league itself was organized by Aristides the Just, a more trustworthy person, with a reputation for incorruptibility which was accepted by the cities of the new league.

So came into being the Confederation of Delos under the leadership of Athens. The purpose and constitution of this league were admirable in theory; but one clause was capable of abuse, and led the way to Athenian domination and empire. In any case Athens was always the dominant power, and could have made the league an empire, with or without the legal rights on her side. But the league itself would probably never have come into being in this dangerous form had the allies not trusted Aristides, who made the naval and financial assessments for each member. The Confederation was more than the offensive and defensive alliance of the Peloponnesian League; it was a full collective security program backed by a joint navy, and under the protection and sanction of the god Apollo. Those members who were wealthy enough to provide ships could do so; the remainder could contribute money proportionate to their means. The money was to be deposited in Delos, a small island sacred to Apollo, and at Delos was to be held every year a congress, in which each state would be equal, each having one vote. Athens guaranteed the independence of each member, including its foreign policy, and freedom to rule itself under whatever form of government it wished. But, no state could withdraw without the consent of all.[10]

The form of this constitution is, of course, democratic enough. But in substance the Athenian veto on withdrawal and the right of the Athenians to make the assessments, combined with her command of the allied navy, gave her a power too great to be opposed by anything except the alliance of all the members together; and this was impossible. In any case most of the members profited by the alliance, and their trade and wealth increased; and they could hope, each individually, that they would not incur the displeasure of Athens nor have their taxes increased. As time went on, almost all the members found it more convenient to pay money instead of providing ships; and this, too, played into the hands of Athens, since the ships bought with the money were built by the Athenians and commanded and manned by them.

In 467 B.C. the Persian navy ventured into Aegean waters and was soundly defeated by the confederation at the battle of the Eurymedon. Thereafter the Aegean became a Greek lake. And though the fleet was used in other imperialist ventures by Pericles later, the real danger was over. It was therefore not unnatural that some of the members should seek to withdraw. The Athenian democracy under all its leaders set itself against this trend with stubbornness and determination, and never in any circum-

---

[10] An instructive modern parallel is the 1834 *Zollverein* of German states under the leadership of Prussia, which emerged as the German Empire.

Bust of Pericles, the Athenian statesman. (COURTESY BRITISH MUSEUM)

stances gave its consent. When a member seceded, the joint navy, partly paid for by the seceding member, was used against it; and the state itself was regarded as rebellious. When the revolt was quelled it was made into a subject state and its taxes were increased. Finding that the revolts were usually the work of oligarchs, the Athenians then insisted upon having democratic governments throughout the Confederation, contrary to their original undertakings when this league was founded. This insistence, however, did not always have the intended results. The members began to realize that Athens was not the lover of liberty in others that she pretended to be; and gradually it came to be said that she was "the enslaver of Greek liberties." However, revolts were few and sporadic until the Peloponnesian War, and on the whole the cities were probably content. Even when the treasure of the Confederation was removed from Delos to Athens in 454 B.C. by Pericles, a specious excuse was made, and it was not Athens herself who proposed it. But the Confederation had clearly become an empire; and Pericles and the Athenians were thoroughly aware of the fact, and prepared to exploit it to the full.

THE PELOPONNESIAN WAR

Though Pericles was a high-minded statesman, and a true democrat as far as his own polis was concerned, his foreign policy was that of a confirmed imperialist. Moreover, his consistent anti-Spartan policy was bound to bring him into conflict with the greatest Greek land power and with the maritime cities in the northern Peloponnesus which found their trade slipping from them. When he tried to interfere in the Peloponnesian League itself, and force and cajole members away from that alliance, it was clear that he was aiming at a complete domination of Greece and that Sparta was indeed in danger. There were several clashes on land before the Spartans could be finally convinced by her allies that war was inevitable, and that she must really enter into it as wholeheartedly as the Corinthians and others who were directly threatened by Athenian aggression. But on the outbreak of full-scale war she sent her incomparable army directly against Attica.

The Athenians knew that it would be impossible to defeat the Spartans in open battle. But the city and harbor were now connected by the Long Walls, built by Themistocles; and as long as Athens maintained command of the sea she could not be starved out and no Greek army could breach the Long Walls until the fleet was conquered. But the policy of keeping all citizens within the Long Walls meant the loss of Attica, and it could not be expected that such a policy would prove popular. In the crowded conditions of the city plague broke out, and Pericles and his policy were briefly repudiated by the people. He failed to be re-elected as general, and peace was considered. However, the tide soon turned, since the people found they could not do without him, and he was given supreme powers to carry on the war as he saw fit. But he died a year later, and soon afterward the Assembly fell into the hands of Cleon, the villain of Thucydides' history, advocate of a strong policy toward the doubtful allies and the counteroffensive against Sparta on land.

Many of the details of this long war remain fascinating and still worthy of serious attention, especially for the light they cast on the workings of a popular democracy in wartime. They are recounted in the matchless pages of Thucydides, continued in a more pedestrian manner by Xenophon who undertook to finish his history, and commented on indirectly by the comic poet Aristophanes. When Cleon criticized the Athenian generals for their failure to win victories, one of them sarcastically suggested that maybe he could do better himself and offered to resign in Cleon's favor. The Assembly applauded the suggestion and at once appointed him. As Thucydides comments dourly, "sensible people" comforted themselves with the thought that they had nothing to lose. Either Cleon would be discredited or even killed, or he would win a victory over the Spartans. As it happened, Cleon chose an experienced general to accompany him and won an outstanding victory. Thereafter he became anxious for more commands, but his luck did not hold. He was killed, largely as the result of his own inexperience and foolhardiness; and since the leading Spartan general was killed in the same campaign, the peace party in Athens gained the ascendancy in the Assembly, and a peace was patched up (Peace of Nicias, 421 B.C.).

Though the peace was intended to last for fifty years, neither side was satisfied with it. A brilliant but unstable aristocrat, Alcibiades, now came to the fore in Athens, and both the Athenians and Spartans soon broke the treaty, thus renewing the war. In 415 Alcibiades proposed that an expedition be sent to Syracuse, a colony of Corinth in Sicily, a strategic concept that might have won the war outright for the Athenians, since they would have been in a position to blockade the Peloponnese. The Assembly, split by party factions, agreed to the plan, but appointed the peace-loving and cautious general Nicias, who had opposed the expedition, to share command with Alcibiades and with Lamachus, a professional soldier. Just before the expedition was due to sail, a sacrilege committed by vandals in Athens cast a superstitious gloom over the city.

Alcibiades' enemies blamed him, certainly without justification, but they did not press any charges until the expedition had arrived in Sicily. Then they brought up the case, and it was decided to recall him to stand trial. But Alcibiades, forewarned, escaped to Sparta, where he informed the Spartans of the Athenian plans for the war. Since Lamachus was soon killed, the sole command of the expedition devolved on the reluctant Nicias, who delayed his main attack until he had received reinforcements. These arrived too late to help, and the opportunity for a quick victory had passed. The Spartans sent out an experienced and intelligent general named Gylippus to take charge of the defense, and the expedition was utterly destroyed.

The Athenian conservatives took advantage of the discredit heaped upon the radical democrats for their failure, and engineered a coup which put a moderate oligarchy in power. The main body of the citizens lost their political rights, for decisions were made by the oligarchs, all of whom were property owners. But even they did not at first have any notion of accepting an unfavorable peace. The Athenian position had nevertheless been seriously weakened, and from this time onward the Persians assisted the Spartans with money and diplomatic support and several Athenian subject states seceded from the League. Alcibiades, who had now left Sparta and was angling for an invitation to return to Athens, also intrigued among the Persians to such good effect that the oligarchs decided he was indispensable, brought him home, and gave him a command. But they were soon overthrown by a democratic uprising when the news leaked out that they were trying to arrange a peace. The democrats, however, though they distrusted Alcibiades, did not dismiss him from his command, since he was proving to be a brilliant leader, winning a series of notable victories. But as soon as he failed in one campaign, a failure for which he does not appear to have been responsible, he felt it to be safer to go into exile, since he had too many enemies in Athens determined on his downfall. Several times during the years of

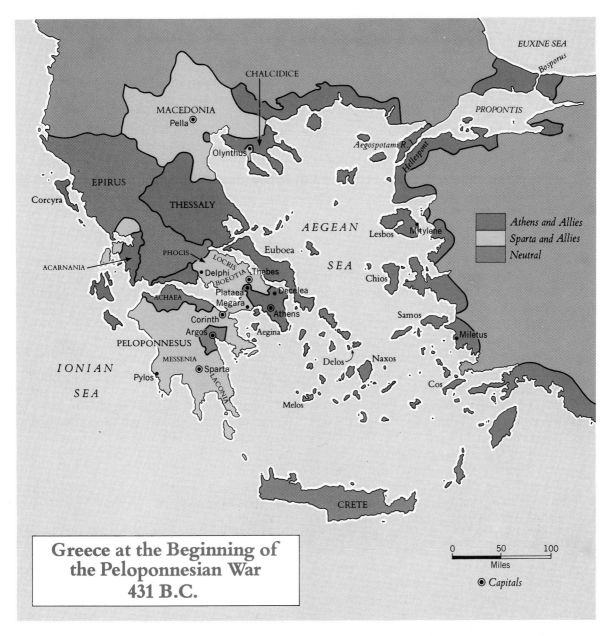

Greece at the Beginning of the Peloponnesian War 431 B.C.

0   50   100
Miles

◉ Capitals

Athens and Allies
Sparta and Allies
Neutral

Alcibiades' success the Spartans sued for peace on terms favorable to Athens, but all overtures were rejected by the Athenians, now led by Cleophon who was determined on outright victory.

In 406 the Athenians, with a fleet in which even slaves were enrolled, won the great naval battle of Arginusae, and the Spartans again sued for peace, which was again refused by Cleophon—the last time he was ever to have the chance. The Athenians following the victory were plunged into an internal crisis. The battle had been brought to an end by a sudden storm, during which the crews had been unable to pick up the wounded. The admirals had pursued the enemy, leaving instructions to subordinates to do what was necessary. But the latter, unable to do anything in the storm, were faced by an irate citizenry when they returned home and in turn proceeded to blame their superiors. In an emotional scene in the Assembly the admirals—or as many as had dared to return to Athens, including the son of Pericles—were condemned to death in an illegal trial, which Socrates, who happened to be its president for the day, had vainly tried to prevent. This suicidal judicial murder of their most experienced leaders sealed the fate of Athens. The inexperienced commanders whom the Assembly now appointed, refusing to listen to the advice of Alcibiades who emerged from his place of exile to give them warning, left the whole fleet exposed to destruction by the Spartan admiral Lysander, who took advantage of the opportunity unhesitatingly. The decisive battle of Aegospotami (405) cut the Athenians off from their grain supply, and the following year they were compelled to negotiate a peace, which amounted almost to total surrender. Cleophon was put on trial for his life, condemned, and executed.

The Spartan allies, Thebes and Corinth, wanted to raze the city, but the Spartans refused. Athenian services to all Hellas during the Persian Wars, they said, had been such that they could never be forgotten (a nasty and typically Spartan reminder to the Thebans of their disgrace in having "Medized"). The terms, however, were severe enough. The Long Walls were to be pulled down, Athens was to lose all her foreign possessions and to keep only twelve ships, and she was to submit to Sparta as a subject ally. Moreover, the democracy was to be replaced by an oligarchy, which afterward became known in Athenian history as the rule of the Thirty, and, in its last stages, the Ten, Tyrants.

These oligarchs, long unused to power, created a reign of terror, and maintained themselves only by the aid of Lysander and the Spartan army. A group of Athenian refugees won some local victories, and other small towns expelled their Spartan garrisons. Sparta, whose losses in the war were serious, realized that it would be either perpetual war or the restoration of the democracy. She chose to permit the latter, and Athens was free again. But she had yielded supremacy in Greece to Sparta, and, though she was able in due course to rebuild her navy, she never again became the leading power in Greece.

CORRUPTION AND DECLINE IN FOURTH-CENTURY
GREECE—HEGEMONY OF SPARTA AND THEBES

Fourth-century Greek history is a sordid tale of intrigues, first by Persia and then by Macedon, that effectively prevented Greek

unity, which in any case few in Greece were looking for. Spartan supremacy was marked by the excesses to be expected of a people only just released from isolation, and whose leaders could not be controlled by the ephors and their social system when beyond Spartan borders. As the price for Persian support Sparta allowed the Great King to take back the Ionian cities in Asia Minor, which remained subject to him till the expedition of Alexander; and he dictated a peace to Greece. His money, however, was spent in intrigues of all kinds. For a time he transferred it to Thebes, and Thebes became the leader in Greece, thanks also to the ability of two of the greatest generals in Greek history, who defeated Sparta decisively in the open field and freed the helots. But Thebes, too, lost Persian support, her generals were killed in battle, and leadership in Greece fell into the hands of the semibarbarian Macedonians. But the fall of all Greece to Philip of Macedon, and the expansion into Asia under Alexander will be left to a later chapter.

▶ The economic basis of Athenian imperialism

AGRICULTURE—COLONIZATION, CLERUCHIES

In the course of the preceding survey mention has been made where necessary of the economic foundations of Athenian society. Though the empire was not of as much benefit to the farmer as to the merchant and manufacturer, and though he was the first to be hit by the war, he must in general have supported the imperial policy of Pericles, or have been unable to vote against it through the requirement of Athenian democracy that he vote in person. Agriculture remained the foundation of Athenian life. There were probably as many small farmers in Attica as there were permanent inhabitants of the city.

The poverty of the soil and the small size of the farms always made living on the land difficult. Large farms were very rare; a farm of sixty-five acres in the fourth century was considered enormous. After the reforms of Solon little wheat was grown in

Attica. More than two thirds of the whole grain supply had to be imported, mostly from the Black Sea area; and 90 per cent of the grain grown in Attica was barley. Vines and olives remained the principal crop. Slavery on the farms was almost negligible. Few farmers could afford the price; and a slave had to eat and could not produce much more than his keep in return for his labor. But though life on the farms was hard, it at least assured economic independence and prevented the working for wages, which was disliked by all Greeks except in the service of the state.

During the imperial period a new policy, already found for the first time at the beginning of the fifth century, was encouraged, which took some notice of the permanent land hunger of the farmer. It has been seen that Athens was backward in overseas colonization because of her late development. But it became the custom in imperial times to establish small colonies called *cleruchies*, in the conquered lands, which played a similar part to the Roman republican colonies to be discussed later. These cleruchies were outposts of the Athenian empire, and their inhabitants retained their Athenian citizenship and, of course, were always ready to support Athenian policy. Pericles sent over six thousand colonists or cleruchs to members of the Delian Confederation which had seceded and required to be disciplined. While some of these cleruchs were traders and merchants, the cleruchies were definite allotments of land, and they were sufficient for the small Athenian farms. As well as helping to solve unemployment in Athens and Attica, they provided a means of military control. The cleruchs were usually well able to take care of themselves and at a pinch could always call on the Athenians for support. All through the Peloponnesian War the policy was continued, and was revived occasionally afterward. It was one of the few uses to which the otherwise usually barren military victories were put.

The agriculture of Attica was, however, not necessarily primitive. Though we do not possess much information on agriculture in classical times, the high production of wine and olives, especially the latter, could not have been obtained without very considerable knowledge and intelligent management of the soil. We know that when the Greeks went into Egypt after the conquests of Alexander they were able to introduce there far more scientific soil management than had been known before. As early as the time of Homer we know that vine management was understood, as a famous descriptive passage in the Odyssey makes clear. It was the grain farming that was inefficient and unprofitable rather than the specialized crops. But on the small farms which were expected to provide a living the cultivation had to be highly intensive, or even this meager living would not have been possible.

COMMERCE AND TRADE

There is no doubt that the Athenian empire was highly profitable to the individual Athenians, and to the state. Empire was not indulged in for the sake of prestige. In spite of their enjoyment of glory, it is improbable that any Greek cities would have thought it worth while to quarrel over which should first set up its flag on a stretch of barren desert or a swamp, or to prove to themselves or their enemies that they were better men than their opponents; least of all would they have indulged in imperialism because they thought that barbarians were entitled to the privilege of being made Greeks, even against their will, or should be made to worship Greek gods. We must remember that the Greeks, though passionate, were rationalists, and modern excuses for imperialism would not have moved them. Greek imperialism was as rational as other Greek activities. They were willing to fight to preserve their independence—meaning, ultimately, for their self-government and social order; and they also fought for material gains without bothering to apologize.

All the Greek maritime cities needed their trade. The country as a whole was not self-supporting in foods; and Athens, after the reforms of Solon, had deliberately chosen not to be, as England chose after the repeal of the Corn Laws in 1846. Grain was mostly imported from the Black Sea area, where

Persia could always be a danger. In addition Athens was dependent on outside sources for hides, for most metals, for timber for ships, and for hemp for ropes. With a constantly increasing population to be fed, grain imports had to be rigorously controlled, and both its price and its sale were regulated. Protective tariffs were unknown. There was only a regular 2 per cent customs and excise duty for revenue purposes. But to encourage the export of grain to Athens, regular quantity shippers of grain were not required to pay import duty on all their other exports to Athens. Cleruchs and metics were not permitted to ship grain anywhere except to Athens. Very heavy penalties fell upon all who speculated in grain, and the officials who regulated imports were made to report ten times a year to the Assembly. These measures show something of the importance of the grain trade for Athens; they show also that the problem was simply to ensure the physical supply of grain rather than to make the trade profitable for the grain merchants. It is true that most of the evidence dates from the fourth century after Athens had lost her empire. But it suggests at least one of the chief reasons for the existence of the Athenian imperial navy and the empire itself.

In order to pay for grain and a large variety of minor imports Athens in the Periclean age had little enough to export. The physical import trade was far larger than the export, and the problem of return cargoes for the grain ships must have been important. Hence the need for some kind of coercion. During imperial days Athens kept a consular officer on the shores of the Hellespont to see that grain ships were headed in the right direction. While she was mistress of the seas, no doubt grain went safely to Athens, and was paid for not only by exports but from the imperial treasury of the Delos Confederation. There was no possibility of substantially increasing the exports, which consisted of olive oil and various olive products, pottery, marble, weapons and armor, artistic metalwork, and similar luxury products, in addition to some wine,

though probably at this time more wine was imported than exported. The only other valuable visible export was silver from the Laurian mines. It is clear, therefore, that with such an enormous trade deficit Athens either had to compensate with an equally large invisible export or had to increase her production of industrial products and sell them. In the age of Pericles she did indeed possess this invisible export—her shipping services, and the protection she extended to the Aegean islands for which she was handsomely compensated by the expropriation of the treasury of the Confederation.

INDUSTRY

As far as we know, if Athens had decided to increase her industrial production by importing raw materials and manufacturing them, as England did in the second half of the nineteenth century, she might well have been able to find a market. But, as in so many other phases of Athenian life that we might wish to criticize, there was a very good social reason why she did not. Every man wanted to control his own business. Not only was it regarded as derogatory to the dignity of a citizen to accept private employment, but if he worked for someone else he was being cheated out of something that gave him great pleasure, namely, running his own business. For a people with such a passion for any form of creative activity to work for another was to work at a disadvantage. Even the building of a great temple, as we know, was carried out by thousands of small contractors, not by one large contractor working efficiently with a gang of workmen, nor by the direct activity of the state. If an Athenian had decided to enlarge his business to make it more efficient and to take better advantage of the division of labor he would have been forced to employ large numbers of slaves, which might have been possible; but he would also need citizen overseers, all of whom would have preferred to be in business for themselves. The largest industrial concern known to us from Greek sources is a shield factory owned by a metic, with 120 slaves;

and the largest for the fourth century that we know of employed only 60. One considerable area of Athens was devoted to the manufacture of pottery, but again in small separate concerns. The marble quarries and the silver mines belonged to the state but were rented out in small concessions. In the fourth century the evidence shows a greater division of labor, a fact mentioned with approval by the great philosophers of the time; but the number of slaves in fourth-century Athens also increased, and examination of the records shows that in the factories both foremen and workers were usually slaves. Probably this fourth-century development was forced on the people by the loss of their empire; but there can seldom have been a city of comparable size which had so many citizens working for themselves. This is just one more aspect of the way in which the Greek polis was able to satisfy, by its peculiar social and economic system, the needs and desires of its citizens. But the result unquestionably was that the total product was remarkably small for such a large population; and in Periclean times there was even less than usual to export because the artisans worked for the city, and almost their whole industrial production was consumed at home. For even the most ardent individualist who would refuse to work for a fellow Greek employer was happy to work for the state. In the next chapter we shall see something of what these men accomplished.

BUSINESS ORGANIZATION AND PUBLIC FINANCE

Most of the improvement in business methods dates from the fourth century, when the need for better methods was greater. There was a considerable development in banking. Not only were more mines being exploited but the subsidies of the Persian kings kept a constant flow of money into the Greek world. In earlier times there were always money-changers who used to sit at a table near the harbor of Piraeus, changing the coins of different states. The value of these coins was largely determined by the intrinsic worth of the coin itself. The Athenian "owls," however, were acceptable almost anywhere in both the fifth and fourth centuries at their face value, for the Athenians were very careful never to debase their currency. It was boasted that foreign merchants were always content to take payment in cash at Athens, knowing they could use it elsewhere. Bankers replaced the money-changers to a large extent, especially during the fourth century, accumulating supplies of money and lending it out, usually at 12 per cent per annum paid by the month. Loans on voyages in which the ship had to face many dangers were at much higher rates. But this was also a kind of insurance, since the money did not have to be repaid if the ship were lost. Bankers also furnished letters of credit, and sometimes financed large transactions and contracts with ready money.

There was no regular tax system in most of the Greek cities. Taxation was on a hand-to-mouth basis. Temple treasures were frequently borrowed, but usually they were carefully repaid. Special assessments were made in times of emergencies, and the rich were expected to make "voluntary" contributions, which in time became compulsory. Athens in imperial days had many extra expenses for public works, but the wage paid by the state was very low, and was the same in nearly all cases for all kinds of work. In later times after the empire, when civic spirit was declining, a new expense had to be met, the pay for the mercenary soldiers who largely replaced the citizen armies. Direct doles to the poor and the unemployed also increased. Moreover, the old system whereby ships were voluntarily contributed by the wealthy was rapidly disappearing, so that recourse to higher taxes was necessary. Sales taxes and a heavy income tax seldom filled the fourth-century Athenian treasury, and the state was constantly in arrears with tax collection, and not infrequently on the verge of bankruptcy. Nevertheless, as soon as efficient and honest administrators were appointed, the city quickly became solvent again, suggesting that some of the tax money went into private pockets.

▶ Athenian society

DAILY LIFE IN ATHENS

The whole social life of Athens, and indeed that of all other Greek cities, reflects, above all, the extraordinary poverty of material resources, which was not only accepted philosophically by the Greeks but regarded as the natural, and even desirable, order of things. The ordinary man remained a frugal liver, both in imperial times and in the fourth century. Even what he considered luxuries would be to the imperial Roman very little indeed. Everything must be judged by Greek standards. When Pericles boasts that luxuries from the whole world stream into Athens we must set this against the background of the known national income, and the known social life as shown by the inscriptions, by the artistic remains as well as by the literature. All Greeks wore clothes of the utmost simplicity at all times, an undergarment fastened with a safety pin, and an outer garment draped about their person. The same garment served as a blanket. Beds were usually planks, without springs. The average house, unlike the temples, was made of sun-dried brick, and houses were built closely together. The walls were not decorated, the furniture was crude and utilitarian. When Pericles insisted that Athenian homes were beautiful and elegant, he may have been speaking the truth, because the artistic decorations that the Greek knew so well how to make may have been in use. If so, we know nothing of such decorations; but a list of the furniture in the house of the most fashionable young man of Athens in his day which we do possess is singularly unimpressive. The houses themselves were adequate for living in, but bear no comparison at all with those of pre-Greek Minoan Crete.

The reason for this utter lack of luxury in the private homes of the Athenians is simple enough. The Greek lived primarily in the open air. More hours of the day were spent in the gymnasium, the agora, or the streets than in his house. When it was dark he went to bed, and at dawn he usually rose and went into the street, without breakfast. We hear nothing from any source of any great mansions of the Roman type in classical times, nor of palatial private gardens and pleasure grounds. Rich men contributed their wealth to the polis, and did not use it so much for their own pleasure; but even their riches were small enough by Roman or Minoan standards. There were no gargantuan feasts; food was scarce and lacked variety. Meat was rarely eaten.

The truth seems to be, hard as it may be for us to believe, that the Greek really did not care for luxury, or not enough to give up his leisure to gain it; and it was frowned upon by public opinion. A contrast sometimes made between Athenian luxury and Spartan simplicity is extremely relative. Both lived simply; but the Spartan cultivated simplicity, wearing only one garment in winter and going barefoot, while the Athenian had sandals. The Athenian was able to decorate his city superbly because he cared for it rather than for his home; and to the service of his gods and his city he devoted all his unparalleled artistic talents. No doubt it was a temptation to distribute, as a dividend to all citizens, the hundred talents unexpectedly gained from a city-owned silver mine; but he was also willing to spend it, as he did on the advice of Themistocles, on a navy instead.

The kind of freedom that resulted from this doing without is one that is unique in history, and can never be repeated. But if one delights in free talk, assemblies, festivals, plays, the development of the mind and the body, self-government, and civic glory, the logical thing to do is to avoid cluttering one's self up with possessions useless to this kind of life. But the loss of the city life—not necessarily even the city itself, for this could be rebuilt—would be irreparable. The life of the expatriated Greek in Alexander's empire was such that he could gain luxury without difficulty; but from the evidence it appears that he was lonely, rootless, bored, inclined to suicide, to the worship of Tyche, goddess of chance, and to mystery religions, even though he tried his best to re-create the forms of the polis around him.

Farewell scene from another gravestone, with a significance similar to that of the scene on the lekythos shown previously. (COURTESY THE METROPOLITAN MUSEUM OF ART)

CLASSES IN ATHENIAN SOCIETY

The classes in Athenian society were definitely marked out on the basis of property, not birth. The three main subdivisions, of course, were the citizens, the metics, and the slaves. From the time of Pericles, citizenship was limited to those Athenians both of whose parents were also citizens. This restriction was later to some extent relaxed, though the officials of the demes who examined credentials were naturally jealous of the privilege of citizenship, which meant much to the citizens and was a considerable expense to the state, for citizens, as a rule, were more lightly taxed than metics. The Assembly, as sovereign body of the state, could, of course, grant citizenship in certain cases, sometimes en masse, as to the inhabitants of Samos who remained faithful to the Athenian alliance under adversity.

About 6 per cent of the citizens were enrolled in the two highest classes of the state, the nobles and the knights. The majority of the population were small farmers (*zeugitae*), a solid middle class which served to balance the radical democrats of the *thetes,* or lowest class, who possessed little or no property, and were mostly artisans and other city dwellers. Some state offices, such as the archonship, always had a property qualification, and the thetes were excluded from them.

Ordinary temporary residents of the city had no rights in it and no privileges. After a certain period of residence an alien could be given the official status of metic, which entitled him to pay taxes, serve in the army, and perform the other duties of citizens. He was not permitted to own land, nor plead in the courts except through citizens. But metics were on a level of social equality with the Athenians, could take part in the festivals, and in certain circumstances could hope to obtain citizenship. Aristotle was never an Athenian citizen, but was able to study and teach there as long as he wished. His ultimate exile as a friend of the hated Alexander could have been imposed with no more difficulty on a citizen.

The position of women in Athenian society has given rise to some controversy among scholars. The literary and legal evidence is clear enough. They could not attend the Assembly or hold office; they could not own property; they could not plead in the courts. In all public affairs a man—her husband or her nearest male relative—had to act on behalf of a woman. If she were an only child and her father died intestate, her nearest male relative could claim her in marriage, even being permitted to divorce his own wife for the purpose, or he became her guardian. The Athenian houses were divided into men's and women's quarters, marriages were arranged between parents without consulting the girl, women were not formally educated; and, finally, Aristotle claims that "by nature" men are superior and women inferior, and Pericles, in a famous passage, advised the women in his audience that their "best reputation is not to be spoken of for good or evil."

But much of the literary evidence can be construed differently. Pericles' advice may mean no more than that women should not provide food for gossip, an unexceptionable and common sentiment in all societies. When Xenophon shows us a middle-aged man giving advice to a young girl while she makes approving and respectful noises in return this may be only a piece of wish-fulfillment on the part of the middle-aged writer. The whole evidence taken literally seems to conflict with the happy pictures of family life shown in the tomb reliefs and on decorated vases; and other indications from the literary sources suggest different conclusions. There are noble heroines in Euripides, and Sophocles' Antigone is one of the great feminine characters of all literature, an ideal of a loving and tender-hearted girl who by her courage and integrity puts all the other characters in the play to shame. There is no suggestion of inferiority here. If women did not vote in the Assembly it was because their menfolk had to make important decisions on public policy which they themselves, and not the women, would have to carry out. Even so, Aristophanes in a famous comedy (*Lysistrata*) suggests that women would be less likely to push the state into unnecessary wars than stupid men.

Probably the explanation of the conflicting evidence is that the spheres of men and women were clearly demarcated in Athens. The woman took care of the home and family, while the man engaged in other work. But the women were not in any way secluded, and there is no reason to believe that family life was not as normal as elsewhere. There is, however, certain evidence that romantic love was not a Greek ideal, at least as between man and woman. Passionate love between men and women is treated by the serious writers as if it were a dread disease, as in the *Hippolytus* and *Medea* of Euripides. On the other hand, there is much evidence that love between members of the same sex was treated as an ordinary and natural thing, and no Greek writer condemns it as likely to lead to the same tragic disturbances as passionate love between man and woman.

EDUCATION

The standard education of the Athenian boy consisted in reading, writing, and practical numbers. This included the learning of much of the best Greek poetry by heart. Musical training was given, especially in the lyre, to those who could afford it. This was accompanied by games, contests, and physical exercises, directed, not as in Sparta, to military ends, but toward the development of a healthy body and physical beauty. Up to the age of fourteen the boy was under the direction of a *paidagogos*, a private tutor, usually a slave, who also tried to instill moral principles into his charges. From fourteen to eighteen the boy's education was primarily physical and conducted in the public gymnasia where athletes were also trained for the games. Here he had his first real opportunity for contact with older men; in the gymnasia he engaged in the public discussions so dear to the Athenians.[11] At eighteen the youth became a citizen by taking an oath to obey the laws and the constitution and not "to disgrace my sacred weapons." From ages eighteen to twenty the first three classes of citizens engaged in compulsory military training from which, as in early Rome, the poorest class was exempt.

This kind of education, it may be noted, was not suitable for women, who received such education as they had privately. Since they were permitted to go to the theaters and take part in festivals, and as the theater, at least, required a considerable understanding, it may be supposed that feminine accomplishment was, in such matters as reading and writing, not far behind that of their sons and husbands. In the matter of education, as in everything else, the polis was realistic. It sponsored what it deemed to be useful, and, for the rest, it left the citizen entirely free. It provided athletic instructors and gymnasia, but private persons contrib-

[11] In the time of Pericles the Sophists also taught for money, much to the disgust of the more conservative Athenians. The subjects they taught were more "practical." But, of course, the Sophists were not sponsored by the polis. Socrates, incidentally, though accused of being a Sophist, was not a professional, and always refused to take pay.

uted the paidagogoi. But the men who talked and discussed in the gymnasia did so from the love of it, and the youths took part if they wished. It was probably entirely possible—but very boring—to be as badly educated in Athens as it is now. What on earth would one do when all that one could see at the theater was a performance of the *Frogs?*

▶ **Suggestions for further reading**

Almost every ancient writer of importance has now appeared in paperbound books. One should probably first examine the translations in the Penguin series which has the most complete list, then consult *Paperbound Books in Print* as necessary. Numerous selections from Greek historians are also available in paperback, which will serve to give some flavor of the original.

When any work is not available in paperback, the Loeb Classics series, published by Harvard University Press, contains the original and a translation of almost every work of antiquity.

PAPER-BOUND BOOKS

Adcock, F. E. *The Greek and Macedonian Art of War.* University of California. Important book on Greek military affairs.

Andrewes, A. *The Greek Tyrants.* Torchbooks.

Burns, A. R. *Pericles and Athens.* Collier. A short and rather simple account of Athenian democracy in the era of the Peloponnesian War.

Boardman, John. *The Greeks Overseas.* Penguin. Deals with the first wave of Greek emigration from the eighth to the sixth centuries B.C.

Claster, Jill N. ed. *Athenian Democracy.* Holt, Rinehart and Winston. Selections from leading historians on the nature of Greek democracy, excellent for the beginning student.

Coulanges, Fustel de. *The Ancient City.* Anchor. In spite of the age of this book (it was published in 1864), modern scholarship has added little to our understanding of its theme— the relation of religion to the life of the ancient city. Covers both Greece and Rome.

Dickinson, G. Lowes. *The Greek View of Life.* Ann Arbor and Collier. A classic, written at the turn of the twentieth century, still unequaled as a presentation of all that we think admirable about the Greeks.

Ehrenburg, Victor. *The People of Aristophanies: A Sociology of Old Attic Comedy.* Schocken. Modern investigation of Athenian social life, with information derived from all sources to throw light on conditions described by Aristophanes. By the same author is the classic *The Greek State.*

Finley, M. I. *The Ancient Greeks: An Introduction to their Life and Thought.* Compass. An introduction by a modern English historian.

Forrest, W. G. *The Emergence of Greek Democracy.* McGraw.

Freeman, Kathleen. *Greek City-States.* Norton. Extremely useful book to read especially in conjunction with the present text, since it contains much information about the Greek cities other than Athens and Sparta which had to be omitted.

Hamilton, Edith. *The Greek Way to Western Civilization.* Mentor. An ever popular account, beautifully written and enriched by many quotations, but not a book to be read by itself. Its catching enthusiasm sometimes blinds the judgment of the reader.

Hatzfeld, J., and Aymard, A. *A History of Ancient Greece.* Norton. A good introduction by a noted French scholar.

Kitto, H. D. F. *The Greeks.* Penguin. This valuable little book, first published in 1951, has deservedly established itself as the most widely read introduction to Greek civilization.

Lloyd-Jones, Hugh, ed. *The Greek World.* Penguin. A series of essays by leading historians on the political, economic, and social history of the Greeks.

Michell, H. *Sparta.* Cambridge University Press. The most useful paperback account of this eccentric society.

Page, Denys. *History and the Homeric Iliad.* University of California Press.

Robinson, Cyril E. *Hellas: A Short History of Ancient Greece.* Beacon Press. One of the best introductions available. Clear, up-to-date, and well organized.

Smith, Morton. *The Ancient Greeks.* Cornell University Press. A useful introduction.

Weil, Simone. *The Iliad or the Poem of Force.* Pendle Hill. Looks at Homer as anti-war poet, stressing his compassion for human suffering. Original and interesting, by important modern religious thinker.

Zimmern, Alfred. *The Greek Commonwealth.* Galaxy. Also Modern Library casebound. This book, though written as long ago as 1911 and revised only slightly until its last edition in 1931, is still indispensable as the only relatively brief presentation of ancient Greece in a topical manner, giving full weight to economic and social as well as political data.

CHAPTER 8

HELLENIC CULTURE

► ## The originality of Greek thought

CONTRAST WITH ORIENTAL THOUGHT

Many efforts have been made to trace Greek thought back to its origins and relate it to its Oriental forebears. The Greeks themselves had a great respect for Egyptian thought and science; certain elements in Greek mystery religion obviously derive from Oriental conceptions. Early Greek art shows traces of Egyptian, and certainly Minoan and Mycenaean, influence; gods and goddesses, myths and legends, are also often of foreign, especially Minoan, origin. But when all is said and done there is something definitely and clearly new in Greek thought, something which is not present even in the profound and important Hindu philosophy (most of which does not in any case certainly antedate Greek thought). The new element is wonder and curiosity about this world and everything in it, particularly man.

The Hebrews, the Hindus, and the Chinese were all interested in discovering what man's position was in this world, and his proper behavior toward the gods. The Hindus saw clearly man's possibility of self-

development; but they lacked admiration for man. They examined his psychology, but their emphasis of his immortal part above his mortal led mature Hindu thought to conceive of earthly existence as *maya,* and the body as a prison house. Self-development therefore to the Hindu was a process of freeing one's self from earthly desires, and becoming as far as possible a spiritual being while still on earth (the *Atman*). The Greeks, on the other hand, respectfully and admiringly inquired into the nature of man on earth, admiring both his body and his mind. The union of body and mind (or soul) was perfection. Hence a culture of *this* world was created, and the next world was pictured as a shadowy existence, hardly imaginable, without solidity, and no substitute at all for the joys and sufferings and growth of this.

THE ATTEMPT TO FIND ORDER AND PATTERN IN EARTHLY PHENOMENA

Since man was anchored securely in this world, everything about this world was of interest and importance to him. The great questions *why* and *what* were always on his lips. No one thing should be examined alone, for this was specialization and meant neglect of all the other good things to which his attention might turn. "We have a happy versatility," said Pericles. All the great Greek philosophers were men of action, or willing to be; all took the whole realm of knowledge for their field of inquiry, or tried to find huge universal explanations which covered all phenomena, and explained the whole, not only the small visible parts. They were fortunate in that a great deal of empirical material existed as the heritage of previous civilizations, and into this they attempted to put order. Later philosophers such as Aristotle tried to put order also into the speculations of their earlier Greek predecessors. But the great characteristic of all Greek thinkers is an attempt, consistently pursued, to find order and pattern, to discover the real harmony in things by the use of their minds, to replace the recalcitrant phenomena of sense perception by the precise and orderly mental conceptions which form their counterpart. In this Plato and Aristotle are at one with the Ionian cosmologists, as well as with Aeschylus and Sophocles, who strove to fit the deeds of men into the framework of human destiny.

THE GREEK LANGUAGE—ITS UNIQUENESS

The Greek genius is reflected in its remarkable language, which is in many ways unique among the languages of mankind, as an instrument for expressing all the different possible shades of meaning. It is the most fully inflected of languages, the inflections being used where we employ the less effective and less precise auxiliaries "to have" and "to be," accompanied by participles. In the Greek language, unlike the Latin, there are no missing forms—there are, for instance, present participles in the passive, and active participles in the past. There are three voices, the active, the passive, and the middle, the last reflecting the shade of meaning required when something is done on behalf of the subject, not unlike the French reflexive verb. There are three numbers, the singular, the plural, and the dual, for every

verb and for every noun, reflecting the shade of meaning which distinguishes acts done in company with many from those performed with only one companion. There are a host of particles used to create an internal balance within a sentence, and to point to the logical connection between one sentence and the one which follows it. Perhaps the most useful feature of the language for all later peoples who have borrowed words from it is the multitude of prepositions, which can be used also as prefixes for verbs and nouns, to reflect slight changes in meaning, as, for instance, between psychology (*psyche*—soul, and *logos*—discussion, both Greek words) and parapsychology (by the side of psychology), a word needed in the English language when the suggestion had to be voiced that certain new theories in psychology did not strictly belong to the original science. The vast bulk of our scientific terminology is Greek in origin, and daily we add new compounds, usually formed from the Greek.

► **General characteristics of Greek thought**

WONDER AS THE PATHWAY TO KNOWLEDGE

The Greeks were the world pioneers in the attempt to apply human reason to the understanding of their world. Few if any of their findings in natural science are found acceptable by modern scientists who have developed systematic methods for organizing knowledge and have a wealth of instruments and intellectual tools that were unavailable to the Greeks. Some of the Greek intuitions, as, for example, the atomic theory of Leucippus and Democritus, may be thought to be astonishingly prescient. But there was no possibility of testing such hypotheses in the fifth century B.C., so they had to remain mere guesses. By contrast some of the observations of the Athenian historian Thucydides on the nature of revolutions and the moral implications of empire may seem as valid today as the day they were written; and Aristotle may still have something to teach us in the fields of ethics and politics, fields which required careful observation and sound reasoning, and could be studied effectively even without the modern paraphernalia of polls, question-naires, and computers.

Plato once remarked that all knowledge begins in wonder. The Greeks wondered about the physical world, whether change was real or apparent and what caused it, whether, like man, it had a soul; they wondered about man, and the relationship between his soul, whose existence they as-sumed, and his body; what was knowledge, how it was acquired, and what was the nature of the human mind; what kind of activities were proper to man, having regard to his essential nature. All these questions were raised by the Greek thinkers, most of them for the first time. Only Aristotle (384–322 B.C.), as far as we know, tried to give an answer to all of them.

PRE-SOCRATIC PHILOSOPHY

It is customary to divide Greek thought into two distinct phases which overlap some-what in time. In the first phase, which begins with Thales of Miletus (late seventh century B.C.), the Greek thinkers, none of whom was Athenian, made extensive speculations about the natural world. The second phase was centered in Athens, and may be said to have opened with the arrival of the Sophist Protagoras of Abdera (a city in northern Greece) in that city early in the second half of the fifth century B.C. Although some of the Sophists were interested in the same type of thought as their predecessors, on the whole they concentrated on more mundane matters and most of them made their living by teach-ing in Athens. It is therefore more convenient to study them in connection with the three great philosophers, Socrates, Plato, and Aris-totle, the first two of whom were Athenian citizens while Aristotle did much of his work in Athens and founded a school there (the Lyceum). The first group of thinkers are usu-ally known as the pre-Socratic philosophers.

No complete work has come down to us from any of the pre-Socratic philosophers. All that we possess are a few fragments drawn from the writings of Aristotle and subsequent philosophers and historians who may not themselves have had access to any of the original works in their entirety. Even Aris-totle's knowledge may have been imperfect, and the long passage in his *Metaphysics* de-voted to the thought of his predecessors may not have accurately expressed what they said. It is also possible that living more than two centuries after him, Aristotle did not under-stand what Thales had been trying to do.

The difficulty is compounded by the fact that until Plato and Aristotle, the Greek language did not have words precise enough to express philosophical concepts. Indeed, much of the work of creating a philosophical language was the work of Aristotle himself. Not only were abstract nouns very scarce—words like "substance" and "material" are derived from Latin, not from Greek—but words like "heat" and "cold" had at first to be expressed by using the neuter form of the adjective, combined with the definite article —the warm thing, the cold thing. Thus when Thales spoke of the "primal beginning" (*arche*) of all things as water, in fact he may have meant "wetness" or "moisture." Anaxi-mander's "boundless thing," which we usu-ally translate as "infinity," may have meant something quite different to the philosopher. When Aristotle himself wished to speak of "substance" he had to use the word for "wood," leaving it to his auditors and readers to know that he was speaking figuratively.

Since modern students cannot escape the necessity of having to come to their own esti-mates of what these ancient thinkers meant, creating a synthesis of the surviving frag-ments, it might be thought that the whole enterprise would not be worthwhile. This might well be true if it were not for the extraordinary importance of the kind of ex-planations these philosophers offered. Perhaps it does not greatly matter if we are mistaken about the exact meaning of what they said. What is quite clear is that they were engaged in a pioneering attempt to understand the world on the basis of reasoning alone without recourse to the traditional teachings about the activities of divine beings. They did not deny divine activity, although some of the later thinkers severely criticized the legends they had inherited. In essence what these men did was to suggest a number of hypotheses that were incapable of verification at that time for lack of the necessary experimental evidence, but which were in principle —unlike hypotheses on the nature and activity of gods—capable of being verified.

As we have seen, Plato held that all knowledge begins in wonder. Aristotle begins his *Metaphysics* with the statement that "all men by nature desire to know." The pre-Socratic thinkers were certainly following Plato's prescription, and "wondering" about the world but they were not doing what, in Aristotle's view, should have "come naturally" to them. They were not searching for new knowledge, but rather trying to explain what they thought they already knew. For this reason it is best not to think of them as scientists, whose task has always been to search for new knowledge, but as philosophers (lovers of wisdom), even though their main interest was in the natural world which is the realm of science. Among the true Greek scientists there were some, like Aristotle, who were also philosophers; but the scientific tradition is better represented by men like the medical doctor, Hippocrates of Cos, and by a considerable number of Hellenistic scientists who will be discussed in the next chapter.

According to Aristotle the question propounded by Thales of Miletus was "what is the primal beginning (or first principle) of everything" and the answer he gave was water. We cannot tell from this single statement whether Thales was wondering whether before the earth came to exist in time there was only water, which by some unknown means became land, or whether he was searching for an underlying substance which changed its form, as water can be condensed into air or congealed into ice. Anaximander, also a Milesian and probably an associate or pupil of Thales (born about 617 B.C.), is said by a late Greek philosopher to have been the first to call "the underlying substance the first principle." However, Anaximander also said that the first principle was "infinite" or "boundless" and therefore not truly a substance at all. Aristotle says with evident disapproval that Anaximander's "infinite" was something different from any of the "elements," which in fact come from it. From these statements we may perhaps conclude that Anaximander was positing a primal undifferentiated chaos before the existence of any of the earthly substances. From other ideas attributed to Anaximander he appears to have been a believer in evolution, on which he speculated in an interesting manner. Man, he said, "at first was like a fish" and he was "generated from all sorts of animals," and "the first animals were generated in the moisture."

With Anaximenes, the third of the great Milesians and a contemporary of Anaximander, we can be fairly certain that what is being sought is an actual substance. Anaximenes chose air as this primal substance, and explained that all change comes about through the condensation and rarefaction of air. However he did not attempt to explain *how* air became condensed, for example, into stone. In other words he did not account for change, a subject that was to occupy Heraclitus of Ephesus who flourished in the later part of the sixth century B.C.

Many fragments have survived from the work of Heraclitus, but all are short and it is extremely difficult to make any kind of synthesis of his thought. From his remark that "you could not step twice in the same river" it may be assumed that he was studying the problem of changes in form; whereas his conclusion that the fundamental substance was an "ever-living fire," which was transformed into "first of all sea," and that "fire lives in the death of air, and air lives in the death of earth, earth in that of water," was a contribution to the same problem studied by Thales and Anaximenes.

Meanwhile other philosophers had been working in southern Italy. Notable among these was Pythagoras (born about 570 B.C.)

who founded a religious brotherhood which interested itself in mathematics, holding, according to Aristotle, that numbers (or mathematical relationships) were the first principles of all things. It was the Pythagoreans who discovered the mathematical basis of musical harmonies by experimenting with a lyre (a truly scientific achievement), from which point of departure they searched for more harmonies in the earth and the universe. Parmenides of Elea, also in southern Italy (born about 540 B.C.), offered a radical criticism of the ideas of his predecessors, who had been looking for a single underlying substance which changed its form. He denied on logical grounds the possibility of any real change. The idea of nothing, or nonbeing, he said, is inconceivable. Thus there could be no coming into existence or passing away, since the one must have arisen in nothing, and the other must end in nothing. It follows that everything must be made up of combinations of already existing things, which merely changed their forms by making different combinations.

Since Parmenides' conclusions were regarded as irrefutable, subsequent thinkers tried to find the basic substance which could be transformed into all the different objects found in the material world. Empedocles of Acragas in Sicily declared that there are four "root" substances or elements, earth, air, fire, and water, but he could not explain how these substances could be transformed without "coming into being and passing away." Anaxagoras, an Ionian who went to Athens at the invitation of Pericles, tried to meet this difficulty by positing the existence of tiny qualitatively different "seeds," of which there was an infinite number. Some of each kind of seed could be found in every kind of material object, with one kind predominating to make it what it was. The seeds were ordered by Mind (*Nous*), which was responsible also for all transformations.

This problem was taken up again by Leucippus and Democritus from northern Greece. Democritus was a contemporary of Plato and Aristotle, who did not like his theories which were taken up again in the Hellenistic Age (by Epicurus) and in Republican Rome (by the poet Lucretius). Neither of them added anything significant to the theory itself, but drew moral conclusions from it. Democritus held—we have no certain knowledge of Leucippus, or what he contributed to the theory—that all things are made up of "atoms and the void," or "filled space and empty space." The word atom means "uncuttable" and was something so small as to be almost but not quite infinitely small. Each atom had its own characteristic shape and characteristic movement, which gave rise to the qualities observed in objects: sweet and sour, hard and soft, and the like. Democritus and his followers tried to account not only for the earth but also for the heavenly bodies through his atomic theory, and he appears to have propounded a detailed theory of evolution which is to be found again in the Lucretian poem *De rerum naturae*.

For lack of any possibility of discovering empirical evidence for his theory, Democritus' speculative venture had to remain unverified in his own day, though it was well known and gave rise to serious discussion in the seventeenth and eighteenth centuries A.D. Pierre Gassendi, a French mathematician (1592–1655) gave it much attention, restating it in much the same terms as it had been put forward by Lucretius in the first century B.C. But no experimental evidence was available even in Gassendi's time, and it could remain only a subject for speculation.

▶ From religion to philosophy

RELIGION—EARLY FORMS

Pervasiveness of religion in all Greek life

In studying Egypt we found it impossible to separate religion from government; and there was almost nothing that could be studied in Egypt without an understanding of the religious framework. The Greeks are usually thought of as a secular people—indeed as the founders of secularism because of their exclusive interest in this life, and their special interest in man. If this interest be conceded, we still should not confuse Greek secularism in this limited sense with modern secularism. All religion is not concerned with the next world, and all religion does not require a canonical book, churches, and priests. The sole necessity for religion is the belief in gods or divine powers which are concerned with man and the universe. And this religion was not only present among the Greeks but suffused all their activities until late in Hellenic times.

Disregard for, and disbelief in, the gods was uncommon before the fourth century B.C. even among intellectuals; and a truly secular attitude to life can be detected only from the middle of the fifth century B.C. at the earliest, concurrent with the rise of individualism and the decline of the polis. At this time art became to some degree emancipated from religion, and the tragic drama, not only religious in origin but providing the deepest of religious experiences for all those privileged to be present, came to an abrupt end. The Sophists questioned the very basis of all received beliefs, and Socrates and his followers Plato and Aristotle tried to build a new ethic upon the ruins. The communal life of the polis, based upon beliefs and rituals held and performed in common, slowly gave place to self-seeking and the pursuit of personal wealth and happiness.

The decay of religion should not be thought of as the *reason* for the decay of civic life and other manifestations of the secularist revolution, but as its necessary accompaniment. It will be misleading, however, to study the religion in total isolation, as if it were kept for Sunday and were not a central element in Hellenic culture. We shall therefore in this chapter study first the early and fifth-century Greek religion, paying special attention to its most mature expression in the tragic drama, and then deal with the Sophists and thinkers of the later period under the general title of philosophy. Then we shall return to Greek art and such of Greek literature as has not

hitherto been considered, and when necessary relate these also to the dominant religious conceptions. It is hoped that this unorthodox procedure will be justified by a greater understanding of the total Greek spirit than is provided by a study of each realm of achievement in isolation.

Our understanding of Greek religion and appreciation for it has been seriously dulled by the way in which most people have learned of it; and this applies to the Romans as well as to ourselves. When the Greek religion ceased to be a living force, the scholars and storytellers began to find it naïve and amusing, and to tell not very edifying stories of the Greek gods on Olympus. Though there was still a substratum of the original myth left, the story was heightened by the art of the teller. We heard of the amours of Ares and Aphrodite, and of the many wives, children, and grandchildren of Zeus, the rape of Persephone, and the story of the pomegranate seeds—there are thousands of them, and most of them appear in the *Metamorphoses* of the Roman poet Ovid. But those stories that become "cute" in Ovid are not cute in Homer or even in Euripides. We have tended to present the story of Greek religion according to the tales of Ovid or the scholarly investigations of the Alexandrians, but not often enough as the Greeks themselves looked upon their gods. It is certain that they never snickered at them. We have said that the common people needed a popular religion, and no doubt they and not the intellectuals believed in the gods of Olympus; but it is too often forgotten that the same common people were able to appreciate the tremendous tragic drama of Aeschylus and Sophocles, and awarded a first prize to that comedy of Aristophanes (*The Frogs*), the heart of which was a technical discussion of the poetry, meter, and thought of Aeschylus and Euripides. Aristophanes continued to win prizes to the end of his days. Can it be imagined that the little people who built the Parthenon and carved the friezes snickered at the stories of the gods and heroes, the subjects of their work?

The nature of Greek polytheism— The gods as powers of nature

As with other polytheistic peoples, the gods were powers. Some of the older myths about the ancient gods and Titans were concerned with the creation of order out of chaos, and the supersession of this order by another, which was more moral than the first. Of such a kind is the story of the ancient sky-god Ouranos, who was defeated by his son Chronos, when Time first came into existence, and then his later defeat by his son Zeus. The vast bulk of the Greek gods were associated with special places; and with the conquests of one people by another it is possible that the old god and the new united, and a myth told of the fusion of peoples as of their gods. Few gods were ousted altogether, for Greek religion was very hospitable to gods; but at all times they were kept in order by Zeus, and belonged to his family—tribal gods, river and place gods, and even abstractions like Themis (Justice), and Dike (Law). All gods were regarded as more powerful than men, like them insofar as they had mortal passions, and unlike them insofar as they were immortal.

We can only write vaguely about the *beliefs* of the Greeks in their gods because such beliefs, as is evident from the dialogues of Plato, vary markedly from man to man. But their ritual and manner of worship did not vary to the same degree, and from them we can realize the general respect in which the gods were held, whatever the individual belief. The god is both a power who can bestow help and a being worthy of man's worship. The Greeks do not seem to have propitiated their gods or even asked favors of them; on the contrary, they honored them, and waited for the blessing of the gods in return, without presuming to make suggestions to them. Temples were built not for worship but as homes for the gods. At a festival the citizens made a solemn procession to the temple, and expressed gratitude for all the god had done for them. They did not kneel, but stood upright, with hands outstretched. The Greeks never abased themselves, before either god or man.

The belief in destiny (*Moira*)

To thinking peoples, however, the gods, even in the time of Homer, were never all-powerful. There is a greater power behind the world, the force of Destiny (*Moira*). To this even the gods are subject. Human life follows an inevitable destiny; man cannot understand it, and neither the gods nor man can change it. This is the true order in the universe. It is not arbitrary, as with the Mesopotamians; it is merely incomprehensible by man. Oedipus had no say in his fatal destiny. It was decreed before he was born; it was foretold, and those who knew of it tried to avoid it—but the destiny was fulfilled. Yet to mature Greek thought Oedipus was in no sense the plaything of the gods. He had to live as a man within the framework of this destiny, and his nobility lay in the human qualities he showed in facing it. In time Moira became incorporated among the powers of Zeus who "orders fate," but this did not alter the conception of fate itself.

Apollo and Dionysus—Mind and emotion

Beneath Zeus were the great powers of Apollo and Dionysus. Apollo was the serene god of light, supreme patron of the arts, of beauty, and of music; his ideal was moderation, self-control through the mind, *sophrosyne*, everything the Greek wished to be. Upon the shrine of Apollo at Delphi were inscribed the words "Nothing too much." Through his knowledge of destiny and of the hearts of men Apollo knew what was to come. At Delphi he could be consulted through a priestess whom he inspired. Any devotee could inquire the future from him and ask his advice. But he could not be petitioned or asked to change the future.

There was an old legend that for three months in the year Dionysus should rule at Delphi, and not Apollo. This was a profound psychological perception of the Greeks, for they knew as well as anyone else that man is not always ruled by reason and moderation, but often by passion. And Dionysus was the god of passion and inspiration. The worship of Dionysus is closely connected with the Orphic mysteries, a form of religion which does not seem, to the traditional way of thinking, characteristically Greek, and was certainly known under various guises in the Orient. Throughout Greece and the Near East were mystery centers where individual human beings were initiated through ceremonies, rituals, and trials, into the knowledge of death, resurrection, and immortality which was otherwise unknown to them. Unfortunately our own information on these mysteries must be inferred from the representations in Greek art, and the type-myths which were enacted during the celebration of the mysteries. Plutarch spoke of the initiation of his own day, centuries later, as an unforgettable experience, after which no initiate could ever be the same again. Innocent happiness dwelt in the darkness, we are told, and no one should receive knowledge which he is not strong enough to bear; hence the preparations and trials before initiation, and the well-kept secrets of the knowledge imparted there.

Dionysus, we know, had a miraculous rebirth after being torn to pieces (reminding us of the Egyptian Osiris myth); Demeter (celebrated at Eleusis) mourns the loss of her daughter Persephone to Hades, king of the underworld; Orpheus goes to the underworld to rescue Eurydice who had died on her wedding night, and by his sweet song so charms the lords of the underworld that he is permitted to rescue her on condition he does not look back. He fails to fulfill the condition, Eurydice returns, and Orpheus is torn in pieces by the Bacchantes. All these myths suggest the trials of initiation and the knowledge of immortality. Pindar, the Theban poet, was deeply influenced by these mysteries, as was Plato, and, traditionally, Aeschylus the tragic poet, who was accused of betraying them in his plays and was forced to take sanctuary and clear himself before the Areopagus by swearing he had never been initiated. We cannot at this date reconstruct the mysteries. From its representation in Athenian art we know of the procession of the initiates along the sacred way to Eleusis, and we know from Pindar of the certainty of immortality given there. It was the only really personal religion of ancient Greece, and to those who could take part it must have offered something that even the most beautiful of civic festivals could not match. But it was at the great annual festival in honor of the god Dionysus that the last great religious creation of the Greeks came to full expression, in which all the people participated to gain that catharsis of the emotions through pity and fear of which Aristotle spoke—the tragic drama of Aeschylus and Sophocles.

GREEK RELIGION AT ITS MATURITY—
THE TRAGIC DRAMA

The beginnings of drama—Relationship of man to the gods—Aeschylus

There is an extraordinary certainty about the drama of Aeschylus and Sophocles that reveals a profound faith in the divine moral order of the universe, and the framework within which man must live, that suggests an accepted and unquestioned faith among the Athenians of their day; though there is nothing of the idea of immortality associated with the mysteries, as found in the poetry of Pindar. Aeschylus is concerned only with the great problem of man on earth and his relationship with the gods; not with man's ultimate fate. The Greek tragic drama had only recently emerged from its beginnings in the dithyramb or sacred hymn to Dionysus, and the sacred dance. But with Aeschylus it has now become a true drama, with few characters and long, beautiful choric odes. For sheer magnificence it has not been surpassed by any later drama. The human beings are drawn on a heroic scale, never individuals such as one would meet on the streets, but types of all humanity. And in what is perhaps his profoundest play, the *Prometheus Bound,* there is no human being at all. A Titan, or demigod, is the hero.

The play, the only one we possess of

the original trilogy, is simple; it is only in its religious implications that it can be comprehended at all. Prometheus has stolen fire from heaven and given it to man; he glories in his deed, refusing to submit, even though Zeus threatens him with endless tortures. He has a secret which Zeus would know. But he refuses to divulge it, though Hermes comes from Zeus with threats, though Oceanos bids him submit for his own good because it is useless to fight with Zeus, and though Io, driven endlessly over the earth from jealousy of the gods, visits him on her journey. The play ends with the descent of Prometheus to the underworld, still defiant, and still glorying in his deed.

At one level of thought Prometheus is the type of rebellious, proud, and independent *man*, who cannot be coerced by threats, though the gods threaten to destroy him. The will of man, sovereign on earth, cannot even be compelled to submission to the gods when they are unjust. But at another level of thought it is also clear that we have not yet exhausted the meaning of Aeschylus, and that the secret that Prometheus knows and Zeus does not is the heart of it. It is impossible to interpret this play in strictly rational terms. It is a long meditation on the theme of the creation of man and his purpose in the world; it has its Hebrew analogy in the story of the Tower of Babel which tells how man tried to ascend to Heaven, and God was jealous and destroyed the tower and confounded the tongues. The thought of Aeschylus seems to be that man, by the use of his freedom, is potentially equal to the gods and can even destroy them; and for this reason they withheld that gift which ensured freedom to man—they withheld fire. So Prometheus stole the fire and gave it to man. The gods cannot take away the gift from man, once he has received it; but they can still punish him for his presumptuousness, and man will remain in the power of the gods—Prometheus will not be freed— until one of the immortals sacrifices himself, giving up his immortality to free him. Though we do not possess the *Prometheus Unbound*, the myth is known, and the play must have

contained something of it. Surely these teachings about immortality and the relationship between the gods and man are close to what must have been imparted in the mysteries; and if tradition is correct this was probably the play which brought the dramatist to trial before the Areopagus.

In the trilogy of the *Oresteia*, the theme is not so much the presumption of man which leads him to madness and destruction, though this is also implied when Agamemnon treads on the purple carpet, forgetting that his deeds of valor are granted him by the gods and are not his own. Returning from Troy, Agamemnon is murdered by his wife, Clytemnestra, her excuse being an earlier crime of Agamemnon in sacrificing their daughter Iphigenia to ensure the success of the expedition to Troy. Orestes, their son, is instructed by Apollo to avenge his father by murdering Clytemnestra and her paramour. He obeys, but is pursued by the Furies, beings whose task it is to pursue those guilty of matricide. Orestes flees over the earth before the Furies, at last appealing to Apollo to save him. But Apollo is powerless. Orestes was indeed right to murder his mother; it was an ancient duty to avenge his father. But by the laws of the universe he incurred the penalty of pursuit by the Furies. The case, however, is tried before the Athenian Areopagus, the votes are equal, and Athena, the judge, gives the casting vote to Orestes. The Furies refuse to accept the verdict until they are pacified by the gift of a new home at Athens, and they are now to become the kindly ones (the Eumenides), and henceforth act as guardian deities of Athens.

Clearly Aeschylus tells here of the passing of an old order. The crime of Orestes has been forgiven, and the sequence of murders is at an end. But it is significant that the avenging deities have now become the guardians of law and order in the city of Athens. The sanctions on a man's actions are still divine; but they are no longer arbitrary. Punishment does not follow automatically; it is no longer a law of the universe, crime breeding punishment and the punishment itself entailing another crime. Order

According to Herodotus, the Persian monarch Cyrus, after conquering Lydia and capturing Croesus, its king, at first intended to put him to death by burning. When Croesus was already on his pyre he suddenly remembered the words of the Athenian sage Solon who had warned him that no man could be considered happy as long as he was still alive. When Cyrus heard Croesus crying aloud the name of Solon, he asked for an explanation. When it was given him he tried to have the fire extinguished, but it was too late. Thereupon Croesus called on the god Apollo who put out the fire by sending a heavy rain. Croesus was then treated kindly by the Persian king who took him along on his campaigns and often asked for his advice. Here Croesus is shown on his pyre with the fire already alight. (From an Athenian amphora. HIRMER)

has been made out of chaos, and the gods withdraw a step, leaving punishment to the laws of the city, sanctified by Athena and the old gods.

But presumption against the gods still earns its punishment as a law of the universe. Man is not a god, and he must not think that he is. In the *Persians*, the history of the Persian War is made into a drama of man's presumption against the gods. Xerxes has been too fortunate, he is king of the world. He experiences *koros* or satiety, and he presumes upon it by attempting to conquer Greece without divine sanction. This is *hybris*. He is led into folly (*ate*) and the result is *nemesis*, or destruction. This theme of the sequence of *koros, hybris, ate, nemesis*, which runs through the bulk of Greek tragedy (it is even implicit in the *Prometheus*), through the poetry of Solon, and through the histories of Herodotus and Thucydides, is essentially the Greek con-

ception of sin. In Herodotus the Persians commit *hybris*, while in Thucydides it is the Athenians. The good fortune of Athens leads her to the sin of *hybris* in barbarously destroying the neutral and unoffending Melians, thus denying the power of the gods to punish, and the common laws of humanity. This leads to the expedition against Syracuse with its grand folly of deposing the general who urged the expedition and appointing as general its chief opponent, and the inexcusable delays out of sheer superstition— this was *ate; nemesis* followed when the entire expedition was destroyed. The dramatic juxtaposition of these events in Thucydides shows the way his mind was working.

Sophocles—The human drama—Search for the meaning of life and purpose of suffering

With Sophocles we are at the height of the human drama. The gods are always present, but no longer on the stage, while man moves within the framework of his destiny. In the *Ajax,* the hero is presumptuous, he thinks he has the better right to the arms of Achilles, which are awarded to his rival Odysseus; he plans to murder his enemies and rivals, but a god sends madness upon him, and he only butchers the animals belonging to the Achaean army. When Ajax recovers he is so ashamed that he dies by his own hand. He had not the right to boast of his own prowess, and *claim* the arms, and it was this presumption that led to his madness and destruction.

In the *Oedipus* trilogy Sophocles moves on to an even more profound problem, the problem of human suffering, and its relation to human destiny. And to this problem he was unable to give any solution until in his old age he completed the trilogy with the *Oedipus at Colonus.* In the *Antigone,* the first of the plays to be written—though the last in the sequence of events—Antigone refuses to accept the right of the tyrant Creon to make a law which infringes "the immutable, unwritten laws of heaven." For this she has to die, and she meets her death nobly. Yet her death is not meaningless, for she has vindicated the sacred rights of humanity and earned a glorious name; while, on the other hand, Creon, in trying to change the divine law, has committed *hybris.* In folly he condemns Antigone and spurns the pleas of his son, and destruction comes upon him with the suicide of his wife and son and the abandonment of his throne.

In the *Oedipus Rex* the hero has been destined to murder his father and marry his mother; but he commits these crimes in ignorance, and in any case he could not have avoided them since they were decreed by his destiny. Nevertheless, after he discovers what he has done he blinds himself, and wanders through the land, led by his daughters. What, asks Sophocles, is the purpose of such a destiny? He gives us the answer in the *Oedipus at Colonus.* Oedipus has now grown old, and is ready to die, and an oracle has foretold that the land in which his bones rest will be blessed. He chooses to die near

Athens, whose king, Theseus, gives him his own tomb. Theseus accompanies him into the tomb and leaves him. And suddenly Oedipus is no longer there, and a great wonder falls upon the messenger who relates that fact. The sufferings are no longer meaningless. The king has been purified by them, and his bones will bring good fortune upon Athens.

These plays have not been described for their dramatic quality, nor has any mention been made of the wealth of imagery in the poetry, nor of the extraordinary dramatic irony, especially in Sophocles, nor of the spectacular effects and the tragic atmosphere created in these masterpieces; rather has Greek tragedy been described here to bring out the religious nature of the whole. The audience knew all the stories, there were no surprises for them; plot was of little importance. The purpose of this drama was, as Aristotle stated it, to win a catharsis through pity and fear; to arouse appreciation of the moral grandeur of the universe, ruled by the unalterable moral laws of the gods. The audience was made up of the ordinary men and women of Athens, but they were present at a festival, the festival of Dionysus, god of inspiration. Time and again they awarded the prize to Sophocles; he gave them the kind of experience they expected of a drama. When Euripides began to exhibit his plays, the Athenians consistently refused to award him the crown. They did not want plays about ordinary people, however pathetic; they did not want to question the gods, doubt the myths, and be generally left with a feeling of mental discomfort. They wanted to appreciate the nobility of man in the face of his destiny. Tragedy is only possible when a good man meets misfortune undeservedly, or beyond his deserts. If a villain receives his just deserts or a good man finds happiness, what of it? And the contrary would be morally repellent, as Aristotle points out. But if a good man suffers, the gods are at work; the laws of the universe are being manifested, and there is a mystery. In short, man can rise above his suffering, and in so doing he shows himself worthy of his position as the crown of creation—a true man.

Transition from religion to philosophy—Euripides, the questioner—Are the gods unjust?

Into this world enters Euripides and he has lost his faith. The gods do play their part in earthly affairs, they do punish man; but without reason. The gods have authority and power but, according to human standards, no justice—and yet this fact appears to be a law of the universe. Heroes do not really suffer nobly. They are human, like you and me, and they rage against the tyranny of the gods. They have to make the best of things, but do not call that justice. There is no such thing, says Euripides, as absolute justice, or god-directed justice. Man is the measure of all things.

But Euripides is a man of deep feeling. He realizes the pathos of a human being who is afflicted by destiny and arbitrary misfortune. He shows how some characters bear misfortune nobly, like Polyxena, Iphigenia, and Hippolytus, while others rage against it like Hecuba, queen of Troy, and Medea.[1] He is acquainted with all the human passions, and does not hesitate to show them on the stage. His plays are problem plays, appealing to the mind, not to religious feeling. Not a single play is really a tragedy in the sense that it purges the emotions, leaving the audience in a religious awe at the nobility of man in the face of his destiny. There may be awe at the gods, as in the *Bacchae;* but the question at the end is always, What kind of gods are these?

The real tragedy is that Euripides himself did not know. His is a work of the critical, rational mind, a destructive work which was necessary in the process of human evolution, and ushered in the age of individualism and reliance on the mind alone, without benefit of gods. His drama concerns the behavior of men in an unknown world, a

world without morality, in which men are not rewarded for their good deeds nor necessarily punished for their evil ones. Heracles in the *Madness of Heracles* is a much-tried man who has been obeying the orders of the gods, but through no fault of his own has incurred the anger of Hera, who sends madness upon him so that he murders his own wife and children. Even Madness herself complains of her task but is forced to perform it. Similarly, Hippolytus is a virtuous young man who wants to devote himself to Artemis, but in so doing incurs the jealousy of Aphrodite; the Trojan women, in the play of the same name, are victims of a war which was none of their making and in which they had no say; Pentheus, in the *Bacchae,* does his duty as king and warns the women of his country not to indulge in the orgies of Dionysus, and after the god has induced a frenzy in him he is torn in pieces by the women; Medea is a violent murderess but escapes through her magic powers. So the list could go on.

Euripides has a vast pity for man in these circumstances, but only very rarely does this become respect. Man, according to his experience, is not dignified by his sufferings; on the contrary, he usually becomes querulous, though sometimes he may have twinges of conscience for evil deeds he may have committed. Indeed, the first use of any Greek word for conscience is found in Euripides—interestingly enough, in a play where we can make a direct comparison with Aeschylus. In Euripides' *Orestes,* after the hero has murdered his mother, he wanders over the earth; but there are no Furies following him. He is just ill at ease. Menelaus asks him why he is troubled, and he replies: "It is my *synesis* [the Latin word *con-scientia* is an exact translation of this word], because I realize I have done terrible things." No longer are there Beings sent by the gods of the universe to pursue him; on the contrary he is inwardly troubled.

The tragedy of Euripides is that he is not an atheist, he cannot deny the gods; he has lost the old faith and has acquired no new one. Though a destructive critic, he can-

---

[1] Polyxena and Hecuba appear in the play called the *Hecuba;* Iphigenia behaves nobly in the play called *Iphigenia in Aulis;* Medea and Hippolytus are in the plays named after them.

not be a complete rationalist. He is still searching for a solution. And to crown the tragedy there seems to be only one immortality that he can recognize—the immortality of the individual man through his children. But children in the plays of Euripides are shown as defenseless, and time and again they are murdered uselessly. There is a vacuum in the thought of Euripides that cannot be filled. It was left for Socrates to fill it, to show that conscience could take the place of external sanctions, that if all the baggage of the old gods were discarded and man searched himself he could find the good and the just; that the intellect was the crown of man's faculties, and man could live and die by his own inner light.

So religion became philosophy.[2]

THE ADVANCE OF RATIONALISM

The criticism of the Sophists

The principal founders of Sophism are Protagoras of Abdera and Gorgias of Leontini (in Sicily). Gorgias arrived in Athens in 427 B.C. on an embassy, and won immediate success as a teacher. If Protagoras was still alive at the time—his dates are uncertain—he was no longer actively teaching. These two teachers must be regarded as the most influential of the Sophists. It was Protagoras who is credited with the fundamental premise held by all later Sophists, "Man is the measuring rod for all things, of things that are, that they are, and of things that are not, that they are not." In other words, all knowledge is subjective and relative, and nothing can be known for certain about either the gods or physical nature; speculation about the nature of things as engaged in by the natural philosophers is futile. The external world as it appears to man must be taken as the only reality he can know. It did not follow, in Protagoras' own view, that man should deny the gods, still less that he should cease to

attend the religious ceremonies revered by Athenians. As far as he was concerned, such ceremonies performed a useful purpose insofar as they helped maintain social cohesion in the city. But men should not believe that other men, their predecessors, had any knowledge of the gods that present-day men no longer had. No one had ever had any real knowledge of such things because such knowledge was unattainable.

Obviously this teaching left the door open for more radical thinkers, such as Gorgias who emphasized much more strongly than Protagoras man's absolute ignorance and who assumed a stance of total skepticism. Nothing exists, he said; if it does it is unknowable by man; if anything is knowable it cannot be communicated. Gorgias' enormous success as a teacher and the high fees he commanded demonstrate clearly how strongly his teachings and methods appealed to the young Athenian intellectuals.

So many other Sophists are known to us that it is difficult to classify them as a school. Some even speculated on physical problems, giving Aristophanes the opportunity to parody them in his *Clouds*. All must be classed as professional teachers who accepted money for what they taught; and it must be assumed that they would not have commanded fees for their services if their teachings did not have a practical value for their pupils. When they were criticized for "making the worse case appear the better," this was because they helped litigants win cases in the law-courts, or taught them to influence the Assembly. The Athenian ambassadors who told the Melians who had refused to join the Athenian alliance in the Peloponnesian War to behave reasonably, and not to expect the gods to help them when they were in a militarily weaker position, were surely influenced by Sophistic thought. "Of men we know, and of gods we can be fairly sure, that they take power whenever they can." Similar arguments are put forward by such a Sophist as Thrasymachus who argues (in Plato's *Republic*) that justice is the interest of the stronger party.

Such Sophistic teachings fell on fertile ground in Athens during the Peloponnesian

---

[2] For this interpretation of Euripides, which, incidentally, necessitated a rereading of all his plays, I am greatly indebted to the masterly monograph by A. Rivier, *Essai sur le tragique d'Euripide* (Lausanne: 1944), which seems to be far too little known.

War. The Athenians were powerful and proposed to have their way, without fear of any disasters except those that could be inflicted on them by men. It was comforting to be told that there were no divine sanctions because there were no gods; that there was no absolute "good," only what convention taught to be good, and convention could be defied. Moreover, in an Assembly in which the common people were the absolute masters, it was helpful for a speaker to have at his disposal all the arts of rhetoric, as taught by the Sophists. Alcibiades, for one example, was able to persuade the Assembly to vote for the Syracusan expedition and to elect him one of the commanding generals in spite of his well known unstable character. When he defected (and went) to Sparta he was able to present his case in such a convincing manner that the Spartans were willing to believe him and take his advice. In fact he had fled to Sparta in preference to returning to Athens to stand trial for sacrilege. But when he reached Sparta he did not content himself with merely requesting asylum. He betrayed the Athenian military secrets, and was thus instrumental in bringing about the destruction of the Syracusan expedition. To the Spartans he pointed out how "natural" it was for any man to be willing to do anything that would help him to return to his city, even if this involved returning in the wake of its conquerors. Apparently he succeeded in convincing the Spartans—a perfect example, at least in our eyes, of "making the worse case appear the better."

Socrates and the Reconstruction of Ethics

It has been noted above that Nietzsche blamed both Socrates and Euripides for the current of rationalism that put an end to the serene intuitive confidence in the world order decreed by the gods, a state of affairs accepted without questioning by the older dramatists. Socrates he regarded as the prototype of intellectual man, accepting nothing on faith, questioning everything, introducing uncertainty and doubt where before there had been certainty and confidence. If blame was due, surely Nietzsche should have blamed the Sophists, not Socrates, whose life task it was to try to repair the damage done by the Sophists, at least in the field of ethics which was his primary, and possibly his exclusive, interest. Unfortunately we do not know what the real Socrates taught. He did not commit any of his thoughts to writing. Aristotle credits him with devising the inductive method and with the definition of universals, which suggests that the "method" always associated with his name was distinctively his. Xenophon provided some valuable biographical details. But virtually all that we know of Socrates has to be gleaned from the dialogues of Plato.

These dialogues are centered around the figure of Socrates, who is shown always questioning, showing up the ignorance of those who laid claim to some knowledge, and striving tirelessly to find the truth after he had first revealed what was not true. We may thus safely assume that it was Socrates who invented the "dialectical" system, always known thereafter as the "Socratic method," and that he offended the sensibilities of the more conservative Athenians by his constant probing. It is also likely that there was a political motive behind his prosecution and condemnation by the restored democracy— perhaps because too many of his disciples had supported the oligarchy which preceded it, including Critias, its leader. What we cannot determine is how many of Plato's philosophical ideas were also held by Socrates, and thus what influence Socrates had on Plato. Plato was only about twenty-eight years old when the seventy-year-old Socrates drank the hemlock. He could not, therefore, have been present in person during many of the years when Socrates was posing his questions in the streets of Athens.

It will be assumed here that Socrates, impressed by the famous dictum of Protagoras and convinced of its general truth, nevertheless could not bring himself to accept all its implications. He thought that men could know something, but that this was not what passed for knowledge in his day. Such knowledge was simply legend or popular opinion, and it could not withstand rigorous

Socrates. This statue suggests the reason why Alcibiades, in Plato's Symposium, *compares Socrates with Marsyas the satyr, the Greek model of ugliness. Yet the artist has also contrived to show the deep seriousness of the master engaged in a problem which requires concentration of thought.* (COURTESY BRITISH MUSEUM)

questioning. The only way to come to real knowledge was, therefore, to discover first what was *not* true, allowing no questionable statement to pass without criticism. What could no longer be questioned and was acceptable to all could alone be true. However small this nugget of truth might be, it was at least something, and therefore preferable to the mere acceptance of popular opinion. The acquisition of this kind of knowledge was necessarily hard work. Socrates therefore called himself the "midwife of knowledge," in that through his questioning he brought knowledge to birth through the labor of the dialectic.

If men can indeed discover the truth by this method, an important philosophical question arises. If men have not acquired this knowledge during their lifetime because all of them have the same knowledge once they have "brought it to birth," then it must be present initially within man, however deeply it may be buried. How and when therefore did man acquire this knowledge? This was a problem to which, as we shall see, Plato turned his attention, whether or not Socrates himself ever did so. Plato even went so far as to demonstrate that an illiterate slave "knew" the Pythagorean theorem, although he was not aware of it until Socrates extorted it from him (*Meno,* 82–85). If, as we are assuming, Socrates' own purpose was to repair the damage done to man's beliefs by the criticism of the Sophists, then above all what he was doing was trying to discover the nature of "the good," as Plato shows him trying in several of his dialogues. If the code of right behavior is not to be derived from tradition, popular opinion, or the supposed will of the gods, the only alternative remaining is that it must be found within man himself. An individual ethic based on man's own knowledge must replace the traditional one. Socrates seems to assume that if man does know the good he will follow it; for no one who truly knows the good and has spent so much effort in attaining this knowledge will deliberately choose to follow evil. If this is true, then ignorance (an intellectual failing) is the root of all moral evil — not an infirmity of the *will*, as Thomas Aquinas and most Christian philosophers were to insist in a later age. Plato, as rational as his master, was later to define courage (for most people a virtue of the will) as a *knowledge* of what is and is not to be feared (*Protagoras*, 360).

Ethical individualism, as taught by Socrates, required the preliminary labor of the dialectic and was most certainly not regarded by him as an excuse for simply doing what one liked. The behavior of some of his disciples, as, for example, Alcibiades, or Critias, tyrannical leader of the oligarchy who carried out a bloody proscription of the democratic leaders after the Athenian defeat in the Peloponnesian War, did him no credit. In Plato's *Meno* there is an incident (*Meno*, 95) which shows how easily an enemy could misunderstand the purpose of his questioning. Socrates had been showing that no virtuous man had ever been able to teach virtue to his son. Anytus, one of the accusers at his trial, at once jumps to the conclusion that Socrates is maligning these men instead of using them to prove his philosophical point. In the political conditions of the restoration of the democracy after the oligarchic revolution, it was difficult to believe that any man could be searching for philosophical truth. Socrates himself was unquestionably a profoundly social being and lover of his polis. He had a high opinion of the truth that lay behind the religious traditions of Greece, though he always interpreted them in his own way, as spiritual rather than physical truths. It was not his task to destroy the law and government of his polis, even though they were based on tradition; he fully accepted the right of the democracy to put him to death under its laws. These laws provided the whole framework of his social life; they were not unchangeable and their ethical content might no doubt be improved. But if it happened that he was the victim of the laws in their present state, then it still behooved him as a citizen to abide by them.

Within himself he only answered to the call of his own inner knowledge. He understood very fully that others might be moved by tradition and prejudice; but this was no excuse for him to follow their example. During his trial he told the jurors about his inner guide, his *daimonion* or little god, who never told him what to do, only what he must not do. This *daimonion* for him took the place of the sanctions of the gods and the traditional piety associated with them.

In 399 B.C. his enemies brought Socrates to trial before a jury of the people on a charge of atheism and corrupting the youth. It was a clever charge, for it was, in appearance, true. Socrates took part in all the festivals and performed all his religious observances, but he certainly spoke of his *daimonion* as his guide, and he did teach—indeed, the whole of his teaching led inevitably to the conclusion—that a new dispensation had come when man was to be free, to rule himself, not be ruled by the gods. And insofar as this was his instruction to his pupils, then he "corrupted the youth."

The account of his trial in Plato's *Apology* shows his moral courage and his confidence that his own path was right. He defends himself against the charges only by affirming them. Convicted by a small majority and asked for a suggestion as to what punishment he deserves, with the same serene confidence he tells them that he ought to have a pension and be supported at the city's expense for the rest of his life. This irony was too much for human endurance, and by a larger vote the jury condemned him to death. Instead of going into exile as his friends urge, an exile which would undoubtedly have been winked at, he accepts his sentence, not in stoical resignation but with dignity, tenderness for his friends, and good humor. While he awaits the fatal hemlock he discourses on immortality, still with the same calm reason that he had shown during his life. There is, he believes, an inner self in man, his divine part; this, being of the same nature as the divine, cannot die, and will dwell forever with the gods. But he will soon know. He shows no fear and no regrets.

So he drinks the hemlock; and by the manner of his dying he truly ensured his immortality on earth.

Constructive philosophy—Idealism of Plato

The heart of Plato's teaching stems from the original conception of Socrates that the human being can know the good; and that, knowing it, he can do it. What Plato seeks to discover is *how* he can know it, and *what* it is exactly that he knows. By using the dialogue form he shows us the whole process by which he arrived at his conclusions; hence the endless stimulation that Plato has afforded to all subsequent mankind.

Assuming then that man can know the good, how can he know it? To this Plato answers that there is a spiritual or nonphysical element in man, his mind or *Nous*, with which he thinks, which is an activity of his soul. The *Nous* is able to perceive the Forms or Ideas, which are likewise spiritual. In his famous parable of the cave (*Republic*, 514–517) Plato (Socrates?) asked his listeners to imagine a cave from which nothing in the external world was visible, only the shadows of the objects outside which were taken by the cave-dwellers to be the only reality. A cave-dweller, going out into the outside world, would see the sun and everything else in this outside world, and know that they were *real*, and would know that what he had hitherto taken for reality was only shadows. By this story Plato wishes to suggest that earthly phenomena are merely reflections of a "higher" nonphysical reality.

Elsewhere in the *Republic* and in many other dialogues Plato developed his theory of knowledge more fully, making it clear that the world of Forms contains the archetypes of all the visible objects on earth. These objects are *particulars,* and none corresponds perfectly to the Form (or universal archetype). No goat or horse, tree, or even table is identical to its heavenly archetype, but all partake of some of the qualities of the archetype. The great abstractions such as "the good," "the beautiful," and "the just" are

archetypes of the same kind, and man may come close to learning their nature through systematic thinking (the activity of the *Nous*), that is, by the use of the Socratic dialectic. This doctrine is known as Platonic Realism (the Forms and Ideas are real, whereas their earthly counterparts are unreal and imperfect). It was still discussed with much ardor in the Middle Ages, the realists holding that the Universal Church was a Platonic Idea or "Universal," whereas individual churches might be imperfect but were entitled to respect because of their relationship, subordinate though it was, to the "Universal." (It may be noted that in our day such a theory would be called Idealism, not Realism, as it was in the Middle Ages.)

According to the Platonic theory of knowledge only particulars were perceptible to the senses, but man was able to recognize a goat, know that a landscape was beautiful, or that an action was good because the Forms of goats, beauty, and goodness were present within his own soul, although he was not consciously aware of them. Plato describes in the *Phaedrus* how the soul before its incarnation in a body passes through the spiritual world and is able to perceive directly all the archetypes, "justice, its very self, and likewise temperance (*sophrosyne*) and . . . the veritable knowledge of being that veritably is." Reason alone can behold it, and all true knowledge is knowledge thereof."[3]

For Plato, holding as he did that true knowledge was to be attained only through thinking, it was more important to try to approach the ideal through his thinking than it was to consider in detail the multifarious phenomena of the sense world, and mundane matters such as the forms taken by historically known constitutions—a study which Aristotle regarded as essential before he could write about politics. When Plato came to write his *Republic* he did have practical

[3] *Phaedrus,* 247. Since the *Phaedrus* is an early dialogue, and Plato does not insist elsewhere on this aspect of his theory of knowledge, it is thought by many scholars that it was Socrates, not Plato, at all events not Plato in his more mature years, who held the theory that all true knowledge is recognition of what had been perceived by the soul before birth.

ends in view, as he is careful to tell us. But since he was aware of the defects of all constitutions known to him he preferred to approach the question from a different angle, namely to try to discover the nature of justice since it was his belief that it was justice that held all societies together. The nearest approximation to a definition of justice that he could find was that it consisted in giving to each man his due. If, therefore, every citizen were to hold a position in the social order that enabled him to do that for which he was best fitted, and if he performed this task to the best of his ability, then the society would be a just one. Since he assumed that justice (as an archetype) would be the same for the state as for the citizen, then the ends of both the citizen and the state would be fully served under such a system as he proposed.

The next step was to inquire into how human potentialities could best be realized within a social framework, and the kind of social institutions that would be needed. There is no need to follow here the logical progression of his thought to his conclusion that the enlightened despotism of a board of professional guardians (philosopher kings and queens) was the best possible form of government. The reason for this preference was that they alone had taken the trouble to try to discover "the good," and had some near to attaining the knowledge. However, such men and women would have to be utterly dedicated to the pursuit of this knowledge. They could possess neither material goods nor family ties, for these would tend to warp their judgment. With such a body of truly scientific professionals there would be no need for laws or for the exercise of power; for at all grades in the society each man would have received the education, and would hold the position, for which he was best fitted.

It has often been pointed out, justly, that Plato makes a number of assumptions which are extremely questionable—for instance, that public and private virtue are identical, and that a state made up of good individuals will be able to function harmoniously as a state. But it will usually be found that these as-

sumptions are the result of his fundamental belief that no one, knowing the good, would deliberately choose to do evil. If the state is a just one, its duties will be just and good; the individual, if he is good, will desire to perform such duties. Duty and inclination must coincide. If they do not, then either the state needs to be corrected or the individual needs to be improved—by development and adjustment, not by repression and force.

Plato may also be accused of neglecting the psychology of man, as it *must* have been known to him from experience. What was the use of theorizing about an ideal state when he knew of its impossibility in real life? Again the answer must be that by showing men the ideal good—which was, for him, not impossible of realization but only extremely difficult—he was pointing out a direction for the aspirations and endeavors of man. That it was not his last thought on the subject is shown by his later works, the *Statesman* and *Laws,* in which he outlines the "second-best state," the state ruled by laws. Laws are directed to the ethical improvement of man, but cannot be as "scientifically" impeccable as the personal guidance of the philosopher kings. Elsewhere he shows that he is not unaware of human psychology. He recognizes the irrational part of man, but does not consider it incurable. The desires can be controlled by reason, which, in the light of its knowledge of the good, will give man the power of evaluating his desires at their true worth, thus helping him to abandon those of which his reason disapproves.

As with the state, so with man. The harmonious functioning of all the parts that go to make up the full man, this is self-realization under the guiding power of the *Nous.* It is a psychology the truth of which would be vehemently denied by both Christians and Freudians, who both deny the power of the mind to control the will unaided. Perhaps to these the psychology of Plato would seem naïve; but it was the fullest and most complete expression of the Greek ideal of harmony and *sophrosyne,* and of the Greek belief in the efficacy of human thinking. If it is a glorification of the one specifically human power, this to the Greeks would have been a recommendation. Oedipus to the Greeks was not a complex but a human being, proud and erring but undefeated; and they were glad to be considered of his company.

Aristotle—the philosopher–scientist

Aristotle was the son of a Chalcidian physician in the service of Philip of Macedon. He studied at the Academy of Plato and was unquestionably his most brilliant pupil. He was tutor of Alexander, son of Philip, for several years, returning to Athens and opening a school himself (the Lyceum), where he taught for twelve years. Forced into exile on the death of Alexander, he died a year later in 322 B.C. at the age of sixty-two.

By the time of his death the great emigration of Greeks to the lands conquered by Alexander had already begun. Aristotle is therefore the last philosopher of the Hellenic period to be studied in this chapter. Since he devoted much of his work to an analysis of the theories of his predecessors, and since in almost all the fields in which they had worked he made original contributions of his own, his death does indeed mark the end of an epoch.

Aristotle was without question the most learned man of his day, but unlike Plato he did not write inspiringly. Indeed, the work of Aristotle that has survived resembles lecture notes rather than finished works intended for publication. Other works that he is known to have written have disappeared, and may well have been more pleasurable to read. His *Rhetoric*, which has survived, is lively and even humorous. His gigantic capacity for systematic thought and careful argument stands out clearly from his surviving works. But some of the sentences are so sparsely constructed that in all subsequent ages when Aristotle has been studied commentaries have almost invariably been utilized. Many medieval schoolmen, as well as Alexandrian and Muslim philosophers, made their reputations by publishing commentaries on Aristotle; sometimes it was these commentaries rather than the original works of Aristotle that were used as the textbooks (a fate that has, to a lesser degree, befallen Karl Marx during the last century).

The world known to the Greeks was a small one, and there were relatively few "brute facts" known to them. It was thus possible for Aristotle to attempt a synthesis of knowledge in all fields of enquiry—a task that would be unthinkable in our world of specialization. Naturally he made many mistakes and sometimes rejected potentially profitable ideas put forward by his predecessors. However, unlike the vast majority of his predecessors, he did engage in much firsthand investigation, especially in biology. But his reputation must rest on the manner in which he tried to use the tool of logical analysis to impose order and pattern on the multifarious phenomena of the external world, insofar as they were known to him. Logic as a systematic discipline was a creation of Aristotle, and it has already been noted that he had to create much of the philosophical language necessary for his analysis. His purpose was always to make the world intelligible to the reason, not to increase the sum of human knowledge—although, in fact, in his biological works he did increase it.

As a Greek his attitude was quite different from that of most modern scientists who hope by their work to add to the corpus of human knowledge some small piece of information in a limited field. He felt no need for improved instruments for observation, such as the telescope or the microscope. It is probable that he believed that all worthwhile knowledge was already known (as did most of his medieval successors). What was necessary was to understand, and to fit all knowledge into a comprehensible pattern, to connect knowledge in one field with knowledge in another. For this task his intellectual tools (which did not include mathematics, a discipline in which he lacked interest) must seem to us inadequate; and his excessive reliance on common sense for many of his theories appears naïve and "unscientific." Many Hellenistic scientists did work that, from our point of view, was far more scientific, notably Archimedes. But none of them attempted to do what Aristotle had done; and his work, for all its weaknesses, faults, and mistakes, was the most nearly complete expression of the Greek desire for an orderly and harmonious whole. His total work is one of the greatest intellectual monuments in the history of mankind.

Whether Aristotle was a true scientist is a question whose answer depends on our definition of science. No one can dispute his preeminence as a philosopher, a searcher after wisdom and understanding. If, however, the primary purposes of science are to discover new knowledge, to bring already verified facts and observations within a framework of general laws, themselves derived from previous observations and verified hypotheses, then Aristotle has some claims to the title of scientist. Nevertheless, from our point of view he falls down because of his penchant for "jumping" to conclusions based on insufficient research, instead of humbly recognizing that he did not have enough facts at his disposal to warrant any conclusions at all. Even so, he did more research than any of his predecessors, not least in his extensive study of Greek constitutions, on the basis of which he wrote his *Politics*. It is unfortunate that for so many centuries Aristotle was regarded as "the master of those who know," and that his work, even in the fields in which he was weakest, was regarded as authoritative. He cannot be blamed because medieval and even early modern university faculties placed his work at the center of their curricula, and in so doing neglected more promising fields of enquiry. But by contrast it can be contended that his influence on medieval theology was beneficent, in that it introduced systematic reasoning into a study not hitherto noted for it.

It is, in short, grossly unfair to criticize Aristotle either for the aberrations of his successors fifteen hundred years later, or for his failure to attempt something that we, more than two thousand years later, think he ought to have done. What he did do was what he set out to do. In the remainder of this section an attempt will be made to give a few indications which may serve to suggest the scope of his genius.

Causality

Fundamental to all Aristotle's thought is his analysis of causation. To explain this it is best to use his own illustration—the work of the sculptor. First, there is the "material cause," the raw material from which the statue will be carved; then the "formal cause," the form of the finished statue; next the "efficient cause," the sculptor who carves it, or, when no human effort is involved, the agency through which something happens. The fourth cause is what Aristotle calls the "final cause," or "that for the sake of which" (there was as yet no word to denote this concept in the Greek language) the sculpture is created. Although only the last two would be considered "causes" by us, Aristotle no doubt meant that all four elements in the making of a statue must be known if the whole process is to be understood.

Now it is clear that nothing would happen to the marble if there were no sculptor to carve it. But at the same time Aristotle recognized that the sculptor would not set to work (the efficient cause) unless he first had an *idea* in his mind. Therefore the final cause precedes the efficient cause in time, while it is at the same time the motivating force without which there would have been no sculpture.

Change

This piece of logical analysis Aristotle carried over into all his other discussions. Everything on earth, he said, is composed of potentiality and actuality. What a being has already become is its actuality; what it has not yet become but is capable of becoming is its potentiality. Change consists simply in the actualizing of potentiality; the operative force behind change is the final cause, which operates not only in the human sphere but in all nature. In the human sphere Aristotle is clearly correct. A student wishing to study history first has the motivation, the final cause, "that for the sake of which" he reads this book. The reading of the book (we may hope) is the efficient cause, which succeeds in actualizing his hitherto unrealized potentiality. In his *De anima* (*On the Soul*) Aristotle generalizes this observation by defining the proper end of man as the fullest possible "self-realization," the actualizing of all his potentialities to the maximum possible in a lifetime. Somewhat less metaphysically in his *Nicomachean Ethics* Aristotle concluded that the final cause in a man's life is happiness, that the search for happiness is the only goal to which man can set himself, having regard to his nature. Since man, according to Aristotle, is a rational animal, this happiness must consist in the final analysis of a kind of intellectual contemplation, since this is the fullest actualizing of that element in man which makes him what he is—his *Nous* or mind.

Aristotle has no difficulty with the question of which came first, the chicken or the egg. For him the whole (the chicken) is logically prior to the egg, because the egg is constituted in the way it is for the sole purpose of becoming a chicken. The egg actualizes its potentiality when it becomes a chicken, the chicken when it becomes a laying hen. The hen itself has its own purpose in the world, and it is what it is so that it may fulfill this purpose. To Aristotle it was an axiom that "nature does nothing in vain," and it was a legitimate intellectual activity to speculate about those purposes as long as the most rigorous logic was employed.

It must be admitted that this "teleology," the explanation of the world in terms of ends, or final causes, does tend to make the world appear a very orderly place, even if it gives too little attention to more efficient causes, which are today regarded as the main subject for scientific study. Medieval Christians with their belief in Divine Providence naturally felt fully at home with this aspect of Aristotle's work. It was at least a "scientific" explanation of what had hitherto been accepted on faith.

Epistemology—the problem of the universals

Aristotle's answer to Plato's problem of the relation between the universal and the particular is typical of his moderation, his belief in the Golden Mean between extremes that he expounds in his *Ethics* as the basis for right human conduct. He could not accept Plato's "realism," still less his (or Socrates') notion that the soul before birth had perceived the universal archetypes and recognized them after incarnation in a human body. On the other hand he could not accept the idea that particulars were the only realities. He preferred to adopt a halfway position, often called Conceptualism. All objects, he claimed, have both a visible part and an invisible part, the visible perceived directly by the sense organs, and the invisible, the object of thought, perceived by the nonphysical *Nous*. Thus the Form or Idea is not in heaven, as Plato held, but is an integral part of the object. However, it requires the cooperation of the soul and the body if an object is to be both perceived (as a particular) and recognized (as a member of a species, or universal). In the Middle Ages Thomas Aquinas used Aristotle's concept of an active nonphysical element in human thinking as his major proof for the existence and immortal nature of the soul. A nonphysical or spiritual element, he said, cannot die, and therefore the human *Nous,* or, as he called it, the "active intellect" must survive death, leaving the sense organs to decay with the body.

As will be seen from the few examples of Aristotle's thinking given above, he showed no hesitation in providing solutions to problems that have exercised philosophers and scientists ever since; few if any of these solutions would be found acceptable today. It is possible that the extraordinary certainty with which Aristotle propounded them was responsible for his enormous reputation both in the Muslim world (where he was called simply "the Philosopher") and in the Christian world of the Middle Ages. Thinkers such as Roger Bacon speculated as to whether he could have received his knowledge indirectly from Solomon who received it directly from God—to which Bacon's contemporary, Albertus Magnus, retorted that Aristotle was only a man and could and did make errors, some of which Albertus noted. Emperor Frederic II of the Holy Roman Empire, whose speciality was hunting with birds, concluded from Aristotle's ornithological errors that Aristotle "rarely if ever" hunted with birds (in which judgment we may agree with Frederic). But these cavils scarcely detracted from Aristotle's reputation or authority as a philosopher or scientist. Before this reputation could be overthrown there had to be not only more knowledge, but also a system of scientific enquiry that used quite different principles from Aristotle's purely logical analysis.

But for his day, with the intellectual tools available to him (most of which he either invented or systematized) his work was a magnificent achievement, typically Greek in its rationalism. If his system had the built-in weakness inherent in all rational constructions not subjected to empirical verification— doomed to be superseded when the facts catch up with them—it was strong enough to withstand all assaults for fifteen hundred years. Even today the books on politics and ethics are not entirely superseded. Even though based on empirical evidence drawn from city-states, Aristotle's generalizations have often a wider application, in much the same way as Thucydides' *History of the Peloponnesian War,* though concerned with a relatively small war and relatively small city-state revolutions, continues to tell us much that is of value about all wars and all revolutions. Aristotle's *Ethics* presents one of the very few nonreligious ethical systems, and was not long ago used as a partial basis for his own "humanistic" ethics by such a well-known psychoanalytical writer as Erich Fromm (in *Man For Himself*). It is difficult to find many other writers from antiquity or the Middle Ages of whom as much can be said—and of these almost all were Greek.

HIPPOCRATES AND THE BEGINNING OF SCIENTIFIC MEDICINE

The age that followed Aristotle was an age of science rather than philosophy. Even the chief philosophical schools were primarily interested in ethics and consolation, and speculation itself became less disinterested. This notable flowering of science will be discussed in the next chapter, and reasons for it will be suggested. With the exception of mathematics, which will be dealt with as a whole under Hellenistic science, only the practical art of medicine can really be said to have flourished in the Classical Age.

It is here called an art (or craft) intentionally since this was what the Greeks themselves insisted it was. They objected very strongly to premature attempts to establish it as a systematic science until enough material was available for proper theorizing. In this they were very much in accord with modern medicine, as were the methods employed. Until very recently medicine always seems to have stood somewhat apart from the other sciences, and owed little to them. This also seems to have been the case in Greece of the time of Hippocrates, although Empedocles the Sicilian, with his four elements derived from his philosophical speculations, provided medicine with a theory of four humors which persisted in various forms even into modern times, and was accepted by the school of Hippocrates.

Early Greek medicine began in the temples, as probably also in Egypt, and much of it returned there in the Hellenistic and Roman ages. Here the patient, under the direction of the priest, lay down to sleep; and while he was asleep the god Aesculapius approached him and healed him. Charms, spells, incantations, and other forms of magic were also practiced by the priests.

Hippocrates of Cos founded in the fifth century an outstanding school of medicine, breaking away from the priestly traditions in which he himself had been reared. His chief principle was that "every disease has a natural cause, and without natural causes nothing ever happens." He and his students and followers made it their rule to study the progress of every disease very carefully, note the symptoms, and use previous experience in diagnosis and therapy. Most of the therapy of this school seems to have consisted of proper care and improved diet; for, as Hippocrates insisted, "nature is the best healer." Nevertheless, most of the herbal healing drugs were known, and presumably used when necessary. A large body of so-called Hippocratic writings have survived, some of which are probably by the great doctor himself; though others are polemical tracts which read more like the work of professional orators with an interest in medicine (evidently this species was a pest then as now). The famous Hippocratic oath, a masterly formulation of the ethics of doctors, is still taken by medical students on their graduation as doctors.

► **Greek art**

ART AS EXPRESSION OF THE GREEK SPIRIT

We have remarked earlier that the Greek ideal was *sophrosyne*, or moderation, although as a people the Greeks markedly lacked this virtue. In the realm of art, however, their search was not doomed to the same failure as in the necessarily imperfect world in which they had to live, and their volatile passions could not be involved in this ideal world as deeply as in the political world of live men and women. In art man is a creator. His materials are at hand but as yet without form. It is for the artist to give form to them. The soul, in Greek thought, is the *form* of the body; it shapes the inchoate mass, the mere raw physical material which decays at death into its original primal matter. So, for the Greek artist, the task is to give form to matter, to give it a soul which makes it live. And it is a curious feature of Greek above all other art that this illusion of life is indeed given to the dead material, marble. This feature can be perceived best in Greek sculpture, but even the Greek

temple does not seem to be altogether dead. We can analyze these temples and see by what technical means certain illusions were created, but the miracle remains. Even with our greatly advanced technical ingenuity, we have not been able to achieve the same results.

This is not to deny the artistic creations of the Greek world in the production of humbler objects than temples or statues. But even these are as perfect as they are because of the dedication of the artist to his task. The Greek did not self-consciously set out to create something "artistic." Though the Greeks are supposed to have a word for everything, they do not have a word for our conception of the "artistic" as something somewhat higher than, and to be distinguished from, the "useful." The Greek word for art is *Techne,* which is nearer to our conception of craft. It was the product of craftsmen, ordinary hand workers. But even in painting a vase for export to a Persian barbarian king the Greek always knew he was creating, giving form to material according to the nature of the material and the purpose for which it was used.[8]

We know that the Greek artisans all received the same low wage when they were at work for the city, just enough to maintain their wives and families for one day; that it was the highest honor to work for her; and that those who scorned private employment as unworthy of free men welcomed the opportunity. And—a very strange thing indeed—the masterpiece among all Ionic temples, the Erechtheum at Athens, dedicated to Athena, protectress of Athens, and to Erechtheus, her first ancestral king, was built in the last days of the Peloponnesian War, when the expedition to Syracuse had been defeated, and there were no longer any spoils of empire and victory available. The love of the Greeks for their polis and their reverence for their gods combined to make the building of a temple the very highest expression of all that was in them as men.

---

[8] Vases and a bow-case destined for export are illustrated in Chapter 7.

A bronze statue of the fifth century B.C. representing Poseidon, the god of the sea.
(RAY GARNER)

The two Homeric heroes Ajax and Achilles playing a game. Detail from a vase dated ca. 540 B.C. (HIRMER)

CLASSICAL ARCHITECTURE—THE TEMPLE AS
HOME FOR THE GODS

At first the Greeks worked within the framework of tradition and inheritance from other cultures. We can see this process with the early Greeks, the Doric temples built like the Mycenaean palaces of the Homeric Age and earlier, the stiff sculptures in the Egyptian style with square shoulders and one foot slightly advanced, and the crude anatomy. Then, suddenly, as early as the tyranny of Pisistratus, the Greek spirit breaks through, and first the detailed representation of hair and drapery and then the human form becomes true to life. Across the Aegean in Ionia the Ionic temple takes shape, and the sculptured figures become mobile and graceful. Then come the Persian Wars, and Athens is sacked and destroyed, leaving to a new generation a new city to be built.

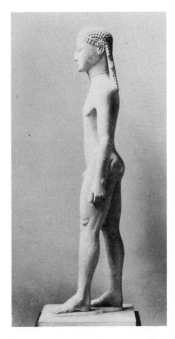

Early Athenian statue, showing marked Egyptian influence (seventh century B.C.). (COURTESY THE METROPOLITAN MUSEUM OF ART)

The city was the work of Pericles and his democracy, the full flowering of the Greek genius in works of harmony and beauty that have been the despair of later ages, imitated but never equaled. The economic resources came from the new commercial prosperity of Athens and her empire, and from the surplus treasure of the Delian Confederacy; the human resources, the architects and the sculptors, were free men of Athens who had experimented and worked on lesser masterpieces until the city could recognize them as the supreme exponents of their art.

The style of the Greek temple was one of the simplest structural forms known to man. Essentially it was composed of the *cella,* a rectangular chamber, the dwelling place of the statue of the god; the columns surrounding the cella and forming a porch; the lintel which rested on the columns and supported the roof; the gabled roof itself; and the pediment, the triangular section under the roof. The difference in the style of temple is determined by the column, of which three were in use—though the third was not known

Athenian head of Heracles (conventional archaic style, sixth century B.C.). (COURTESY AMERICAN SCHOOL OF CLASSICAL STUDIES AT ATHENS)

Model of the Parthenon, now a semi-ruin, constructed by The Metropolitan Museum of Art. Note the Doric columns. (COURTESY THE METROPOLITAN MUSEUM OF ART)

The Hephaesteum in Athens, the best preserved of all Greek mainland temples, built in the years immediately preceding the Peloponnesian War during the ascendancy of Pericles.

Students learning to play the lyre and recite poetry. Detail from a fifth century B.C. vase.
(STAATLICHE MUSEEN, BERLIN)

The Discus-Thrower. Roman copy of one of the most famous sculptures of antiquity by the fifth century artist Myron. (JOAN MENSCHENFREUND)

in Periclean Athens. The Doric column is a strong, heavy, sharply fluted column, crowned with a plain capital. The Ionic is more slender and graceful, with flat flutings, and a scroll or volute capital; while the Corinthian has similar flutings and a very ornate capital. The Corinthian order, although developed in the Hellenic period, appealed more to the Hellenistic Age and to the Romans.

The temple, then, is the house of the god. Unlike the medieval cathedrals, it is not intended for worshipers, who had full access to the temple only on special occasions, and the god or goddess is not lighted except by such sunlight as penetrates through the transparent marble of the roof. The frieze and the pediments of the temples are decorated with scenes from mythology or history, and it was in these reliefs that the sculptor joined hands with the architect to build a fitting home for the god.

Though his work was not confined to the Acropolis of Athens, the hill which stood in the center of the city, it was the restoration of the Acropolis temples that was the crowning work of Pericles—above all the Parthenon, the temple of Athena, the protecting goddess of Athens. This unique building is constructed entirely of marble, with eight Doric columns at the ends and seventeen along each side. There are also six internal columns at each end. But the Doric columns are more graceful and slender than is usual in this order. One of the wonders of the Parthenon, noble still in its ruins, is that it is made to *live* by the slight curves given to every part of the building, from the columns which lean slightly inward and taper toward the top, to the steps leading to the temple. The temple itself was the work of Callicrates and his younger contemporary Ictinus, the bulk of the work being ascribed to the latter. The sculpture was directed by Phidias; and the marvel of his work lies not only in the general design, which is a long continuous theme in glorification of Athens and her goddess, but in the way in which each part fits so perfectly into the whole. There is no dullness or monotony in it, with the horses prancing, and their young riders in perfect control,

Volute of Ionic column, showing detail. (COURTESY THE METROPOLITAN MUSEUM OF ART)

Athena springing in full panoply from the head of Zeus while the other gods are calm and commanding, having not yet heard the momentous news. Some of these reliefs many feet above the ground were not meant to be seen by any mortal, but they are all executed with the utmost honesty.

SCULPTURE—HARMONY OF BODY AND SOUL

The human body for the first time was appreciated, indeed loved, by those sculptors, great and small, of the Hellenic Age. Every muscle is perfectly rendered, whether in tension or repose. There was no striving after effect, as indeed there was no realism in the sense of contortion and strain as we find it in real life. Everyone who examines any of the smaller sculptures—the large sculptures for this age are all lost—is at once struck by the way the artist has been able to suggest life, and somehow conjure it out of his marble or ivory. Originally almost all the sculpture as well as the buildings themselves were painted, and it is difficult to imagine the effect the whole must have created, especially when we always view what remains to us in the cold white of the original marble.

Phidias is generally considered the greatest sculptor that Greece produced. In addition to his statue of Athena for the Parthenon,

he is known for his forty-foot figure of a seated Zeus at Olympia in Elis in the Peloponnese, which is described in detail by Pausanias, a Greek traveler of the Christian Era. No work known to be by him survives, though the Parthenon friezes give some indication of his style of work, and some of them may be by the hand of the master. The only sculpture by one of the really great Greek sculptors which is certainly identified is the Hermes of Praxiteles, an Athenian of the fourth century B.C., when art had been modified from the complete idealism of the Age of Pericles. This is a real youth, alive, though in repose. Though he is called a god, no one could mistake him for one. Many of the great sculptors, however, are known through Roman and later Greek copies. These at least serve to suggest the kind of sculpture and the methods and character of the sculpture of a particular artist. From them we know how great a loss we have sustained in having none of the genuine work of Lysippus, whose

Marble relief of a Maenad. Classical period, fifth century B.C. (COURTESY THE METROPOLITAN MUSEUM OF ART)

Two slabs from the Parthenon frieze known as the Elgin marbles after the English lord who carried them off to England. Note the mastery of the riders in the Panathenaic procession, and the absence of any sense of the strain which is noticeable in some of the realistic sculpture of the Hellenistic Age shown in the next chapter. The riders are caught in a moment of eternity rather than individualized as riders taking part in one particular procession at one particular moment. The frieze was designed by Phidias and carried out at his direction though by different craftsmen. (COURTESY BRITISH MUSEUM)

Head of an athlete. Roman copy of a Greek statue dating from the third quarter of the fifth century B.C. (METROPOLITAN MUSEUM OF ART, ROGERS FUND, 1911)

portrait of Alexander the Great, known in a copy, has fixed his features and demeanor indelibly upon later generations.

PAINTING

Of painting, as such, unfortunately we know only what Roman and Greek tourists have told us. We know of the great Polygnotus of Thasos, who was invited to Athens before the time of Pericles to do frescoes, and who depicted scenes from the Trojan War with Athenian notables in the likeness of their Achaean forebears; and we know that in the individualist fourth century was the beginning of portrait painting, with stress on fidelity to nature. Zeuxis and Apelles were the great masters in this genre.

But though all the great painting is lost we possess thousands of examples of vase painting from the earliest times, examples which are of great value for the information they give of life in the Greek cities, as well as for incidents of mythology and religion. It was a kind of specialized miniature painting, and often done with great skill. But this art was already decaying before the fourth century, and the later pottery was more strictly utilitarian; but, as always in Greek art, a special effort was made to draw each figure with full regard for the group in which it appeared, and for the shape of the vase itself. The vases are painted in red and black, and are made of clay turned on the potter's wheel.

The famous Hermes of Praxiteles, the only almost complete statue extant from the fourth century B.C. Note how the god is given truly human features, which should be contrasted with the less differentiated features of the participants in the Panathenaic procession shown in the Parthenon frieze (Elgin marbles).

▶ Literature

LYRIC POETRY—THE CHORAL LYRIC

In the classical Greek period there was, as far as we know, no literature produced for the sole purpose of entertainment, and none that was not intimately connected with the social and political life of the polis. There were no self-conscious "men of letters" until the breakdown of this social life after the conquest of Asia. Several of the more important writers have therefore already been dealt with in the course of this chapter, leaving only formal classification and a few supplementary remarks for this section.

Epic poetry inevitably suffered a decline after Homer. The heroic deeds which it celebrated were now far in the past, and new forms of poetry were better fitted to express the great deeds of the present. There was no attempt to recover it until the Hellenistic Age, when some scholars made the effort to tell the legends of the past again in a manner fitted for contemporary consumption. Hesiod's poems, of which mention has already been made, have value for us principally because of the information they contain, especially on Greek mythology. The poems themselves have few graces of style and to us lack poetic feeling.

Greek lyric poetry, as such, reached its apex in the period before the Greek genius reached its full maturity. In later centuries it was replaced by the great choral lyrics incorporated in the tragic dramas and comedy. Few of these earlier lyrics survive in their entirety. Most of them are known to us only through quotations by later scholars and critics. These have been assembled by modern Western scholars into a collection substantial enough for us to have some idea of the richness and variety of the treasures that are lost.

This poetry can be best classified into elegy and personal lyric. The elegy used many varieties of meter, but it was not primarily musical. Solon and Theognis used the elegiac form to voice their social criticisms and calls to action in the sixth century B.C. Later it was used for epigrams, especially epitaphs, which were usually short and packed with feeling, especially when they were composed to honor the glorious dead.

The personal and choral Greek lyrics were sung to the music of the lyre or cithara. Many of them, such as the passionate poems of the sixth century poetess Sappho, sing of love; others, of the beauties of nature. These poems have given inspiration to thousands of poets in other tongues who have copied their meters, themes, and images without ever being able—with the possible exception of the Roman Horace—to approach the perfection of the originals. One development of the personal lyric was the great odes celebrating the winners in the various Greek games. These reached their climax in the Theban poet Pindar, who was able with a wealth of images and often profound thought to elevate the whole theme of glory and victory into a paean of praise of man and the gods, and the life of man upon earth among the beauties of the natural world.

THE PERSONAL LYRIC—PINDAR AND THE EXALTATION OF THE GREEK GAMES

The choral lyric found its early home in Sparta, and was designed to express the spirit of a civic festival. Usually it glorified the mythical or historical past of the city, its ancestral hero, and its god; and for this reason was specially suited for martial Sparta, though it was equally at home at Athens in the days of her glory. It found a natural continuation in the tragic drama and the Old Comedy; both Aristophanes and the great tragic dramatists were all wonderful exponents of the choral lyric, the singing and the dancing enhancing the atmosphere of the festival, and the lyrics themselves giving the poets the opportunity to point to the universality of the solemn themes which were the heart of their plays.

THE OLD COMEDY—ARISTOPHANES

Of Greek drama, which has already been dealt with extensively, it only remains to treat more fully Aristophanes, the master of the Old Comedy. Fragments exist from other writers of comedy, although insufficient to

A youth being instructed in how to play the aulos (a double flute), and how to write with a stylos. Detail from a fifth century B.C. vase. (STAATLICHE MUSEEN, BERLIN)

enable us to form a judgment on his competitors; but Aristophanes failed to win the first prize at the annual festivals often enough for us to surmise that the works of other dramatists were of the same high standard as the extant works of the master himself. To appreciate Aristophanes today it is absolutely necessary to re-create in the imagination the circumstances of the time. Notes on the meanings of the great number of allusions to current events can hardly take the place of this knowledge. He was an extremely acute social critic, with a love of Athens which shines through all his work. He has been called an arch-conservative, incapable of understanding the changing times; but this is a one-sided judgment. He understood the changing times only too well, and he did not like the change. Spending his youth in the bright days of the Periclean empire, and living through the Peloponnesian War and the oligarchic revolution, he was in a position to estimate the magnitude of what was being lost; and his comedies should be read in conjunction with the history of his contemporary Thucydides, as a parallel picture of the disintegration of the democracy under the scourge of war—and Thucydides is not usually accused, after his famous Periclean Funeral Speech, of being a hater of democracy.

Aristophanes saw Euripides destroying the tragic drama (the *Frogs*); he saw Cleon and the demagogues destroying the balance and order of the Periclean democracy (again the *Frogs*, but especially the *Knights*); he saw the dignity of the law courts being destroyed by corruption and blackmail (the *Wasps*); he saw faith in the old gods and the old unquestioned basis of society being destroyed by the Sophists (the *Clouds*); and he saw from the beginning that imperialism was not worth the price and would lead to what in fact followed (the *Acharnians*). With an unsurpassed gift for caricature and comic invention and a rich sense of verbal repartee, he brings forth his satires, one after another, criticizing his polis and its leaders unsparingly—and yet the Athenian comedy was produced out of public funds. The plays make use of dozens of different meters chosen with such obviously meticulous care for the effect they create that we could recognize a master poet in spite of his medium, even if we could not see this from the exquisite choral lyrics.[4] They were rich entertainment for a politically alert citizenry; but once the social and political conditions of the old polis had changed, this kind of comedy had outlived its purpose and there was never any serious attempt to revive it. In the so-called Middle Comedy of the fourth century B.C., the old uproarious satire takes on gentler tones, and the ordinary foibles of private life come increasingly to the fore, to emerge in the comedies of manners and character which reach full fruition in Menander and the New Comedy of the Hellenistic Age.

PROSE

The historians—Herodotus and Thucydides

Prose writing finds its beginning in the two great histories of the Classical Age. Enough references have already been made to Herodotus, the "father of history," for the reader to be already familiar with his work and methods. Ostensibly his book (the *Persian Wars*) deals with the Persian Wars; but he was also so much interested in the peoples who took part in them, even remotely, and he traveled so extensively and made so many inquiries, that his work is almost a universal history. The customs and history of Persia and Egypt, as far as he was able to ascertain them, fill a large portion of his work, which

is a mine of interesting stories as well as material for social and cultural anthropology. For the age in which he wrote, before the advent of rationalism and the critical spirit of the Sophists and their followers, he was not especially credulous, as has sometimes been stated. The trouble was that he had as yet no proper tools for criticism. When a story was told him, he either accepted or rejected it on the grounds of its own inherent credibility or lack of it. He could not check it by comparing and evaluating sources, but only by making more inquiries from more people, so that the problem of credibility remained unsolved. The story of the Persian Wars itself is told in a masterly narrative form, and primarily as an example of the destruction that awaits the presumptuous. From this point of view the Persian Wars were indeed a tragic drama, and Aeschylus used them as a theme for one of his own. Written in the days when faith in the justice of the universal order was still unshaken, and with an incomparable theme to celebrate, the later part of his book has unity and solidity; and with its charming style and the fund of delightful as well as heroic stories, it is a work of perennial interest, and has never failed to find appreciative readers in all the ages since.

But with Thucydides, son of Olorus, we are in the presence of one of the great minds of the world, one of the greatest that has ever turned to the writing of history. The defects, from a modern point of view, are easily stated, and detract little from its value. His book (*History of the Peloponnesian War*) is too little concerned with economic and social life, and too much occupied with politics and political psychology; and it says nothing of the great Greek art and the flowering of Athenian culture. And occasionally the style is artificial and crabbed (a characteristic also of his great English pupil Gibbon). But it was not the purpose of his work to deal with Athenian culture. He was not even writing a formal history of Athens during the Peloponnesian War; but of the Peloponnesian War itself, the interstate rivalry and imperialism that caused it, and the defects and virtues of Athenian

---

[4] The reader in need of a translation should use those of B. B. Rogers, who, in spite of his sometimes overdelicacy, catches beautifully the spirit of Aristophanes, as well as rendering the lyrics into the same meter as the original.

democracy that caused it to take the course it did. If we grant this framework as the legitimate field for a historian, and further take into account that he was writing the most difficult form of history, the study of the contemporary scene, the magnitude of his achievement remains without parallel in the whole field of history.

Thucydides himself was at one time an Athenian general, but because of ill success in a campaign and suspicions arising from it he was exiled, and while still in exile he wrote his *History*. He made it his business to gather together all the information he could, and he is severely critical in his use of sources. But most of the facts he recounts were quite familiar to him, and only needed his interpretation. As a true Greek he always tries to see the universal in the particular, and on almost every page we find magnificent generalizations which have remained permanently true, and make his history a treasure of wisdom for the politician and the soldier and the citizen. He is so impartial and objective in his descriptions and criticisms that he sometimes seems like the voice of the Greek gods themselves commenting on the presumptuousness of man, the overconfidence born of success, and the madness and destruction that follow. Intensely dramatic in the structure and emphasis of his writing, Thucydides, as no historian has ever done since, laid bare the psychology of a whole people perfectly—the Athenian ideal as proclaimed by Pericles, the cold realities of the rule by the people, the oratory that moved them and the considerations of power that shaped their imperial policy, the party strife between oligarchs and democrats that destroyed the polis from within and was finally responsible for the follies of the war.

The drama is revealed especially in the speeches, not heard by Thucydides himself; but the emotions felt and the arguments used are those of the occasion, re-created by the imaginative understanding of the historian, heightening the drama and relieving the somber realism of the narrative. The Peloponnesian War may have been a small one between small states of little political importance in the history of the world, and (unfortunately) later wars greater in magnitude have sometimes suggested that this was a lot of fuss about little; but it was, like other Greek experiences, an archetype, the history in miniature of all other wars. And because it found its historian of genius it has remained till our own times, with its warning and its lesson, as vivid as in the day it was written.

The orators—Demosthenes, Isocrates, Aeschines

Another form of prose writing sprang up in the fourth century, the written and published speeches of professional orators. The Sophists, as has been seen, first showed the value of careful professional training in speaking, which already with them in practice meant the careful planning of the effects of the speech, the use of a carefully calculated diction, the building up of dramatic effects as well as the employment of doubtful arguments of the kind satirized by Plato and Aristophanes. The effect of this self-conscious examination of what had always no doubt been applied half-consciously in practice is to be seen in Thucydides; but the full impact of this new education was not felt until the fourth-century schools of oratory attained their maturity and their resounding success. No longer could a pleader hope to win his case in the law court or a speaker command the attention of the Assembly without the assistance of planned artifice; and by the second half of the fourth century almost every politician of note had been trained by the orators. But in addition to public speaking the demand also arose for publicists, men who could make their appeal to an informed public by the written word.

All fourth-century prose writing was dominated by the art and craft of the orator. It was apparently impossible to find an audience for anything except fine writing, artificial, perhaps, but carefully balanced and elaborated, thoroughly orderly in the Greek manner, and thought out, rather than merely poured out, in words. Even the appeal to the emotions was planned, though with such an orator as Demosthenes the fire of his patriotism and the real emotion behind his words removed any hint of the artificial. Because he himself and his art were so intermingled that the masterly technique is concealed, he has been regarded as the greatest exponent of political oratory in history; and his speeches remained the model for Romans and Western Europeans until very recent times.

Isocrates is the great example of the scholarly orator, who wrote his speeches and rarely delivered them because, as he explains, his voice was too weak to be effective in public. His was for the greater part of the century the most influential school of oratory, and the most promising students of the Greek world came to study with him. While not aloof from politics he strove to look at them with a detached eye, and he alone of Greek publicists recognized that the future of the world did not lie with the individual polis, and that the necessary unity of Greece could best be attained by a joint expedition under Greek leadership against the barbarian world of Persia. From early in his long life till almost the end he urged this policy and his *Letter to Philip*, in which he exhorted the Macedonian king to undertake the leadership of the Greeks against the Persians was an act of political courage in the days of the ascendancy of the superpatriot Demosthenes. Isocrates always seems to have had a circle of friends around him who held similar views, though they were men of little political influence. But their very existence and the way in which the independent politicians were able to find thoroughly respectable arguments to justify the appeasement of Philip are a commentary on the detached and excessively rational attitude of the Athenian democracy in its declining days.

A considerable number of orations, private and public, are known for this period, but most of them are hardly to be classed as literature, valuable though they are for the insight they give us into the social conditions of the time. Aeschines was a brilliant writer and a brilliant speaker, though lacking sincerity and without profound political insight.

If he had not been a contemporary of Demosthenes he, instead of his implacable enemy, might well have become the model for later times. When we read his speech against the man who had proposed a crown for Demosthenes, we marvel how he could have failed to win his case. Then when we read Demosthenes afterward we see why there could have been no other verdict. Demosthenes had every art of the orator at his finger tips in addition to a burning sincerity. On whether his policy was a wise one in the circumstances there can be difference of opinion; but on whether he was a worthy exponent of it, and of his passionate love of and belief in the idea of the polis and of Athens there can be none at all. But of this the reader will better be able to judge when the struggle between Demosthenes and Macedonian imperialism has been considered in the next chapter.

▶ Suggestions for further reading

No recommendations can be given here for the numerous translations from the individual Greek writers now available in paperback. Among the most useful selections are W. H. Auden, ed. *The Portable Greek Reader* (New York: Vintage) and T. F. Higham and C. M. Bowra, eds. *The Oxford Book of Greek Verse in Translation* (New York: Oxford University Press, 1938), and an invaluable selection with commentary from the works of pre-Socratic philosopher-scientist. M. C. Nahm, *Selections from Early Greek Philosophy* (New York: Appleton-Century-Crofts, 1947). Books of criticism, sometimes with extensive selections, are listed below with other suggestions.

PAPER-BOUND BOOKS

Barker, Ernest. *The Political Thought of Plato and Aristotle.* Dover. A fundamental study by a student of ancient and modern politics. Better on Aristotle than on Plato.

Boardman, John. *Greek Art.* Praeger.

Bowra, C. M. *Ancient Greek Literature.* Galaxy. By the author of *The Greek Experience.*

Bowra, C. M. *The Greek Experience.* Mentor. Excellent modern synthesis of the Greek cultural achievements to 404 B.C. Especially good on the role of religion in Greek life and the development of religious ideas in the fifth century.

Cornford, Francis M. *From Religion to Philosophy: A Study in the Origins of Western Speculation.* Torchbooks. Short but suggestive and stimulating study, throwing much light on the Greek beginnings of philosophy.

Dodd, E. R. *The Greeks and the Irrational.* Beacon. Explodes the point of view, still too frequently held in spite of the evidence to the contrary, that the Greeks were a calm and restrained people.

Graves, Robert. *The Greek Myths.* 2 vols. Penguin. By a learned English poet, profoundly interested in mythology and religion. Interpretations often farfetched, but argued with such overwhelming erudition and determination that they are often difficult to refute by those less learned than Graves. To be treated, like all this author's works, with caution.

Grube, G. M. A. *Plato's Thought.* Beacon. A good summary.

Guthrie, W. K. C. *The Greeks and Their Gods.* Beacon. Good discussion for serious students.

Hadas, Moses. *Ancilla to Classical Reading.* Columbia University Press. An informative and helpful guide. Also by the same author, *A History of Greek Literature.* Columbia.

Harrison, Jane. *Prolegomena to the Study of Greek Religion.* Meridian. Very thorough study, not recommended for beginners, but rewarding for serious students.

Jaeger, Werner. *Aristotle: Fundamentals of the History of his Development,* trans. by R. Robinson. Oxford University Press. Epoch-making work which changed the whole trend of thinking about Aristotle. Though not accepted *in toto* by many, no student of Aristotle and Greek philosophy can neglect it.

Kitto, H. D. F. *Greek Tragedy.* Penguin. Since Kitto's interpretation differs so markedly from that given in the text and is written from a quite different viewpoint, it should be used to complement it.

Nietzsche, Frederich. *The Birth of Tragedy and the Geneology of Morals.* Anchor. Early work of the German philosopher, the key to much of his later work. Uses the contrast between pre-Sophist and post-Sophist writing to condemn the latter as no longer in accord with the true Greek spirit. Stimulating and original thesis used with modifications in the present text.

Norwood, Gilbert. *Greek Comedy* and *Greek Tragedy.* American Century. These two books are more concerned with the technical aspects of the products of Greek plays than with their interpretation.

Randall, J. H., Jr. *Aristotle.* Columbia. Interpretation of Aristotle by a professional philosopher, with many stimulating insights into the continuing value of his thought.

Rose, H. J. *A Handbook of Greek Literature.* Everyman.

Rose, H. J. *Gods and Heroes of the Greeks.* Meridian. By a noted scholar of Greek mythology and religion.

Taylor, A. E. *Aristotle.* Dover; *The Mind of Plato.* Meridian; *Socrates: The Man and His Thought.* Anchor. Three separate studies by a renowned classical scholar, all well-written and interesting, all controversial. Taylor's estimate of the influence of Socrates on Platonic thought, however, is widely accepted, especially by those who have read little but Taylor.

Windelband, W. *A History of Ancient Philosophy.* Dover. Very substantial nineteenth-century study by a man who was a distinguished philosopher in his own right. His classic work includes interpretations that often reflect his own philosophical viewpoint.

Zeller, Eduard. *Outlines of the History of Greek Philosophy.* Meridian. A good introduction by one of the best of the earlier historians of philosophy.

CASE-BOUND BOOKS

Jones, W. T. *A History of Western Philosophy.* Vol. I. New York: Harcourt, Brace & World, Inc., 1952. Well-organized modern history of philosophy with very fair summaries of the Greek thinkers.

Warbeke, J. M. *The Searching Mind of Greece.* New York: Appleton-Century-Crofts, Inc., 1930. In my opinion, one of the best introductions to Greek thought, especially good on the nature of the problems Greek writers were trying to solve.

CHAPTER 9

THE HELLENISTIC AGE

▶ The end of the independent polis in Greece

DIVISIVE CITY-STATE POLITICS VERSUS THE
UNIFIED IMPERIAL STATE

The struggle between the polis and Macedonian imperialism deserves more space than is usually given it in a textbook. Looking back from this distance of time it is clear that all the advantages were on the side of Philip, and that Demosthenes and his party were always fighting a losing battle. The polis as a unit of government had outlived its usefulness, and as a social unit it had outlived its creativeness. The weakness of the barbarian empires, possessed of a potential power that the Greek poleis could not command, had allowed the latter to make their outstanding contributions to civilization. Now again it was the turn of the great empires, and the future lay with them, until once again the civilization of Europe was destroyed by primitive barbarians unfitted to manage their inheritance of empire.

All this may be so, but it did not seem so to Demosthenes; nor even, so far as we can tell, to Aristotle, who, as tutor of the young Alexander, ought to have known better. The social organization of the polis was dear to its inhabitants; the collaborators with Philip were probably not pining for a great strong master and an enlightened or powerful despotism. They were merely shortsighted self-seekers who failed to see the danger. And in fact the polis in Greece did survive for a couple of centuries more, even though it had lost its full political autonomy. It is thus as a case history of unpreparedness, political ineptitude, and the willingness of a democracy to be hoaxed that this period has a melancholy interest, rather than merely as a struggle for an inevitably lost cause.

The Greek political genius had not been fully spent, even if the leadership of Greece had passed from Athens. There are sporadic attempts at federations and leagues of cities, each maintaining its social autonomy and yielding some of its political autonomy. The problem was again not dissimilar to our own in the twentieth century, with the political unit in ancient times being the polis, and in modern the national state. The heart of the matter in ancient times was that the cities wanted to eat their cake and have it; they wanted to remain the arbiters of their own destiny and at the same time to have the advantage of "collective security"; they did not want a different social organization from that of the polis, nor to give up the patriotism associated with it. As it turned out, events were too strong for them, and the more hopeful leagues had only brief moments of growth and prosperity before being destroyed from within by traitors or unredeemed polis patriots, or from without by armed force.

THE RISE OF MACEDONIA—PHILIP II AND THE PIECEMEAL CONQUEST OF GREECE

One of the most interesting of these attempts at intercity organization led directly to the rise of Macedon, and so is worth a brief mention here. About 387 B.C. the democracy of the city of Olynthus in the Chalcidian peninsula at the borders of Macedonia suggested to the local smaller cities that they hold certain well-defined rights in common, in particular those of property and intermarriage. There should also be a league citizenship in addition to the citizenship of the individual polis. All citizens would therefore hold a dual citizenship, one of their own polis and one of the league. The league and its new idea quickly spread outside the original peninsula and began to incorporate other local cities against the will of their governments. It also began to make military advances with a joint army, capturing the Macedonian capital of Pella. Macedonia at that time was only a semibarbarian kingdom with a weak army and constantly beset by dynastic feuds. The two Greek cities with oligarchic governments within the sphere of influence of Olynthus naturally appealed to the chief upholder of oligarchies and the leading power in Greece at that time—Sparta.

The Spartan government decided to take action, backed as usual in the early fourth century B.C., by Persian gold, proceeded to besiege Olynthus, and after four years forced her capitulation. The league was nominally dissolved. Shortly afterward, however, Sparta

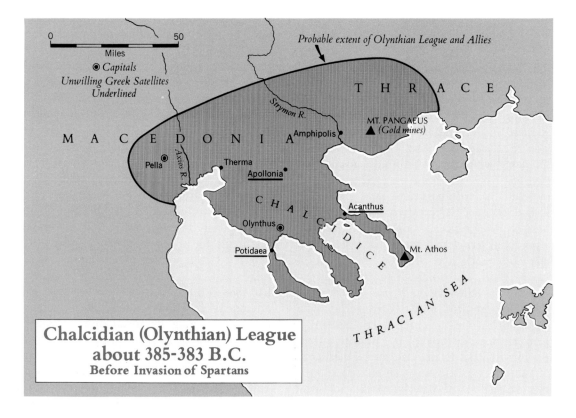

Chalcidian (Olynthian) League
about 385-383 B.C.
Before Invasion of Spartans

herself was defeated by Thebes, and the league came to life again. But the Macedonian king, Amyntas, a minor victim of the Olynthian expansion, had learned his lesson and proceeded to re-establish his kingdom, build up an army, and try to ensure that he would be able at least to defend his kingdom against a few aggressive cities of Greece. At his death the kingdom was rent for another ten years by internal struggles until his third son, Philip, came to the throne in 359 B.C.

In his youth Philip had been taken to Thebes as a hostage and there he had taken careful account of the Theban improvements in military organization, and had gained a firsthand knowledge of the internal weakness of the Greek city-states. This knowledge he was to put to good use in his drive for supreme power in Greece. This remarkable man, who has never received from history a fame commensurate with his achievements, succeeded, in the comparatively short reign of twenty-three years, in converting Macedonia from a weak, disunited, and unimportant kingdom which had remained on the fringe of Greek civilization and taken no part in its affairs, into the dominating power in the Greek world, with every state save Sparta submissive to him, and with a strong, well-trained body of troops which under the leadership of Alexander was to conquer Asia. All his life Philip seems to have been a genuine admirer of Hellenic culture, though he had nothing but contempt for its outmoded government. Time after time his knowledge of Greek political weaknesses enabled him to divide and rule; but even when he had won his final victory he imposed easy terms on Athens, and did not even demand the banishment of his unyielding opponent Demosthenes. He seems genuinely to have desired the cooperation of the Greek states in his Asiatic venture, and probably hoped for it till the end. Even though he knew the lukewarm nature of Greek support he took the trouble to organize a league for the conquest of Persia and had himself elected its leader.

In his dealings with the Greek city-states he showed himself master of the art of power politics.[1] He was completely faithless, he regarded a treaty as a move in the game, to be abandoned whenever it seemed advisable; he knew equally the value of a well-placed bribe and soft and soothing words. He knew exactly what his ultimate aim was, and, being one of the most brilliant opportunists in history, he could always take advantage of a momentary weakness or division among his opponents. To assist him he had a personally trained professional army, by far the finest in the Western world of his day but small in size; he could use it exactly when and where it was needed, confident of its loyalty. He was altogether too formidable an opponent for the Greek cities, even though the material means were usually in their favor, and at any time in his career until the last, a united front must have overwhelmed him. Even after the Athenian defeat by land at Chaeronea in 338 B.C., the Athenian navy could and did defeat singlehanded any navy he was able to put together.

Philip's first need was money to pay his army. He looked covetously at some gold mines which belonged to Amphipolis, a city which did not exploit them properly. Some shrewd diplomacy to hold off interference from Athens, a lightning blow of his army, and the gold mines were his. With these funds he organized the famous Macedonian phalanx, a new and effective formation which remained the master military unit of the Western world until the Roman legion defeated it. The Chalcidian cities and Olynthus barred his way to the sea, and with the considerable resources of the revived league, they presented probably the most formidable single opposition in Greece, far too strong for a direct attack at this point. Thebes was still a strong land power, with the best army. Athens had the best navy. But Athens in the fourth century had grown accustomed to using mercenary soldiers under generals of fortune, and her reputation for regular payment was not of the best.

The Athenian, in fact, at this time had

[1] It will be realized by the student that the detailed account of the strategy of Philip given here is intended to draw attention to an instructive modern parallel.

a good reputation for nothing. When the Assembly, under the influence of some war-minded demagogue, decided to engage in a military expedition, the usual procedure was to appoint a general and tell him to go out and raise some troops on credit. This he might do if he were otherwise disengaged; then someone else would offer a higher rate or more swift payment, and Athens would suddenly find herself at war but without an army. And as the war was usually to be fought with some ally, the ally would then be left in the lurch. Even the navy was semi-professional and dependent upon spasmodic outbursts of generosity by the citizens or upon a good orator to urge its support. The ready cash accumulated in the city treasury from the good years, which were rare enough, was put into a so-called festival fund which was sacrosanct, not to be touched; for out of it the poorer citizens were given money to attend the festivals, and the poorer citizens were in full control of the Assembly by the late fourth century B.C.

The incessant struggles between the city-states brought Philip actively into Greece for the first time. Thebes accused Phocis, the custodian of the Delphic Oracle and its treasures, of some sacrilege, and proceeded to invade the small state. The Phocians, who no doubt thought they might as well be hanged for the sheep as the dog, then became really sacrilegious, and stole the god's treasure, with which they purchased the bulk of the unemployed mercenaries in the country. They started to expand northward; and Thebes, frightened at the hornet's nest she had stirred up, appealed to Philip for assistance. Delighted to oblige, he descended with an army and inflicted a decisive defeat on the Phocians. At this point he was almost in the center of Greece; and the Athenians, suddenly scared, sent an army to Thermopylae. Philip, not having secured his rear and not yet ready to take on a major foe, retired gracefully. His services to the god Apollo were rewarded by an invitation to take the place of the sacrilegious Phocians on the Amphictyonic Council,[2] which meant

[2] See page 211, above.

that Philip was now a Greek by adoption—and, more important, if another "sacred" war could be incited, he was the proper agent to defend the god and his property.

At this juncture Athens found herself a leader—Demosthenes, who had realized before his countrymen what a danger the Macedonian king represented to all Greece and her cherished liberties. He proposed in his first *Philippic* (his speeches against Philip have received this name from posterity) the creation of a national army, citizens as well as mercenaries, and a policy of uncompromising hostility to Philip, and he gave exact indications as to the number of men required and how they should be financed. But the Athenians thought he was taking the situation too seriously. No one questioned his figures, but they said that Philip was just a kind, cultured gentleman; in any case he was "far away"—and, besides, he might die.

Back in Macedonia, enriched by a little privateering against Athenian vessels, Philip suddenly struck at his real enemy, Olynthus and the Chalcidian League, in the meantime fomenting a small rebellion in another Athenian dependency nearer home. Demosthenes in his *Olynthiac* orations now urged the use of the festival fund for troops; the opposition, some of its members now probably in the pay of Philip, countered with the usual arguments. Philip made short work of the confederate cities and laid siege to Olynthus. At this point Demosthenes had his way, and some two thousand troops went north. But they were too late. Philip had some well-placed traitors in the city, and it fell without too long a resistance. It had been too dangerous to Philip, with its constructive ideas of federation, it had shown too marked an ability to recover. There must be no mistake this time. It was razed and its inhabitants were sold as slaves, shocking all Greece into the realization of Philip's power and ruthlessness. This was not the kind of thing that happened in the enlightened fourth century.

But Philip had calculated correctly. The shock was not enough to awaken the Athenians to activity, but it was just enough to scare them into good behavior. When he

► chronological chart

The end of the independent polis

Expansion of Olynthus in Chalcidice	400–379
First conquest of Olynthus by Spartans and Macedonians	379
Philip II becomes king of Macedon (Macedonia)	359
Olynthiacs of Demosthenes	351
Destruction of Olynthus by Philip	348
Sacred (Phocian) War	355–346
Philip conquers Phocians	346
Philip invited to take part in further Sacred War	339
Demosthenes, *Third Philippic*	339
Battle of Chaeronea	338
Congress of Corinth and foundation of Hellenic League	338–337
Murder of Philip	336

The career of Alexander the Great

Alexander crushes revolts in Greece	335
Alexander invades Asia—Battle of Granicus	334
Battle of Issus	333
Expedition to Egypt and submission of Egyptians	332–331
Battle of Gaugamela (Arbela)	331
Murder of Darius—Alexander becomes Great King	330
Indian campaign of Alexander	327–324
Death of Alexander	323
Deaths of Demosthenes and Aristotle	322

Results of the conquests

Ptolemy I Soter seizes Egypt	321
Civil War between the generals	322–301
Battle of Ipsus—Final division of Alexander's kingdom	301

Hellenistic Age in Greece

Formation of the Aetolian League	290
Formation of Achaean League	280
Revolution and reforms in Sparta	245–235
Philip V of Macedon engages in first hostilities with Rome	215

Hellenistic Age in Egypt

Foundation of Museum of Alexandria	286
Romans intervene to save Alexandria from Syrians	168
Cleopatra (VII) on Egyptian throne	51

Hellenistic Age in Asia

Seleucus I founder of Seleucid dynasty	305–280
Eumenes I founds independent kingdom of Pergamum	263
Antiochus III defeated by Romans at Magnesia	190
Revolt in Palestine against Antiochus IV (Judas Maccabaeus)	168
Attalus III of Pergamum bequeaths kingdom to Rome	133
Syria made a Roman province by Pompey	64

Dates are before Christ.

invited them to discuss a peace treaty, he played the charming host at his Macedonian capital, and convinced them that he was a good, cultured Greek after all; and they signed the peace. But Demosthenes had now made his influence felt in the Assembly. *He* had not been charmed by Philip, and he was backed by a strong party who had realized the danger presented by Philip and that only force would defeat Philip. Backed by the Assembly Demosthenes proceeded to organize a pan-Hellenic league against Philip. But most of the cities were powerless and were hardly capable of making any appreciable contribution to a joint army. Only Thebes had such an army, and Thebes was still in uneasy alliance with Philip. At this point an opposition leader in the Assembly committed either an inexcusable blunder or deliberate treachery.

Philip, it will be remembered, was now in the Amphictyonic League of all Greeks. It was thus very probable that there would somehow be another extremely profitable "sacred" war. No one ever could prove that the fine hand of Philip was behind the "Second Sacred War," and perhaps he was just in luck.

At all events, Athens gratuitously and publicly insulted Thebes on the old matter of Theban collaboration with the Persians a century and a half before, and was herself accused in the Amphictyonic Council of sacrilege by Amphissa, a small city friendly to Thebes. Athens replied by the counter-charge that Amphissa had been committing a much worse sacrilege by cultivating the lands of Apollo (she had been doing so with impunity for at least a hundred years). The Athenian orator Aeschines was so effective in the ensuing debate that the Council declared war against Amphissa. Philip was invited to undertake the job, which he accepted with alacrity.

With an unnecessarily powerful army he moved into central Greece past the gates of Thermopylae, was welcomed as the defender of the god of Delphi, and took up a position commanding the road to Thebes. The Athenian Assembly, apparently not having ex-

pected this, now turned once more to Demosthenes. He personally went to Thebes, armed with full authority and funds from Athens, and succeeded in persuading the Thebans at last that they must either fight together or be picked off separately. By his eloquence he persuaded the Thebans to throw off their long-standing alliance with Philip, and just at the moment when they were in the greatest danger. Philip, now safely in central Greece, was in no hurry. He took a trip to Amphissa and settled the affairs of the god in a swift and relentless campaign; then suddenly turned on the army of the alliance and routed it at Chaeronea in 338 B.C. The Theban Sacred Band, the crack troops of the city, fell to the last man, and the harshest terms were imposed upon her—a Macedonian garrison in the citadel, and slavery or death for her leaders. Athens was spared, either for the sake of her glorious past and her culture or because she still had a navy.

PHILIP AS THE GREEK LEADER AGAINST PERSIA— HIS MURDER

Philip then proceeded to call a congress of all Greek states to which only Sparta, now almost impotent, who had not fought in the recent war, refused to go. He dictated his terms. No state should be allowed to go to war on its own, and each must contribute troops and arms for his projected war against the barbarian Persians. In return Philip offered them his protection. No one was interested in his campaign, and, as the sequel showed, the hope was general that he would overreach himself, and perhaps be put out of the way by some barbarian.

As it happened, within a year he was murdered, probably in a family quarrel; and his son Alexander succeeded him. Demosthenes sprang to the attack again and persuaded the Athenians to send envoys even to Persia for support. Thebes expelled the Macedonian garrison. But Alexander in a lightning march took Thebes by assault, razed it, and enslaved the inhabitants. The Athenians, faced with a similar fate and not knowing what to expect of this terrible young man, passed a motion of congratulation on

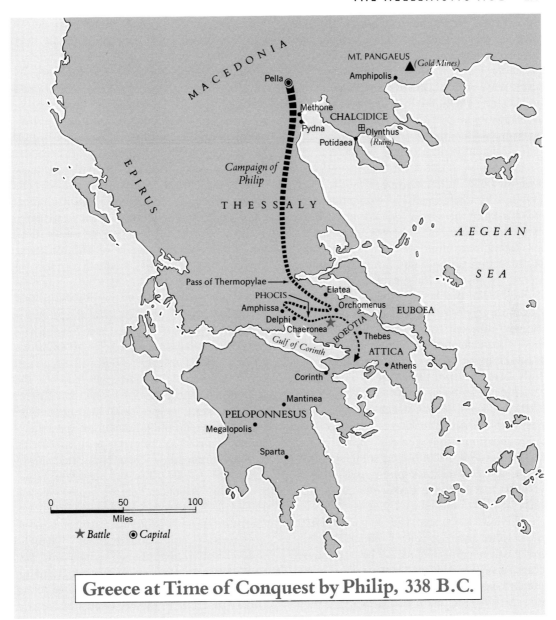

Greece at Time of Conquest by Philip, 338 B.C.

his punishment of Thebes! Alexander was reinstated as leader of the Greeks, and prepared for his expedition to Persia.

▶ The career of Alexander the Great

THE INFLUENCE OF ARISTOTLE

Alexander the Great was one of the most remarkable conquerors in history. Yet he was much more than a conqueror. A man of wide learning and genuine enthusiasm for all that was Greek, something of a poet and a very

considerable idealist, he seems to have been imbued with a sense of mission, and an exact knowledge of what he was going to do and how he was going to do it, even before he started on his expedition. It is tempting to ascribe at least some of this to his association with Aristotle, who had tutored him privately for at least three years—and Aristotle, as we have seen, was both the most learned man in the world of his day and the best exponent of all things Greek that could have been found. The evidence shows that Alexander and Aristotle were in close contact with each other all through the campaigns, and that the association was not broken even when Alexander found it necessary to execute his tutor's nephew. But, at the same time, Aristotle in his *Politics* is critical of monarchies, and regards the polis as the only fit form of government for human beings. How can these apparent contradictions be reconciled?

Alexander's regard for reason and balance, his belief in the control of the body by the mind, his disinterested love of knowledge, and his spirit of inquiry could have been instilled into him by his tutor. Alexander's first thought in entering a foreign country was to visit the shrines and initiation centers, and to inquire into the customs and beliefs of the people. But he persistently refused to regard the conquered as barbarians and in any way different from Greeks, much to the annoyance indeed of his own soldiers. In this he might appear to be ahead of Aristotle. The truth seems to have been that as a practical man he needed a policy, and that he used what he could of his teachings from his master, put them into effect wherever possible, and improvised the rest of his policy on the basis of his growing understanding of the problem of an empire builder in a territory in which the Greeks would necessarily be outnumbered by foreigners.

Though, as we shall see, he consolidated the empire under a central administration, this governmental technique he took over intact from the Persians; but in addition he founded new poleis wherever he went. To these he gave the institutions exactly as they were found in Greece itself. And though in many respects these cities could not function effectively as political entities, as social entities they were far nearer the Greek ideal than anything formerly to be found in Persia. A king over barbarians, Aristotle had said, must at least pretend to an interest in public welfare, avoid the exhibition of a tyrant's vices, and rule as little like a tyrant as possible. As far as his imperfect control over his own temper permitted him—for unhappily, like too many Greeks, he lacked moderation (*sophrosyne*)—this is what Alexander seems to have attempted. He did not accept

Aristotle's more cynical suggestions as to how the tyrant could rule without the consent of his people and still maintain himself in power. For the rest he did his duty by his old tutor by taking along with him a corps of specialists, collecting specimens of strange plants and animals and sending them back to him. No military campaign in history has been so much like a scientific expedition. But the question remains: Did Aristotle know of the expedition in advance, and did he approve of it? If so, why did he not give his pupil special instructions on how to carry it out, and why did he not give more attention to the special needs of the situation, giving more detailed instructions, for instance, on monarchy?

While there is always the possibility that Aristotle's works on this subject are lost—tradition says that he was asked for books on colonization and monarchy—even if we assume these books were not written, it can hardly be doubted that Aristotle knew of the planned expedition. Everyone in Greece knew of it for a considerable time before, and it was certainly known at the Macedonian court. Probably the best conclusion is that the expedition itself was the plan of Philip, inherited by his son Alexander. Isocrates, the Athenian orator and political philosopher, had urged it upon Philip. When the latter chose Aristotle as tutor for his son, he may have only wanted him to have the best education that money could buy. But Aristotle succeeded in giving his pupil an enthusiasm for Greek culture that was later to bear much fruit, though details of his personal advice on how to conquer and rule a barbarian people are missing and probably were never committed to writing.[3] For Aristotle was hoping to return to Athens, and public support of the policy of the Macedonian king was hardly likely to endear him to Athenians.

Aristotle was a student of politics, and particularly of the Greek polis as a form of government and as a medium for social life; he probably hoped that something of

[3] Plutarch, writing four centuries later, declared that Aristotle did give Alexander such private personal advice. But we do not know whether Plutarch had any definite information on the subject.

A mosaic from Pompeii showing the artist's conception, several centuries later, of Alexander the Great and Darius III at the battle of Issus (333 B.C.) (ALINARI)

the values of the polis, as he saw them, could be transferred to an alien territory. And Alexander, as we have seen, tried his best to transfer the polis to Asia, and it was no personal fault of his if it failed to take root within a monarchical system, and in a foreign land permeated by Oriental culture. What Alexander seems to have appreciated, and Aristotle did not, were the values of Oriental culture in themselves. This was the result of the conqueror's own experience, which, of course, Aristotle lacked.

FLEXIBLE POLICY TOWARD THE CONQUERED PEOPLES

Alexander was a consummate master not only of military strategy and tactics but of publicity. This was of vital importance, especially in the initial stages of his campaign. For though Philip had made nearly all the preliminary preparations for the campaign, he had not yet taken care of financing it. The Persian treasury was a more formidable enemy than the Persian native manpower, for it meant that he would be opposed by Greek mercenaries who were as tough fighters as his own Macedonians, and originally more numerous. There seem to have been, in fact, more Greeks fighting

against Alexander at the beginning than were fighting for him. However, they were scattered throughout Persia, and not all of them could be brought to bear upon him at the same moment. Alexander's policy, as it revealed itself, was therefore to pose as a champion of Hellas, and to try to arouse Hellenic patriotism. Moreover, if he could demonstrate to the world that he was an invincible conqueror the mercenaries might be persuaded to desert. And above all if he could acquire the treasury of Darius, the Macedonian himself could hire troops and put them in the field against the Persian king. Alexander's policy, with a force vastly inferior in numbers, though of excellent quality, varied in each country he entered. He had to pose as the champion of liberty in a country such as Asia Minor which appreciated that pose; he had to pose as a god-king appearing in majesty in Egypt where god-kings were acceptable, and for this purpose he had to win over the priesthood; and in Persia proper he had to be an invincible conqueror and appreciative of Persian valor and traditions. His brilliant propaganda seems to have been an important element in his success. His policy and campaigns have always been of great interest to students of the Greek mind and civilization because not only did he have the physical appearance of an ideal Greek, but in every act that he performed, except when he could not control his passions, we see the evidence of a trained and logical Greek mind, master of itself and its environment.

THE CONQUESTS

He started on his conquest of Asia with only thirty days' provisions for his army and with only seventy talents in his treasury; and he was already heavily in debt. He dared not leave Greece without an effective garrison, so that he had to leave nearly half his army behind in Macedonia to keep order and prevent revolt in the Greek cities. As it happened, the garrison was very necessary since Sparta suddenly revived, and for a while tried to unite the cities against him. The revolt caused considerable trouble to the regent, but was ultimately suppressed. The Greek "volunteers" in Alexander's army amounted to fewer than eight thousand men, and he only had enough cash and credit to hire a further five thousand. The "Hellenic League," so carefully provided by Philip, was of little use to him until it could be seen that he would be successful. The Macedonian nucleus is estimated at about eighteen thousand infantry and three thousand cavalry, with a valuable unit of Thessalian cavalry which had really volunteered and was of inestimable value to him. His fleet was very small and made up of undependable allies. The Persians, on the other hand, possessed almost unlimited gold and silver, which was, however, virtually useless to Darius once his original mercenaries were expended, since he could not hire any more foreign manpower after Alexander had secured the coasts. Darius also had the services of a large Phoenician navy. Potentially he had a very large Persian army made up of feudal levies, but these were not, for the most part, well trained, as he had relied in recent years too heavily on Greek mercenaries, and could not organize an effective army from his polyglot empire in the short time available to him.[4]

The first battle in Asia Minor was a resounding victory for Alexander (Granicus, 334 B.C.). The propaganda was working well enough for most Greek mercenaries to be doubtful, and so take little active part in the battle. Those who did take part and were captured were sent as slaves to Macedonia, causing some consternation among the remainder. They finally chose their sides; but the remnant that opted for the Persian king and his treasure was too small to be effective, and was wiped out by Alexander's victorious troops in a local engagement. The Persians retired from Asia Minor, and most of the non-Persian inhabitants offered their submission, the Ionians naturally hailing Alexander as liberator. The remainder were quietly mopped up, and suitable forms of government granted to them.

Darius by this time had assembled what he could of the Persian armies, including Greek mercenaries from his Persian provinces, and advanced to meet Alexander in Syria; and though Alexander's army had also increased in size it was no match in numbers for the Persian. This time everything seemed to be in Darius's favor. His Greek mercenaries, knowing that Alexander would show them no mercy, fought loyally and stubbornly. But Alexander's cavalry won the day and Darius himself fled into the interior (battle of Issus, 333 B.C.). Alexander captured his camp and enough spoil to be able to pay his troops, hire more, and still have something in hand. In no hurry about pursuing Darius, he proceeded to capture the Phoenician coast and secure the sea; then he went on what was largely a triumphal tour into Egypt, sacrificed to the Egyptian gods, rebuilt a number of temples, and founded the city of Alexandria, destined to become the greatest city of the world. Greek architects, artists, craftsmen, and plain immigrants flocked to it. At last Alexander had the support of some of the Greeks. His tolerant and Hellenizing policy was beginning to pay off. He made a state visit to the Greco-Egyptian oracle of Zeus-Amon

[4] See also Chapter 4 for the organization of the Persian Empire.

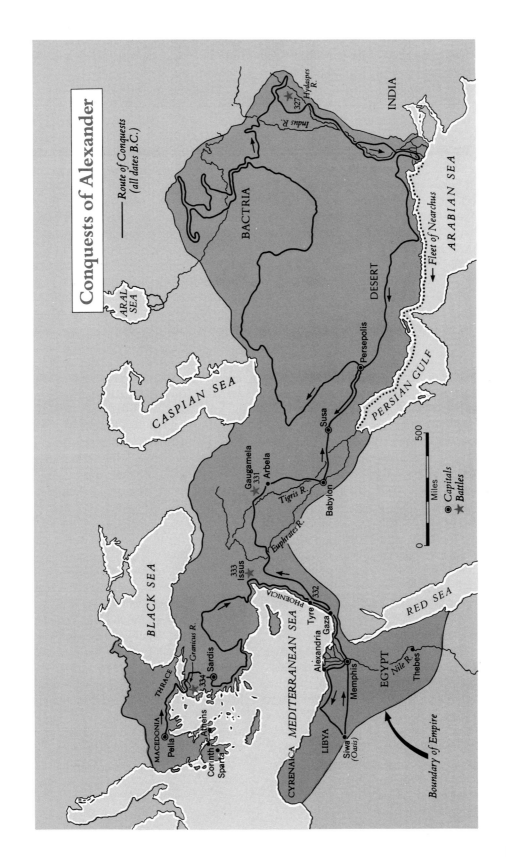

Conquests of Alexander

—— *Route of Conquests*
  (all dates B.C.)

ARAL
SEA

CASPIAN SEA

BLACK SEA

BACTRIA

INDIA

Hydaspes R.

327

Indus R.

DESERT

Fleet of Nearchus

ARABIAN SEA

Persepolis

PERSIAN GULF

500

Miles

◉ *Capitals*
★ *Battles*

0

Gaugamela
331

Arbela

Tigris R.

Susa

Babylon

Euphrates R.

333
Issus

PHOENICIA

332

Tyre

Gaza

Alexandria

Memphis

Nile R.

Thebes

EGYPT

RED SEA

Siwa
(*Oasis*)

LIBYA

CYRENAICA   MEDITERRANEAN SEA

THRACE

Granicus R.

334

Sardis

MACEDONIA

Pella

Corinth
Athens
Sparta

Boundary of Empire

away off in the desert, and left everyone to this day speculating what the god told him that was so "agreeable to his desire."

Having settled Egypt to his satisfaction without opposition, he took up again the pursuit of Darius, who had now gathered together his motley troops into another powerful army, which still greatly outnumbered anything Alexander could muster. But again by superior tactics and discipline he was successful on a battlefield chosen by his opponents, a wide plain near Nineveh, former capital of the Assyrian Empire (battle of Arbela, 331 B.C.). Alexander now adopted the Persian title of the "Great King," successor to the "abdicated" Darius, who had again fled into the interior, and took possession of the remaining three capitals of Persia, together with their enormous hoards of treasure. The avenging of the ancient expedition of the Persian Xerxes, the official reason for the war, was now complete, and Alexander dismissed all his allied Greek forces with thanks and handsome rewards. He then took steps to capture his predecessor, who was still at large; instead he found Darius's corpse, slain by the latter's own satraps. Furious that these men could have committed such sacrilege upon his own predecessor Alexander proclaimed a man hunt for the murderers. After burying Darius with all the honors befitting a Great King, he adopted Persian court ceremonial, and began to treat Persians as his subjects rather than as his enemies, much to the annoyance of the Macedonians. They also disapproved of his man hunt for the murderers, since this meant a further campaign into far-distant lands. Before he was able to catch up with them he had to cross the mountains of the Hindu Kush and conquer Bactria, developing new tactics as he went along to cope with a kind of warfare he had never known. He was, however, uniformly successful. He assumed Oriental manners more than ever before, demanded the Persian custom of prostration before him even from his Macedonians, and married Roxane, a native princess. Callisthenes, nephew of

Aristotle, refused to prostrate himself and was later put to death for plotting against the king.

Pushing south, Alexander made his way next into India, and again won a desperate battle with a formidable force, including elephants, by developing other new tactics, and the Punjab was his (battle of the Hydaspes, 327 B.C.). But at this point his exhausted army refused to go any further, and at last Alexander decided to return to Susa and Babylon. The homeward journey was made very difficult by Alexander's insistence on returning by way of the deserts of Baluchistan, apparently for scientific and exploratory reasons only. At last, however, he reached Susa, where he held a five-day marriage festival with ninety of his leading Macedonians marrying Persians, and he himself taking as an extra wife the daughter of Darius. All previous Greco-Persian marriages, amounting to about ten thousand were registered, and the bridegrooms rewarded with royal presents. Alexander also distributed some thirty thousand noble Persians throughout the Macedonian army, causing a revolt which was settled after an eloquent speech by the commander. After a few months he went to Babylon, where he contracted swamp fever and died at the age of thirty-three (323 B.C.). He had changed the face of the ancient world and never lost a battle.

Since he had left no provisions for a successor, and he had as yet no children—though Roxane later gave birth to a son—the inheritance was disputed among several of his more capable generals. There were a few attempts to hold the empire together; but no one general was strong enough to take over the whole, and the efforts ultimately collapsed. Egypt fell to Ptolemy Soter, the greater part of the Asiatic provinces to Seleucus, and Macedonia, after a long struggle between several contending generals, was consolidated under Antigonus Gonatas. Each of these men founded dynasties, and such of their history as is necessary will be recounted elsewhere in this chapter.

▶ **Results of the conquests**

THE FUSION OF GREEK AND ORIENTAL CULTURE

The effects of the conquests of Alexander were momentous in world history, not so much politically as culturally. The empire did not last as a single unified governmental unit, but the rule of Macedonians and Greeks over Oriental peoples was secured. Extensive immigration from Greece made the conquest more real than if an alien power had established political control only, as has happened in other periods of history. The barriers between Greek and barbarian had been broken down forever, and the resulting interpenetration of cultures determined the future pattern of all later civilization in the West. It is impossible to estimate whether Greek or Oriental culture predominated in the resulting complex. Both Oriental and Greek civilizations were already developed, and neither could be said to have absorbed the other; on the contrary, both contributed to a new, distinct amalgam. And it was left to the Romans, who entered this world in the guise of semibarbarians with a gift only for law, government, and military science, to spread this amalgam into a Western Europe which had been largely untouched by the Greeks and the Orientals themselves.

The period following the death of Alexander (usually called Hellenistic, as distinct from the earlier Hellenic) is therefore one of the great formative periods in the history of mankind, and should require extensive study. But since we have studied separately the elements that went to make it up, it is only necessary here to discuss the fusion, and the new trends in human civilization that resulted from it. Thereafter we shall move to the beginnings of the Roman state which inherited it, though it would have been quite possible, and perhaps even preferable, to have discussed Rome as a late comer in the Hellenistic civilization to which it contributed a few distinctive features.

The outstanding element making for unity in the whole Hellenistic world was the penetration of the Greek language as the common language of all educated men and of all those engaged in any form of commercial or trading activity. The old cuneiform and hieroglyphic writing quickly disappeared. The Greek language lost its ancient purity and became hospitable to any useful Oriental expressions that were needed. The language in which the New Testament, for instance, is written is the *Koine,* the "common language," which could be understood from Central Asia west to Italy and beyond. Other languages and dialects were, of course, spoken, especially Aramaic in the Near East, as has already been described; but the possession of a second language made it possible for the Italian and the Bactrian to carry on commercial and literary activities together. We find Armenian and Parthian kings as connoisseurs of Euripides and even writing plays in Greek, and we find a king of far-off Ethiopia having at least a nodding acquaintance with the language centuries after the conquests of Alexander. This powerful instrument of cultural fusion was perhaps the greatest single Greek contribution to the Hellenistic world civilization.

COMMERCIAL AND INDUSTRIAL CIVILIZATION OF THE HELLENISTIC WORLD

The Greeks had always been good traders, though the peoples of the Near East had been no novices. But the Greeks had developed more useful devices for the furthering of trade, and these now appeared in the Hellenistic world and were developed on a far larger scale than had been required before. Greek traders made themselves at home in the new world-cities founded by Alexander and his successors and were often granted special privileges. The greatest stimulus to trade was the release of the enormous hoards of gold and silver accumulated by the Persian kings, but never allowed to enter circulation. The chronic shortage of precious metals was therefore relieved, with a remarkably fructifying influence upon all trade and industry. For the first time throughout a large area taxes were paid in coin, and the states paid out their own wages in coin, especially to the armies. Banks sprang up everywhere, credit expanded far beyond anything previously known, and the check became a usual method of payment, though Egypt was ahead of the Asiatic empire in this. The new, largely money, economy, however, had a serious effect upon the poorer classes, as will be seen.

Insofar as the economic situation can be generalized, it may be said that the numerous new cities and the greatly expanded old cities were characterized by a commercial and industrial civilization more like our own than in any period prior to the sixteenth century. However, as was to be expected in an economy where slaves were present in large numbers, there was a very distinct cleavage between rich and poor. Profits were very high, while wages remained extremely low. The upper classes had access to all the luxuries of the ancient world and took full advantage of it. The poor, with the price of their labor determined by supply and demand, and the latter determined by the available slave labor, found themselves at the mercy of economic forces over which they had no control. Slaves actually declined in number, but this was no advantage to the poor freeman; slavery declined only because slave labor was more expensive than free labor. Slaves had to be fed and housed and treated as a valuable property, while the free laborer could be exploited without limit and it was of no interest to the employer whether he lived or died. The upper classes in the early period were predominantly Greek and Macedonian, but increasingly local nobles and traders were admitted into their company. Intermarriage continued in Persia, though in Egypt it was not so common and was hedged by restrictions. The distinction between rich and poor was far more important than that between Greek and barbarian. The peasant continued to work as from time immemorial, he gave crops and services to the state under the Seleucids and the Ptolemies as he had given them to Persian kings or Egyptian Pharaohs. The money economy of the cities hardly affected him; nor did the cultural radiation from the Greek cities, with their imported political institutions and their literature, philosophy, and science. The improved agricultural practices of the Greeks were passed on to him and when he was compelled to do so, as in Egypt, the peasant adopted them.

But there were several important differences, both political and economic, between the different parts of the Hellenistic world, and these require some separate mention.

▶ The Hellenistic Age in Greece

CONTINUED POLITICAL EXPERIMENTATION—THE NEW LEAGUES

The cities of Greece were usually politically subject to Macedonia, but Macedonia did not interfere with their economic activities. Indeed, the Macedonians performed a notable service to them by protecting them from barbarian invasions from the north, and by insisting that they keep the peace. Corinth, however, now far surpassed Athens in trade, being a more important industrial and manufacturing city, while the Aegean islands and ports on the Hellespont and in Asia Minor knew their greatest period of prosperity during the Hellenistic Age. But there was a constant drain of the population of the mainland into Asia and Egypt, and the prosperity was on a small scale, enjoyed mostly by the upper classes. On the land, owing to the depopulation, the estates became much larger than in classical times, with severe consequences to the small farmer, who could not compete with them and was often evicted for debt and lost his land permanently. There was a great increase in agricultural unemployment, and many parts of the country became desolate. Free distributions of grain became the rule in those cities which could collect enough in taxes to afford them.

Two promising political organizations were developed during the centuries after Alex-

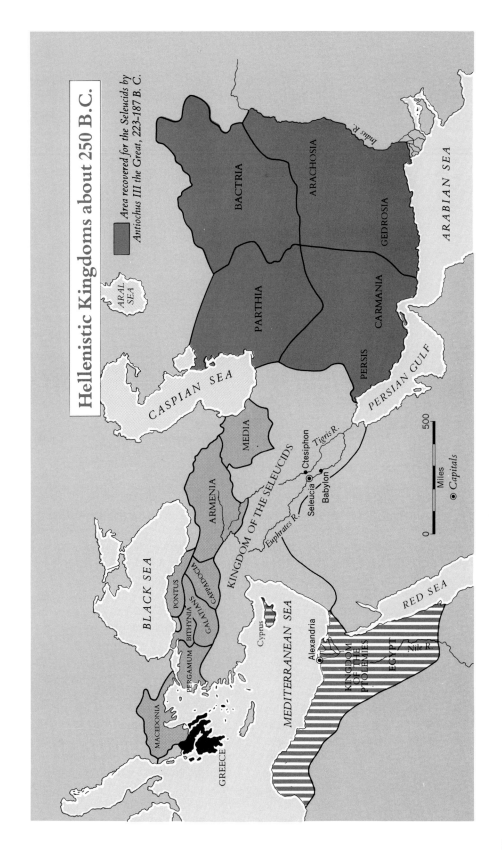

Hellenistic Kingdoms about 250 B.C.

Area recovered for the Seleucids by Antiochus III the Great, 223-187 B. C.

ARAL SEA

BACTRIA

ARACHOSIA

Indus R.

GEDROSIA

ARABIAN SEA

CASPIAN SEA

PARTHIA

CARMANIA

PERSIS

PERSIAN GULF

MEDIA

Tigris R.

Ctesiphon

Babylon

Seleucia

Euphrates R.

KINGDOM OF THE SELEUCIDS

ARMENIA

500

Miles

Capitals

0

CAPPADOCIA

GALATIA

BITHYNIA

PONTUS

BLACK SEA

PERGAMUM

MACEDONIA

GREECE

Cyprus

MEDITERRANEAN SEA

Alexandria

KINGDOM OF THE PTOLEMIES

EGYPT

Nile R.

RED SEA

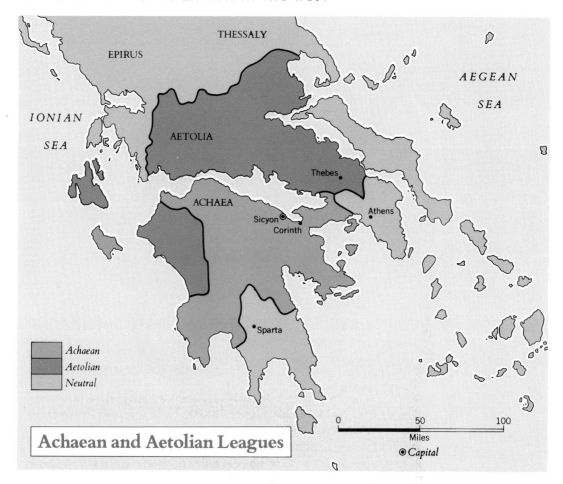

THESSALY

EPIRUS

IONIAN

SEA

AETOLIA

ACHAEA

Thebes

Sicyon
Corinth

Athens

Sparta

AEGEAN

SEA

Achaean
Aetolian
Neutral

Achaean and Aetolian Leagues

0   50   100

Miles

⊚ *Capital*

ander, but unfortunately they were usually antagonistic to each other. Moreover, the superior power of Macedonia in the north was a disturbing factor, since it tempted the leagues to apply for help to Macedonia when they quarreled with each other. But these leagues had genuine federal, or confederate, constitutions, and were the nearest approach the Greeks ever made to any organization larger than the polis. Their special contribution to federal unity was the abolition of the leadership of the most powerful city, leadership which had been the downfall, for instance, of the otherwise promising Chalcidian League of Olynthus. The capital cities of both the Achaean and the Aetolian leagues were small and unimportant. The constitutions of the two leagues were substantially similar. In their most advanced forms they had a federal

council on which each constituent city was represented on a proportional basis and to which had been delegated the power to take joint action without referring back to the cities. There was also an Assembly of all the citizens of all the cities, who voted by city, each of which had only one vote. The vote cast by the city was determined by a majority of all the citizens attending the Assembly who belonged to it. This Assembly elected officials and had to decide on peace and war and a number of other important questions concerning its own league. A general of the whole league was elected, but he could not succeed himself in office, though he could be elected in alternate years. The Achaean League at its height was made up of more than half of the cities in the Peloponnesus; the Aetolian League was made up of the cities of central Greece with the exception of Athens and some cities of Thessaly.

The only other power of importance in Greece was Sparta, where the old spirit reasserted itself and found expression in the division of the land, cancellation of debts, reform of the army, and re-establishment of discipline. The distinction between rich and poor that had grown up during the period of Spartan imperialism was abolished, together with the ephorate and council. But when the kings, under whose leadership these reforms were instituted, tried to expand their power in the Peloponnesus they came into contact with the Achaean League, which appealed to Macedonia rather than to the Aetolian League, which thereupon joined Sparta. The superior alliance squeezed out Sparta for the time, the revived Spartan kingdom was abolished, and the old constitution was restored. The Aetolians, left to the mercies of Macedonia, appealed to Rome, which ultimately conquered both Greece and Macedonia. As always, the internal strife in Greece prevented any chance of an all-Greek government, until, with the conquest by Rome, their liberties were lost for good.

▶ The Hellenistic Age in Egypt

MACEDONIAN EFFICIENCY IN AGRICULTURE

Egypt under the Ptolemies was for several centuries probably the most prosperous area in the world, at least as far as the upper classes were concerned. We are exceptionally well informed on the period because of the continuous discovery in recent years of Greek papyri preserved by the dry climate of the country. With the exception of Alexandria, which became a metropolis of more than half a million people and lived a full and relatively independent life of its own, the whole land of Egypt was the personal estate of the new Pharaoh, who made it a definite policy not to found any new Greek cities, preferring to exploit the political and economic heritage of ancient Egypt, which, as will be remembered, was accustomed to a god-king. First, however, it was necessary to restore the agricultural system to prosperity.

An extensive program for the improvement of irrigation and cultivation was put in hand for the benefit of both ruler and sub-

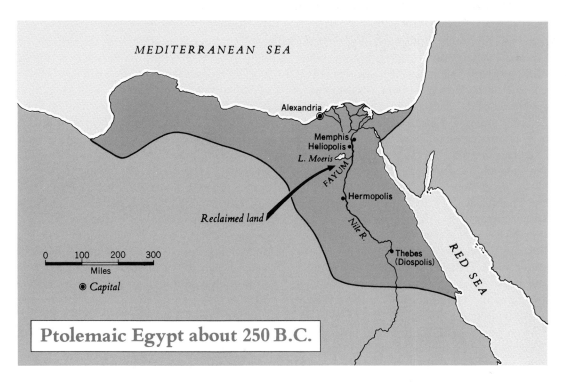

Ptolemaic Egypt about 250 B.C.

jects. Most of the best soil in the country was farmed as the Pharaoh's personal estate through royal appointees or by tenants of the crown, who were not permitted to leave their land and had to supply services and produce in exchange for the right to farm and for seed. In the reigns of the earlier Ptolemies this did not bear too hard on the tenants, but later the taxes and exactions were raised so high that it was almost impossible to make a living. Moreover, each village was collectively responsible for the taxes and had to make up any deficit on the part of individual tenants. Though we hear of several strikes and attempts to leave the land, the police and the military system were in every case strong enough to suppress them and enforce obedience. The lands let out by the Pharaoh, including temple lands, were farmed in the same way. Loyal soldiers, generals, nobles, and other favorites were sometimes freed of all taxes and allowed to exploit their tenants so long as they kept the land in good condition in case the king-god should have need of it himself. This was one of the methods used for pensioning soldiers and ensuring a new supply when required.

The Ptolemies also maintained a tight monopoly of all industry. Either directly or indirectly through concessionaires, usually Greeks, and carefully supervised by the state, all important businesses were under royal control, with gangs of inspectors checking to see that the established price was maintained. Even retailing was controlled, with the individual retailer buying the right to sell at a fixed rate of profit. The crown also subsidized voyages and exploration, and transportation was a royal monopoly. Directly or indirectly the Pharaoh had his hand in everything; his subjects were allowed to make a living, but only by his permission and under his control. Though there were organizations of workers, these were mostly for social and religious purposes, and not for the purpose of coercing their rulers. The theory of ancient Egypt was now put into thorough practical operation as it probably had never been, even in ancient times, under the efficient management and with all the necessary police control

of a dynasty descended from a Macedonian general who had once more appeared as a god on earth.

▶ The Hellenistic Age in Asia—Pergamum and the Seleucid Empire

On the conditions in Asia we have less information. One important part of Asia, northwest Asia Minor, was separated from the Seleucid Empire very early and became an important and very prosperous small kingdom, the kingdom of Pergamum, more urban than the other Hellenistic kingdoms, and better situated for maritime trade, with royal monopolies in the key industries and private enterprise in the others. This was almost a model small kingdom under the Attalids, who were great builders and patrons of art. Many of the finest specimens of Hellenistic art and architecture come from Pergamum. The whole kingdom was bequeathed to Rome by the last of the Attalids, as we shall see.

Central control in the Seleucid Empire was far less effective than in Egypt, for the rulers had continuously to fight with pretenders to their throne, with military adventurers, and, by the second century B.C., with the Romans. Their kingdom increased and decreased in size according to the fortunes of war. The old kingdom of Persia was largely worked by royal serfs, and temple lands were added to the royal property. The kings also made it a policy to dispossess nobles when possible. The Seleucid monarchs established royal monopolies in several industries, but private enterprise in industry was far more widespread than in Egypt, owing to the difficulty of central control in such a vast country. The royal post roads and the postal system of the Persians were expanded and improved, and for the first time many of the Asiatic rivers were made navigable; fleets of ships under royal protection and supervision carried the products of industry over long distances in shorter time than before.

Most of this system in the western part of Asia was taken over intact by the Romans. Internally, as in the Persian days, the area was usually at peace; the warring armies of

Ruins of the temple of Zeus at Pergamum as they appear at the present time. The size of the ruins will give some indication of the scale of the work of the Hellenistic monarchs of this commercial state. (COURTESY TURKISH INFORMATION OFFICE)

the monarchs did not affect the ordinary life of peasant and trader. Ships regularly plied the seas and rivers all the way from Persia to Italy, some armed with catapults against enemies and pirates. There was already substantial peace in this part of the world before Rome, with fanfare of trumpets, established her Pax Romana.

▶ Hellenistic culture

GENERAL CHARACTERISTICS—COSMOPOLITANISM AND INDIVIDUALISM

The cosmopolitanism of the Hellenistic world is the dominant characteristic of all Greek thought and society during this period. We have seen the rise of individualism in the fourth century, B.C., and how this tended to break down the old, close-knit social organization of the polis. Although the polis was now transferred to new surroundings and many formal elements of self-government were retained, the self-determination of the state was irretrievably lost, and with it community duties and responsibilities. In fifth-century Athens a citizen was content to live in a humble house on a tiny income because he valued participation in the social life of the community more than individual wealth and "self-expression"; his religion was part of the life of the community rather than a means of individual comfort, much less salvation. His art and his architecture were expressions of his love for his city and were the result of great communal efforts. When the polis life disintegrated, everything the earlier Greek had valued disappeared with it. The transition was, as we have seen, gradual through the fourth century. The conquests of Alexander only put the seal on the already accomplished fact.

It is useless to try to discover whether

individualism was the cause or the effect of the social breakdown. Both were always present at the same time. And, since there no longer was a community, it became necessary for each man to take care of himself, whether he liked it or not. A great temple of Zeus built by a monarch was not his, and he felt no civic pride in it. But he could still feel pride in a piece of fine craftsmanship of his own making. He could hope to get rich by struggling, necessarily to some degree at the expense of his neighbor and fellow citizen. If he were wealthy, he could take advantage of the good things, the luxuries offered by this cosmopolitan civilization. He could be entertained in the theater by amusing slices of life, seeing other people fighting to reach the top like himself; he could read books of an entertaining nature, not the kind to make him think, but worth reading to keep himself from contemplating the fact that something was missing in life that his ancestors had known, some secret of happiness withheld from him. Or, if he were a scholar, he could try to discover what it had been that these ancestors had had, he could diligently peruse their works, editing them with fine fidelity, taking care to catch the exact wording of the original, and write ponderous histories about them. If he were practical he could try to increase the sum of useful knowledge instead of speculating about things that could never be known. Or, finally, he could decide that life was not worth living anyway, with this vacuum at the heart of things, and so he could turn to the Persian religions or the religions of the mysteries, or he could become a Stoic philosopher.

All these different manifestations of individualism we find in the Hellenistic world; it only seems to have needed the Industrial Revolution, which was already well on the way with the latest technical developments of the Greek scientists, to transform it into our own society. But the creativity of the early Hellenistic civilization gradually spent itself for reasons which still elude the investigator. There was too much revolt perhaps against the relatively new individualism, too little real interest in the workings of the material world, too much respect for nature to wish to interfere with it for the satisfaction of the material needs of human beings. Too recently had these peoples emerged from the belief that they were powerless against the gods for them to be able to take the whole step of usurping the position of the gods without drawing upon themselves *ate* and *nemesis*. They had to go through a long apprenticeship before they could come to believe that man was the lord of creation, and that only the individual human being and his welfare on earth counted in all creation, and explain satisfactorily to themselves that this indeed was the intention of the gods. In the Hellenistic Age they lacked the compelling assurance of the value of this life for the individual man that proved to be the great strength of Western civilization in its struggle to understand and control nature; and so when the new religions promised salvation in the next world after a period of trial and testing in this, their teachings fell on willing ears. When Bishop Theophilus in A.D. 390 destroyed the bulk of the library of Alexandria, the greatest collection of Greek books ever assembled, he was only symbolizing a choice that had been made centuries earlier in the Hellenistic Age.

PHILOSOPHIES OF DOUBT AND PESSIMISM

The Cynics

The thought of the Hellenistic Age is in strong contrast with that of earlier days. The Academy of Plato and the Lyceum of Aristotle continued their work, the latter patiently assembling more facts and writing histories of special fields, the former moving at first into some of the more mystical aspects of Platonism and then into Skepticism. But the original philosophies of this age were more directly influenced by the new social experience of individualism and cosmopolitanism.

The earliest of these was Cynicism, founded by Antisthenes; its most notorious early member was the famous Diogenes, who lived in a tub and cultivated rudeness and self-sufficiency. Though it arose out of the discontents of the fourth century before the conquests of Alexander, the germ of developed Stoicism is already to be found in this philosophy. Everything in society, said the Cynics, is foolishness; nothing in life is worth having. What men pursue is not worth the trouble; whether you are rich or poor, Greek or barbarian, is of no importance to the wise man. Only the wise man can appreciate the uselessness of possessions. He alone can be self-sufficing, and his own thought and character are all that count. He can think and he can be moral only if he is completely indifferent to possessions. The wise men in the world form a world community, a city of the world, as Diogenes called it, based on contempt for everyone and everything.

The Cynics did not form an organized school of philosophy but became wandering beggars and preachers, often cultivating uncouthness and rudeness in order to show their superiority to all conventions. The only positive action that the wise man would take would be what his personal sense of duty dictated, for he was bound by no social convention nor by any other of man's inventions for leading people away from the philosophic life. The equality in Cynicism, the world-city of wise men, and the cultivated indifference to worldly things were all to be found later transformed in Stoicism; therein lies its only permanent importance, for the philosophy was obviously not designed to attract a numerous following.

Epicurism

The philosophy of Epicurism was founded by Epicurus, who began to teach in Athens about 306 B.C. Though Epicurus took over the atomistic science of Democritus, the core of his teaching was his insistence on indifference (*ataraxia*—literally the condition of not being shaken). "Be happy with little, for being interested in, and needing, much, brings unhappiness." The goal of men is the attainment of happiness. But for Epicurus and his disciples happiness consisted primarily in freedom from physical pain, worldly cares, and fears. Since congenial friendship was one of those pleasures

which can be obtained with the least difficulty, the early Epicureans especially cultivated it, living a simple life and discoursing on philosophy in the famous "Garden of Epicurus."

In Epicurean thought everything was subservient to the pursuit of happiness. It was better to cultivate the virtues than the vices because the latter usually involved pain—which should be avoided. But there was no need to cultivate virtue too assiduously, since this would lead to self-denial—which was unnecessary and prevented enjoyment. In general the philosophy in its original form was more negative than positive—a tired man's travesty of Aristotle's Golden Mean—and a mild asceticism was the usual practice of the personal followers of Epicurus.

In order to justify such a worldly philosophy the gods were relegated to a far-off sphere, primarily to provide man with an example of how to live perfectly. They paid no attention whatever to man, and all religion was simply superstition. Astrology, divination, and other outgrowths of religion were the result of man's ignorance. The truth was, according to Epicurus, that we live in a purely material world of atoms in constant motion, and the whole world has come into existence by chance and not by divine decree. It is not known whether Epicurus himself, or his Roman disciple Lucretius, introduced the famous "swerve" of the atoms so that they would move from their regular perpendicular downward path and strike each other; at all events this swerve was also fortuitous in the atoms, though its occurrence made free will possible in human beings.

The philosophy of happiness, although with Epicurus it led to a gentle asceticism, in later times, especially in Rome, became a simple philosophy of hedonism, or the pursuit of pleasure, even of the grosser varieties—likely to lead to pain. The same lack of interest in social responsibilities was maintained, and the same indifference to worldly success; but happiness was considered to be attained best by enjoyment of all that the

The Stoic philosophers were so called because they congregated in the great stoas of Athens to discuss philosophy. One of these stoas is at present being restored by the American School of Classical Studies in cooperation with the Greek government. This picture shows a corner of the restored stoa, originally built by King Attalus II of Pergamum about 150 B.C., and gives an impression of these long porches frequented not only by the Stoics but by earlier philosophers such as Socrates. The size of such a stoa can be gauged from the reconstruction of the whole Agora shown in Chapter 7. (COURTESY AMERICAN SCHOOL OF CLASSICAL STUDIES AT ATHENS)

world offered, even to excess, rather than by the moderate enjoyment of Epicurus, and the consequent lack of the penalties of excess.

Stoicism

Stoicism was unquestionably the greatest philosophy of this age, and in its many aspects went far toward answering the difficult problems arising out of the new social experience. It was a philosophy that continually grew in scope as the centuries passed; much of it was woven into the fabric of Christian philosophy and ethics, and much also into Roman law. As a philosophy it was still vital in the last centuries of the Roman Empire, and at times it provided the only moral anchor for those who could not accept the salvationist religions, and yet would not lapse into the negative or hedonistic indifference of Epicurism, or complete Skepticism. Its founder, Zeno of Citium, supposedly a "Phoenician," founded a school at Athens about 300 B.C., but Stoicism was never centered on a single school, and never held deep roots in old Greece. It was from the beginning Hellenistic rather than Hellenic. Zeno, like the Cynics, his forebears, taught that there is only one world-state, with all men equal in it, united by no race or class but only by virtue—as with the Cynics, a world of wise men united by their wisdom. We know very little about Zeno himself beyond his teaching on the ideal state, for his writings have not survived. Indeed, most of our knowledge of the Stoics comes from Roman sources.

Chrysippus, a Cilician who taught at Athens some seventy years after Zeno, is regarded as the second founder of Stoicism. He it was who gave it its systematic theology and its ethics. The purpose of Stoicism, as with Epicurism, is to give man individual well-being and self-sufficiency. It is therefore primarily a philosophy of *this* life. Throughout the history of Stoicism there are many who interpret the ideal of self-sufficiency as justification for the withdrawal from life, including even suicide in certain circumstances. But Chrysippus taught resolution, fortitude, and devotion to duty, combined with indifference to all temptations of ordinary earthly pleasure and enjoyment. Every man on earth has his part to play, assigned by Divine Providence, and this he must seek to play with dignity, answering only to his own conscience for his lapses from rectitude. The world order is created by God and it is working for good; the wise man should understand the goodness and seek to work in accordance with the divine plan. Not only man, but the animal kingdom, is part of this great world order, and animals also have their part to play. But man is different because he has reason; and reason is an attribute of God. Hence the world order is reasonable, and it is man's duty to discover this Divine Reason as far as he can, and try to make his human laws approximate to it. Therefore above the laws of any earthly state are the divine laws, or what is henceforward to be called Natural Law. Every man possessed of reason is equal to every other man; there are no natural inequalities. A slave is a "laborer hired for life," and should be treated accordingly, not as a subhuman implement.

This dogmatic teaching, so much at variance with earlier Greek rationalism, laid itself open to practical criticism, which it received primarily from Carneades, the Skeptic who devoted the greater part of his life to attacks on Chrysippus. The chief ground for criticism was that the wise man indifferent to things of the world, inhuman in his attempts to get rid of all natural feeling, could be found nowhere in nature. And Carneades complained that there was no evidence for divine justice whatever, and there could be no agreement even between reasonable human beings on what justice is. On the contrary, Carneades insisted that on the evidence man is governed by self-interest only; and it is nothing but fear of the consequences that prevents him from pursuing his own interests altogether without regard for others. He disagreed that this could be called justice. This and other criticisms led Panaetius of Rhodes to modify the early Stoicism into the philosophy of the so-called Middle Stoa, restating it in a form palatable to the Romans, among whom Stoicism was now finding most of its adherents. The Romans were imperialists; and the Stoic idea of a world-state, the old Stoic virtues of devotion to duty and public spirit, and the idea of natural law were able to appeal to them, once Panaetius had brought the philosophy down to earth by eliminating the superhuman wise man, and replacing the asceticism by public service and humanity. But this aspect of Stoicism in the Roman world will be briefly discussed in a later chapter.

In the East, Stoicism became more religious in tone, with Divine Reason being exalted almost to the status of a God. Cleanthes in his famous *Hymn* petitions this one universal God not for anything worldly but for a virtuous mind. The traditional gods were also absorbed into the Stoic system as attendants upon the Divine Reason, even astrology and magic finding their home in it. But in whatever form it appeared, and whatever religion it influenced, always the central ethic remained—be indifferent to worldly success and strive to cultivate the moral life, for man's first duty is to fulfill the demands of his moral nature. Externals can never be worth anything in comparison with the self-sufficiency of the consciously upright man. This was clearly a thought to which all religions that stress morality could be hospitable.

The Skeptics

The Skeptical school was founded by Pyrrho as early as the end of the fourth century B.C. We know little of the founder beyond the fact that he seems to have been the first to make criticism of other theories the goal of his philosophy, denying that knowledge was possible. All sense perceptions are illusions, and against every statement that can be made an opposite is equally probable. The wise man therefore will make the best of the world of illusion, and by suspending all judgment not strive after the impossible, but take the world as he finds it. Later Skeptics continued to emphasize criticism, which in a world of superstition and dogmatism was necessary enough; and their work was on the whole salutary, as we have seen from its effect on Stoicism. But Skepticism as a philosophy made little impression on the less rational philosophies and religions. It was too austere to command much general success, though for a while its spirit dominated, of all places, the Platonic Academy at Athens. A philosophy without positive content can be a valuable tool for the reform of others, but in a religious age even the indifference which Skepticism preached found more arguments in its support within other philosophies than Skepticism alone could offer.

THE RELIGIOUS VACUUM—MYSTERY RELIGIONS

In philosophy Greek thought still predominated, but Greek religion of the Classical Age was so closely associated with the polis that it could not be expected to survive in the Hellenistic world. The religious vacuum was filled by the mystical Oriental religions; and the mystery religions of old Greece, which themselves had developed out of an earlier Oriental tradition, received a new lease on life. The more intellectual upper-class Greek probably despised the new "barbarian" religions, and many of them took refuge in atheism and skepticism, or in the Greek philosophies. The goddess Tyche or chance, which indeed seemed to rule Hellenistic life, was widely worshiped, and astrology from the Chaldeans was both believed in as a science and used as the basis for a kind of star worship. On the whole, even when the Greeks accepted the Oriental religions they were inclined to make the gods abstract, representing universal principles rather than the *persons* they were to their Oriental adherents. The Stoic god, for instance, was never a person, which has led students to characterize the philosophy as pantheism. For the Greeks there were divine persons, but they did not fulfill the functions of Oriental gods. The Greeks had no objection to deifying kings, especially after they were dead. It was even explained in the Hellenistic Age that this was what had happened to the Olympian gods: they were ancient kings who died and had been deified (Euhemerism).

A more extended discussion of the Hellenistic mystery religions of this time will be deferred to Chapter 12, when they will be considered as part of the background for Christianity.

SCIENCE

In classical Greece, as was noted in the last chapter, there were very few scientists in the modern sense of the word, even though mathematics had made some progress and Hippocrates of Cos had laid the foundation of scientific medicine. By modern standards even Aristotle must be regarded as more of a philosopher than a scientist. In the Hellenistic Age, by contrast, there is a considerable roster of scientists. Among these the mathematicians and astronomers take pride of place. They are separated from each other only with difficulty, since the great majority of mathematicians known to us were also astronomers. It is in the Hellenistic Age that astronomy first became a real science weaned from astrology, its Babylonian parent. Although few of the findings of the Hellenistic astronomers are still acceptable in our day, most of them were based on observation and calculation. These astronomers showed a marked willingness, on the whole, to revise their hypotheses in accordance with their empirical findings. Much less than medieval men did the Hellenistic scientists insist on clinging to older notions that had been hallowed by time but in fact rested on subjective, nonscientific beliefs.

When Aristarchus of Samos, in the third century B.C., put forward the hypothesis that the earth moved around the sun it was criticized by Hipparchus of Nicaea (who did most of his work on the island of Rhodes) and by later Hellenistic astronomers, not because it upset the old idea that the earth, as the qualitatively basest body in the universe, must be stationary while the lighter and "more perfect" heavenly bodies were able to move in "perfect" circular orbits, but because his hypothesis did not "save the phenomena," in other words because it did not fit the observed facts. Hellenistic astronomers naturally knew from their observations that the geocentric hypothesis presented difficulties that had to be overcome, but these difficulties seemed less weighty, especially since the solutions they put forward enabled them to predict with considerable accuracy.

It was a common fact of observation that planets sometimes appear larger than they do at other times, from which it was a simple deduction that their distance from the earth must vary at different times. It was Apollonius of Perga (ca. 220 B.C.) who suggested a solution to this problem that was accepted in its main outlines until the sixteenth century A.D. He suggested that the planets might move in a circular orbit (known as an epicycle) around a center which was not the earth. This center, however, was itself on the orbit of another circle (known as the deferent) which did circle around the earth.[5] Either Apollonius or one of his contemporaries also suggested that the planets, even if they did circle around the earth, might circle around a point on the earth which was not its center. Hipparchus, who did his work during the following century, made use of both these hypotheses, explaining the periodic movements of the heavenly bodies by means of the system of

epicycles and deferent, and the apparent motion of the sun and the motions of the moon by the hypothesis of the eccentric movement of these bodies. In his finished system Hipparchus was able to explain satisfactorily all the periodic movements of the heavenly bodies insofar as they were known to him. There was therefore no need, from a scientific point of view, to give serious attention to the alternative heliocentric hypothesis of Aristarchus.

The work of Hipparchus and other Hellenistic astronomers was systematized by the astronomer and mathematician Claudius Ptolemy in the second century A.D., and it was his work rather than that of his predecessors that was available to the Muslim world and was translated into Latin in the Middle Ages. Indeed the entire geocentric system was in later times called by his name (the Ptolemaic system). By Ptolemy's time it was necessary to postulate no fewer than eighty epicycles to account for the periodic movements of the heavenly bodies. One of the features of Copernicus' sixteenth century heliocentric hypothesis was his reduction of the number of epicycles to 34, though he could not yet do without them altogether. Meanwhile Aristarchus' work on the movements of the heavenly bodies was neglected, and his book on the subject (if he ever expressed his ideas in writing) has not been preserved. Knowledge of his hypothesis was fairly widespread in the ancient world, as is evidenced by occasional casual references to it by classic writers. But the evidence on which it was based, and his mathematical calculations, were not available to Copernicus.

The advance in astronomy in the Hellenistic world was in large part made possible by the records that had been kept by the Babylonians, mostly in pursuit of their astrological aims. However, there were some serious Babylonian astronomers, notably Kidenas (about 340 B.C.) and Diogenes of Babylon (about 160 B.C.), the first to teach the correct position of the planets in relation to the earth. Babylonian mathematics was well known to the Greeks, especially algebra. Indeed, in many ways Babylonian

[5] For this system see the diagram of the heavens taken from the medieval textbook of John of Sacrobosco, which appears on page 627.

290 CLASSICAL CIVILIZATION IN THE WEST

mathematics remained superior to that of the Greeks, who did not develop some of the best Babylonian ideas. The Babylonians had invented a positional notation based on the number 60 (as our decimal system uses a positional notation based on the number 10). The Greeks took from Babylon the sexagesimal (60) numerical system, but by using letters for numbers abandoned the positional notation of the Babylonians. The number 60 was indeed an excellent choice because of the many factors into which it can be divided, a marked weakness of the decimal system. The Romans used letters, following Greek practice, making necessary the reinvention of a positional notation in the West in the later part of the Middle Ages.

Many calculations of the distance of the sun and planets from the earth, and of the circumference of the earth itself, were attempted in Hellenistic times. Eratosthenes (ca. 275–195 B.C.), the chief librarian of the Museum of Alexandria and probably the greatest geographer of antiquity, arrived at a figure of 252,000 stades for the circumference of the earth. His method was to measure the arc of the sun's rays at Alexandria on a midsummer day, and the distance from Alexandria to Syene, where the sun at the same moment was directly overhead. We do not know the precise equivalent of the Greek stade, but the best modern opinion holds that 252,000 stades equaled 24,662 miles. Since the true mean circumference by modern calculations is 24,857 miles, this was an amazingly close approximation, and it would have been even closer if Eratosthenes had known that Syene did not have exactly the same longitude as Alexandria. Hipparchus recognized the enormous size of the sun and its great distance from the earth, calculating that the sun's mass was 1880 times that of the earth and 1245 earth diameters away. Although these figures are still far short of modern estimates (other Greeks, such as Poseidonius of Apamea made still higher estimates than Hipparchus) the authoritative Ptolemy reduced these estimates considerably, thus giving early modern astronomers and mathematicians the impression that the Greeks were

further away from the truth than they were. Since Ptolemy also adopted a much lower figure for the circumference of the earth than had Eratosthenes, he may be said to have contributed to the discovery of America by Columbus in 1492. If Columbus had believed Asia to be as far away as Eratosthenes had held, he might never have attempted his voyage! Eratosthenes himself realized that Europe, Asia, and Africa constituted an island, and that it was possible to sail from Spain around Africa to India, and also that India could be reached by sailing westward from Alexandria.

Perhaps the two most familiar names in Hellenistic science are those of Euclid and Archimedes. Euclid, whose geometrical propositions and proofs remain perfectly valid for three-dimensional space, may not have been responsible for many of the theorems in his great textbook. It was his supreme merit to have collected in a single work the achievements of many of his predecessors and to have transmitted them to posterity. Archimedes of Syracuse was the most distinguished of a long line of Greek engineers and mechanics (some of whose findings were committed to writing in Alexandria), but he was at the same time a mathematician and physicist, the most all-round scientist of antiquity. His work On Method shows also that he was a clear and systematic thinker, and that he made use in all his work of geometrical principles and the deductive method first systematized by Aristotle. The lever had been known in remote antiquity, but Archimedes found new uses for it and made it his business to deduce mathematically from self-evident axioms why it behaved as it did. In this he used the syllogism; in other words he combined two pieces of known information to demonstrate a new conclusion. The idea of specific gravity he is said to have discovered in his bath when he noticed that he displaced water equal in volume to his body. The legend has it that he cried "Eureka" (I have found it), and ran out into the streets naked to proclaim his discovery. After discovering specific gravity he then proceeded to deduce his discovery mathematically. Legend also tells how he was able to detect frauds on the part of the gold-smiths of Syracuse when the supposedly golden crown of his patron King Hiero of Syracuse was found to displace more water than an equal weight of gold. Cicero, the Roman orator and man of letters, tells us that Archimedes made a planetarium that repro-duced the movements of the heavenly bodies, and was even able to show eclipses. Lastly, he was able to keep the whole might of Rome at bay for three years during a siege of his native city, and was killed by a Roman soldier who was said to have been wholly ignorant of who he was. His fertile imagination con-stantly invented new devices for use in siege warfare, especially grapnels and catapults. But such achievements did not rank in his own mind with discoveries in the realm of geometry. By his command it was recorded on his tombstone as his greatest achievement that he had discovered the ratio of the volume of a cylinder to that of the sphere inscribed in it. Neither the ancient nor the modern world would be inclined to agree with his typically Greek judgment.

Several important advances were made in biology, largely because of the abandonment of the old taboo against the dissection of cadavers. Herophilus of Chalcedon, who worked mostly in Alexandria, was apparently the first to dissect human bodies in public. He discovered the nerves, previously un-known, and determined that the arteries car-ried blood, not air, as had hitherto been thought. He was the first to distinguish be-tween veins and arteries. Unfortunately Erasistratus of Iulis, who founded his own school of medicine in competition with Herophilus, disputed the conclusion that the arteries carried blood because he found that the arteries of dead animals were empty. He held that the blood escaping from a severed artery entered it only after the air had been expelled. The supposed air in the arteries carried "vital spirit" to the heart and brain. The vital spirit became "animal spirit" in the brain and was thence distributed through the nerves. Erasistratus was the first to distin-guish motor and sensory nerves.

The findings of these schools of medicine

and biology, together with the earlier teach-ings of Hippocrates and his school, were in-corporated into a medical encyclopaedia by the Latin Aulus Celsus, possibly in the time of Augustus early in the first century A.D., and carried forward by Galen of Pergamum, who lived in the second century A.D. and became physician to the Roman Emperor Marcus Aurelius. Galen disssected barbary apes and other animals (though not human bodies) and was able to show conclusively that the arteries, contrary to the opinion of Erisis-tratus, did indeed contain blood. However he made use of his predecessor's distinction be-tween "animal spirit" and "vital spirit" to ex-plain how venous blood was transformed into arterial blood by the infusion of the "vital spirit" contained in the air, which he sup-posed flowed down the pulmonary vein from the lungs into the left chamber of the heart. Galen did not discover the way in which the blood actually circulated, but his theories fitted the facts known in his day, and his work was so authoritative that his theories were not abandoned until well into the sixteenth century.

HELLENISTIC LITERATURE

The Hellenistic Age was not one of great literature, and there is nothing extant that can compare with the works of the classical age on the Greek mainland. Perhaps it was the political and cultural conditions of the old polis that had called forth the deep and pas-sionate involvement that is the hallmark of the greatest literature. It is certain that such an historian as Thucydides would not have flourished in Alexandria, nor could the tragedy or the Old Comedy of Athens have grown readily out of such soil. Euripides was by now by far the most popular of the older tragedians, almost certainly because his char-acters were recognizable men and women. The New Comedy of Menander and others in Athens was popular, but it was a comedy of manners, with stock characters and often romantic plots with happy endings. Menander himself handled his material with a sure touch, and his comedy became a model for that of the Roman comic writers, Plautus and

Terence. Today it is valuable primarily for the insights it gives into the social life and customs of Athens in its most tranquil period when the former imperial city had become a peaceful backwater, its inhabitants living in the genteel poverty to which they had become accustomed, attractive to tourists and students, but no longer playing an effective part in world affairs.

The one great figure in Hellenistic literature is Theocritus, a Sicilian Greek who spent some years in Alexandria. Theocritus was the inventor of pastoral poetry and almost always is regarded as the greatest poet who ever worked in this genre. His exquisite idylls of shepherds and shepherdesses are filled with perceptive impressions of natural beauty. Perhaps unhappily, Theocritus has been imitated

The temple of Zeus at Içel (Mersin) in Asia Minor. Note the ornate Corinthian columns of this temple of the Hellenistic period. (COURTESY TURKISH INFORMATION OFFICE)

The Altar of Zeus (restored) as it looked in the prosperous commercial city of Perfanum in Asia Minor, early second century B.C. (STAATLICHE MUSEEN, BERLIN)

so often in later centuries that it has been forgotten how delicately the original master handled this kind of material. His most eminent imitator, the Italian Vergil, who imitated Theocritus in his *Eclogues*, is usually regarded as inferior to his Greek master. In spite of the undoubted charm of some of his *Eclogues*, Vergil has undoubtedly helped to generate an acute dislike for pastoral poetry in numerous schoolboys, to whom Theocritus was only a name.

HELLENISTIC ART

It is wholly natural, in view of the new conditions in the Hellenistic world, that Hellenistic art presents many contrasts with the Hellenic art of the classical period. As was noted in the last chapter, almost all classical Greek art had a religious basis. With the decline of civic religion Greek artists and craftsmen had other patrons than the polis. The new Greek cities in Asia, and the older Greek cities of Ionia, many of which enjoyed a greater prosperity than in earlier times, desired the services of Greek architects for their building programs and many of them vied with each other in creating beautiful new civic buildings and temples. The kings had more money available for such purposes than had ever been available to the mainland cities, and their building programs were planned to reflect their wealth and power. The architects therefore found their services much in demand, as did the sculptors. Not only did every Hellenistic city desire to decorate itself with the finest sculptures available, but wealthy private persons were also able to afford statues of themselves and their families. Although the older vase painting soon died out there was a new demand for painted portraits, and fresco painting in the temples, civic buildings, and even private homes became an important industry.

The result was a commercialization of all Greek art, with the natural result that in time its quality began to decline since there were simply not enough first-rate artists to satisfy the demand. The great works of art, including those of the classical period, were duplicated

A beautiful sculptured eagle poised and ready to fly, dated ca. 200 B.C. and found in Egypt, is as suggestive of movement as the more famous Nike of Samothrace, pictured on page 294. (NATIONAL GALLERY OF ART, SAMUEL H. KRESS COLLECTION, 1952)

many times over, and it is only through their Hellenistic and even Roman copies that many of them are known to us at all. Nevertheless, many of the greatest Greek artists worked in the Hellenistic period, including the unknown sculptors who carved such masterpieces as the Aphrodite of Melos ("Venus de Milo") and the Nike of Samothrace, a winged victory in the form of the prow of a ship.

Whereas in the earlier period the human body was always idealized, and even such processions as the Panathenaic procession in the Parthenon friezes have a static quality, the Hellenistic artists tended toward realism and were sometimes, as in the Nike, remarkably successful in suggesting movement. Some later artists consciously strained after effect as is particularly noticeable in the striking Laocöon

The Nike (Victory) of Samothrace, a statue (now in the Louvre) in the form of the prow of a ship. Note how the Nike suggests speed and movement, unlike the static figures of the Parthenon. (COURTESY THE LOUVRE)

group, in which the artist portrays the struggle of the Trojan priest and his sons with the serpents sent by the gods to destroy them after Laocöon had warned the Trojans not to admit the wooden horse into the city. The victories of the kings of Pergamum over the Gauls were commemorated in some remarkable statuary in which the artists made a serious effort to show the heroic barbarians as they were in life, and succeeded in differentiating them for all eternity from the Greeks who conquered them. Such figures as the old market woman, probably looted from Greece by the Romans, who is shown in full realism would have been unthinkable as a subject for the artist in classical times.

Clearly the Hellenistic Age was one of the great artistic ages in world history, even though opinions will always differ as to the comparative virtues of classical Hellenic and Hellenistic art, and whether the latter constitutes a decline from the undisputed greatness of the former. Idealism and realism, classicism and romanticism, and other conflicting schools all have their champions, and a preference for religious or secular art need not prevent a just appreciation of both. Objectively a Corinthian column (especially favored in the Hellenistic Age) is more ornate than the older Doric and Ionic orders, but who can say that it is more or less beautiful? The Hellenistic and Roman tendency to include ornate columns in their buildings even when these columns were not required for support may be criticized on the grounds that a column has only one legitimate purpose—to support a structure. But clearly Hellenistic architects found them aesthetically pleasing, and thus included them for purposes of decoration, as was done also during the neoclassical revival of the eighteenth and nineteenth centuries.

No doubt classical Greece would have considered this practice reprehensible as a waste of scarce resources. But the Hellenistic world no longer had to consider such mundane matters. It could afford to be experimental and daring, and it could tolerate the waste that necessarily accompanies such a policy. So the artists were daring, experimen-

tal, and often wasteful, and, especially in later times when most of the patrons were newly rich Romans, they were frequently slipshod. When resources were scarce in classical Greece, and the building of a new temple to the tutelary god or goddess of a city was not to be undertaken lightly, the building was a common undertaking of the whole city and had to be as perfect as its creators could make it. If the original Parthenon has never been equaled, but has been endlessly imitated in inferior copies, the circumstances of its build-

Hellenistic realism. This statue of an old market woman, discovered at Rome, dates from the second century B.C. and was perhaps looted from Greece by the Romans. (COURTESY THE METROPOLITAN MUSEUM OF ART)

Portrait head of a man, late Hellenistic period (second to first century B.C.). (COURTESY THE METROPOLITAN MUSEUM OF ART)

Goddess Aphrodite of Hellenistic period discovered at Smyrna. The statue was broken when found, but most of the parts were retrieved and assembled as shown here. (COURTESY TURKISH INFORMATION OFFICE)

Opinion has varied remarkably at different times on the merits of the Laocoön, a late Hellenistic group showing the priest Laocoön and his two sons grappling with snakes. The impression of strain and power has appealed to many as one of the finest expressions of Hellenistic realism, while others have found the whole composition theatrical and forced and, from the Greek point of view, "bad art."

Bronze figure of Eros (god of love) sleeping; third to second century B.C. (COURTESY THE METROPOLITAN MUSEUM OF ART)

ing may go far to explain this undoubted fact. Yet it would also be difficult to point to a more perfect statue of a woman than the Aphrodite of Melos, and she was a Hellenistic creation.

The best Greeks, in short, had not lost their skills; they even developed them further in the Hellenistic Age. But the social setting for their art had changed. In colonizing what they called the "inhabited world," the *Koinon* of the Hellenes, they spread their skills more widely and more thinly. So there was never again for the Greeks a century like the fifth century B.C., when all their talent was concentrated, mostly in Athens. But their world influence dates from the conquests of Alexander. The Greeks in southern Italy would surely have influenced the Romans if Alexander had never been born. But the Romans would not have taken over by force a living and active culture and civilization in the east and become partly Hellenized if the major work had not been done before them. This world the Romans never Latinized; on the contrary they learned Greek in order to understand and rule it. Even the conquest of much of the Near East in the seventh century A.D. did not put an end to Greek influence. Muslim philosophy owed an incalculable debt to Plato and Aristotle, and Muslim science was built on Greek foundations.

The vast bulk of the Western heritage from the ancient world is Greek, Roman, and Hebrew. If the Greek segment is as large as it is, this was due to the Hellenization of the "inhabited world" in the centuries following the conquests of Alexander, and the assimilation of the Hellenistic culture by the Romans. If the Greeks had never expanded, their culture might well have remained a local one, important in its time but without world influence. Almost surely the Muslims would never have discovered it. And the Romans themselves might not have felt it necessary to conquer the Near East if the way had not been opened for them by the Hellenistic rulers who could not unite to resist them, and thus allowed the Roman policy of "divide and conquer" to prevail.

▶ Suggestions for further reading

PAPER-BOUND BOOKS

Baron, J. *Greek Sculpture.* Dutton/Vista.
Burn, A. R. *Alexander the Great and the Hellenistic World.* Collier. Popular short presentation.
Farrington, Benjamin. *Greek Science.* Penguin. This book, first published in 1949, was long the only available work on Hellenistic

The Aphrodite of Melos (so called because the statue was discovered on the island of Melos) is widely regarded as the finest statue of a woman ever made. The artist is unknown, but the figure probably dates from the second century B.C. No photograph can do justice to this masterpiece. Located in the Louvre, it is displayed to perfection—especially at night, when it is most effectively lighted. (COURTESY THE LOUVRE)

science. Still useful, but explanations often simplified too much. Supplement with less technical parts of Sarton and Neugebauer.

Grant, F. C. ed. *Hellenistic Religions: The Age of Syncretism.* Liberal Arts Press. A book of readings.

Scranton, R. L. *Greek Architecture.* Braziller.

Tarn, W. W. *Alexander the Great.* Beacon. One of the best biographies of the great conqueror.

Tarn, W. W. (revised by G. T. Griffith). *Hellenistic Civilization.* Meridian. Comprehensive study of all phases of the civilization, the best single volume treatment, but fairly difficult and with an organization that is not always easy to follow.

Wilcken, U. *Alexander the Great.* Norton. Good standard biography of the conqueror.

CASE-BOUND BOOKS

Bell, H. I. *Egypt from Alexander the Great to the Arab Conquest.* London: Oxford University Press, 1948. Interesting specialized study on Egypt, including the influence of Hellenism on native Egyptian culture. A pioneer work.

Ferguson, W. S. *Greek Imperialism.* Boston: Houghton Mifflin Company, 1913. This old classic is still useful and stimulating; even if its point of view is not always acceptable, it is always brilliantly stated.

Hadas, Moses. *Hellenistic Culture: Fusion and Diffusion.* New York: Columbia University Press, 1959. Most recent study of the intermingling of Greek and Oriental cultures.

Jouquet, P. *Macedonian Imperialism and the Hellenization of the East.* New York: Alfred A. Knopf, Inc., 1928. Thoughtful and analytical study.

Neugebauer, Otto. *The Exact Sciences in Antiquity,* 2d ed., Providence, R.I.: Brown University Press, 1957. Excellent on Hellenistic science, made more useful still by careful study of its debt to Mesopotamia.

Rostovtzeff, M. I. *Social and Economic History of the Hellenistic World.* Vols. I and II. New York: Oxford University Press, 1941. The most comprehensive and interesting work on the age. Exceptionally well written, it is not as formidable as it looks. Judgments often controversial.

Pickard-Cambridge, A. W. *Demosthenes and the Last Days of Greek Freedom.* New York: G. P. Putnam's Sons, 1914. For an adequate account of the struggle between Demosthenes and Philip it is necessary to go back to 1914. This book, possibly available only in the larger libraries, is a lively and accurate account of this rather neglected subject.

Sabine, George H. *History of Political Theory,* 3d ed. New York: Holt, Rinehart and Winston, Inc., 1962. Throughout this text Sabine should frequently be used when studying ancient and medieval political thought. He is specially good on the Stoic thinkers.

Sarton, George. *History of Science: Hellenistic Science and Culture in the Last Three Centuries* B.C. Cambridge, Mass.: Harvard University Press, 1959. Though much of this comprehensive and well-written book is technical, the remainder is excellent even for the beginning student.

Zeller, Eduard. *Stoics, Epicureans and Skeptics.* New York: Russell & Russell, Inc., 1962. Reissue of a famous classic, still of great value.

CHAPTER 10

THE ROMAN REPUBLIC

▶ **Divisions of Roman history—Republic and empire**

Roman history proper can be said to begin only with the expulsion of the kings, about 509 B.C. Previous to this date it can only be reconstructed with difficulty from archaeological remains and such facts as can be tentatively inferred from later Roman legend. Imperial Rome fell to a barbarian ruler in A.D. 476; and thereafter a Roman emperor ceased to rule in the West.

A natural dividing line during the period 509 B.C. to A.D. 476 occurs in 31 B.C. with the battle of Actium. Previous to 31 B.C. the form of government was *republican;*[1] after 31 B.C. it may be called *monarchical* (Greek *monos*—one, *arche*—rule = rule by one man). Traditionally we speak of the earlier period as the period of the *Roman Republic,* and of the later as the period of the *Roman Empire.*

It should be clearly understood that this division into republic and empire refers to the *form* of government. Confusion is often

[1] The Latin word *respublica* means only the "state." It is we who have given our word "republic" its modern meaning of a state without a monarch.

caused by the fact that it was the Roman Republic that conquered most of the lands beyond Italy which were later administered by Roman emperors; and this rule of foreign peoples is in modern times called an empire. But, to avoid confusion in this text, the word "empire" will not be used in this modern sense, and will only refer to the *period* and *form* of government after 31 B.C. The word "expansion" or other words suitable to the context will be used to refer to the conquests of the Romans which took place primarily under the republic.

▶ **Roman history as the classical case of a democracy destroyed by its own imperialism**

THE INVOLUNTARY NATURE OF THE MARCH TO EMPIRE—CONTRAST WITH GREEK POLITICAL FORESIGHT

During the whole of the period from 509 B.C. to A.D. 476 the Romans were never subjected to domination by others. On the contrary, it was the rulers in Rome, whether the people, the senatorial oligarchy, or the emperor, who made their will felt and respected by others. In studying Roman history we are frequently struck by the fact that there seems to have been something inevitable about the march of the Romans to domination of the Mediterranean world, and that the individual men responsible for Roman policies never seem to have planned anything the way it turned out. The Senate did not want to expand beyond Italy, but the relentless pressure of events forced that expansion; the citizens of the Roman republic did not want to destroy their republic, any more than did the soldiers of fortune who made its fall inevitable. We who live so many centuries later can see the majestic sequence of cause and effect, how each change in the form of government, each province added, was dictated by necessity, so that these self-governing, responsible, dominating Romans appear almost as puppets, doing what had to be done and nothing else. The Christian Fathers regarded the Roman Empire as a necessary preparation for their establishment of the Catholic Church; and we can see how they were able, even with far less evidence available to them than we have and working with a preconceived notion of Divine Providence, to reach such a conclusion and defend it. The Athenians *thought out* a constitution, logical and appropriate to themselves, which they proceeded to make work; Alexander *thought out* the policy appropriate to his empire, which had been quite self-consciously planned by his father and himself. The Greeks imposed mind upon matter, in their political life, in their art, and in their philosophy; the Romans *felt* their way along, modifying, adapting, improvising. Conservative to the core, they tried to retain every old form they had ever known far beyond its limit of usefulness, responding to each challenge as it presented itself to them. Thus the Romans remained empirical, practical, illogical, but uniquely effective, without producing a truly creative mind throughout the whole of their history comparable to any one of a dozen Greeks. It was no wonder that the Roman augurs consulted the gods every day, for no great people ever owed less to their own minds and more to their

gods than they. That they should have conquered the Greeks was the triumph of character over intellect, and it is salutary for us to remember that fact. That it should have been Plato and Aristotle who took over the theology of the Roman church, and the Greeks and the Syrians who developed the Roman law in the final form in which it could be transmitted to posterity, is an ironic commentary upon the ability of even character, important though it is, to substitute for mind in the long sweep of history.

The history of the Roman Republic is the classical case of a potential democracy destroyed by its own imperialism. The Roman Republic was never a true democracy as Athens was, for the people never used the power that formally belonged to them, although it had taken centuries of struggle to acquire it. They were not really interested in participation in the government so much as they were anxious to secure equality of rights due to citizens, an equality which was taken for granted in Athens and never became a problem. The Roman oligarchy, the ruling class (a conception foreign to the Athenian polis altogether), was interested in government and extremely competent in it, and did not want to give the less competent masses any opportunity of acquiring it. Instead, the oligarchy made way for competent and distinguished *individuals* to enter its ranks. But the expansion beyond Italy which necessarily followed the expansion within Italy had such momentous results for the now enfranchised people and for the oligarchy that the former were compelled to use their voting power against the oligarchy to ensure their rights; while the oligarchy in defending itself won the day, but lost its morale and the respect of the people. Thereafter, as the problems of the expansion remained unsolved, both yielded power to the military, and the republic itself yielded to the one-man rule of the emperor.

In studying Roman history, therefore, the foregoing is the sequence of events to be observed. At no time in the history of the republic does it seem possible to say that if A had been wiser or B more conciliatory or C had had a bright idea, the republic would have survived. The very form of the republic carried within itself the seeds of its downfall. The Roman Republic, with its oligarchy and its magistrates and its solid farmer-soldiers, proved itself incompetent to rule beyond Italy; competent though it was in conquering, it could not manage its conquests. If we are to discover the reason for this fact, we must examine the nature of Roman institutions and how they functioned, and watch the influence that the Roman possessions beyond the seas had on the home government.

THE REPUBLIC AND ITS SUCCESSES AND FAILURES AS THE NECESSARY PRELUDE TO WORLD RULE

And yet without the republic there would have been no effective empire. An Oriental empire which had never known free institutions might have conquered, but it could not have consolidated its possessions into a form of government as stable as that of the Romans. The heart of the empire was its self-governing cities; the means of government was the professional army and its officers, and the administrators with their long tradition of public service. These carried over from the great republic, the builder of character and the developer of institutions. Without the republic the empire would have been just another despotism, not a world organization that called forth such an unexampled loyalty from its citizens. When that organization fell, it seemed even to Christians who hated its gods and deplored its morality that the world itself had lost its foundations.

► Early Italy

PHYSIOGRAPHY

The land of Italy is a peninsula extending southeast into the Mediterranean, divided by the Apennine chain of mountains, high in the north and dwindling away into foothills only in the extreme south. The largest fertile area in the country suitable for grain growing is the Po Valley in the northeast; but as this is separated by the moun-

tains from the coastal plains of the west, communications have never been easy between the two areas, and in republican days the region of the Po was not regarded as a part of Italy at all but as the separate province of Hither Gaul. The second largest expanse of fertile land in ancient times was in Latium and Campania, though the surface soil was early exhausted, and the land became more suitable for vineyards and orchards than for grain. The greater part of Italy was best suited for pasture, either of sheep or cattle; but the basic agricultural unit, except when political and social conditions prevented it, has always been the small mixed farm.

There are many variations in climate, from the Po Valley, which has cold winters and warm summers, to the semitropical climate of the southwest. The east coast in ancient times was almost barren of seaports; Italy is not too well blessed with them, even now, in spite of her long coast line. The best harbors in the country were in the south and southwest. Ostia, the harbor of Rome, was never a good one, and needed constant dredging to keep it usable. The Tiber, which leads from Rome to Ostia, is a swift-flowing river, and suitable only for small boats and lighters. Rome, disadvantageously situated for water traffic, never became a great commercial or industrial city.

Italy on the whole was far richer in agricultural resources than Greece, and Greek travelers to Italy in early imperial times always emphasize the abundance of produce, the fine timber, especially the hardwoods, and the animals pasturing on the rich lands. But she was and is short of metals, with iron in significant quantities only to be found on the island of Elba, and small deposits of other metals scattered throughout the country; and even in arable and pasture land she is greatly inferior to France, and was inferior to almost any land in her empire in ancient days.

Rome itself was situated on the left bank of the Tiber, about fifteen miles from the sea, with the fertile hinterland of Latium to the south, and the more broken but still fertile land of Etruria to the north. Her famous Seven Hills are really three separate hills with four adjacent spurs. Rome at its most extensive filled the whole space between the hills and had a settlement on the right bank of the river. The only real advantage of the situation of Rome was that it was in central Italy and could usually prevent the northern and southern areas from uniting against her. The immediate neighborhood of Rome was unhealthful, and even the land covered by the city had to be artificially drained before it was habitable. It was primarily her man-made system of roads, all leading out of Rome, that enabled her to keep military control of Italy. It was, then, the work of her people that made her mistress of Italy rather than any special advantages of geography. In the Middle Ages, and in modern times, Milan, with a far better natural situation, has always tended to grow naturally and surpass Rome; it has always required special man-directed efforts, almost contrary to nature, to build Rome up to equal or surpass her upstart daughter in the north.

PREHISTORIC SETTLEMENTS IN ITALY

Several prehistoric cultures are known in Italy. Skulls of Neanderthal man have been found not far from Rome, and Neolithic settlements of a people who domesticated animals but did not yet know agriculture have been excavated. An extensive Bronze Age culture of people who lived in pile dwellings similar to those found in Switzerland (the so-called Terramare culture) was followed by the "Villanovan" people who used iron. These last two groups are generally supposed to have been migrants from the north who mingled with the neolithic inhabitants to form the Italic people of the peninsula in historic times. But there is as yet no final certainty on the matter, and excavations may still turn up enough evidence to establish the original homes of these settlers and to determine whether the Terramare and Villanovan cultures are distinct, or the latter developed from the former. It seems quite possible that some tribes of Indo-European people went into Greece, where they found the advanced Mycenaean civilization already existent, and so were able to progress more quickly themselves till they ultimately became the Hellenic peoples of history. At the same time another offshoot went into Italy, but were slower in developing a characteristic culture of their own, having less to build upon. At all events by 1000 B.C. the Italic peoples were already speaking the language that ultimately became Latin, though they could not yet write it. About 1000 B.C. also the first settlement on the Palatine Hill of Rome was founded.

THE INVADERS OF ITALY—CELTS AND ETRUSCANS —INFLUENCES ON ROMANS

Into the Italic peninsula during the next three hundred years came three groups of invaders: Celts, who formed a permanent settlement in the valley of the Po and were called Gauls by the Romans; Greeks, who came from the mainland from the eighth century onward, as we have seen, whose settlements were for the most part in southern Italy close to the sea; and a group of people called the Etruscans, "people of the sea," probably coming from Asia Minor after the destruction of the Mycenaean civilization by the invading Dorians. These Etruscans were considerably more advanced culturally and militarily than their Italic neighbors, and they maintained contact by sea not only with the Greek cities in southern Italy but with Carthage. They gradually expanded northward in Italy to control the Po Valley, as far as the Alps, and through Latium to Capua, ruling Rome itself intermittently. Though their language is almost unknown to us, archaeologists have made very extensive finds, so that we are familiar with the material elements in their civilization. We know that they had developed urban life to the extent that their nobles had fine houses and enjoyed athletic contests, feasts, and dancing, that the women had elaborate dresses with considerable ornamentation, and used cosmetics and make-up. In material comfort and luxury the civilization was far ahead of anything the Romans or Italians achieved for

An Etruscan biga, a kind of chariot, dating from the sixth century B.C., the period of the Etruscan domination of Rome. (COURTESY THE METROPOLITAN MUSEUM OF ART)

many centuries afterward. There was, however, no single centralized Etruscan state, but many self-governing cities which frequently engaged in intercity warfare. We cannot, therefore, speak of an Etruscan Empire so much as of the expansion of the Etruscans, though there is evidence that the Etruscan cities sometimes united into leagues. From the Etruscans the Romans learned the use of hewn stone for their public buildings, temples, and walls, and probably gladiatorial games. One feature in Roman religion, divination from the entrails of animals and augury from the flight of birds, was taken from the Etruscans, but the principles were apparently never fully understood by the Romans, for even in Cicero's time (the first century B.C.) Etruscan diviners were employed by the priests and augurs of Rome. Some Roman gods take their names from their Etruscan counterparts.

Etruscan influence on Roman political development was crucial, but not long lasting. Rome was conquered by the Etruscans and dominated by them for a period of uncertain duration. During this time the small villages which occupied the area of the Seven Hills were consolidated into one city. Naturally the Romans never gave credit to their conquerors for this creative act; the city in Roman tradition had been founded in 753 B.C. by Romulus, who had come from Alba Longa in Latium. The founder of that city had himself come from Troy as a child with his father, Aeneas, one of the Trojan heroes mentioned in the *Iliad*. Romulus, according to this tradition, was the first king of Rome. But, as we have seen, there was already a settlement at Rome by 1000 B.C., and though there is some evidence that emigrants from Alba did found it, the famous date of 753 does not seem to represent any event of significance. The tradition, in fact, is not older than the fourth century B.C. The last king, and possibly the last three kings, of Rome were Etruscans; they did not endear themselves to the Romans, who hated the name of king forever afterward.

► Early political evolution

EXPULSION OF THE KINGS

About 509 B.C., according to tradition,[2] the kings were driven out of Rome. Again, it is not certain that the Romans themselves drove them out. Some scholars are of the opinion that it was the neighboring Latin cities who were ruled from Rome by the Etruscan monarchy who united to defeat the Romans and the Etruscans together. It is also probable that Rome was retaken by the Etruscans for a time after the fall of the monarchy. However this may be, the Romans did soon succeed in gaining their independence, but found themselves at war with the Latin League, a league of cities of Latium. Presumably Rome was trying to assert her rule over these cities on her own account, as during Etruscan days. This war was brought to an end by a Roman victory at Lake Regillus in 496 B.C., and a treaty was signed under which Rome and the Latin cities entered into a virtual partnership which lasted for nearly 150 years, and which enabled Rome to become the recognized leader of all central Italy.

THE ASCENDANCY OF THE NOBILITY

In addition to making the villages of Rome into a city from which it dominated Latium, the Etruscan monarchy had been able to keep order between the classes in Rome. Almost every Roman was a farmer, for though the Etruscan kings tried to support industry, there was very little, and most manufacture, for instance of weapons and pottery, was done in the home. Three kinds of land were available to the farmer, his own plot belonging personally to him, public land which he might rent, and common

[2] Roman tradition is represented to us above all by the first historian of the Roman Empire, Livy, who makes no secret of his purpose to show how the gods guided the destiny of Rome from the beginning, and to remind his generation of Romans of their glorious past. In line with this purpose he quite consciously exalts the heroic virtues of the Romans to more than life size. The tradition, of course, is older than Livy, but does not go back to within even two centuries of the Etruscan kings.

land where he could pasture his flocks and herds. But certain customary rights were held by the old noble families; and when they had the power they constantly encroached on the rights of the smaller farmers, who had no means of defending themselves. The noble families, or patricians, jealously guarded their rights, and were divided from the plebeians, the remainder of the population, by a rigid class distinction. While the kings ruled in Rome the nobles were kept in check. But when the kings were expelled from Rome and the nobles ruled the state in their place, the latter held arbitrary power over the plebeians which they abused to the utmost. Public land was sold to the highest bidder as long as he was a patrician, or let out at a nominal rent; or it was pre-empted for the sole use of the patricians. Thus the poorer farmer fell into debt or was driven from his land. Moreover, with the wars that followed the breakdown of the monarchy and with the ill success that often attended Roman arms at the beginning, especially when the Etruscans tried to retake the city, the farmers would go on the annual campaigns and return to find their land ravaged and their property ruined by the war.

THE STRUGGLE OF THE ORDERS—FIRST STAGE

Revolt against the patrician power seems to have been ill organized at the beginning, and took the form of occasional acts of violence, which were avenged speedily by the more powerful patricians, armed with all the authority of the state. The magistrates were able to inflict any legal penalty at will, and creditors were entitled to sell the debt-ridden farmers across the Tiber; if there were several creditors, under primitive custom they could divide the debtor's body in pieces.

There was only one recourse for the more numerous plebeians. In one thing their numbers counted, even though the machinery of the state was controlled by their enemies. They were needed as soldiers—the patricians could not fight the Etruscans or the Latin League all by themselves. So about 494 B.C., according to the story in Livy, the plebeian troops, called out for a campaign, marched to the Sacred Hill where they presented demands, in particular for some security against arbitrary acts of magistrates. They were granted the right to have their own assembly of plebeians which would elect two tribunes (later increased to four, then to ten), whose persons were to be sacrosanct, i.e., anyone offering violence against them could be put to death without trial. The tribunes could forbid any act of the magistrates by pronouncing the word "veto" (I forbid).

THE GOVERNMENT OF EARLY ROME—PRIMITIVE DEMOCRACY—MAGISTRATES, SENATE, AND ASSEMBLIES

In order to understand how the nobles had acquired such power after the expulsion of the kings it is necessary to examine the institutions of the Roman state during and after the kingly regime, and then to see how they were modified by further acts of the plebeians through their assembly and officers, and through further use of their potent weapon, the military strike.

The early government of Rome was probably a Primitive Democracy of the kind previously described in the chapter on Mesopotamia. But, as in the case of the Greeks, the king ceased to hold his position instead of developing into an absolute monarch, as in the East. The Council in Rome was known as the *Senate*, and was composed originally of the heads of clans (*gentes*), and the Primitive Assembly was the *Comitia curiata*. In this Assembly each man had a vote; but the whole Assembly was divided into thirty *curiae*, and it was the majority of the curiae rather than the majority of the total vote that counted. In the time of the kings, the Senate was an advisory body only, and in the event of the death of the king administered the state until the new one was chosen. The Assembly chose the king and conferred his authority (*imperium*) upon him, and would occasionally be consulted, if called by the king, on important matters of legislation. The

king was the sole executive, leader in war, chief priest, and judge.

These bodies and their functions, then, were substantially similar to those discussed in earlier chapters. In Rome all the later governmental organizations retained their basic character, and in fact, long after it had been superseded by other assemblies which had real powers and could use them, even the old Comitia curiata continued to exist, with no powers beyond solemnly meeting to confer the imperium upon magistrates. The Senate always remained in theory an advisory body, could be called only by the magistrates, and had no power of legislation. Although it encroached upon the powers of the other governing bodies of the state so that it became for a long time the actual ruling body, these powers never belonged to it in theory, and could be taken away from it by determined action by the Assembly and magistrates as soon as the Senate lost its indirect control over them.

The first great change in this system was, of course, the expulsion of the kings. Their place was taken by two magistrates, first called *praetors*, then *consuls*. The important feature of the supreme magistracy in the state was that, as the name suggests, they consulted together; to prevent arbitrary and absolute power from going to either, each had a veto on the acts of the other. These consuls were primarily leaders in war, and they alternated authority in the field; in practice this did not make for too much difficulty as there were usually two armies in the field at once. The consuls were elected annually by the Assembly, and they appointed the members of the Senate from among those who were eligible. In important matters it was customary for them to consult the Senate; but it was with them and not with the Senate that responsibility rested. Consuls at this time were always chosen from the number of existing senators, and they returned to the Senate after their year of office; this fact no doubt was of considerable influence on their behavior while in office, as they would not wish to antagonize unduly their future colleagues. The consuls could also call the Assembly when necessary, and neither Senate nor Assembly could be called by anyone else except in the case of a dictatorship. The only appeal against the decision of a consul was in a case involving capital punishment of a citizen; then custom permitted an appeal to the Assembly.

In times of grave danger to the state a *dictator* could be appointed for six months, with a *master of the horse* as his second in command. For this period the dictator had supreme power, and his appointment was therefore the equivalent of six months under martial law, unless the crisis was over before this time, in which case the dictator automatically retired.

It will be seen at once how this election of consuls instead of the king would work to the detriment of the plebeians. The consuls always came from the noble class, and were to some degree responsible to their class owing to their annual term of office; whereas the king held his office for life and was above the nobles, and thus need not be in any way subservient to their interests.

The priestly power of the king was not transferred to the consuls, but to a college of priests and augurs, also patricians, who were headed by a chief priest (*Pontifex Maximus*) who was elected by the Assembly. The priestly function was of considerable importance since most public acts were preceded by religious ritual. Knowledge of this ritual was necessary, and ignorance of it kept plebeians from transacting public business on their own account.

Almost at the same time as the election of consuls—the exact date is uncertain—the need for a new kind of Assembly became apparent. The old Comitia curiata was not, however, reformed or abolished. Instead, an altogether new Assembly was formed to which the powers of the old were assigned, together with some new ones. This was the Assembly by centuries (a military formation), the *Comitia centuriata*. The whole population of the state was divided into various classes, according to the military equipment each could provide. Thus the first class, which could provide horses, weapons, and armor, was superior to the second class,

which could not provide horses; and so on. The largest number of centuries was allotted to the first class; the propertyless citizens of the lowest class, who were excused from fighting except in cases of extreme danger to the state, were all put into one century. The centuries of the first class, who provided most military equipment and paid the highest property tax, amounted in number to 98 out of a total of 193 centuries. Since voting went by centuries and not by numbers of individual soldiers, the wealthy classes were able to dominate the Assembly if they voted together (see the chart on opposite page).

To this Assembly were transferred the right to make war and peace, the right to elect magistrates, the right to hear appeals of citizens against the death sentence, and the right to accept or reject proposals for legislation offered by the magistrates. It could not, however, discuss or amend such proposals; no Roman Assembly ever had this right. The vote was always taken in Roman Assemblies by the presiding magistrate's calling for the vote of each century (or, in the Tribal Assembly, to be discussed later, of each tribe) one by one. When a majority was obtained, the bill was declared passed, and the opinion of the remaining centuries was not taken. So the poorer classes were virtually disfranchised, their opinion not being heard and their vote not counted. The only way open to them to make their voice heard was to acquire enough wealth to enable them to be enrolled in a superior century. This Assembly, though it lost much of its power later to the Tribal Assembly, remained throughout the Roman Republic a factor making for conservatism; even when it was re-formed about 240 B.C. and its composition changed, it was still largely a vehicle for the men of property.

THE STRUGGLE OF THE ORDERS—SECOND STAGE

Tribal Assembly

We have seen how the plebeians* first seceded about 494 B.C. and demanded some

---

* The plebeians were men who were not of noble birth, though they might be wealthy. In time plebeian officeholders became a kind of plebeian nobility, often allied by marriage with the noble families.

check upon the arbitrary power of the magistrates. The result of their action was the right to appoint tribunes. The tribune was a new civilian official who held no military powers and only the limited civil authority (*potestas*) already described. These tribunes were to be elected by the plebs alone, in an assembly of their own (*Concilium plebis*). This Assembly was also allowed to legislate in matters that concerned the plebs alone (*plebiscita*). Very soon afterward—though the details of the operation are not clear—the composition of this new Plebeian Assembly was regularized by its conversion into an Assembly of the People by Tribes (*Comitia tributa*), of which three tribes were urban and seventeen were rural, later rising over the course of the next 250 years to four urban and thirty-one rural. The new Assembly could be called into session either by the tribunes or by the consuls. Later, when the title of praetor was revived and praetors were elected to undertake some of the duties of the consul, these magistrates could also summon the Assembly of the Tribes.

The result of these changes was that the Romans now had three Assemblies; obviously there was no real need for all three. The Comitia curiata of the kings fell into disuse, retaining no powers but a few minor duties, mostly of a religious nature. The Comitia centuriata controlled by the wealthy classes gave place to the Comitia tributa, theoretically controlled by the majority of citizens. This change was accomplished by the Valerio-Horatian laws of about 448 B.C., under which all legislation passed by the Comitia tributa became binding on the people if ratified by the Senate. Thus the Comitia centuriata lost its powers of legislation but retained its other powers, especially the election of magistrates and the declaration of war. It remained the last court of appeal in death sentences.

The first codification of the law— The Twelve Tables

The appointment of the tribunes and the enlargement of their numbers were a help to the plebeians but not enough. Presumably the arbitrary acts continued and the magistrates interpreted the customary law as they wanted. Moreover, the wealthier plebeians felt themselves discriminated against in the matter of magistracies, which were still confined to the patrician class. And they were not allowed to intermarry with patricians. Around the middle of the fifth century several advances were made under severe pressure from the plebeians. First came the appointment of a body of decemvirs (ten men) to codify the hitherto unwritten law. Since they did not produce a law code within their first year of office, the plebeians agitated very violently, and perhaps staged a second full-dress secession. The result was the issue of the Twelve Tables, which was followed by the Valerio-Horatian laws just described, giving the power of legislation to the Comitia tributa. By then or even earlier this Comitia also enrolled the Roman patricians in its ranks, though of course they were numerically inferior to the plebeians in this Assembly. Agitation for the consulship was settled by a compromise under which a new office, military tribunes, was substituted for the consulship, and to this office plebeians could theoretically be elected. When the number of military tribunes reached six, and the Romans were engaged in a deadly conflict with the Etruscans at the end of the fifth century, a few plebeians were at last elected by the patrician-controlled Comitia centuriata. But the agitation still continued for the return of the honored consulate, and for the election of plebeians to it.

Piecemeal concession of rights and offices to plebeians

Meanwhile a gain had been registered by the plebeians in the first important breach of the social stratification of the classes. Permission to intermarry with patricians was granted a few years after the codification of the law. At the same time the patricians created a new office for themselves, that of *quaestor,* an assistant to the consuls, whose duties were mostly financial, including the administration of the treasury and the division of war booty. The office, however did not remain for very long exclusively in patrician hands, no doubt because the booty was being unfairly divided. The plebeians obtained the right to be elected to the quaestorship about twenty-five years after it had first become an elective office.

By the end of the fifth century, then, the plebeians had obtained some important concessions. They could be elected military tribunes, though they were not often in fact elected; they could be elected quaestor. They had an Assembly which could legislate, though the Senate had a veto; they had succeeded in obtaining a written law code; and they were allowed to intermarry with the patricians. But they were still far from

---

► chronological chart

THE ETRUSCAN MONARCHY

Internal history			External history	
Terramare culture	*ca.*	2000		
Villanovan culture	*ca.*	1000		
First settlements in Rome	*ca.*	1000		
Etruscans appear in Italy	*ca.*	900		
Traditional date of founding of Rome		753	Greek colonization in southern Italy	760
Traditional first four kings of Rome		753–616		
Tarquinius Priscus (Etruscan king)		616–578		
Servius Tullius		578–534		
Tarquinius Superbus (Etruscan king)		534–510		
End of Etruscan domination		509		

THE ROMAN REPUBLIC

Internal history

First secession of plebs—Election of tribunes and establishment of Concilium plebis (plebiscites binding on plebs)	494
Establishment of Comitia tributa (Assembly of Tribes)	*ca.* 460
Twelve Tables	450–449
Valerio-Horatian Laws (legislation by plebs binding on state if accepted by Senate)	448
Intermarriage permitted between plebeians and patricians	445
Suspension of consulship, substituted by military tribunes, open to plebeians	444–367
Licinian-Sextian Laws—Consulship opened to plebeians	367
First plebeian dictator	356
One of consuls *must* be plebeian	340
Censors to give preference to ex-magistrates in drawing up list of senators	310
Loss of senatorial veto on all legislation	287
Reorganization of Comitia centuriata (electoral assembly)	*ca* 242
Tiberius Gracchus elected tribune	133
Murder of Tiberius Gracchus	132
Re-election of tribune made legal	125
Tribunate of Gaius Gracchus	123–122
Death of Gaius Gracchus	121
Marius elected consul	107
Reorganization of army on volunteer basis by Marius	106
Sixth consulship of Marius	100
Return of Sulla to Italy—Proscriptions	83
Sullan Constitution	83–80
Pompey given extended command against pirates	67
Pompey given extended command against Mithridates	66
Consulate of Cicero and conspiracy of Catiline	63
Return of Pompey to Rome	62
First Triumvirate	60
Caesar appointed to command in Gaul	58
Return of Caesar to Italy	49
Caesar as dictator	46–44
Murder of Caesar	44

External history

Battle of Lake Regillus—Roman victory over Latin League	496
Treaty with Latin League—Promulgation of Latin rights	493
Rome leader of Latin League—Gradual expansion	490–430
Conquest of Veii (southern Etruria)	396
Invasion of Italy by Gauls—Sack of Rome	387–386
Wars with various Latin and other local cities	362–345
War with Latin League	340–338
Defeat of Latin League—Roman Confederation	338
Samnite Wars	327–290
War with Pyrrhus and Magna Graecia	281–272
First Punic War	264–241
Sicily becomes first Roman province	227
Sardinia and Corsica become second Roman province	227
Second Punic War	218–201
Spain divided into two provinces	197
Defeat of Antiochus III (king of Syria) at Magnesia	190
Wars with Macedonia	200–197; 171–168
Third Punic War	149–146
Destruction of Carthage and sack of Corinth	146
Macedonia becomes Roman province	146
Jugurthine War	112–106
Marius defeats Cimbri and Teutones	102–101
Social War in Italy	90–88
Murder of all Romans and Italians in Asia by Mithridates VI	89
Sulla undertakes war with Mithridates	87
Wars with Mithridates (Lucullus)	75–66
Slave War in Italy	74–71
Conquest and reorganization of Asia by Pompey	66–62
Caesar conquers Gaul	58–51
Crassus defeated and killed in Parthia	53

Dates are before Christ.

being first-class citizens. And, as we shall see, whenever the patricians made a concession, they tried to recover their lost power by other means. The background of the struggle remained primarily economic. The successful fifth-century campaigns of the Romans added a great deal of public land to the state, which was divided unfairly by the patricians as long as they had a monopoly of government. And, since the possession of land also determined the position of the owner in the Comitia centuriata, which elected magistrates, the plebeians still had no legal redress. To reduce their agitation for reform there were occasional land divisions which helped them, and in conquered territory colonies were planted in which the poorer citizens could take part.

But after the sacking of Rome by the Gauls in the early fourth century B.C. and the extensive wars in Italy that followed, it became clear that the patricians could no longer maintain their complete monopoly of government. So in 367 B.C. the Licinian-Sextian laws were passed admitting plebeians to the consulship, which was now restored, and limiting the amount of public land that could be held by any citizen. The land law, however, seems to have remained a dead letter, as we find land tenure still a problem for the next two centuries. Following these laws there was intensive agitation for a scaling down of debt, and by the end of the century, after a few minor reforms, slavery for debt was abolished.

The patricians, as usual, had another card up their sleeves. Two new magistracies were instituted after 367 B.C., the *praetorship* and the *curule aedileship*, the latter occupied primarily with the administration of the city of Rome, the former undertaking some of the civil, and if necessary, military powers of the consul. The praetor became the chief judge in Rome, but he could also command armies in the absence of the consul and could summon the Senate and the Assemblies. Needless to say, these offices were reserved for patricians, as some compensation for the loss of their exclusive right to the consulate.

The plebeians realized that it was useless to have the right to be elected consul if the Centuriate Assembly never elected them, though in practice a few wealthy plebeians were elected who were acceptable to the patricians and who usually had intermarried with them. So in 340 B.C., since the election machinery could not be tampered with, a law was passed that one of the consuls *must* be a plebeian; two years later the praetorship was opened to the plebeians, and at the same time a law was passed that the highest dignity in the state, the *censorship*, must be shared between plebeians and patricians.

A word is now necessary on the censorship, which had been established soon after the Twelve Tables. Every five years two ex-consuls must be elected by the Military Assembly to take a census of the citizens, and decide on the property classification for this Assembly. This work usually occupied about eighteen months, after which the censor (or census taker) laid down his office. During the expansion of Rome the censors came to exercise many important financial functions, including the auctioning of tax contracts and the letting out of contracts for public works. In the early days senators had been appointed by the consuls, but this duty soon devolved upon the censors, who had, in any case, all been consuls. It was, of course, impossible for plebeians to be censors until they had obtained entry into the consulate; but when one consul had to be a plebeian, one of the censors could be a plebeian ex-consul. In 310 B.C. the censors were instructed by the Ovinian Law to give preference to ex-magistrates in drawing up the list of senators, so that it became the custom for all magistrates to enter the Senate automatically. The censors, however, assumed as part of their function the right to purge the Senate for breaches of public decorum and for other offenses (hence our word *censorious*).

In 300 B.C. the last patrician stronghold fell with the admission of plebeians into the college of pontiffs and augurs, thus giving them access to the secrets of religious ritual necessary for the management of the state.

Abolition of senatorial veto on legislation

Only one victory now remained to be gained—the abolition of the senatorial veto on legislation. Again it was the question of public land and the pressure of debt during the Samnite War that fanned the agitation that was to lead to the concession. Under the leadership of the plebeian Hortensius, a third secession of the plebs was staged in 287 B.C. Hortensius was made dictator, and the final authority in legislation was handed over to the Tribal Assembly. All laws passed by this Assembly became law with or without the consent of the Senate.

It might appear that the constitution was now well balanced, as the Greek historian Polybius thought it, with a fairly even division of powers between the patricians and plebeians. Yet in fact for the next 150 years the balance was only on paper; in practice rule was by a senatorial oligarchy in spite of the fact that the Senate remained in theory what it always had been—an advisory body.

▶ ## The ruling oligarchy of the mature republic

INDIRECT SENATORIAL CONTROL OF THE ASSEMBLIES

The two potentially democratic elements in the constitution, the tribunate and the Tribal Assembly, were both indirectly controlled by the patricians; and such strife as we hear of during the next centuries, not even excluding altogether the revolt of the Gracchi, was more an interfamily struggle for power among the patrician families and their respective plebeian connections than a true struggle between patricians and plebeians. It was, on the whole, only the richer plebeians who were interested in obtaining office; and these were frequently allowed to marry into the patrician families, not only because of their wealth but because they could, as plebeians, be elected tribune. As tribunes they were extremely useful to the

ruling classes because they were able to veto legislation introduced into the Tribal Assembly. There were now ten tribunes, and the veto of any one of them was sufficient to hold up legislation for a year. The tribunes, moreover, now sat in the Senate and had gained the privilege of calling it. So the practice grew up of calling the Senate first and consulting it before taking any measure to the Tribal Assembly. Unless it were called by a magistrate, the Assembly could take no action, and it could neither debate nor amend. So through the control of one or more tribunes the Senate was able to gain an indirect power at least the equal of what it had lost in 287 B.C.

But the patricians had a further indirect control of the Assembly. In the Tribal Assembly the votes were distributed inequitably. It has already been mentioned that there were originally twenty tribes. Over the years the number had been increased to thirty-five, only four of which were urban, while the remainder were rural. Moreover, all new citizens were enrolled in the urban tribes, where their votes counted for little or nothing. It might be thought that in a system where votes could only be cast in person the urban vote would swamp the rural, since genuine farmers could not afford the time to come to the city to vote except on rare occasions. This, however, was not the case; for anyone who had been born in the country retained his vote in a rural tribe even after he had come to live in Rome and the tribal vote could be cast by the few members of the tribe who were able to be present. The votes for the rural tribes were therefore cast by rich landowners whose interests lay with the senatorial oligarchy, and by the clients of these landowners who were evidently organized into an effective political machine, no doubt being paid their expenses for living at Rome in exchange for their vote. Only when the small farmers themselves were dispossessed or had such an important grievance that they thought it worth while to make their journey to Rome to vote could this machine be broken, as it was in the time of the Gracchi.

DIRECT POWERS OF THE SENATE

In addition to these indirect powers which enabled the senatorial oligarchy to control legislation, the Senate also had important powers of its own. Being the only deliberative body in the state, and made up of all those who had held office and high command in the army, it discussed foreign affairs, appointed and received ambassadors, appointed commissions to discuss treaties and ratified them, allotted military commands to the consuls and praetors, and later prolonged the commands of consuls (with the title of proconsuls) and praetors (propraetors). It had to approve the public contracts let out by the censors, and it had almost complete charge of finance. Later it claimed to be able to decree martial law when the state was in extreme danger, and to call upon the consuls to enforce it. Though the Senate did not formally have the right to declare war, its policy could make war inevitable, aside from its general control of the Assembly.[3] Finally, the Senate could always refuse to finance any legislation, so that such legislation would remain a dead letter. Thus the Senate had still another means of preventing the execution of the popular will.

SENATORIAL CONTROL OF THE REPUBLIC DURING THE PERIOD OF EXPANSION

The whole result, therefore, of the plebeian agitation for reform was that certain plebeians were now admitted to office and its rewards, while the people were in the same position as before, though they now had the formal power to break the oligarchy if they could gain sufficient cohesion within their class and find the necessary leaders. But, although a few such leaders did arise, they were rare, for they had to resist all the blandishments that were available to the oligarchy for their seduction. A tribune who wanted to fight on behalf of the people would need to organize the farmers' vote to

___

[3] There are, however, at least two important cases where the Senate did not wish for war, but the consuls were willing to defy it and cajoled a declaration out of the Assembly.

break the political machine, he would have to ensure that all his colleagues were of the same mind and could not be corrupted or persuaded to veto his measures, and he would have himself to possess a private income, which in the early days meant the possession of land—for officers of state were not paid. Finally, he would probably be called upon to resist temptation in the form of a marriage into one of the best families, who were quite willing to use their daughters as pawns in the political game, marrying and divorcing them with alarming suddenness to cement a political alliance. It is not, therefore, surprising that most of the tribunes who did in fact espouse the cause of the people were themselves aristocrats or allied with the aristocracy already, even though they might still be classified as "plebeians."

From this account it should not be concluded that the Senate was unworthy of its responsibilities and position of power. For several centuries it was really the only possible government of Rome, containing, as it did, all the men with experience in public office, military command, wealth, and education. It retained its position primarily because of its enormous prestige, its long series of victorious wars, its successful diplomacy, and its real sense of responsibility and tradition of public service. Not only was the Senate unpaid; members were not allowed to engage in commerce or industry or to contract for provincial taxes. It was only when it failed in war and later when it lost its prestige through corruption and mismanagement in the conquered provinces, and when a new class arose which was wealthier than the landholding Senate and willing to use its wealth to promote its material interests, that the Senate began to lose its grip and become a jealous and embittered oligarchy fighting every inch of the way against all reform.

But for nearly 150 years of expansion the Senate's power was unchallenged by any other class in the state, and during this time Carthage was defeated and destroyed and the bulk of the Mediterranean world was added to the possessions of Rome. Some of the material proceeds of this expansion filtered down to the people who fought the wars, and for a long time no Roman citizen had to pay any tax, since the whole state was financed by its booty from wars and its taxes from the unfree provinces.

▶ External history*

THE UNIFICATION OF ITALY

General Italian policy—Roman, Latin, and allied rights

The constitutional development has taken us forward by several centuries in time, and we must now return to the external history of Rome, which had so much influence upon this development. Here again Rome showed the ability to compromise and improvise which made her capable of ruling so many foreign peoples with efficiency and considerable success, at least until she went beyond the borders of Italy.

After the treaty with the Latin League following the battle of Lake Regillus she was quickly able, with the assistance of the Latin cities, to subdue the local hostile tribes until at the beginning of the fourth century B.C. she had extended her dominion over southern Etruria. Toward the peoples she conquered she adopted a military and civil policy which became the model for all her conquests in Italy. She never made permanent peace with an enemy before she had put herself into a position to dictate terms. The terms were always of the same type. A colony of Roman citizens with a garrison was to be established on land ceded to Rome, and a treaty was signed regulating the status of the conquered. Some cities near to Rome were granted full citizenship, including the right of trade and marriage, and the right to vote. This status, however, was rare. The so-called Latin rights were the usual concession, which left the city in full possession of its self-government (*municipia*), with the exception of its foreign policy, of which Rome thereafter took full charge. The city provided Rome with specified numbers of troops under

their own commanders to fight in the Roman wars, and a comparatively low tax. Trade and intermarriage with the Romans were permitted, but not the right to vote. This last lack was not felt to be of importance in early days, though later full Roman citizenship meant the first share in the spoils of victory, while the Latin allies only received what was left. Even then it was not the right to vote, as such, that was appreciated so much as the other privileges that belonged to the full Roman citizen. The allied Latins were allowed to send out special Latin colonies within Italy after Roman victories, and these colonies, as well as the cities themselves, were always protected by Rome.

On the whole the arrangement was a distinct gain for these Latin allies. No longer were they in danger of defeat and destruction at the hands of local enemies; and the cost of protection was far less than the maintenance of a separate army capable of self-defense. And for a long time they retained all the important elements of self-government. The cities were united with Rome by the famous network of Roman roads. Each city was bound to Rome by a separate treaty, but the cities themselves did not have treaties with each other; frequently the rights of one Latin city were not enjoyed by all other Latin cities. The purpose of this direct connection with Rome was, of course, to prevent alliances from springing up against her; already the principle of "divide and rule" had been adopted with success.

The third type of treaty was the treaty for federate allies, substantially a defensive alliance. Again the cities were in direct relationship only with Rome; they also kept their self-government but lost the right to make war on their own. They furnished troops to the Roman army under local officers. The Romans paid for their subsistence when on campaign, and they had a share of the booty; they were not otherwise taxed.

If we consider this general policy more carefully we shall see that in the wars for the control of Italy Rome was in an exceptionally favorable position. For Rome had a policy, while the Italian cities were fighting only for complete independence without any

---

* The chronological chart (page 311) for this chapter is of special importance for the understanding of Roman expansion and its effects on the internal organization of the republic.

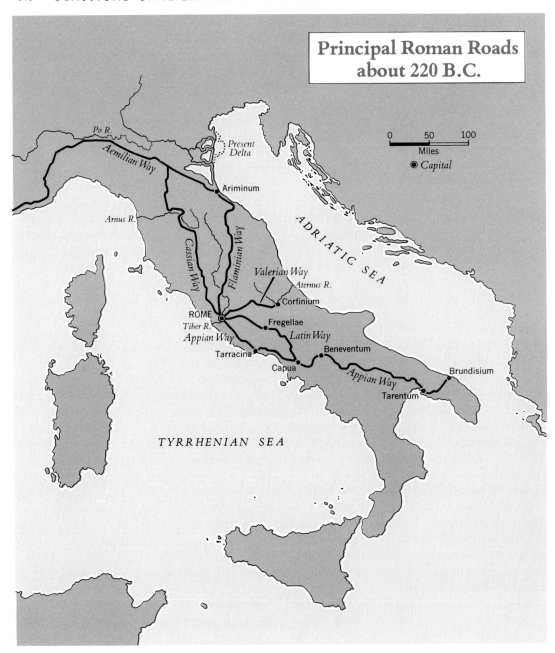

Principal Roman Roads about 220 B.C.

dictation from Rome—a rather intangible good, when it is remembered that this in substance only meant the right to make war and run their own foreign relations. And it was soon learned that when Rome fought, she would never give up, short of outright victory. Her enemies knew that they had only to submit and they would receive her usual terms. So Rome was never without allies; there were always cities that were content with their position and did not want to make foreign wars at the high cost of having to fight Rome for the privilege. Moreover, her enemies had no comparable policy; if they defeated Rome, even captured her, what could they do that would be of permanent value? It is significant that the Samnites, the most persistent of Rome's enemies in

Italy, had to form another confederation of their own to oppose her, with a similar constitution and with similar rights. So it became merely a question of confederation under the Samnites or confederation under Rome. In either case complete independence was over for the cities in Italy.

Wars with Gauls, Etruscans, and Samnites—The Latin League

In 387–386 B.C. the terrifying Gauls descended upon Rome from Gaul and the Po Valley on a plundering raid. The Roman armies panicked at the battle of Allia, and the city was captured except for the fortified Capitol. The Romans were forced to ransom their city, and the Gauls retired, having no further use for the territory. But it was a

considerable blow to Roman prestige and leadership; the Etruscans revolted, as did some of the Latin cities. But more important than these was the competition for leadership in Italy offered by the Samnites, a fierce and determined group of fighters from southeastern Italy, more numerous than the Latins. When the Samnites threatened Campania and its capital Capua, the Campanians appealed to Rome and the Latin League for help. This was given, and in the first round the Romans and Latins were successful. But the Romans annexed the territory themselves and did not share it with the Latins; whereupon the latter revolted, demanding full Roman citizenship and their share in the spoils that went with it. Rome refused concessions and was able, with the aid of some

The Appian Way, the most famous road in Italy, built by the censor Appius Claudius during the fourth century B.C. (COURTESY ITALIAN STATE TOURIST OFFICE)

0   100   200
Miles

⊙ Capital
★ Battles

CISPADANE GAUL

Po R.

ADRIATIC SEA

Lake Trasimene

ETRURIA
280

UMBRIA
290

PICENUM
302

Tiber R.

396 Veii

AEQUI
303

290
SAMNIUM

Rome

338
LATIUM

Beneventum

Cannae

Capua

APULIA
312

Cumae
Naples

Brundisium

Tarentum

CAMPANIA
338

272   Heraclea
MAGNA GRAECIA

Thurii

TYRRHENIAN SEA

Rhegium

Messina

SICILY

MEDITERRANEAN
SEA

Carthage

Syracuse

★ Zama

Italy about 200 B.C.
Dates (B.C.) Indicate Final Conquest by Romans

loyal allies, to defeat the Latin League before the Samnites were ready for the next round. By not reducing the Latin rights and making a few minor concessions, Rome pacified her ancient allies and was able to use their help when the Samnites attacked again in full force. At times the Etruscans and at times the distant Gauls helped the Samnites in the long wars that followed, which became almost the final struggle for Italian independence. Often the Romans lost battles, but their persistence finally wore the Samnites and their allies down, and at last, by 290 B.C., the war was over—the Romans victorious.

The conquest of Magna Graecia— The confederation of Italy

Too late the cities of Magna Graecia in southern Italy, which had been giving desultory aid to the Samnites, realized their danger. These ancient Greek colonies had enjoyed independence and prosperity for centuries, but they were never united and, as usual with Greek cities, they frequently indulged in petty wars with each other. During the course of one of these, some cities had appealed to Rome, and one city, Thurii, had been taken into the Roman Federation. The very year after the final defeat of the Samnites, in 289 B.C., Thurii was attacked by its neighbors who were allied with the chief city of Magna Graecia, the old Spartan colony of Tarentum. Having no force of her own, Thurii appealed to Rome, but the Senate, weary of the Samnite Wars, refused help. The consuls, however, refused to accept this senatorial decision as final and called the Assembly, which then authorized the war.

The operations of the Romans soon brought them into conflict with the Tarentines, who invited Pyrrhus, the Greek king of Epirus, a military adventurer, to help them. Pyrrhus agreed, and with a formidable army including elephants, crossed to Italy and defeated the Romans in two battles but lost so many men that he became discouraged (whence our term "Pyrrhic victories"). Unable to get much assistance from the unwarlike Italian Greeks, Pyrrhus left Italy for Sicily, whose cities were appealing for his aid against Carthage. This brought Carthage, a maritime Phoenician city of North Africa, and the greatest power in the western Mediterranean, by chance onto the same side as the Romans, and a treaty was signed which called for Carthaginian financial and naval aid to the Romans. Pyrrhus was now in difficulties. He was at first very successful in Sicily, but the Romans began to capture the Greek cities in Italy one by one. So he decided to return to Italy, and on the way the Carthaginians sank half his ships. Rome meanwhile improved her army, adopted new tactics to withstand the elephants, and was able to defeat Pyrrhus comfortably at the battle of Maleventum ("ill chance"), thereafter called Beneventum ("good chance"). In 275 B.C. Pyrrhus went home to Epirus, intending to return some day, but he was killed by a skillfully (or luckily) aimed tile from a woman's hand while he was besieging a small town in Greece a few years later. Tarentum gave up the struggle in 272, entering the Italian Federation with an obligation to provide ships to Rome when required, and Carthage quietly gobbled up most of Sicily again without too much difficulty.

Consequences of Italian conquests— Infiltration of Greeks—Beginnings of money economy

Rome was now mistress of the whole of Italy, with a confederation of free cities, especially among the last series of acquisitions, which enjoyed wide contacts with the Mediterranean and Oriental world. From this time on, the influence of Greek culture on the Romans was gradual but persistent. The nation of farmers now had contact with all the riches of Hellenic and Hellenistic culture. Greeks began arriving in Rome, and Roman literature appeared for the first time, a poor imitation of Greek, but at least in the Latin language. Roman primitive religion was gradually transformed, the Greek gods receiving Roman names, and some of the Greek ritual even penetrated into the Roman festivals. But these developments will be discussed in a later chapter.

Economically Rome began for the first time to live in a money economy. This was a considerable hardship to the poorer farmers, who had already suffered enough from the encroachments of the nobles, and had already ceased to grow much grain. Land was no longer the only form of property. Various plebeians who preferred wealth to office began to enter into trade relations with southern Italy. But this was a cumulative process, and became more marked with

Ruins of the temple of Mars in the Roman Forum. (COURTESY ITALIAN STATE TOURIST OFFICE)

the organization of the first Roman province of Sicily after the First Punic War.

THE CONQUEST OF THE MEDITERRANEAN LANDS

Reasons for expansion beyond Italy

A few words are necessary on the reasons for the expansion of Rome beyond Italy which was to have such momentous effects for Rome and the whole world. Rome was now one of the two great powers in the western Mediterranean, and she was bound by certain treaty obligations to her allies by reason of the fact that she had prevented them from defending themselves and their interests. One of the unpalatable facts that all powerful states, however isolationist in sentiment they may be, have to learn is that it is impossible not to use their power. The southern Italian cities which had trading interests with the rest of the world could not be simply left to their fate and not permitted to defend themselves though they had a defensive alliance with Rome. Moreover, the very existence of Rome as a great power meant that she would be constantly appealed to for protection and arbitration between smaller warring cities. In the next centuries Rome was often anxious to spread no further; she tried to grant self-government to conquered peoples and to the leagues of Greece. But when the leagues quarreled with each other, one of them would always appeal to Rome or to one of the other great powers in the East for assistance. Rome had either to refuse or to allow the other great power to come too close to her borders for comfort.

Carthage in the third century B.C. was the second great power in the western Mediterranean. A Phoenician colony, she had obtained her independence when Phoenicia fell, first to Assyria and then to Persia. Expanding into the hinterland of North Africa, commanding the North African coast, part of Spain and Sicily, and controlling Corsica and Sardinia, she had a formidable naval and military as well as financial and commercial strength. However, she remained primarily a sea power. Her trade policy was mercantile, that is, she maintained a monopoly on all overseas trade, and taxed even her own colonies and dependencies mercilessly. With the resulting financial resources she could afford to hire huge armies of mercenaries, whom she paid fairly well but whom she allowed to supplement their wages with booty. The Greek cities which also lived by trade objected very strongly to Carthaginian policy, especially in Sicily, which had usually been ruled by Greek tyrants with a more lenient trade and tax policy. It is probable, therefore, that sooner or later these cities would have tried to enlist Rome in an effort to weaken the Carthaginian hold on their natural markets.

The First Punic War

It is unlikely that the Roman Senate fully understood all the implications of Rome's defensive alliances with the southern Italian cities, since we find it refusing to entertain a request for help from some Italian mercenaries besieged by the Carthaginians in Sicily in 265 B.C. It is true that this incident in itself was an insufficient cause for outright war with Carthage, but Rome could not look with equanimity on the presence of Carthaginian troops in Messina, which commanded the strait leading to Italy. The consuls, in any case, went to the Assembly and secured a declaration of war in which the Senate acquiesced. So began the First Punic War, which lasted for more than twenty years and started Rome on the path to world empire.

Carthage proved at first too strong for the Romans, who had no navy of importance and who did not altogether trust the Greek cities they had so recently conquered. So the Romans built a special kind of navy with ships which could grapple with those of the enemy at close quarters, turning what should have been a sea battle into a hand-to-hand fight on the decks of the ships. By these tactics they so disconcerted the Carthaginians that they defeated them in every battle but one that was fought at sea during this war. On the other hand, the Romans had very little idea of navigation and apparently did not take full advantage of the skill and experience of their allies in the confederation. They lost more than a hundred thousand men in storms, a far greater number than they lost in battle, and were forced to modify their system of annual commands to some degree when they found that admirals did not all come from the best families, and in any case could not be trained in a year. Though Rome's allies were extremely restive at the losses, they remained loyal until the Carthaginian mercenaries, depressed at the lack of booty provided by the Roman farmer-soldier-sailors, and not receiving their pay from Carthage regularly, began to fight with diminishing enthusiasm as the war progressed. When the Romans finally defeated these soldiers of fortune and Carthage made peace, ceding Sicily to the Romans, the mercenaries decided to take matters into their own hands by sacking Carthage, where there was certainly enough booty; and the Carthaginians were hard put to it to defend themselves.

The first provinces—Organization and tax system

Rome now was faced with the problem of what to do with Sicily, whether to incorporate it into the confederation, annex it, or make some other arrangements. She finally decided on a combination of all three plans. Some cities were given to a loyal king of Syracuse, a few were incorporated into the confederation, and the remainder were organized as the first Roman *province*. Since the provincial system was used for the bulk of her later conquests, it needs a brief description here.

The most important person in the province was the Roman governor, at first holding the rank of praetor; then, when it became the custom to send out magistrates after their year of office at Rome, he was called a propraetor. Other provinces were governed by ex-consuls, called proconsuls. The governor was head of the state and chief judge; he was commander in chief of the Roman army which was permanently stationed there. He held office for only one year unless he had to undertake a prolonged military campaign. In this case his command could also be prolonged. As always with Roman magistrates, he was unpaid. The individual cities in the province were allowed municipal self-government under Roman protection, but they had to pay taxes to Rome. The governor, however, had no staff capable of assessing the taxes and making the collections. This task was therefore handed over to private enterprise in the persons of *publicani*, tax contractors who bid for the provincial tax contracts in Rome from the censors, who made the assessment for each whole province. Sometimes the provincial city itself bid for its own tax contract, and this was the usual custom in Sicily. If the contract fell to the publicani, they were supposed to make only a profit of 10 per cent on the contract price. The publicani had the support of the governor and his army in case of necessity. If the provincials thought the governor had been extortionate, they could prosecute him in the Roman senatorial courts.

Now this system made considerable demands on the character of the governor and the courts to which he was responsible; and it is a tribute to the still honest senatorial class that complaints in early years were so few. It need only be pointed out here that there was a natural community of interests between the publicani and the governor, which might be made to pay off at the expense of the provincial. And since the courts were composed of men of the same class as the governor, who hoped to govern a province themselves later, it might be difficult to secure a conviction. And even if a conviction were made for the sake of public appearances, the ex-governor was always permitted to live in some other part of the world, comforting his declining years with his ill-gotten gains. Moreover, when it is considered that for only two years in his life, the year following praetorship and the year following the consulate, could he hope for a province to govern, there was an undoubted temptation to make the most of those years. We shall see how this system did indeed tend to ruin the morale of the senatorial class after we have briefly followed the progress of the imperial expansion.

The Second Punic War

Carthage, having with difficulty beaten off her rebellious mercenaries, soon returned to the war again, this time with a new and brilliant leader. Hannibal, one of the great generals of history, came through Spain over the Alps into Italy, defeating every Roman army that was sent against him. But he did not take Rome, even though after the battle of Cannae he came almost up to her gates. He took Capua and ravaged Campania, remaining in Italy for over fifteen years. But he could not gain many allies in Italy, and he was insufficiently supported by reinforcements from Carthage. Ultimately the Second Punic War was decided by a brilliant young Roman general, Scipio Africanus, who with a prolonged command conquered first Spain, and then landed in Africa with a new army. He first defeated the local Carthaginian army, and then defeated the returning Hannibal decisively at the batta of Zama (202 B.C.). Carthage received severe terms, losing all territory except the capital and surrounding areas. Rome became the protector of the North African coast, and Spain was made into a province.

Interference in Greece—Conquest of Macedonia

The war with Hannibal involved Rome in another war with Macedonia and interference in Greece. Even before the Second Punic War the Romans had been forced to intervene on behalf of the traders of Italy to put a stop to piracy on the Adriatic Sea. When the pirates were cleaned up, the Romans naturally had to prevent their reappearance by occupying the coastal area of western Greece (Epirus and Illyria). This annoyed the Macedonian king, who regarded this as his sphere of influence. So when Hannibal appealed to him for help he joined the alliance against Rome. The Romans, however, in spite of their preoccupation with Carthage, were still able to spare enough troops to force Philip v of Macedon to make peace.

Meanwhile the Hellenistic kingdom of Seleucia had been extending its boundaries in Asia under Antiochus III (the Great) and was beginning to look westward. Antiochus entered into a private agreement with Philip of Macedon to partition Asia Minor (the kingdom of Pergamum), the Ionian cities, and possibly Egypt. The important commercial city of Rhodes and the king of Pergamum at once sent envoys to the only power capable of preventing the partition. They arrived at Rome with a request for help in the last year of the Second Punic War; and this time it was the Senate who wanted to go to war with Philip v and Antiochus, while the people hesitated. The Senate quite correctly pointed out that the Romans might be able to defeat Philip before he could get help from his ally, and thus stop the whole scheme before it had started. The people allowed themselves to be persuaded, and Rome, with the assistance, for once, of both the leagues of Greece,[4] defeated Philip decisively. The Roman consul Flamininus, amid scenes of great enthusiasm, solemnly proclaimed freedom for all the Greeks for the first time since the conquests of Alexander.

[4] See above, page 280.

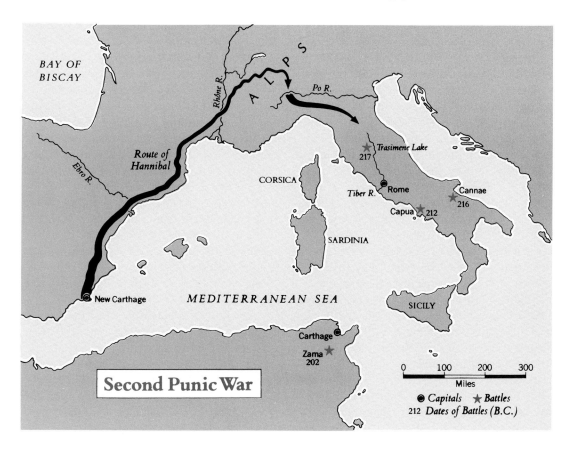

Second Punic War

The gesture, unfortunately, was useless, for the leagues began quarreling again soon afterward, and the Aetolian League invited Antiochus into Greece. The Romans, now freed from the war with Carthage, defeated him, chased him back into Asia, took Asia Minor from him, and added the bulk of the northern part of the old kingdom of Seleucia to the territories of their allies, Pergamum and Rhodes. The Aetolian League surrendered, and Greece was now in Roman hands. But again Rome did not annex, preferring to keep all the existent governments too weak to present a threat to herself, but unfortunately, also too weak to maintain order. Macedonia, which had remained neutral during the war with Antiochus, soon began to intrigue against Rome until she was defeated decisively at the battle of Pydna in 168 B.C. Still she was not annexed, being divided into four "autonomous" republics, with newly devised constitutions.

It is not likely that this Roman policy of making no annexations was dictated by any special concern for Greek liberties; it seems to have been simply a refusal to take the responsibility of maintaining order in these countries as she kept order in Italy. The problem was not so simple for the Roman ruling class as it might seem to us. It was already clear that the Roman armies were not as well disciplined and efficient as they had been in the past. The Romans now fought with considerable superiority in troops and resources at their disposal, but the campaigns were no longer sharp and decisive. What had happened was that both the soldiers and their generals now realized the great profits to be won from the conquests, and too frequently they went as plunderers rather than as disciplined soldiers. The booty gained from the battle of Pydna was enormous, but it had taken several years to defeat the greatly inferior Macedonian army, and even the disunited Greeks could not be overcome in one short campaign. And at the other end of the Roman territory, Spain, inherited from Carthage, was very far from subdued, even though its armies were composed of poorly armed barbarians. If Rome then annexed these territories outright, they would have to be governed; and experience elsewhere showed how difficult it was to keep the governors under proper control by the Senate.

Hardening of Roman imperial policy— Destruction of Corinth and Carthage

After Pydna there is noticeable a definite hardening of the senatorial policy under the influence of men like Cato the Elder, who hated foreigners, and especially Greeks, and no doubt also of the capitalists who had so much to gain from the conquests. The lack of a clear policy combined with exploitation soon drove the Greeks to rebellion again, and at last they were defeated for good in 146 B.C. The chief commercial city of Greece, Corinth, was ruthlessly sacked and Macedonia was annexed and made into a Roman province. In the same year Carthage was razed and the site cursed, even though she had scrupulously respected her treaty obligations, and even aided the Romans with troops and ships. Trade competition cannot explain it, for Rome was still not greatly interested in commerce; this destruction has always been difficult to account for rationally, though we know that it was the ultrapatriotic party of Cato that urged it tirelessly until it was accepted as a policy. Greece was made into a protectorate under the governor of the new province of Macedonia. At last Rome had accepted responsibility for Greece's defense; but it was a looted and declining country that remained. Spain also was finally pacified a few years later, after barbarous cruelties, and in callous disregard of treaties.

By 133 B.C., therefore, when the Roman Republic entered on the last century of its existence, the whole state was already far on the road to complete demoralization. It is time now to deal more systematically with the effects of the expansion upon the Roman people and their constitution.

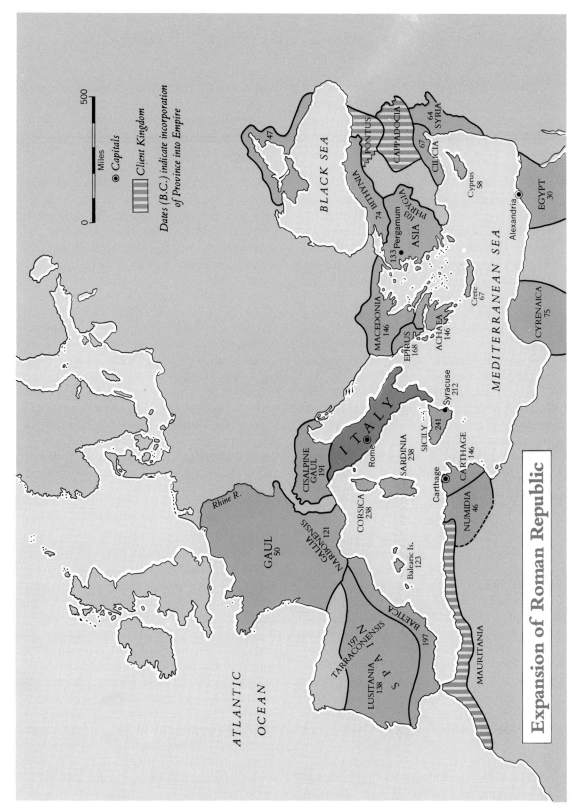

Expansion of Roman Republic

500

Miles

● Capitals

Client Kingdom

Dates (B.C.) indicate incorporation
of Province into Empire

ATLANTIC
OCEAN

Rhine R.

GAUL
50

GALLIA
NARBONENSIS
121

CISALPINE
GAUL
191

TARRACONENSIS
197

LUSITANIA
138

BAETICA
197

S
P
A
I
N

Balearic Is.
123

MAURITANIA

CORSICA
238

SARDINIA
238

ITALY

Rome

SICILY

Syracuse
212

241

Carthage

NUMIDIA
46

CARTHAGE
146

MEDITERRANEAN SEA

EPIRUS
168

MACEDONIA
146

ACHAEA
146

Crete
67

CYRENAICA
75

BLACK SEA

BITHYNIA
74

PONTUS
47

PHRYGIA
103

ASIA

Pergamum
133

CAPPADOCIA

CILICIA
67

SYRIA
64

Cyprus
58

Alexandria

EGYPT
30

325

EFFECTS OF THE EXPANSION ON ROME

The profits of empire

Rome still remained a city without much industry beyond the supply of goods necessary for the maintenance of the armies and ordinary daily needs of the citizens, and she suffered from an extremely unfavorable visible balance of trade. The exports consisted of some wool, wine, olive oil, and iron implements, and very little more. The Romans were not in the least interested in the carrying trade, never inserted any commercial clauses in their treaties, and allowed other seafaring peoples to attend to all the details of shipping the necessary grain and other imports to Rome. But the profits of empire were so enormous in the form of booty and regular tribute that the city and its more prosperous inhabitants had a handsome surplus, some of which went into new buildings and private estates. By 133 B.C. Rome was beginning to look somewhat like a Greek city; for the contact, first with southern Italy, and then with the Hellenistic world, brought thousands of Greeks, both free and slave, into Rome, where they made themselves useful to their masters in organizing more businesses, especially the retail trade, and introducing Hellenistic financial improvements. At the same time the stolid Roman began to be influenced by Hellenistic culture, which took on a new lease of life in Rome. Greek and Oriental luxuries began to flow into Roman hands, causing old puritans like Cato to bemoan the decadence of the old Roman character and the loss of old Roman manners. Some of the Roman families became educated in the Greek style, and even studied Greek philosophy, especially the circle around the Scipios, who were strong patrons of all forms of Greek culture. More and more interesting things could now be bought for money than in the hard old days. Cato was certainly far from wrong when he viewed this taste for luxuries with alarm; for it did indeed play an important part in the ultimate downfall of his republic.

The rise of the equestrian order

The class that profited most from the expansion was the group of wealthy plebeians, never very many in number, who did not seek office but preferred wealth and the indirect influence that went with it. These men, who belonged to the first class in the Centuriate Assembly and therefore could have been enrolled in the cavalry, were called *equites,* or knights. These were the men who bid for contracts for public works on which they made profits, but their main source of income was from handling the provincial tax contracts. Most governors could be bribed, for reasons to be discussed shortly, with the result that taxes were stepped up far beyond the permissible rate. When the provincials were unable to pay and faced eviction or worse at the hands of the governor, other capitalists, called *negotiatores,* offered to lend them the money at high rates of interest, thus ensuring double profits for the equites of Rome. These capitalists soon began to exercise a sinister influence on Roman imperial policy, partly through suborning the senators, and partly through political influence over magistrates and the Assemblies by means of well-placed bribes.

Dispossession of the peasant proprietors —Latifundia

Meanwhile the senators themselves, forbidden by law to handle tax contracts or, indeed, to engage in any other business, could increase their wealth only by capitalizing in some way upon their monopoly of office. They had three methods open to them: winning booty in military campaigns, exploiting the provinces in cooperation with the equites during their terms as governors, and by increasing their landholdings, mostly in Italy. The Punic Wars, while ruinous to the small farmers, had helped the large landholders. Much land had been devastated, especially in southern Italy, and only wealthy men could bring it back into cultivation and make it pay. They were able to buy this land at very low prices, or rent it at a nominal figure, and thereafter work it profitably with slaves on a plantation basis. The resulting large estates, called *latifundia*, were mostly given up to sheep, which required the least labor, though olive orchards and vineyards also lent themselves to large-scale cultivation.

The growth of the city proletariat

The social results of the growth of these large estates were catastrophic. The poor farmers who found themselves ousted could only go to Rome, where there was very little employment for them. The Latins and Italians, who were the chief victims, were not permitted, as noncitizens, to bid for the public land even if they had had the money to do so. These allies had won no rights for centuries even though they had loyally supported Rome in all her wars. They began to agitate for Roman citizenship, and the poorer among them went to Rome, where they had an even more precarious existence than the impoverished Roman citizens.

In Rome there was little to do. For those who were skilled there were new public and private buildings to work on, others might be able to pay court to the rich, citizens could sell their votes when the oligarchy needed them. With the influx of slaves, often better educated and more capable than the Roman farmer in the city, wages fell till it was barely possible to live on them. The total result was the creation of a vast proletariat, most of whom had the vote and full rights but felt no responsibility for the state. They were, however, potentially very dangerous to the oligarchy; for many of them came from the rural tribes, and could at any moment break the senatorial political machine in the Tribal Assembly if they were not fed and amused and otherwise bribed.[5] The office seekers began to provide them with great public games and spectacles, and the state began to supply them with grain at very low prices. But all these distractions did not prevent the ex-farmers from agitating

for the breaking up of the large estates and for the founding of colonies where they could start life again. For the majority of them there was nothing else; the army still required some property qualification, so that even this last resort was closed to many.

▶ The Gracchan revolution

THE LAND LAW OF TIBERIUS GRACCHUS—
THE CONSTITUTIONAL ISSUE

This was the background of the Gracchan "revolution." There had been several attempts in the years before 133 B.C. to have the land redistributed, often sponsored by members of the Claudian family, which had always cultivated the proletariat for political purposes; but Tiberius Gracchus, the elder of the two reforming brothers, though connected with this family, was undoubtedly sincere himself. In 133 B.C. he was elected tribune, after a campaign in which he promised the redistribution of the land.

When he brought forward a comparatively mild law in the Tribal Assembly, the senatorial party, now generally called the Optimates, played its usual card: a tribune, one of the colleagues of Tiberius, vetoed the bill. Legally Tiberius had no recourse. He could only wait for the next year and hope to have a full board of tribunes elected to support his program. But he himself could not be elected tribune two years in succession. Rather than abandon his program he chose to appeal to the people to depose the recalcitrant tribune. The people backed him, but the deposition was undoubtedly illegal. The law was then declared duly passed.

In ordinary circumstances the Senate could have resisted further by refusing to provide funds to put the law into operation. But, as it happened, it was just at this moment that the last king of Pergamum, in Asia Minor, left his entire kingdom to Rome in his will. Tiberius summoned the Assembly and instructed it to accept the gift on behalf of the people of Rome. This act was not illegal, but for centuries this had been regarded as the task of the Senate and not of the people, and thus was deeply offensive to that august body, which saw a future in which a determined tribune with the aid of the proletariat could wrest from it all its long-cherished privileges. Only one safeguard remained—the tribune could not be re-elected. But Tiberius did not have time in his year of office to put his law into execution, and he chose to stand again for office the second year. On the election day the Pontifex Maximus, a Scipio and an opponent of the Claudian faction, led an armed band of senators and their clients against Tiberius and succeeded in murdering him and three hundred of his followers. Some reaction against this violence followed, and the law of Tiberius was put into effect, showing perhaps that the opposition was rather against rule by the proletariat than against the law itself. And a law seems to have been passed during the next ten years that a tribune could succeed himself in office.

THE TRIBUNATE OF GAIUS GRACCHUS—
SENATORIAL RESORT TO DEMAGOGUERY AND
VIOLENCE

In 123 B.C. the younger brother of Tiberius, Gaius Gracchus, was elected tribune with a much more comprehensive program than his brother had sponsored. But it was not uniformly popular with the people, thus giving the Optimates a chance to defeat him by strictly legal means. The first item on Gaius's program was to provide grain for the people below cost price. This was probably not new, and was of no special importance, except that Gaius also made careful administrative arrangements for the import and distribution of this grain. All later tribunes who tried to persuade the people to pass laws included such bills in their program. Gaius also proposed an extensive colonization scheme in the conquered lands, including one on the "cursed" but incomparable site of Carthage. The colonists, however, had to possess some means, as the sites were often, like Carthage, capable of commercial as well as agricultural development. This was therefore not very interesting to the quite penniless proletariat. He proposed a program of public works, especially roads; and he also

re-enacted his brother's land law, although there was by then not much land available for distribution. To gain the support of the equites he made special arrangements for a graduated tax system in the provinces, and he handed over the new rich province of Asia to them alone as taxgatherers; although this system was already substantially in effect elsewhere, the new law gave it official sanction. The whole provincial tax was now let as a unit at Rome, and not to separate groups as had been the earlier custom in Sicily, thus necessitating the formation of large and profitable corporations in Rome. Gaius also substituted equestrian juries for senatorial juries to try cases of corruption in the provinces, a move which involved the recognition of the equites for the first time as a separate order in the state. The new juries were certainly no improvement on the senatorial juries, since both classes were equally engaged in the fleecing of the provincials.

Gaius now stood for re-election and was successful, though far from the top of the poll. As one of his colleagues he had an Optimate sympathizer, one Livius Drusus, who had discovered a new and effective weapon against Gaius. For Gaius wanted to introduce, and may have already introduced in his first term, a bill which he was certain would not be popular—the full enfranchisement of the Italians. This could never please the Roman proletariat, which saw various treasured privileges shared with "foreigners," especially such minor but personally important matters as good seats at the games and festivals. Drusus proceeded to veto this bill, even though it probably had little chance of passing, and proposed instead a bill which might have passed and would have removed one important grievance of the Italians, namely, discrimination between Italians and citizens when on military service in the matter of discipline. But Drusus went on to show his real intentions by playing upon mass superstition, warning the people of the terrible results that would come from settling a cursed site; and he proposed also that the new colonies should be opened equally to propertyless citizens. There was doubtless no

ON THE PRECEDING PAGE: *Fifth century bronze showing Athena, goddess of wisdom and patroness of Athens, with her symbol, the owl.* (METROPOLITAN MUSEUM OF ART, HARRIS BRISBANE DICK FUND, 1950)

BELOW: *A Grecian cylindrical container (Pyxis) of the fifth century B.C. This superior example of Grecian vase art depicts a scene from the Judgment of Paris, with Paris in the center and the attendant god Hermes on his left (the third figure has not been identified with any certainty).* (METROPOLITAN MUSEUM OF ART, ROGERS FUND, 1907)

RIGHT: *This fresco was painted on the walls of a cubiculum, part of a villa excavated in 1900 at Boscoreale, about a mile from Pompeii in southern Italy. The entire villa was buried in the eruption of Vesuvius in A.D. 79, in which the Elder Pliny, the naturalist, lost his life. It is not known for certain why the Romans painted such vistas as this one on the interior walls of their houses, but the Roman architectural writer Vitruvius tells us that scenery suitable for tragedies, comedies, and satyr plays was sometimes used for interior decoration. The satyr at the top of the picture suggests that this fresco may well have been the scenery for a satyr play.* (METROPOLITAN MUSEUM OF ART, ROGERS FUND, 1903)

Roman mosaic from Tunisia, probably from the second century (A.D.), found in an atrium at El-Djem, Tunisia. This mosaic, possibly an allegory of a muse, shows the Romans' outstanding capability, in this medium, for design, execution of detail, and the use of shadings and tints of color. (INGE MORATH, MAGNUM)

intention whatever of putting such a proposal into effect, but he was successful in defeating Gaius, who was not elected for the third year.

As his term neared its end the Optimates made obvious preparations to deal with Gaius personally as soon as he had ceased to be sacrosanct. Incidents were numerous, and Gaius surrounded himself with a body-guard drawn from his own political party, the Populares, as they were called. When one of his followers was tricked into murdering an opponent at the end of the year, the Senate declared martial law and called upon the consul, a ruffian elected for the special purpose, to take steps to defend the state. The consul did so by killing a large number of Populares, and Gracchus himself was either killed or committed suicide. Three thousand more were condemned to death by a senatorial judicial commission without allowing the traditional appeal to the people and without even a trial. The Senate had declared publicly its moral bankruptcy; and though it did not take further steps against such of the Gracchan laws as had passed, it had set the example of violence which was to be followed by senators, demagogues, and generals alike until the republic itself collapsed.

▶ **The collapse of the republic**[6]

THE ENROLLMENT OF A VOLUNTEER
PROFESSIONAL ARMY—MARIUS

The instrument which was to destroy the republic was forged by a general who certainly had no idea of the ultimate future consequences of his handiwork, and was directly due to the corruption and rapacity of knights and senators. A young African prince named Jugurtha, who was well acquainted with Rome, decided to use the venality of the governing classes in Rome to carve himself out a large independent kingdom in Africa. Since this meant the deposition of

[6] This section is given in considerable detail for its value as a case study of the dangers to free institutions of refusal by an entrenched oligarchy to grant timely reforms which could perhaps have preserved them.

an ally of Rome, he evidently hoped that the judicious placing of bribes would persuade the Senate to wink at his activities. Unfortunately for him, an eloquent tribune succeeded in keeping the issue before the people, or Jugurtha might well have been successful. Several armies were sent against him, but all met with unexplained difficulties, and Jugurtha openly proclaimed that everything in Rome was for sale. Though our only account of the war is from a source unsympathetic to the Senate, there can be little doubt that the earlier generals were bribed; at last Metellus, a member of the ruling clique, himself went out and made some progress in the war. But even he was unable to finish it, thus giving the opportunity to one of his subordinates, C. Marius, to suggest that his superior, too, was lagging for private reasons, and to insist that he himself should be given the command as consul.

Marius was a man of the people, a rugged soldier, no doubt; and with the ability to win popular support in Rome, where his friends prepared the ground for his consul-ship. When all was ready he demanded a leave from his superior officer to go to Rome and stand for the consulship. This ultimately had to be granted, and Marius was duly elected. But the Senate, which, by custom, distributed the commands, refused to appoint him to Africa. The Assembly, working smoothly under his supporters, passed a special law giving it to him, and the Senate had to acquiesce. It was now that Marius adopted the military policy that led to the downfall of the Republic. He abolished the property qualifications for military service altogether, and proceeded to recruit his army from the proletariat. This army was now made up of volunteers, men who looked to their general for payment of their wages, as well as for booty, and for pensions when they had completed their service.

It is hard to overestimate the importance of this innovation. Property qualifications had been consistently lowered for centuries, and this was only the final logical step; but the soldier-citizens now recruited were those for whom the Roman Republic meant nothing but a hostile oligarchy and "bread and circuses" on occasion. They had no loyalty to it, and only contempt and dislike for the ruling oligarchy which made such a good thing out of it. Now they could recover their self-respect in the army; it was not, however, the army of the Roman Republic but the army of the general. One thing only was necessary as qualification for this general. He must be successful, capable of delivering pay, booty, and pensions—or the equivalent of pensions, land. This last could only be secured at the expense of the republic, by political activity.

It was easy for a general with an army at his back to cow the Senate and the people once he was in command; but he had first to be appointed to this command. And he had to be sure that there was no rival general of equal power with him. So it became necessary for the prospective general to maintain a political machine which would ensure him his first and subsequent commands, and would see to it that his rivals did not surpass him. And in order that there might be suitable commands available, the conquests must be expanded, with or without causes of war.

It was clear that the Assembly was now a more suitable instrument than the Senate for this purpose. If the Senate was favorable, well and good; but if not, the Gracchi had shown where the real power in the state lay. And the army belonged to the proletarian class. The power of the Senate rested on the acquiescence of the people and its willingness to abide by the constitution; the new army, being an extraconstitutional power, was hampered by no constitutional inhibitions, and needed to have no compunction about intimidating a few hundred senators and their clients. From this time onward the government of Rome was to be in the hands of the tribunes and the Assembly, aided by such funds as were necessary for bribery, and by the threat of the return of the army commander to enforce his will on any opponents of his regime. While the commander was away the Senate was still able to function, and even assert itself on occasion.

But the oligarchy knew well enough that the power in the state had gone elsewhere; its only hope was to be able to persuade a successful general to lend his support to it, rather than to the people. But the Senate was never able again to function as an independent, responsible body, without the support of some general; it could be a nuisance to the general who wanted to act constitutionally, but it could no longer overrule him if he decided to act in opposition to it.

Doubtless none of these consequences were foreseen at the time that the army was organized on a volunteer basis, but they followed inevitably. The republic was doomed.

Marius himself with his new army made considerable headway in his campaigns against Jugurtha. But the latter had gained an important ally in his father-in-law, another African ruler, and it was not until one of Marius's own officers, Sulla, persuaded the father-in-law to betray Jugurtha that the war could be finished. Marius flew into a jealous rage against Sulla; but since the people gave Marius credit for the victory and since he, not Sulla, celebrated the triumph over Jugurtha, the consul remained the most popular man in Rome. At this moment Rome was suddenly threatened by an invasion of German barbarians from the north. Marius stood illegally for re-election as consul, and was successful, receiving the supreme command against the Germans. It took him several years to recruit and reorganize a larger and more effective army, and finally defeat the enemy, and during this time his supporters in the Assembly continued to elect him every year as consul. But when the war was over, he needed lands for his veterans and he wanted to be elected consul for the sixth time. He had to obtain some political support, for he was no longer an indispensable man; the Senate was anxious to put an end to his illegal consulships, and the proletariat was not interested in his program of lands for veterans.

The only party possible for him was the Populares, led at this time by a pair of unscrupulous demagogues whose price was high. By grain doles and wholesale bribery he was duly elected consul for the sixth time, but his supporters proceeded to rule Rome by violence and open murder. When the Senate called upon him to suppress them and declared martial law, he decided to disown the demagogues, who were themselves murdered by supporters of the oligarchy. Marius, his usefulness to the Senate over, and naturally deserted by the populace, retired to exile in Africa, where he plotted how to obtain revenge as well as how to achieve the seventh consulship promised him by a soothsayer.

DISCONTENT OF THE ITALIANS—THE SOCIAL WAR

Meanwhile the Italians, who had fought loyally against the Germanic invaders, were subjected to new indignities and discriminations. Italian soldiers in the armies of Marius had not been permitted to take part in the colonization schemes put through for them by the Assembly; and civilian Italians found that some of the colonization, as usual, was at their expense. For years they had been trying to overcome this discrimination by the use of the vote, since they were allowed to vote if they came to Rome to live. But the Senate and people were united in their desire to prevent this, and in 95 B.C. a drastic law was passed expelling all Italian noncitizens from Rome. From this moment the Italians began to plot a rebellion, actual secession from Rome, and the setting up of a new confederacy independent of Rome.

In 92 B.C. new evidence of the debasement of justice, one of the few remaining reasons for Roman pride and Italian loyalty, gave further ammunition to those agitators who claimed that Rome had outlived its usefulness. A certain Rutilius, who had refused to allow the equites to exploit his province of Asia, was himself accused of extortion and bribery and convicted by the equestrian jury as an example to governors to keep their hands off the capitalists. On conviction he went into exile in the province that he was supposed to have exploited, which supported him in comfort for the rest of his days.

In 91 B.C. the last effort was made to satisfy the Italians by a tribune named Drusus the Younger, who brought in a bill for their enfranchisement. Knowing that it had no chance of passing by itself, he included it in an omnibus bill which also contained provisions for cheap grain and new colonies for the proletariat. The Senate claimed that he had ignored the auspices, that earthquakes and other portents showed divine displeasure, and declared the legislation invalid. The people refused to re-elect him, and the next tribune proposed to prosecute him and all his friends. Drusus was murdered, and the Italians, their last hope of succeeding by peaceful means gone, rose in revolt.

With armies the equal of any the Romans could command in Italy, they won several victories, and set up a new state called Italia. But the Romans were no longer exclusively dependent upon the Italians. They recalled Marius and sent for veterans from the provinces who knew nothing of the grievances of the Italians. With these, and under the generalship of Marius and Sulla, his rival and lieutenant from African days, they began to make headway. But progress was slow, and the Romans at last decided to take some action on the grievances in the hope of dividing the Italian ranks. They passed a law giving citizenship to all Italians who had not revolted, and followed it up by another law offering citizenship to anyone whose home was in Italy and who would lay down his arms within a stipulated period. This move was successful, for the Italians had never been fully united in their desire to leave Rome altogether. Indeed, the upper class among the Italians had sometimes profited from Roman rule, and had from the beginning opposed Italia. The Roman armies were now able to make much better progress and at last, with the death of the Italian leader, the revolt was suppressed. But, as usual, the oligarchy had a card up its sleeve. The new citizens were all enrolled in eight tribes out of the thirty-five, and, though they gained some privileges, they were unable to make their influence felt in the Assembly.

Crassus and Caesar would have been impotent. As it was, Pompey was forced to look to these two for political support, and he had much to offer in exchange for it. His land-hungry veterans would naturally follow him in any venture which he demanded from them, in spite of the fact that they had been formally disbanded.

Nevertheless the price of Caesar and Crassus was high, though Pompey seems not to have realized at the time what would be the personal cost to himself. The money of Crassus had partially undermined Pompey's previously unchallenged popularity with the voters, and the banker's support was pledged to his protégé Julius Caesar, whose year it would ordinarily be for the consulship. But there was a legal obstacle to Caesar's election. He had just returned from his first command of importance in Spain, and he desired a triumph for his work there. But, if he were to have his triumph, then legally he could not enter Rome and stand for the consulship. Reasonably enough, he asked the Senate for permission to stand for the consulship by proxy. Cato filibustered the proposal out, and permission was refused. Caesar abandoned his triumph, which had social rather than political value, and was duly elected consul with the support of Crassus. The Senate, still rushing on blindly to its destruction after the manner of a Greek tragedy but well aware of Caesar's military ambitions and believing that it still wielded the powers of ancient days, gratuitously insulted him by allotting him as his proconsular command, to which he was entitled after his year as consul, the sinecure of control of the forests and roads of Italy. This drove Caesar into the arms of the only man who could get him what he wanted.

Pompey needed ratification of his acts in the East and he needed lands for his veterans, Caesar needed a command to satisfy his newly discovered military genius, Crassus needed a pay-off from Caesar whom he had financed so faithfully while waiting for this moment. All these needs were taken care of by an unofficial and extralegal agreement known as the First Triumvirate (60 B.C.). When Caesar proposed that the Senate should satisfy Pompey's demands and it refused, Pompey offered the consul the use of a few of his veterans. The Senate house was surrounded and of course the Senate had to give way. When Caesar asked for a five-year proconsular command in Gaul, Pompey, not fearing any danger from such a recent and militarily unknown rival, supported him. Crassus was entirely happy at the distribution of land to Pompey's veterans, as he had been quietly buying up all the good land in Italy which he could now sell to the state at substantial profit to himself; while for good measure a tribune was permitted to propose that there should be a one-third reduction in the price of all tax contracts for the year (the tribune was paid off in shares of Crassus' corporation). Finally, Caesar and Pompey accepted a gift of six thousand talents from King Ptolemy of Egypt in return for a senatorial resolution that he should be allowed to keep his throne! But Caesar also had what he wanted most, a five-year command in Cisalpine Gaul where there were a few local disturbances. Later Transalpine Gaul was added to his command when a more real danger appeared from invading northern tribes. The year ended, and Caesar went on his epoch-making command, while Pompey and Crassus stayed in Italy.

CIVIL WAR—THE DICTATORSHIP OF CAESAR

The story of the next ten years is the story of the gradual supplanting of Pompey by Caesar. In the early years of the triumvirate Pompey was still supreme, but his veterans were aging, while Caesar was building up a strong army of disciplined legionaries loyal to himself. Crassus was eliminated from the triumvirate when he insisted on being appointed to a military command against the Parthians in the East and was killed in a disastrous defeat at Carrhae (53 B.C.). For most of the time Pompey held no official position, though his services were occasionally called upon to suppress riots in Rome and to organize the grain supply. He was in command of troops in Spain and elsewhere, and the navy was under his control, but he did not rule these forces personally, preferring to stay in the vicinity of Rome. When reports of Caesar's successes reached Rome, for a long time he took no action to sustain his earlier supremacy over all rivals. And the Senate, realizing that it was now in greater danger from Caesar than from Pompey, proceeded to woo the older man away from his partner. In 51 B.C. it tried for the last time to make use of constitutional republican safeguards against an aspiring general, and this ill-timed maneuver precipitated the civil war which destroyed its independence forever.

Caesar spent nearly ten years campaigning in Gaul. The Gauls or Celts were by no means a barbarian people, but had developed a distinctive civilization of their own, though they retained their primitive tribal governments. They were, however, seriously disunited, and it had been Caesar's task to take advantage of this disunity to offset his comparatively small army. He never had to fight with many Gauls at the same time; and though, even so, he was usually outnumbered, he always emerged successful in the end. There was very little excuse for the whole campaign, since the Gauls were not troubling the Romans; but once Caesar had intervened, the disunity of the various groups made possible the exercise of the customary Roman imperial policy of divide and rule. By slow degrees Caesar was thus able to conquer the whole country. In the process he built up a very strong body of legionaries, personally devoted to himself, though several of his senior officers later deserted him as soon as they had the opportunity, and a number of them joined in his murder. His administration of the province and his military acumen were clearly of a very high order, although our only account was written by himself.

At this crisis of the Roman Republic in 50–49 B.C., one thing stands out clearly. Caesar, in addition to being a slightly younger man than his rival Pompey, had obviously a greater resolution; he had tasted supreme military power for ten years and was at the height of his glory and self-confidence. He had no intention of allowing himself to be dictated to by the constitution,

by his rival, or by the Senate, though he would probably have preferred to avoid civil war, especially when he had little strength beside his own legions in Gaul. He was not sure how strong Pompey and the Senate would actually prove; for on paper Pompey had the Spanish and African legions, a legendary reputation in the East which could be converted into troops, and undisputed command of the seas. Clearly it was better to behave legally if possible.

But the Senate seemed determined to drive Caesar to illegal action, evidently with the intention of summoning Pompey to take drastic legal steps against him. Pompey, who could have taken supreme power for himself earlier, had refrained from doing so. He might therefore as a last resort be relied upon to defend the republic against Caesar, who might well be intending to destroy it. There were many charges that could be made against Caesar. There were undoubted illegalities in the conduct of the war in Gaul. He had extended his authority without permission, he had massacred prisoners contrary to accepted rules of war, and if these real crimes were not enough, many others could be manufactured, quite sufficient to ensure his exile and punishment should he ever permit himself to be tried by Roman courts. Caesar, of course, was well aware of what was planned against him; hence his insistence that he must continue to keep his command or another one which would carry with it immunity from prosecution. But the Senate had no intention of permitting him such immunity; on the contrary, before he even returned to Italy, it declared martial law and called upon Pompey to defend the republic, thus forcing Caesar's hand. Caesar, hearing the news, is said to have cried, "Alea jacta est!" ("The die is cast!") and crossed the river Rubicon, the boundary of Italy, with his army, thus putting himself at once legally in the wrong, as no general was permitted to enter Italy with an army.

Pompey did his best. But when he summoned troops to his standard, too few responded. His active legions were far away, and his reputation was no longer what it had been. The bulk of the senators and the aristocrats in general were with him; but in the campaign that followed they were a hindrance rather than a help, forcing him into battle before he was ready. With a properly planned campaign he should have won, but he was never allowed to plan his strategy; the navy, which was entirely on his side, was used to poor advantage. Leaving Italy for Greece, he tempted the impetuous Caesar to follow him, but then allowed the rebel to escape from the consequences of his rashness. In the end Pompey was defeated at the battle of Pharsalia (48 B.C.) and escaped to Egypt, where he was murdered. Caesar followed him there and was nearly brought to an untimely end by a sudden uprising of the Egyptians under the last of the Ptolemies. Surviving this misadventure by the fortunate arrival of reinforcements, he defeated and killed Ptolemy and spent the winter with his widow, a young beauty named Cleopatra. The following year he set out again in pursuit of the last supporters of Pompey. Though some of the campaigns were strenuous and hard fought, Caesar was uniformly successful, and was able to return to Rome at the end of the year 46 B.C. and turn his attention to affairs of state.

ESTIMATE OF THE WORK OF JULIUS CAESAR— ADMINISTRATIVE REFORMS AND POLITICAL INEPTITUDE

Caesar spent the last two years of his life in trying to create order in the empire of which he was now undisputed ruler. Unquestionably he had a very considerable grasp of the administrative problems involved in this task, and his administration, as far as it went, was enlightened. He extended Roman citizenship to many provincials and he stopped the tax-farming system, making the governors responsible only to himself. He put the municipalities of Italy on a uniform basis. He planned and put into execution an extensive program of public works, draining of marshes, and building of roads; and he planned an immense program of colonization in the provinces. He reformed the calendar, putting into use the Egyptian solar calendar of 365¼ days. He

took measures to diminish the population of Rome, and he instituted a public works program for the remainder, which was greatly superior to the privately sponsored building programs of his predecessors in that it was better planned and less haphazard. He undertook an important reform in the free municipalities of the empire in the hope of ensuring a regular supply of officials to undertake public duties, he substituted a graduated land tax in some of the provinces instead of the much-abused irregular collections. He was able to carry out these reforms because, for the first time, there was a real public authority in Rome in the person of himself. Rome was, in his day, on the verge of becoming, for the first time, a true state.

It was a good beginning, and a very considerable body of achievement for the short time that he held absolute power. There is no doubt that Caesar was a military man of immense energy and outstanding attainments, and as an administrator he was equal to any in Roman history, though perhaps not surpassing his great-nephew and successor. He was, of course, also one of the best military writers of all times, and a master of the Latin tongue. It is, however, doubtful if he deserves the enormous reputation that he has acquired in the centuries since his time, as a kind of universal genius. If he had survived longer than two years after his final return to Rome, we would be better able to come to an informed judgment. It was to the interest of Augustus, his great-nephew and adopted son, to exalt the reputation of his "martyred" predecessor, as we shall see; and it may well be that this propaganda and the use of the name Caesar by all the imperial rulers of Rome have tended to obscure the real defects in the vision as well as in the character of the great dictator.

For Caesar, above all, lacked political insight. The visible and tangible problems of Rome and the empire were clear to him but not the more subtle political realities of which the founder of a stable regime must take account. What was so vitally important in his time was the regularization of his own position, and about this he seems to have had no ideas whatever. He had himself elected dictator for life, but, unlike Sulla, he made no attempt to reform the constitution, and then abdicate his emergency power. He accepted every honorific title offered him by a cowed and obsequious Senate, and even suggested more. He did not know whether to make himself king—a few trial balloons were sent up on this notion—or stay in his present position. He allowed no one to approach him in power, and was content to hand over administrative tasks to his military subordinates. It would seem that the only thought he had on the matter of his position was that he should become something like a Hellenistic king, with divine attributes, ruling by divine right.

This, in a city which had known self-government for nearly five centuries and had risen to be mistress of the world by her own efforts, and especially by the activities of her noble families, a city, moreover, as conservative and enamored of tradition as Rome, was certain to arouse all classes against him. The Senate was "reformed" by the introduction of recently enfranchised provincials and by some of his own veteran soldiers, down to the rank of centurion. This "reformation" may have improved the quality of the Senate, but it is far more likely that Caesar instituted it in order to satisfy his own sardonic sense of humor, since he pointedly gave the Senate nothing to do. But why waste such an institution? Though it had fallen on evil days it still counted for something, and a statesman, like Caesar's successor, Augustus, was able to put it to work. The result of Caesar's tactlessness, which could easily have been foreseen, was that the senators were furious, even though they had to conceal their feelings, and the Senate became the focal point for the conspiracy which cost Caesar his life. Sulla had been much more careful. Though he knew as well as anyone else how feeble the Senate had become, he tried to make use of it, striving to improve its quality by increasing the number of officeholders and making entry into the Senate mandatory for officeholders. Caesar, of course, realized that the time had come for one-man rule, and that a reform of the Sullan variety was no longer feasible. But a dicta-

torship, based on military power alone, could never have been permanent. And it was the height of folly to plan a new campaign in Parthia, on which he was to take his intended heir, leaving a city full of enemies behind him. As it happened, the conspirators against his life seized the opportunity to murder him before he left.

Caesar always prided himself on his "clemency," and it is true that he did not proscribe his enemies as did Sulla and Caesar's own successors. He could be ruthless on occasion, while at other times even his enemies admitted his personal charm. There can, however, be little doubt that Caesar did regard himself as in some degree superhuman, not subject to human failings, and altogether removed from the ordinary run of men. He trusted his destiny, and in all his career never bothered to take elementary precautions. Probably it was for this reason that he did not care to trouble himself with the subtle arts of the statesman. His treatment of his enemies must have wounded them in their dignity; there are different ways of forgiving one's enemies, and even Caesar's most determined apologists have never credited him with tact. When he returned from his victories over Roman citizens in Spain he celebrated a triumph, and forced the Senate to vote him a thanksgiving. Several of his most trusted officers deserted him, even when he was victorious, and the conspiracy against his life included such soldiers as Decimus Brutus and Cassius, who had served through long campaigns with him. It would seem, then, that in the end it was his inhuman or superhuman arrogance that was responsible for his death, and prevented him from being the founder of the empire.

On the Ides of March in 44 B.C. Caesar was murdered in the Senate house as he sat listening to petitions. Marcus Brutus, his longtime friend, and reputed illegitimate son, led the conspiracy, and, according to Suetonius, Caesar gave up the struggle with the famous words, "Et tu Brute!" when he saw Brutus among his enemies. The conspirators had no program, and it was an act of folly to murder the man who had become the state without any idea of what was to replace him; but on personal grounds the act was entirely understandable. It can hardly be denied that Caesar in a sense invited his own murder. If, like Augustus, he had taken the Senate into partnership, or even spared its dignity by pretending to do so, he would probably never have been murdered. Something new had to be thought out, some way of ensuring continuity between the dying past and the future not yet born. In this Caesar failed, and it was left to the political genius and the unsurpassed tact of Augustus to achieve this result in the forty-five years of absolute power that he enjoyed. Certainly Augustus profited by Caesar's mistakes and untimely end. But nothing in Julius Caesar's career or in the ideas that he revealed during his few years of supreme power suggests that he could have founded an empire that would last for five hundred years, even if he had had twenty more years to live and had returned victorious from Parthia with the eagles lost by Crassus at Carrhae.

▶ Suggestions for further reading

As in the case of Greece, as much as possible should be read of what the Romans themselves wrote, and most of the material from the Republic is now available in paperback. A selection from Cicero's letters is available from Norton, nine orations in a Mentor edition, and other selections appear in Modern Library and Penguin editions. Sallust's two histories are available in Penguin. Part of Livy's history is also in Penguin, while Plutarch's *Lives* of Roman leaders are available in several different editions. Caesar's *Gallic Wars* have been published in several editions, and the *Civil War* is available in a Penguin edition. However the best selection of Roman documents is the case-bound book covering both the Republic and Empire, which includes material from inscriptions, Naphtali Lewis, and Meyer Reinhold, *Roman Civilization*. 2 vols. (New York: Columbia University Press, 1951, 1955).

PAPER-BOUND BOOKS

Adcock, F. E. *Roman Political Ideas and Practice*. Ann Arbor. Useful short summary.

Barrow, R. H. *The Romans*. Penguin. A good first chapter on the Roman character and an excellent summary of Roman law and juris-

prudence; otherwise not especially distinguished.

Cowell, F. R. *Cicero and the Roman Republic*. Penguin. The book is far from exclusively concerned with Cicero. Presents a vivid and factual picture of the last century of the Republic, but interpretation is traditional.

Hamilton, Edith. *The Roman Way to Western Civilization*. Mentor. Similar to her more famous *The Greek Way*.

Jones, A. H. M. *History of Rome through the Fifth Century*. Vol. 1. The Republic. Torchbooks. By a leading specialist in Roman government and law.

Mattingly, Harold. *The Man in the Roman Street*. Norton. Covers very effectively the social conditions of ancient Rome.

Mommsen, Theodore. *History of Rome*. Wisdom and Meridian. This classic history of the Republic remains the finest single work in its field.

Rostovtzeff, M. L. *Rome*. Galaxy. By one of the greatest authorities, covering both the Republic and the Empire in a relatively short survey.

Starr, Chester G. *The Emergence of Rome as Ruler of the Western World*. Cornell University Press. Valuable short survey on the period of expansion.

Syme, Ronald. *The Roman Revolution*. Oxford University Press. Argumentative and opinionated (but extremely valuable) work on the last century of the Republic.

Taylor, Lily Ross. *Party Politics in the Age of Caesar*. University of California. An excellent book which complements while sometimes disagreeing with Syme.

CASE-BOUND BOOKS

Jones, A. H. M. *Studies in Roman Government and Law*. New York: Frederick A. Praeger, Inc., 1960. Specialized study, partly on the Republic.

Marsh, F. B. *The Founding of the Roman Empire*. New York: Barnes & Noble, Inc., 1960 (originally published in 1927). Should be read in conjunction with Syme's *The Roman Revolution*. Covers the fall of the Republic as well as the beginning of the Empire under Augustus.

Smith, R. E. *The Failure of the Roman Republic*. New York: Cambridge University Press, 1955. Interpretative study tracing the failure to the work of the Gracchi.

Showerman, Grant. *Eternal Rome*. Vol. I. New Haven, Conn.: Yale University Press, 1924. Well-written and well-illustrated history of the city of Rome.

CHAPTER 11

THE FOUNDATION
OF THE ROMAN EMPIRE

▶ **The Civil War and the establishment of one-man rule**

Caesar had been successfully murdered, but the murderers had no idea how they were to replace him. There is no evidence that any of them had grasped the magnitude of the difficulties with which the republic had to contend if it was to survive. Only Cicero, a lifelong supporter of constitutional government, showed any real signs of leadership in the crisis. But even Cicero, who was not himself one of the actual conspirators against Caesar, had no positive policy for dealing with it. He seems to have hoped vaguely for an end to the military dictators and a restoration of the republic through a new concord between the warring classes. Though he gave leadership to the senators, his practical policy was one of opportunism, trying to play one leader against the other. He failed to appreciate the real abilities of Caesar's adopted heir, and this underestimation cost him any chance he might have had of success, and ultimately his life.

The murder of Julius Caesar was not greeted with any enthusiasm by the proletariat, who had always regarded Caesar as their champion, and who naturally appreciated his openhandedness. But their sullenness presented no immediate danger to the conspirators. The danger was from the Caesarian armies led by Mark Antony the consul, and by Lepidus who held the title of master of the horse, second in command to Caesar as dictator. Another important army in northern Italy was commanded by Decimus Brutus, one of the conspirators. If these commanders could hold the loyalty of their troops, a new civil war was inevitable. Lepidus succeeded in escaping from Rome and joining his army, but Antony was trapped at the time of the murder, being forced to barricade himself in his own house. In spite of the realization by some of the conspirators that Antony ought to have been murdered with Caesar, they failed to secure him. Instead, they negotiated with him, and he at once came to terms, hoping for time to come to his aid. But no sooner had an agreement been patched up when an opportunity presented itself to Antony for getting rid of them. On the occasion of Caesar's funeral he made an impassioned speech which was followed by a riot, and the conspirators suddenly found Rome too hot to hold them. They fled across the Adriatic, and began to recruit armies in Greece and the Near East among those who had been supporters of Pompey and were willing enough to put an end to the Caesarian rule. Pompey's son Sextus, who was in Spain, also proceeded to raise an army and a formidable fleet. But Antony was left with the priceless advantage of possession of the capital and control of the machinery of government. Lepidus went off to Spain on a lucrative command.

Cicero and the Senate were for the moment helpless. It was not therefore surprising that they gave a warm welcome to a new candidate for power who showed promise of becoming the only possible champion against Antony. Gaius Octavianus, Caesar's great-nephew, had been adopted as the dictator's personal heir by the terms of his will, and the will had been proclaimed and accepted by Senate and people alike. Antony had disregarded many of its terms, and embezzled for his own use part of the money. He had also hesitated to fulfill the bequests of lands to Caesar's veterans until the situation was easier. It was natural that Antony had paid little attention to his chief's adoption of a young and unknown man of eighteen, although the consul had hoped to be made Caesar's heir himself. But Octavian was no ordinary young man. Caesar had paid sporadic attention to him and provided for his education. But he too could have had little idea of his qualities, having had little opportunity for personal contact with him. Octavian was known to be sickly and he had had little military experience. His father's family was an obscure one, and if he had not been adopted by Caesar, he would have been regarded as an Italian rather than a true Roman. At the time of Caesar's death he had been undergoing training in preparation for accompanying the dictator on his Parthian campaign.

But Octavian in fact possessed certain personal assets of his own which were in most respects wholly contrary to those of Caesar, and would probably have failed to rouse the latter's admiration if he had known of them. Octavian had political gifts of the first order, a natural tact and understanding of people, an appreciation of their strengths and weaknesses, including his own, and he seems to have been entirely free from the arrogance that was the undoing of his great-uncle. At the same time he had great personal courage, and at this period in his career he could be as ruthless as any of his opponents, with a farsightedness and flexibility in action denied to them.

With an astonishing resolution and grasp of the realities of the situation and of the possible sources for his own power Octavian proceeded to capitalize on his only real asset, the act of adoption in Caesar's will which enabled him to add the names of Caesar to his own. Realizing that Antony had lost the loyalty of some of Caesar's troops by not carrying out his bequests, Octavian proclaimed that he personally would honor them, and indeed he paid some of them out of his own pocket in the name of Caesar. The gamble succeeded. On his arrival in Italy from Greece, where he had been in training, several legions joined him. In due course others deserted to him, even from Antony. Cicero offered him the support of the Senate. Antony, occupied with preparations for the campaign in northern Italy against Decimus Brutus, treated him with disdain, but did not take effective measures against him, and ultimately left for the north. This was Octavian's chance. Cicero delivered a series of orations against Antony (the *Philippics,* so called from their resemblance to the famous speeches delivered by Demosthenes against Philip of Macedon). Antony was declared a public enemy, and the consuls of the year, with the aid of Octavian and his legions, took the field against him. The consuls were killed in the fighting, but Octavian was left in possession of the field. Antony escaped across the Alps, where he defeated Decimus Brutus and recuperated from his losses.

The Senate under Cicero's leadership then repeated the mistake it had made on Pompey's return from the East. Octavian was slighted and refused the consulship on

► chronological chart

The Civil War and establishment of one-man rule
Second Triumvirate—Proscriptions and death of Cicero	B.C.	43
Battle of Philippi—Death of Brutus and Cassius		42
Antony goes to the East		42
Defeat and death of Sextus Pompeius		37
Renewal of triumvirate for five years		37
Battle of Actium		31
Death of Antony and Cleopatra		30

The work of Augustus
Augustus given *proconsulare imperium* and *tribunicia potestas* for life		23
Augustus becomes Pontifex Maximus on death of Lepidus		12
Danube frontier established for empire		15
Rhine frontier accepted after defeat of Varus	A.D.	9
Death of Augustus		14

The successors of Augustus
Reign of Tiberius	14–37
Reign of Caligula (Gaius)	37–41
Reign of Claudius	41–54
Reign of Nero	54–68
Year of the Four Emperors	69
Vespasian and the Flavian dynasty	69–96
Nerva chosen emperor by Senate	96
The "Good Emperors"—Nerva, Trajan, Hadrian, Antoninus Pius, Marcus Aurelius	96–180

technical grounds, while the conspirators, who had now prepared a formidable force in the East, were honored with official commands. But these forces were not in Italy, where Octavian still had his loyal and victorious legions, which he did not hesitate to use against the Senate. Rebuffed by the Senate, Octavian decided to make advances to Antony and to Lepidus, who still had troops under his command which could not be ignored. The three met in northern Italy, and on the first day of the year 42 B.C. began a triumvirate which, unlike the first private agreement of 60 B.C., was proclaimed the official government of Rome.

The first act of the Triumvirate was the proscription of three hundred senators and two thousand knights. While the private vengeance of the triumvirs was sated against the murderers of Caesar and their own political enemies, the chief purpose of the proscriptions seems to have been to secure money for the necessary campaign against Marcus Brutus and Cassius. Estates of the proscribed were confiscated and the proceeds used to recruit an army. Even this was insufficient, and the triumvirs resorted to arbitrary requisitions and forced loans. But at last the army was ready, and in the brief campaign of Philippi, Brutus and Cassius were defeated and committed suicide. The credit lay mostly with Antony, for Octavian showed poor generalship and was intermittently confined to his bed by sickness.

There was now only one formidable enemy left, Sextus Pompeius, who had a fleet of ships active in the Mediterranean with which he was able to threaten and at times cut off the grain supply of Rome. Antony had allied himself with him before the Triumvirate, and afterward tried to use him against Octavian; and even Octavian several times was forced into an agreement with him. It was not until 37 B.C. that Octavian, by then in sole command in Italy, was able to dispose of this naval menace and restore Italy to normal life.

After Philippi (42 B.C.), Antony, still the leading partner in the Triumvirate, was given the chief command in the East to undertake the Parthian campaign projected by Caesar, while Octavian had to be content with Spain, and Lepidus with Africa. Control in Italy was divided between Antony and Octavian. But Octavian did not find it necessary to go personally to Spain and was actually present for several years in Italy, while Antony left for the East. His absence from Rome proved to be the older man's undoing.

It will never be known whether it was the infatuation of Antony for Cleopatra, queen of Egypt, that destroyed them both, or whether Antony had a coherent and potentially successful plan for an Eastern Roman Empire with its capital at Alexandria, in the most prosperous area of the empire. But it is certain that his absence from Italy during the crucial period of his rivalry with Octavian presented the latter with an opportunity for the display of his unique political gifts, which at this moment in history were more necessary than any possible military talents. Octavian had at least one first-rate general in Agrippa, but it was not Agrippa's talents that won Caesar's nephew the empire. His gradual ascendancy over his rival was due to his building of an effective political party loyal to himself, and to an unexampled use of propaganda to which Antony had laid himself open by his own policy.

Cleopatra had become queen of Egypt in her own right when her brother (and husband) Ptolemy had been killed in the time of Julius Caesar.[1] But her country's independence was only nominal while the Romans ruled the Hellenistic world. She was a woman of great ability as well as beauty, she was thoroughly conversant with Roman politics, and she had unbounded ambition. A useful asset was a son Caesarion, who was presumed to be the son also of Julius Caesar, and therefore a real rival for Octavian, who was only the adopted son of the dictator. She was not, however, of Egyptian ancestry, being descended on both sides from Ptolemy Soter, the general of Alexander who had taken Egypt after the untimely death of his master. She was therefore a Macedonian princess who happened to be queen of Egypt. But the Roman people looked upon her as an Oriental, an Egyptian, and there is no doubt that the vast majority of the Roman people were made to believe by Octavian that she was a foreigner who had captivated Antony and charmed him out of his senses.

Antony met her first at Tarsus when he set out on his Parthian campaign. He followed her to Alexandria, and thereafter with brief intervals of military activity which was far from successful, and occasional visits to Italy to renew his alliance with Octavian, he remained in Egypt, formally marrying Cleopatra and divorcing Octavia, the sister of Octavian, whom he had married in 40 B.C. He proclaimed Caesarion as "King of Kings," joint ruler of the East with Cleopatra, while kingdoms were also given to her two children by Antony. This procedure was not in itself unprecedented. Many Roman territories for years to come were ruled by "client kings," nominally independent, with many real duties to perform but under the overlordship of Rome. Herod the Great held such a position in Judaea at the time of the birth of Jesus. But it was easy for Octavian to represent these administrative arrangements as gifts of Antony to his lover and to frighten the Romans with stories that An-

[1] Soon after the death of this brother, she had married another younger brother, but after a short time had him murdered.

tony intended one day to conquer Rome itself with the aid of Egyptian resources, and to make Cleopatra queen of the Roman Empire with himself as king. Italy would be dethroned from her proud position as the seat of empire.

It should be remembered that Egypt possessed vast resources, but its troops were now Roman. Antony could not rely upon foreign or Oriental troops alone in any trial of strength with Octavian. It was essential to him to keep both officers and men loyal to himself, or they would desert to the enemy; and not all his superior generalship could help him against Octavian if he had no troops to support it.

Evidently Octavian saw that this was his supreme chance. He did not dare to challenge Antony for many years, during which he was patiently building up his own strength in Italy. Though Antony was suspicious, he also could no longer afford to quarrel with his rival, and the Triumvirate was always formally renewed until the end of 33 B.C.

Antony then made his bid for power in Rome, but now it was too late. Octavian had the support of the people, inflamed against Antony by the publication of his acts in the East, colored by the young triumvir's own interpretation of them. And though perhaps even a majority of the Senate still supported Antony, they soon began to desert to what was clearly to be the winning side. The conclusion was by this time inevitable. Cleopatra dared not let Antony venture too far from Egypt lest he make terms with Octavian which would be insupportable for her. On the other hand, if she accompanied Antony in a military attack on Octavian, then the Roman troops would believe the propaganda of Octavian that Antony had fallen victim to the wiles of an Oriental princess. The naval battle of Actium, therefore, in 31 B.C., such as it was, was a foregone conclusion. The bulk of Antony's forces deserted him, and shortly afterward both he and Cleopatra committed suicide.

Octavian was now in all but name the supreme ruler of the Roman world. That he

had matured greatly and that his early ruthlessness had been softened can already be seen by his immediate acts. There were no more proscriptions. Where the triumvirs had mercilessly expropriated land in Italy for Caesar's veterans, Octavian now gave his veterans land outside Italy. The administrative arrangements of Antony in the East he disturbed as little as possible, though Egypt was annexed as his personal property. A subservient but perhaps also grateful Senate, purged of some of its less reliable members, a few years later voted Octavian the title of Augustus, by which he will henceforth be known in this book. One-man rule had begun, and the new ruler was faced with the enormous task of making it permanent, in spite of the five-hundred-year tradition which had been too strong for all previous aspirants.

▶ The problems facing Augustus and his solutions

THE SCOPE OF THE PROBLEMS

The magnitude and scope of the problems facing the young ruler (he had been born in 63 B.C. and was thus thirty-two at the time of the battle of Actium) can hardly be overestimated. The old Roman Republic had clearly failed to live up to the responsibilities of empire, and had collapsed from its own weaknesses. Yet some form of government must replace it which was capable of enduring. And this government, whatever it might be, must also be able to keep under control the vast territories which had fallen to Roman arms during the previous three centuries. Rome had a responsibility to them also. It was impossible simply to decree their freedom and independence, even if the idea had ever occurred to Augustus. Their earlier forms of government had been destroyed beyond recall and could not be restored by a mere imperial fiat. In the last century of the republic the governors of the provinces had been political appointees of the Senate, anxious only to make their fortunes and return to Rome. By corruption and extortion they had advanced themselves; moreover, they were in league with the equestrian class of Rome which had milked the provinces for the sake of its own financial interests. The provinces had suffered abominably from this regular regime, and in many cases had been driven into bankruptcy by the more recent civil wars and irregular extortions by would-be rulers of Rome. There was little encouragement to honesty or efficiency, qualities rarely found in the governors. Was it possible for Augustus to reward these qualities and so improve the provincial system that they would become the rule rather than the exception?

We have seen that the enrollment of volunteer armies by Marius had led directly to the fall of the republic, since the troops relied upon their generals for pay and pensions, and their loyalty was given to these generals rather than to Rome. Moreover the various armies had swollen to such an extent in the civil wars that there were probably at least half a million men under arms at the time of the battle of Actium. Augustus had to consider what was the real purpose of an army in the Roman Empire, where the various legions should be stationed, how they were to occupy themselves during peacetime, how they could be persuaded to be loyal to Rome rather than to generals; and yet at the same time the armies must continue to have those professional military virtues, the absence of which in the earlier armies had compelled Marius to introduce long-term volunteer service.

Behind the great political and administrative problems was the ever-present social and economic background. Rome was not a great manufacturing city, not even a trading center of importance comparable to its size and population. There were far too many people in Rome unable to make a living and requiring public support. Yet these men were citizens and possessed the right to vote. The votes of this urban proletariat had always been for sale to the highest bidder in the last century of the republic. Could they be made into a self-respecting citizenry by any means available to a capable administrator? How could the numerous slaves live side by side with a free citizenry without depressing wages? In spite of the fertility of much of the soil, Italy had never really recovered from the depredations of Hannibal nearly two centuries earlier. The small estates had been swallowed by senators and capitalists and made into large specialized agricultural units worked usually by slaves under overseers. Moreover, the small landholders who survived suffered from chronic insecurity of tenure, their properties often being sequestrated for the benefit of veterans. And throughout the length and breadth of Italy, especially near Rome, rich men built their villas, too often neglecting the land itself and its cultivation.

The cleavage between rich and poor had undermined the old Roman traditional virtues, and the search for ever-increasing luxury among the upper classes had replaced the stern frugality of the earlier republic. Family life in the upper classes had almost disappeared, with divorce to be had for the asking and marriage used for political and financial advancement. The birth rate among the free Romans had naturally been declining. Was it possible to arrest this process, at least the decay of public morality, even if the ancient virtues had disappeared forever?

These were a few of the problems with which Augustus had to contend. If he did not solve them all, at least he perceived their existence, and made an attempt to solve them. And the organization of an empire which endured for many centuries, the most enduring indeed that the Western world has yet seen, is almost entirely his work. The essential administrative structure was built by him, though the conquests themselves were bequeathed to him by the Roman conquerors of the republic.

THE WORK OF AUGUSTUS

The establishment of a legitimate government

The most difficult problem of all was undoubtedly the reorganization of the government: and it was the most fundamental. Julius Caesar's inability to make any constructive contribution to this problem marks his inferiority to his successor as a statesman. Not even a provincial reorganization, the establishment of an equitable system of taxation, nor the enlargement of the conception of Roman citizenship, all of which were in the mind of Julius and well within his capacity, would have been of any permanent value without a governmental system which was capable of controlling the empire and which was at the same time acceptable to the people. Any dictatorship or arbitrary military rule can be cut short by assassination, as Caesar's own career had shown. It was a measure of the genius of Augustus that he made his government both acceptable and legitimate. Though he did not solve permanently the method of succession, this may only be because, as will be discussed later, the problem may well be insoluble within the framework of absolute monarchy.

According to the tradition believed by the Romans, Rome had existed as a city for more than seven hundred years. For almost five hundred it had been free and self-governing. Though occasionally defeated in individual battles, it had never lost a war and had never been compelled to sign a peace with an undefeated enemy. For five hundred years magistrates had been elected and the noblest of the citizens had sat in the Senate and given their advice to the magistrates. It was a body of incomparable prestige, even though in the last century, often through its own incompetence, it had been forced to bow to arbitrary military men with armies at their backs. And the people of Rome had accepted its supremacy and shared in the glories won by their arms under its leadership. Though Rome was not a state, the Romans were truly a people, and Roman citizenship was prized by everyone who possessed it; and those who did not possess it valued it and sought to win it for themselves. During all these years the name of *rex* or king had been detested. The Romans no less than the Greeks regarded it as an office fit only for barbarians.

Yet Augustus realized that he must be king in fact, even though he did not hold

Bust of Augustus at the prime of his manhood.
(COURTESY BRITISH MUSEUM)

the title. It would never have occurred to him —nor indeed would it have been possible— to have ruled the empire with its many different peoples of varying degrees of culture, through any kind of representative government. The empire was too vast and heterogeneous for any such experiment. But if the government had been returned to Senate and people as under the republic, the same weaknesses would have led to the same breakdown of government. Only a monarch could hope to hold it together.

Augustus solved his dilemma by one of the great creative compromises of history, a species of legal fiction which bridged the gulf between the fallen republic and the monarchy which had to come. In time the republic was forgotten, the monarchy supplanted it, and the necessity for the fiction disappeared. But in the competent hands of Augustus, who understood it, the reasons for it, and the behavior required of him to maintain it, the fiction worked. Though thinking Romans of course knew that he was the sole ruler and that his power was ultimately based on the army and the treasury, nevertheless to the mass of the people the republic still survived. They felt at home in the new Roman state. The magistrates were still elected by the same procedure as before, though no candidate would even have run for office without the approval of Augustus; the Senate and the Assemblies still met for debate and legislation; and though there was now a Princeps, or first citizen, a title and office unknown to the republic, he was not obtrusive, he scrupulously respected all the old republican forms, and his public and private life were beyond reproach in the best tradition of the early days of the Roman Republic.

Augustus confined the offices held by himself personally to the minimum required for his possession of the reality of power. He had a permanent proconsular military power (*proconsulare imperium*) conferred upon him, giving him supreme command of the army; he was granted a permanent civil power as previously exercised by the tribunes (*tribunicia potestas*), which gave him the power to introduce legislation and veto it. He became chief priest (*Pontifex Maximus*), giving him authority in religious matters; but, characteristically, he did not assume this office until the death of Lepidus, who had been ousted from his position as triumvir in 36 B.C. and consoled for his loss of power by appointment to this honored position. Occasionally Augustus allowed himself to be elected consul in the early years of his rule, feeling that he needed the civil as well as the military power inherent in this office. But consuls, praetors, aediles, and even tribunes were elected as before to perform the specific duties of these offices under the guidance of the Princeps.

Augustus tried his best to maintain the dignity of the Senate. He encouraged it to give him advice, and he presided over it personally as *Princeps Senatus*. The judicial functions of the Senate were maintained and even increased under his rule. By setting aside certain provinces to be ruled by ex-magistrates under the direct control of the Senate and not of himself, he made it worth while moving through the full sequence of offices (*cursus honorum*) to the exalted position of consul. The Senate also had its own treasury. As under the Constitution of Sulla, the quaestors on being elected automatically became senators, though under Augustus their duties lay primarily in the provinces. From the equestrian order he recruited a body of public officials, paid out of the imperial treasury (*fiscus*) but with the same duties as taxgatherers and tax assessors that they had performed in their own interests under the republic. Under later emperors these men became part of the imperial civil service.

When it was proposed that he should be worshiped as a god (his adoptive father had already been deified), he refused the honor, but permitted his Genius to be worshiped instead. According to old Roman belief every man had a guiding Genius, and the Genius of the head of a family guided the fortunes of that family. In allowing a cult to be set up to his Genius, Augustus was therefore directing Roman worship toward the state of which he was now the controlling Genius. Later this indeed became the worship of the living emperor as god, a state cult to which all had to subscribe on pain of treason. But Augustus in his lifetime never claimed to be a god except in the Hellenistic world, which had for centuries been accustomed to a divine monarchy.

The greatest difficulty inherent in his position as sole ruler, the difficulty of the succession, Augustus never solved. There were only a few possibilities open to him. Since the Roman ruler had to be a supremely capable man, the vagaries of heredity made this natural and traditional method of succession dangerous for the welfare of the state. Augustus himself had no sons, and his one daughter Julia was the scandal of Rome, from which Augustus was ultimately forced to banish her. He had grandsons and several relatives by marriage, but all died before him. He also had two stepsons, both extremely competent men, the younger of

Mausoleum dedicated to Gaius and Julius Caesar, grandsons of Augustus who died before him, to the great grief of the ruler, who had hoped that his position would be inherited by members of his family (St. Rémy, France).

the right was an empty one, never independently exercised during the empire except when the Senate was called upon for an election by its military masters. So for the first two dynasties the succession was hereditary within the Julian and Flavian families. The so-called "Good Emperors," Nerva, Trajan, Hadrian, Antoninus Pius, and Marcus Aurelius (A.D. 96–180), were all childless except the last-named, and adopted the best men they could find in the empire as their successors. Marcus, however, chose his son, who happened to be incompetent and a wastrel, and under him the empire declined precipitately. It always remained true that the ultimate power to choose an emperor rested with the army. But there was not only one army. The legions stationed in different provinces favored their own particular leaders, and as early as the death of Nero in A.D. 68 these legions joined battle with each other on behalf of their respective choices.

If, therefore, an emperor chose his successor and granted him military power while he was still alive, then this successor would probably accede to the throne without difficulty as long as he had taken the precaution to promise suitable bonuses to the army. When, however, an emperor died before nominating his successor and without having transferred to anyone a part of his power, a free-for-all usually resulted, and the most powerful army leader won the throne. If the hereditary principle had been strictly observed, as in modern monarchies, there would have been no doubt in anyone's mind as to who was the rightful succcessor. But in that case the risk of having an incompetent ruler, and the chance of the death of an emperor without sons, would have to be run. Even under a strict hereditary monarchy, the possibility of a civil war over the succession is not avoided altogether, but it is greatly minimized. On the whole, therefore, it would seem that the hesitancy of Augustus to face the problem of succession was inevitable in the circumstances of his time, and the combination of adoption and heredity was as good a choice as any available to him.

whom was accidentally killed while on campaign in Germany. The surviving stepson, Tiberius, did indeed succeed him, but not by virtue of his own relationship to the Princeps. Tiberius was forced first to divorce his wife and marry the profligate Julia. Later Augustus adopted him as his son, and conferred on him the two great powers held by himself as Princeps. So on his death there was no doubt as to who had been designated as his successor; and Tiberius, already possessing proconsular and tribunician power, could have mastered any possible rival with ease.

But the principle of adoption or heredity was not yet established. Theoretically the Senate was entitled to elect the ruler; but

The reorganization of the provinces

The reorganization of the provinces was a further example of Augustus' efficient use of such opportunities as existed. He saw at once that it was not necessary to keep armies in every province, as had been the custom in the later years of the republic. Those that had long been pacified and had no frontiers to be defended against barbarians needed no more than enough troops to ensure local discipline. These provinces (see the map for details) he entrusted to the Senate, which was given the power of appointing governors and administering the tax monies. These provinces, as under the republic, were reserved for ex-magistrates, and constituted a reward for those who had progressed through the cursus honorum. In addition the arrangement gave the Senate some real work to do and served to maintain its prestige as a body. And though Augustus exercised a final supervisory jurisdiction over these provinces, he left them largely to themselves. Those provinces, however, which needed legions of trained troops, and whose frontiers had continually to be defended against enemies, were under his direct control, which he exercised though the appointment of salaried legates, personally responsible to him, who could hold their positions as long as they proved efficient. This arrangement gave them the opportunity to gain a real knowledge of their provinces and to win the loyalty of their troops, but in later times it proved a serious danger to the state in the event of a disputed succession to the throne. Egypt, as the richest province, the primary source of the grain supply for Rome and Italy, was given a special status in keeping with its history as well as its present importance. As in the past, the ruler was divine and the owner of all the land. Augustus, therefore, was a Pharaoh in Egypt, with all the privileges of this office, although he did not perform his duties as king-god there himself, but entrusted them to a prefect of equestrian rank, responsible to himself. The country, however, was farmed as an imperial estate rather than as a province with a certain degree of self-government, and its revenues accrued directly to the ruler. No one of senatorial rank was permitted within the territory without the permission of the Princeps. Finally, a number of kingdoms on the outskirts of the empire were permitted self-government

Triumphal arch of Augustus, set up near the present St. Rémy de Provence, in southern France.

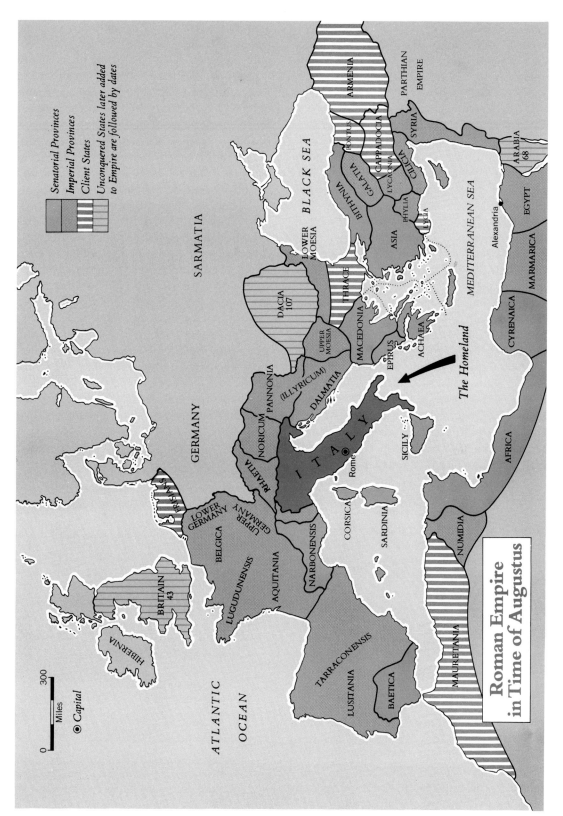

Roman Empire in Time of Augustus

Senatorial Provinces
Imperial Provinces
Client States
Unconquered States later added to Empire are followed by dates

Capital

Miles
0   300

ATLANTIC OCEAN

HIBERNIA

BRITAIN 43

FRISIA

GERMANY

LOWER GERMANY

UPPER GERMANY

BELGICA

LUGUDUNENSIS

AQUITANIA

NARBONENSIS

RHAETIA

NORICUM

PANNONIA

(ILLYRICUM)

DALMATIA

TARRACONENSIS

LUSITANIA

BAETICA

CORSICA

SARDINIA

SICILY

ITALY

Rome

The Homeland

MAURETANIA

NUMIDIA

AFRICA

CYRENAICA

MARMARICA

EGYPT

Alexandria

MEDITERRANEAN SEA

EPIRUS

ACHAEA

MACEDONIA

UPPER MOESIA

THRACE

LOWER MOESIA

DACIA 107

SARMATIA

BLACK SEA

BITHYNIA

ASIA

GALATIA

PAPHLAGONIA

CAPPADOCIA

LYCAONIA

PAMPHYLIA

LYCIA

CILICIA

PONTUS

ARMENIA

SYRIA

PARTHIAN EMPIRE

ARABIA 68

351

under their kings, who became clients or vassals of Rome.

The provinces of the Roman Empire had always been made up of more or less self-governing municipalities, city-states on the Greek model, together with a number of other communities whose position had been defined by treaty, usually without full self-government. Augustus encouraged as much local administration as was compatible with the imperial relationship, thus saving the burden of direct administration. The corrupt tax system of the republican period was not abolished by Augustus, probably for lack of any alternative method of collection. His successors, especially Claudius and Hadrian, developed a regular civil service which gradually supplanted the tax companies. Meanwhile the abuses of the system were checked through more efficient supervision by the Princeps, even in the senatorial provinces. Penalties for extortion were severe, and even senatorial governors were far too much under control to be able to lend the efficient aid to the tax farmers that had been the custom under the republic in its last years. And the nucleus of the later civil service was formed with the inclusion of treasury officials in the staff of the governors.

The entire system of provinces was reorganized thoroughly by Augustus, with new boundaries, chosen for the sake of efficient administration and defense (see map). In the process a number of minor conquests had to be undertaken to round out many territories which had been acquired haphazardly by the republic according to the needs of the moment. Augustus always hoped to make the northern boundary the Elbe rather than the Rhine, as shorter and more easily defensible. Such a boundary, however, would have necessitated the conquest of a large part of Germany. Though progress with this conquest was made in the earlier years of his reign, his armies suffered a severe defeat toward the end of his life, and the conquest was abandoned. The Rhine became the northwestern frontier, while Augustus maintained the Danube in the East, refusing to move into Dacia to the north of the Danube

(the modern Rumania) on the grounds that it was indefensible. This policy was maintained until Trajan (A.D. 98–117), who not only took Dacia but engaged in extensive wars in the East, the spoils of which had to be abandoned by his successors, as Augustus had predicted. The empire was held together by the great Roman roads, which were constantly extended throughout the imperial period and over which the imperial post traveled, bringing news to the emperor and his instructions in return.

The provincial system proved to be the most enduring of the reforms of Augustus. Whatever happened at Rome, the life of the provinces went on much as usual, under good rulers and bad alike. Only when the burden of taxation was heavily increased and prosperity declined in the third century A.D. with the continuous civil and foreign wars was the strength of the provinces slowly sapped. But while the Roman peace (*Pax Romana*) gave them a respite from war they had never previously enjoyed, their prosperity increased and with it the ability to pay the taxes which ensured the continuance of that rule.

Two bronze plates of a military diploma granting citizenship to honorably discharged soldiers and their wives. (COURTESY THE METROPOLITAN MUSEUM OF ART)

Augustus himself, as has been said, was an Italian rather than a Roman, and always regarded Italy as the center of his dominions, the homeland with special privileges, with Rome as first the capital of Italy and then of the empire. The inhabitants of Rome, however, were no longer exempt from all taxation as had been the case under the republic for all Roman citizens. But their taxes always remained lighter than those of the provinces. Every native freeborn Italian was a Roman citizen with all the privileges attached to the position. The provincials could achieve Roman citizenship, but Augustus regarded it as a privilege to be earned and not a right to which they were entitled by birth. This policy was gradually abandoned by his successors until in A.D. 212 citizenship was granted to every free inhabitant of the empire.

The reform of the army

By virtue of his proconsular power the Princeps was naturally commander in chief of the army. Augustus, drawing upon the experience of his predecessors and especially of his adoptive father, laid down a permanent basis for recruitment and for the composition of the army, which survived in its essentials throughout the whole empire. The regular troops or legionaries were drawn from Italians and the most Romanized provincials, who received citizenship on enlistment if they did not already possess it. They served for twenty years, receiving a regular salary and a pension on retirement. In addition to these were auxiliary troops who received citizenship only on retirement. These were also salaried men, but drawn from the less Romanized provinces, and serving primarily within these provinces. Their officers also were originally drawn from the same territory, but later, after it had been shown that these troops were capable of rebellion in the interests of their own provinces, Italian officers were substituted. The armies were by no means always engaged in active warfare, although the legions might at any time be transferred to a danger spot on a distant frontier. During the first two centuries, however, the general practice was for the legionaries to live in camps behind permanent fortifications which were built by themselves. There were strategic roads to be built, ditches and moats to be dug, walls to be erected, and many of the troops necessarily became skilled artisans as well as soldiers, not unlike the modern corps of Army Engineers. These men, holding Roman citizenship, speaking Latin, imbued with Roman tradition, enjoying even on the frontiers the comforts of Roman civilization, such as warm baths, naturally mingled with the peoples among whom they were stationed, and served therefore as an important instrument for the Romanization of the empire. The army, however, in its own estimation, was rarely well enough paid in proportion to its value to the state. Its chronic dissatisfaction and its sporadic insistence on bonuses gave ambitious generals the opportunity to make lavish promises in exchange for support of their candidacies to the throne.

In Italy itself no regular troops were stationed except the Praetorian Guard, which in the early centuries was drawn from Italians alone. This was a body of about nine thousand men under its own prefect and living in special barracks just outside the city of Rome. Being the only body of troops with easy access to the capital, it was often instrumental in the elevation of an emperor, and its prefect at all times wielded an authority far greater than could be justified by his actual position. As early as the reign of Tiberius the praetorian prefect, in the absence of the Princeps himself on the island of Capri, was the virtual ruler of Rome, with actual power quite sufficient to dominate the Senate. Nevertheless at this time the power of the Princeps was hardly to be challenged if he cared to exercise it, and a letter of Tiberius to the Senate with a concealed threat was enough to ensure the fall of the ambitious prefect.

Social and economic policy

Rome had never been an important industrial center, and even as a commercial

Reconstruction, by the Metropolitan Museum of Art, of a bedroom from the southern Italian city of Boscoreale, which was buried by the famous eruption of Vesuvius in A.D. 79. Note the frescoes on the three walls. The room is furnished with authentic pieces from the same city dating from the period of the eruption. (COURTESY THE METROPOLITAN MUSEUM OF ART)

city its usefulness was impaired by its lack of a good harbor. The muddy Tiber had constantly to be dredged to keep the harbor of Ostia at its mouth open for commerce at all. Puteoli, where Paul landed on his journey to Rome, became the regular seaport for Roman trade, and developed into a great city, largely peopled by Greeks and other foreigners, who remained the leaders in maritime commerce as under the republic. But in spite of the absence of large-scale industry, there were innumerable small manufacturing shops in Rome and throughout Italy. For centuries Italy was the chief manufacturer for the Western world, though its products were far surpassed in quality by those of Alexandria and the East. Nevertheless, the Italian balance of trade was always

unfavorable, if Rome is included with Italy, since Rome remained a parasite on the economy.

Augustus did not take any active interest in the economy as such. Except for Egypt, industry in the Roman Empire was overwhelmingly in private hands. There was no state industry, nor monopolies of the kind that later developed in the Eastern Roman Empire of Constantinople. But indirectly the establishment of the Pax Romana, with its network of roads and safe transportation, increased prosperity for all classes throughout the empire. And Augustus used the tax money that came from the provinces to pay for an enormous program of public works, chiefly temples and other public buildings, gardens, and baths; and in this the majority of those emperors who had the money available and were not too heavily engaged in unproductive warfare followed his example. These public works provided a market for numerous products made by small industry throughout the empire, and direct work for the large army of unemployed in Rome itself. The provincial municipalities also engaged in similar programs on their account, and it became a matter of civic pride for wealthy citizens to improve their cities with gifts of parks, gardens, temples, and other public buildings.

But social and political conditions throughout the empire and especially in Rome itself militated against any real and lasting prosperity for all. In a world without machines, hand labor must be efficient indeed to produce any surplus for luxuries over and above the ordinary daily needs. Agriculture, the backbone of the imperial economy, improved in efficiency, it is true, with the introduction of rotation of crops and the use of leguminous plants. But it was severely hampered by many disabilities, especially absentee ownership; and it had to feed an enormous urban population. The real life of the Roman Empire, as life had been in the Hellenistic world, was concentrated in the cities, and every encouragement was given by the authorities to create ever more and more municipalities. The inhab-

The excavated site of the old Roman harbor of Ostia, at the mouth of the Tiber. The harbor constantly had to be dredged to keep it free of silt, but was still used as late as the third century A.D., thereafter being abandoned. It is one of the most studied of ancient sites, since it provides an excellent opportunity for appreciating the layout of an ancient city. (INGE MORATH, MAGNUM)

itants of the cities never produced by their inefficient industrial techniques goods proportionate to the large number of people engaged in their production, and these goods in any case were luxuries rather than essentials. Moreover, there were large numbers of people who did no productive work at all, but lived on the proceeds of farms and small industrial establishments owned but not worked by them. In addition there was a growing army of public servants engaged in important work but not contributing directly to production. The reason why it was possible for so many men and women to be idle from the point of view of production was that there was also a large army of slaves, manumitted slaves, and freemen, all of whom consumed far less than they produced. Most slaves in the imperial period could look forward to being manumitted (freed) by their masters as a reward for good service, and in many cases they could earn enough to buy their own freedom. On ordinary farms the slave was also to some degree protected as a valuable property and at least fed enough to live on. But slaves engaged in mining and contract labor were in a different category. They cost less to buy than domestic and agricultural slaves, whose skills were appreciated. The work of these men and women was supervised by overseers who drove them mercilessly to obtain the maximum work from them. In the last days of the republic enormous numbers of slaves were captured and sold (Caesar sold 53,000 as the result of one campaign alone, the proceeds from slave sales forming an important item in his estate), but with the decline of foreign wars this source gradually became less productive. More slaves at most periods of the empire were probably obtained by natural increase (the child of slave parents being a slave himself) than by capture.

Nevertheless, in the time of Augustus a large part of the population of Rome and indeed of the whole empire was made up of slaves who, as always, served to depress the wages of free labor, which had to compete with them. But at the same time the low wage rate for free workers also served to promote the manumission of slaves, since a slaveowner not only had to buy and support his slave throughout his lifetime, but also by custom had to allow him to keep some of his earnings for himself. On the other hand, a free laborer could be laid off work in slack times and left to fend for himself, and his employer had to make no initial investment in him. Economic causes therefore worked in the direction of free labor rather than slave, and slaves became fewer. Furthermore, with the decline of prosperity in the upper slaveholding classes, fewer men could keep the armies of domestic slaves retained for prestige purposes in the early days of the empire. But, however socially desirable the freeing of slaves may seem to us, it should be emphasized that it was only because free labor was so cheap that slavery declined, and that emancipation did not result in any economic improvement in the lot of the ex-slave or of the laborer in general.

For social and political reasons Augustus attempted to place some restrictions on the manumission of slaves, as part of his general effort to make Roman citizenship a privilege and prevent the Orientalizing of the Roman populace. But it seems to have been impossible to halt the natural process by imperial decree.

For the poor of the city of Rome, who were grossly underemployed, he found no remedy beyond his public works programs and a continuance of the republican practice of providing them with cheap or free food. In addition he, and more particularly the later emperors, provided lavish public spectacles to keep them amused. This program was called by the later satirist Juvenal "bread and circuses." Since the elections were arranged and laws were now really made indirectly by the Princeps, the Roman people, so powerful in the last century of the republic when their votes were necessary for the election of magistrates and army officers, lost their power. Riots could be dangerous on occasion, but they could now be easily suppressed. On the other hand, all the rulers were anxious to keep the people as contented as possible, and tried to provide for their needs. Augustus, recognizing the irresponsibility that went with their unemployment and dependence on imperial handouts, tried to give them some status in the community and in their own eyes by incorporating them formally into an order, the plebeian as distinct from the equestrian and senatorial orders. But since they had no real duties in addition to their privileges, it is probable that the gesture remained an empty formality. We are not told what the plebeians themselves thought about it.

The city in the time of Augustus was efficiently policed, and a fire brigade was established, first under elected officials and then under appointees of the Princeps.

In agriculture Augustus strove to increase the number of small farmers. He gave security of tenure to those who had farms already, and he made an effort to instill a real love of the Italian countryside into the free peasantry. In this effort he was ably assisted by the poet-farmer Vergil, whose *Georgics* are a long paean of praise of the rural life. But the tendencies of the time were against Augustus. It was difficult to arrest the growth of large farms and estates which could be more economically worked than the small unit. The exodus of farmers to the cities which had been such an important feature of the last years of the republic continued. Not all the praise of the rural life could prevail against the hard necessities of making a living. Though there was, as has been seen, chronic underemployment in Rome, at least the citizen could scrape a living somehow, and free bread and circuses were available, as nowhere else. Not until the Industrial Revolution in modern times did it become possible to work farms efficiently with a small labor force, and at the same time keep millions employed in the large cities through the production of machine-made goods and the provision of multifarious services. The problem of Rome itself was almost certainly insoluble by Augustus, however great his power and intelligence.

Cultural and religious policy

There is no doubt that Augustus thoroughly understood the Roman ideal and the Roman tradition. Though in his earlier days he was no model of virtue, in his principate he strove by example and legislation to revive the old Roman virtues which had made her great. Seriousness, hard work, frugality, piety, family solidarity, public spirit—these were the traditional virtues, and Augustus did not believe they had disappeared forever. The desire for luxury and ostentation, overeating and overdrinking, skepticism, public and private immorality had been no part of the earlier Roman tradition. But it was quite another matter to try to put the clock back and revive the old virtues against all the cultural pressures of the age. Still less was it possible to do this by legislation, although Augustus has had some distinguished successors in the attempt in many times and places. His cultural and religious policy, therefore, though partially successful in some directions, must on the whole be accounted a failure. Trying to restore the sanctity of private life, he decreed compulsory marriage at a certain age, and for all citizens. Later, when he was forced to modify this decree he laid special disabilities on the unmarried and he offered preference to certain state offices to fathers with three children. He legislated on the size of houses, and the quantity of food and drink to be consumed at banquets. He even encouraged informers against those who offended against his laws. Naturally these laws were extremely unpopular, especially among the upper and middle classes who could afford luxuries, and they were completely ineffective against the other social evils at which they were directed. And, as far as we know, bachelors remained as numerous as ever, and the birth rate was not increased.

The more positive aspects of his policy, however, seem to have had some effect. He tried to revive some of the old Italian rural religious festivals, and regenerate the old primitive religion of the countryside, which had never altogether died out. And he undoubtedly succeeded in reviving patriotism and a reverence for the Roman heritage, as evidenced by the success of his great patriotic poets, especially Vergil and Horace, and even of the old republican historian Livy, whose history exalts the Roman virtues at the expense, it is feared, of historical accuracy. The court poets and writers, dealt with in the next chapter, for the first time found a patron in Maecenas, who subsidized and encouraged them with the full backing of the Princeps. But, above all, the imperial cult really did take hold of the people and persisted for several centuries in the form of emperor or state worship. It does not seem to have been the empty formality that we, with our higher religions concerned with the relationship between man and God, might have expected. It was building on traditional foundations, both the reverence paid to the gods of the household and family, and to the Genius of the father of the family. What Augustus did was enlarge the conception to include the whole Roman family and state, and institute rituals designed to capture this reverence for the protective deities of the state and the ruler himself. In addition he exalted the older gods Apollo, Mars, and, above all, Jupiter, building great temples for them in their capacity of protectors of the state. The new era of peace was his greatest helper in the program; for it did seem to all at this time that the gods had indeed had the protection of Rome within their care, and brought her through a long age of civil war and anarchy to a secure haven. And though Livy's history was designed to show that the gods had always protected those Romans who had kept their virtue, every reader could see for himself that it was for this purpose, for the purpose of bringing into being the Roman Empire, that the Romans had been tried and purified—that it was their *destiny* to rule, as Vergil had stated more explicitly in his *Aeneid*, and had always been since the day when Aeneas completed his long journey to Italy and his descendant Romulus laid the foundations of Rome.

Estimate of the achievement of Augustus

It is difficult to find in the records of all history a greater political and administrative genius than the first Princeps of Rome, the "architect of Empire," Augustus Caesar, and there are few who have approached him. He has suffered in comparison with his great-uncle, who was undoubtedly a more impressive personality with more spectacular and captivating qualities. He has also suffered from his biographers in ancient times, who could not appreciate at their true worth his farsightedness and understanding of the real problems involved in the transition from republic to monarchy, and who paid too much attention to minor failures, such as his sumptuary legislation.

He was conservative, cherishing the old virtues and the old institutions, and appreciating their value; and he devised means to continue what seemed good in them. He did not try to set back the clock in his governmental reforms, nor yet leap forward rashly into impossible experiments forbidden by the nature of the times. The most difficult and rare art of the statesman is to see the limits of the possible and pursue only the possible. And his monument was the Roman peace and the Roman Empire, which endured for hundreds of years in the framework which he had invented. The empire did not collapse after his death as did Charlemagne's, nor fall to pieces by military overextension as did Napoleon's.

Augustus had a tremendous job to accomplish in which all his predecessors had failed; and yet once he had achieved supreme power he substituted, almost without friction, a legitimate and acceptable civil government for civil warfare and domestic anarchy. There is a tale that a man was brought before him who had attempted a conspiracy against him. Augustus reasoned with the man, asking him how he proposed to replace him, and succeeded in convincing him of the impossibility of any alternative. Thereupon he forgave the would-be murderer and even promoted him in the public service. Perhaps Augustus was fortunate in that he was still a young man and had many years of life in front of him to make full use of the opportunity with which he had been presented. But he was never a healthy man, and it is one of his titles to greatness that he was able to overcome the handicap. He lived without ostentation, and never let anyone believe that he had any other ambition than to be first citizen in a restored and transformed republic. He is the most eminent disproof in history of the famous dictum of Lord Acton that "all power corrupts, and absolute power corrupts absolutely."

▶ The successors of Augustus

TIBERIUS AND THE DECLINE OF THE SENATE

It is not necessary in a book of this compass to go into detail on the achievements of the successors of Augustus. The reign of Tiberius (A.D. 14–37) was marked by excellent provincial administration but a growing disharmony between the Princeps and the Senate. Our chief authority for this period is the great Roman historian Tacitus, a man of senatorial rank who lived almost a century later, who, in the opinion of many scholars, described the conditions of his own time but placed them earlier in the age of Tiberius, as this was less dangerous to himself. But Tiberius most certainly lacked his step-father's tact, and he was already a morose and disillusioned elderly man when he became Princeps. It was not surprising that the senators for the first time now realized the potentialities for an *imperial* tyranny that had been masked under the principate of Augustus. And many of them began to look back nostalgically to the lost republic, viewing it through rose-colored glasses since few of them had actually experienced it. Brutus and Cassius, the tyrannicides, became their heroes, for they had defended with their lives the dignity of senators. Throughout the reign of Tiberius there were constant intrigues over

the succession, even while his son, later poisoned by the orders of his favorite, the praetorian prefect Sejanus, was still alive. Betrayed by the one man he had trusted, Tiberius countered the opposition to him with new laws against treason, and new rewards for informers, setting a precedent followed by too many of his successors. There were many real conspiracies against him, but, more than anyone else Sejanus, master of Rome when Tiberius retired to Capri for a little peace in his old age, betrayed him; and though Tiberius was strong enough to crush this conspiracy, the aftermath of treason trials and executions was always remembered against him by later historians and posterity.

The position of the Senate was indeed unenviable. It had had a long tradition of power under the republic, and its position even at its worst was always one of dignity. Augustus had given the senators work to do, but there was no doubt that all real power had been taken from them, and they were deeply offended. Tiberius would preside over the Senate; and though even the anti-imperial historian Tacitus admits that, at least in the early part of his reign, he encouraged the senators to speak freely, most of them were careful to catch every sign of approval or disapproval, so that they would not be found on the wrong side, in opposition to the Princeps, with all the danger that this entailed. This subservience wounded them in their dignity. They were forced out of fear to agree, and their true opinions were not valued. As long as any republican tradition remained, as it did at least until the death of Nero, A.D. 68, they were bound to regret their lost freedom, human dignity, and respect. Not all the outward dignity of a special toga could compensate them. Only the Stoics in the reigns to come provided any real resistance to the rulers, since they had a philosophy to sustain them, and at the last a sword to fall upon; and it was no accident that the tyrannous emperors especially singled out the Stoics as their enemies and treated them accordingly.

At last Tiberius died, and was succeeded by Caligula (A.D. 37–41), a young man of no ability and no experience who soon became insane, his insanity revealing itself in an undisguised tyranny and sadistic cruelty. When he was murdered in a praetorian conspiracy he was succeeded by Claudius (A.D. 41–54), an able administrator and student of history who effected many valuable reforms in the provincial administration but was unable to keep order in his own house, being ruled by his successive wives. He was murdered by his last wife, who thus succeeded in securing the succession for her son Nero (A.D. 54–68), who was only the stepson of Claudius. Nero lost no time in getting rid of his stepbrother, who was a real son of Claudius, but for five years he allowed his praetorian prefect Burrus and his tutor Seneca to exercise the actual rule of the empire. Thus the first five years of Nero's administration became proverbial for excellent administration at home and abroad. Then Nero began to show himself as the misfit he was on the throne, a second-rate artist, anxious only for the plaudits of the crowds for his theatrical performances and careless of his administration. The people loved him for his spectacular games and gladiatorial shows, but he degraded the imperial dignity, emptied the treasury, and won only contempt and enmity from the upper classes, contempt which culminated in conspiracies against his life. Thereafter no one in Rome was safe from his vengeance, and especially not his former friends. His tyranny in his last years equaled that of the madman Caligula. When he was overthrown by an open revolt and perished at the hands of a freedman when he lacked courage to take his own life, no provision had been made for the succession and no direct heir remained of the Julian house (called Julian after Julius Caesar). First the commander of the Spanish legions took the throne, then the praetorian prefect, then the commander of the German legions, none surviving the year (A.D. 69). Finally the commander of the Eastern legions, a plebeian general of rural ancestry, gained the throne and restored order.

Vespasian (69–79) ruled sensibly and restored some of its earlier dignity to the principate. He was succeeded by his two sons (the Flavian dynasty), one of whom died after two years, while Domitian, the second son (81–96), a suspicious tyrant but a good administrator, fell to a conspiracy. This was the end of the hereditary principle for nearly a century. For the first time no obvious candidate was available for the throne, and the choice fell into the hands of the Senate, which selected Nerva (96–98), a mild, elderly man whose most important act was the adoption of the best general in the empire as his son. Thus the adoptive principle superseded the hereditary, and the result was the period known as the era of the "Good Emperors." Each of the four emperors who reigned between 98 and 180 was a good administrator, and Trajan (98–117) was a great general, though it is not certain that his policy of enlarging the empire was altogether a wise one. The province of Dacia, north of the Danube, acquired by him, in addition to territories in Asia had to be abandoned before most of the rest of the empire, but not before it had been civilized by the Romans. The old Roman province of Dacia, the present-day Rumania, still has a language based upon Latin. Hadrian (117–138) was one of the ablest of the Roman emperors as an administrator. He it was who systematized the civil service, the most competent body of bureaucrats outside China in the ancient world, recruiting its members almost exclusively from the equestrian order, which was now entirely dependent upon himself. Hadrian also gave impetus to the study and codification of the Roman Law by abolishing the edicts of the annually elected praetors (see the next chapter). By Hadrian's time it was recognized that the word of the emperor was the true source of law for the empire, and it may be said that with Hadrian disappeared the

Bust of the Emperor Antoninus Pius. Note the Greek influence and the careful attention to detail characteristic of this period, as shown in the treatment of hair and beard. (COURTESY THE METROPOLITAN MUSEUM OF ART)

remnants of the old republican tradition. Antoninus Pius (138–161) further improved the law and provided a long reign of almost unbroken peace. Marcus Aurelius (161–180), the Stoic writer of the *Meditations*, was compelled to spend most of his reign defending the empire against barbarian tribes who were threatening the frontiers, but maintained the record of his predecessors in the administration of the empire.

All these emperors were chosen by their predecessors and adopted as their sons. The Augustan title of Princeps, though still formally used, no longer seems appropriate for these absolute rulers. Unfortunately, as has already been mentioned, Marcus Aurelius was not, like the others, childless, and chose as his successor his worthless son Commodus (180–193), whose reign marked the beginning of the serious decline of the empire, as will be narrated in a later chapter. But, whatever the principle of succession used, there was no thought now of restoring the antique republic. The monarchy as an institution had proved itself; the republic was a fit subject only for historical study.

THE PROVINCES IN THE FIRST TWO CENTURIES

The Empire in its first two centuries consisted of a great number of city-states with limited self-government, each controlling a rural area around it. This had been the system in the Near East during the Hellenistic age, and it was taken over intact by Rome. When the Romans organized the West, which had of course never come under Greek influence, they created municipalities on the Italian model. The Roman Empire itself may therefore be thought of as a gigantic federation of city-states under the authority of the capital city of Rome.

For the first two centuries of the Empire little was changed. The cities all had their assemblies, councils, and elected magistrates, but office holding and voting were confined to property holders. Moreover the magistrates were unpaid, and it was a considerable financial burden to serve. When elected they were expected to make a special money donation to the city or provide it with some new public building or monument. Cities indeed competed with one another in this respect, and for well over a century there was no difficulty in obtaining wealthy candidates for office, willing to spend their money for this purpose. Some opportunities for exploiting their position existed, but most of the emperors, especially the Antonines, kept a sharp eye out for irregularities. The lower classes, ruled by a local oligarchy, often suffered from their helpless position and we know of appeals sent by them to the emperors. Whether for the sake of greater efficiency, or simply because the ever-growing imperial bureaucracy needed work to do, the emperors began more and more frequently to interfere in provincial affairs and take over more of the governing functions of local officials and councils. This process reached its culmination in the early fourth and later centuries, as will be discussed in Chapter 14.

Nevertheless Roman rule not only bore lightly on at least the upper and middle classes for at least two centuries, but there were many compensations for all. There was complete freedom of movement and trade throughout the Empire and unbroken peace, as well as a uniform law code for freemen. The eighteenth-century English historian Edward Gibbon's belief that never in the history of mankind, before or afterward, were so many people secure and contented has undoubtedly some justification in fact—even if the lower classes and slaves ruled by an ever-narrower oligarchy with little opportunity to share in the prosperity might have vehemently disagreed with him.

Life in the provinces was rarely affected by the disturbances in the capital. The chief annoyance undoubtedly was the arbitrary increases in taxation necessitated by the spendthrift habits of some of the early emperors, especially Caligula and Nero. Imperial governors usually remained over from one regime to another, and senatorial governors continued to be appointed as before unless the emperor was especially interested in the appointment. The Roman peace was maintained in almost the whole empire without a break. The only power in the first two centuries that presented any danger was the Parthian Empire in the Near East. But it was already on the decline in the second century, and Trajan inflicted several severe defeats upon it, altering the Augustan settlement in this region by annexing several new provinces. But his successor recognized the great difficulty of holding them, and the fact that the expense involved could ill be afforded. For this reason he returned some of the new provinces to client kings. Not until the reign of Marcus Aurelius was the Roman peace seriously threatened by the first movements of barbarians against the frontiers; and even this was of no moment to the interior provinces, save for increases in taxation to pay for the wars.

The first two centuries of the empire were characterized by an increasing centralization of the government, above all through the growth of the bureaucracy or imperial civil service. Hadrian brought every Roman official under direct imperial control, including those in Italy, even in some cases nominating the governors of senatorial provinces, who were in any case by now the prisoners of the bureaucracy provided for them by the emperor. Though the "Good Emperors," including Hadrian, were not personally tyrants, and indeed kept on very good terms with the Senate, being themselves drawn from the senatorial class, their policies tended toward an increasing absolutism which was ultimately recognized by the formal changes in the nature of the monarchy brought about by Diocletian at the end of the third century A.D. It should be added, however, that the Senate no longer provided any opposition to the absolutist tendency, for it had been itself enrolled by previous emperors, and the old qualification of nobility of birth alone had long ago disappeared. The tyrants Caligula, Nero, and Domitian had paid careful attention to see that it should.

The Romanized provinces by the end of the second century had become the real heart of the empire, though Rome, of course, remained the capital. The rank and file of the legions was made up exclusively of provincials, and the officers now came as much from the Romanized provinces as from Italy. One of the reasons why Trajan's wars in the East were ultimately so dangerous to Rome was that the most thoroughly Romanized provinces, Gaul and the two Spanish provinces, provided so many of his troops, who too often did not return to their homelands; if they were not killed in the East they were likely to settle there. All the emperors after Nero had had long experience in the provinces and recognized their importance; Trajan and Hadrian were both Spaniards. The Italian patriotism of Augustus was therefore slowly replaced by the wider patriotism of the citizen of the Roman Empire itself. This reality was ultimately recognized in the famous edict of the Emperor Caracalla in 212, which granted Roman citizenship to every freeman of the empire.

INFLUENCE OF THE ROMAN IMPERIAL IDEA

The Roman Empire, then, by the end of the second century had become fully established and accepted as the natural order of things. Internal opposition had disappeared, and the idea of the Roman Empire now had such a hold on the hearts and heads of men as no empire in the past had ever achieved, with the possible exception of the Chinese Empire under the Hans. There was some excuse for the belief that it was eternal, that it had even been willed by the gods. It was in this atmosphere of eternity and impregnability that the foundations of the Christian Church were laid, and this Church, the spiritual successor of the Roman Empire, was deeply influenced by it.

The achievements of the empire had already been enormous. It had always given tolerable and often excellent administration and an equitable law to a vast area, and it had given this area a peace it neither knew before nor has known since. If liberty was missing, this was a lack not felt by the people of the time. No one alive had known it from experience. It survived, at most, as a philosophical ideal. In the next chapter we shall see the other contributions to the cultural heritage of the world made by this hardheaded, efficient, practical, but hardly inspired people who first unified and ruled the Western world.

▶ **Suggestions for further reading**

Sources for this period are available in different editions. Penguin has published the *Annals* of Tacitus, and *Agricola* and *Germania* under the title of *Britain and Germany*. These are the most important works of Tacitus for the student. The *Satires* of Juvenal which throw light on the social conditions of the second century A.D. are available in Mentor, Indiana University, and Penguin editions. *Satires and Epistles* of Horace are published in a Phoenix edition, useful for a picture of Roman society in the Augustan Age. Penguin has an edition of *The Lives of the Twelve Caesars* by Suetonius. The *Satyricon* of Petronius (probably reflecting society in the time of Nero) is available in Ann Arbor, Penguin, and Mentor paperbacks.

Other documents available in case-bound books in addition to *Roman Civilization* by Lewis and Reinhold mentioned under Chapter 10 are Victor Ehrenberg, and A. H. M. Jones, eds., *Documents Illustrating the Reigns of Tiberius and Augustus*, 2d ed. (New York: Oxford University Press, 1955), and M. McCrum, and A. G. Woodhead, eds., *Select Documents of the Prin-*

cipates of the Flavian Emperors (New York: Cambridge University Press, 1961).

PAPER-BOUND BOOKS

Carcopino, J. *Daily Life in Ancient Rome*, trans. by E. O. Lorimer. Yale University Press, 1960. Lively and detailed picture of Roman life in the time of the emperor Trajan.

Charlesworth, M. P. *The Roman Empire.* Galaxy. Brief but valuable summary of the Empire, with cultural achievements.

Dill, Samuel. *Roman Society From Nero to Marcus Aurelius.* Meridian. An old classic (1904), still in many respects the best on the subject.

Grant, Michael. *The World of Rome.* Mentor. Topical treatment of Rome during the early Empire, preceded by a short historical survey. Illustrations in the original version (Cleveland, Ohio: The World Publishing Company, 1960) are superbly chosen and excellently reproduced).

Graves, Robert. *I, Claudius.* Vintage. This novel and its sequel, *Claudius the God*, (Vintage) present a colorful and accurate picture of the early principate.

CASE-BOUND BOOKS

Buchan, John. *Augustus.* Boston: Houghton Mifflin Company, 1937. Masterly biography, very favorable to Augustus.

Marañon, Gregory. *Tiberius: The Resentful Caesar.* New York: Duell, Sloane & Pearce, Inc., 1957. Interesting psychological portrait of this controversial emperor.

Marsh, F. D. *The Reign of Tiberius.* New York: Barnes & Noble, Inc., 1960. Masterly attempt to rehabilitate the second Roman princeps, especially by acute criticism of Tacitus. Reissue of a book originally published in 1931.

Mattingly, Harold. *Roman Imperial Civilization.* New York: St. Martin's, 1957. Thorough modern survey using all latest findings, handled topically.

Mommsen, Theodore. *The Provinces of the Roman Empire*, 2d ed. New York: Charles Scribner's Sons, 1909. An old classic, still not superseded.

Rostovtzeff, M. L. *Social and Economic History of the Roman Empire*, 2d ed. Revised by P. M. Fraser. New York: Oxford University Press, 1957. Standard work, though judgments often controversial. Excellent illustrations.

CHAPTER 12

ROMAN CULTURE

▶ **General characteristics of Roman culture**

CONTRAST WITH CREATIVENESS OF THE GREEKS

It is one of the ironies of history that, in spite of our admiration for the Greeks, Western civilization has always been nourished far more by Roman ideas and institutions than by Greek. With the recovery of Greek literature in recent centuries and the opportunity to study some of the masterpieces of Greek art in the original we have been able to make a comparative estimate of Greek and Roman contributions; and few would today claim the Romans to have been qualitatively superior in any single field of cultural endeavor to which the Greeks turned their attention. Roman architecture made use of far more forms than the Greeks had found necessary for their simpler needs, Roman engineering solved practical problems that were outside Greek experience. But though we are impressed by the grandeur of the Pantheon in Rome and admire the excellence of Roman roads, bridges, and aqueducts, it is to the Athenian Parthenon that we go for an ideal of architectural beauty. Yet our own public buildings are copied from the Romans, we are inclined to use the Corinthian rather

than Doric or Ionic capitals, and our columns, like Roman columns, too often support nothing and are merely superfluous decorations. But remove a Greek column and the building will collapse. To us the Greek world is remote, to be admired but not imitated, whereas the Romans are close to us. We feel we understand them. They are people like ourselves. To enter the Greek world requires an effort of the imagination; but the Romans, nearly as far away from us in time, can be understood, it seems, without any such rare and difficult mental activity.

It would appear that even to the Romans themselves the Greeks were a people apart. They admitted that in every branch of cultural activity the Greeks were their teachers and masters, and they did their best to imitate them. But they never seriously tried to think in the way the Greeks had thought. It is impossible to conceive of any Roman with whom we are acquainted taking time out to consider the fundamental problem of the early cosmologists, what it is that is stable in a world of changing appearances. No Roman could speculate like Plato or reason like Aristotle. The more simple ideas of these masters they could understand, at least in part. But whenever they tried to explain

The Pantheon at Rome, a much-imitated building, where the deified emperors were buried. Note the combination of dome and Corinthian columns. (COURTESY ITALIAN STATE TOURIST OFFICE)

One such imitation—the Low Library at Columbia University, New York. (COURTESY COLUMBIA UNIVERSITY)

what they had read—and many Romans, notably Cicero and Seneca, made a real effort to cope with the problems of philosophy— the result always appears as oversimplification, not touching the root of the matter, in some way debased. The truth seems to be, however it may be explained, that the Roman mind simply *could* not think in the Greek manner. Not that such thinking died out in the Roman period. The Greeks, Claudius Ptolemy the astronomer and Galen the physician are recognizably Greek in their thinking, though they lived in the second century of the Roman Empire.

PRACTICAL NATURE OF THE ROMAN GENIUS

The great Roman contribution to world culture therefore lies not in the field of thought, but in the application of thought in the ordinary world of men. In this way they served as a complement to the Greeks. They reaped the harvest of whatever had been thought before them, putting it to practical use. Where the Greeks had been concerned with ethical speculations, the Romans translated these into practical everyday morality; where Democritus had speculated on the constitution of matter, and Epicurus had drawn the conclusion that in such a cosmology there was no need for gods, the Roman Lucretius makes a passionate attack on religion and superstition as the prime causes of human suffering; where human morality is conspicuously missing in the adventures of Odysseus as told by Homer, the Roman Vergil in his *Aeneid* emphasizes the filial devotion of his hero, and the glorification of Rome and its destiny—the purpose of the voyage of Aeneas—breathes in every line of the poem.

ASSIMILATION AND TRANSMISSION OF GREEK CULTURE

The Romans, then, were the greatest transmitters of culture the world has yet seen, though to a lesser degree the Arabs later performed the same function. But the Roman spirit is nevertheless imprinted on every line the Romans wrote, every idea they took up and put to use. They should not be regarded as mere copiers. Moreover, when the Greeks left no model, the Romans showed themselves quite capable of developing new forms of their own, as in satire, epigram, letter writing, and perhaps even fiction. If anyone had ever had the temerity to translate a Roman work into Greek, it would at once have been recognized as Roman handiwork.

What is especially worth studying, therefore, in a survey of civilization is the process of cultural assimilation from the Greeks, the working of the Roman genius upon the material, and then the advances, if any, made by the Romans themselves in the same field. This chapter, then, will take the various fields of cultural activity one by one, and try to show this process at work rather than attempt a strictly chronological account of republican, Augustan, and Silver Age (the second century A.D.) achievements; external circumstances surrounding particular works will be mentioned only when they have a special relevance. In this way it is hoped that the student will perceive something of the nature of cultural assimilation in general, since every culture, now and in the future, will necessarily build upon the achievements of its predecessors, adding, like the Romans, the impress of its own distinctive genius, and thus carrying it forward into the future.

THE LATIN LANGUAGE

A word, however, is first necessary on the language of Roman literature. The Latin language is a native product of Italy. Though it has many virtues, it cannot compare with the Greek for flexibility, variety, and subtlety. It has comparatively few tenses, it lacks the middle voice, the dual number, and above all it lacks the Greek particles and prefixes which make Greek a language capable of expressing so many different shades of meaning. In this it shows itself as a suitable vehicle for Roman expression. The Romans did not make fine distinctions, they were not subtle; they, like their language, said what they meant, clearly and distinctly, with no nonsense about it. Moreover, the Latin language also lacks the invaluable auxiliary verbs, "to have" and "to be," which are so useful in the modern languages. It is defective in many parts, lacking, for instance, the present participle passive and past participle active in transitive verbs. Classical Latin makes use of what seem to us awkward circumlocutions when dealing with reported speech and past events (this defect was remedied in medieval Latin). And while it has one useful case, the ablative, unknown to the Greeks, this hardly compensates for what is missing. However, it has a wonderful terseness and brevity which make for precision and clarity, and in the course of time it developed a wealth of abstract nouns, which made it in medieval times an admirable vehicle for the formal logical philosophy of the scholastics. It also has the qualities of dignity and stateliness which made it especially suitable as the language of church and government. Medieval Latin, though derided by the humanists of the Renaissance, had gone far toward remedying the language's earlier defects, and out of medieval Latin developed not only all the Romance languages of the West, but much of the English language in its present form. For more than a thousand years it was the universal language of educated men, and until the present century was probably read by more people in Western Europe than any other. It is still, in its medieval form, the official language of the Roman Catholic Church.

▶ Religion

NATIVE AND ETRUSCAN

Native Roman and Italian religion reflects the social structure of the primitive Romans, but it is difficult to look upon it as in any sense a religion in our sense of the word. If the Romans had not become in later times a great people, few students of religion would probably have troubled to examine their religion. It conforms very closely in its primitive beliefs and rituals to those discovered by modern anthropologists working with uncivilized tribes. It explains, however, much in the early Roman character, and makes it easy to understand why the Romans were always so hospitable to im-

A lar, one of the household gods of the Romans. (COURTESY THE METROPOLITAN MUSEUM OF ART)

ported religions which made a greater appeal to religious feeling.

The early Romans evidently regarded all nature as animate, and gave names to the spirits, of particular areas and of natural phenomena such as rivers, as also to various agricultural functions such as plowing and sowing. These natural forces were called *numina,* or spiritual powers, and the farmer had to propitiate these powers by sacrifice. In addition there were certain protective deities, especially the *lares,* protectors of the home, the *penates,* protectors of the household stores, and the *genius,* protector of the family itself who worked through the head of the family. There was no kind of morality or ethics in this religion, as the spirits merely required specified attentions from members of the family. If these duties were fulfilled then the spirits were bound by a kind of bargain to support the family. Ironically enough, this binding contract is the original meaning of the word "religio," from which comes our word "religion." After death the spirits of human beings survived, but apparently without any individuality, and wandered in a featureless underworld, similar to the Babylonian Irkalla. In addition to these nature spirits, Jupiter, god of the sky, and Mars, god of war, were worshiped from an early time and seem to have been native Italian deities. They possessed greater power than the lesser spirits, but the latter were closer to the individual man, like the personal gods of the primitive Sumerians and Babylonians. The household gods, especially the *lares* and *penates,* served to keep the Roman family together, and were very close to all its members, while the greater gods only came into prominence when the Romans became a real people, and families acquired a wide loyalty to Rome itself.

The Etruscans influenced the early religion in several important ways. The father of the family was originally the only priest required for household worship. But as the state grew in importance, especially under the Etruscan monarchy, it became necessary to know more about the will of the gods of the state so that they might be propitiated in times of danger. Hence developed, as in Babylonia, the art of reading the future through the inspection of the livers of animals, and later the interpretation of various omens such as lightning and the flight of birds. For these specialized functions colleges of priests came into existence, whose duty was to keep officials advised of the will of the gods. This gave the college of pontiffs and augurs a considerable political power in later days, for the Romans were legally unable to transact any business on unlucky days. Bibulus, the colleague of Julius Caesar in his first consulship, refused to take any part in the triumvir's transactions, and laid the legal basis for nullification of his laws by retiring to his house to watch the omens every day the Senate sat. Since these omens were all declared by the stubborn consul to be unlucky, the laws were officially null and void.

When Caesar decided to cross the Rubicon rather than face as a private person charges of illegal acts committed during his consulship, no doubt he remembered the process by which they had been made illegal. Under Etruscan influence the gods of the state were first furnished with temples, and these gods gradually became established in public esteem, with the addition of Juno, as a wife for Jupiter, Minerva, goddess of the artisans, and others. Temple building, however, was slow to take hold in Rome, and several gods were worshiped only in the open air until a late date in Roman history. The state religion was looked after by a college of pontiffs, under the chief direction of the Pontifex Maximus, an official elected for life, and exact rules were drawn up for public ceremonial and worship.

GREEK INFLUENCE

With the conquest of the Greek cities in Italy a great change came over this primitive religion. Perhaps the first effect was the acceptance of one of the Greek oracles, the Sibyl of Cumae, as inspired. Her prophecies were contained in the sacred Sibylline Books, which were consulted by the pontiffs in times of crisis. The Greek gods were early grafted onto their Roman counterparts, and the Romans took over intact the very considerable Greek mythology and applied it to their own gods. By the end of the third century B.C. the new Hellenistic religions were already flourishing in the Near East, the worship of Cybele, the great Earth Mother, and various mystery religions. It was not long before these penetrated into Italy, and the greater requirements of the new gods seemed to meet a need on the part of many Romans. The Sibylline Books aided in this process, for when they were consulted the advice usually was to introduce a new cult from the Near East. Since consultation coincided with an actual crisis in Roman affairs, the entry of these new gods was greeted with emotional fervor and elaborate festivals were held. The older and more conservative Romans looked upon these innovations with disgust, and Cato the Elder (234–149 B.C.) led a special campaign to drive all Greeks from the city. But he was behind the times and never met more than a temporary success. On the whole the Romans remained tolerant of all religions unless they presented, like later Christianity, a danger to the state or offended Roman conceptions of morality.

ORIENTAL INFLUENCE

As we have seen already, when Augustus became princeps he tried vainly to revive the old agricultural religion. But he was only successful in the countryside, which had never fully abandoned its old primitivism. Bringing rural deities to the city was hardly sufficient to satisfy the now apparent emotional needs of many Romans. Only emperor-worship among Roman cults took any real hold of the people, and even this was supplemented by other more emotional religions which offered more to the individual worshipers. All the religions imported during the empire taught individual immortality and purification of the soul in this life in preparation for the next. It is therefore clear enough that many Roman men and women by the time of the principate were thoroughly dissatisfied with the old traditional ceremonies and the cold formality of the state religion. The worshipers themselves did not take part in these ceremonies but only watched them, whereas in the new Oriental religions the worshipers themselves were initiated with mystic rites and ceremonies. Moreover, with the assumption by the emperor of so many of the duties of private citizens in earlier times, local patriotism began to die out, together with the religion that had sustained it. For some few the semi-religious philosophy of Stoicism with its high ethical content (dealt with in the next section) was sufficient, but the new Oriental religions claimed far more adherents.

The two earliest and most important of these were the revived religion of the Egyptian Isis and the Persian Mithraism. The Egyptian religion now included more definite teachings on immortality, initiation ceremonies, and festivals of mourning for the dead Osiris. It was also highly organized into a cult of priests and worshipers, providing a sense of community missing in both Stoicism and the state cult. Mithraism had developed out of Zoroastrianism, and retained its central belief in the two great spirits, Light and Darkness. But now it was made clear that the worshiper must struggle against the Spirit of Darkness. In the struggle he is aided by the god Mithra, who is nearer to man than the original Sun-god, Ahura-Mazda, with whom indeed Mithra intercedes for the human soul. This religion, which has so many striking elements in common with Christianity, made tremendous advances within the empire in the early centuries, especially through dissemination by the Roman legions. But it suffered from one handicap that was insuperable. Unlike the religion of Isis and of Christianity, it did not admit women, whose influence in early Christianity was so strong. Very similar to Mithraism was the worship of the Unconquered Sun, of which very little is known, in spite of the fact that one emperor (Elagabalus, 218–222) was a priest of the cult, and another (Aurelian, 270–275) established it as the official religion of Rome. The rival of Constantine for the throne, A.D. 312, fought under the banner of the Unconquered Sun (*Sol Invictus*) but lost to Constantine, who had chosen before the decisive battle to fight under the sign of the cross of Christianity. Thereafter Christianity, discussed more fully in the next chapter, became the official religion of the emperors, and before the end of the fourth century the only permitted religion in the empire. The competitive religions gradually died out, though elements of Mithraism survived in Manichaeism,* which influenced many important Christian thinkers, especially St. Augustine, and Manichaeism itself survived in various heretical groups in Bulgaria and later in southern France, where we shall meet it again among the Cathari or Albigensians, suppressed by Pope Innocent III in the thirteenth century. The essential element in these religions of Persian origin was always dualism, or the almost equal power of good and evil, and human life as the scene of the struggle between these powers. Christianity, while admitting Satan into its religion, nevertheless always stressed his complete inferiority to God, and denied him any part in creation.

* Founded in A.D. 242 by Mani, a Persian, put to death by the Persian government about 276.

▶ Philosophy—Transformation of Greek thought by the Roman spirit

STOICISM

Until the introduction of Greek thought into Rome there was no philosophy among the Romans, and they found no need for it. As an active and practical people they were inclined to despise all forms of speculation. However, in the first flush of enthusiasm for all things Greek in the second century B.C. a number of Greeks were invited to Rome by a distinguished Roman gentleman of the highest rank, Scipio Aemilianus, around whom formed a circle of young Romans interested in Greek culture. Among those who came to Rome was a Stoic philosopher Panaetius, who had already done much original thinking on the traditional Stoic material of which mention was made in Chapter 9. Stoicism, it will be remembered, postulated a Divine Reason which pervaded all nature and was indeed identical with it. All human laws are attempts to legislate in accordance with the Divine Reason, which must be discovered by men. Thus arose the persistent belief in the existence of a natural law in accordance with which positive law on earth must be made. No law is really just unless it conforms with this natural law. All men are equal and brothers, said the Stoics, and this fact necessitated full equality before the law, a lasting principle of Roman jurisprudence. These ideas exercised an enormous influence upon Roman jurists, the greatest of whom were thoroughly at home with Stoic philosophy, which thus found practical application in Rome rather than in its own Hellenistic world.

It will be remembered also that Stoicism taught that the task of man was to achieve indifference to worldly success, and emphasized the dignity and worth of the individual human being, standing alone and without support from the gods, but secure because his wants were few and he could willingly relinquish all earthly desires. Though such a thought was no doubt too demanding for most Romans, and indeed for most human beings of any national origin, it nevertheless did appeal to something deep-seated in the Roman character, his willingness to undertake unpaid public service as a duty laid upon him simply by virtue of the fact that he was a Roman. Throughout Roman history we find many such self-reliant men, devoted to the service of their family and of the state, willing to expend themselves in it without hope of material reward. Such men found their philosophical justification in Stoicism. It was a philosophy only suited to the strong, for it offered no hope of reward in this world or the next. It is no accident that the greatest opponents of the absolute power of the emperors were the Stoics, whose regard for human dignity made them also willing to commit suicide rather than submit to indignity and loss of freedom.

We possess the writings of several Roman Stoics, but none is of first-rate quality. Too often lacking the capacity for sustained original thought, they are inclined to fall into platitudes, and little moral sermons. Cicero interprets Greek Stoicism fairly effectively, but makes no claims to originality. Seneca in the early empire sometimes utters ethical teachings worthily and has a few moving passages much appreciated by the early Christians, who believed him to have corresponded directly with Paul. But too often he lapses into commonplaces; and when we remember his own personal fortune acquired in public office, his sincerity is too often open to doubt, spoiling the effect of some of his preachments. On the other hand, the lame freedman, Epictetus, born Greek but thoroughly Romanized, neglects philosophical speculation altogether and concentrates his attention on how to lead a good life on earth in accordance with Stoic principles. All through his work the sincere moralist is evident. In the *Meditations* of Marcus Aurelius we see the effect of Stoicism upon a man who happened to be an emperor but would have preferred to be an ordinary humble human being. Possessed of a true humanitarian spirit, and really imbued with the theoretical Stoic love for all mankind, there is no doubt that he felt the burden of empire a heavy one. But Stoicism helped him fulfill his imperial duties, and the *Meditations,* written (in Greek) for the most part when he was on campaign and under the most difficult circumstances, shows both the man and the philosophy at their best.

EPICURISM

In the hands of the republican poet Lucretius, Epicurism appears as one of the great scientific philosophies of history. Lucretius, however, had a practical aim, to save human beings from their unreasonable fear of death, and free them from the bonds of superstition and religion, which he regards as synonymous and tending to destroy what little happiness is possible in life. Basing his science upon the teachings of Democritus and Epicurus—that the world is made up of atoms which come together by a chance swerve—Lucretius concludes with his masters that gods are unnecessary. Even if they do exist, they live apart at ease, and take no account of human affairs. It is therefore irrational to fear them, or to worship them. Death is not an evil, but a rest from earthly suffering. It is man's task to live without fear, and without any particular hope for happiness.

The beautiful poem *De rerum natura* is unique in all literature in that the greater part is true poetry, with many imaginative passages of great power, especially in the account of the creation of the world and all living creatures; yet it remains thoroughly scientific according to the best scientific principles of the time. It achieved wide popularity again in the European Enlightenment before its science was fully outmoded. Even Lucretius' science was taken seriously for a time, especially by Gassendi in the seventeenth century.

The form of Epicurism as found in Lucretius was not the form in which it was accepted by most Romans. Always implicit in the teaching, "Be happy with little, for desire is likely to bring unhappiness, and we shall all soon be dead"—the teaching of Epicurus himself—is the further thought that we ought to be happy now while we can, and not trouble about tomorrow. And it was in this form that the Romans accepted it as a philosophy of eating, drinking, and being merry. Horace, the Augustan poet laureate, is a gentle Epicurean, content with his loaf of bread and his bottle of Falernian wine on a Sabine farm, and many are the praises he sings of the harmless life of simple pleasures. Others were not so restrained, and ultimately it became the fate of Epicurus to act as the philosophical sponsor for Roman hedonism, the cult of excessive eating and drinking for which Rome is too often remembered.

ECLECTICISM

It was the custom for many centuries for upper-class Romans to go to Greece for the completion of their education. Here they came in contact with many schools of philosophy, and, as in modern universities, they had the opportunity to develop their own philosophy after listening to the best that was offered by their predecessors. The best example of this eclecticism, or choosing parts from various philosophies as one's own personal philosophy, is to be found in the great lawyer Cicero, who was a thoroughly educated man, but not himself a thinker of the first order. He did not even claim to be, preferring to consider himself as an interpreter of the Greek schools, putting their ideas into attractive Latin dress. It is characteristic of Cicero, as of Romans in general, that Plato and Aristotle are, on the whole, beyond his comprehension, though he admired them greatly. He prefers the later Hellenistic thinkers and philosophies, and again he is more interested in the practical side of their work. He discusses virtue at great length, but the more profound thoughts of Plato and Aristotle on the subject of the Good he lays aside in favor of discussions on how to live a happy life. On the whole, Stoicism seems to be interpreted with the greatest sympathy, and Cicero is one of our best sources for the Stoic teachings current in his day. He pays special attention to the later Stoic idea of divine providence, thus endearing himself later to the Christian Fathers. But he always remained to some degree skeptical, and he appreciated Greek Skepticism, but in a busy life it was natural that that philosophy never engaged his full attention.

Cicero's philosophical writings have had a career far beyond their intrinsic merit, for they were well known throughout the medieval period, and were still appreciated in the Italian Renaissance. Their simplification of the more profound problems of human life has always appealed to those who do not wish to struggle with the metaphysical issues involved, and his practical advice can be appreciated without excessive mental strain. The clarity of his language, even in his philosophical writings, is always a delight; indeed, he was responsible for the development of a philosophical Latin language capable of conveying Greek thought to posterity.

► Science

In pure science the Romans contributed not a single figure of any importance. In mathematics they were encumbered with numerals which present insuperable difficulties to any advanced calculations. Although they understood techniques based on mathematics and were extremely competent engineers and surveyors, they had no interest whatever in the fundamental Greek science of geometry, the theoretical basis of these techniques. Indeed, science actually degenerated in Roman hands and the few works written by them were far inferior to work already done before their time.

The elder Pliny was a man of considerable scientific curiosity but no talent. And even though he is said to have lost his life in an attempt to investigate at firsthand the eruption of Vesuvius which destroyed Pompeii, his enormous encyclopedia of *Natural History* betrays no critical sense. It is nothing but a repository of all the information available to an inquiring Roman in his day, without much serious attempt to discover whether it is true or not. Yet this work remains extremely valuable to us, as it is the primary source for Roman scientific knowledge in all the many fields it covers. The book was also greatly valued in the Middle Ages, since, with the Bible, it provided most of the information available to that period before the more advanced Muslim science and the works of Aristotle became accessible in Latin translations.

The Romans were diligent astrologers but had little interest in astronomy. The Greek Ptolemy in the second century A.D. wrote a highly competent synthesis of the work of previous astronomers, but no Roman name is known in the history of astronomy. When Caesar needed a competent astronomer for the revision of the Roman calendar, a Greek had to be hired for the purpose.

The history of medicine among the Romans is typical of their attitude. Theory was almost entirely neglected, though Galen, a Greek contemporary of Ptolemy, summed up earlier Greek theory and added much of his own. But the Romans were greatly interested in public health and sanitation. The emperors also established a hospital service for soldiers and officials in the provinces. If, however, the remedies used in these hospitals were those described by Pliny, it would seem probable that the doctors who served in them played but a small part in the eventual recovery of the wounded.

In technology the Romans made progress beyond their masters. Even in early republican days they developed a new technique for making roads, the best ones paved with stone, while secondary roads were surfaced with gravel. They built their roads up carefully from a depth of several feet below the surface of the surrounding country, using small stones and even concrete. It seems to have been by accident rather than through any scientific knowledge that the Romans discovered how to make a real concrete composed of lime and a volcanic ash which happens to contain the necessary ingredients. This discovery enabled the Romans to construct their public buildings out of a readily available material instead of using only the always expensive marble, which was then freed for use as a veneer.

The Romans knew how to construct strong bridges through the extensive use of the arch; they made tunnels through difficult

This famous Roman aqueduct, the Pont du Gard in France, gives some idea of Roman engineering skill and the gigantic size of Roman public works of the imperial period. Such construction is even more impressive when one realizes it was carried on with only the most primitive machinery.

mountain terrain; and they understood, but rarely used, the principle of the siphon for their baths and aqueducts. The many Roman remains, not only in Italy but throughout Europe, are an ample testimony to the strength of the materials used and the effectiveness of the Romans as engineers.

▶ Art

ARCHITECTURE—CULT OF HUGE AND
GRANDIOSE, CONTRAST WITH GREEK HARMONY

Oswald Spengler, when he put forward his theory of the rise and fall of cultures and their different stages of development from "spring" to "winter," suggested that the winter stage was characterized always by the cult of the gigantic, the mania for huge buildings and engineering projects rather than the more delicate, beautiful, and truly artistic works of the earlier stages. Since he regarded the Roman civilization as the "win-

ter" phase of Greco-Roman culture, one of his most important pieces of evidence was Roman architecture (the colossal buildings of Rameses in Egypt and American skyscrapers were others). Whether this preference for the huge may be better explained by other theories or not, it is certainly true that the Romans had a taste for the large and ornate rather than for the simple and unpretentious. Whereas the Greeks excelled especially in temples and other religious buildings which were intended only to house the god, much of the best Roman architecture has more practical uses. The greatest successes of the Romans are to be found in their public buildings, baths, theaters, and amphitheaters, and in their monumental imperial architecture.

It was the Etruscans who first taught architecture to the Romans, and Etruscan influence always persisted. It was they who instructed the Romans in the use of stone

373

and brick, and they who gave them the arch. But the Etruscans had themselves been influenced by the Greeks, and they used Greek columns in their public buildings and had houses of Greek design. After the Punic Wars, Greek influence became predominant in Rome, and during this period Roman buildings, public and private, were usually copies of those in Hellenistic cities. But even in this copying the Romans knew what they liked, which was invariably the ornate and the grandiose. The Corinthian column was preferred to the more severe Ionic and Doric, and the post and lintel construction was abandoned as unsuitable for large buildings constructed for practical needs, for which the dome, vault, and arch were more suitable. Gradually the Greek forms which the Romans, like ourselves, felt to be "artistic," became merely decorative on Roman buildings. They solemnly inserted useless columns, supporting nothing, they carefully fluted their columns although the fluting served now no practical purpose. The volutes at the top of the columns became more and more luxuriant and decorative, the Corinthian and Ionic capitals now being welded into a new composite. Not until twentieth-century architecture was the Roman practice looked upon with disfavor, and even now it is far from ousted, as a glance around any of our large cities will confirm.[1] But it is now believed by architectural theorists that the function should dictate the form and not the reverse. This principle, of course, had been fully understood by the Greeks.

When the spoils of war began to flow into Rome during the last century of the republic, private houses, often built by successful bankers and generals, became larger and more ostentatious, and still for the most part constructed by Greek architects, and often furnished with Greek works of art looted during the successful campaigns. Pompey built the first permanent Roman theater out of his spoils, Julius Caesar from his Gallic booty built a new Forum and repaved the old. Roman taste at this time, as usual with the new rich, ran to the extravagant and splendid, with elaborate ornamentation and

statuary (copied from the Greek, of course) in wild profusion.

With the advent of Augustus, Roman architecture came into its own, and we begin to hear of Roman architects and engineers, even though Greek influence was still strong and perhaps predominant. The rebuilding of Rome by Augustus, and the construction of vast new temples in accordance with his religious policy, influenced provincial cities also to take advantage of the new prosperity and rebuild their cities. In the imperial period every city of any importance had its baths, and even the smaller cities were able to build theaters, amphitheaters, and basilicas which were used for public business and to house the law courts. The best known of the Roman amphitheaters is the Colosseum, constructed by the first two Flavian emperors, much of which is still standing today, a huge round structure with a great arena for the spectacle. Underneath the arena is a network of passages, enabling performers—beasts and men—to reach any part of the arena as required. The basilica is a typical Roman structure, the plan of which, with nave, aisles, and clerestory windows, was adapted by the Christians for their early churches.[2] The cross-vaulting of the Romanesque cathedrals seems to have been a Roman invention, and allowed far greater size to the buildings.

Roman architecture reached its zenith in the time of Hadrian in the second century A.D. Thereafter there are still many huge and impressive buildings, especially the Baths of Caracalla, the Basilica of Constantine, and the palace of Diocletian at Split on the Adriatic Coast. But these only showed that the Romans had not forgotten how to construct. The materials, as was natural at a time when prosperity was declining, were now inferior, and there is no significant architectural innovation. Diocletian's palace was more of a fortress than a royal residence of the earlier ages, and indeed many of the villas and palaces of this declining period paid more attention to strength than to style.[2] It is true that in the Constantinople of Justinian there

[1] For example, New York General Post Office.

[2] A Christian church in the style of a Roman basilica is illustrated in Chapter 20 (Cathedral of Pisa), while the palace of Diocletian at Split is shown in Chapter 14.

Detail from Trajan's Column in Rome, built to celebrate the emperor's victory over the Dacians in the early second century A.D. (ALINARI)

Aerial view of the Colosseum at Rome, built by the Flavian emperors for the display of such public entertainment as gladiatorial fights. (COURTESY ITALIAN STATE TOURIST OFFICE)

Two portrait busts from the last period of the Republic. Note how the Roman sculptors of this epoch strove to express character in their subject's faces, thus confirming the belief, expressed in Roman literature, that character showed in a man's face. It is noticeable that busts are found in Rome more often than full-sized statues. (LEFT: MUSEUM OF FINE ARTS, MOSTON; RIGHT: METROPOLITAN MUSEUM OF ART)

Detail of one of the most famous of Roman sculptures, the so-called "dying gladiator," artist unknown. (ANDERSON)

Roman mosaic from Capua, south of Rome, probably of a girls' school, with the male teacher in the rear. (R. SCHODER)

was a real rebirth of architecture, but this can no longer be called Roman, and will be considered in its place under Byzantine art.

SCULPTURE—REALISM

Like architecture, Roman sculpture was first influenced by the Etruscans and then by the Greeks. Indeed, the Romans had such a high opinion of Greek (almost exclusively Hellenistic) sculpture that to the end of the empire many sculptors were employed simply at making copies of Greek statuary for the Roman market. But aside from these copies there is a pronounced difference between Roman and even Hellenistic sculpture, which is in full keeping with the Roman character

as we know it. The Romans liked their sculpture to be realistic, thus completing what was only a tendency in the Hellenistic world. In this preference they followed the Etruscan tradition also. The Romans therefore developed the art of realistic portraiture far more than the Greeks. When the Greeks, even Hellenistic Greeks, carved a portrait they were always conscious of the harmony between body and mind or soul, between life itself and the material it informed. So the Greeks preferred to carve the whole body, of which the head and face were only a part. When, at the request of the Romans, who usually desired merely a portrait bust, Greek artists took to portrait sculpture, they remained aware of the mind which lay behind the mere features, and thus strove to reveal character through the features and the harmony of the whole composition. The details thus fitted into place as part of the whole, but were not insisted upon, and perhaps the Greek sculptor did not care too much whether he caught the actual features to be observed on the model. This tendency is what is usually meant when we speak of the idealism of Greek sculpture.

The Romans, on the other hand, as always, were preoccupied by the outer appearance, which they carved exactly as they saw it, including lines of anxiety and unruly hair, which in most cases had no relation at all to what the Greek was trying to portray. For a period in the early empire the two tendencies fully harmonized, the realistic detail being combined with the psychological penetration of the Greek. Then the tendency again disappeared, and this time it was the Greek spirit alone which triumphed, late imperial and other portraits often being only suggestive of the subject rather than realistic likenesses. In noting the insistence of the Romans on this detail in the portrait busts, one is reminded of the way in which Tacitus describes the senators watching the emperor Tiberius for any change of facial expression, trying to discover what he was thinking from the outward appearance. It is clear that the Romans believed that the outward face was the true expression of a man's individuality, lines of anxiety and the set of the eyes included, and they probably did not wish any detail to escape them, however apparently unimportant. Hence this emphasis on what we call realism.

The same tendency is carried over into Roman sculpture en masse, the enormous reliefs of the imperial triumphal monuments. One has only to look at the Elgin marbles and then at, say, Trajan's column or the arch of Titus, to perceive at once the difference, though again the tendency toward realism was already visible to some degree in the Hellenistic world. The horses and riders in the Elgin marbles are magnificent, but they are not individualized. Though a mythical story is told, it is done in a series of scenes of a certain static beauty. But Trajan's column tells a true story, with real men fighting and dying. One can follow the Dacian campaign from beginning to end—and indeed the column has been used to supplement the historical accounts. The Romans tried also to add a third dimension to their relief sculpture by carving in depth, unlike the Greek reliefs where the background is flat and the figures are merely carved on it, all parallel to each other. The Roman technique in reliefs is sometimes very effective. No one would imagine an actual procession in motion from the Greek reliefs, while the best Roman work succeeds in creating this illusion.

Sculptural skill seems to have been lost by the Romans in the troubled third century A.D. Constantine, when building his famous Arch of Triumph, was forced to steal panels from the work of his predecessors Trajan and Marcus Aurelius, and these present a marked contrast to the figures made by his own workmen on the same arch. All illusion of movement has gone from them, and they are stiff, badly executed and designed figures of no artistic merit whatever. Constantine fared no better when he sought for a sculptor to make a statue of himself. The statue is huge but we do not know what the first Christian emperor looked like nor even whether the sculptor was attempting to make an ideal image. An ideal image may have been in his mind, but, though he was presumably the best sculptor in the empire, he lacked the skill to execute it.

▶ Rhetoric

INFLUENCE OF RHETORIC ON ROMAN LIFE AND CULTURE

Roman rhetoric deserves a section to itself as the art which the Romans most diligently cultivated, and a full study of its rise, influence, and decline would be a comment on the whole history of Rome. In the world of the republic words were powerful. A man could sway the Assembly, the Senate, or the law courts by his oratory, which could mean both a lucrative private profession or election to a magistracy, with a possible command of an army and a fortune awaiting him at the end. It could even mean the control of the republic itself. The Greeks, too, had been noted orators, and toward the end of the period of Athenian independence all the orators had studied carefully how to compose their speeches. But whenever a speech is carefully composed, it may tend to overemphasize its calculated psychological effect on an audience, while true sincerity may be lacking. The Sophists had been the first teachers of rhetoric in Athens, and the tradition they began was carried to perfection in the fourth century B.C.

When, therefore, the Romans began to be self-conscious about their speeches and ceased to speak directly out of their momentary inspiration, they naturally turned to the Greeks, whose schools were already established. Even the conservative Cato the Elder studied the speeches of Demosthenes for self-improvement. The Greeks soon began to teach rhetoric for the new market, and the Romans were apt pupils. Unfortunately there are many dangers in the art, dangers of which too few Romans were aware. Demosthenes had possessed such a burning sincerity that his speeches were relatively free from ornate and studied elaborations. Isocrates, on the other hand, had never delivered his speeches, and flowery phrases and circumlocutions abound in them. Too many of these airs and graces slipped into Roman rhetoric, especially when the speeches were intended for publication and not for delivery. In the empire, when the most effective of spoken speeches could have had no practical effect, since the real decisions were always made by the emperor, rhetoric became ever more polished and artificial and entirely concealed any possible sincerity of the speaker.

Indeed, rhetoric, the principal subject in Roman education under the empire, found its way into all Roman writing of this period. Lucan wrote an epic, with Pompey as its hero, in which a theme that could have been nobly presented was utterly spoiled by the striving after effect. A few passages are still noteworthy, even many, for Lucan had the makings of a first-rate poet, but the whole is now almost unreadable. A further danger exists in the too thorough study of rhetoric. The student goes back to the great speeches of the past and examines carefully the form, the pregnant pauses, the rhetorical questions, the moments of drama. And, since it is impossible really to reimagine the circumstances of the original speech, he painstakingly analyzes the form and then tries to use the same form in his own compositions and prepared orations. He is thus working at secondhand, and all sincerity and directness of his own are lost, and his speech becomes merely a lifeless artifice, convincing to no one, but polished and worked over to the last comma. The too exclusive study of rhetoric in the schools of imperial Rome has often been given as one of the most potent reasons for the general decline of Roman culture. And though the study of rhetoric may have been primarily a symptom rather than a cause, it certainly reacted upon the writers, and helped prevent the emergence of a new style suited to the times and more expressive of the spirit of that age.

CICERO, THE MODEL ORATOR

Cicero, of course, was the model for all later would-be orators. He himself had studied in Greece and claimed that his speaking style was based on both Demosthenes and Isocrates. But however powerful these formative influences may have been, he used a different language and his speeches were dictated by the needs of his own day, so that his work was truly original. Fifty-seven full orations and many fragments have come down to us, a greater bulk of work than from any other orator, Latin or Greek. Until very recently these were the possession of every educated man in the Western world, especially the well-known ones, such as those on Catiline. Cicero was not at his best in legal argument, and in this many great lawyers have surpassed him. But few in any language have equaled his capacity for irony and invective, carefully controlled rhythm, and the use of the telling word. He was the complete master of the Latin tongue, and it is not to be wondered at that his works became classics in the empire and again in the Italian Renaissance, which looked back to him as the master who should be imitated, while despising the medieval Latin which was still in daily use.

RHETORIC UNDER THE EMPIRE—SENECA— QUINTILIAN

Perhaps the best example of false rhetoric is Seneca, whose writings are consistently bombastic and always striving for effect, especially by the use of antithesis. Against the tendency of Seneca, the greatest teacher of rhetoric, his fellow Spaniard Quintilian, set himself. Quintilian looked to Cicero as his model, and regarded rhetoric from an ideal standpoint as part of a whole liberal education. To him rhetoric was rather eloquence, which is something not to be produced solely by technical training but by study of the humanities. His work on oratory therefore is a treatise more on education than on oratory, and is the only first-rate Roman contribution to this subject.

Orators in the next century turned more and more to artificial diction, archaisms, and stilted mannerisms, and reacted against Cicero, returning to even earlier writers for inspiration. Their work, however, need not detain us here.

▶ History

UNDER THE REPUBLIC—SALLUST AND CAESAR

History was one of the earliest forms of writing to be attempted in the Roman Republic, but mostly in the form of annals, factual accounts of events written for information. The earliest histories known to us were written in Greek, though evidently for Roman consumption. But in the middle of the second century B.C. Polybius, a Greek hostage in Rome, wrote one of the great histories of the ancient world, analytical, thorough, containing an admirable analysis of the Roman republican constitution, which he greatly admired (he did not grasp the fact that the form of the constitution in 150 B.C. bore little relation to the way in which it functioned in practice).

The first strictly Roman historian of the first importance was Sallust, whose history was clearly modeled on that of Thucydides, showing the same interest in human and social psychology, and using fairly effectively Thucydides' device of introducing speeches verbatim, even when he had not heard them. We possess only two monographs of Sallust, enough to show the quality of his work, but the *History* on which his Roman reputation was based is lost.

Contemporary with Sallust was Julius Caesar himself, whose two monographs on the Gallic and Civil Wars are masterpieces of their kind. Caesar writes about his own exploits in a clear, lucid, military style, speaking always of himself in the third person in an effort to appear impartial. No more effective propaganda device could have been invented; for his reputation, at least as a soldier, has been secured primarily on the evidence of these works. Although few would deny the military prowess of the great dictator and the thought and care that he put into his campaigns, it is possible to remain unconvinced that he was always as justified and unerringly right as he claims—possible, but difficult.

THE AUGUSTAN AGE—HISTORY WITH A PURPOSE—LIVY

Mention has already been made of Livy, the prorepublican historian of the Augustan age. Not all his *History of Rome* survives, but enough for us to realize how valuable the work would have been if complete. It was the first systematic attempt at covering all republican history; and evidently Livy had a real enthusiasm for his subject. Unfortunately no one in his day knew any certain facts about the kingdom and early republic, nor had any histories been written within centuries of this early age. What Livy gives us, then, is the tradition as it was known in the Augustan period, and this tradition centered round certain great heroes, whose lives had conformed, or were made to conform, to the best republican ideals of seriousness, courage, fortitude, and selfless service to Rome. The work thus served as a kind of supplement to the *Aeneid* of Vergil, which showed how the gods had, from the end of the Trojan War, always planned for the greatness of Rome and her imperial destiny. Livy shows how the virtues of the Romans had made them worthy of this high destiny. Its republican bias was therefore all to the good in a work of this kind. Livy was in no sense a scientific historian like Polybius or Thucydides, and was barely indebted to them at all, and he had done no research beyond studying the works of his predecessors. But it is his picture of republican Rome that captured the minds and hearts of posterity rather than the more difficult and thoughtful Tacitus, who was not known in the Middle Ages, and has never attained a tithe of Livy's popularity in the centuries since.

TACITUS—THE PSYCHOLOGIST AS HISTORIAN

Tacitus was a republican at heart, but born out of his time into the age of the Flavians and early Antonines, and his experience as a senator in this difficult period for men of his class undoubtedly embittered him. He made no real attempt at objectivity (though he did not realize his bias himself), but his work is nevertheless one of the world's historical and literary masterpieces. Tacitus had evidently been trained in rhetoric and he wrote in a terse epigrammatic style which is extremely effective in Latin, though it would be entirely unsuited to Greek. Time and again his thumbnail personality sketches hit the mark, summing up an emperor or an official with deadly accuracy.[3] For Tacitus is primarily a psychologist writing history. His *Annals,* as far as we have them, cover the reigns of Tiberius, Claudius, and Nero, while the *Histories,* of which we have only the first part, cover the Year of the Four Emperors. In addition there is a famous and often-quoted monograph on the primitive Germans, whom it was his intention to contrast with the effete Romans of his day. There is also a biography of his father-in-

law, a Roman official whom he greatly admired, and who served in Britain.

Tacitus' thesis throughout his work is that the decay of public and private morality in his age was due to the absolutism of the emperors and to the suppression of human freedom. As far back as Tiberius this tendency was visible, and it is inherent in the very nature of absolutism. Tacitus movingly describes the way in which the moral fiber of the senators must have been undermined by their subserviency, and describes how as members of the highest law court in the land they were forced to agree to the condemnation of entirely innocent men by Domitian, on pain of having to suffer the same fate. Nowhere do we get such an impression of what it was really like to be a noble in the days of the tyrannous emperors. Yet it is only fair to point out that this was not the whole story of the empire, and that Tacitus quite intentionally blinded himself to any merits the system might have had in other respects. But for a modern reader these passages nevertheless remain the vital parts of his work, and Tacitus can be read with profit in our own age, even by those who have no other interest in Roman history.

THE LATE EMPIRE

Suetonius, who lived in the reign of Hadrian, may be classed as a historian only by courtesy. His gossipy biographies of twelve emperors have been very influential in forming later opinion of these men and usually stress the facts about them that are of the least historical importance. The information may be reliable as far as it goes, since for a time he had access to the imperial archives. But his selection of what was important leaves almost everything to be desired, and there can be little doubt that the scandalous anecdotes which fill his work are precisely those that would *not* have appeared in the imperial archives, and were probably selected from Roman gossip, in many cases more than a hundred years after the events described. The reliability of this part of the work may therefore be seriously questioned.

[3] Well known is his characterization of Galba, for a few months emperor in A.D. 69: "Omnium consensu capax imperii nisi imperasset." ("By universal consent he was fit to rule only had he never ruled.")

Ammianus Marcellinus, the last Latin historian of importance (there were other minor historians who wrote in Greek) lived in the fourth century A.D. His history starts where Tacitus left off, but we possess only that part which covers the second half of the fourth century. Accurate and painstaking, there are several vivid passages describing the corruption of the period, though he did not seem to appreciate sufficiently the fact that the empire was doomed, and so sometimes conveys an air of unreality to the modern reader.

Epitomes of history were also written in considerable number, and are sometimes of considerable value, since they digest passages of historians now lost. One of the best of these is Florus's *Epitome of Livy.*

▶ **Law**

CONTRASTS WITH EARLIER SYSTEMS OF LAW

The greatest of Roman glories, and Rome's supreme legacy to mankind, is the Roman law, the development of which we are fortunately able to trace almost from the earliest times, owing to the extant writings of so many great jurists, and to the firsthand description of the working of republican courts derived from such men as the practicing lawyer Cicero.

As was seen in an earlier chapter, the first codified law of Rome was the Twelve Tables, drawn up by a committee of ten in 449 B.C. under the stimulus of the second secession of the plebs. This committee is said to have visited Greece to study existing systems of law and especially the constitution of Solon. But if the visit was ever made (it is recorded by Livy many centuries later), it was singularly unfruitful, for the Twelve Tables bear no evidence of Greek influence, being an extremely primitive document as far as we are able to judge from what has survived. They remained the basic statute law of the Romans. In addition, statute law was made from time to time by the Assembly. These laws, however, covered primarily constitutional and criminal law, which have only

limited importance. They were applicable only to Rome herself and her citizens. Since no principles were involved they were incapable of wider application.

To understand the epoch-making character of the Roman contribution to the science of law, it should first be contrasted with what went before it. Until late times the Egyptian law was the word of the Pharaoh as revealed to him by the gods (*Ma'at*). In other words, each case was decided by a person, whether the Pharaoh or a judge appointed by him, not necessarily in accordance with any law or legal principles. Personal justice of this kind is common throughout the East, even to the present time. It has nothing to do with law in the Roman sense.

The Hammurabi Code of Babylonia is a series of statute laws, some criminal and some social and commercial, which name definite penalties for their contravention. Individual judges could no doubt decide whether to enforce the full penalty, but since the penalties were clearly stated, the minimum room was left for the exercise of their personal discretion. The code, in fact, was clearly designed for the purpose of preventing judges from making arbitrary decisions. The Hebrew codes were of the same nature, with the addition of certain prescribed religious practices.

The Greek city-states, in addition to possessing basic constitutional laws, had a number of statute laws of the same kind as those mentioned above. But in ordinary private litigation each particular case was decided on its merits by appeal to a jury. The jury did not have to take into account decisions made by earlier juries in similar cases. There was as yet nowhere any science of jurisprudence or principles of law which could be applied to each case as it arose, regulating the decisions of the judges. Nor did the Romans have it at the time of the Twelve Tables, which was a primitive code of the type of the Code of Hammurabi, though much simpler, as befitted a primitive society.

THE RIGHTS OF THE ROMAN CITIZEN— JUS CIVILE

But the Romans did have a new and quite original conception of citizenship, which covered certain well-defined rights, already discussed in Chapter 10. The rights belonged to the man who was a citizen, they were inherent in his person, wherever he might happen to be. This is the first time these particular rights, which in earlier times accrued to a man only by birth, were believed to be vested in a *person*. In Athens the city gave certain privileges to its citizens, but there was no kind of contract between them and the city, and naturally they possessed no privileges unless they were living in the particular city which gave them. But the Romans guaranteed certain definite rights to their citizens, and these they retained even when abroad. These rights collectively were known as *jus*, and a Roman citizen was entitled to have any case tried under the *jus civile*, or civil law.

Now this law was rarely affected by statutes (*leges*) passed by the Assembly. It was built up ordinarily in early times by the priests, who stated on authority what the law was. This task then passed to a special official called the *praetor urbanus* (city praetor). The praetor, however, was an elected official, probably a would-be general rather than a jurist. It was hardly possible for him to state what the law was, or to decide all cases personally, and it was not his duty to do so. He had as assistants judges who came from noble families, and who were in charge of the actual trial. But even these judges were not as a rule trained lawyers, though they had more experience than the annually elected praetor.

When, therefore, a civil case was brought to trial, it was necessary for the parties to the case to have some knowledge of what the law was likely to be in their case. So it gradually came about that the praetor every year on assuming office made a public statement of the law that he would use while in office. This was called the *edictum*, and it was made up largely of the instructions that he proposed to give to the judges. These instructions were called *formulae*. And the edict was made up, for the most part, of decisions that had been made by his predecessors in office.

It will be seen, then, that in this way a collection of decisions would be built up which would really have the force of law, even though no statutes had been made on the subject. Statute law would, of course, be taken into consideration by the praetor, but even this he could interpret, as our judges and higher courts interpret law today. And this interpretation would probably be incorporated in the edict of the next praetor and so be binding for the future, unless a praetor for good reasons decided to depart from it —as our judges may also on occasion depart from interpretations of their predecessors.

THE RIGHTS OF FOREIGNERS—JUS GENTIUM

This, then, was the system for public and private law for Roman citizens, and it lasted for a considerable length of time. But cases also arose where one party to a lawsuit was a Roman citizen and one was not, and where two resident noncitizens might engage in litigation with each other in the Roman courts. If the case concerned a foreigner's personal status, it would clearly be impossible to settle it through the *jus civile*, applicable only to citizens. So in 242 B.C. a *praetor peregrinus* or foreign praetor, whose task was to look after such cases, was elected for the first time. Thus the idea arose that foreigners also had rights, and the new law under which they were judged was called the *jus gentium*, or law of peoples. Both praetors now issued annual edicts covering the cases for which they were responsible.

INTERPRETATION OF THE LAW—BEGINNINGS OF JURISPRUDENCE

As the Roman state grew in importance and undertook more and more responsibilities, and legal decisions of wide significance had to be made by unqualified persons, an innovation was made which proved to be the real foundation of Roman jurisprudence. It became the custom for certain skilled lawyers, who had also held high office in the state, to assist the praetors in drawing up their edicts and in answering questions put by judges. They could also give advice to litigants. These men were not paid, nor did they hold any official position, but undertook the work from a sense of duty and for the prestige involved. Since these *juris prudentes* (men skilled in the law, hence our word "jurisprudence") were appealed to for advice, especially in cases where the law was doubtful, they became specialists in interpretation, and theirs was now the chief responsibility in the building up of new law for the future. It was among these men that the conception of equity (*aequitas*) grew up as a principle which could override a strict interpretation of the law. In time, especially under the empire, certain individuals among them became known for the excellence of their opinions, as certain Supreme Court Justices of the past may still be quoted and accepted in the United States even though they have been long dead.

INFLUENCE OF PHILOSOPHY—JUS NATURALE

Many of these *juris prudentes* were strongly influenced by Stoicism, with its conception of the natural law of divine reason (*jus naturale*), which became a commonly accepted ideal, a kind of ideal law in accordance with which all statute law should be made and all legal decisions should be rendered. The strongly humanitarian viewpoint of the Stoics thus became incorporated into Roman law.

Under the early principate the same system was maintained. But naturally the edict of the praetor and the opinions of the *juris prudentes* had to take account of the new influence of the princeps; and with the increasing absolutism of the emperors the decisions in public law tended to reflect the increasing importance of the state. There was also far more statute law in the empire than under the republic. The Assembly declined as a lawmaking body after Augustus,

but the Senate now became for the third time since 509 B.C. a real legislative body, though its laws were naturally in accordance with the emperor's wishes. The emperors after Augustus also issued decrees which had all the force of law. Under Hadrian the praetors' edicts were codified into a perpetual edict, leaving the *juris prudentes* and their interpretations of still greater importance than before. After Hadrian many of them began to hold official positions in the imperial service, often serving as advisers to the emperor, who now felt in need of skilled legal assistance. The law continued to develop, often in accordance with newer Greek and Oriental philosophical ideas.

By this time there was virtually no distinction between the *jus civile* and the *jus gentium*, since the vast majority of the inhabitants of the empire by the time of Hadrian, and all by A.D. 212, were Roman citizens. It was the principles of the *jus gentium*, which had always been more universal and thus more in accordance with philosophical principles, as well as more in accordance with contemporary requirements in law, which prevailed. In the last stage of the empire, the great codification of the law began. Creativeness declined under the absolutist emperors, and the opinions of the great *juris prudentes* of the past were taken as actual law, and a number of dead jurists were named whose opinions must prevail. In the event of a tie, the opinion of the supposed greatest, Papinian, was to be decisive.

THE GREAT CODIFICATION OF THE LAW AND ITS INFLUENCE

The Theodosian Code of A.D. 438 was a collection of imperial edicts binding in the Eastern and Western Empires. This was followed in the sixth century by the great definitive code of Justinian, drawn up by Trebonian and a group of distinguished jurists in Constantinople. This code, known as the *Corpus Juris Civilis,* had four parts: the Code, which consisted of the imperial edicts of all the emperors *(constitutiones);*

the Digest, which contained the decisions of the great *juris prudentes;* the Institutes, primarily a manual on legal principles for use in schools; and the Novels, a series of new laws which Justinian found necessary to complete the whole structure. Naturally the Digest was the most important part of the code for posterity, since these opinions, based on the best thought of the greatest jurists in accordance with their conceptions of the natural law, were to a large extent free from limitations of time and place. This law code, however, differed from earlier ones in that Christian influence had now been admitted to it. Religious crimes, such as heresy, were included, but on the whole the Christian influence was a gain, especially the legislation on slavery.

The influence of Roman law is almost incalculable. It is not so much that codes of law in many modern countries are still largely Roman, nor that the canon law of the Church is almost exclusively Roman; but that this civilizing work was done by the Romans once and for all, and there was no need ever to do it again. The primitive laws of the barbarian invaders of the empire were so far behind Roman law in principles and sheer intellectual grasp of the problems involved in any law code that all took freely from the Romans, and no code in the Western world has not been influenced by it. It was used as a political tool to help the development of the national state by medieval monarchs. It was so patently superior to feudal law that when the king's justice was modified Roman, and the local law was feudal, every litigant, if he had the choice, would prefer the king's justice. When Napoleon needed a new law code for France in the early nineteenth century, it was to Roman law that he went for a model.

And, as we shall see in a later chapter, the great tradition of the *juris prudentes* was carried on by the jurists of the University of Bologna from the eleventh century onward. Indeed, the university itself only came into existence as a law school with the rediscovery of the *Corpus juris civilis* of Justinian, which had been lost in the ages of barbarian domination of Europe.

▶ Literature

POETRY

In the field of literature as such the influence of the Greeks was for a long time paramount. But three new fields were exploited by the Romans—satire, the satirical epigram,[4] and letter writing. They may also have invented the novel, of which the earliest example known to us is the *Satyricon* of Petronius, though among the vast lost literature of Alexandria, much of it written for pure entertainment, there may have been precursors.

THE EPIC

Much has already been said of the great epic of Vergil, the *Aeneid.* The story is concerned with the voyage of Aeneas to Rome after the fall of Troy, but the real purpose is to extol the glory of Rome, founded by a descendant of Aeneas. It thus becomes a patriotic poem, the first in history, and perhaps still the greatest. Since Aeneas is also a wanderer, and several of the scenes in the poem are direct imitations of Homer, the whole poem is bound to invite comparison with the *Odyssey.* This, in view of his purpose, is unfair to Vergil, for his work is on the whole original, with most of its best episodes not even paralleled in the *Odyssey.* The work is very uneven—Vergil himself intended to polish it if he had lived—and the hero is by all standards a failure, never holding either our interest or our sympathy. But the incidental scenes, and especially those in which the hero is forced to wrong innocent people in the pursuit of his mission, are moving. And there is a great grandeur in the poem, especially in the account of the fall of Troy. Vergil was a great literary artist, certainly a master of the Latin lan-

---

[4] The Greeks had also composed epigrams, but these were, as a rule, short panegyrics of famous people and events, rather than the pointed, usually witty and often biting thumbnail sketches of Martial.

guage. But the *Aeneid* is not an easy poem to appreciate in any language but the original, and without some understanding of and sympathy for his purpose. The medievals, with their special feeling for Rome, regarded Vergil as not only the greatest of the pagans, but as almost superhuman, a prophet as well as poet, and in Rome itself he was a classic as soon as he was dead, to be studied by every Roman schoolboy. His influence until the present century was probably greater than that of any writer of the ancient world.

LYRIC POETRY

The Greeks had been such masters of lyric poetry that the Romans never escaped fully from their influence, and many excellent Latin lyrics are little but paraphrases of Greek originals. Yet the subjects chosen are frequently Roman, and it was early found that the Latin language could be effectively used for lyric and that the principal Greek meters could be turned easily into Latin. Catullus is the greatest early master of the Latin lyric. Much of his work is on conventional Greek subjects, but his odes to Lesbia, a noble Roman lady who was probably also the most profligate and notorious of her generation, are deeply felt. Horace, a poet of the age of Augustus, composed his odes very carefully, and they are not always entirely successful as poetry. But most of his odes, composed both in light and serious vein, are highly polished and apparently sincerely felt. Horace's remarkable felicity of phrase has made him perhaps the most translated of ancient poets, and his poems render well into any language. The Greek influence is mostly to be found in his choice of meters, which are nearly always of Greek origin.

PASTORAL POETRY

Theocritus, the Hellenistic Greek, was the model for all pastoral poetry, and, in the opinion of many critics, he has never been surpassed. But Vergil composed a number of poems in this style, which are collectively called the *Eclogues,* though they are not all concerned with shepherds and shepherdesses and the usual material of the pastoral. Several of them are charming, though recognizably imitations. But the fourth eclogue is of a different kind, containing a prophecy of the birth of a child who was to usher in the Golden Age. Christians, of course, took this to be a prophecy of the birth of Jesus, and this was probably the chief reason they looked upon Vergil as inspired. The details of the prophecy as they appear in the eclogue do not apply very closely to any child known to us, but it expresses clearly Vergil's semi-mystical temperament, and the hopes that had been aroused in him by the era of peace inaugurated by Augustus, his patron.

DIDACTIC POETRY

The most original didactic poem in the Latin language is certainly the *Georgics* of Vergil, a long, sustained hymn of praise of the rural life, which really succeeds in recapturing the atmosphere of the Italian countryside in which the poet was reared. The occupations of the farmer are accurately detailed, but always with the halo of romance upon them. The poem is more finished than the *Aeneid,* and within its chosen compass in many ways more effective, and much of the poet's best work is in it.

Ovid, after Vergil the most popular of Latin poets in the Middle Ages, was the most versatile and facile of all poets in his versification. In view of the variety of his subjects, he cannot be easily classified. Amongst his didactic poems are the *Fasti,* in which he takes up the various feast days of the Roman year and tells of the rites celebrated and their origin. His most famous, or notorious, work also falls into this classification, the *Ars amatoria,* or the art of loving, in which he explains the art of seduction, with many witty and intentionally sententious digressions. His *Metamorphoses,* one of our chief sources of information on the subject—and sometimes our only source— is a handbook of Greek mythology. These Greek stories he tells very entertainingly. His *Amores* are love poems addressed to passing loves, written as ever, without any real feeling, but with great facility. Ovid was finally banished from Rome by Augustus, perhaps for his *Ars amatoria,* which was hardly in keeping with the Princeps's policy for restoring the sanctity of family life, but possibly for a more than usually outrageous exploit with Julia, the daughter of the Princeps, who was banished about the same time.

DRAMA

The Romans had no sense of tragedy in their make-up, and it is not surprising that there are no first-rate writers of tragedy in Latin. The tragic dramas of Euripides, however, as the reader will realize after recalling the discussion of this writer in an earlier chapter, lent themselves to imitation fairly well. Early in the republic various writers tried to adapt Euripides to the Latin stage, and the first important Roman poet, only fragments of whose work remain, wrote a few plays based on Roman history. The only poet whose tragedies are extant, Seneca, was not eminently fitted for his task as a tragedian, as he was unable to rid himself of his sententiousness and his addiction to false rhetoric. Occasionally a speech rings true, and there is some verbally dexterous dialogue, but very little that can be called truly tragic. And it was almost ludicrous to attempt, as he did, to imitate the Greek paraphernalia of gods when in his day no one had any belief in them. Unfortunately his influence was strong in European tragedy before Shakespeare, and the medievals, knowing nothing better, admired him. He is seldom admired now that we have the Greek tragedians in the original, and never performed.

COMEDY

The Romans do not seem as a people to have been gifted with a natural facility for laughter. There was always some cruelty in their wit, and they did not possess the urbanity required for comedies of manners. Doubtless a people who could be entertained by gladiatorial shows would not take so easily to the more polite entertainment of true comedy. The only comedies extant were written in the first days of Greek influence under the republic, and both the playwrights, Plautus and Terence, are heavily indebted to the New Comedy of Athens. The scenes and characters of Plautus are invariably Greek, but to make a greater appeal to his Roman audience he combined elements from the Roman society of his day. They were written solely for entertainment, and in this they are on the whole successful, and revivals and adaptations of Plautus have even been successful in modern times. Shakespeare and Molière were indebted to him for some of their plots, though these, of course, also came from the New Comedy of Athens. Since we possess only fragments of the New Comedy, the plays of Plautus have a certain additional value for us. The other writer of comedies, Terence, who belonged to the circle of Scipio Aemilianus at Rome, was not interested in adding Roman characteristics to his plays, since his audience was made up of pronounced Grecophiles. They are therefore simply adaptations of the New Comedy in Latin. His style was more polished than that of Plautus, and he is more quotable. And he is believed to have added a new feature to the drama, the use of plot to sustain interest. Though this device may have already been used in some plays of the New Comedy of which we know nothing, all the plays prior to Terence of which we have knowledge, tragedy and comedy alike, used only plots and situations to which the audience possessed the key. The audience knew, and the characters did not, what was going to happen, so that the entertainment consisted in watching the characters make errors which full knowledge would have avoided. The use of a plot which was unknown to the audience provided it with a new interest to hold its attention to the end of the play.

CHARACTERISTIC ROMAN FORMS

Satire

The same qualities which made the Romans unsuccessful at comedy, their seriousness, their interest in moral questions, and their caustic wit, led them to develop a new form of literature unknown to the

Greeks. A man like Aristophanes could criticize his society bitterly enough, but beneath it all there was a real love of Athens, in addition to a wild and irreverent inventiveness and boisterousness altogether alien to Roman character. When the Romans wished to criticize their society they did it as moralists and realists, and with full seriousness, and they were really indignant at what they criticized, however they might sweeten the pill with wit and even humor. The form most suitable for this is satire, which was developed for the first time by the Romans. An early satirist of whose work we possess only fragments is Lucilius, who presented scenes from the life of his time in verse, usually criticizing its vices, though some of his satires are merely descriptive of contemporary life. This simple descriptiveness disappears in the more developed form of the satire as it appears later. Horace, who acknowledges himself as the follower of Lucilius, is still genial and without personal bitterness. But most of his satires are concerned with the follies and absurdities of mankind, though some are also devoted to incidents in his earlier life. Vivid and often extremely funny, they lend themselves well to translation. Perhaps the best known is the satire about the bore who tried to coerce the poet into introducing him to his patron Maecenas, and Horace's attempts to get rid of him.

The satirists of the Silver Age of the early second century A.D. had far more, it would appear, to criticize in their society than had Horace. Persius seems too often to be insincere and his themes are stock ones. But Juvenal, unquestionably the greatest of Roman satirists, whipped himself into a continual fury at what he saw around him, and he did not hesitate to put it on paper. No doubt his portrait of Roman society, with its clients, its legacy hunters, its gluttons, and its crooked contractors, is overdrawn, and Juvenal was a bitterly disillusioned man who took little joy from his life. But the portrait is vivid and convincing as far as it goes. It is from Juvenal that we get the famous expression "bread and circuses" for the life of the proletariat, and from Juvenal that the stereotype of the decadent society of the imperial capital has been taken by subsequent writers. He has been the model for satirists ever since.

Epigram

The Latin language was eminently suitable for epigram, and in Martial, an earlier contemporary of Juvenal, it found its master. Most of his epigrams are extremely witty and pointed, and defy translation with the same condensation in any other language. They were usually composed to order for anyone who would pay him, or hold out the hope of paying him. His picture of the decadent society of Rome coincides in all essentials with that of Juvenal, and all classes of Roman society came within range of his biting wit. Like Juvenal, he succeeded in making himself the model for later generations in his particular field.

Letter writing

The Greeks, for want of a postal system, did not take naturally to letter writing, although some letters attributed to Plato are extant. So this art can be credited to the Romans, and above all to Cicero, whose voluminous correspondence, which also includes some of the replies he received, presents an extremely valuable picture of the Rome of his day and of Roman politics of the late years of the republic. More than this, it presents a picture of Cicero himself which is unequaled by that of any other man in all Roman history. For Cicero did not intend the letters to be published, and he made no effort to edit them. So they reveal him with all his faults, which are apparent on the surface, while the virtues are more concealed, but still visible to the discerning reader.

In contrast, Pliny the Younger's letters seem a little precious, having been carefully edited by the writer to show off his virtues, and more polished than is usual with people who write letters in the ordinary course of the day's activity. But they, too, give us a valuable picture of the life of the early second century A.D. in Rome and the provinces and are especially important in that this is the same period covered by the satirist Juvenal. Curiously enough, none of the vices castigated by the satirist are so much as mentioned by Pliny. His letters to the Emperor Trajan show him as an honest official, who in accordance with the conditions of his appointment as a "trouble shooter," consults his master on every point and elicits replies that are a model of imperial patience. Among these is the famous letter from Trajan telling him not to seek out the Christians and punish them although the laws against them are still in effect, but rather to leave them alone until they are accused and then only to take appropriate action in punishing them.

Fiction

Though the *Metamorphoses* of Ovid, already dealt with, might be classed at least as storytelling, the only real novel we possess is by a writer named Petronius, who is thought by most critics to be a friend of the emperor Nero mentioned by Tacitus as sharer of Nero's pleasures. This man was ultimately made to commit suicide by his master, and sent him a detailed list of his imperial crimes in revenge. The incident provided the inspiration for the famous novel *Quo Vadis* by Sienkiewicz, twice used as the basis for spectacular motion pictures. However, there are dissenting opinions as to the authorship of the *Satyricon*, and the novel could also describe the society of a much later age than Nero's. The novel relates the experiences of a trio of adventurers wandering around southern Italy. The largest part of the *Satyricon* that has survived is concerned with a gargantuan feast given by Trimalchio, a new-rich freedman. Petronius tells his story in an urbane, detached manner, quite unlike the fury with which Juvenal describes a not dissimilar scene, and the book is also notable for its effective use of conversation, giving us our only real knowledge of how Latin was spoken among the people of Rome and Italy in the early empire.

This brief account of Latin literature, which is far from inclusive, may fittingly end with a mention of the *Metamorphoses* of Apuleius, a prose writer of the second century A.D. The writer was a professional orator who turned his hand to the composition of tales based on subjects taken from the Greeks. The famous *Golden Ass* and *Cupid and Psyche* are still known and still retranslated today, and have never lost their popularity. But the Latin scholar is amazed at the work of Apuleius, wondering how it could be possible as early as that day for such antiquarian zeal to be employed in the writing of anything designed to be read by contemporaries. It is full of strange words, still stranger turns of phrase, and other exhibitions of what seems to be simple verbal fantasy. He coined words and phrases which we find in no other writing of his time, and no other extant writer has imitated him.

It would look as if the virtuosity of Apuleius was carefully calculated to attract the interest of the bored Roman of his day (like some *avant-garde* writers in the 1920's), which would not have been excited by an ordinary composition in a tongue familiar to readers. Most of the verbal ingenuity is lost in translation into any tongue, though many translators have made the attempt, in part, perhaps, accounting for his continued popularity with them, for they were thus enabled to play amusing tricks with their own languages also. The highly sophisticated and calculated artificiality of the tales of Apuleius renders them sometimes most charming in translation, but is certainly a sign that the creative period of Roman writing was over. Latin literature did not recover its vitality until the descendants of the invading barbarians took up the use of a greatly modified Latin once more in the early Middle Ages.

▶ Suggestions for further reading

Latin classics in paperback not yet mentioned in the last two chapters are the *Aeneid* of Vergil (Bantam and Rinehart editions), Horace's

Odes and Epodes (Phoenix), and four of Seneca's tragedies, in Penguin. The long poem of Lucretius *On the Nature of Things* is available in five different editions. The Greek satirist Lucian, whose works are valuable for his picture of second-century Rome is published in Penguin and Norton editions. *The Golden Ass* by Apuleius, discussed in the text, is available in Noonday and Collier editions. Lastly, for late Stoicism Epictetus and Marcus Aurelius should both be read. They are available in Liberal Arts Press editions, Marcus Aurelius also being available in several other editions and translations.

PAPER-BOUND BOOKS

Clark, M. L. *Studies in the History of Thought from Cicero to Marcus Aurelius*. Norton. Gives a fairly full picture of the modest efforts of the Romans in this field.

Duff, J. W. *Literary History of Rome*, ed. by A. M. Duff. 2 vols. Barnes & Noble. Reissue of what is still the best complete history of Roman literature to the death of Hadrian.

Hadas, Moses, ed. *The Stoic Philosophy of Seneca*. Norton. Useful selection, showing how Roman Stoicism had developed by the time of Nero. Another selection of Stoic works including others beside Seneca was compiled by the same editor, *Essential Works of Stoicism* (Bantam).

Highet, Gilbert. *Juvenal the Satirist*. Galaxy. Excellent study, well-written and often very entertaining. By the same author, a fine classical scholar, *The Classical Tradition* (Galaxy) is another good study of what we owe to both the Greek and Roman worlds.

Laistner, M. L. W. *The Greater Roman Historians*. University of California. A comparative study of the work of the four major Roman historians.

Mackail, S. W. *Latin Literature*. Revised by Harry C. Schnur. Collier. An old but still valuable survey.

McKendrick, Paul. *The Mute Stones Speak*. Mentor. Excellent book on imperial architecture.

CASE-BOUND BOOKS

Anderson, W. J., and Spiers, R. P. *The Architecture of Greece and Rome*. Vol. 2. New York: Charles Scribner's Sons, 1927. A very substantial account of the Roman feats in building and engineering. See also Showerman, *Eternal Rome* in suggestions for further reading at the end of Chapter 10.

Declareuil, J. *Rome, the Law-Giver*, trans. by E. A. Parker. New York: Alfred A. Knopf, Inc., 1927. This excellent work which explains the uniqueness and importance of Roman law is unfortunately scarce, but the effort to find it is worthwhile, as it remains by far the best book on the subject.

Greene, W. C. *The Achievement of Rome*. Cambridge, Mass.: Harvard University Press, 1933. Useful general survey.

Grenier, C. *The Roman Spirit in Religion, Thought, and Art*, trans. by M. R. Dobie. New York: Alfred A. Knopf, Inc., 1926. Interesting attempt to isolate the "Roman Spirit" and distinguish it from the "Greek Spirit."

CHAPTER 13

THE RISE
OF CHRISTIANITY

► **Religious conditions in the Roman Empire at the beginning of the Christian Era**

THE GREEK AND ROMAN BACKGROUND

In order to understand the setting for the new faith that is to be considered in this chapter, a faith that was destined to supersede the numerous religions current in the Roman Empire, it is first necessary to consider the religious conditions in the Augustan Age, especially in the Hellenistic world in which Christianity arose. The general political, social, and economic conditions in the centuries that followed the conquests of Alexander were considered in Chapter 9. It was noted that once they left their polis to try to make their fortunes abroad, the emigrant Greeks lost the security they had enjoyed at home and with it the old traditional polis religion. The religious vacuum was filled for some by the Stoic philosophy, which was almost as much a religion as it was a philosophy. Its austerity appealed, in particular, to the Roman nobility. But the oriental religions seem to have made a much greater impact, not only on the Greeks in the Hellenistic world but also on the Romans. Long before the fall of the republic some of these religions had reached Rome, and from time to time laws were passed in an attempt to check their growth. The Egyptian cult of Isis was especially popular, and during the Empire so was the Persian cult of Mithras. The native Greek mysteries of Eleusis and Samothrace experienced a revival.

Common to all these religions was the appeal they made to the individual, especially those religions which offered him initiation. After a neophyte had undergone various tests in preparation for initiation, he was granted a mystical experience and was assured of the immortality of his soul. In Mithraism, which was fairly widespread throughout the Hellenistic world before the Christian era but which did not make its impact on the West until the end of the first century A.D., the sun-hero Mithras was depicted as the great mediator for mankind, who gives man not only all the good things of the world but also assures him of salvation in the afterlife. Mithraism was later to become the great competitor of Christianity, and was vanquished only after the emperor Constantine I (312–337 A.D.) gave his support to Christianity. At the turn of the Christian era there was no such competitor; no Hellenistic or oriental religion, with the possible exception of the Isis cult, was making such progress that it could be thought of as a potentially universal religion, with a series of beliefs and teachings that could appeal to individuals everywhere. It is impossible for us to think of any of these religions as in any sense a "higher" religion, as Buddhism and Judaism clearly were and are. Buddhism had not yet spread to the West, and Judaism was as yet the religion only of a single people, the Jews, who at this time made no attempt to convert others, even though they accepted converts if they offered themselves.

THE JEWISH BACKGROUND

By the opening of the Christian era the Jewish religion had absorbed various elements from the other oriental religions. Some orthodox Jews now believed in the future life, and in the Satan and angels and demons that had always formed part of Zoroastrianism. But the Jews also held fast to their own ancient law and ritual which, with the ascendancy of their priesthood, had become ever more strict and rigid. They remained monotheists, believing that all other gods than Yahweh were either demons, idols, or nonexistent. Above all they were looking for a Messiah who would come to redeem the faithful people of Israel; for him they must remain apart, a chosen people, the only righteous ones on earth, the only ones ready to greet him when he came.

The center of the Jewish religion was the holy city of Jerusalem, which had retained a precarious independence under the Maccabees only to fall to the arms of Pompey, and thereafter submit, first to a client king, Herod of Idumaea, and then to the direct government of Rome under an equestrian procurator. The Romans had never been able to understand the Jews. From sad experience they knew that they could not drive them into making any compromises with polytheism, not even the formal acknowledgment of the divinity of the emperor. So at last they accepted the fact and let them alone, giving them religious privileges withheld from any other subjects of Rome, for the Romans felt that the Jewish faith did not constitute any real danger. It seemed impossible that such a small and exclusive sect could

expand so far that it could undermine the loyalty of the vast population of the empire.

But the Jews in Jerusalem were by no means the only Jews in the Hellenistic world. Elsewhere, in every city of importance, there was a Jewish colony which sent representatives to the great festivals at Jerusalem, willingly acknowledged the temple there as the headquarters of their religion, and from their greater wealth often sent donations for the poorer Jews of the religious capital. The widely scattered Jews of the Diaspora (Dispersion) lived in Greek cities, and were subject to the all-pervading influence of Greek culture. They could not all be so strict in their religious observances as their brethren of Jerusalem. Though they studied and loved the Hebrew law, they also studied Greek philosophy at Greek schools; they were familiar with all the intellectual currents of the Greek world. Such a one was Saul of Tarsus, who was to become the first great Christian missionary.

In Jerusalem, and to a lesser degree in the Diaspora, two important groups had arisen within Judaism, the Sadducees and the Pharisees. The Sadducees, mostly drawn from the upper classes in Jerusalem, denied the existence of angels and demons, and did not believe in the future life—all of which were accepted by most Pharisees. At the time of the Crucifixion the high priest was a Sadducee, and the Sadducees were also probably in a majority in the Jewish council (the Sanhedrin or Synedrion), which was entrusted with local government by the Romans, subject only to the general supervision of the Roman procurator. As a ruling group the Sadducees felt it necessary to play a very careful game with the Romans. If they did not perform to the satisfaction of their masters their task of keeping order locally, there was an obvious danger that the Romans would do the job themselves, and all Jews would suffer from the change.

A serious problem was presented to the Jewish authorities by the frequent appearance of self-proclaimed Messiahs, mainly in the desert areas. These men gathered around themselves fanatical and devoted bands of disciples who were too often determined that

The "Antioch Chalice" the earliest known Christian chalice used in the sacrament of the Eucharist, dating probably from the fourth century A.D. The intertwined design consists of grapevines with birds and animals. In the center is shown Christ surrounded by his apostles. (METROPOLITAN MUSEUM OF ART, CLOISTERS COLLECTION, PURCHASE 1930)

Ntrauit autem rex ut uideret
discumbentes & uidit ibi homi
nem nonuestitum ueste nuptiali &
ait illi amice· quomodo huc intras
ti nonhabens uestem nuptialem
at ille· obmutuit· Tunc ait rex
ministris ligatis pedibus & manib;
& mitte te eum intenebras exteri
ores ibi erit fletus & stridor dentiū
multi autem sunt uocati pauci uero
electi
Tunc abeuntes pharissaei con
silium fecerunt ut caparent
eum insermone· & mittunt ei dis
cipulos suos cumherodianis dicen
tes· Magister scimus quiauerax es
& uiam dī inueritate· doces &non

LEFT: *The eighth century Book of Kells, from which a page is shown here, is a beautifully illustrated version of the gospels in Latin, and is the finest known example of Celtic illumination.* (LIBRARY, TRINITY COLLEGE, DUBLIN)

BELOW: *A mosaic from the Church of the Hagia Sophia at Constantinople, showing Christ in the center, and the eleventh century empress Zoe on the right. The figure on the left was originally her first husband Romanus, who was murdered while she was a fairly young woman. Her third husband, Constantine IX, who survived her, in due course substituted his own head for that of his predecessor.* (ERICH LESSING, MAGNUM)

ON THE FOLLOWING PAGE: *The Sanskrit book of animal fables known as the* Panchatantra, *probably first compiled about 500 A.D., became popular later among the Muslims. This illustrated page from these fables shows a man, with a saddled horse and a boar, and comes from a fourteenth century Egyptian version.* (FREER GALLERY OF ART)

وكان يقال اذا رايت نفس الكذاب قد تشتتها عالم اللذ والفساد لكلها

اليه فانه لا يوثق بها للفساد تركيبها والليل على تركيب انما مضرته معرضه

عن الحقيقة في الحوادث وتراعة الى العدم المحل فيصور العدم وجودا

مساده

٢ نفس الكذاب

their Messiahs should prevail, if necessary by force. The authorities had therefore found it necessary to suppress all these messianic groups; there can be no doubt that they were deeply concerned with the danger presented by the activities of Jesus. Most of the Sadducees presumably were also awaiting the coming of the true Messiah, but they could not afford to take the chance that Jesus might be a false one like the others. The reign of the true Messiah would necessarily involve the destruction of the all-powerful Roman Empire. The acid test of whether or not a self-proclaimed Messiah was the true one would be his willingness to use his divine power to put an end to Roman rule. Jesus' refusal to do this must have been the final proof, to the Sadducees as well as to most of the Pharisees, that he was not performing a mission entrusted to him by Yahweh, but was a troublemaker who would undermine their position with the Romans. He must, therefore, be put to death.

► The Biblical Story of Jesus

We do not know as much as we should like about the early history of Christianity or the actual life and work of its founder, for reasons not unlike those already discussed in connection with the Hebrews. Almost all that we know is gathered from the four Gospels (the Greek word is *evangelion*, meaning "good news," hence the writers were called Evangelists). But the Evangelists were highly selective, choosing only those parts of the story which each felt to be essential. They were not systematic historians or biographers. Their purpose was to "preach the good news." Thus, to a later historian, there appear to be contradictions and even discrepancies, as, for instance, in the differing accounts of the birth of Jesus and the events immediately following the birth which are recorded by Matthew and Luke. Yet these Gospels are all that we possess in the way of external record, and from them must be constructed such consecutive history as is possible.[1] At this point in time it is clearly

impracticable for any historian to establish an exact history of the events in Palestine at the beginning of the Christian era. All that can be attempted is to give a brief narrative of the events that came to be believed by most Christians, with a few words on the most important of the teachings of Jesus, paying particular attention to the divergences from orthodox Jewish teaching which made it impossible for most Jews to accept him as the Messiah for whom they had been waiting.

Matthew, Mark, and Luke describe the events in Palestine from substantially the same viewpoint (hence they are known as the "synoptic" Gospels, i.e., Gospels which see the events from the same point of view), and the weight of critical opinion certainly inclines to the view that these Gospels represent the tradition as it was believed by the early Christian communities. The Gospel of John was written very much later under the influence of Hellenistic and Jewish philosophy. Thus John's Gospel already contains a clear concept of Jesus as the Christ, the Son of God, whereas critical opinion is still divided as to whether Jesus made this claim for himself. In the synoptists he is almost always called the "Son of man," and in any event they do not emphasize that he was the Son of God, as John did.

Many critics are also inclined to be extremely selective in what they accept as genuine and belonging to the original text of the Gospels, sometimes accepting or rejecting various passages simply because they are or are not consistent with the opinion they have already formed of Jesus and his teachings. Thus the passage in Matthew, a synoptic writer (16:16), in which the apostle Peter tells Jesus that he is "the Christ, the Son of the living God," a wording used also by John (6:69), has to be rejected by those critics who believe that Jesus, who on this occasion commanded Peter not to reveal what he had discovered through his intuition, did not himself claim to be the Son of God. This passage, and similar ones in Mark and Luke (8:29; 9:20), in which Peter calls him the Christ, but not the Son of God, have therefore to be rejected as later interpolations, inserted under the influence of the early Christian communities.

Lastly, it may be worth noting that only John of the four Evangelists claims to have been actually present at many of the events that he describes. If this was indeed so, then his testimony, even though it was—as may be conceded—written after the others, and after the writer had pondered during a long lifetime over the events that he had witnessed, merits at least as much credence as the writings of the other Evangelists. It remains possible that Jesus taught his more intimate disciples (of whom John, by his own account, was one) in a different way from the way in which he spoke to the twelve apostles—in which case John's record of his sayings may be a most valuable and authentic supplement to the work of the synoptists.

[1] Biblical critics, especially in recent centuries, have been struck by the fact that the Gospels of

Since the subsequent dating of the Christian era was almost certainly erroneous it is probable that Jesus was born in 4 B.C., in Bethlehem of Judaea. His mother was Mary, whose husband was Joseph of the lineage of King David. According to the Matthew account it was Joseph who was informed by the archangel Gabriel that his wife was with child and that the child was "born of the Holy Spirit." According to Luke, Mary herself was informed by an angel that the child was to be born and was to "be a son of the Most High." Thereafter, according to the account in Matthew, the infant Jesus was visited by three wise men or kings, an event which excited the suspicion of King Herod, who commanded that all newly born children should be put to death. Joseph and Mary, warned in

a dream, took the child to Egypt, returning to Nazareth to live after all danger was over. As the story is related in Luke, the child was visited by shepherds and adored by them, but thereafter returned peacefully to Nazareth, the home town of his parents. Only one further incident of the childhood of Jesus is recorded in the Gospels: a visit to the Temple in Jerusalem at the age of twelve, when he escaped from his parents and was later found by them disputing with the Rabbis, both hearing them and asking them questions.

Thereafter there is a break in the narrative until all four Evangelists record a visit to a desert prophet, John the Baptist, who had been preaching the imminent coming of the Messiah and urging the people to change their way of thinking in preparation for this

The Evangelist St. John writing his gospel. The eagle, always associated with St. John, symbolized, according to the inscription, the evangelist's yearning toward the heights. From a book of gospels (Anglo-Frankish), ca. 850. (COURTESY THE PIERPONT MORGAN LIBRARY, Ms. 862, folio 144)

► chronological chart

Birth of Jesus	(probably)	4 B.C.
Mission of Jesus Christ	(probably) A.D.	26–30
Crucifixion of Jesus	(probably)	30
Missionary journeys of Paul	ca.	34–60
Paul appeals to Roman emperor		60
Fire of Rome—First Martyrdom of Christians		64
Pliny's correspondence with Trajan about Christians		111–112
Rescript by Marcus Aurelius against Christians		169
General persecution of Christians by Emperor Decius		249–51
Diocletian persecution [Diocletian and his immediate successors]		303–13
Constantine succeeds to throne		312
"Edict of Milan"—equal rights granted to all religions		313
Council of Nicaea		325
Conversion of Goths to Arianism (Bishop Ulfilas)		340–348
Rule of St. Basil	ca.	360
Julian the Apostate		361–363
Theodosius I forced to do penance for massacre at Thessalonica		390
Proscription of pagan religions by Theodosius		392
Death of Augustine (*City of God, ca. 425–430*)		430
St. Patrick's mission to Ireland		432
Invasion of Italy by Attila the Hun		452
Western bishops subjected to Pope Leo I by Emperor Valentinian III		455
Rule of St. Benedict		529
Irish monasticism of St. Columbia		533–597
Columbia founds monastery of Iona and Scottish Church		563
Missionary work of St. Columban in Europe		590–615
Pope Gregory I the Great		590–604
Conversion of England to Catholic Christianity		597
Synod of Whitby—Submission of Irish Church		664

event.[2] John had already declared that he himself was not the Messiah. When he saw Jesus coming, he immediately recognized him as the one who should come, "the latchet of whose shoes I am unworthy to unloose," and baptized him in the river. A voice was heard from heaven saying, "This is my beloved son in whom I am well pleased," and the Holy Spirit was seen descending from heaven in the form of a dove.

[2] The Greek word *metanoeite* means literally "change your outlook" or "change your way of think-thing." This conveys a different sense from the word *repent*, by which it is usually translated, here and elsewhere in the Gospels.

For the next three years Jesus preached to the people and healed the sick. Sometimes he taught straightforwardly, attacking above all the strict Pharisees, whose religion was mere outward show. At other times he hid his true message within parables, sometimes, even as he gave one interpretation, adding the words, "Let him hear who has ears to hear." He chose twelve men to be his special aides, and these were called apostles; around him gathered many more who came to listen to him. Those who decided to follow him were called disciples.

Throughout his teaching there is always the emphasis that true religion comes from the heart, and that "the Law and the prophets" are comprised in two commandments, the love of God and the love of one's neighbor. Though these teachings, with their evident wealth of hidden meanings, have inspired Christians ever since, nevertheless it is not the teachings of Jesus, but his life, death, and resurrection, as recorded in the Gospels, that have been regarded by the Christian Church and Christian believers as the best evidence for the divine origin of his mission and for the divinity of his person. Clearly such a record is unverifiable by any means available to the historian, and Christians themselves have always regarded the acceptance of this record as an act of faith. They believed that the Son of God had actually been incarnated in a human body (or, as John puts it, the Logos (or Word) became flesh) and had, as man, been crucified and resurrected after three days. This belief that the central figure of Christianity had actually lived on earth, and had been seen and could be remembered by his followers, gave Christianity an appeal denied to such religions as Mithraism or any of the oriental mystery religions, whose central figures were gods, but not at the same time men.

On the other hand the teachings of Jesus have been expressed by others almost equally well, and there is nothing profoundly *new* in them. Many Jews had in recent years been emphasizing "love of one's neighbor" as a commandment of God, which had indeed been incorporated in the Torah (Leviticus 19:18 commands the Hebrews to love their neighbors as themselves). Some Hebrew prophets had spoken out against hypocrisy scarcely less vehemently than Jesus. Absolute obedience to God's will was stressed as much by Jesus as by the Jews. An important segment of the Jews (the Pharisees) accepted the future life. But Jesus' attitude to the law was not that of the stricter Jews, and there can be little doubt that he gave far less importance to formal prayers and ceremonials than did the Jews. His concept of the Kingdom of Heaven was different from theirs; there is no sign that he ever believed that in this Kingdom there would be a special place for the Jews as a chosen people.

What was striking in the ethical teachings of Jesus was not that they were new or revolutionary, which they were not, but the manner in which he proclaimed them, with, as one of the Evangelists expressed it, "authority," as if he were indeed inspired by God and proclaiming what he *knew* to be God's will. If there had been no martyrdom, no death and resurrection, he might well have seemed to his followers to be in the direct line from the great Hebrew prophets, perhaps greater than they because of the public manner in which he performed his mission—and the miracles that accompanied it—but not superhuman, not the "Son of God." It was his resurrection that placed the seal on his life and death, and this was fully grasped by St. Paul, the first great Christian missionary. "If Christ be not risen, then is our preaching vain and your faith vain" (I Corinthians, 15:14).

The Gospel accounts are in substantial agreement with each other on the death and resurrection. After three years of preaching and healing Jesus had aroused the resentment of many Jews, who had not been convinced by his signs[3] or his teachings. But it was one of his own apostles, Judas Iscariot, who betrayed him to the leading Jews, who thereupon sent a guard to take him prisoner. Jesus made no attempt to defend himself, and indeed forbade his disciples to use any violence against the guard. He had already warned them that he would be put to death and raised from the dead after three days, but they had not understood him. When they saw that he was captured and would not defend himself, they deserted him. The leading apostle, Peter, even went so far as to deny publicly that he had ever known him, thus fulfilling another prophecy of his master.

Jesus was then examined by the High Priest. The Evangelists give different versions of the question he was asked and of his answer, but the synoptists agree (John omits altogether the details of the scene, at which

---

[3] The Greek word *semaion* or "sign" was translated into Latin in the authoritative Latin Bible of St. Jerome as *miraculum*; hence our word *miracle*, which probably gives the wrong impression of these symbolic acts.

The crucifixion of Jesus Christ painted by the Dominican Friar, Fra Angelico (fourteenth century). (COURTESY THE METROPOLITAN MUSEUM OF ART)

he could not have been present) that the High Priest and Council took the answer to be a blasphemy and wished to put him to death in accordance with Jewish law. But to do this the sentence had to be confirmed by the Roman procurator, Pontius Pilate. Pilate then questioned him, but finding that his offense seemed to be only a religious one, was anxious to release him. However, when the Jews insisted that Jesus had wished to make himself "King of the Jews," Pilate realized at once that the situation was dangerous. Tiberius was on the imperial throne, and he had recently been increasing the severity of the treason laws and enforcing them. When the Jews insisted that they "had no king but Caesar," and that he himself would not be "Caesar's friend" if he let Jesus go, he gave way and allowed him to be crucified. A rich follower of Jesus claimed his body and buried it in the tomb prepared for himself.

At this point it must have seemed to anyone alive at the time that Jesus had failed in his mission. He had been put to death, like other Messiahs before him, and his followers, mostly men and women of the lower classes and of no influence, had deserted him. He would soon, like the others, be forgotten.

► The early Christian Church

THE CONVERSION OF ST. PAUL AND THE NEW MISSIONARY IMPULSE

This time, however, there was a strikingly different outcome. On the third day after Jesus' death Peter, John, and a woman follower of Jesus named Mary Magdalene went to the tomb and found it empty. Then they saw their master once more alive in the body, and he showed himself to his disciples several times. This experience gave them new hope and energy, and, according to the only account of these events that has come down to us, the New Testament book known as the Acts of the Apostles (presumably written by the evangelist Luke), they began to remember the promises that had been made to them by Jesus both before and after his resurrection. After forty days on earth, during which he had given new teachings about the future, he was taken up to heaven and "a cloud received him out of their sight." But the disciples were left with his promise that the Helper or Holy Spirit would come to them and remain with them always.

One day, when the apostles had gathered together in an upper room and after they had chosen by lot a twelfth apostle to replace Judas Iscariot, who had, in remorse, hanged himself, there was suddenly "the sound of a rushing mighty wind." They were all filled with the Holy Spirit, and began to prophesy, and speak each in the tongue of the land of his origin. The onlookers thought them drunk, but with new inspiration they began to proclaim the resurrection of Jesus and to make converts. One of the disciples, Stephen, addressed an assembly of Jews, accusing them of always having maltreated, rejected, and put to death their prophets. The Jews, goaded beyond their endurance, stoned him to death, making him the first Christian martyr (Greek for "witness"). Apparently the Roman officials looked the other way and did not interfere.

Present at the stoning was Saul of Tarsus, a Roman citizen, an orthodox Hellenized Jew of the sect of the Pharisees, who at once saw the danger from these new fanatical believers in a Messiah who had failed and died without fulfilling the mission expected of him. Saul therefore, with a band of determined helpers, proceeded to lead an expedition of extermination against the Christians, presumably with the aid, or at least the connivance, of the Roman authorities, since the Jews did not have the right to inflict capital punishment themselves. Having done his best in Jeru-

salem, he set out on a journey to Damascus in Syria to continue the persecution of converts in the north. On the road to Damascus he had an experience in which the crucified Jesus appeared to him in a vision. This experience gave him an absolute conviction from which he never afterward wavered, leading him to regard and speak of himself as an apostle called out of due time. At first, however, he was paralyzed and struck blind; his servants brought him to Damascus, where his faculties were restored by a Christian. From this moment Saul, whom the records thereafter call Paul, was as strongly for the Christians as he had previously been against them. After a period of retirement during which he was apparently coming to an understanding of his experience on the road to Damascus and the realization of his mission, he went to Jerusalem, where he was naturally received with some distrust by his late enemies. But, even without any real authorization from the body of Jewish Christians who had now formed a church in Jerusalem as headquarters of the new religion, he set out on a missionary journey. During the course of this journey he took the epoch-making decision to baptize Greeks and other non-Jews as Christians without making them become Jews first, sparing them the Jewish rites and ritual which Peter had been insisting on in Palestine.

Returning to Jerusalem, Paul reached a compromise with Peter that Gentiles outside Palestine need not become Jews, while the church in Jerusalem would continue with the requirement. Then Paul set out again, making converts everywhere, especially among the Greeks to whom he, with his Greek education, was able to speak in their own language and in their own terms. At Athens itself, finding an altar dedicated "To the unknown God," he showed the Athenians who this God was, and why he hitherto had been unknown to them. With rare organizing ability and drive, he founded churches in all the places he visited, and kept in touch with them afterward by correspondence. His letters, the earliest authentic Christian documents, expounded the new Christian theology, which seems to have been almost entirely his own work, and answered the numerous questions put to him. In all the cities Paul visited in Asia Minor and Greece, his most determined opponents were, at least according to the account in the Acts of the Apostles, always the Jews. Indeed, it is from this book that all our information on the apparently systematic opposition of the Jews to Christianity is drawn.

OPPOSITION OF THE JEWS TO CHRISTIANITY

According to the writer, Paul and his fellow-missionaries invariably went first to the Jewish synagogues in the Hellenistic cities, and tried to make converts. They always succeeded in making some, but at the same time excited the hostility of others. Some of the hostile Jews made it their business to warn in advance those communities which Paul was expected to visit next. As a result there were numerous riots which the Romans were forced to suppress, apparently with considerable irritation and distaste since from their point of view the riots stemmed from religious quarrels among the Jews. They could scarcely be expected to distinguish between Christians and Jews. According to the Acts of the Apostles the hostile Jews even pursued Paul to Jerusalem and roused their fellow-Jews there, including the official leaders of the community, against Paul, making it necessary for the Romans to rescue him once more.

Although there is no reason to doubt the details of the story—Luke himself accompanied Paul on some of his journeys—it does raise the question of the extent of the opposition of the Jews to Christianity. Even in this account the attacks on Paul and his fellow-missionaries look like the work of a determined minority of Jewish militants, who were quite capable of exciting the passions of their fellow-Jews even though the latter may have had little idea of the reasons for the quarrel. Devout Jews could hardly be blamed for objecting to the use of their synagogues for the purpose of preaching and winning converts to a religion in which Gentiles also participated. The one specific accusation recorded by Luke was that Paul brought a Gentile Greek into the synagogue, a charge which Paul denied. His Jewish accusers brought this

charge up again when Paul was brought before a Roman governor, though they naturally added that he was disturbing the peace by sowing dissension among "Jews all over the world."

From the Jewish point of view the Christians were a serious threat to Jewish unity. It was an article of faith among Jews that they should remain together as a people, obeying the law and observing the rituals and practices prescribed for them in the Torah, and that Yahweh had often punished them in the past because of their infidelity. When Jews converted to Christianity they widened the schism in Jewry. There was, therefore, every reason to forbid their synagogues to such effective missionaries as Paul and his companions. Some Jews, especially the official leaders, were seriously disturbed also because the Romans at first looked upon Christianity as a Jewish sect, in which case Jews would be held responsible for the deeds of Christians over whom they had no control. The Christian zeal for conver-version, in particular, would be likely to offend the Roman authorities who tolerated Judaism only because it was virtually confined to a single small people.

It is clear from Luke's account that the missionaries felt that they had every right to preach to Jews, because it was their belief that the promises formerly made to the Jews had been fulfilled when Jesus appeared on earth as the promised Messiah. If Jews did not accept this truth the reason was that they had been insufficiently informed. It was necessary, therefore, to preach the "good news" to them. However, it was also part of Paul's message that though the Messiah had appeared among the Jews, as had been promised, he had died for all mankind, and not for the Jews alone. There can be no doubt that this teaching was bitterly resented among those Jews who had been most deeply attached to their notion that they were a people set apart by Yahweh, and bound together by their common observances. Now the Christians were making light of these observances. Paul taught that the law had been given to them "because of offenses," that is, because they had not until then known what God required of them. The law, he wrote in a letter to the Galatians, is a "schoolmaster to bring us to Christ." Under the new dispensation, human beings were no longer children, needing to be kept under discipline, but "sons," with their knowledge of right and wrong no longer dictated to them by the law, but by their own intuition, guided by faith and love. Such a teaching might be deduced from what the Hebrew prophet Jeremiah had said, that the law would one day be "written within their hearts" (see page 128), but the majority of the Jews could not bring themselves to abandon the practices of their religion, which were also a part of the law.

PAUL AS THE FOUNDER OF CHRISTIAN THEOLOGY

On the whole Paul met with little opposition from Greeks and Romans unless, as at Ephesus, he offended the priesthood of a powerful Greco–Oriental mystery cult, or unless he was responsible for the outbreak of riots. When he eventually returned from his journeys to Jerusalem the riots were so bad that the Romans had to take him into protective custody to save him from a plot against his life. Later, in a hearing before the Roman authorities, Paul gained the impression that he would be put to death by them, a penalty which could not be inflicted on Roman citizens except by permission of the emperor. He therefore claimed his right as a Roman citizen and appealed to Caesar (Nero). The local governor was thus forced to send him to Rome, where, according to Luke, no one had heard of him and he was allowed full freedom to preach. Tradition has it that he was beheaded during the first organized persecution of Christians in Rome about A.D. 65.

Paul was the real founder of Christianity as a universal religion. If the other apostles, who wished to confine Christianity to the Jews, had been successful it hardly seems possible that the religion could have survived. Paul also deserves to be considered as one of the most influential thinkers of history. It was no mean feat to transform what was, to external eyes, nothing beyond the life and death of a great prophet into a system of theology which remains the fundamental teaching of all Christian churches, Catholic and Protestant alike.

Nevertheless, this theology is not stated systematically, but has to be gleaned from Paul's letters to the various Christian communities. There is a noticeable difference in the way in which he writes to Gentiles, such as the Ephesians, who had converted to Christianity, and to converts from Judaism. In his letter to the Ephesians he passes quickly over the question of the relation of the law of Moses to Christianity, merely saying that it has been "voided," whereas the letter to the Jewish converts in Rome is almost entirely devoted to the subject. It should therefore be understood that not only have there always been differences of opinion among Christians on what aspects of Paul's teaching should be emphasized, but even on what he actually did teach. Many of his letters were evidently written in reply to specific questions that the different communities had asked him. As a result there are important shades of difference in his replies. What follows, therefore, is a very brief resumé of those aspects of his teaching which he himself appears to have emphasized and which come under the heading of theology, as distinct from advice on moral behavior of which his letters are full.

To Paul, who of course had not known Jesus in person (although he claimed to have seen him after the resurrection), Christ was the Son of God, and yet at the same time he was also "an earthly man." Paul never uses the name Jesus by itself. To him Jesus is either the Lord Jesus, Christ Jesus, or simply Christ, or the Christ. It is therefore appropriate to use the word Christ in connection with the teachings of Paul. It was as an earthly man that Christ passed through death, and he was the first earthly man to have been resurrected. In Paul's teaching sin and death had come into the world through Adam, the first man.[4] Thereafter all men had sinned, and as a result

[4] This refers to the Hebrew story of the sin of Adam (Genesis, 3). Because he had disobeyed God at the instigation of "the serpent" and had eaten of the tree of knowledge, Adam was driven out of the Garden of Eden before he could eat also of the other forbidden tree, the tree of life. Thus, because Adam sinned, he lost the possibility of eternal life.

all had been condemned to die without the possibility of resurrection and eternal life. God then gave man the law so that he would know the difference between right and wrong and would no longer sin through ignorance. But God had given it only to the Hebrews, and even they had not been able to refrain from sinning because of "the domination of the body." So man continued to sin, and to die without hope of resurrection.

But in the fullness of time, God, who loved man and did not want him to go on sinning and who wanted him to have eternal life, sent his son to the earth as a "ransom" for man, to live on earth as a man and to suffer death on the cross. Man had done nothing to deserve this; it was an entirely gratuitous act on the part of God, an act of mercy, not justice. Sin is justly *recompensed* by death, but God's *gift* is eternal life. Christ was the "first to be raised of those that slept," and for this reason Paul calls him the "last Adam." "As in Adam all die, so in Christ shall all be made alive."

Although Paul does not make his teaching entirely clear on the matter, and there are passages in his works which apparently teach the opposite, one important passages states that those who "die in Christ" will remain peacefully asleep until the last day, the day of the Second Coming of Christ. No one knows when this will take place, because he will "come like a thief in the night." According to his first letter to the Corinthians (15) Christ will be the lord of the world until the Second Coming, and he will then yield up his kingdom (this world) to his Father. After this there will be no more death—"the last enemy to be destroyed is death"—and the living, together with all those who died in Christ and "belong to him," will be granted eternal life. According to Paul they will then have "spiritual bodies" and no longer physical bodies because "flesh and blood cannot share in the Kingdom of God, and decay will not share in what is imperishable."

Paul states clearly that what Christ asks of man is faith. "Everyone who calls upon the name of the Lord will be saved." "If with your mouth you acknowledge the Lord Jesus,

and if you believe in your heart that God raised him from the dead you will be saved."[5] He never tires of repeating that his message was proclaimed for all men, Jews and Gentiles alike. It had become the custom in the Christian communities for conversion to be symbolized by baptism. The synoptic writers, Matthew and Mark, state that this sacrament had been established by Jesus after his resurrection, whereas John tells us that Jesus himself had never baptized, though his disciples did so. Paul tells the Corinthians that he had not been sent by Christ to baptize but to preach the good news, though he admitted he had baptized occasionally. However, in two passages he makes clear that baptism allows the believer to "die with Christ," and because he dies with Christ, he may hope to be resurrected like him. This has been interpreted by many, but far from all, Christian theologians to mean that baptism frees man from original sin (the sin of Adam), and that therefore the baptized person will not die as other sinners die. Hence the importance of baptism as a sacrament of the Catholic Church, even though it has ceased to be the symbol of conversion, and is now ordinarily performed in infancy.

THE APPEAL OF CHRISTIANITY IN THE ROMAN WORLD

Christianity, as it emerged from the mind and heart of St. Paul, was eminently fitted to make the deepest appeal to religious men and women throughout the world. It promised salvation in the hereafter to all who would accept Christ, and this acceptance was simply an act of faith. Thus, in spite of its complex theology, perhaps never understood by more than a small minority of its adherents, it was basically simple. It was no respecter of persons. The

[5] Romans 10:9. The translations used in this section have been taken from several English translations, but the author has in each case checked with the Greek text since almost all the translators of the New Testament have taken some liberties with the original, either for the sake of added clarity or possibly because of religious commitment. For example, the Chicago Bible, which was recommended for the Old Testament, translates the above words as "If with your lips you acknowledge the message that Jesus is Lord and with your mind you believe that God raised him from the dead you will be saved."

meanest slave was eligible for salvation, and to him it also offered the fullest compensation for his hard life on earth—which was merely a testing ground for the hereafter. No distinction was made between men and women, and there were no difficult trials or initiation ceremonies to be undergone by the convert. And in early days there was a belief in the imminent Second Coming of Christ to judge the world, so that the faithful Christians might not even see death. No religion in the world of the time, not even the mystery religions, could offer as much to its converts—community fellowship, a sense of mission and urgency, a promise of a blessed immortality, and a theology and philosophy capable of satisfying even the Greek mind when later it set to work on it. If at first Christianity lacked gorgeous ceremonial, this was later added in full measure by the Church. And in the recorded sayings of Christ it had a fund of ethical and moral teachings which could satisfy even the Roman feeling for active morality.

Yet it did not appeal in early times to the upper classes among either the Romans or the Greeks; indeed, for centuries it was primarily a religion of Greeks and Orientals, with comparatively few Roman converts, and hardly a single Roman martyr. The Romans, even when they were correctly informed about it, regarded it as a religion for slaves and foreigners, and it was difficult for men who considered themselves morally superior to the rest of the world and destined to rule to accept as a redeemer a man who had belonged to a despised people and had suffered a slave's death in a remote part of the empire. His origin and manner of dying offended their class consciousness and pride of race, while the Greek intellectuals at first considered his teachings philosophically negligible. In time, however, as the Greeks learned more about the religion, many of them began to take an active role in the formulation of Christian theology, and, especially in the early days of the Byzantine Empire, entered passionately into theological controversy.

Physical conditions in the Roman Empire, however, were ideally suited for the spread of Christianity. The establishment of the Pax Romana made it possible for missionaries to travel in perfect safety from one end of the empire to the other, and the strategic Roman roads provided an ideal means of communication. The common languages of Greek and Latin could be understood everywhere. Roman protection was extended to all, without discrimination, at least until the new religion was proscribed as a subversive organization. And, as we have seen, any missionary like Paul who happened also to be a Roman citizen had special privileges in addition to the general protection extended by the Roman Empire to all its subjects.

The Romans, in general, were hospitable to all religions. But the religion of emperor-worship, which was the official cult of the empire, was both more and less than a religion. On the one hand, it was not expected to command the religious devotion of the people, but on the other hand no one, save only the Jews whose uncompromising monotheism was well known to the Romans, was exempted from paying at least formal tribute to the emperor as a god. This allegiance the true Christian was unwilling to give, since he regarded worship as the prerogative of God alone. Roman attention was first officially drawn to the Christians when they were accused in the reign of Nero of having set fire to Rome (A.D. 64). At that time Christianity became a proscribed religion, and the first Christians were put to death by the Roman authorities. The steadfastness of the martyrs, whose number traditionally includes Peter and Paul, probably aided the Christians more than the laws against them harmed them. The religiously indifferent Romans had never been treated to such a display before; and even while the majority ridiculed, it is certain that a minority was impressed. When the immediate persecution died down, the laws against Christianity remained on the statute book, presenting a difficulty to Roman officials who regarded them with distaste. An interesting correspondence between the Younger Pliny and the emperor Trajan is extant, in which Pliny asked for advice about enforcing the laws. The emperor instructed him to take action only when Christians were denounced to him and refused to pay the required worship to the emperor.

This indifference remained the official Roman policy until the middle of the third century A.D., by which time Christianity had become a powerful organized religion, whose leaders commanded more respect from their followers than did the often shadowy emperors of that epoch from their titular subjects. Several emperors revived and strengthened the laws against Christians, but they were only sporadically enforced until the reign of Diocletian, who, as we shall see in Chapter 14, was able to secure his own position and rule as an absolute monarch. A part of his program for the reestablishment of imperial authority was the revival of emperor-worship. In this aim he naturally came into conflict with Christian beliefs. The persecution, however, in spite of creating many martyrs, ultimately failed and a few years later (312) Constantine, opposed by a sun-worshiper who was competing with him for the throne, called upon the Christian God for support in his struggle. When the victory was won, he and his coemperor in the East authorized the toleration of Christianity and during the course of his reign he himself was converted. Thereafter all the emperors but one (Julian the Apostate) acknowledged themselves as Christians, until in 380 the emperor Theodosius I made Christianity the official religion of the Empire. Twelve years later he proscribed all other religions.

▶ **The organization of the Church**

IN THE PROVINCES

As the Church grew, so naturally did the complexity of its organization. St. Paul himself, as we have seen, kept in touch with all the congregations he had founded, giving them advice and visiting them when he could. As yet there were no priests or Church officials of any kind, and the simple ceremonies and meetings did not require the services of men set aside for purely religious duties. The affairs of the churches were managed by elders, active men in the congregation who took the initiative in matters of religion. But as ever more congregations were organized and it was realized that they might drift apart both in doctrine and in practices if left to themselves, it became clear to the leaders that some kind of more elaborate organization was necessary to keep them united. Living as they did, within the Roman Empire, there was obviously one particular pattern of organization that could best be imitated, the organization of the empire itself. Within the congregations three hierarchies differentiated themselves in the process of time: deacons, whose task was to give help to Christians in their ordinary daily affairs and especially to take care of the administration of charity; presbyters, who looked after religious affairs of the church; and then an individual leader, called an overseer or episcopus, from which comes our word *bishop*.

In early times neither presbyters nor bishops were in any way superior to the ordinary layman, nor did they go through any special ceremony when they were elected to their position. But by the end of the second century, with the elaboration of the ceremonial of the Church and the growth of the belief that its services were needed for salvation, these clergy became set apart as a class of real priests who were *ordained* by the bishops. Ordination, like baptism and the Eucharist, had now become a *sacrament*, while the ceremony of ordination became a ritual conferring special sanctity upon the holder. For several centuries more it was the congregations who chose their bishops; but once chosen, these men had full monarchical power within their churches. As time went on, it became necessary to have archbishops whose seats were usually in the Roman capitals, or chief cities, and who were in charge of all the churches in their respective provinces. These men were called metropolitans. The bishops in the whole empire met from time to time in ecumenical (universal) councils, presided over by the metropolitans or by the bishop of Rome (later called pope[6]), to consider doctrinal problems and to discuss matters which concerned the Church as a whole.

IN ROME—THE BISHOP OF ROME— PETRINE SUPREMACY

The bishop of Rome had a peculiar position as the head of the church in the capital city of the empire. Probably as early as the second century A.D. the Roman congregation was the largest in the empire. The church in Rome, according to tradition, had been founded by the apostle Peter, who had become its first bishop and been martyred and buried there.

But it was a long time before St. Peter's position was supposed to confer any supreme authority upon his successors. Other bishops claimed to be the equals of the bishops of Rome, and it was usually the reputation and personality of individual bishops which gave them whatever authority they might possess in spiritual matters. Ambrose, bishop of Milan in the fourth century, was clearly the most influential bishop of his day, and was able to force the emperor himself to do penance for a massacre he had committed. But in the course of time it gradually became accepted doctrine that Peter, who had been entrusted by Christ with the task of founding the Church, had delegated his authority to his successor, and the latter to his successor, right down to the present time. This theory of the Petrine (or Apostolic) succession is still the basis for the authority claimed by the Catholic Church.

As long as an emperor ruled in Rome, the bishop's authority was naturally limited to his spiritual domain. But when Honorius, Emperor of the West, removed his court to Ravenna at the end of the fourth century the bishop was left as the chief dignitary in Rome, and at times he performed the functions of a Roman ruler in the city. One great pope, Leo I, negotiated with Attila the Hun and succeeded in diverting him from the city; and

[6] The Latin word *papa* merely means "father," a title given by courtesy to other priests than the pope. It is not known for certain when the word *pope* was first applied exclusively to the bishop of Rome.

the same pope negotiated for the safety of its inhabitants during the sack of Rome by the Vandals. As the Roman provincial administration gradually collapsed in the fifth century, under the impact of the barbarian invaders, the bishops in many of the provinces took over from the helpless Roman governors and tried to protect the interests of the people as best they could. They now started to look to the pope (as we may now call the bishop of Rome) for guidance in political policy as well as for spiritual leadership. Pope Leo I was given official recognition by Emperor Valentinian III of Ravenna, who conferred upon him full authority over all the bishops in the empire. Pope Leo did not hesitate to use this authority, demanding implicit obedience from them and pronouncing final decisions in matters of doctrine.

► The establishment of Christian doctrine

THE QUESTIONS NOT ANSWERED BY ST. PAUL

St. Paul, as mentioned previously, was the founder of Christian theology; but his teachings, usually given in response to definite questions put to him by his churches, were very far from being satisfying to all inquiring minds. Early in the history of the Christian Church his authority was accepted as that of an apostle chosen by the resurrected Christ to explain the nature of his relationship to God the Father and other mysteries of the religion; and by A.D. 170 his letters, together with the letters of the other apostles, the four Gospels (though there was still some dissent about the authenticity of the Gospel of John), the Acts of the Apostles, and most of the present books of the New Testament, were accepted as canonical or inspired books. In 367 Athanasius, the influential patriarch of Alexandria, declared that all the present New Testament books should be accepted as canonical, leaving the many other early stories of Christianity without authority. Nothing excluded from the New Testament or written later has quite the same authority. Other men might add to Paul's theology, but such men were not apostles, and there was no inherent reason why one man's ideas on the subject should be better than any other man's. Yet clearly all the questions that could be asked had not been answered by Christ, Paul, or the other apostles. And it was equally clear that some questions really did need answering. Moreover, many men came into Christianity after earlier experience in the mystery religions, and they were not all ready to abandon what they had been taught before conversion.

There were questions of doctrine, in particular one concerning the relation of the Son of God to the Father and the relation of both to the Holy Spirit, which were to exercise theologians for many centuries; and there were practical questions, such as the respective roles of faith and good deeds in the winning of salvation, and the effect of God's infinite foreknowledge and omnipotence upon man's free will. Many differing opinions on these matters had been stated publicly by the time of the conversion of Constantine, and there was no evident way of establishing the truth. Yet the truth must be established if Christianity were not to divide into many competing sects, each holding its own beliefs as established truths.

THE ESTABLISHMENT OF ORTHODOX
DOCTRINE

The question of heresy

In 325 Constantine himself summoned a council of Nicaea, over which he presided in person. Here the bishops of the empire assembled and a statement of beliefs, or a creed, was agreed upon. The teachings of an elderly presbyter named Arius, who claimed that Christ was sent from God, possessed divine substance, but was in no sense coequal with God the Father, were condemned. The teachings had been making considerable headway, especially among the barbarians who were in the process of being converted to Christianity. Indeed, this simpler belief appealed to some of the emperors subsequent to Constantine, and they continued to permit Arianism to be preached by the missionaries in their domains. The consequence was that all the Germanic barbarian peoples who later penetrated into the empire, with the single exception of the

Franks, had already accepted Arianism before the fall of Rome. They were thus hostile to the papacy, which adhered to the teachings of Athanasius, whose teachings were pronounced by the papacy to be "orthodox" (the "right opinion"). Arianism was termed a "heresy" (Greek word for "choice"), and true Christians were forbidden to hold it.

Arianism, however, was far from the only heresy of the early centuries of Christianity.[7] Especially in Constantinople there were numerous heresies, sometimes supported by the emperor and his nominee, the patriarch who was the chief Church official in the East. In the eleventh century the Eastern and Western Churches were finally split over a doctrinal difference. But in the West, as the doctrine of the Petrine supremacy gained acceptance, it was agreed also that the pope, by virtue of his authority as the successor of St. Peter, could declare the true doctrines of the Church which must be held by all believers. He could also state which of the early Christian writings were authoritative, and contained truths inspired by the Holy Spirit. Thus grew up the authority of the Fathers of the Church, whose teachings were to be regarded as orthodox. Indeed, the Catholic and other Christian Churches teach many dogmas that are not to be found in the Bible, but have been derived from the inspired writings of the Greek and Latin Fathers.

The teachings of St. Augustine

Most influential among these Fathers was St. Augustine (354–430), bishop of Hippo in North Africa (to be distinguished from the later St. Augustine of Canterbury, who was sent by Pope Gregory I to convert the English), who devoted his life not only to the duties of his bishopric but also to evolving a theology which became in its essentials the accepted doctrine of the Church,

[7] Two other important heresies were Monophysitism, still held by the Coptic Church, which denied the humanity of Jesus Christ claiming that he was of wholly divine nature; and Nestorianism, which won many successes in Asia, including, for a time, in China. Nestorians objected to calling the Virgin Mary the Mother of God. In their view she should be called only the Mother of Christ. The Nestorians therefore emphasized his human above his divine nature.

even though some of his most extreme views were not stressed owing to their momentous consequences for human free will. Augustine has left us in his *Confessions* a complete account of his intellectual and spiritual struggles before his conversion, which are of the greatest importance for our understanding of the conflicting intellectual currents of the time. Always conscious of his own guilt and sinfulness, like Martin Luther, who resembled him in so many respects, he could only believe in a real conversion of the heart. But for a long time he could not bring himself to accept Christianity, which he was inclined to despise because it left too many questions unanswered. Tempted by the dualistic doctrine of Manichaeism (see page 369), he never really freed himself from it, believing most fervently in the power of evil, which he had experienced within himself. Then he immersed himself in the last great pagan philosophy of Neoplatonism,[8] which also taught the evilness of matter, and the necessity of overcoming all material desires for the purpose of attaining a mystical union with God. This also finds its place in Augustine's theology; and there is an extraordinarily moving passage in the *Confessions* where he describes such an experience, which came to him as the result of his conversion.

The real question, therefore, for Augustine was what need there was for a Church as mediator between man and God, and why there should be a Church at all. Indeed, Martin Luther, a deep student of Augustine, did break away from the Catholic Church, while not deviating from St. Augustine save in this one matter. The human

will, said Augustine, following St. Paul, is not free, and the human being is bound by original sin. He cannot even acquire any true knowledge merely out of himself. But Christ's sacrifice had redeemed mankind, and thereafter it had become possible for man to receive grace, as a heavenly gift. Grace alone can enable man to know the truth, and to do good. This line of reasoning led Augustine to accept the Church teaching that grace can be obtained only if a man truly believes and receives the sacraments. The Catholic Church alone can administer these sacraments. Where did the Catholic Church receive this power? Directly from Christ to St. Peter, as we have seen, and so through the succession of popes.

This, however, does not mean that man is necessarily saved by faith or by receiving the sacraments, for God has infinite foreknowledge and infinite power. Augustine therefore comes to the conclusion that God has predestined some men for salvation and some to damnation. Man can never know for certain whether he is saved, since this is entirely in God's hands, and within his knowledge alone. In logic this position is irrefutable, and Thomas Aquinas and the medieval scholastics were forced to wrestle with the problem again. But predestination was never stressed in the Catholic Church, and not until John Calvin in the sixteenth century was it stated in this extreme form again. The remainder of the doctrine—the powerlessness of human thinking and willing, and the necessity for grace—became part of orthodox Christian thought.

As an indefatigable polemicist Augustine spent much energy in combating the teachings of a certain Pelagius, who claimed that man could be saved by his own good deeds. It may well be that he gradually worked out his teachings on the necessity for grace and the powerlessness of the human will in response to what he regarded as the dangerously heretical teachings of Pelagius, whose belief that there is no original sin, that man is free and responsible and not in need of any special grace because he had already been given enough grace by God to enable

---

[8] This philosophy, whose founder was an Egyptian named Plotinus, was derived from Plato, but it is a far more systematic idealism than that of the Greek. Fundamentally it is an attempt to bring mysticism within the scope of philosophy, and is both a philosophical explanation of the experience of the human soul when it finds union with God (called by Plotinus the One), and an "otherworldly" ethic which emphasizes the desirability of this union. It is impossible in a brief space to do any justice to the philosophy, which had an immense influence on both Christian and Muslim thought, though a few further remarks will be devoted to it in later chapters.

Unlike the Greeks and Romans, who cremated their dead, the Christians insisted on burial, and were permitted by the Romans to bury their dead as long as their burial places were outside the city walls. They therefore constructed extensive catacombs outside many of the more important cities, where they buried their dead in closed vaults. These catacombs also served as places of refuge during the earlier persecutions since Roman law forbade the arrest of persons in holy places, including cemeteries. It was not until the third century persecutions that the sanctuary was taken away from them. From the very early times the catacombs were decorated with frescoes, initially only of Christian symbols and later with more elaborate paintings. The picture above, from the second century tomb of St. Domitilla, shows the altar, a barely decipherable fresco, and burial niches. The lower picture, from the catacomb of St. Priscilla, shows three youths in the fiery furnace, a symbol of redemption and resurrection. (TOP: EDITORIAL PHOTOCOLOR ARCHIVES; BOTTOM: R. SCHODER)

him to perform good deeds, was formally stigmatized as heresy by the Council of Ephesus in 431.

Augustine was also a pioneer in another field of thought at least as influential as his theology. An earlier Christian Father, Eusebius, had written an *Ecclesiastical History* which interpreted all the events of his own and earlier times in the light of the Old Testament, and especially of Hebrew prophecy. But Augustine went much further, and in his *City of God* produced a philosophy of history designed to show that with the coming of Christ an entirely new phase had opened. Attacking the pagans who claimed that the sack of Rome by Alaric was due to the desertion of the old gods by their worshipers, Augustine declared that this was part of God's scheme. Rome belonged to the "City of Man," which was only temporary and must pass away, to give place to the "City of God" on earth, which would endure forever. The beginnings had already been made under the Hebrew theocracy, and now from the coming of Christ must be continued by the Christian Church. Augustine with great passion and power described God's whole plan for the world, the creation and fall of man and the old dispensation, followed by man's redemption in the new age and the building of the City of God. It need hardly be pointed out how much this conception owes to the Hebrew interpretation of history, already discussed in an earlier chapter.

In Augustine's own thought it is clear that the perfect City of God can never exist on earth; but it is the ideal to which all Christians should aspire, and the beginnings of the building can be made in the here and now. Christians in subsequent ages, however, took it to be the ideal of Christendom, a working plan for all Christians to follow, justifying the extirpation of heresy as treason to the City of God, and later justifying also the extermination of infidels as a fulfillment of God's plan for the unity of all men on earth in the Christian religion. The *City of God* was perhaps, after the Bible, the most influential book in the medieval world.

▶ The persistent ideal of poverty and holiness—Monasticism

From very early times there was opposition to the Church as an organized institution, and especially in the East, where Roman organization had not been so greatly admired as by its inheritors in the West. These dissenters could point to the teachings of Christ himself on poverty and its spiritual value, and to his advice to the young man who asked him what was necessary to salvation. Christ had replied that he should sell all his goods and follow him, "but the young man went away sorrowful because he had great possessions." These men were deeply influenced by Oriental thought, and indeed by the mystery religions, which taught that the true path of salvation was by purification on earth and an inward acceptance of the Divine. They did not believe in the machinery of salvation, as propounded by the Church, regarding it as too complex and too legal, too much in the nature of a Roman contract to be the real path to salvation. Yet at the same time they fervently believed in Christ and the central truths of the Christian religion as taught by Christ himself. Determined on self-purification, some went alone into the desert, fasted and prayed and inflicted tortures upon themselves, trying to mortify their evil nature. Others lived in small communities, holding their possessions in common, and aiding each other in their self-mortifying practices. These ascetics were regarded by all the people as holy men, so that it was difficult for the official Church to say that they were heretics.

But they did present a real problem for a Church which had chosen a different path, one that entailed organization, material resources, and political power. Their lives were a standing reproach to such a Church gradually becoming immersed in worldliness. Both in the East and in the West, however, the Church proved flexible enough to accept popular opinion of these hermits and anchorites, sometimes canonizing them as saints, even the famous St. Simeon Stylites, who lived on a pillar for more than thirty years without even space to lie down. But it did attempt also to organize them. By the end of the fourth century the moderate Rule of St. Basil was adopted, which prescribed an orderly, regular life for these monks, as they were called. They no longer lived in the open air or in the desert or in caves, but in a communal dwelling house or monastery, in which each did a share of the work required for their subsistence. Most monks of the Eastern Church still live under the fourth-century Rule of St. Basil.

In the West asceticism of the kind possible in Egypt and the East was more difficult, as the climate in most parts is not conducive to a solitary outdoor life throughout the year. But the ascetic practices found favor with those who wished to devote their whole lives to prayer and worship, and we know of many solitary hermits and hermits already living in communities in the time of St. Jerome, who spent much of his eloquence in defending the practice. It met severe opposition from those who objected to the monks on the ground that they were too often merely escaping their social responsibilities; and when women also began to organize themselves into monasteries or nunneries

Jerome had to take up the cudgels on their behalf also. St. Martin of Tours (316–397), who spent most of his life destroying the last remnants of paganism in France after the decree of Theodosius forbidding the practice of any religion but Christianity, was criticized sharply by his superiors for his own personally ascetic regimen, although he never was a monk. But in time the monasteries became institutionalized, both for men and for women; and it became a recognized sign of holiness that a man or woman should submit to mortification of the flesh while on earth, even if such people did not live according to a recognized Rule. If they lived by a Rule they were called "regular" clergy, or sometimes just "religious," since they devoted their whole lives to religion. They were distinguished from the "secular" clergy, whose duties lay in the outer world.

At the beginning of the sixth century an acceptable Rule which was applicable to all Western monasteries was drawn up by St. Benedict, who had begun his religious career as a hermit. When, however, his fame as a holy man began to attract many followers, he changed his manner of living and founded the monastery of Monte Cassino, instituting an orderly regimen which was blessed by

The monastery of Monte Cassino, in southern Italy, as it was before it was destroyed during World War II.

Pope Gregory the Great. The monks at Monte Cassino and all those who lived by the Benedictine Rule had to take vows of poverty and obedience to the abbot, the head of the community. They had to cut off all ties with their families and their previous lives before entering the monastery. Periods were set aside each day for prayer and worship; the rest of the day was to be spent in manual labor, either in the fields, which were cultivated with great care and made to yield all the food required by the community, or in the monastery itself. No monk was permitted to own anything at all; everything was to be handled by the abbot, whose word was law within the monastery. Monks slept in a common dormitory and ate in a common dining room.

By the eighth century the Benedictine Rule was adopted by the vast majority of monasteries in the West except the Irish, and for centuries it was the model life for the religious, and faithfully observed by those who had chosen it. Even when abuses began to creep in, all those who undertook reforms returned to the Benedictine Rule or some modification of it, as the ideal Rule for a religious community. There was no doubt that in spite of its initial reservations the Church was wise to permit and ultimately take the lead in organizing these communities of monks. For if it was necessary to institutionalize the Church, and the papacy had no doubts on this necessity, then it was also necessary to take care of those deeply earnest men and women who wished to devote all their lives to their religion, and to live a communal life of poverty that seemed to them more in accordance with the teachings of Christ. As long as the monks continued to live holy lives they were a standing example of the virtues of Christianity; they troubled no one, and at the same time they absorbed into their communities all those who might have attacked the Church for its institutionalism and worldliness. It is surely no accident that those later medieval heresies which stressed poverty and asceticism as the true Christian ideal never arose while the monasteries were still truly religious communities

and practiced poverty and abstinence; but that when they no longer fulfilled this function and the monks became notorious for laxity in morals, idleness, and luxurious habits, such a heresy as that of the Poor Men of Lyons obtained numerous adherents and for a long time constituted a real threat to the Church, calling forth a St. Francis and a St. Dominic to set the example once more of saintly lives spent in the earliest tradition of Christianity.

The Irish monasteries alone did not conform to the Benedictine Rule and some monasteries founded by Irish missionaries persisted for a long time on the Continent. The reason for this situation is to be found in the manner in which the Irish had been converted to Christianity. Ireland had been a land of clans, with a very primitive system of government; it had never been conquered by the Romans. St. Patrick, who had been attracted by Oriental monasticism before going to Ireland, succeeded in converting many of the savage chieftains and with them their clansmen. Instead of setting up a church on the Roman model, he allowed the clan to become the congregation. There were no priests except monks, and these did not live in the same isolation from their fellow men as in Western Europe, since they had also to perform the same functions as the secular clergy. They undertook the task of converting the other clansmen who had remained heathen while at the same time they lived in monasteries, practicing austerities, and gaining a great reputation for both piety and learning. Remaining for centuries unconnected with the Church in Rome, they were unaware even of many of the newer teachings of the Church. The result was that they developed a Christianity that was never institutionalized in the Roman manner, and they retained a fervor, especially in missionary activity, that had begun to disappear from Europe. St. Columba converted some Celtic tribes in Britain before they had yet been visited by official emissaries of the Church, St. Columban penetrated into Gaul and made converts in places where Christianity had as yet no foothold and founded monasteries there; another Irishman founded the great monastery of St. Gall in what is now Switzerland. Moreover, once the first monks had gained a knowledge of Greek, it continued to be taught in the monasteries, and was never allowed to die out in Ireland. The most learned philosopher of his day (*ca.* 810–880) in Europe, John Scotus Erigena, was an Irishman.

But this progress was rudely checked in Britain. Pope Gregory I (the fourth and last of the officially recognized Latin Fathers of the Church), of whom more in the next chapter, at the end of the sixth century sent a missionary to Britain named Augustine, who succeeded in converting the South. As this Catholic Christianity progressed northward it came into contact with the communities converted from Ireland, which had quite unknowingly adopted a different form of ecclesiastical usage. Both sides agreed to accept the decision of a synod at Whitby (664), presided over by the king of Northumbria. The question hinged upon the Petrine supremacy. The Irish could point to no such authority as that of the pope, descended from St. Peter. Their failure was decisive. The Roman Church received the award, the new English Church was organized after the Roman manner and the monasteries accepted the Benedictine Rule; in time even the Irish themselves accepted the inevitable, and adopted the discipline and organization of the central Church in Rome.

▶ Suggestions for further reading

The New Testament is available in paperback in several modern translations, including *The New English Bible: New Testament* (Oxford University Press & Cambridge University Press), *The New Testament in Modern English*, trans. by J. B. Phillips. (The Macmillan Company), *New Testament, Revised Standard Version* (Bantam), Official Catholic Versions (Guild and Image). A case-bound edition is Edgar J. Goodspeed's translation, *The New Testament: an American Translation* (Chicago: University of Chicago Press, 1923).

Augustine, Saint. *City of God.* Tedious and rambling but extremely influential book, available in an abridged Image edition. Also selections in an Ungar edition.

PAPER-BOUND BOOKS

Augustine, Saint. *Confessions.* A moving account by the great churchman of how he came to Christianity via Neoplatonism and Manichaeism, a masterpiece of autobiography. Available in two different modern translations—Penguin and Image. A useful selection of St. Augustine's writings, edited by Roger Hazelton, is available from Meridian.

Bettenson, H. S., ed. *Documents of the Christian Church*, 2d edit. Oxford. Valuable collection of primary documents.

Burckhardt, Jacob. *The Age of Constantine the Great.* Anchor. Interesting study by the nineteenth-century Swiss historian, who gives little credit for sincerity to the first Christian emperor.

Bultmann, Rudolf. *Primitive Christianity in its Contemporary Setting.* Meridian. Brief, but scholarly and up-to-date work (1956).

Butterfield, Herbert. *Christianity and History.* Scribner. Already recommended for chapters on prophetic Judaism, this little book by an English professor of history has many stimulating insights into the place of Christianity in the history of religion.

Cross, Frank. *The Ancient Library of Qumran.* Anchor. An important scholarly study of the Dead Sea Scrolls.

Cumont, Franz. *Oriental Religions in Roman Paganism.* Dover. Classic account by a French scholar. Published first in 1911, it lacks material from more recent discoveries. More detailed account of Mithraism by same author is *The Mysteries of Mithras* (Dover).

Daniel-Rops, Henri. *The Church of the Apostles and Martyrs.* Image. Important study by the foremost French Catholic historian of the Church.

Davies, John G. *The Early Christian Church.* Anchor. A good introduction.

Davies, W. D. *Paul and Rabbinical Judaism: Some Rabbinic Elements in Pauline Theology.* Torchbooks. Difficult but rewarding.

De Burgh, W. G. *The Legacy of the Ancient World.* Penguin. Several chapters on early Christian thought, including the heresies, attempting in particular to show how Christianity placed the capstone on Greek and Hebrew philosophy and religion.

Deissman, Adolf. *Paul: A Study in Social and Religious History*. Torchbooks. Scholarly estimate of St. Paul and his influence, using all available sources, including papyri.

Dupont-Sommer, A. *Essene Writings from Qumran*. Meridian. Valuable collateral material from the sect to which John the Baptist belonged.

Enslin, Morton. *Christian Beginnings* and *Literature of the Christian Movement*. Both Torchbooks and both excellent.

Frend, W. H. *Martyrdom and Persecution in the Early Christian Church*. Anchor. Important scholarly work.

Glover, T. R. *The Conflict of Religions in the Early Roman Empire*. Beacon.

Goodspeed, Edgar J. *Paul*. Apex. By a distinguished scholar, who also translated the New Testament.

Grant, Frederick D., ed. *Hellenistic Religions: The Age of Syncretism*. Liberal Arts Press. Documents bearing on the religious background of Christianity in the Near East.

Grant, Robert. *Gnosticism and Early Christianity*. Torchbooks. See Jonas below. Covers somewhat the same material.

Jonas, Hans. *Gnostic Religion*. Beacon. The Gnosis, which was condemned by the early Christian fathers in unmeasured terms, regarded Christ as God rather than man. This book describes what little is known of the Gnosis, almost all of the writings of which have been lost.

Jones, A. H. *Constantine and the Conversion of Rome*. Collier. Important study by a leading English historian of the ancient world.

Ladner, Gerhart. *The Idea of Reform: Its Impact on Christian Thought and Action in the Age of the Fathers*. Torchbooks. One of the rare books on the social ideas of the early Christians.

Laistner, M. L. W. *Christianity and Pagan Culture in the Later Roman Empire*. Cornell. An important book by a leading American scholar.

Latourette, K. D. *Christianity Through the Ages*. Harper. A standard history of Christianity, good on the early period.

Loisy, Alfred. *Origins of the New Testament*. Collier.

McCann, Justin. *Saint Benedict*. Image. The Benedictine Rule with commentary by a present-day Benedictine monk.

Mattingly, Harold. *Christianity in the Roman Empire*. Norton. By a distinguished historian of Rome.

Nock, Arthur D. *Early Gentile Christianity and its Hellenic Background*. Torchbooks. Short but difficult, as is the same author's *St. Paul* (Torchbooks).

Schürer, Emil. *A History of the Jewish People in the Time of Jesus*. Schocken. Useful collateral reading.

Scott, C. A. *Christianity according to St. Paul*. Cambridge. This book is not easy, but for an appreciation of Paul's influence on Christian thought, this, or another book on this list should be attempted.

Waddell, Helen. *The Desert Fathers*. Ann Arbor Books. A classic account of the Greek Fathers of the Church who escaped from organized Christianity into lives of solitude.

CASE-BOUND BOOKS

Duchesne, Louis. *Early History of the Christian Church*. 3 vols. New York: Longmans, Green & Co., Inc., 1922–1947. Standard, very full history, includes all the early heresies.

Pegis, Anton C., ed. *The Wisdom of Catholicism*. New York: The Modern Library, Inc., 1949. Contains important selections from the writings of the Church Fathers and others.

Shotwell, J. T., and Loomis, L. R. *The See of Peter*. New York: Columbia University Press, 1927. Documents on the growth of the papacy and gradual acceptance of the bishop of Rome as head of the Church.

PART IV

THE CENTURIES
OF TRANSITION

CHAPTER 14

THE END OF
THE ROMAN EMPIRE,
AND THE ESTABLISHMENT
OF SUCCESSOR STATES

▶ The beginning of the end

THE MILITARY AUTOCRACY OF SEPTIMIUS SEVERUS (193–211)

The murder of Commodus in 192 was the signal for the opening of a period of outright domination of the Roman emperor by the army, which was to last till the fall of the empire. The first half of this period, up to the accession of Diocletian, was characterized by the increasing disintegration of the civil government under a series of military usurpers whose chief, and sometimes only, ability lay in the military sphere. The empire itself was, on the whole, successfully defended against external pressure on the boundaries, but at tremendous cost to its internal stability. The second half was characterized by the development of a totalitarian state under a civil administration backed by a usually obedient professional mercenary army, directed by an absolute emperor. Without going into the question at this stage of whether wiser policies on the part of the emperors could have prevented this sequence, which culminated in the fall of the empire and the survival of a truncated East-ern Empire under absolutist government, it is clear that it was the policies of the early third-century emperor, Septimius Severus, that set the process in motion.

He himself owed his position to his military ability alone, which was sufficient to enable him to defeat several other contenders. African by birth but Roman in education, and with a Syrian wife, he had no personal or sentimental attachment to Rome and her institutions. He frankly despised the Senate, and showed no understanding of the political and economic basis of the empire. Certainly the pretense that the government was a principate with himself as first citizen, that it was a partnership between ruler and people, had long been outmoded. And it was demonstrably true that the ruler was made and unmade by the various armies of the state. But the armies still had to be fed, paid, and clothed; and if their requirements were not to be always forcibly taken directly from the people that provided them, then some basis of consent must be retained. Moreover, since the empire's prosperity, such as it was, was based to such a large extent upon the production of the cities, and it was the cities which provided the bulk of the tax money for the troops, it was not wise to destroy the urban middle classes for the sake of the army, the peasants, and the urban proletariat. Whether the policies of Severus had any such intention or not, their result was to set in motion the process which led inexorably to the impoverishment and ultimate destruction of the middle classes and the independent municipalities which had provided the solid substructure of the older empire.

To pay for his increased army it was necessary both to increase taxes and to take more active steps to see that they were paid. Severus therefore kept a very strict watch upon all provincial governors, brought many provincials into the imperial service, and in this respect his administration was superior to those of his immediate predecessors. His object, however, was not in any way to lighten the burdens of the provinces and municipalities, but to see that his treasury was full. For this purpose he initiated the policy of making municipal magistrates personally responsible for the collection of the taxes. If they were not paid in full, the magistrates themselves had to make up the difference. To see that all sources of income were tapped and that all officials were kept to their duty, he inaugurated a secret police to report directly to himself on any failure to fulfill obligations and to warn him of any tendencies toward treason. On the other hand, he won the approval of the proletariat by increasing its dole from the state, and passed other special legislation which protected its interests.

THE ASCENDANCY OF THE PEASANT ARMY

But the real danger of the policy of Severus was in the favoritism he showed to his legions. Their pay was considerably raised, and many concessions were made to them which had the effect of impairing their usefulness to the state, while incidentally lowering their efficiency. Married soldiers were allowed to live with their wives in towns behind the lines, auxiliary divisions were given permanent lands, and social clubs in the army were encouraged. This policy made the troops relatively immobile and unfit for service on an endangered frontier. It also made them less willing to fight and less amenable to discipline. Time after time in the third century we hear of mutinies and of the assassination of military leaders when they called upon the troops to fight in defense of the frontiers or tried to instill some discipline into them. Moreover, Severus now made it possible for all provincial soldiers to rise to the position of centurion, which carried with it equestrian rank. Since this was the class favored both by Severus and by his successors for all posts in the imperial bureaucracy, the result was that a military career became the best means of entry to the highest positions in the state, and civilian rule was gradually replaced by military. The very highest offices in the imperial service brought their holders within the senatorial aristocracy, which carried special privileges. Thus the senatorial order became increasingly filled with successful soldiers who acquired large tracts of land and settled down, unencumbered by taxation, having in their progress from the ranks avoided any payment of taxes whatever, and having acquired a vast contempt for those more productive members of society upon whom fell the whole burden of their upkeep. Thus the army became a privileged career, and the military caste, pampered and favored by Severus and all the third-century emperors, became a state within the state, entirely irresponsible, and giving its support only to those rulers who perpetuated its position and catered to its demands.

By opening to soldiers from the ranks the way even to the crown itself, the emperors might have attracted into the army men from the upper and middle classes. But, though Italians and provincials of equestrian rank did continue to provide some of the officers, the bulk of the army was recruited, by design, from the peasantry. It has even been suggested that this was a deliberate policy to increase the class struggle between the peasantry and the urban middle classes. It would seem more probable, however, that the conscript army could only find recruits in sufficient number from the peasantry, and that the concessions made to them were of the kind more likely to appeal to a largely illiterate and semicivilized peasantry which had always found it difficult to make a living from the land. The result of the whole policy, as doubtless intended, was to undermine the position of the upper classes and infiltrate them with uncouth but able soldiers; but it was probably not foreseen that the army itself would become progressively barbarized, nor that it would prefer its privileged life behind the lines to defending the state. The soldiers preferred to follow only those leaders who promised them the most at the least cost to themselves in military activity. So many emperors were assassinated by rebellious troops during fifty years of the third century that only one of eighteen such "emperors" died peacefully in his bed.

FIFTY YEARS OF ANARCHY—THE "BARRACK EMPERORS" (235–284)

There is no need to dwell on the lives, activities, and sudden deaths of these "barrack" emperors. No real rule of succession was observed, though on a few occasions fathers were in fact succeeded by sons who had made appropriate donatives to the legions; frequently there were several competing emperors supported by their own troops but not accepted by any others. On several occasions the Germans penetrated into Gaul, once even passing the Alps and only meeting ultimate defeat in northern Italy. For ten years there was a separate kingdom of Gaul with complete independence. Without effective central administration, tax collecting was by the rough-and-ready method of requisition of supplies and forced levies of money. Almost the whole of Roman Asia acquired a virtual independence for a time (267–273) under the leadership of a desert city named Palmyra, and its queen, Zenobia. The middle classes and active peasants were progressively impoverished; it hardly seemed worth while to plant crops or to engage in any commercial activity when so little could be kept from the insatiable maw of the army.

Near the frontiers the Germanic barbarians at times were able to enter the empire and plunder at will.

But at last a succession of emperors from Illyria was able to re-establish discipline in the armies. And though the greatest of these, Aurelian, was himself murdered (275) after enjoying only five years of supreme power, it was not before he had restored Asia to the empire, defeated the Parthians, brought Gaul back to her allegiance and unified the old Roman Empire almost within her ancient boundaries, though the province of Dacia added by Trajan had been lost forever.

▶ Re-establishment of discipline— Totalitarianism

THE ESTABLISHMENT OF ABSOLUTE GOVERNMENT—DIOCLETIAN AND HIS ASSOCIATES

When Diocletian (285–305) became sole ruler of the empire in 285, having vanquished his only serious rival, he was faced with problems beyond the capacity of any ruler to solve. The years of anarchy had impoverished the middle classes to such an extent that desperate measures to ensure their continued service to the state and payment of taxes had already been put into effect; the industrial and agricultural workers were already being regimented in a similar manner. Trade had been meeting increasing difficulties, not only because of the insecurity of transport but because of constant depreciations of the currency. The Illyrian emperors had been driven to the expedient of inviting warlike barbarians to serve in the imperial armies for pay, and even in the ranks of the officers barbarians were rapidly becoming as frequent as Roman citizens. But at least these barbarians were usually willing to serve; and, being professional soldiers, they fought better than the peasantry of the earlier part of the century and were better disciplined, not having yet grown to look upon the army as a privileged existence, entitling them to live indefinitely off the civilian economy without giving services in return. On the other hand, they owed no

► chronological chart

Roman Empire

Murder of Roman Emperor Commodus	192
Reign of Septimius Severus	193–211
Edict of Caracalla—Extension of Roman citizenship to virtually all free inhabitants of the empire	212
Murder of Emperor Alexander Severus	235
"Barrack Emperors"	235–284
Palmyra declares independence under Queen Zenobia	267
Capture of Zenobia and sack of Palmyra by Aurelian	273
Murder of Aurelian	275
Accession of Diocletian	284
Diocletian chooses Maximian as colleague (Augustus)	285
Appointment of two "Caesars"	293
Edict limiting prices of goods and labor	301
Persecution of Christians	303–311
Abdication of Diocletian and Maximian	305
Galerius emperor of the East, Constantius of West	305
Death of Constantius in Britain, Constantine saluted as emperor	306
Death of Galerius	311
Battle of Milvian Bridge, death of Maxentius	312
Constantine emperor of West, Licinius of East	312
"Edict of Milan"	313
Execution of Licinius	324
Constantine sole emperor	324–337
Council of Nicaea	325
Foundation of Constantinople	330
Conversion and death of Constantine	337
Advance of Huns into empire, defeating Goths	372
Goths permitted across Danube by Emperor Valens	376
Battle of Adrianople—Death of Valens	378
Stilicho the Vandal becomes imperial master of troops	400
Honorius moves Roman capital to Ravenna	*ca.* 400
Sack of Rome by Alaric and Visigoths	410

Roman Empire (cont'd)

Aetius becomes master of the troops under Valentinian III	430
Aetius defeats Visigoths in Gaul	436
Rise of Attila to power among Huns, moves west	445
Battle of Chalons—Partial victory of Aetius over Attila	451
Aetius defeats some Franks, remainder permitted into Gaul	451
Attila invades Italy	452
Death of Attila	453
Murder of Aetius by Valentinian III	454
Sack of Rome by Vandals under Gaeseric	455
Puppet rulers in Rome	455–476
Odoacer deposes last emperor ("Fall of Rome")	476

England and France

Roman legions leave England	407–442
Franks penetrate into Gaul	431 onward
Aetius defeats some Franks, remainder permitted into Gaul	451
Clovis consolidates Franks into kingdom	481–511
Merovingian kingdom	481–754
Conversion of Clovis and Franks to Roman Catholicism	486
Invasions of England by Angles, Saxons, and Jutes	5th and 6th centuries
Mission of St. Augustine of Canterbury to England	596–597
Conquests of Angles, Saxons, and Jutes completed by	615
Influx of Celtic Christianity into England from Iona	633 onward
Synod of Whitby—Triumph of Roman Catholicism over Celtic Christianity	664
Charles Martel "mayor of the palace" in France	714–741
Pepin crowned king of the Franks (Pepin the Short)	754

loyalty whatever to the empire. Serving for experience and pay alone, they were loyal to their paymaster the emperor, but to no one else.

Finally, there was no acceptable method of succession to the throne, and no apparent way of preventing usurpation by the strongest commander.

Diocletian was in no sense an innovator. But he was a disinterested ruler, with no personal ambitions—he abdicated later in accordance with a plan he devised for a succession without bloodshed—and he had many years of life in front of him in which to accomplish his reforms. His general plan was to accept conditions as they were and to create formal institutions in keeping with them, and, by instituting a strong government, try to preserve the empire at least from the anarchy of the previous fifty years. In this he was, on the whole, successful, in spite of the failure of his new principle of succession. The empire did survive in form for nearly another two hundred years, and a substantial part of it, the later Byzantine Empire, ultimately gained a new lease of life and survived for a further thousand years.

In a word, his plan was to make of the whole empire one centrally administered state of the kind now called totalitarian.[1] This necessitated the final abolition of the principate in theory as well as in fact. But Diocletian also realized that the administration of the empire and the defense of its boundaries against the increasingly dangerous barbarians were far too much for one man. He therefore invited Maximian, another Illyrian general, to act as his colleague in the empire, sharing the title of Augustus. Maximian and he then chose two seconds-in-command, with the title of Caesar. The two Augusti were to retire after twenty years in office, to be succeeded by the two Caesars, each then naming a pair of Caesars who would in turn succeed them. Unfortunately

[1] The system has often been called "oriental absolutism," but the latter is a very vague term, since the Orient has known many different degrees of absolutism, while the analogy with modern totalitarian states, with their emphasis on guns instead of butter, is clear.

not all these potentates were as disinterested as himself, nor were the sons of the Augusti willing to be discarded in favor of generals of greater experience, even under parental pressure. The scheme actually never worked at all except when Diocletian was able to compel the Augusti to keep to their agreement, and civil wars continued until Constantine (312–337) established for good the hereditary principle, in spite of the danger that the empire might fall into childish or incompetent hands.

The division of the empire into two parts, however, survived the abdication and death of Diocletian, though without the refinement of the two added Caesars. And the scheme of the two Augusti and the two Caesars proved effective enough in his own lifetime to enable him to put into effect the necessary administrative reforms that made the empire into a totalitarian state. The frontiers were guarded, a number of minor revolts were quelled, and the expanding Persian Empire was held in check.

REORGANIZATION OF ARMY AND PROVINCES UNDER IMPERIAL CONTROL

The army was considerably enlarged, friendly barbarians were allowed to settle in frontier districts with an obligation to military service, companies of barbarians, sometimes even under their own chiefs, were welcomed, while the more warlike sections of the empire provided further conscripted recruits; if not of high quality their discipline and training were better than they had been for years. Diocletian also organized a force of picked men who could be moved from one part of the empire to another as danger threatened, helping to stiffen the resistance of the resident legions. The army was under the direct command of the emperor and his associates, who were all experienced generals, so that there was less opportunity for local armies to revolt and try to set up a new emperor.

The number of the provinces was increased by subdivision to 101, with every governor an appointee of one of the emperors, and subject to control by vicars who had about seven provinces each (dioceses), who in their turn were responsible to four prefects, personal representatives of the four rulers. The vicars, however, had the right of direct appeal to Diocletian, as senior emperor, against decisions of the prefects. Thus was established a graded hierarchy responsible to the emperor and his associates alone.

Diocletian and Maximian as Augusti now took divine titles although they did not call themselves actual gods. They withdrew as much as possible from direct participation in public life, instituting an elaborate court ceremonial of an Oriental kind, including prostration and kissing the hem of the emperor's robe when the privilege of an audience was granted. The persecution of Christians which accompanied the elevation of the monarchy has been discussed in the last chapter. Many new temples were built to the old gods, while there was an insistence on greater observance of the imperial cult.

REGIMENTATION OF PUBLIC AND PRIVATE LIFE

The imperial bureaucracy and its task

It was clear at once that the expenses of the new administration could not be less than the old. The increased burden of the army and the building program could be met only by increased and more efficiently collected taxes. And this collection must also entail an increase in the unproductive army of imperial bureaucrats whose task it was to see that the taxes were paid. Diocletian's solution was simply to use his army and his bureaucrats, including secret police and paid informers, to ensure the collection, and hope to keep up the necessary agricultural and industrial production by all the legal weapons available to him, enforced by his officials and his army.

Compulsory agriculture—The *coloni*

The armies during the period of anarchy had been accustomed to requisition supplies. Diocletian now took away the arbitrary and casual requisitioning and made it regular and legal. Having little idea of the productive value of the various lands in his empire, he assessed them in accordance with

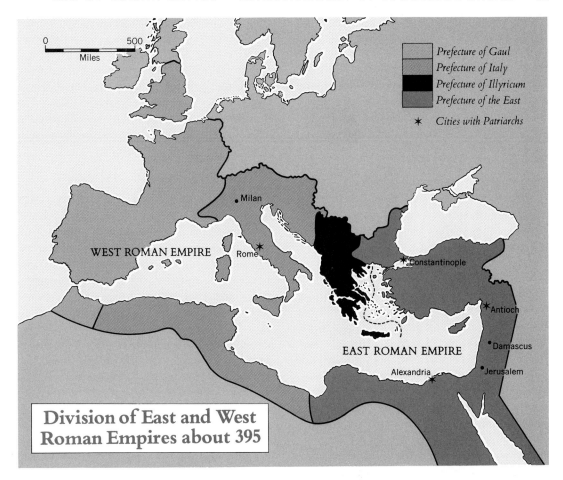

0   500
Miles

Prefecture of Gaul
Prefecture of Italy
Prefecture of Illyricum
Prefecture of the East
＊ *Cities with Patriarchs*

Milan

WEST ROMAN EMPIRE   Rome

Constantinople

Antioch

Damascus

EAST ROMAN EMPIRE

Alexandria

Jerusalem

Division of East and West Roman Empires about 395

the numbers of cultivators employed and the land under cultivation, irrespective of the fertility of the soil and the probable yields, which were more difficult to measure. This tax was then collected by his officials, regardless of the actual ability to pay or the hardship payment entailed upon individual farmers. Since many farmers tried to escape their obligations and left the land, by the time of Constantine they were forced to remain on it, whether they were owners, tenants, or sharecroppers. If they left they were still liable for the tax on the land they had left, and if found they were returned to it. Though still theoretically freemen, they were practically serfs. These farmers were called *coloni*. Manumitted slaves were now free only in name also. They remained tied to their masters and bound to work for them. If they did not pay their masters due "reverence," a phrase which could be made to cover

any refusal to obey instructions, they could be returned to their status of slaves.

The privileged landowners

On the other hand, the large landowners who still employed some slaves, and had always a number of *coloni* on their lands, were often able to avoid taxation altogether, as they were in many cases too powerful for the imperial officials to dare to antagonize them. During the period of anarchy these landholders had often been able to increase their estates when the small farmers had fallen irretrievably into debt or had had their livestock driven off by the rapacious armies. From this time onward the large landowners were the only people to profit by the imperial policy, and many of them, who had been soldiers or imperial officials themselves, had obtained legal immunity from taxation. Assisted by slaves and *coloni* who were completely dependent upon them, they were rarely forced by even the strongest emperors to pay taxes commensurate with their income, for a squadron of troops would have been needed to enforce the collection. Many of the luxurious villas of these privileged aristocrats still survive, especially in France, some of them with their own manufacturing establishments which produced a variety of goods, even luxuries, with large storehouses for provisions, the whole fortified as if for security against possible imperial emissaries as well as against invading barbarians. These villas are the forerunners of the medieval manors.

Compulsory state service—The *curiales*

We have already seen that Septimius Severus inaugurated the system of making municipal magistrates personally responsible for the collection of taxes. Naturally few wished in these circumstances to become magistrates, however much prestige the position might bring them. Diocletian made it compulsory for men of a certain property qualification to hold these positions. In addition to taxes to the emperor, they were compelled to pay for local games, public buildings, and their repairs, and were personally responsible for seeing that all such work was carried out satisfactorily. Constantine laid the burden of this taxation upon the whole body of people eligible for these offices, who were called *curiales,* once a title of honor but now a badge of municipal serfdom.

The only way for the *curiales* to escape their onerous position would have been to rise to the senatorial class and receive tax immunity. But this also was made impossible by decree in the century after Diocletian. If they left their class, then their children would have to undertake the curial obligation instead. If they tried to escape by joining the army, they were summarily returned to their previous duties. And, forced to find means to pay the taxes and other obligations, they naturally tried to obtain as much as they could from their own tenant cultivators or *coloni;* thus the class struggle was intensified more than ever. With no chance of escaping

their involuntary servitude, faced on the one side by the imperial officers and on the other by a bitterly hostile peasantry, and with a complete lack of incentive, this middle class, which had previously been the backbone of the empire, was mercilessly crushed. Its gradual disappearance was one of the chief causes for the economic decline and ultimately the fall of the empire.

Compulsory industry—The *collegia*

The regimentation in industry was equally severe. As early as the second century urban workers had been encouraged to form themselves into guilds or *collegia,* according to the particular goods produced or services rendered. An early third-century emperor organized into monopolies under state control all collegia suplying goods to the capital. The same control was exercised over merchants and manufacturers engaged in purveying supplies to the army. Under the Illyrian emperors and Constantine, all city workers were finally organized into castes under strict state control, with each worker bound to follow the trade of his father. We know of hereditary castes of bakers, shippers, millers, and others, but it is not known whether all industry was thus regimented or if any escaped. None, however, escaped the ubiquitous tax collectors.

Thus with *coloni, curiales,* and artisans all forbidden to change their occupations and unable to improve their status, the entire class structure of the state was stratified, and the totalitarian empire firmly established. The only way of avoiding one's obligations was to bribe the tax collectors; and we hear of numerous cases of such corruption in the following two centuries. But even bribery amounted to nothing more than an irregular alternative to taxes, and could only modify the impositions for a brief period.

CONSTANTINE AND THE PERFECTING OF TOTALITARIANISM

Economic and military policy

After his prescribed twenty years of rule Diocletian celebrated a jubilee in 305, and

A reconstruction of the huge palace which the Emperor Diocletian built for his retirement after he abdicated. The palace is at Split, Yugoslavia. (COURTESY YUGOSLAV STATE TOURIST OFFICE)

then retired, dying much later in 313. His colleague Maximian, however, was not yet tired of power. Diocletian at last persuaded him to relinquish it, but Maximian preferred to hand it over to his sons rather than to the properly appointed Caesars. An intermittent civil war then broke out which was concluded by a great victory in 312 won by Constantine, son of a man who had been Caesar while Diocletian was still on the throne. Diocletian, who survived these brief wars, contented himself with exhortations issued from his huge fortress-palace at Salona (now Split, in Dalmatia). For a further twelve years after Constantine's succession to the empire in the West the new emperor tolerated an Eastern colleague, Licinius, in charge of the empire in the East. Then they came to blows, in part because of the latter's studied policy of persecuting Christians and trying to restore the old religion. Constantine prevailed and in 324 became sole emperor.

The policies of Constantine were in full accord with those of Diocletian, but after over thirty years of experience it was now possible to see in what respects they had failed. Constantine concluded only that they had not yet been carried far enough. He increased the imperial bureaucracy still further and clamped the machinery of repression still tighter. By the end of his reign the totalitarian state was complete, and the hereditary caste system no longer had any loopholes in it. Each man was securely fixed in the position in which he had been born; and his obligation to fulfill his quota of work and provide a surplus for the ever more insatiable needs of the army was absolute. The police and the bureaucracy were ubiquitous in ferreting out any source of income, returning escapees to their duty, and requisitioning food and supplies when money was unavailable.

Though Constantine reformed the coinage it is clear that there was not enough precious metal available even to keep the wheels of trade and industry revolving, much less to provide the agricultural workers with hard cash. As we now know, some of it had left the empire altogether for distant places such as India, which had always had a favorable trade balance with the empire. Increasingly taxes were paid in kind, and there was a gradual return to a barter economy and self-sufficiency on the large estates. The surplus of raw materials thus collected by the emperors presented a further problem, which was solved in the classic totalitarian manner. The emperors set up industrial establishments of their own with conscripted hereditary workers manufacturing for the needs of the emperor and the army. These factories were under the control of imperial bureaucrats, and formed the pattern for the great imperial monopolies of the later Byzantine Empire.

Constantine completed the barbarization of the army by carrying Diocletian's policies to their logical conclusion. The old frontier legions which had been at least recruited from Roman citizens, even though they had been little enough influenced by Roman civilization, were now degraded to a local militia, and troops still drawn from the citizen body were made inferior in status to the German mercenaries. The real army was a mobile field army, recruited from the neighboring barbarians, chiefly the Germanic tribes in the West, and the Sarmatians on the Danube. The elite corps of cavalry, the crack troops of the empire, were entirely composed of German mercenaries. It was possible for the foreign mercenaries to reach the highest position in the army and become *magistri militum,* or masters of the troops. From the time of Constantine onward, and especially in the fifth century, we find German masters of the troops far more powerful than their puppets who wore the purple and were still called emperors. As a rule the barbarian leaders did not aspire to the throne themselves—a possible reason for the choice of barbarians for the supreme military position. But this army, at least in the hands of Constantine, was the most efficient instru-

ment the Romans had possessed in centuries for its two primary purposes—the defense against unauthorized barbarian immigration and armed attacks into the empire, and the enforcement of discipline upon the civilians who paid for its upkeep. Always increasing as defense needs grew more imperious, it devoured the substance of the civil population, laying its heavy, unproductive hand upon all enterprise until the Roman empire collapsed from within under the impact of foreign peoples with a population almost certainly far short of theirs. But the army at least served to introduce many of the most able barbarians to the civilization of the empire, which trained them and gave them military experience—which many of them used in later years against the empire itself.

New Rome on the Bosporus

The most significant act of the reign of Constantine, however, was the founding of a new capital near the incomparable site of ancient Byzantium on the Bosporus at the entrance to the Black Sea. This city, called Constantinople, quickly grew to surpass Rome. The eastern provinces of the empire, though equally ground down by taxation, never sank to the level of the more agricultural West. Some cities continued to thrive and trade continued, if less luxuriantly than in the past. It was certainly for this reason that Constantine founded his new capital in the midst of this area. The western provinces hardly served to support themselves and their defense, while the defense needs in the East were not so vast. Moreover, the provinces themselves provided some surplus for luxuries appreciated by the now entirely Orientalized court of the first Christian monarch.

Constantinople was also a port, which Rome had never been; it could be made impregnable by sea and strongly fortified by land. Not very far from the capital was the river Danube, more easily defended than the distant Rhine. Time and again the barbarians threatened the Danube, and on some occasions they crossed it and reached almost to

Constantinople. But faced with the formidable bastion of the city itself, they realized they could hardly conquer it with their crude weapons. When, therefore, the emperors suggested to them that the West was an easier target, Alaric, Theodoric, and other barbarian leaders took the hint, and Constantinople was left in peace. Not until the barbarian "crusaders" from the West took it in 1204 against what was little more than a token defense did it ever succumb to an external invader.

For the adornment of his new capital Constantine sent for the best artists and craftsmen of the empire. But their talent proved to be far from adequate to the opportunity. Constantine then proceeded systematically to pillage Greece. The ancient Greek shrines were made to yield up their sculpture of the glorious age of Hellenic art. Trophies of the battle of Salamis, marble columns from temples to the Greek gods, possibly even the Olympian Zeus of Phidias, by all accounts the noblest sculpture the world has yet seen, priceless manuscripts from Alexandria and other Hellenistic cities were brought into Constantinople, where they survived for many more centuries, cheek by jowl with the inferior, badly built, and artistically tasteless artifacts of the age of Constantine. The bulk of these works was destroyed in the early thirteenth century by Latin "crusaders" ignorant of art and interested primarily in the precious metals of which so many of these works of art were made. What was not stolen at this time was largely destroyed by fires set by both the "crusaders" and their victims.

Constantine himself ruled over the united empire, and he ensured the succession of his sons to the throne. But he realized it was too vast for efficient rule by one man; and, having two sons, he divided it. Thereafter, though in theory they were each co-emperors of the whole, the empire was in fact divided between two emperors, one resident in Constantinople, the other with an official residence in Rome, but more often living in Milan, Trier, or Ravenna, an impregnable city in the marshes of north-eastern Italy where, amid the invasions of the Goths, the emperor felt safe enough to neglect the interests of the empire with impunity.

▶ ## External dangers to the empire

BARBARIAN INFILTRATION

The Germanic tribes, general characteristics

We have already had occasion to refer to the infiltration of barbarians into the Roman Empire. Naturally this description of the invaders is not the preferred term in Germany and Northern Europe where the whole process, which occupied several centuries, is known as the *Völkerwanderung*, or the migration of peoples. Without attempting to pronounce on the native excellences of these peoples, it is clear that they were imperfectly versed at this time in the practices of civilization which had grown up in cities, of which these peoples had none.

Julius Caesar and Tacitus among the Roman historians had described the manners and customs of the German peoples in their day—Caesar briefly from the point of view of an alien conqueror; Tacitus actuated, in part at least, by a desire to contrast the noble savage with the effete and decadent Romans of the capital at the beginning of the second century. These accounts, valuable as they are, need to be treated with some caution. Tacitus himself had probably never been in Germany, and his picture, convincing though his incomparable style makes it, is only based on information received from others. Nevertheless the facts of his *Germania* coincide in essentials with later records based on the firsthand observations of later times.

In physical characteristics the Germans were, as a group, taller than the Roman peoples from the Mediterranean area; many of them had reddish or blond hair which they wore long. The country which they inhabited was infertile, swampy, and heavily forested; to the Germans, therefore, life was a constant struggle for survival. Their chief joy in life appears to have been fighting, and many of them knew no other occupation. Though by the fourth century they had moved from "savagery" to "barbarism," and cultivated some crops, their chief occupation remained hunting and food gathering. They possessed large numbers of domestic animals, especially pigs and cattle with which they supplemented their food supply. Their agricultural practices were wasteful. When one piece of land was exhausted they moved on to another. However, like the Dorian peoples who invaded and conquered Greece, they had the use of iron, and the weapons of at least the leading warriors were made of that metal. Both in their manner of living and in many features of their political and social organization they strongly resembled the North American Indian as he was known to the Americans of the colonial era.

As in all primitive societies, their basic unit was the family, and a number of families composed a clan or tribe. The clan had a hereditary chieftain who was the leader in war and peace. There was also a tribal assembly of all free men who met in council to decide policies suggested by the chief. If they agreed they showed their assent by clashing their shields. In later times many tribes would unite under a king; as a rule when the Romans came in contact with them it was with the king they had to negotiate, and the kings and the tribes consolidated under them with whom they had to fight. The only distinctive organization not to be found in the other primitive peoples studied in earlier chapters was the *comitatus*, or league of companions. In a fighting people it was to be expected that powerful warriors would sometimes arise who held no hereditary position. These men would attract around themselves others who looked to them for leadership. Such organizations were encouraged by the Germans. They fought together, and if necessary died together. The leader looked first to the needs of his men, and they in turn were bound to him by the strongest ties of loyalty. In this institution we evidently have the germ of the later feudal relationship between lords and the vassals who were tied to them by an oath of fealty, and owed military service to them.

Such law as these peoples possessed was based upon the tribal relationships. It was the duty of a family or tribe to avenge the death of its members or exact monetary compensation for it. The tribal council might act as arbiter but without considering so much factual evidence as the number and quality of the oaths taken by supporters of both sides. In cases of doubt, single combat might be prescribed, the loser thus being proved guilty; or, in the case of men of inferior status and women, an ordeal would be called for, from which if the victim emerged without serious damage he could safely be presumed to be innocent.[2]

The men of the German tribes spent most of their lives in fighting or looking after the animals, the women stayed home and looked after the household, while the slaves, who had some personal freedom though tied to the land, looked after such crops as the tribes possessed. Not being closely attached to any piece of land, it was not difficult for whole tribes or nations to migrate, either in search of better pastures or crop land or from simple restlessness. None of the Germanic peoples had moved very far from the nomadic life; while other barbarian peoples who now began to endanger the empire were still truly nomads, who pushed the more settled peoples before them, and, as a result, set an even larger migration in motion.

These migrations of people are as old as history. We have already noticed the Achaean, Ionian, and Dorian invasions of Greece. In the fourth century B.C. the Celts migrated all over Europe and into Asia, and

---

[2] It has been thought by some that the institution of compurgation (joint swearing) by "oath-helpers," mentioned here, was the origin of the modern jury, especially since twelve was the number of oath-helpers most commonly used. However, it is now generally believed that the jury system in England originated in the medieval French practice of sending out officials to inquire into various matters of interest to the kings, about which evidence was taken on oath.

were defeated by the Romans only with great difficulty, not before Rome itself had been thoroughly sacked. At the turn of the first century B.C. the Germanic Cimbri and Teutones had penetrated far into Italy, and could not be defeated until the Romans had reorganized their army. The rulers of the early Roman Empire after a few abortive efforts, decided that it was impossible to civilize and conquer the barbarians beyond the borders of the empire, and contented themselves with building fortifications to defend its boundaries. For several centuries this defense was successful.

When at last new groups of barbarians began to threaten again, the danger came from Eastern Europe rather than from the land known to the Romans as Germany. But the threatening peoples were still Germanic in origin. By this time they were a far more formidable enemy than the earlier primitive Germanic tribes, having learned new methods of warfare from contact with less primitive peoples. Many of them now fought on horseback and used the lance and improved armor. These were the Goths, Vandals, Burgundians, and Alemanni. They in turn were followed by native Germanic groups who had never migrated to Eastern Europe, and were armed with pikes and battle-axes, with wooden shields carried on their left arms, fighting on foot and lacking mobility, but powerful in defense, and terrifying when they appeared in large numbers. These peoples were the Franks, and the Angles and Saxons who conquered Britain. Among them only the leaders rode on horseback; and they lacked the ability to produce the superior military equipment used by their less primitive predecessors.

Behind the Germanic groups were the Sarmatians, a warlike people who gave much trouble to the Byzantine Empire with their raids into the Balkans, but who for the most part remained in southern Russia; and the Slavs, who at this time lived in a more primitive manner than any of the other groups, but whose capacity for resisting and absorbing conquerors enabled them to survive when most of the more warlike groups had disappeared. These Slavs moved into eastern Germany and Central Europe in the wake of the migrating Germanic peoples, and stayed there, many of them to this day, as well as infiltrating into the Balkans. Behind all these peoples, again, were the Asiatic Huns who relentlessly moved westward, pushing the other peoples in front of them.

The Goths

Relations with the empire—A great island of civilization into which they were not permitted to penetrate naturally exercised a powerful fascination on those barbarian peoples who were closest to the Roman frontiers. Within the empire were settled towns, law and order, luxuries, and a way of living entirely alien to them but nonetheless attractive for that. The disciplined legionaries of Rome were always more than a match for them save in exceptional circumstances, and they hesitated to try conclusions with them unless pressure from the rear forced them to violate the Roman boundaries in spite of themselves. On the other hand, they fiercely defended themselves against attacks from the Roman side. While they may have at all times expressed contempt for the civilized Romans on the other side of the barrier, great numbers of them seem to have hungered for a different kind of life, and not only for the plunder of a successful raid. When the Roman emperors found that they could no longer rely upon the empire and the citizen body to defend their boundaries, and especially during the half century of anarchy when individual Roman generals seeking the supreme power would take troops wherever they could find them, then it was natural to turn to these barbarians whose trade it was to fight, who were strong and warlike, though lacking the training which would enable them to defeat the Roman legionaries.

So from the third century we find individual barbarians and whole tribes being enrolled into the army, receiving training, and acquiring some knowledge and understanding of Roman civilization. They were not, of course, at first loyal to Rome or to the empire, impersonal entities quite alien to their experience, which was always of men rather than institutions. Few indeed can ever have grasped the idea of the Roman Empire. But they did take to disciplined military life, and did not lose their warrior spirit; and they were far more loyal to their new leaders than most of the Roman peasants who had been conscripted into the army, were scarcely more literate than the barbarians, lacked warlike spirit, and yet looked upon themselves as a privileged caste.

It was, therefore, natural for the Roman soldier-emperors to look more and more to the barbarians, especially to the Goths, and, in the East, to the Sarmatians, for the real core of their armies. As long as they needed troops there were unlimited numbers of barbarians available to them, who served for pay, who obeyed orders, who did not want to set themselves up as emperors, and who in their simplicity would put up with more hardships than would the citizen conscripts. Thus arose the military policy of the late emperors, especially Constantine. They were managers of a totalitarian state which had to be kept down by an iron rule, and whose citizens had to be forced to work and to pay taxes. Many of these emperors no doubt believed in the Roman Empire, believed that no price was too high to pay for its formal preservation. And few indeed probably realized what the result would be: that instead of the Romans civilizing the barbarians and making them into good civilized servants of the empire, it was the empire that would be barbarized by the Goths and their successors, and that the whole superstructure of an imperial universal state would collapse from within, when the real cement that held it together, the free municipalities and the economy and culture based on them, finally crashed and gave way. The Romans, as has been said, were not an imaginative people, and few were their thinkers who perceived the inevitable end even when it was almost upon them.

The policies adopted by the emperors were dictated by the immediate circum-

stances of each case. There never was a settled, agreed policy for keeping the barbarians in check. The earliest Goths were recruited for the army as individual soldiers, perhaps a comitatus, or even a tribe. When in later times large bodies of barbarians clamored for entry into the empire, with their wives and children, they were allowed to come in as *coloni,* were given land to cultivate which they were not permitted to leave, and agreed to give military service for the privilege. When in the late fourth and fifth centuries the boundaries became increasingly difficult to defend, whole tribes and even nations with their kings violated the frontier openly and settled down in land that had been Roman territory. When the emperors got around to it they legalized the position by giving these peoples the status of allies, *foederati,* bound by treaty to Rome and expected to defend their newly acquired lands against the next comers. This they often did, the Goths having little friendship for the Franks, and even the West Goths (Visigoths) little enough for the East Goths (Ostrogoths), and vice versa. And all united, as we shall see, against the Huns. Other groups applied for permission to come in as allies in advance, and were allowed in, upon the signing of a treaty; but these in many cases found the Roman officials unbearably patronizing and predatory, reluctant to carry out the terms to which their masters had agreed.

Gradual barbarization of the Romans— It was to be expected that once the boundaries were defended by barbarians, some at least of their kinsmen would be admitted without formalities, and that gradually the frontier provinces would become predominantly barbarian. As a privileged caste also the soldiers would have little respect for the Roman citizens who were living in virtual slavery under constant threat from themselves, the emperors, and the imperial bureaucracy. If they were not paid promptly they could always loot a few cities, for which they had little respect but much envy. The Romans, whose cities had been destroyed by the Goths, could not hope to recover in the circumstances of the fifth century. Thus, gradually, and especially after the invasion of the Huns which forced ever more peoples over the imperial boundaries, the peoples of the empire became themselves barbarized, sometimes joining the hordes and plundering their neighbors, protected only by some of the assimilated barbarians who now regarded themselves as Romans and by those few landholders who could still maintain their independence in spite of barbarian infiltration.

Conversion of the barbarians to Christianity—One softening influence, however, should be noticed. For much of the fourth century Bishop Ulfilas (*ca.* 311–383), of partly Gothic ancestry himself, but educated in Constantinople, had been working in the Gothic vineyard. He gave the Goths their first writing, including a Gothic Bible, and converted great numbers of the West Goths, who passed the new religion on to many of the East Goths and Vandals who were in close contact with them. The type of Christianity, however, to which he converted them was Arianism, which had been the accepted doctrine in Constantinople during the good bishop's period of study, and which in any case was far more likely to be acceptable to the simple barbarians than the more mysterious teachings of orthodox Christianity. Thus all the earlier barbarian peoples who invaded the Roman Empire were converted to Arian Christianity, ultimately bringing upon themselves difficulties when an orthodox pope and an orthodox emperor used their heresy as an excuse for the invasion of Italy and the destruction of the East Gothic kingdom. The organization of the Arian Church in the areas inhabited by these peoples was also of material help during the most severe period of the barbarian invasions when the imperial government broke down. In Gaul, later Frankland, however, most of the bishops remained orthodox, giving great help to the orthodox Frankish King Clovis at the end of the fifth century in the establishment of his authority over most of the territory which had been Gaul.

THE BARBARIAN INVASIONS

The advance of the Huns (372–451)

While the first stage of the entry of the barbarians into the West is marked by slow infiltration, with the agreement, if not always active support of the emperors, the second stage consists of true invasions, not intentional on the part of the invaders, but forced by the westward advance of a central Asiatic people, the Huns. These people, according to the records of their enemies, were a group of short, squat, strong warriors who came riding into Europe on horses, which they seldom left, being believed by the Goths even to sleep on them. Their numbers do not seem to have been overwhelming; but they could move very rapidly, giving the appearance of great numbers. They were yellow-skinned, beardless, and to the Westerners incredibly ugly, and terrifying. They showed no mercy.

Involuntary advance of the barbarians into the empire

The Goths and other Germanic peoples were unable to hold their own against the assaults of the Huns, and many of them became vassals and fought in the Hunnish armies when summoned to do so. Other Huns who moved further westward were enrolled in the Roman armies as mercenaries. The Ostrogothic kingdom was completely subdued by the Huns and confined in an area close to the Black Sea, though some Ostrogoths escaped to the Carpathian mountains. Large numbers of the Visigoths, pushed by the Huns, congregated on the Danube, the boundary of the empire, and petitioned the Eastern emperor to allow them to cross into safety. The emperor, Valens, faced with such massive immigration, was uncertain what policy to adopt. At last he made up his mind to accept them as *foederati;* but as soon as the Goths were in Roman territory the imperial officials proceeded to plunder them, carrying off some of their people as slaves, and refusing to supply the remainder even with food. The fiercely independent and numerically superior Goths finally took matters into their own hands and made their way towards Constantinople, plundering and ravaging as they went. The emperor called to the West for aid. But his young nephew Gratian, who had succeeded to the throne in 375, was fully occupied with a campaign against the Alemanni. After a few successes won by his generals, Valens became more confident and rejected the advice of his nephew, who urged him to wait for the arrival of his own force. Taking the field himself, Valens was disastrously defeated in the battle of Adrianople, and was killed shortly afterwards while trying to make his escape (378). His successor promptly made terms and tried to carry out the original treaty. But the Goths were now firmly ensconced in the empire, with their own kings and leaders, a constant menace to the emperors, sometimes paid salaries and serving in the imperial armies, sometimes taking the law into their own hands, wandering up and down Europe.

But the Eastern emperor held two trump cards denied to the emperor in the West. The heart of his territory was defensible. His important towns were strongly fortified, and Constantinople itself was impregnable to barbarian arms. And the emperor, commanding the resources of the only remaining prosperous area in the empire, had access to ready money. The combination of these two was sufficient to enable the Eastern Empire to survive the worst that the barbarians could do. The emperor was willing to take them into the army and pay them well; and they could not, on the other hand, hope to conquer him unless he should be as foolhardy as Valens. There can be no doubt also that the Oriental splendor of the imperial court made a deep impression on the barbarians and convinced them that the emperor possessed power greater than he actually had at his disposal. At all events, it was possible for him to convince the ambitious barbarians that pickings were easier elsewhere.

The barbarians invasions in the West— Visigoths, Vandals, Franks, Burgundians, Bretons—So it was upon the now greatly enfeebled empire in the West that the Goths concentrated their attacks, opposed for a few years by a Vandal general in the service of Rome, then on his death marching into Italy and sacking Rome, as will be described in more detail in the next section devoted to the fortunes of Italy. From Italy they moved into Gaul and thence into Spain, where in 419 they were allowed to form their own kingdom as allies of the empire. They were later driven from Gaul by the Franks.

At the beginning of the fifth century the Vandals, themselves driven relentlessly by constant pressure from the westward advance of the Huns, moved into Gaul without meeting much opposition, plundering and burning as they went. From the fact that the Roman prefect a few years earlier had been transferred to southeastern Gaul it seems clear that the empire had given up hope of defending the Rhine and the North. It took three years (406–409) for the Vandals to eat up the resources of Gaul ("the whole of Gaul burnt like a torch," as a contemporary poet described it) and cross over into Spain. After a few years in Spain, they were driven by the Roman armies and their Gothic allies into the extreme south. Here they found in Gaiseric a great leader who, through the treachery of the Roman governor in Africa, was allowed to cross the strait of Gibraltar into Africa, where he founded a kingdom (429). This kingdom was later recognized by the Roman emperor as another ally. But by this time the emperor exercised hardly even a nominal sway over his numerous barbarian allies.

Behind the Vandals came the Franks and the Burgundians. The last great Roman general, Aetius (*magister militum*, 430–454), permitted the Franks to stay in northern Gaul, again as allies; while the Burgundians moved, also with his assent, into southern Gaul along the valley of the Rhone, and into the area now known as Savoy. Taking advantage of the general movement, a group of Celts, severely harassed by the activities of another Germanic group, the Saxons, who had sent expeditions to Britain

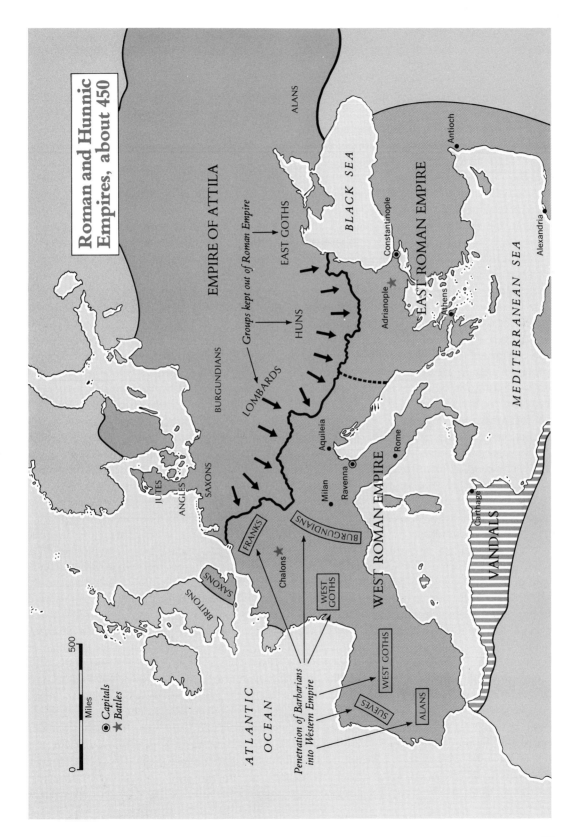

Roman and Hunnic Empires, about 450

Miles
⊙ Capitals
★ Battles

0   500

ATLANTIC OCEAN

BRITONS
SAXONS
JUTES
ANGLES
SAXONS

FRANKS
Chalons ★

BURGUNDIANS

WEST GOTHS
SUEVES
WEST GOTHS
ALANS

WEST ROMAN EMPIRE

Milan
Ravenna
Aquileia
Rome

VANDALS
Carthage

Penetration of Barbarians into Western Empire

EMPIRE OF ATTILA

BURGUNDIANS
LOMBARDS
HUNS
EAST GOTHS
ALANS

Groups kept out of Roman Empire

BLACK SEA

Adrianople ★
Constantinople ⊙

EAST ROMAN EMPIRE

Athens
Antioch
Alexandria

MEDITERRANEAN SEA

from about 440, passed over from their home in Britain into northwest Gaul, the land now called Brittany.

The lifting of the Hun menace

In the first half of the fifth century the Huns became united in a formidable kingdom under the leadership of Attila, an indefatigable warrior and organizer of genius, who took possession of much of east-central Europe and compelled all the barbarian tribes in the area to become his vassals. For a few years his power in Europe surpassed that of either of the Roman emperors, and both were forced to pay him tribute. When the Eastern emperor Marcian felt himself strong enough to discontinue the tribute, Attila, rather than fight him, turned westward in search of an alternative. He was the more ready to do this, since the Western emperor's sister, Honoria, had written to him, soliciting his help to save her from an undesired marriage. Attila chose to regard the request as an offer of her own hand, and a dowry from imperial lands.

In 450 he invaded Gaul at the head of an army composed of his own Huns and a considerable number of Germans. But the Roman general Aetius, himself allied with other Germans, checked him at the battle usually called Chalons in 451—although the battle seems to have been fought many miles from that city. Though neither side won a clear-cut victory, Attila decided to retreat. The next year he invaded Italy, but for reasons still unknown he withdrew at the request of an embassy headed by Pope Leo I. The emperor continued to refuse Attila the hand of his sister, of whose fate nothing is known. Attila himself died the following year. On his death his German vassals revolted and were able to defeat the Huns in a decisive battle, which put an end to the short-lived Hunnish confederation. Some of the Huns settled down in Europe, while others returned to Asia, where later they became part of the Avar horde. Their only

permanent settlement in Europe was in Hungary, later to be peopled by another nomadic group, the Magyars.

Thus was the Hun menace lifted, leaving the now freed Germans at last able to move against the Roman Empire.

▶ Barbarian conquest of Italy

NOMINAL IMPERIAL RULE FROM RAVENNA

After the death of Constantine, as we have seen, the Western half of the empire had its own co-emperor, but, without access to the more prosperous part of the Roman dominions, it fell into a swift decline. For brief periods during the century the East and West were again united, and the façade of empire was successfully maintained for most of the fourth century until the pressure of the Huns started the barbarian movements again. When the dangers became acute at the end of the century, Honorius, the western emperor, moved his capital to Ravenna (ca. 400), leaving the pope as the real ruler of Rome. Thereafter most of the emperors were either children, feeble-minded, or both. They lived in a hothouse atmosphere of intrigue, surrounded by eunuchs, courtiers, clergy, and women. But they were still officially rulers of the empire, and it was with them that the barbarians negotiated. Secure in their stronghold of Ravenna, which, fully fortified and surrounded by marshes, could not be conquered with the resources available to the barbarians, many of these emperors behaved with an astounding lack of foresight and sense of responsibility. Beset by fears of treachery and even ignorant of what was going on in their territories, they still imagined themselves the potentates that earlier emperors had actually been. They treated the barbarians, including their own generals, too often with a lordly disdain. The result was that the generals were forced to take matters into their own hands, and do the best they could to preserve the empire. And yet the emperors, on at least two occasions, rewarded them, in the one case with execution, and in the other with assassination. By the end of the fifth century the last of these successors of Constantine was deposed by the barbarian general of the day, who merely assumed the kingship without opposition. This was the so-called fall of Rome in 476.

ROME UNDER PAPAL RULE

The position of the pope

In Rome itself the pope was the real, but not the nominal, ruler of the city. Only his influence was able to temper the ferocity of the barbarians who invaded Italy three times during the century, twice sacking Rome. The imperial generals were away from Italy, defending the northern provinces. On each occasion it was the failure of these generals that allowed the barbarians to enter the defenseless peninsula. The popes organized such defense as there was, negotiated with the enemy, and superintended the reconstruction. The old Senate, now only a municipal council of Rome, gave occasional aid; even consuls continued to be elected, but they were not allowed to exercise any real power. The only well-organized and effective body in Rome was the clergy, under the authority of the pope.

Sack of Rome by Alaric (410)

The first attack came from Alaric the Visigoth, who had marched over from the Danubian provinces. The barbarian imperial general Stilicho twice defeated him; but the emperor Honorius suspected his general's loyalty, and had him executed. The Goth was thus given a free passage into Italy. No army was there to meet him, the emperor remaining safely defiant in Ravenna when Alaric asked him for land in Italy for the settlement of his people. The Roman citizens offered Alaric a ransom for their city, but he wanted land, not cash. Exasperated with the stubbornness of Honorius, Alaric then ap-

pointed an emperor of his own, a Roman noble. But when this gentleman also was either unwilling or unable to grant his demands, Alaric and his troops lost patience and sacked Rome for three days. But the Gothic king died within a year, and the emperor patched up a treaty with his successors. The Visigoths moved off to greener pastures.

Sack of Rome by Vandals (455)

The invasion of Italy by Attila in 452 has already been noted, and the role of Pope Leo I in persuading him to retire. Only three years later, at a moment when Aetius, the Roman victor of Chalons, had just been assassinated by the emperor Valentinian III (a murder quickly avenged by friends of the general), Gaiseric, the terrible king of the Vandals, sailed from Carthage with a fleet of barbarians bent on plunder. Sailing unmolested up the Tiber in their shallow-bottomed boats, the Vandals entered Rome. Again Pope Leo interceded, but was able to win nothing but the lives of the citizens. The Vandals then sacked the defenseless city for two weeks. When their ships left, laden with booty, Rome was little but a desolate ruin, her temples pillaged, her palaces sacked and burned, and everything of any value that had not been hidden from the barbarians was on the way to Africa.

THE BARBARIANS IN ITALY—THE END OF IMPERIAL RULE ("FALL OF ROME," 476)

For another twenty years the imperial rulers in Ravenna exercised a nominal sway over Italy. But the real rulers were the barbarian chieftains who bore Roman titles and commanded the army, which was still Roman in name. Emperors were made and unmade at will until one of the generals, Odoacer by name, finally decided to put an end to the solemn farce. The last emperor, a child rejoicing in the name of Romulus, the little Augustus (Augustulus), was formally deposed, his imperial insignia confiscated and sent to Zeno, the shrewd emperor of the East, as a token that there was no further emperor in the West. Though he proclaimed himself king of Italy, Odoacer thus showed himself willing to acknowledge the overlordship of the Eastern emperor, who was theoretically still lord of the whole united empire. Doubtless Odoacer thought him sufficiently far away and sufficiently occupied to be of no danger to his Italian sovereignty. Thus was the fall of Rome, which had stood for almost a thousand years in proud independence, consummated by the simple act of a barbarian general, without fighting, and with little noticeable change even in the form of the government. For a long time the imperial officals had been powerless, with the clergy alone keeping their Roman-inspired organization intact. Even under Odoacer, the Senate still sat as the municipal council of Rome, a position of honor but no authority; and even consuls continued to be solemnly elected. But all real power was now in the hands of the army and its generals. The army itself was made up of various Germanic tribesmen under the leadership of Odoacer himself, whose origin is unknown. He has been thought by some scholars even to have been a Hun, though he is usually called a Herulian. High positions in the state were reserved for the barbarian rulers. Relations with the papacy were correct but not cordial, for these barbarian peoples were all heretical Arians and thus unacceptable to orthodox Christians. Not until Justinian's reconquest of Italy, to be described later, was the papacy to be freed from its difficult position as an island of orthodoxy within a sea of heresy.

OSTROGOTHIC KINGDOM OF ITALY—
THEODORIC (493–526)

But Odoacer was not to enjoy his new crown in peace. His army, though loyal to him, had no united body of tribesmen behind it. It was a formidable enough body of military men, but not strong enough to defend itself against a powerful united people. And such a people under Theodoric, prob-

ably the greatest of all barbarian generals and administrators, this army was now to be called upon to meet.

We have seen that the Ostrogoths (East Goths) had early submitted to Attila, and had been penned into a territory near the Black Sea. When this menace was lifted the Ostrogoths began to stir again and look for land for settlement. They made a treaty with Constantinople under which they became allies of the empire, and a young prince named Theodoric was sent to the capital as hostage. Thus he was educated in Constantinople, learned to understand and respect Roman institutions and even Roman law, and gained military experience. When his father died and he became king of a section of the Ostrogothic people he continued friendly relations with Zeno, emperor at Constantinople, was made a Roman citizen, and a master of the Byzantine troops. But later, when Theodoric consolidated all the Ostrogoths under his rulership, the emperor began to worry, and thought it would be safer to divert Theodoric and his people to the West, where he had no objection to the expulsion of Odoacer. Theodoric, taking the hint, led his people over into Italy and drove his opponent into Ravenna, from which, however, he found it impossible to dislodge him. Resorting to treachery under cover of peace negotiations, Theodoric was able to murder his rival, and became sole ruler of Italy, with a united Ostrogothic people behind him (493).

His reign of thirty-seven years was a remarkable example of the importance of good government to the prosperity of a country, even one as ill-used as Italy had been in the last centuries. Unencumbered by an imperial heritage, facing no enemies who could not be easily handled, keeping Constantinople at a safe distance and without cause for complaint against him since he scrupulously acknowledged the overlordship of the emperor, Theodoric gave a government to the Italians such as they had not known for centuries. The Goths were assigned land in Italy, apparently by the simple expedient of dispossessing a few large pro-

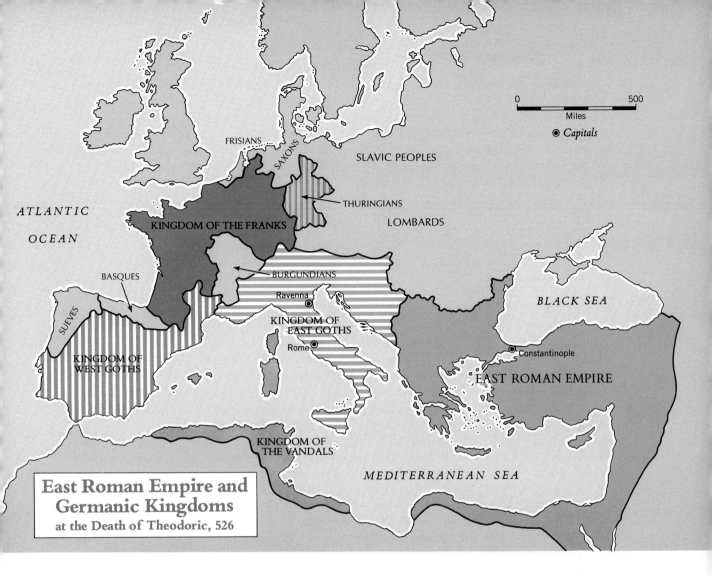

ATLANTIC
OCEAN

FRISIANS

SAXONS

SLAVIC PEOPLES

THURINGIANS

LOMBARDS

KINGDOM OF THE FRANKS

BASQUES

BURGUNDIANS

Ravenna

KINGDOM OF
EAST GOTHS

Rome

BLACK SEA

Constantinople

EAST ROMAN EMPIRE

SUEVES

KINGDOM OF
WEST GOTHS

KINGDOM OF
THE VANDALS

MEDITERRANEAN SEA

0   500
Miles
◉ *Capitals*

**East Roman Empire and
Germanic Kingdoms**
at the Death of Theodoric, 526

prietors and repopulating land that was not being worked for lack of cultivators, while those who were not in the army settled down as farmers. The Roman administration of government and justice was maintained, the Senate remained, on the whole, loyal to the king, and taxes were drastically reduced, as there was no longer such need for them. Agriculture and commerce revived; even private enterprise began to appear. Theodoric dredged the harbors, rebuilt aqueducts, and restored the cities as far as he could with his limited means. No longer having a vast empire to maintain, and with a greatly reduced population to support, Italy became the self-supporting territory that she has always had it in her power to be. The pope continued to maintain correct relations with the king though he was an Arian; and Theodoric in

return made no attempt to convert his orthodox Roman subjects to Arianism.

There was even a brief revival of culture, with the two great scholars Boethius and Cassiodorus the chief ornaments. Boethius, foreseeing correctly the certain loss of all Greek culture in the West under the barbarian monarchy, spent much of his life translating the logical works of Aristotle into Latin, and writing textbooks based on the dying Greek knowledge, but suitable for the barbarians and barbarized Romans who alone would remain to study them. Unfortunately he became suspected of treasonable designs against the throne, and was cast into prison. Here he wrote the *Consolations of Philosophy,* which has been read ever since, and was especially popular in the Middle Ages. Ultimately he was executed by order of Theodoric. His shade, however, may have been compensated by the knowledge that his textbooks and translations did indeed survive to become the chief intellectual diet of generations of medieval students. Cassiodorus, however, long outlived the Gothic king, supervising the translating and copying of manuscripts in a monastery which he founded on his own estate. He also wrote a *History of the Goths.*

RECONQUEST OF ITALY BY THE BYZANTINE EMPIRE

Italian policy of Justinian

Theodoric's kingdom, however, did not survive his death. It was evidently only his personality that held it together. Civil war disrupted the kingdom, the succession, as so often in the Germanic kingdoms, being disputed between several contestants; in 535, Justinian, the emperor of the East, decided that the time was ripe for the restoration of the old Roman Empire, as it had been and always ought to be. The emperor Justinian was also a strong zealot for the orthodox faith as long as he was allowed to interpret it himself. In the laudable aim of extinguishing Arianism, he had the moral support of the papacy in Rome, and whatever more tangible support it could give him—at least until the popes recognized that Justinian's authoritarianism extended to the field of religion also.

Destruction of Ostrogothic kingdom— Economic and strategic consequences

In a long-drawn-out and ruinously expensive war, Justinian's generals, Belisarius and Narses, reconquered Italy piecemeal. Behind them came the imperial bureaucracy and the tax collectors from whom the fortunate Italians had been free for a generation. The Ostrogothic nation resisted to the last, and was virtually destroyed, Italy was devastated; twenty years of warfare in which neither side showed any mercy was the final crippling blow to a country which had been able to recover from so many in the past. From this she never recovered for centuries.

Justinian, leaving an *exarch,* an imperial official, to rule Italy from Ravenna on his behalf, and a pope grateful for his orthodoxy but disliking intensely his autocratic manner of dealing with spiritual matters which he had acquired in his own capital, turned his attention to other affairs. He died soon afterward, having saddled his empire with a territory almost useless for exploitation, and incapable of self-defense against any barbarian horde that wished to enter.

INVASION OF ITALY BY LOMBARDS (568) —PARTITION OF ITALY

The Lombard conquests (568–605)

This was not long in coming. Justinian had not been in his grave three years before the Lombards, another Germanic people, but by far the least civilized of any that had hitherto penetrated into Southern Europe, nominally Arians also, but in fact nearer to heathenism, swept into northern Italy, where there was no one left to oppose them. This time they made no compromises with the emperor, nor were they interested in Roman civilization. The Italians lost their estates, which were simply sequestrated by the Lombards. Northern Italy was consolidated under their rule in seven years, and they began to push southward. The exarch of Ravenna maintained his stronghold, still theoretically the ruler of Italy under the emperor; but neither he nor the rest of Italy could obtain any support from the various emperors of Constantinople, who were fully engaged elsewhere. Nor did the emperors give any aid to the other isolated areas in Italy under their nominal rule. And there was no such partly civilized king as Theodoric over the Lombards. They were united only for conquest and plunder. Thereafter their separate leaders (dukes) took what they could, and maintained it as their own private possession. By 605 all Italy except Ravenna, Naples, Rome, and parts of the extreme south were in the hands of the barbarians.

Remnants of Byzantine rule

What remained to the empire from the

warfare of Justinian was the isolated and useless Ravenna, and the south. Rome acknowledged the overlordship of Constantinople on the principle that a distant overlord is better than a local one, especially if he is powerless to intervene. Since such acknowledgment carried with it no obligation to obedience, the popes were content to make it for centuries to come. And the pope of Rome was now at last in fact its temporal lord also. He was the spiritual lord of all Christendom, the owner of many scattered estates in Italy which had been given to the Church in the troubled times, and the defender of Rome against the barbarian Lombards from whom he had managed to keep his city intact.

Position of the papacy—Gregory I (590–604)

This was the work of one man, one of the greatest of the popes, a Roman by descent, a saint, and a gifted administrator and diplomatist, Gregory I, the Great.

It is possible that the Lombards, vastly superior in numbers as they were, could have taken Rome by force if they had united against it. But they seem to have respected the person of the pope, and perhaps the sanctity of the city, in spite of the fact that they were only nominal Christians, and a heretical sect at that. At all events, they never made any serious effort to do so, perhaps in part because of their internal disunity. Thus for centuries the popes were able to exist, often isolated and always precariously, until they were rescued in the eighth century by the orthodox Frankish kings. Gregory, who had at an earlier stage in his life been an official agent of the papacy in Constantinople, knew how useless it was to look for help from this quarter. He therefore accepted the position, and negotiated directly with the Lombards, while the emperor continued to bid him resist, and for many years refused to accept his arrangements. Ultimately the empire recognized the conquests; and Gregory through the negotiations was allowed to keep his city and the territory around it.

Such a position, in spite of its precariousness, had certain manifest advantages. As a temporal ruler the pope continued to owe a nominal allegiance to Constantinople, an allegiance which could not be enforced, but still gave him legal title to his position, and perhaps served to keep the Lombards away from his city. As a spiritual and temporal leader he had just shown himself as a true shepherd of his people, thereby greatly enhancing his prestige. He began to improve his position still further by directing missionary enterprises, especially the successful mission of St. Augustine to England (596), and a further mission to Spain, where the Visigothic king was at last converted from his Arianism to orthodox Catholicism. Gregory took careful thought for the position of the clergy in Christendom, and wrote several works giving them guidance and practical advice on the care of souls. His instructions to bishops remain the fundamental work on the subject, explaining in a simple manner the different kinds of cases with which they would be called upon to deal, and how the instruction varied in each case. As explained already, he also fully supported the work of St. Benedict in his reform of the monasteries.

Perhaps the most important of Gregory's work was his insistence that all the clergy of Europe should obey the papacy and receive instructions from it. He was not too successful in France, where the appointment of the clergy was largely in the hands of the Merovingian kings, but the bishops nevertheless listened to him with respect, and later popes could quote Gregory as authority for their own claims. Newly converted Spain and England accepted the overlordship of the papacy from the first. And wherever there were orthodox clergy in Italy, they too accepted his supremacy. Though Gregory could not actually alter the domination of the Church by the state in Constantinople, he constantly repeated his claim that all the Eastern bishops and the Patriarch of Constantinople were subordinate to the Holy See by virtue of the Petrine supremacy. In all these things he gave a lead to the popes

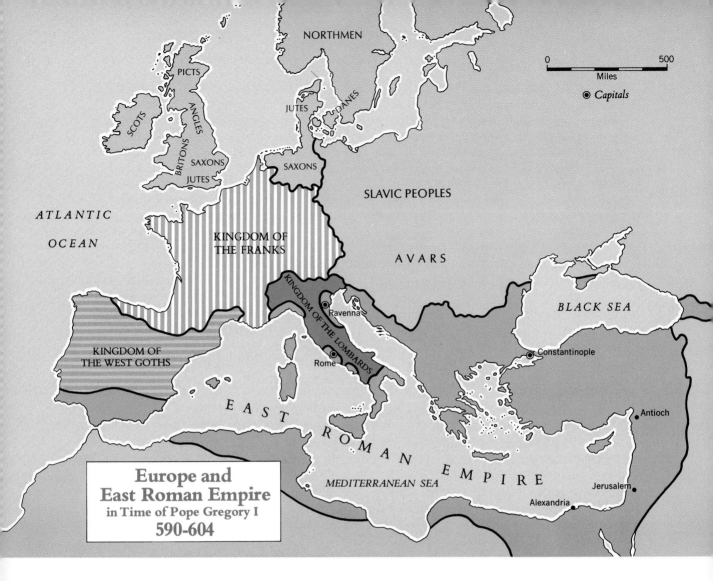

Europe and
East Roman Empire
in Time of Pope Gregory I
590-604

who followed him. For, though the practice of appointing bishops by lay rulers was never abandoned in France and Germany, and discipline could hardly be enforced, the clergy nevertheless did look to the papacy for guidance in spiritual affairs when they felt the need for it; and this dependence largely remained even when the papacy fell into weak hands, and when Constantinople and the Eastern Empire drifted entirely away from papal rule.

▶ Barbarian kingdoms in the West

THE ASCENDANCY OF THE FRANKS

Conquest of Gaul by Clovis (481–511)

When we last mentioned the Franks, they were following the Vandals into the land that was then called Gaul but thereafter was to be known as Frankland or France. Meeting little opposition from the few remaining Romans, the Franks first set up several kingdoms in the north under separate kings. But in 482 a young prince named Clovis became the ruler of one small kingdom clustered around the modern Tournai. Able and ambitious, he began to expand his kingdom to the south by judicious murders, treachery, and open warfare. France at the time was peopled by Visigoths, Burgundians, Alemanni, as well as the old Gallo-Romans, including a Gallic noble who called himself king of Rome. Defeating this pretender first, Clovis then drove the Alemanni back across the Rhine into Germany (to which they gave their name, Allemagne in the French language) and incorporated their

438

kingdom into his; then he turned south and drove the Visigothic remnants into Spain to join their fellow tribesmen; and at last, having disposed also of his fellow Frankish kings, he consolidated a kingdom not much smaller than the present-day France (481–511).

Conversion of Clovis to orthodox Catholicism

Clovis, as it happened, had a Christian wife, Clotilda, who was orthodox and not Arian; after his victories he allowed himself to be converted by her clerical adviser and with him his Franks, thus being the first barbarian group to deviate from the otherwise universal Arianism. Publicly baptised at Rheims by a Catholic bishop, by this act he gained the support of the entire clergy of France, who now rallied to his aid. This was no mean help, since they controlled what was left of the old Gallo-Roman administration, while the remainder of the old Gallo-Roman population, also orthodox Christians, offered Clovis at least their moral support. From this time onward the Frankish monarchy remained the papal favorite among secular powers, and it was to the Franks that the papacy looked for help and military aid when it became involved with the Lombard kings, in preference to the official overlord of Italy away in Constantinople who was too prone to lapse into heresy and was inclined to treat papal claims to supremacy with disrespect.

The Merovingian kingdom

After the death of Clovis, his kingdom, according to Germanic custom, was divided between his four sons, who spent most of their lives fighting against each other, though they united against all non-Frankish outsiders, consolidating their total dominions by the addition of almost all the remainder of modern France. The Merovingian kingdom (418–754, so called after Meroveus, grandfather of Clovis) was sometimes under the rule of one member of the family and sometimes subdivided. But until the eighth century at least one of his descendants occu-

pied the throne, though in later years the authority of the kings was only nominal and the real power was in the hands of hereditary officials, chief stewards, who are usually, and incorrectly, called mayors of the palace (*major domus*). Ultimately, as we shall see, one of these officials deposed his titular master with papal approval and became king of the Franks himself.

It is difficult to generalize about the state of the country in Merovingian times. Some of Gaul had been thoroughly Romanized, and remained so, even under alien monarchs. On the whole, it can be said that the Latin element tended to prevail. The French language has barely four hundred words of Germanic origin, all the remainder being of Latin origin. Much of Roman law and even Roman governmental system remained, especially in the center and the south, while in the north German customs prevailed. On the other hand, the barbaric habits of the kings; their addiction to murder, wholesale and retail; their lack of care for commerce and trade so long as they were able to have the Oriental luxuries, especially of dress and ornament, in which they delighted; their general propensity to treat their territories as if they were private estates to be exploited for their own gain; and their failure to control the rapacity of local, semi-independent chiefs called counts—all these tended to push the unhappy country further into barbarism, which historians have politely called a fusion between German and Gallo-Roman culture. This fusion undoubtedly existed, and the result, after many centuries, was the modern kingdom of France, but far more Latin than Germanic—in this showing once again how the superior culture tends to absorb the lesser, if the lesser, like the Frankish culture of this period, has less to offer. The best that can be said for the Merovingian monarchy is that, by providing government of a sort and by not interfering too drastically with institutions they were incapable of understanding and with a culture that meant nothing to them, they preserved France for a brighter future when the Dark Ages which had fallen

**Territory of the Franks
under the Merovingian Kings, 614**

on all Europe at last should come to an end.

As in all other matters the Merovingian kings were dictatorial and arbitrary in their policy toward the Church. They insisted on making all higher appointments themselves, or at least in supervising them. The result was that the choice was not always suitable, and morality does not seem to have been one of the more important qualifications for office. However, there were many good choices among the bad, and there can be little doubt that, on the whole, the bishops were several degrees better than the counts, with whom they shared the authority within the territories under their control. While we hear of bishops who publicly boasted of their adulteries, who adopted the trade of highwaymen in addition to their spiritual duties, who daily used to drink themselves into a stupor and celebrate Mass without taking the trouble to recover their sobriety, of bishops who went to war in full armor and of at least one who admitted to regicide, the record would be incomplete without mention also of many who spent their lives looking after the poor and humble and defending them against the secular power, many who administered justice faithfully, and many who were true shepherds of their

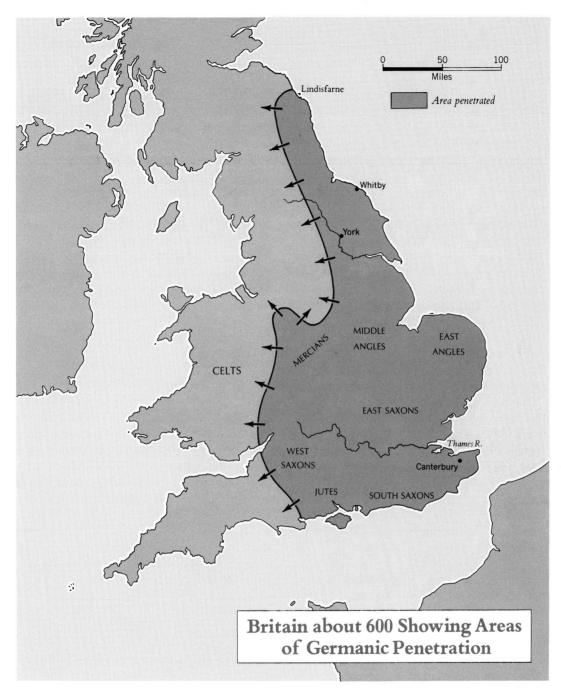

0   50   100
Miles

Area penetrated

Lindisfarne

Whitby

York

MIDDLE
ANGLES

EAST
ANGLES

MERCIANS

CELTS

EAST SAXONS

Thames R.

WEST
SAXONS

Canterbury

JUTES

SOUTH SAXONS

Britain about 600 Showing Areas of Germanic Penetration

flocks. The bishops and clergy were a reflection of the times in which they lived and of the monarchs who appointed them.

THE ANGLO-SAXON KINGDOM OF ENGLAND— INVASION (440–615)

In the early fifth century the Roman legions in Britain revolted, and finally left the country to its fate (442). The northern walls which had protected the country from the Celtic Picts were promptly overrun by these invaders, while other Celts from Ireland, called the Scots, came over by sea. Saxons from Germany, and later a people called Angles, usually collectively known as Anglo-Saxons, together with some Jutes from Denmark, invaded Britain from the east, driving the Celtic population, including the recent arrivals from Ireland and Scotland, into the west of the country, and setting up kingdoms of their own, the Angles and Jutes in the north and east, and the Saxons in the South. These conquests were completed by 615. The original Celts, who had never fully accepted Roman culture, though they had been, for the most part, converted to Christianity, fled into the extreme west of the country, and relapsed into barbarism, retaining their Celtic language to this day (Welsh); they were not reclaimed into England until the fourteenth century. The Celts (Britons) who remained in England were thoroughly Germanized by the invaders, and the country became in all essentials a Germanic one. This Anglo-Saxon realm was even able to survive the fierce raids of the Northmen, who invaded repeatedly from the late eighth to the eleventh century, and at one time gave England, as the country came to be called, one of the greatest of its kings (Cnut). The Irish and Roman Churches soon competed for converts among the English, as described in the last chapter, the Roman Church finally obtaining one of its most constantly faithful clergy and people, subject to discipline from the papacy. The English kings made no attempt to defy the Church or interfere with clerical appointments until after the Norman Conquest in the eleventh century. This was the most successful and permanent of the Germanic kingdoms, of all that the barbarians invaded during these migrations the only country which survived as a truly Germanic entity.

THE VISIGOTHIC KINGDOM OF SPAIN (507–711)

The Visigothic kingdom of Spain, conquered after many efforts in other directions by the Visigothic people, remained under Gothic control until the beginning of the eighth century, with the exception of a small area in the south which was conquered by Justinian in 554 and held by the Byzantines for a few years. Being the most civilized of the German barbarians, they fused more easily with the Romanized Spaniards than did the Franks with the Gallo-Roman peoples of France. This was especially true after the conversion of the Visigoths to Catholic Christianity in the late sixth century. Roman law was maintained as well as elements of the Roman government, with the Goths providing the ruler, though they remained a small minority in the country. The Spanish language has very few words of Germanic origin, remaining almost as close to Latin as is Italian.

But the Goths declined in military ardor during their two centuries of rule, and were no match for the invading Muslims under Tarik (711), even though the latter were only one comparatively small unit among the numerous Muslim armies. As soon as the Muslims brought over their first reinforcements the kingdom succumbed without serious resistance. The consolidation of this kingdom by the Muslims will be described in Chapter 16.

THE VANDAL KINGDOM IN AFRICA—ITS EXTINCTION BY JUSTINIAN

The Vandal kingdom in Africa, founded by Gaiseric, survived only until the early sixth century. After the death of the great leader the government disintegrated, with civil war and disputed successions among the chiefs. One such dispute gave Justinian, the Emperor of Constantinople, the opportunity to interfere and add this Arian kingdom to orthodox Christendom. This was accomplished in one expedition under the brilliant Byzantine general Belisarius (533).

▶ The end of an era

With the fall of the Roman Empire we reach the end of an era. Though the successor-state in the East, known as the Byzantine Empire, survived for almost a thousand years longer, this civilization was so different from the old Roman Empire that it will be discussed separately in the next chapter, together with its own offshoots.

The achievements of Greco-Roman civilization were far from lost, even in the West; but the destruction of its political system and the decline of its culture as a living creative force threw Europe into a condition of political, social, and cultural degradation which used to be called the "Dark Ages." If these centuries are not believed by modern scholars to be as dark as earlier historians thought them, the term remains not altogether inappropriate. It was a period of fermentation which ultimately proved to have in it the potentiality for new life and creativity; but while the fermentation was in process life was dark indeed, and no one could have foretold what would arise from it. Other countries which have had great cultures in the past have never emerged from their stagnation, and it was possible that Europe might have followed their example.

The conditions which made possible the Greek and Roman achievements had disappeared, as it proved, forever. The Roman Empire had survived as long as it had because it was able to make use of the old city-state culture which was the distinctive achievement of the Greeks. The empire had succeeded in the one field in which the Greeks had failed; it had provided a political framework under which the ruinous intercity warfare was no longer possible. But the later empire had destroyed the basis for its own government when, by relentless pressure, it undermined the ability of the cities to survive as independent entities. It was not possible to force them to produce in the same way as they had produced under their own impetus; and though the peasant has always been ready to work his land under the most tyrannous oppression, either by landlords or by monarchs, Europe was too vast to treat as if it were an Egypt, and no emperor could be strong enough to keep every landlord in Europe directly subject to him and obedient to his orders. So no basis remained for absolute government; the army could not be maintained with the cities refusing to work, and with the peasants out of the control of the absolute monarchs. The army was merely an instrument for compulsion, and it could not itself produce.

With the destruction of the cities, land alone remained; and for the next few centuries the rule of Europe was in the hands of landlords, sometimes nominally subject to monarchs, but actually exercising almost independent control of comparatively small areas which were not beyond their capacity to rule. With the subsequent rise of cities it again became possible for monarchs to unite with them and subject the landlords to control; but it has never been possible up to this time to exercise this dominion in areas as large and with as wide and varied a culture as the territory ruled by the Roman Empire.

This is not to say that this fact was ever understood by contemporaries. To the people who could remember, or whose institutions had been formed by the Roman Empire, it seemed that the natural form of government was a huge universal state ruled by an emperor who, at least according to Christian thought, was responsible to God, or perhaps to God's spiritual representative on earth, the pope. If this no longer suited the new condition of Europe, then it must be imposed by force. Charlemagne, as we shall see, succeeded by the force of his personal genius in subjecting most of the landlords to discipline in his day and compelling them to acknowledge his authority. But all they had to do was to sit out his lifetime and throw off his out-of-date despotism as soon as he was dead. In this they were backed by all the effective force of the times.

The papacy, seeking a similar restoration of the empire in a different form, would probably have liked an emperor, obedient to itself in spiritual matters but exercising supreme authority in the secular sphere. This arrangement would have been more convenient, but the basis for such an authority was nowhere to be found. The emperor of Constantinople before the division of the Eastern and Western Churches refused to accept the overlordship of the papacy, even in spiritual matters. And the Holy Roman Empire was usually only a shadow empire, unable to maintain undisputed authority even within Germany, and could not even aspire, after Charlemagne, to the rulership of Europe.

So the papacy had to fall back upon the dream of a spiritual dominion, its ruler trying to dictate to the separate governments of Europe in spiritual matters, the only universal authority in a Europe split into many separate and warring states. But in the Middle Ages, when the Church fulfilled so many functions now considered the prerogative of secular governments, it was impossible to draw a dividing line between the realms of each. The secular governments, trying to establish their own power within their states, could not tolerate what came to seem foreign intervention in domestic matters, and conflict ensued between them and the spiritual authority exercised from Rome. And the latter, in an age of declining faith and increasing interest in worldly matters, was, at the last, unable to substantiate its claims.

So there was no restoration of the Roman Empire, either by secular or religious powers. It had served its purpose in history. Its achievements had been many; it had given to the Western world its first long experience of peace, it had spread Greek culture, with its ability to deal with abstract thought, its thirst for experimentation and explanation, and its tendency to think of life in terms of this world; and it had itself introduced mankind to the idea that each human being has rights which should be embodied in a law which ought to be just, clear, and not arbitrary, and as far as possible in accordance with what man could discover about the Divine Reason. It had given hospitality to an Oriental religion which gave man hope of a blessed hereafter, and explained this life as a proving ground for a world to come; and it has been contended that it also laid the impress of its own thought on the ancient Hebrew idea of man's atonement for sin by making it into a contract between man and God with salvation as the reward; and it certainly gave the organization of this Church as a gift to the religion. And it provided a language for this Church which could be understood throughout Europe, and has remained its chosen language to this day.

If little that was authentically Roman survived outside the Church in the Dark Ages Roman and Greek rationalism was not lost forever. When the human mind awakened again—when, with Anselm, it was first found necessary to *prove* the existence of God—the process was set in motion that led to modern Western civilization. And the work of the Greeks and Romans, gradually recovered and assimilated, had no mean share in it.

▶ ## Suggestions for further reading

PAPER-BOUND BOOKS

Bede, The Venerable. *The History of the English Church and People.* Penguin. The finest historical work of the seventh century, by an English monk.

Boethius. *The Consolation of Philosophy.* Ungar and Liberal Arts Press. A dialogue concerning the merits and values of philosophy, written when the author was in prison awaiting his execution by Theodoric.

Bury, J. B. *The Later Roman Empire.* 2 vols. Dover. The pioneer work in English on the period, covers also early Byzantium to the death of Justinian. Not all interpretations now acceptable, but the work should be known.

Chambers, M., ed. *The Fall of Rome: Can It be Explained?* Holt, Rinehart and Winston. As in the Kagan book on next page, this problem of perennial interest is discussed by several authors.

Davis, Charles, ed. *Eagle, Crescent and the Cross: Sources of Medieval History, 250–1000.* Appleton. Useful source book for this period.

Dawson, Christopher. *The Making of Europe.* Meridian. This popular book, by a Catholic historian, is excellent on the heritage of the Roman Empire. In the later chapters he sees more light in the "Dark Ages" than is commonly acknowledged.

Duckett, Eleanor S. *Alfred the Great: The King and his England.* Phoenix. By a fine medieval scholar, very familiar with the few sources available for the period. By the same author is a fascinating book *The Wandering Saints of the Early Middle Ages* (Norton). See also in case-bound section.

Gibbon, Edward. *Barbarism and the Fall of Rome.* Vol. II of *The Decline and Fall of the Roman Empire.* Collier. The section of Gibbon's eighteenth-century rationalist masterpiece printed in this paperback may whet the student's appetite for more. To be treated cautiously as history. The interpretation is one-sided, but the book is still part of every man's literary education.

Kagan, Donald. *Decline and Fall of the Roman Empire; Why Did it Collapse?* Heath. Contains judicious extracts from several modern historians from Gibbon onward, stating the various points of view on this most controversial of subjects.

Katz, Solomon. *The Decline of Rome and the Rise of Medieval Europe.* Cornell University Press. Brief treatment.

Laistner, M. L. W. *Thought and Letters in Western Europe,* A.D. *500–900.* Cornell. Difficult but important, the only full study available in English.

Latouche, R. *The Birth of the Western Economy.* Torchbooks. A standard economic history.

Lewis, Archibald. *Emerging Medieval Europe,* A.D. *400–1000.* Knopf.

Lot, Ferdinand. *The End of the Ancient World and the Beginning of the Middle Ages.* Torchbooks. The most adequate analytical account in English of the fall of the Empire and the establishment of successor states.

Momigliano, Arnaldo. *Studies in Historiography.* Torchbooks. Contains an interesting study of the important transitional figure of Cassiodorus, with sidelights on the period.

Moss, Henry S. *The Birth of the Middle Ages, 395–814.* Galaxy. Good brief general picture of the last period of the Empire, the barbarian invasions and the new European states, clearly written.

Sullivan, Richard. *The Heirs of the Roman Empire.* Cornell. A good brief introduction.

Tacitus. *On Britain and Germany,* trans. by H. Mattingly. Penguin. Contains the *Agricola* and *Germania,* the last named our only important literary source for early Germany.

Wallace-Hadrill, J. M. *The Barbarian West: The Early Middle Ages, 400–1000.* Torchbooks. An excellent synthesis.

Whitelock, Dorothy. *The Beginnings of English Society.* Penguin. A competent survey of Anglo-Saxon England.

CASE-BOUND BOOKS

Dill, Samuel. *Roman Society in Gaul in the Merovingian Age.* New York: The Macmillan Company, 1926. Exhaustive study of Merovingian society rather than an analysis of the remnants of Roman culture in Frankland.

Dill, Samuel. *Roman Society in the Last Century of the Western Empire.* New York: Macmillan, 1899. A classic, especially valuable for its long quotations from contemporary writers who were ignorant of the impending fall of the Empire.

Duckett, Eleanor. *The Gateway to the Middle Ages.* Ann Arbor: University of Michigan Press, 1961. Extremely well-informed study, with useful detail and good judgments, especially valuable for its use of the literary sources dealing with relations between Romans and barbarians.

Gregory of Tours. *History of the Franks,* trans. with an introd. by O. M. Dalton. New York: Oxford University Press, 1927. Colorful account by an observant Merovingian bishop, on which all historians have had to rely for the social and political history of the time.

Rostovtzeff, M. L. *Social and Economic History of the Roman Empire.* See *Suggestions for further reading* at end of Chapter 11.

INDEX

(Note: Page references to maps are given in italics)